DATE DUE

4/29/99		
JUN 1 8 2003		

DEMCO 38-297

McGRAW-HILL SERIES IN EDUCATION

HAROLD BENJAMIN, Consulting Editor

THE EDUCATION

OF

EXCEPTIONAL CHILDREN

THE EDUCATION

OF

EXCEPTIONAL CHILDREN

*Its Challenge to Teachers, Parents,
and Laymen*

BY

ARCH O. HECK

*Professor of Education, College of Education
The Ohio State University*

FIRST EDITION

McGRAW-HILL BOOK COMPANY, Inc.

NEW YORK AND LONDON

1940

THE MAPLE PRESS COMPANY, YORK, PA.

TO

My Father and Mother

DAVID STOUT HECK

AND

MATILDA ANGELINE (Davis) HECK

PREFACE

American educators have accepted, in theory, the principle that children should have, in terms of their abilities, equal educational opportunities. Actually, this principle has been and is being violated; this violation is particularly flagrant when the education of exceptional children is considered. Most states, even yet, exempt children from school attendance for physical and mental defects. Thus local districts are encouraged to ignore the cripple, the deaf, the blind, and the mental defective, instead of being required to establish the special facilities needed by such children. Instead of establishing local schools that help the truant and the delinquent to make a happy social adjustment, they too frequently send them to state institutions, penal in character. Even the gifted child is ignored, as such, and, except as he forces himself upon our attention by his superior work, is permitted to do merely the work of the regular curricula with the resultant mediocre achievement.

Through the author's interest in pupil-personnel work, these exceptional children were most forcibly called to his attention, and the very practical problem of what to do for them arose. This book presents a point of view as to what should be done for them and how it should be done. In general, the book undertakes to do five things: (1) It aims at setting the challenge which educators face in properly caring for and educating exceptional children. (2) It develops those basic principles to be observed in the education of exceptional children. (3) It considers in some detail the various practical problems encountered in caring for and educating these children. (4) It presents accounts of how various cities and states are actually handling these problems. (5) It outlines in great detail the responsibilities that parents, teachers, principals, superintendents, and laymen must assume if mental, physical, and social handicaps are to be prevented.

In addition to its use as a text in college and university courses, it should serve as a handbook for teachers, principals, and superintendents. An attempt has been made to present material sufficiently nontechnical so that laymen and parents not only can profit from its reading but will have some pleasure in that reading.

The problem of selecting the cities and the state schools whose programs were to be included was handled most arbitrarily. Accounts of these programs were sought by examining educational magazines, city and state school reports, and material received directly from cities and from state schools. Many cities and many state schools had very little, if any, printed data that describe what they are doing. This fact automatically eliminated from consideration a great many city and a great many state schools which unquestionably are doing good work. After data had been assembled from a large representative group of cities and schools, reductions had to be made in order to keep the book within printable size. In general, these reductions were made upon the basis of three principles: (1) quality of program, (2) programs that emphasized different phases of the problem of educating a given type of exceptional child, and (3) cities and state schools representing different sections of the United States.

The author felt that pictures might portray even more effectively than words the special educational programs of various cities. Cities were asked to provide pictures. Between 200 and 300 photographs were received. Forty of these appear in the book; they were selected upon the basis of (1) clearness and quality of the picture, (2) appropriateness to the discussion, and (3) avoidance of duplication of concepts already presented by other pictures.

As the manuscript was being prepared, it was read by many teachers, principals, superintendents, and laymen. These critical readings gave the author many needed suggestions for revision; parts of the manuscript have gone through eight revisions; all parts have gone through at least three revisions. As far as possible, statistical data were brought up to date as of 1939.

A preface would not be complete without a word of gratitude to particular individuals who have given unusual aid and encouragement as well as helpful criticisms and suggestions. Dr. Charles S. Berry kindly read the entire manuscript and gave helpful suggestions on content. Dr. J. W. Larcomb, M.D., read all sections dealing with prevention of physical handicaps and gave valuable professional advice. Professor Marie K. Mason of the Speech Department at Ohio State University read the chapters dealing with the deaf, the hard of hearing, and the speech defective and gave material assistance in the later revisions. Professors John Lee, Director of Special Education of Wayne University, and Ruth Heavenridge, Supervisor of Special Education of Butler University, have both urged the need of such a volume and have encouraged me to complete the manuscript at an early date. My wife, Frances A. Heck, read each revision and gave innumerable suggestions on organization, style, and English. And it is to my student groups, each spring and summer quarter for the past 12 years, that I owe a great deal of my inspiration for undertaking and completing the work involved in the preparation of this book.

ARCH O. HECK.

OHIO STATE UNIVERSITY,
COLUMBUS, OHIO,
    April, 1940.

CONTENTS

PART III.   EDUCATION OF MENTALLY EXCEPTIONAL CHILDREN

EDITOR'S INTRODUCTION

To judge the true eminence of an educational institution it is necessary to find out how much its operators know about the learners within its gates. Wise administration, helpful supervision, effective instruction, adequate curriculum—all these things are required, but they seem often to be added automatically unto that school whose teachers really know their pupils. It would be foolish to try to isolate cause and effect in what is a great complex of causes and effects, but it is safe to say that teachers who study their pupils from every available angle and with every useful device are far more likely to find themselves in a well-administered, well-organized, and well-taught school than will those teachers who regard their particular bit of teaching as a potent nostrum good for any child, provided always that he has been properly instructed by his previous teachers.

The reason for this relationship between knowledge of the learner and general excellence of the system of education is not far to seek. Instruction, curriculum, supervision, and administration are all based squarely upon understanding of the learners, or they have no adequate basis. This is the rock upon which a good educational system must rest. To erect it upon any other foundation is to build it upon the sands of ignorance. The stability of the structure is not improved, moreover, by giving that ignorance a number of academically genteel titles.

This is why the most forward-looking and effective school systems are commonly those which make most adequate provision for the education of exceptional children. The more they study their pupils the more they recognize that every learner is unique and that those who deviate most markedly from the mental, social, and physical norms must be given a special type of education. They see that exceptional children must be given special education not only in their own interest but also in the interest of the no less individual but more nearly average children.

The present book offers a comprehensive and thorough treatment of the field of special education. It presents the principles and reviews the practices which modern school systems employ in this field. It gives a wealth of specific suggestions for the successful establishment and operation of educational programs for exceptional children. It is both a guide book and a field manual for any teacher, supervisor, or administrator who is interested in this field.

No one is more thoroughly conversant with the facts, materials, and techniques of special education or more competent to present them to the profession than is the author of this book. The results of his wide scholarship, extensive practical observations, and experience in teaching are here given form and substance in what the editor believes will be a landmark in the development of educational services for exceptional children.

HAROLD BENJAMIN.

UNIVERSITY OF MARYLAND,
April, 1940.

THE EDUCATION
OF
EXCEPTIONAL CHILDREN

CHAPTER I

THE FIELD AND THE CHALLENGE

1. INTRODUCTION

Child study is today the basis of good instructional procedure. Pupil cumulative records are being kept more widely, and prospective teachers are being trained more generally in the proper use of such records; guidance programs are being established and trained technicians are being placed on the pay rolls of boards of education to assist in the study of pupils; attendance departments are beginning to accept the idea that more can be done for a child when he is understood than can be done by ignorance and force; many of these agencies are passing on to the teacher the information secured; bureaus of tests and measurements are encouraging teachers to use objective tests and are showing them how to apply the results of these tests in the diagnosis of pupil ability; private foundations are promoting children's clinics and are co-operating with public school systems in an attempt to give teachers a training that will help them in analyzing more carefully the physical, mental, social, and moral attributes of their pupils. All these programs are being promoted in the belief that such study will make it possible so to adapt both the contents and the methods of instruction that the child will be better taught.

Individual Differences.—Such programs for the study of children imply a decided change in our educational psychology from that of an earlier day; child study would hardly be necessary if all youths were alike in ability, capacity, and interests. Such similarity would make the problem of educating them relatively simple. We know today that pupils differ one from another in mental, social, physical, and moral attributes. It is only recently, however, that the extent of these differences has been fully recognized.

1

Two developments during the past three decades have tended to emphasize these differences. (1) The development of the standardized examination made it possible to get a clearer and more objective picture of the extent to which pupils differ in their ability to spell, read, write, and cipher. Few good schools now fail to use such tests; as a result, they have a better picture of the differences in ability among pupils. (2) The development of better compulsory school-attendance legislation made for more effective enforcement of attendance in the various states; thousands of children in recent years have been brought into schools or have been caused to want to attend school who, during the preceding century, would either never have attended or would have attended for so short a time that their inabilities to progress would never have been recognized. These two developments have so encouraged the study of children that we now have numerous agencies so interested in child study that innumerable differences in their abilities have been discovered.

These differences do not apply to scholastic or academic abilities alone; they apply just as definitely to mechanical, physical, and social abilities. Examinations of hearing and of sight show variations that are extreme; tests of the ability of pupils to deal with tools and machinery show large individual differences; close observation of any unselected group of fifth-grade pupils would disclose to the teacher great differences in ability to adjust to new social situations and to exert appreciable control over the group to which they belong or have been attached.

Correlation vs. Compensation.—Not only do we find pupils differing within a single trait but we find that those who show considerable ability in one trait may be quite low in another. Caution needs to be urged at this point, for it is undoubtedly true that human abilities generally are governed by correlation instead of compensation. This is shown by the positive correlations found when various traits of unselected groups of individuals are measured and these measures correlated. While it is true that most individuals who are low in ability in one trait are likewise low in other traits, instead of being exceptionally able in these other traits in compensatory fashion, yet we do find the so-called law of compensation occasionally at work.

A few years ago, tests given in a large city high school revealed the fact that one girl in the tenth-grade class was of very low-grade mentality. The girl was physically very mature, talked well though not as informingly as one would wish, was very likable and socially acceptable in her age group, and was, in fact, a leader socially. Extensive subject-matter examinations showed that she did not have a mastery of even sixth-grade work and yet she, because of other well-developed traits, had been passed into senior high school. Numerous instances could be cited of individuals who have done poorly in school and who have even risen to eminence. This happens frequently enough to warrant psychologists in classifying mental ability as abstract, mechanical, physical, and social.

2. THE FIELD OF SPECIAL EDUCATION

Although correlation is accepted as the rule in the place of compensation, yet the fact that correlation is not perfect, and is far from being perfect between many traits, makes more complex the problem of dealing with exceptional children. If correlation were perfect, the gifted children would be the most fit physically, the most adjustable socially, and the most dependable morally; likewise, the feeble-minded would be our cripples, blind, deaf, and delinquent. But the problem is not so simple. Our gifted child may be crippled or deaf; the feeble-minded child may have no physical handicaps. All kinds of combinations of handicaps and lack of handicaps will be found when any considerable number of children are examined.

The Mentally Exceptional Child.—The exceptional child, by implication, has just been described as one who deviates or varies from the normal by a considerable amount in respect to any one of a number of traits. Table I, for example, shows how Terman classifies children upon the basis of I.Q. According to this classification, children with an I.Q. of 120 or higher are very superior, or in the genius class; those below 70 are definitely feeble-minded. Terman also says that 1 per

TABLE I.—TERMAN'S CLASSIFICATION OF CHILDREN UPON BASIS OF I.Q.[1]

I.Q.	Classification
Above 140	Near genius or genius
120–140	Very superior intelligence
110–120	Superior intelligence
90–110	Normal, or average, intelligence
80–90	Dullness, rarely classifiable as feeble-mindedness
70–80	Border-line deficiency, sometimes classifiable as dullness, often as feeble-mindedness
Below 70	Definite feeble-mindedness

[1] LEWIS M. TERMAN, *The Measurement of Intelligence*, p. 79. This table is applicable to the original Terman, Stanford Revision of the Binet Scales, 1916. Used by permission of, and special arrangement with, the publishers, Houghton Mifflin Company, Boston.

cent of any unselected group of children will have I.Q.'s of 130 or better and that another 1 per cent will have I.Q.'s of 70 or less. Five per cent have I.Q.'s of 122 or above, and another 5 per cent are of 78 or below.[1] The group, in fact, is normally distributed.

Not all cities accept the same standard in deciding which of their children are mentally exceptional. Some cities consider them exceptional if they have an I.Q. of 130 and above or of 70 and below; the former constitute the gifted children, the latter the feeble-minded. Other cities include children of I.Q.'s of 120 and above in classes for the gifted; they may also include children with an I.Q. in the seventies in their exceptional group at the other end of the distribution.

The Physically Exceptional Child.—In a similar fashion, the deaf and the hard-of-hearing children belong to the lower extreme of a distribution based upon some measurement of the hearing ability. Children who have superlatively good hearing are not school problems, but those who have no hearing or relatively very little are. This latter group is, therefore, exceptional with respect to ability to hear; if we had a good measuring instrument, moreover, it is probable that it would be discovered that the ability to hear is normally distributed. It is quite possible that if adequate measurements were had for determining the amount of ability children have for seeing, speaking, walking, and any other physical attribute needed for school attendance, we should discover that these abilities follow the normal curve. In all cases, it is those children at the lower end of the distribution who are known as exceptional.

The Socially Exceptional Child.—The social and moral traits of children would doubtless fit a similar curve were we able to make adequate measurements. It is not true, however, that we uniformly accept just those children at the lowest extreme of the distribution as exceptional. It is entirely possible that a boy or girl might rate normal on such a scale and still be brought into the exceptional group because of having been found out, whereas there might be hundreds of youths much worse but undiscovered who would be classed with the normals or superiors. It should be recognized that, in dealing with truants and delinquents, we have in our group of apparently exceptional children many who would rate near normal by any accurate and true measuring stick of morality. If there is need, therefore, for individual attention to the requirements of other types of exceptional children, there is a triple need for giving this attention to truants and delinquents.

The Education of Exceptional Children.—The term "exceptional child," as has been indicated, applies to all children who are handi-

---

[1] Lewis M. Terman, *The Measurement of Intelligence*, p. 78, Houghton Mifflin Company, Boston, 1916.

capped physically, socially, and mentally, as well as to those who are gifted according to some scale of mental measurement.

The field of special education is defined, therefore, as the educational program which is planned by private or public agencies for the education of these various groups. The fact that the exceptional child, by definition, deviates so far from the normal makes it obvious that many difficulties will be encountered in attempting to teach him in a regular class group, where reactions are so different from his own.

In this text, the field of special education will be limited to the delinquent boy and girl among the socially exceptional. Among the physically exceptional, it will include the cripple, blind, deaf, speech defective, hard of hearing, children with defective vision, and delicate children. The mentally exceptional includes the feeble-minded, the specially gifted, and the gifted.

3. THE CHALLENGE OF SPECIAL EDUCATION

The very definition of the field of special education sets the challenge. We find 11 groups of exceptional children. These groups are not small; they reach deeply into that great mass of youths whom we have considered normal. Our difficulty, in the past and even at present, is that we have failed to recognize, among the normals, those thousands who have been and are suffering from various and serious social, physical, and mental handicaps. The more pronounced cases we could not fail to observe but, due to their seemingly insignificant numbers, we have tended to ignore them; by exempting them from attendance at school, we have even "washed our hands" of the entire problem of caring for and educating them. It is only as we are now faced with the great number of exceptional children that the challenge has become apparent. It makes itself felt in three ways. Educationally, socially, and individually these handicapped youths constitute a real challenge.

Educationally.—The committee on special education of the White House Conference of 1930 estimated that there was a grand total of 13,521,400 handicapped children in the United States. How this number was computed is shown in Table II. Excluding some possible duplication, we still have an enormous number of children needing a special program of education. This committee reported that of the 13,521,400 only 210,802 handicapped youths were enrolled in special schools and classes. Either handicapped children in vast numbers are being held in the regular classes or they are being entirely deprived of an education.

Many handicapped children fall within the latter category; they vary so much from the normal that the regular schools cannot take care of them.   Each of the 48 states exempts or even excludes children who are so handicapped physically or mentally that they cannot "profitably" attend school; only by the establishment of special schools and classes is it possible for this group to be educated properly. Handicapped children who attend the regular school seldom have an adjustment made in care and instruction which greatly benefits them. It is the aim of special education to make such an adjustment and to develop the abilities of exceptional children just as the abilities of normal children are allowed to develop.   Special education means that the ideal of an "equal educational opportunity" for all is in the process of being achieved.

TABLE II.—HANDICAPPED CHILDREN IN THE UNITED STATES[1]

Type of Handicap	Number
Blindness (children under 20)	14,400
Partial sight	50,000
Impaired hearing	3,000,000
Defective speech (5 to 18)	1,000,000
Crippled condition (calling for special education)	100,000
Tubercular condition	382,000
Suspected tuberculosis	850,000
Weak or damaged heart	1,000,000
Malnourished state (school age)	6,000,000
Behavior problems (3 per cent of elementary)	675,000
Mentally retarded condition (2 per cent of elementary)	450,000
Grand total	13,521,400

[1] White House Conference, *Special Education: the Handicapped and the Gifted*, pp. 5–6, The Century Co., New York, 1931.

Educationally, the challenge is far greater than just that of properly educating the handicapped; it calls attention to our responsibility for providing the best possible setting for educating normal children. When the handicapped voluntarily attend a regular school, they at once become problems for the regular teacher; they must be given special help and attention.   This special help will involve (1) much individual instruction and (2) preparation of special materials.   So much of the teacher's time is utilized in helping the handicapped that she finds she has neglected the normal group.   Special education tends to reduce the load carried by regular classroom teachers and thus makes it possible for them to do a better job of instructing normal children.

Socially.—Special education is a challenge, socially, to laymen as well as to school men.   The whole program is by no means limited to that of educating children who have become handicapped; the most significant aspect of such a program is its effort at prevention. We are no longer just interested in remedial work; we want to prevent handicaps, so that remedial work will be less and less necessary.

This social challenge has two aspects; one relates to social well-being and the other to financial savings. Where prevention is emphasized, socially handicapped children have their customary responses so changed that they early become adjusted to normal living conditions. This protects society from those depredations that now result where a policy of neglecting these incipient cases of delinquency is followed. If the psychology of learning has anything to teach us, it is that habits of response to given stimuli are modified or are eliminated much more easily in the early stages of habit formation than they are after those habits of response have once become firmly fixed. The greatest problem met in dealing with socially handicapped pupils is that even now their habits are so firmly fixed; we are failing to reach such children soon enough.

With regard to the second aspect, workers in the field believe that special education saves society considerable financially. If the mentally handicapped can be so trained that under a plan of supervision they become self-supporting, if the physically handicapped are so educated and trained that they need not become wards of the state or community, if the socially handicapped are so stabilized that they become industrious working members of society, and if preventive measures so operate as to reduce materially the number of handicapped children of all types, then surely the program of special education does result in a real financial saving to society.

Individually.—When one observes the effects of a good program of special education upon the handicapped youth himself, the challenge is even more impressive. Self-confidence is developed. As long as they are members of a normal class group, children who are slow to learn seldom have that feeling of success which comes from accomplishment. They are trained to accept failure; they come to accept themselves as failures. Under such circumstances it is not to be wondered at that they show so little initiative. One is rather surprised that they should show any at all. A program of special education provides the child with work that he can do; he is permitted the "feel of something accomplished."

For the plan of supporting the blind, the crippled, or the deaf at home or in institutions, the program of special education substitutes the development of any capacity that the child may have; he is thus educated and trained to be self-supporting. The realization of ability to support himself brings to the child a feeling of freedom, which in turn begets self-confidence.

4. ACCEPTANCE OF THE CHALLENGE DELAYED

Thus far the acceptance of the challenge that special education presents has been delayed. We have either ignored it entirely or we have taken only those steps that have been forced upon us. We have said the problem is small and unimportant; we have insisted that our big duty is to educate the masses. There are several reasons for this continued refusal to face the challenge.

Need Not Realized.—First, the need is not clearly recognized. Workers in the field have, for the most part, a clear picture and a deep realization of the need. Unfortunately, many workers have this vision only for those exceptional children with whom they are working. It is not uncommon to find special-education groups opposing one another's programs before legislative committees; each group feels that if the other's program is accepted his own will be curtailed. We need more co-operation and understanding among these groups; until there is such co-operation and understanding, we cannot expect to find legislatures backing proposed programs with adequate appropriations. If workers in one field do not recognize the size of the problem in other fields, it is not surprising that teachers, principals, and superintendents of schools fail to see the need. It is even less to be wondered at that the public generally is not informed concerning the needs of special education.

Few know the number of children with different types of handicaps that are to be found in a given city or county. Surveys to determine the number within a given school district are difficult to make. The report of the White House Conference on Child Care and Training ought to help the general public to see the need. One is almost staggered by the suggestion that there are 1,000,000 children with speech defects, 1,000,000 with damaged hearts, 3,000,000 with defective hearing, and 6,000,000 who are malnourished.[1] If data from the White House Conference can be made common knowledge, the next decade ought to see a great advance in properly caring for and educating exceptional children.

Costs.—A second very practical difficulty in accepting the challenge is the fact that the costs are so great. Cleveland annually prepares an analysis of per pupil costs of different types of education both special and regular. Table III presents cost data for 3 different years; it also gives the average daily enrollments; it shows that the

[1] See Table II, p. 6.

costs for the school year 1928–29 at the Sunbeam school for cripples were $442.57; the costs at Alexander Graham Bell school for the deaf were $456.67; the costs at Thomas A. Edison school for boys were $188.02; the costs in special classes for mental defectives were $203.71; and the costs of Braille and sight-saving classes were $451.55 in the elementary schools. In general it will be noted that all types of special education were uniformly more expensive than elementary education and that six of the types were more expensive than regular senior high-school work.

TABLE III.—PER PUPIL COSTS OF SPECIAL EDUCATION IN CLEVELAND[1]

Types of special education	School year					
	1928–1929		1933–1934[2]		1937–1938[3]	
1	2	3	4	5	6	7
	A.D.E.	Costs	A.D.E.	Costs	A.D.E.	Costs
Alexander Graham Bell...	147.1	$456.67	137.9	$321.16	140.0	$439.13
Sunbeam (cripples).......	149.1	442.57	102.5	443.16	197.7	375.69
Thomas A. Edison (boys)..	986.7	188.02	939.8	133.39	766.0	223.48
Jane Addams (girls' trade).	393.1	152.32	818.9	76.79	1,193.3	143.20
Blind and sight-saving classes (elementary)....	197.1	451.55	225.3	300.00	211.9	405.10
Blind and sight-saving classes (junior high school)................	90.5	384.21	92.9	310.04	111.4	438.23
Mentally defective........	1,489.0	203.71	2,013.4	107.37	2,181.4	138.44
Open- air................	694.1	152.86	659.1	111.11	521.5	154.53
Gifted (major work)[4].....	318.9	157.92	596.2	108.28	474.4	162.46
Regular elementary, I–VI.	70,380.9	92.61	52,408.4	65.49	46,421.2	97.81
Regular junior high.......	32,865.3	127.29	33,044.5	81.10	31,649.9	116.11
Regular senior high.......	18,514.4	164.49	28,947.3	91.32	28,832.4	137.86

[1] Received from Office of the Superintendent of Schools, Sept. 8, 1939.
[2] Year of severe salary reductions after nearly as severe reductions in 1932–33.
[3] Much of salary reductions restored Sept. 1, 1937.
[4] Data cover elementary only.

The committee on special classes for the White House Conference[1] reported the following costs per pupil per year: (1) educating blind in state institutions $630; (2) Braille classes in the public schools

[1] *White House Conference*, 1930, pp. 233–234, The Century Co., New York, 1931.

$120 to $590; (3) sight-saving classes $132 to $331; (4) day schools and classes for the deaf $204 to $517; and (5) open-window and open-air schools and classes $100 to $305.   These costs are all materially higher than the costs of regular elementary education.

Unquestionably it is difficult to establish an adequate program for educating exceptional children when costs are so great.   Workers in the field must show that such a program is effective and make sure that the money spent is efficiently used.   If evidences of success and of efficiency can be definitely produced, greater costs will not be severely criticized and the challenge will be more readily accepted by the general public.

Outside the Regular Program of Education.—A third hindrance to accepting the challenge is the fact that special education is thought by so many to lie entirely outside the community's regular program of education.   The fact that state schools for the deaf, the blind, and the delinquent are so often governed by state departments of public welfare instead of by state departments of education is indicative of this point of view.   Parental schools organized for the care of truant and delinquent boys and girls are often controlled by civil instead of educational authorities.

The thesis herein proposed is that when the function of an institution is primarily educational, then it should be supervised and controlled by educational authorities.   This principle will be referred to constantly as various types of institutions are discussed.   If, therefore, a state institution for blind children is primarily for the instruction of these children and only incidentally houses them in order to educate them, the state department of education should by all means control and supervise the school.

This thesis would seem to be one that could be readily accepted by all; yet so strong is custom that the old idea, that the deaf and blind cannot be educated for self-support but must be cared for permanently at public expense, still holds and many states have not yet seen fit to place these state schools under the control of educators.   Housing is still made the primary issue and education is secondary.

We believe today that these handicapped children can be educated; we believe that many of them can be made self-supporting by means of this education; and we believe that so educated they will be able to make their own real contributions to society.   As soon as this concept is accepted and as soon as it is recognized that educational leaders should supervise and be responsible for all state or local educational activities, just so soon will this third handicap to the proper development of special education disappear.

Scarcity of Data on Results.—Another handicap to the acceptance of the challenge is the fact that there are available very few data that give objective evidence of the worth of special education. Special schools and classes have been operated in some cities now for two decades or more; many claims are made concerning their effectiveness; workers in the field believe in their work. Claims and beliefs, however, are daily becoming more and more futile as arguments for costly programs of education. Special education can be no exception to the rule. If, during the next quarter of a century, workers are to see their programs expand widely enough to meet the problems facing them, they must produce the facts.

We need extensive studies concerning what has happened, after 10 or more years, to young men and women who have spent considerable time in these special schools; we need to contrast these findings with findings from a study of similar individuals who have not had the advantages of such schools. Such studies are difficult to make, and this undoubtedly accounts for the scarcity of these data. Information of this kind is needed, however, and it is hoped that the next decade will find many workers checking carefully the results of their programs.

5. SOME GUIDING PRINCIPLES

A Point of View.—A program of special education is governed by the same aims and ideals and guided by the same philosophy as the regular program. If the special educationist holds that the vocational ideal is the proper starting point for developing an educational program for normal children, he then insists that special education be guided by the same ideal. If the cultural ideal is his lodestar, courses are likely to be required of these handicapped children without any inquiry into the special needs of individuals who deviate so widely from the normal.

The modern educator refuses to accept such specialized goals as *the* aim of education. He recognizes that the vocational is not all of life, just as the cultural is not. He recognizes that cultural subjects may be distinctly vocational in nature; on the other hand, the vocational subjects may be made truly cultural. The aim of education, therefore, becomes one of giving meaning to all of life in such a way that the child will have the ability to find new meanings as new experiences come to him. Facts of a course of study are so taught that they have a living relation to daily life, so taught that they develop the ability in the child to relate to his constantly enlarging vision of life all new data as they come to his attention. This is the aim of special education.

Child Study.—The preceding point of view requires upon the part of the teacher a knowledge of subject matter; it requires a familiarity with life problems and world conditions; but it also requires an intimate knowledge of forces governing the responses of each pupil within her class.   It is a bit futile to try to help a boy catch the meanings of a lesson assignment when he is emotionally wrought-up over home disagreements, when he lacks sleep due to nightwork, when he is weak from lack of food, when he is disturbed emotionally because of the rough treatment he receives from the school gang or because of the teacher's crossness, which throws him into confusion.   Every teacher ought to know each of her pupils.   Such knowledge implies a knowledge of his past school record, of home conditions, of playtime activities, of his extreme likes and dislikes, and of his mental, physical, and emotional maturity.   This applies particularly to teachers in special education.

An Equal Educational Opportunity.—Only when aims are the same will exceptional children have the same educational opportunity as normal children.   Tendencies, therefore, to train these children for specific trades at the expense of other courses that they have the ability to pursue should be discouraged; in teaching trade courses, the subject matter should be so treated that more than skills or tricks of the trade will be learned.   The aim in work with the handicapped is not to give them just a training that will make them self-supporting, unless this implies a broad understanding of life and a seeing of relationships between what they study and extensive life situations.   If only special training is to be provided, then handicapped children are not being provided an equal educational opportunity.

If this principle is to apply with equal force to all children, special schools and classes must be established.   As long as mentally handicapped children may be excluded from attendance at school, as long as the mentally and physically handicapped may be exempt from school attendance, and as long as school districts fail to provide special schools and classes for their handicapped, just so long do they fail to apply the principle of equality of educational opportunity to all groups of children.   The school or classes should be provided at public expense, and never should poverty stand in the way of any child's securing an education that will enable him to develop to the maximum whatever ability he has.

Develop Good Citizens.—If the point of view suggested at the beginning of this section is adhered to, we have the general concept necessary for the development of good citizenship.   The truant or the delinquent boy or girl, for example, has not the true meanings of things; he has failed to note relationships properly. The meanings and relationships that he has gathered have been warped and distorted. The special-education teacher has the task of trying to look at the world through the eyes of the delinquent child and trying to discover wherein that child's interpretation of life situations is erroneous on account of his failure to see the whole picture.

Such a program of special education will not herd truants and delinquents together in mammoth colonies; it will not treat all these socially handicapped children alike; it will not assume that delinquents are all inherently bad; and it will not assume that severe physical punishments and a regime of military discipline are basically the only means of curbing the behavior of delinquent children. Such a program will provide each child with an opportunity to put into practice those actions that are a part of and help to develop good citizens; it will curb the reaction of each individual only to the extent necessary to enable him to master the handicap from which he suffers and which has been the occasion for placing him in the special school or class.

A Chance to Enjoy Life.—If the saying, "Ignorance is bliss," indicates a state of enjoyment, then we do not need a program of special education in order that the handicapped may enjoy life. If, however, enjoyment comes from the increased ability to understand the points of view of others, and in an increased ability to understand and interpret the phenomena of life that go on about us continually, then a modern program of education is necessary. Since it is with this latter point of view that we agree, it is necessary that the education provided handicapped children be such that for them more extensive meanings will become attached to the incidents of life that surround us.

The understanding that can be secured may be quite limited, as in the case of feeble-minded children; such a handicap, however, should not deprive the child of the degree of understanding that might be his. If he can be taught the few simple words necessary for reading simple primers, give him that, though to teach even so much may take several years. The child should not be deprived of any training that holds the possibility of giving him some pleasure, however minute.

Training Necessary to Offset Handicap.—A very common suggestion is that the children should be so trained that their handicap will be offset to the maximum. In conforming to this suggestion, some schools insist that the blind be given musical education; others suggest piano tuning, shorthand, typing, weaving, and chair caning. The deaf are encouraged to become printers or factory workers in jobs where hearing is unnecessary. Cripples are encouraged to take training for jobs where they will not need to move about much.

The suggestion has an essential truth in it; to educate a blind boy to teach in the public schools would be unwise, without informing that boy of the great difficulty he will face in attempting to secure a position. Even though the lad be an exceptionally capable teacher, his handicap will be a decided hindrance in public school work. If the boy can enjoy a vocation where his handicap will have little or nothing to do with his success on the job, that will be an ideal arrangement.

On the other hand, the road to teaching should not be definitely closed to the blind if they choose to enter it with a clear understanding of the difficulties they will encounter. If the deaf boy likes the printer's trade and has some ability in that direction, he should be encouraged; his education should not, however, be limited to the specific skills of the trade, but he should be given an opportunity to catch the essential spirit and meaning of life by contact with as many of life's situations as possible; this contact may be direct or vicarious and any course may be used to contribute toward this end.

If workers in special education will not forget that their task in educating handicapped children is governed by the same general principles that govern the education of normal children, some of the errors that have been made in the past in educating them will not be repeated. Handicapped children are the same qualitatively as normal children; they have the same traits and characteristics. They differ in that they do not have a given trait or characteristic to the same degree; the difference is quantitative, not qualitative.

6. SUMMARY

Modern psychology shows that individuals differ greatly in any mental, social, or physical trait which it has been able to measure. These differences at the extremes are great, so great in fact as to permit us to call these extreme deviates exceptional children. The program of education adapted to the education of such exceptional children is called special education.

The need for special education is not clearly understood. Some even suggest that the work to be done for handicapped children is not properly educational work but a public welfare responsibility. The costs of a program of special education are heavy and scant evidence is available concerning the effectiveness of such work. All these things tend to delay the development of an adequate program in special education.

Workers in this field need help if handicapped children are to be cared for properly. Teachers in regular schools can help materially in reducing the problem of special education, if they have a proper understanding of their own job. There is need in administrative offices for principals and superintendents of schools who have understanding. As soon as they have acquired full information of the requirements, officials of the kind needed are usually available. Finally, the public must have similar information, and it is the responsibility of the administrator to see that the public is informed.

Principles underlying a program of special education do not differ from those that guide our work in a regular program of education. More emphasis must be given to a study of the child in the light of his handicap, but essential principles are the same; the child is to be studied in such a way and the courses are to be so taught that the child will grow from a more or less self-centered individual into one who is able not only to adjust satisfactorily to his present environment but to find ways and means of adjusting to whatever new situations may face him in the future.

Problems and Questions for Discussion

1. What is an exceptional child? What is the field of special education?

2. What relation has the concept of individual differences to special education?

3. What is the challenge of special education? Who is challenged and why?

4. Why is the acceptance of the challenge of special education so generally delayed?

5. Why is special education usually so costly?

6. What conditions must exist before the challenge of special education can be fully accepted?

7. Debate the thesis, "Handicapped children should be educated at public expense."

8. Should special education be administered by a department of public welfare of the state?

9. In what ways can classroom teachers aid in reducing the problem of special education?

10. Would the principles governing special education differ from those governing the regular program of education? If not, why not? If so, explain.

11. What do we mean by saying, "All children should have an equal educational opportunity"?

Selected Bibliography

Amoss, Harry, and DeLaporte, L. Helen. *Training Handicapped Children*, pp. 1–16. The Ryerson Press, Toronto, Canada, 1933.

Discusses special education as the normal development of the larger movement to "completely democratize education." It is an effort to meet the problem of individual differences at the elementary-school level.

Berry, Charles S. *White House Conference* 1930, pp. 231–245. (Report on Special Classes by Chairman of Committee.) The Century Co., New York, 1931.

Reports the number of handicapped children in the United States and gives the recommendations of the White House Committee on means of providing special education more adequately.

BODE, BOYD H. *Fundamentals of Education*, pp. 1–21. The Macmillan Company, New York, 1922.

Sets forth his general concept of what is meant by education; he identifies it with growth and then amplifies upon the meaning of growth.

SCHEIDEMANN, NORMA V. *The Psychology of Exceptional Children*, Vol. II. Houghton Mifflin Company, Boston, 1937.   460 pp.

Considers 10 types of unusually exceptional children, such as the Enuretic, Albinistic, and Eidetic.

TERMAN, LEWIS M. *The Measurement of Intelligence*, pp. 78–104. Houghton Mifflin Company, Boston, 1916.

Discusses the significance of various intelligence quotients; the quotients are classified.

White House Conference, *Special Education: The Handicapped and The Gifted*, pp. 3–16.   The Century Co., New York, 1931.

Presents in detail the size of the problem and gives a summary on training of teachers, costs, legislative shortcomings, prevention, and recommendations.

PART I

EDUCATION OF THE SOCIALLY HANDICAPPED CHILD

CHAPTER II

THE LOCAL PROBLEM

1. INTRODUCTION

Ignore children who are physically sick and they will probably die; ignore the mentally sick and they may starve to death; ignore the socially sick and they will spread a contamination of unrest and vice to vast numbers of their associates. No other group of handicapped children presents so many serious problems to society as do the socially handicapped; this chapter and the six that follow will discuss ways and means of more adequately caring for and educating members of this group.

Definitions.—The term "socially handicapped" includes children who are usually spoken of as truants or delinquents and who often are educated in parental or farm schools or in state industrial schools; it also includes those who are potential truants or delinquents. This term is used for the sake of avoiding others that have in the popular mind a very unsavory connotation; also, because of the current usage of the terms "physically handicapped" and "mentally handicapped." Youths classed as socially handicapped have been unable to accept and live up to the social standards set by society; they may be intellectually bright and physically fit, but they refuse to conform to the customs and modes of their group. This includes youths who are truants, who are incorrigible, who steal, and who get into sex difficulties; these groupings may be subdivided into an incalculable variety of specific acts.

The local problem of caring for the socially handicapped is defined as including more than whatever is done in local special schools or classes; it will include the work that the regularly constituted authorities of the school system could and ought to be doing in order that the number of children requiring the special school or class may be reduced. It would seem quite important that the problem should be thus broadened. Unless this is done the emphasis of the entire program will be remedial, from the point of view of the local district, whereas it should be preventive. The re-educating of these children becomes a very discouraging problem when none of the obvious steps are taken that might prevent much of this social maladjustment.

19

Guiding Principles.—In the process of locally caring for and educating the socially handicapped, three principles can well apply.

1. Every plan proposed should be evaluated in terms of whether or not it will help the child in question. If this principle is observed, there will be no place for punishment for the sake of punishment. A child will not be punished because he stole; he will be punished only if punishment seems, after a study of the youth, to be what he needs. Regular teachers, child clinics, special teachers, and trained house-fathers and housemothers will work out with these youths a program of study, work, and recreation that will re-educate them in their social outlook upon life and society.

2. The home should be preserved as long as such preservation will not interfere with the operation of principle 1. If this second principle is in operation, a child will not be sent to a permanent boarding school as long as there is a possibility that he can be helped while still kept at home.

3. There is also the idea that society must be protected. If the other principles have operated, we have the best possible assurance that society is being protected. If, however, when everything has been done that trained workers can do, there are still no signs of improvement, it may become necessary to lock up certain individuals. There is the argument, of course, that such a procedure might be best for them; it might perhaps save them from a death penalty, later, for committing murder.

2. HISTORY

The principles just discussed are of recent origin. McDonald[1] characterizes the change in attitude toward juvenile delinquency by four successive aims: the punitive, the deterrent, the reformatory, and the socioeducational. A few schools at present may be operating under the last of these aims, but many are not. A comparatively recent survey[2] of 30 institutions showed aims that varied seemingly from the mere punitive to the educational. Some institutions practically ignored the individual and others based treatment wholly upon individual diagnosis.

Houses of Refuge.—Local communities in this country did not attempt to make special provision for socially handicapped children until about the close of the first quarter of the nineteenth century.

[1] Robert A. F. McDonald, *Adjustment of School Organization to Various Population Groups*, p. 17, Teachers College, Columbia University, New York, 1915.

[2] Miriam Van Waters, "Where Girls Go Right," *Survey* (May 27, 1922), Vol. 48, pp. 361–376.

The first local institution to be established was the House of Refuge founded in New York City. Judge G. S. Adams of the Cleveland Juvenile Court, writing in 1913, says that "On January 1, 1825, the New York City House of Refuge formally opened its doors."[1] Within the next 3 years a house of reformation was established in Boston and a house of refuge in Philadelphia. During the following half century a number of other cities organized truant schools; these schools were under city control. Some of them were later discontinued and a few were transferred from the control of the city to the board of education.

Local Public Schools or Classes.—Just what local public school system was the first to organize a school or a class for these children we do not know. There is evidence that Cleveland had a school for incorrigibles as early as 1876 and that Chicago had a class for delinquents in 1892. Providence and New York City organized similar classes in 1893 and 1895, respectively.[2] In 1898, Indianapolis, Philadelphia, and Newark, N. J., organized classes for truants and delinquents. A recent survey[3] showed 41 cities in the United States that reported day schools and classes of this type, enrolling 5,462 pupils. In 1937, the Office of Education reported 45 cities, enrolling 12,653 truants and disciplinary cases.

Public education did not take much interest in such special schools or classes until compulsory-attendance laws came into being. These laws forced all children of given ages into school; this brought to the attention of educators a group of children who for various reasons had previously been eliminated at an early age; they had not, therefore, caused the schools any trouble. In the last decade of the nineteenth century, the problem of helping these children was new only in the sense that it could no longer be ignored; it had always existed.

Parental Schools.—The parental school came into existence at the opening of the twentieth century, according to McDonald; the first school he reports is the Chicago Parental School, which was opened in 1902.[4] Hiatt says, "The first real parental school was established in Boston in 1896. Buffalo followed in 1897, the Jefferson

---

[1] GEORGE S. ADAMS, *Recent Progress in Training Delinquent Children*, p. 491, Report of Commissioner of Education for the Year Ended June 30, 1913, Vol. I, 1914.

[2] MCDONALD, *op. cit.*, pp. 18–22.

[3] ARCH O. HECK, "Special Schools and Classes in Cities of 10,000 Population and More in the United States," p. 5, *U. S. Office of Education Bulletin* 7, Washington, D. C., 1930.

[4] MCDONALD, *op. cit.*, p. 22.

Farm School at Watertown, N.Y., was founded in 1898, the Seattle school in 1900, and the Chicago Parental School in 1902."[1] Hiatt also reports that Kansas City, Baltimore, Spokane, and Tacoma started schools in 1907 and 1908. Both writers report that the New York school opened in 1909. In recent years a number of cities have established similar institutions, but they are not always called parental schools.[2]

3. SPECIAL LOCAL ORGANIZATIONS THAT OPERATE

Special local organizations have been set up in various communities with the announced purpose of doing what they can to remedy cases of social maladjustment as these cases come to them from the regular school organization. They also represent a unique piece of preventive work, in that they attempt to keep the children sent to them out of state institutions; they thus constitute an attempt upon the part of the locality to solve its own problems. These local organizations consist of special classes, day schools, and the parental, or twenty-four-hour, school.

The Special Class.—Special classes for truant or delinquent children are frequently called disciplinary classes; problem children of a regular school building are segregated for special schoolwork. The class is under the supervision of the building principal, just as the regular class groups are under her supervision. A survey[3] in 1929 shows that only 16 states had cities of 10,000 population and over which reported classes of this type; since the reports came from 96.6 per cent of all cities in the United States of this size, it would seem fair to conclude that this type of class is unknown in approximately two-thirds of the states.

Of the 762 cities of 10,000 population and above according to the 1920 census, 736 reported in this study and only 28 cities had organized the special class for the socially handicapped child. Only five cities reported an enrollment of 100 or more in their classes; the median enrollment for the 28 cities was 33 pupils. Obviously, the special class does not accommodate a great many of our problem children. The total enrollment for the 28 cities in all their special classes was 1,950. If the special class proves to be an excellent method of dealing with this type of child, there will be an abundant opportunity to develop it.

---

[1] JAMES S. HIATT, "The Truant Problem and the Parental School," p. 20, *U. S. Bureau of Education Bulletin* 29, Washington, D. C., 1915.

[2] They will be described in detail in Chap. IV.

[3] HECK, *op. cit.*, p. 5.

The Day School.—The day school, sometimes called a "disciplinary school," is not common. The survey just mentioned showed, out of 736 cities reporting, only 16 that had schools of this type. The movement to establish such schools, however, is not dead; two of the very best have been organized since the date of making the survey.[1] Three cities in California and three in Ohio reported schools of this type; the remaining 10 cities were scattered throughout as many states.

There were 26 disciplinary schools reported in this survey, their total enrollment being 3,512. The largest enrollment for a single city was 788, the smallest was 25, and the median for the 16 cities was 113.5. Schools of this type are caring for more youths than classes are; they also seem to be increasing, whereas similar evidence about the classes is not reported.

Parental Schools.—Parental, or twenty-four-hour, schools are not maintained in many cities. Reporting in 1924, Horn says there were in the United States 11 cities with a population of 100,000 or more that had established the parental or residential school. In my own study, only eight of Horn's group of cities reported parental schools; in addition to these, 15 other cities, varying in size from 15,197 to 1,950,961 population, reported parental schools; 8 of these 15 had a population of 100,000 or more, according to the 1930 census.

Observations.—The scarcity of special day classes and schools and of parental schools for taking care of the socially handicapped youth suggests that most immediate aid must for the present come from those agencies of the regular school organization that have contact with pupils.

The use of these regular school agencies is to be recommended as the most nearly ideal method of dealing with truancy and delinquency. This method allows the work to be done at less cost; it includes all the advantages that come to the child from having had overt acts prevented; it keeps all children having fit homes with their families; and it tends to prevent the setting apart of certain groups of children with the label *bad* attached to them.

Not all children, of course, can be handled by the regular school agencies, and special arrangements have to be made for the more extreme deviates. Much more emphasis, however, ought to be placed upon the necessity of the public schools' solving their own problems, instead of having extreme emphasis laid upon the necessity of establishing a vast number of special agencies to care for the socially handicapped.

[1] For a description of some of them, see pp. 37–43.

4. REGULAR SCHOOL AGENCIES NOW AT WORK

A Teacher at Work.—This teacher secured from the principal's office at the opening of each semester the office record of each of his pupils. The record was a good starting point for discovering the interests and abilities of the members of his class. The principal provided the mental tests and allowed the teacher to give them. The home of every child who presented the possibility of being a problem was visited during the first week of school; previous teachers were consulted; and numerous personal contacts were made, both in and out of school, with the small group of potential problem children.

The following illustration is typical. The teacher discovered a fifth-grade boy who had an I. Q. of 120; the lad, while not a truant or a delinquent, had caused previous teachers considerable trouble; the school record showed that the boy's attendance record had been far poorer the year before than at any other time in his school career. When asked why he had been absent so much, the boy in a half-defiant manner said he "hated school."

Conferences with the parents and with earlier teachers and incidental talks with the boy showed that he liked machinery and was proud of his gang leadership. Instead of the boy's being held to regular classwork, he was given special assignments; he was not required to take part formally in class discussion but was free to enter it whenever he felt that he had a contribution to make or whenever he wanted help from the discussion. Bill was also allowed to spend two half days per week in a junior high school shop class; this privilege was given with the understanding that he was to keep up with all of his regular schoolwork.

The boy never again so much as approached being a problem; his adjustment took time from the teacher's leisure hours, as it was a harder task to solve the difficulties involved than this short sketch might imply. Bill's treatment was typical of the teacher's approach to all problem cases; some were worse and some were much simpler. This teacher never had to report a child to the principal's office. When all teachers are trained for and interested in this type of pupil management, we shall doubtless find a lessening need for special classes and schools for the socially handicapped.

A Principal at Work.—One principal enjoyed basketball and played with the boys. When they asked to be permitted to play evenings, the principal called a group meeting of all interested in basketball and invited several others who had an interest in clubs of various kinds. A suggestion was made that it hardly seemed fair to plan just for the boys who cared especially for athletics. They were asked if they could not devise some plan that would make it possible for all boys to participate in some type of activity.

The discussion that followed eventually resulted in the organization of a club that included many more than simply those concerned with basketball. Some had a special liking for cabinetmaking; some wanted to read in the library, since they had no books at home; some enjoyed free play in the playroom; some liked dominoes, rook, and many other simple games and wanted a room that could be properly equipped for that purpose; others enjoyed dramatics and wished to put on a play occasionally; and still others needed a place where they could do extra work on one or more of the regular school subjects. Officers were elected; rules governing membership were formulated. The boys were made responsible for the care of the building during the hours of meeting. Only members were permitted to attend. Those who refused to abide by the rules were summarily dropped from the membership roll.

It soon became an honor to belong to the club. Since the boys were made responsible for all that happened in the building on meeting nights, they realized that new members must take admission to membership seriously. The club grew in popularity. The boys enjoyed their evenings at school and were not slow to tell their friends; these friends were made to feel the importance of proper behavior if they were to become and remain members.

The principal reported that, whereas his district had formerly had from 12 to 15 cases before the juvenile court each year, during the past year not one of its boys had come before the court. This principal is confident that his club has been the means of preventing such truancies and delinquencies.

Not all schools need this program, but it would seem that every principal ought to study his district, know the needs of his boys and girls, and then plan a program that would supplement the wholesome out-of-school activities already in existence within the district. If his pupils have no chance for home reading and study and if the community does not provide it, then a program of greater utilization of the school plant would be decidedly in order.

A Fieldworker in a Rural Community.—This fieldworker was responsible for a county school district. She was handicapped in her first year's work because she had to assume responsibility for all attendance problems as well as other problems; the county superintendent took over the attendance cases that she was unable to handle without going into court. She was occasionally embarrassed in her work by teachers and principals who were used to the ways of a "hard-boiled" attendance officer. Her first year was a program of education for teachers and parents alike. Her procedures represented nothing new in high-type field service; what she did can be found described in any one of a half dozen books describing the activities of visiting teachers.

It has seemed worth while to mention the activities of this worker because she served in a rural school district, was confronted with almost all possible hindrances, and yet was able to show material reductions in nonattendance, in the number of youths brought before the juvenile court, and in the number of other problem cases it seemed necessary for her to handle. A recounting of her success in dealing with individual cases would materially strengthen the case for the newer type of field service.

A Fieldworker in a City School System.—This man was head of the attendance workers of a large city system. He insisted that, in order for him to improve attendance, he must know the name, age, and address of every child of school age in the city. He, therefore, kept a continuous census which enabled him at the opening of the school year to contact immediately all children who had not yet enrolled. This quick check brought increased respect for attendance workers and tended to reduce the number of pupils who needed to be brought before the juvenile court for nonattendance.

He instituted a preliminary and unofficial court of his own, to which parents were called before any case of nonattendance or truancy was taken to the juvenile court. He secured the permission of the juvenile court to send a formal summons to parents and children to appear before this unofficial court. The fieldworker agreed to send to the court only those cases demanding drastic action; in return, the court agreed to co-operate in seeing that drastic action was taken. As a result, very few cases went to the juvenile court, whereas formerly it had been overcrowded with cases from the schools.

This procedure had distinct advantages. In the intimacy of the informal court, parents came to realize that the school was their friend. Sometimes a principal or a teacher, obviously in the wrong, was given an opportunity to correct his error without the publicity of a court's criticism. The child realized that the attendance office wanted to do what was right, and this had considerable to do with changing his attitude toward schoolwork. Of greater importance was the fact that so few of these children were given court records; most of them were kept free from being labeled truant or delinquent.

Pupil-personnel Departments at Work.—With great profit one might review at this point the task of capable workers in each of the agencies doing pupil-personnel service. Such a résumé would only re-emphasize principles already clearly shown in this section. It would show (1) that we are seeking to help the child, not punish him; (2) that we realize there are specific causes for the problems with which we are dealing; (3) that we must know the child, his home life, play life, and school life if these causes are to be discovered; and (4) that any program for helping the child must first seek the removal of these causes.

5. THE LOCAL PROBLEM

We are now able to point directly to the problem that every locality faces in dealing with its socially handicapped children. The regular school organization, through its teachers, principals, and pupil-personnel agencies, may so operate as to reduce to a minimum the number of youths who need to have a special educational program provided for them; it may ignore those youths entirely and by refusing to do either preventive or remedial work send great numbers of social degenerates to the state for permanent keeping; or it may ignore the preventive measures but spend a great amount of money locally on special schools and classes for the socially handicapped. The local problem is to know where to draw the line between preventive and remedial procedures.

6. SUMMARY

The socially handicapped are defined as truants and delinquents. Special attention was not given to them until about the opening of the twentieth century. Methods of dealing with them should emphasize prevention. The chief aim should be to make treatment individual. The detailed study of each youth is therefore emphasized.

More attention to this group must be demanded of local school people if prevention is to be successful. The teacher, the principal, and the superintendent have an opportunity to prevent many of our present cases of truancy and delinquency. The local schools need to develop various pupil-personnel activities much more adequately before the best of preventive work can be done. The local problem is to decide just how far local workers can go in developing a preventive program and at what point in such a program it would be more expedient, socially, to cease depending upon individual efforts and to provide special education—local special schools and classes.

Problems and Questions for Discussion

1. Who are the socially handicapped?   Argue, pro and con, the appropriateness of the term.

2. What aims should govern our work in educating the socially handicapped?

3. Trace the development of the community's work of educating the socially handicapped.

4. Describe in detail your answer to a teacher who asked, "What can I do to help problem children in my class?"

5. What can the regular school organization do to prevent truancy and delinquency?   Illustrate.

6. What are pupil-personnel agencies?   How are they related to this problem of preventing delinquency?

7. What types of special education does the locality provide for the socially handicapped?   How widely are they provided?

8. What is the big problem each local school system faces in dealing with the socially handicapped?

Selected Bibliography

GRAVES, FRANK PIERPONT. *The Administration of American Education*, pp. 138–161. The Macmillan Company, New York, 1932.

A brief account of modern attendance and census service which will help combat truancy and delinquency.

HEALY, WILLIAM, and BRONNER, AUGUSTA F. *New Light on Delinquency and Its Treatment.* Yale University Press, New Haven, 1936. 226 pp.

Emphasizes the new orientation in dealing with delinquency. We are to shift from seeing it as merely wrongdoing to seeing it as a form of human behavior aimed at better satisfying the individual's needs. We, therefore, seek causes as a means of changing the behavior rather than putting "a stop" to wrongdoing.

HECK, ARCH O. "Pupil-personnel Services in the Public Schools," reprint of articles in *Educational Research Bulletin*, Ohio State University, Vol. 14, pp. 57–61; 98–102; 155–161; 182–191; 214–216. Ohio State University, Columbus, 1935.

An account of pupil-personnel services available in cities of 100,000 population and over throughout the United States; these services are modern means of preventing truancy and delinquency.

HECK, ARCH O. *Administration of Pupil Personnel*, pp. 1–124. Ginn and Company, Boston, 1929.

Describes modern attempts at improving school attendance and thereby preventing truancy and delinquency.

HECK, ARCH O. "Special Schools and Classes in Cities of 10,000 Population and More in the United States," pp. 3–6. *U. S. Office of Education Bulletin* 7, 1930.

Detailed reports concerning cities of the United States having parental schools and local classes and schools for the socially handicapped.

HORN, JOHN LOUIS. *The Education of Exceptional Children*, Chap. VIII. The Century Co., New York, 1924.

A discussion of the extent to which American city schools made special provision for incorrigibles and truants and an analysis of their characteristics.

McDonald, Robert Alexander Fyfe. *Adjustment of School Organization to Various Population Groups*, Contributions to Education 75, Chap. III. Teachers College, Columbia University, New York, 1915.

Gives a brief history of the development of provisions for the juvenile delinquents, unruly and truant; it also presents data concerning the status of these provisions in 1913.

Reeder, Ward G. *The Fundamentals of Public School Administration*, pp. 301–326. The Macmillan Company, New York, 1930.

Discusses briefly several important pupil-personnel services that are necessary if truancy and delinquency are to be prevented.

Van Waters, Miriam. "Where Girls Go Right," *Survey* (May 27, 1922), Vol. 48, pp. 361–376.

Discusses adjustment and education as the purposes of correctional schools for girls, rather than punishment. Her ideas are based upon the visitation of 30 state correctional schools.

17691

CHAPTER III

THE SPECIAL CLASS AND SCHOOL

Violation of the accepted social code immediately stigmatizes the violator. The placement of youths in schools for the socially handicapped automatically brands them as violators. The school can say that such children are not bad; that they are there to be helped, not punished; that circumstances they are powerless to control have forced the violation; and still they suffer from the stigmatization attached by the general public to being placed in such a school. This attitude will probably continue to exist as long as we wait until the code has actually been violated before placing the child in the school and as long as none but violators are placed in it.

When and if preventive measures of the kind suggested in the previous chapter are put into operation, we ought to be able to select children needing the special-education program before overt acts are committed. This would make possible a better school placement of pupils. Children needing the special program could be singled out and placed just as a child is placed in the academic curriculum instead of the commercial. When this goal has been achieved we can hope to disperse the stigma now attached to attendance at schools and classes for the socially handicapped.

1. THE SPECIAL CLASS AND ITS PROBLEMS

The special class is the simplest of all proposed plans for educating the socially handicapped and can be put into operation in the smaller school districts.

The Purpose.—Actually, the special class is often organized in order to relieve regular teachers of their "bad" boys. These boys have demoralized instruction; they have been centers about which all class problems seemed to focus; they have been a constant source of irritation to the teacher. A strong arm is needed, it is said, to deal with such youths and so a special class is formed for them; they are to be taught to respect authority, and the strong arm of authority falls upon them. The reason why the child misbehaved is ignored.

The special class should be organized in order to make it possible for the special teacher to discover the causes of the child's misbehavior

30

and, having a clue to the causes, to make it possible to work with him in an attempt to remove those causes. The aim of such a program of individual study and work is the elimination of the child's social handicap so that he can adjust normally to the social group.

Organization and Administration.—The plan under which such classes may be organized is very simple. If the schools are large, with enrollments of 1,500 or more, each could organize its own class; the class would be a regular part of the school unit and the teacher would be directly responsible to the principal. If the school is small, it could co-operate with near-by schools for the purpose of organizing a special class.

Such a class should not be called the disciplinary class or the "bad" boys' class; it might be given a special name; it might be known as a placement class, finding class, or some other appropriate designation; it is not necessary, however, that it be given a name; it could be known as Mr. Jones's class and thus related to a given teacher, just as any regular class is.

If several classes are organized in the city, there should be a supervisor of the work, to function in the same way as the supervisor of music or of art. He is to be responsible for developing, with his special teachers, a tentative program which he will undertake to "sell" to the superintendent and the principals. When and if they accept the program, the principals carry it to the special-class teachers, and the supervisor aids the principals in putting it into effect. This avoids conflict in authority between principal and supervisor.

Admissions.—The admission to these special classes should be by placement and not by commitment. Every teacher in the building or buildings from which pupils may come should clearly understand that the worst offense they could commit would be to threaten a boy with commitment to or placement in the class. Placement is not to be thought of as a matter of punishment; it should mean an opportunity for more complete diagnosis and more scientific treatment.

A pupil will be placed only after the teacher and the principal have reached the limit of what they can do for him in regular class-work; all means available to the teacher will have been used in trying to make an adjustment; when these have failed the pupil will be placed in the special class. This will be done with the understanding that the placement is made in an effort to help the pupil find in school that program which will be of most value to him.

Size of Class.—The size of class depends upon many factors; if the pupils are of approximately the same grade, if they require little or no home visitation, and if the teacher is an understanding person, approximately a normal pupil load can be carried. These conditions, however, rarely exist in so ideal a combination. The problem facing the teacher is usually so complex that a small pupil load is imperative if these youths are to be helped. An average teacher load of 15 to 20, in the usual school situation, should represent the maximum. If the load is so lightened that the teacher has time to work with and help individuals to the extent that they can be returned to regular school classes, this lighter load will be the more efficient.

Curricula.—The schoolwork to be done should depend upon the group. If it contains pupils of normal ability or better and if their troubles are not those of curricular maladjustments, the regular course of study may be quite satisfactory. This would simplify the problem greatly. Many of these special-class pupils, however, will be problems of just such a maladjustment. Every class should be so organized, therefore, that its pupils will have an opportunity to try out various courses; this can be managed if all classes are located in large schools where a variety of courses would be available as a part of the school's regular program of studies.

Teachers.—Too frequently teachers have been selected because they were strong and "hard-boiled." Such a selection, as has already been indicated, is based upon a false notion of their function; they are not instruments of punishment, but social doctors, whose duty it is to diagnose and to help effect a cure.

The first essential in such a teacher is that he be interested in working with pupils who are socially nonadjusted and who need the help that an understanding teacher can give. He should be an alert, capable individual of the "he-man" type, not a sentimentalist, and yet with enough of the dreamer in him to help him see the possibilities within the make-up of each pupil with whom he makes contact.

The teacher, ideally, should have a rich background of social, professional, and technical study. He needs to know the subject matter he is to teach, something of case work and social investigation, the laws of social psychology, and the possibilities for educational adjustment. He will be not only a teacher but a social worker, a psychologist, and a social diagnostician all in one.

Recreation and Spare Time.—The activity of the pupils outside school hours may nullify all the teacher's efforts within the school. The social attitude of a child can hardly be changed by 6 hours in school, if no adjustment is made in his conditions of living during the other 18 hours. In describing the classes in Detroit, the annual report of the superintendent says, "Because the matter of recreation and spare time seems to be a large factor in the problems of the ungraded boys [socially handicapped],[1] efforts have been made to have all become active members of organized boys' clubs. During the year ending June, 1930, over half of the boys joined some club. There are twenty-five clubs receiving these boys, many of them at churches or settlement houses."[2] No program that may be worked out for a given pupil can be considered complete unless it makes some provision for recreation and for the proper spending of his spare time.

2. DAY SCHOOLS AND THEIR PROBLEMS

The Name of the School.—No title should be used that refers in any way to the type of child placed in the school. A title such as "truant school," or "disciplinary school" stigmatizes it and the pupils who attend it. Titles of that kind are relics of the day when youths who defied social customs were considered bad and when it was thought necessary to punish the bad if they were to change their ways. We know today that they are not inherently bad, but they have not had a proper opportunity.

"Industrial school" is a title that does not properly describe the day school. At least, it ought not to do so. The title emphasizes the industrial courses to the exclusion of the regular academic work and therefore gives a wrong impression of what is taught. The latter type of work will be just as important as the former, and sometimes may be even more important.

Recent practice tends to name these schools just as all regular schools are named, with no thought of attempting to describe their function. The Montefiore School in Chicago, the Moore School in Detroit, and the Thomas A. Edison School in Cleveland are examples of this tendency.

Organization and Administration.—If one or more day schools are to be organized within a city school system, they should be under the supervision of the local school official who is responsible for the special-education program,[3] just as an elementary school or a secondary school is under the supervision of the officials responsible for those types of education.

If the city maintains both a school and classes, the school may be established in that section of town where most of the socially handicapped are located; the classes would then be distributed where the

---

[1] The author's explanation in brackets.

[2] *Eighty-seventh Annual Report of the Detroit Public Schools,* p. **77,** Detroit, Mich., 1930.

[3] The details of such a proposed local organization are shown in Chaps. VIII and XXXI.

need exists.   This would reduce costs of transportation.   The school may, however, receive only those pupils who are suspected of having curricular maladjustments; it could then be located so as to be reached conveniently from all parts of town, without being too far from the center of present and future pupil groups and without being located in too unfavorable an environment.   In this case, the special classes would contain no pupils with serious curricular maladjustment and the likelihood of their being able to help the pupils would be greatly increased.

Admissions.—The same principles should apply to the admission of pupils to the school as apply to the classes.   It will do no harm to repeat that (1) placement, not commitment, should govern admissions; (2) no pupil should be threatened with being sent to the school; and (3) the decision to place a child in the school should be based upon the fact that all evidence indicates that such placement will be of material benefit to him.

At the time of admission the school has a very important function to perform.   The youths who enter have been serious behavior problems in their home schools.   If they are to profit more in the new associations than in the old, better adjustments will have to be made. Such adjusting requires accurate and detailed knowledge of the pupil; it requires that a confidence be built up between the new pupil and at least some one individual in the new school; it requires close personal supervision of the pupil by someone in whom he has confidence; and finally it requires such a placement of the youth within the school that he will be happy and contented.

Many schools claim to do this type of service for all pupils admitted. When their work is examined carefully, however, it is often discovered that the extent to which this work is carried is no more than a half-hour or an hour interview.   No abiding confidence between pupil and interviewer is built up and no understanding of the pupil's difficulty has resulted.   The effect of the interview may even be to produce an actively hostile rather than a merely indifferent attitude in the pupil.

There are being developed at present plans for scientifically studying these youths as they enter the special schools; records from previous schools are received; interviews with the boy are held, not by numerous individuals, but by the person responsible for the receiving of all new pupils; tests are given to determine special mental and educational ability; and an opportunity is allowed the pupils to visit all departments.   The office of the receiving teacher is headquarters for the youth, and he returns to report his findings at given intervals. Through questions and discussion the teacher tries to help the new arrival analyze and discover his own difficulties. Between them a program of work is set up. It may take a half day or again it may take a week for the new arrival to find himself. Rarely does he fail to get an entirely new conception of his relationship to and responsibility for the social group. The satisfactory handling of this first step more often than not proves to be the beginning of the end of the new pupil as a disciplinary problem.

Discipline.—Discipline should be no different from that which would be found in the best of our elementary or secondary schools. Courts and paddles are just as much out of place as they are in the regular schools. A system of penalties and credits whereby the length

ILLUSTRATION 1.—A day in student court at the Thomas A. Edison School, Cleveland. The student court in action.

of stay is determined would be most vicious, in that it implies commitment to the school as a punishment for wrongdoing; no such purpose should govern the conduct of these schools.

The following principles are illustrative of the type of discipline that ought to govern local schools for socially handicapped pupils. (1) "Compulsion will hold a child's body in school, but his mind must be kept there by interest." (2) "There are stronger forces within than without a child, to impel him to right behavior." (3) "The problem of child control is chiefly one of helping him to discover values he has not seen before." (4) "Rewards are better than punishments. Punishments may stop a child who is going in the wrong direction. They have no value in leading him in the right direction."[1] Some schools have student courts. Illustration 1 shows a student court in action at Cleveland's Thomas A. Edison School.

Curricula.—One of the causes of poor social adjustment is lack of curricular adjustment in the regular school, due to lack of interest or to lack of ability. These special schools, therefore, provide a variety of offerings. Academic work is given in English, mathematics, science, and social science. Industrial arts courses include woodwork, general metalwork and sheet metalwork, general mechanics, furniture finishing, weaving, printing, sign painting, upholstering, applied and illustrative art, cartooning, and basketry; other courses are gymnasium, music, and assembly. The gymnasium work includes gymnastics, athletics, games, swimming, physical examinations, and corrective exercises.

One school says that the aim is to cover the minimum requirements of the regular course of study; in addition, the pupils have woodworking, sheet metal, machine work, printing, and electricity. All the boys go to the shops; they make the kitchen equipment, such as supply closets, tables, benches, trays, and drainers. The boys are taught to cook; this course has interested them in catering and in restaurant and hotel work. They wash and iron their own caps and aprons. Gardening is an important part of the work of the school; the vegetables raised are cold packed by the boys for winter use.

Teachers.—The requirements for teachers are the same as for those of special classes.[2] Teachers in the arts and trades should be expert workmen as well as good teachers. Too frequently teachers are secured who are excellent craftsmen but who have little or no ability as instructors; the reverse situation is just as bad, since the pupil can have little respect for the teacher whose workmanship is inferior.

Guidance.—Every teacher in the school will have a share in the work of guidance. If a receiving room is operated, the initial work is begun by the receiving teacher. His work must be closely followed up by classroom teachers. Each teacher should act as counselor for a given group of students; each would have individual plans for keeping constantly in contact with his guidance group. This is imperative if worth-while guidance is to be given, since the receiving teacher will not be able to work with the entire school. If the school has a receiving teacher, he may be the co-ordinator of all guidance work and should

---

[1] *Eighth Annual Report of Thomas A. Edison School*, p. 6, Cleveland, Ohio, 1929.
[2] See p. 32 of this chapter.

hold himself ready to advise with the teachers constantly with respect to individual pupils.

If the teachers are to serve as counselors, the records of pupils should be readily available to them for inspection and study. Each teacher should endeavor to know his boys intimately. He may arrange hikes, picnics, excursions, or tours of inspection; these should be managed by the student group, with the teacher setting a situation that will supply the pupil drive necessary to carry the project through successfully.

Placement and Follow-up.—The weakest point in the entire program of developing local schools for the socially handicapped is that of placement and follow-up. We have too little knowledge of what happens to pupils after they leave the school. It is, of course, difficult to set up machinery that can reach out and keep track, over a period of years, of all youths who have been in the school.

There are certain steps, however, that officials in these schools might take. They might ask principals of schools to which they transfer pupils to report informally each semester. They ought, upon the basis of their study of a given pupil, to assist in his placement in industry, if he is not to continue his schooling; this aid ought to give them a right to expect the boy to report to his counselor or school principal from time to time. Someone in the school should be responsible for keeping an alphabetical file of former students; as data are received by any member of the staff about former pupils, they should see that such material reaches the teacher in charge of the file. Some individual should be given the task of following up all former pupils, every four or five years. Data concerning the youth's residence and position, and his apparent success in making a satisfactory social adjustment would be pertinent.

3. DESCRIPTION OF SELECTED DAY SCHOOLS

The Montefiore School.[1]—This school was organized by the Chicago Board of Education in September, 1929, under the direction of Edward H. Stullken, as the result of a survey he made of how larger cities were caring for and educating their truants, delinquents, and incorrigibles. It is located in a modern, fireproof building with ample shop and laboratory equipment, at 655 W. 14th St.; it is approximately in the center of the district that it serves and is provided with adequate transportation facilities. At the present time it has 625 pupils and

[1] Based upon second and seventh annual reports of the school, plus typed material received from the Office of the Superintendent of Schools late in 1936.

28 teachers. The day is 6½ hours long and the year 12 months. Recently, grades 9 and 10 have been added, although they are offered on an elementary level.

The school has a nurse, dentist, psychologist, psychiatrist, personnel officer, special speech teacher, remedial reading teacher, and truant officers, doctors, and carefully selected classroom teachers. The program of the school is enriched and modified so that it fits education to the needs of problem boys. The boys spend approximately three-eighths of their time on academic subjects, four-eighths in various kinds of activities, and one-eighth in organized recreation. Considerable emphasis is given to the proper placement of the boy when he enters. Mental, educational, aptitude, and personality tests are given; physical examinations are made; conferences with the boys are frequent; and all possible data concerning the past life of each youth are assembled. In every case placement depends upon the findings; moreover, each boy is encouraged to have a real part in deciding that placement.

The school has electric and metal shops, equipped with machine lathes, motor generator, drill press, grinder, benches, and gas and electric furnaces; there are two well-equipped wood shops and a household mechanics workshop. A print shop offers training to those interested in learning the fundamentals of printing. Three general science laboratories supplied with aquariums, germinating tables, demonstration tables, and necessary apparatus are provided. Mechanical drawing and freehand drawing are not neglected. A regular art studio is available to those who have ability for art. A reed- and rug-weaving laboratory also forms a part of the equipment. Not the least interesting is a library which co-operates with the Chicago Public Library. The school has an adequate auditorium. Much attention is being given to remedial reading.

All boys who attend Montefiore are provided with a hot noonday lunch at the expense of the board of education; since its introduction, the general health of the boys seems to be better, their attitude has improved, and the problem of apparently pauperizing those unable to provide their own lunches has been removed. The general result has been a better school spirit.

The school has shower baths with an attendant in charge at all times. The bathers average 50 a day. The school is furnished with two directors of recreation, who spend all their time teaching boys how to play and how to get along together successfully in groups. In addition to the gymnasium, a game room assures ample opportunity for play of all kinds. This playroom also serves as the boys' clubroom.

The Montefiore, the Moseley (which is a similar school for colored boys), and four truant rooms in the elementary schools constitute what might be considered a screen through which certain truants, delinquents, and incorrigibles are separated out and kept out of court. That the screening process is successful is indicated by the fact that during the school year 1935–36 more than 1000 boys who otherwise would have been referred to the juvenile court were rehabilitated and kept in the special schools, or returned to their home schools.

The Moore School for Boys.[1]—A day school for the socially handicapped boy has been in continuous existence in Detroit since 1925. It

ILLUSTRATION 2.—Science class in the Moore School, Detroit. A study of birds and small animals is in progress.

was first housed in the Clay School, then in the Roberts, and finally in the Moore, where it has been since 1934. Previously, practice in educating truant boys had alternated between classes and a central school. Classes were first organized in 1899; from this date "the work passed through several stages, isolated classes, central school, isolated classes again, then housed in the building with the juvenile court, disbanded again into isolated classes,"[2] and in 1915 placed under the supervision of the attendance department. In 1921 the department

[1] Taken from pp. 1–6 of bulletin material entitled "Ungraded Schools and Classes," received from the office of the Director of Special Education of the city of Detroit in January, 1937.

[2] *Ibid.*, p. 1.

of special education was made responsible for the supervision of such classes or schools.   In addition to the Moore School, there are seven ungraded rooms near the outskirts of the city and located in six different school buildings.

The school has an auditorium, clinic, gymnasium, library, lunchroom, metal shop, print shop, wood shop, and nine classrooms.   The boys have 2½ hours of academic work and a shop period daily; they have an auditorium and a library period twice a week; there is work in art, music, and science; excursions are arranged.   See Illustration 2, showing a science class studying birds at the Moore School.   The boys assist in the lunchroom and some of them elect the cooking courses.

Though they come from almost every part of the city and some from a considerable distance, an effort is made to assist them in happily occupying their leisure hours after school, on week ends, and during vacation time.   Recreation centers, boys' clubs, church activities, public libraries, and Y.M.C.A. facilities are called to their attention. Visits are made to some of these centers and boys are introduced to the activity as well as to those responsible for it.

The most unusual feature of the work is the provision for a free summer camp; it is called Boytown Camp and is located on Mill Creek near Chelsea, Mich.   In the summer of 1936, there were 200 boys in attendance.   Local authorities hope that the camp "will be financed so that it will become an established unit in the education of these boys."[1]

The Thomas A. Edison School.—This school was first organized in Cleveland in the fall of 1921; it was organized to care for "truant and problem boys."   Its aims and program in the past have not differed essentially from those of the schools just described.   Beginning with the school year 1938–39, however, a change in general policy took place.   Instead of having boys entered in the school by the attendance department, enrollment has been placed upon a voluntary basis.   It is no longer a school for "bad boys," but a prevocational school for boys of the public schools who cannot find in regular elementary and secondary schools a program of studies adapted to their needs.   Under the former plan, boys have been known to commit an offense deliberately in order to be allowed to attend Thomas A. Edison; now they can be transferred to the school whenever they discover that it best meets their needs.

This is just the school that is necessary if special education for the socially handicapped is to become preventive in the sense of providing

[1] Director of Special Education, Detroit, *op. cit.* p. 6.

youths with a school program adapted to their needs, before they have committed that overt act which in the past has caused them to be placed in the special school. In order to make it truly preventive, however, there must be a thorough understanding of the school's objectives by all members of the regular school staff; they must give their pupils sufficient study so that they are in a position to give guidance. If they have 50 youths who need this new Thomas A. Edison, these 50 should not only be given an opportunity to attend but they should be given assistance in deciding upon the transfer.

ILLUSTRATION 3.—A foundry class at work, Thomas A. Edison School, Cleveland.

The program offered does not differ essentially from the one provided by the school during the past few years. There are academic courses and shop courses; there is a great amount of pupil study and diagnosis; programs are adapted to individual pupils; and there is a constant attempt to develop health, moral, and social ideals. Illustration 3 shows a foundry class at work.

4. A CITY PROGRAM

Los Angeles[1] started its first "special school" for truant boys in the spring of 1906, some 2 or 3 years after California adopted its

[1] Data received directly from the Office of the Superintendent of Schools of Los Angeles in January, 1937.

compulsory education law; that fall, 2 more "special schools" were opened. In May, 1917, special classes were organized in 8 different school buildings, enrolling 156 pupils under 11 full-time and one half-time teachers. By 1923, there were 11 schools with 11 teaching principals, 24 other teachers, and 714 pupils. In 1936, there were 9 schools with 3 teaching and 6 full-time principals, 60 full-time and 1 part-time teachers, and 986 pupils.

At present there are 8 special schools and 14 branch centers. There are 5 elementary and 3 secondary schools. Of the branch centers, 10

ILLUSTRATION 4.—Boys' shop class, Union Avenue School, Los Angeles. One of the City's welfare classes.

are for boys and 4 are for girls; 6 of those for the boys are elementary and 4 are secondary. The centers are located throughout the city for "socially maladjusted pupils who have been transferred from the regular schools." They are called "Welfare Schools and Centers." Illustration 4 shows a shop class in one of these centers.

The entire program is most modern and social. Causes are important to the workers; they recognize the need for knowing well the youths whom they are trying to help. Offenses mean little to them except in the light of all the background data related to the offenses.

5. WHY AND WHERE ORGANIZE LOCAL SCHOOLS

Why Organize?—The preceding descriptions should help to clarify for the reader certain reasons for the organization of local schools. A brief enumeration of these reasons may be helpful. (1) The school with its larger enrollment makes possible a much better classification of pupils. (2) The larger enrollment makes it possible to provide a great variety of course work which usually is not provided by the regular schools and which these pupils must have if the best work in adjustment is to be done. (3) Better guidance and study of the individual can be provided. (4) If the regular schools begin to assign pupils to the special schools before overt acts against society are committed and on the basis of pupil needs, this special school will soon be accepted as a specialized school of the regular school system, just as are trade schools and commercial schools in many city systems. (5) With a system operating thus, the present stigma attached to local classes and schools for the socially handicapped will be removed. (6) When operated in this way, the entire city program of dealing with the socially handicapped will begin to emphasize and demand real preventive work.

Where Organize?—Obviously, a large city of 100,000 population or more could organize one or more such special schools. What, however, is to be done for rural districts, villages, and smaller cities where the emphasis is upon an academic school program? The small school unit has found it impossible to provide a greatly differentiated program of study. These units exist because of difficulties of transportation; children cannot travel far over mud roads. But such roads are being rapidly eliminated. When and where this has taken place, the basic foundations have been laid for the development of large school units and for a greater differentiation in the school program. Such a situation will make possible the provision of special schools for the socially handicapped that will reach every school district in the country. Every county could then have one or more special schools by co-operating with the smaller cities of the county.

6. SUMMARY

Special schools and classes for the socially handicapped at present have a stigma attached to them. This may be removed by placing in the school a pupil who needs help, before he commits the overt act. Problems of organizing such schools and classes involve (1) determining the purpose, (2) proper naming, (3) the manner of admitting, (4) size, (5) the program to be offered, (6) the kind of teachers needed, (7) discipline, (8) guidance, and (9) follow-up. Classes can be organized at once in smaller places; they can be made very effective. Schools have a distinct advantage over classes on account of the number enrolled. The larger cities only are now organizing schools of this type. Cleveland, Chicago, and Detroit have schools that are typical. Ultimately, such schools should be available in some way in every district.

Problems and Questions for Discussion

1. Why does stigma seem to be attached to attendance at a school or class for the socially handicapped?

2. Is it possible to remove the stigma now attached to these schools and classes? Give reasons for your answer.

3. What are the problems involved in organizing these schools and classes? What seems to you to be the solution of each?

4. Argue the relative advantages of the class and the school as a means of educating the socially handicapped.

5. Describe one or more special day schools other than those described in the text.

6. How widely should day schools be established? Defend your answer.

Selected Bibliography

DOLTON, ISABELLE. "Laying the Foundations for the Enrichment of Adult Life among the Problem Youth of Chicago," p. 113. *Proceedings of the National Education Association*, 1930.

A description of Chicago's experiments in trying to cope with truancy and delinquency in the public schools; considerable attention is given to an account of Chicago's newly developed Montefiore School.

Montefiore School, Chicago. *Second Annual Report of Montefiore School*, 1930–31, Board of Education, Chicago, 1931.

Describes the aims of the school, types of problem boys received, special activities carried on, and academic work and shopwork provided.

Montefiore School, Chicago. *Seventh Annual Report of Montefiore School*, 1935–36, Board of Education, Chicago, 1936. 107 pp.

Presents a brief historical sketch, describes the numerous activities of the school, presents data descriptive of the pupil group, and outlines a few new proposals for the further development of the school.

Thomas A. Edison School, Cleveland. *Eighth Annual Report of Thomas A. Edison School*, Board of Education, Cleveland, Ohio, 1929. 60 pp.

Presents a brief history of the school; describes the process of enrolling the boys; outlines in some detail the activities provided; and outlines plans for the future.

Thomas A. Edison School, Cleveland. *Eleventh Annual Report of Thomas A. Edison School*, 1932–33, Board of Education, Cleveland, Ohio, 1933. 37 pp.

Presents a brief discussion of the needs of problem boys, of the effects of the depression, of the work done in the auditorium, and of what becomes of the Edison boy.

CHAPTER IV

THE PARENTAL SCHOOL

1. INTRODUCTION

Given social agencies are frequently too deeply impressed by the sense of their own importance. The public schools are by no means exempt from this generalization. Much was said in the preceding chapter concerning the worth of special day schools and classes for combating and preventing truancy and delinquency. Considerable emphasis was given to the idea that truant and delinquent children can be helped by properly adjusting their school program. The suggestion is important. We must remember, however, that there are other social agencies that may be influencing the child far more than either regular or special day schools; we must remember that the child is in attendance at them only 5 to 6 hours out of a total of 24.

We find pupils whose basic difficulties lie not within the school but outside. A boy's home relations are unsatisfactory or even vicious; his gang life may be controlling him; or the general atmosphere of his community may be unnerving him. If such be the case, nothing the school can do is likely to solve the problem until these conditions are remedied; often the school is utterly helpless to better such conditions. In these cases it becomes imperative that the youth be removed entirely from such out-of-school influences.

There are two ways of meeting this problem. (1) The proper authorities may place the youth in a foster home in new surroundings. (2) The locality may, if it has not already done so, organize what has come to be known as the parental school.

Definition.—The parental school is an institution for lodging, boarding, and educating those socially handicapped youths who, because of unfortunate out-of-school conditions, cannot be successfully treated by local public education officials. It is generally located upon a farm some distance from the city. It has many variations. The parental home in Detroit,[1] for example, makes no claim of being a parental school in the sense that the term is used here. The same

---

[1] Mimeographed bulletin published by the Department of Attendance, Detroit, Mich.

types of boy are received and they live at the home, but they attend the public school that is located closest to them. The "24-hour" school,[1] which has been advocated by certain Californians, is for truants and delinquents and is very similar to the parental or farm school. The farm, however, does not seem to be an essential feature.

The Purpose.—The ultimate purpose is to develop a program that will help the socially handicapped child to find himself; its advocates are not interested in punishment for punishment's sake. These youths are no more hardened than are the boys in the local special class or school. Both the special day school and the parental school take children of the same general type as far as abilities, capacities, and character traits are concerned. The dividing line depends upon social and home conditions. If the youth is from a vicious home or if he is linked up with a degrading gang in the home neighborhood, he needs the constant supervision and care given by the parental school. He is not necessarily worse than the boys in the day school. The parental school is no place for the hardened vicious criminal type; his place is in the state industrial school or the state reformatory.[2]

2. ADMINISTRATIVE CONTROL

Two Methods.—The parental school is managed on two distinctly different bases. One places the institution under the control of the city council and makes the board of education responsible for providing teachers and school supplies; the other places the school entirely under the control of the board of education.

The advocates of the first method argue that the management of an institution where children are housed and fed is not an educational problem and that the money for these functions should not come from the educational budget; the institution, therefore, should be under the control of civil, not educational, authorities.

The advocates of the second plan insist that the fundamental function of the parental school is educational; they insist that the whole program of caring for the child must be so related to the strictly school program that the whole life of the child as he lives it at the school is his education; they claim that any attempt to separate his life into two compartments by having a few teachers responsible for his academic training and another group of individuals, under separate control, responsible for the remainder of his activities is setting up

---

[1] JOHN WESLEY HARBESON, "The Twenty-four Hour School," *The Journal of Delinquency* (March, 1926), Vol. 10, pp. 330–333.

[2] The purposes of the special class should be reviewed at this point (the class and the school have similar purposes). See pp. 30–31.

barriers to the successful handling of the problem of assisting him to return to normal social reactions.

An Argument for Educational Control.—Administratively, of course, a dual system of control is never desirable; there is too much opportunity for friction. Politics, moreover, has a chance to work havoc with the school's program of work. The city council more generally represents the professional politician than does the board of education. The professional politician must give attention to certain cliques and gangs; failure to do so may mean a blocked political career. The members of boards of education more generally represent the citizens' group and have no higher ambition than to help provide the best schools possible; a defeat for office is not a serious matter.

Since the fundamental objective of the institution is that of providing a setting in which these youths can be re-educated socially and since social, academic, and trades education must go hand in hand to be effective, the administration of the institution ought to be directed by educational authorities rather than by civil authorities. The time ought to come when all institutions whose primary function is educational will be controlled and administered by educational authorities.

3. ADMINISTRATIVE PROBLEMS

Admissions.—Some schools require court commitments for all pupils admitted; other schools permit court commitments only as the last resort. The latter method is much more in keeping with the idea that the purpose of the parental school is educational and not penal. A recommended procedure is that boys and girls be designated for transfer from a public school to the farm school only after a careful study. If the principal, the social investigator, and the psychological bureau believe the transfer to be to the advantage of the pupil, it should be recommended. In this case, the child's parents are consulted and the reasons for the transfer are given. The parents are then asked to approve the proposal. Their approval is necessary, since such a transfer in schools involves taking the child temporarily from his home. Usually a fair presentation of the facts is the only thing needed. The parents see the necessity for the transfer and give their approval. This procedure has been used successfully.

Occasionally parents are defiant; then, if the case is clear and no doubt about the necessity of the transfer exists in the minds of the transferring authorities, the parents are told frankly that if they do not consent voluntarily, the case will be taken before the judge of the juvenile court. The reasons for the proposed change are again set forth and it is explained that if the child is sent voluntarily, no court record will exist against him; very few parents, it has been found, continue to withhold their consent. As a result, very few court commitments need reach the parental schools. This procedure may well find universal acceptance as soon as the parental school is accepted as strictly an educational institution.

The School Plant.—There are two methods of housing pupils in parental schools. In one, which is called the congregate system, the entire plant is under one roof in the form of a huge institution; in the other, the cottage system, the school plant is composed of a number of buildings and the children live in groups, each group having its own cottage.

There is a distinct trend in favor of the cottage system. The new school for girls in Cleveland is on the cottage basis; the Cleveland Farm School at Hudson, Ohio, houses its boys in cottages. These schools have relatively small cottages. The capacity of the cottages reported by various cities ranges from 15 or 20 to approximately 50 occupants.

If the original object of the cottage system is to be retained, it would seem necessary to keep the enrollment as small as possible; a group of from 10 to 15 is perhaps ideal. The housefather and housemother can hope to develop an informality in the cottage life that will approximate home life. Such an ideal is not attained when 50 or more pupils are housed together. They then cease to have a cottage.[1]

Schooling.—The minimum essentials of the regular course of study are usually required of all pupils. As in the day schools, industrial work is given considerable attention; basketry, carpentry, electricity, laundry, masonry, plumbing, printing, weaving, and woodwork are taught. Many parental schools find that the boys are interested in farming, gardening, stock raising, and poultry raising, in addition to shopwork. Much of the housework is done by the pupils; cooking and baking are taught; and occasionally the boys wash and mend their own clothes. There is an opportunity for every boy to be interestingly employed; this fact alone is all that is needed to help many of them adjust satisfactorily.

Placement in the Schools.—Upon his admission to the farm school, some provision should be made for the proper placement of the boy. In some cases, the school has a receiving cottage. At the Bellefontaine Farm, maintained by the city of St. Louis, there is such a cottage. The principal or some teacher of the school talks to each boy on his arrival; the faculty come to know every boy by name.

[1] For a definition of the "cottage," see pp. 71–72.

Their theory is that if a boy goes wrong there is some unnatural influence at work; they try to find out what the influence is. Following up a medical examination by a competent physician, an effort is made to cure defects and set the youth right physically. After careful study he is classified as: (1) the nearly innocent child of tender years; (2) the mischievous, yet easily tractable; (3) the more hardened; or (4) the vicious type, needing most stringent methods of discipline.

Discipline.—No one thing denotes the fundamental policies of the school any more quickly than its disciplinary procedure. The superintendent may theoretically hold the most modern ideas relative to the management of socially handicapped children and actually allow disciplinary practices that negate his entire theory. As would be expected, procedures vary considerably. The disciplinary measures at the Spokane Parental School are described by the city superintendent thus: "The boys learn discipline through a well-regulated daily program. The merit system and the self-government plan are used. The boys' court works well. It is held each Friday."[1]

The Chicago Parental School does not use corporal punishment. Deprivation of play, granting special privileges, longer stay at school, and silent moments are the usual means of disciplining. The school works "upon the plan that it is more profitable to spend time upon training the good that is found in everyone, rather than to attempt continually to repress the bad."[2]

Writing in 1915, McDonald asserted of the parental school that "Discipline is usually military in form, and drill instruction is given by boy officers under direction of family officers. Penalties consist in deprivation of privileges."[3] This type of discipline is not being used in some of the more recently established schools and one hopes that it will soon have no advocates among those interested in the development of parental schools.

Costs.—Costs vary greatly; it is difficult to determine how comparable reported costs are. The items included are not always the same. Hiatt in 1915, before school costs had reached their recent peaks, reported that the average was $243.35 per pupil per year. The Bellefontaine Farm School for 1919–20, reported a per pupil cost of $385.95. This did not include interest on the original investment or depreciation. Superintendent Milliken estimated the per pupil cost

[1] *Fifty-fifth Annual Report of the Spokane Parental School*, p. 16, Board of Education, Spokane, Wash., 1930.

[2] O. J. MILLIKEN, *The Chicago Parental School Review* (1927), p. 13.

[3] ROBERT A. F. McDONALD, *Adjustment of School Organization to Various Population Groups*, p. 22, Teachers College, Columbia University, New York, 1915.

of the Chicago Parental School at $580; the state paid $190 per pupil.[1] These figures indicate how necessary it is that some accounting be made of the effectiveness of parental schools in remaking boys and girls.

4. RESULTS SECURED

The Follow-up.—An attempt to follow up and thus keep in touch with all pupils who are transferred from the school is probably the most ineffective part of the program of dealing with the pupils of the parental school. , A given child may make such excellent adjustment that he is transferred back to the public schools; however, those who have had a part in helping him make his new adjustments then lose sight of him and have no part in helping him to carry these adjustments over to his old home environment.   Consequently, old life situations bring to the surface past reactions with such force that the youth all too frequently responds as formerly to them; as a result, he is soon a candidate for transfer back to the parental school.

This special school might have fieldworkers attached to its permanent staff; these workers would have firsthand contact with all pupils in the school and would keep in touch with them after they were transferred back to the regular school.   An even better arrangement would be to permit each large elementary school its own fieldworker. She would then keep in constant contact with all the pupils of her school who were transferred to the parental school; upon their return, she would be present to assist each child as needed.   She would be responsible for all follow-up work.

Effectiveness.—Only by the best of follow-up procedure can the effectiveness of these schools be adequately determined.   At present the question of effectiveness is an unsolved problem.   We have many opinions.   We have numerous instances of individuals who have left the parental school and who have made good for a short period.   We need more information as to how many make good over a long period of time.   We also need to know, in respect to those who really make good, whether attendance at the parental school worked the change, whether a chance meeting with some one of influence in the school did it, or whether the youth's continued development physically and socially did it, irrespective of the parental school.[2]

---

[1] O. J. MILLIKEN, "Cost of Chicago Parental School," *Chicago Principals' Club Reporter*, Vol. 19, pp. 7–9.

[2] Detailed data concerning the effectiveness of parental schools might well be collected by some foundation interested in the prevention of truancy and delinquency.   These schools have been in operation for many years.   Many believe

5. SELECTED PARENTAL SCHOOLS FOR BOYS

Bellefontaine Farm. [1]—The Bellefontaine Farm is the successor of the old house of refuge in St. Louis, which was first given permanent quarters in 1860; the city council authorized the establishment of a house of refuge in 1853, but it was housed in temporary quarters until 1860. In 1905, the board of education took charge of the school department and the name of the institution was changed to Industrial School. In 1910, the mayor appointed a commission to draft a new plan for caring for delinquent children; in 1912 the city council passed an ordinance covering the recommendations of this commission and the mayor appointed members of the Board of Children's Guardians to manage the new school for delinquents.

In September, 1915, three cottages were ready for occupancy and 90 boys were transferred from the old industrial school. In 1918 two more cottages were ready; two more were opened in 1919; and the last two were occupied in 1920. The Industrial School was then abandoned. The nine cottages cost approximately $25,000 each; they are two-story brick buildings. This new school, the present Bellefontaine Farm, is located on a high bluff on the south banks of the Missouri, just a few miles from the juncture of that river with the Mississippi. It consists of 359 acres and is beautifully located, overlooking those two magnificent rivers.

Thirty boys can be accommodated in each cottage. They take their meals at the cottage, with their foster parents; the boys eat at tables for four. In each cottage, there are two small dormitories. They are on the second floor at either end of the building. Between these rooms are bedrooms for "Dad" and "Mother," as the boys call their foster parents, and for the teacher of the cottage. The boys have their lessons in a large room that is used as a living room in the evening. There is no central school building.

No walls surround the grounds; no watchman is hired to guard the boys; no bars are in front of windows; and no locks fasten the boys in at night. "Bellefontaine Farm is the incarnation of judicious freedom and lenience." [2] Beautiful driveways run through the grounds. Shrubbery, trees, and flowering plants make the farm a very attractive place to live in. All buildings for the farm stock are

they are very effective; if they are, we need more of them for our smaller cities and rural territories. The foundation could serve the socially handicapped very effectively by making such a detailed study.

[1] "Bellefontaine Farm—St. Louis Home for Delinquent Boys," *St. Louis Facts, A Municipal Record* (July, 1924), Vol. 1.

[2] *Ibid.*, p. 5.

in the rear and away from the river; these consist of a barn, a tool shed, a garage, silos, hen houses, and pig houses.

The boys take care of the cows; they milk, separate the milk, make the butter, and keep a record of the amount of milk and cream from each cow. Any cow that does not pay for her keep is sold. The boys similarly take care of the hens and keep a record of the efficiency of each hen; any hen that is not self-supporting is eaten. The boys are not only taught carpentry but are allowed to put their knowledge into practice; they build almost everything that is to be built about the farm. Vegetable gardens and fruit orchards are cared for by the boys, who prepare the products for the table and can some for winter use, as well.

For 3 hours each day, the year round, each boy from seven to sixteen years of age attends school at his home cottage. He can continue academic schoolwork through the ninth grade. The course of study parallels that used in the city schools. Part of the boys have schoolwork in the forenoon and vocational work in the afternoon. Other groups reverse this order. The vocational work includes farming, gardening, dairying, bee raising, poultry raising, fruit raising, shoemaking, keeping a greenhouse, and numerous kinds of shopwork, such as cabinetmaking, carpentry, clothing production, and automobile, sheet-metal, and farm-implement repair shops. Listing these types of work falls short of telling the true story; one must see the fruit, vegetables, chickens, grain, and flowers raised and the milk, butter, honey, shoes, clothing, and furniture produced to gain a true picture of what the boys do.

During playtime the boys are under the supervision of a physical education instructor, but they are free to do very much as they like. They play tennis, baseball, football, basketball, or soccer. Each boy takes a shower daily; during the summer he takes two a day. There is a clinical inspection daily and a physical examination twice a week. The boys arise at 5:30 A.M. in the summer and at 6:00 A.M. in the winter. The registration at the close of the year 1936 was 199, of whom 81 were white and 118 were colored.

The principal of the school has immediate supervision over the boys. He has had excellent training. Through a study of the individual, interesting work, physical care, social development, religious training, development of leisure-time interests, and vocational training, these youths are helped in making the needed social adjustment. A recent report shows that many of the boys are making good upon transfer from the school; it does not present exact data with respect to all youths in attendance. We need such facts.

The Boys' Farm at Hudson.—The city of Cleveland has established a parental or farm school near Hudson, Ohio. The farm is under the control of the municipal government; the board of education provides teachers and all school supplies. Hiatt claims that Cleveland had the first boarding school for truants; it was founded in 1850, but was in no sense a farm school.[1] The present farm school was not established until 1903.

A central school building is provided. Every boy of compulsory school age, six to sixteen, is required to attend school; if he is sixteen and has not passed grade 7, he must attend. If the boy has completed the grade 7 and is sixteen years old, he may be released from school attendance to work on the farm. In addition to an opportunity to work in the fields and in the gardens and to care for the livestock, the boys are given instruction in manual training, carpentry, general metalwork, molding, baking, laundry work, all kinds of power-plant activities, electrical work, dairying, animal husbandry, and automobile mechanics.

On the farm proper the boys help with the planting and harvesting of corn, oats, and wheat; they take part in the haying; they care for the horses, cows, pigs, and poultry. Gardens and orchards are planted and cared for. There is healthy outdoor activity for these boys throughout the year. All this work is done under close and constant supervision by farmers who are on the staff and in the employ of the school.

The boys live in small cottages housing from 15 to 20 boys each. Meals are served in the cottages, although the food is prepared and cooked in a large central kitchen. A housefather and housemother in each of the cottages supervise the boys. The administration building and the hospital are modern buildings. A full-time nurse is employed to care for the hospital. Medical service is provided by physicians on part time.

The superintendent of the school does not believe in a militaristic regime; his plan is to allow the boys a great deal of freedom in play; he considers that boys who have all but lost their self-confidence and self-respect are more "sinned against than sinning"; he feels that they need someone to help them understand themselves and to assist them in discovering and adjusting their difficulties. Several visits to the farm—some of them unannounced—have always found a number of the boys at free play, with no direct supervision. The boys have the run of the farm. They know their hours of work and know that they must take care of their assigned chores.

[1] JAMES S. HIATT, "The Truant Problem and the Parental School," p. 20, *U.S. Bureau of Education Bulletin* 29, Washington, D. C., 1915.

In these visits, the feature that was of greatest interest was the perfect freedom with which the boys would approach the superintendent to ask questions about their work, to make requests for privileges, or to report some fact in which a boy was personally interested. In the attitude of these boys no feeling of suppression or of fear was in evidence. All of this is indicative of the fact that the staff is maintaining a school and not a penal institution.

6. DESCRIPTION OF A PARENTAL SCHOOL FOR GIRLS

Parental schools for girls do not differ greatly from such schools for boys. Perhaps, the cottage ideal is stressed more; manual labor on the farm is confined chiefly to gardening, caring for hens, and housework; shopwork is in the form of handcrafts; and the care of livestock is not made one of the girls' responsibilities. In other ways such schools for boys and for girls are quite similar. For this reason, only one parental school for girls will be described.

The Blossom Hill School.—Blossom Hill is under the control of the Cleveland municipal authorities. The Cleveland Board of Education provides school supplies and teachers. The school is located on a beautiful elevation south of Cleveland, about 17 miles from the center of the city. From the front lawn, one can see on a clear day wooded hills and valleys for miles and miles in the distance. One would have to look far and wide to find a more beautiful spot. The visitor on his first trip there never fails to remark on the beauty of the landscape.

The welfare department, the attendance department, and the juvenile court co-operate in the transfer of girls to this school. All are taught to cook and to serve, but the program of work is adjusted to each girl. The academic work of the regular city schools is adapted to the vocational training provided. An attempt is made to enable every girl to become economically independent.

There are four cottages housing 15 girls each; two teachers are resident in each cottage. Every cottage has a sun porch, a dining room, a living room cosily furnished, and a kitchen with all electric equipment. The kitchens and dining rooms are classrooms for the students in the cooking and serving classes. The second floor has a room for each of the two teachers and a private bath. The three bedrooms house five girls each.

The administration building houses the offices and living rooms of the superintendent and other members of the faculty, in addition to the dispensary; the schoolrooms are located here. A fifth cottage, with a dormitory for 13 girls, is located on the third floor. In the basement is an assembly room where entertainments and church services are held.

7. THE BERKSHIRE INDUSTRIAL FARM

A Private School.—The Berkshire Industrial Farm is a private institution, but recent accounts of it illustrate so well some of the idealism of parental schools that a brief description does not seem out of place. It is supported chiefly by private subscription, but parents who are able are asked to pay. "The Farm was founded in 1886 by Mr. and Mrs. Frederick Gordon Burnham."[1] It is located in the Berkshire Hills, 150 miles north of New York City and 30 miles east of Albany. The Farm contains 1,100 acres of farm, garden, pasture, and timberland. Until December, 1925, the capacity was 120 boys; at that time it was increased to 150. Each cottage can house 30 boys.

Ages of Admission.—Boys twelve, thirteen, and fourteen years of age are admitted. The management believes that these boys need a long period of training if social habits and attitudes are to be changed; it believes that they should be self-supporting on leaving, so that they need not return to their old home surroundings. The school provides a 2-year course in trades. This makes it possible for every boy to complete the work by sixteen years of age; he can then go to work supporting himself. The program of work and the method of management at the school are not adapted to older boys; it is necessary, moreover, to refuse admission to boys over fourteen if they are to benefit from the 2-year course and be ready to leave the school at sixteen.

The Admission.—Border-line defectives are not encouraged to enter and feeble-minded are not admitted. Boys with physical conditions that hinder them from taking part in routine farm work are not admitted. Admission takes place any time during the school year. The boy is kept in isolation for 2 weeks upon admission to the school; during this period he is examined physically and mentally; his behavior and personality are studied by the staff of the clinic and the school nurse. The new entrant is told why he is at the school. It is made clear that the school is "for boys who have found it difficult to adjust in other schools, their homes, or their neighborhoods." The school, he is shown, is not a penal institution, but neither is it a "fancy boarding school."

Management.—The Farm is controlled and managed by a private board of directors, which hires the staff that has direct management of

[1] "Facilities for Treatment of the Problem Boy," p. 7, *Bulletin* 2, Psychiatric Research Department, Berkshire Industrial Farm, Canaan, N. Y., January, 1927.

the Farm.   This staff is composed of a superintendent, an assistant, a business manager, house matrons, teachers, physicians, psychologists, clerical help, and manual help.   Each cottage of 30 boys has a matron, or a matron and a master.

Instruction.—Academic instruction is in charge of teachers who have done college and normal school work; these teachers have shown a particular interest in the handling of problem children.   The instruction is individual; placement is based upon the work a pupil does, his previous record, and the results of standard tests.   Schoolwork is made very informal and no child is forced beyond his ability.   This informality and individual attention discover in pupils interests that were never brought to light in the regular school.   Many boys complete with some success the eighth-grade Regents' examination and go on to high school.   In the 1930 report the superintendent stated that eight boys had "shown such good scholastic ability that we are sending them to a neighboring high school."[1]   Shopwork, farm work, and recreation similar to other parental schools is provided.

Disciplining.—"The discipline most usually practiced and which is most effective is the deprivation of special privileges and the occupation of free time by work for which the boy under discipline is not paid."[2]   The boys at Berkshire are paid for all their work during free time at the rate of 10 cents per hour.   Free time is defined as "all time before school in the morning and following school in the afternoon."   Each boy is thus permitted to earn money; he uses it to buy clothing and luxuries.   This plan, the superintendent believes, teaches "the principle of earning" what one gets.   There is no physical restraint; doors are not locked; roll is called at intervals during the day; at night a watchman is on duty.   Boys are free to come and go within prescribed limits.

Placement.—When the boy leaves, an attempt is made to place him in a new city if his old home environment was poor; if not, the follow-up agent for the school prepares the home for the boy's return. The agent finds the boy a job and helps him secure new jobs as occasion seems to demand.   Social agencies in the community are contacted for the purpose of making a closer follow-up.   It is reported that 83 per cent of the boys discharged over a 5-year period are making good.

8. EXTENDING THE CONCEPTION OF PREVENTION

The prevention of truancy and delinquency was emphasized repeatedly in Chap. II.   It was suggested that, if all regular school officials

[1] Berkshire Industrial Farm, *Annual Report*, 1930. Canaan, N. Y., Vol. 39, p. 9.
[2] Taken from material dated Mar. 13, 1937.

such as principals, teachers, and pupil-personnel workers did their work effectively, the community's need for special local schools and classes would be considerably reduced.

We have now reached the point where all the agencies described in the past three chapters may be thought of as agencies of prevention. They represent the efforts of local communities to solve their own problems without being forced to call upon the state for help. Insofar as they succeed, they prevent youths from being sent to state agencies for re-education and control and are, therefore, doing preventive work. The succeeding three chapters will deal with the state's remedial programs for those youths that the locality was unable to help adjust socially.

9. SUMMARY

Despite the work of regular school officials and special day schools and classes, some youths will find adjustment impossible as long as they remain in the old home locality. Parental schools that house them 24 hours a day are organized to care for such cases. The cottage system, control by the board of education, admission based upon transfer, discipline governed by regular school practice, and a careful follow-up of these youths are recommended. The costs are high. The Bellefontaine Farm and the Hudson Farm are typical of good parental schools for boys. Blossom Hill represents well such a school for girls. The Berkshire Industrial Farm is a representative private school. These schools aim at a readjustment so complete as to make their pupils worthy members of society.

Problems and Questions for Discussion

1. What is a parental school? Why is it needed?

2. How do the aims of the parental school differ from or agree with those of the special school or class?

3. What are the pros and cons of the two types of administrative control?

4. Enumerate the administrative problems involved in organizing a parental school. Give your own slant on how these problems should be solved.

5. What do you know about the pupils who usually attend parental schools?

6. What evidences, if any, are you able to find that show the extent to which parental schools are successful?

7. How do costs of parental schools compare with costs for other types of schools?

8. How extensively should parental schools be organized in your home state?

9. Describe in some detail one or more parental schools in addition to those described in this chapter.

10. Is it feasible to establish parental schools for girls? Defend your point of view.

Selected Bibliography

"Bellefontaine Farm—St. Louis Home for Delinquent Boys," *St. Louis Facts— A Municipal Record.* (July-August, 1924), Vol. I, No. 1, pp. 4–9.

A good description accompanied by illustration of the Boys' farm at St. Louis; describes the boys admitted, the work they do, the way they live, and the way they are studied.

Berkshire Industrial Farm. "Facilities for Treatment of the Problem Boy," *Bulletin* 2, Psychiatric Research Department, pp. 1–44. Canaan, N. Y., 1927.

Gives a good description of the aims of the farm, its organization, its growth, its activities, and its psychiatric work.

HIATT, JAMES S. "The Truant Problem and the Parental School," *U. S. Bureau of Education Bulletin* 29, 1915.

Summarizes data concerning parental schools in 13 cities; deals with costs, school plant, staff, pupils, curriculum, physical care, discipline, after care, and so on.

CHAPTER V

THE STATE'S PROGRAM

1. INTRODUCTION

"Give youth a chance" is a modern slogan in dealing with the socially handicapped; there comes a time, however, when we have to say, "Give society a chance." When all aid fails to change the individual's mode of response and when that mode of response begins to have a decidedly detrimental effect upon other individuals, society must demand for its own sake that the youth be incarcerated. Such drastic action may, of course, be the stimulus needed to change his social response; regardless of the effect, however, there comes a time when the state must act.

Definitions.—The socially handicapped who become state charges should be restricted entirely to delinquents; local districts should be able to manage all truants. A state program for these delinquent youths will include the management of schools that the state establishes for such children. It will not include the management of penal institutions that are maintained for adults, even though such institutions provide some schoolwork; it will merely supervise their educational program. It will include those steps which the state must take in order to facilitate work done by local communities for the socially handicapped.

Guiding Principles.—These principles are identical with those governing the work of the local community; there is, however, a different emphasis.

1. The nature of the institution implies that now the chief objective is the protection of society. The youth is withdrawn from the social group because his attitude is so perverse that he is having a detrimental effect upon other individuals. This principle has important corollaries, far-reaching in their effects. Punishment has been eliminated from the category of purposes. Release will depend upon the changes that take place in the attitude of the youth. For the same outward delinquency one youth may remain 2 months, another may stay 5 years, while another may be retained until twenty-one years of age if the vicious social reactions that caused his incarceration continue.

59

2. The administrative regime of the state institution should have as its goal the giving of all possible aid to its inmates. Such a principle has obvious implications, which will be discussed in this and the two succeeding chapters. These implications apply to the training and character of supervisors and teachers; to the means provided for studying the capacities, abilities, and interests of these boys; to the provisions for giving each youth the type of educational program that will best fit these capacities, abilities, and interests; and to the number of youths that each teacher or housefather and housemother must supervise.

2. HISTORY

The ideals just set forth may cause the reader who is familiar with some of our state institutions considerable alarm; he may have seen schools that fall far short of achieving these ideals. One needs only to note the great changes in the treatment of juvenile delinquents during the past century to realize that the attainment of these ideals is well within the range of future possibilities.

English Beginnings.—Judge Hall, describing conditions during the middle of the nineteenth century, tells us that children, seven years of age and above, were dealt with by the criminal law of England just as were adult criminals.

We accordingly read [he says] of a child of eight years, who had "with malice, revenge, craft and cunning" set fire to a barn, being convicted of felony, and duly hanged.[1] [He says that children charged with crimes were] flung into the same gaol to await the same trial under the same conditions as the most hardened criminal.

The child, when committed, might be perfectly innocent of any crime whatever. He had no one to bail him, and so remained in prison awaiting his trial; in the country districts it might be for many months. If, when finally arraigned before judge and jury, he was declared innocent, there can have been little innocence left after his prison experience; if found guilty, he returned to the prison to be made guilty indeed of every vice and depravity which such a hell could breed.[2]

There were, during this period, between two and three thousand children who were annually sent to prison.

England's first reformatory school act was passed in 1854, and its first industrial school act in 1857. The reformatory was for youths from twelve to sixteen years of age who had committed a penal offense, or for youths under fourteen who had been convicted before or who

[1] CLARKE W. HALL, *The State and the Child*, p. 1. The Pelican Press, London, England, 1917.
[2] *Ibid.*, p. 2.

were too incorrigible for the industrial school. The industrial school admitted two types of children under fourteen years of age: (1) children who were convicted of criminal acts for the first time and who were younger and less hardened; (2) children who, through no fault of their own, but because of bad environmental conditions, could not be properly cared for at home or elsewhere.[1]

Beginnings in the United States.—In the United States, municipalities first attempted to care for this problem by the establishment of houses of refuge or similar institutions.[2] The first state institution to care for the socially handicapped was organized in the state of Massachusetts in 1846.[3] It was the Lyman School for Boys and was located at Westborough, Massachusetts.[4] The school was named for a former mayor of Boston, the Honorable Theodore Lyman, who proposed its establishment and who gave considerable money for its maintenance. The school originally received boys under fourteen years of age and boys under sixteen who were specially approved by the board.

Ohio in 1856 opened a state school at Lancaster. The school represented an entirely new type of institution; it had no walls, was built on the cottage instead of on the congregate plan, and established what has come to be known as the family system. This pioneering effort of Ohio was copied by many other states, both in the reorganization of their schools and in the organization of new schools.

3. CONTROL

State institutions for the juvenile delinquent have not in the past been considered primarily educational; they have attempted the reformation of youths, not so much by means of a well-rounded educational program based upon detailed analyses of the needs of these youths, as by means of a program of repression and punishment. Today we believe that these state institutions should be schools where the youth is reformed by teaching him to adjust to social requirements and by helping him to meet those requirements in actual life situations.

These ideas demand that state schools should be under the complete control and supervision of the state department of education; their

[1] *Ibid.*, pp. 2–3, 57–60.

[2] See pp. 20–21.

[3] This date is in dispute. Folks, in his *Care of Destitute, Neglected, and Delinquent Children*, reports 1847. McDonald, in his *Adjustment of School Organization to Population Groups*, reports 1848. The date given in the text was reported by the trustees of the school in 1928.

[4] Report of the Trustees of Massachusetts Training Schools, 1928. Department of Public Welfare, Public Document 93, p. 3.

immediate supervision should be in charge of the state director of pupil personnel.[1]   These schools at present are too often under the control and supervision of state departments of public welfare.   This is unfortunate, because it tends to classify them as penal institutions; it places them under the control of men who do not have an educational point of view.

4. STATE FUNCTIONS

Survey of Need.—The state should be responsible for the maintenance of a continuous survey of the needs of these state schools; this would involve determining the number of children within the state for which provision should be made.   The co-operation of all local agencies interested in the socially handicapped would have to be secured.

Supervision.—If the state is to educate those youths who have become too hardened for the locality to help, it must be given authority to supervise the type of preliminary care which the locality sees fit to provide for socially handicapped children.   It should not be possible for one community to send all its juvenile offenders, regardless of type, to the state school, merely because it has refused to make any local provision for caring for them.

The state department of education through its bureau of pupil personnel should, therefore, supervise local communities in their establishment of special schools and classes for the socially handicapped; it should assist them in planning a co-ordinated program of co-operation between juvenile court, probation officers, the local pupil-personnel department, and the local public school teachers and principals to meet more effectively the needs of socially maladjusted children.

The State School.—Pupils at the state school should be entirely under the control of the state department of education.   This control is to be exercised through administrative officers which the department has selected to manage the school.   The department will set up qualifications for administrative and supervisory officers, teachers of academic subjects, shop instructors, home supervisors, and other workers.

The programs of academic study, shopwork, agricultural work, institutional help, health supervision, recreation, and individual analysis will also be under the general control of this state department.   This will make possible a unified program, which is hardly possible where the department of education is made responsible for

[1] For a description of the recommended organization, see Chap. XXXI.

academic studies only and where the department of public welfare manages all other departments.

The Follow-up and Placement.—At present there is very little evidence of what happens to these youths after they are educated. Provision for adequate care, study, and education is costly. There ought to be some means provided for securing data, over a period of several years, upon the basis of which one could judge the success of state schools in fulfilling their purposes of social readjustment.

Placement is necessarily an important part of any program of social rehabilitation. Jobs are not always available to youths who have been in a state school; a popular prejudice exists against them and is likely to continue to exist for some decades. It is necessary, therefore, to help place these youths in jobs that will make them self-supporting; if nothing is done and if they do not find work, the groundwork is all laid for their return to the unsocial attitudes that caused them to enter the school originally. The state should see to it that adequate help is given in order to make follow-up and placement effective.

Legislation.—The state department of education should take all steps necessary for securing the legislation needed to put these general proposals into effect. Until the state is willing to organize upon some such basis as has just been outlined, it cannot hope to have a unified program of caring for its socially handicapped.

5. RELATION OF THE DEPARTMENT OF EDUCATION TO PENAL INSTITUTIONS

Since the reformatories for youths from eighteen to thirty, or thereabouts, are strictly penal institutions and provide schoolwork only incidentally, they are logically placed under the control of the department of public welfare. The same is true of state penitentiaries.

It seems wise, however, to suggest that the schoolwork that is given by these institutions should be supervised by the state department of education. Two considerations prompt this suggestion: (1) the department of education has directed the whole program of attempted social re-education up to this point and is familiar with the needs of this group; (2) the department knows good educational procedure and is in the best position to aid in the development of a program of education for this criminal group. Under its direction the necessary courses of instruction could be worked out, the best experience of the public schools in curricular reconstruction could be called upon to help solve the institution's curricular problems, and good methods of certification of teachers could be devised.

6. THE PROBLEM

The big problem that the state faces in dealing with its socially handicapped children is now clearly evident; it is a problem of when and where to place responsibility in caring for and educating these youths.   How much should the local district be expected to do by way of preventing social handicaps?   When these handicaps occur, how much should the locality do before sending the children to the state? When they are sent to the state, is the problem to be considered primarily one of education or of reform?

If prevention is to be given major emphasis, the local public school system must assume the responsibility for searching out its problem children and its potentially problem children and giving them all the aid possible.   If this is to be done, it cannot be left to chance; responsibility for the program must be assumed by a specific agency.   The assistant superintendent of schools in charge of pupil-personnel work[1] is the logical man.

If the local districts are to care for all the socially handicapped until they become a menace to the social group, sufficient state supervision must be given so that practices with respect to sending children to the state school will be more uniform; also, local special schools and classes, or parental schools, would need to be provided widely enough to care for all children needing their services.   At present we find some communities doing a minimum of preventive work and having no special schools or classes; they are sending many relatively minor cases to the state school or they are ignoring them until they become so vicious that they must be sent.

If these youths under eighteen constitute a real educational problem to the state, the state school should forthwith be placed under the control of state educational authorities.   These are the problems that the state must solve in working out a complete program for helping the socially handicapped youths of the state to make satisfactory social adjustment.

7. SUMMARY

There comes a time when the socially handicapped must be taken out of the social group, for the protection of the latter.   They then enter the state school.   The program at this school should be educational, not penal.   Only in later years has the state seen fit to provide schools for juvenile criminals, in place of sending them to the penitentiary for adults.   The first state school in the United States was organized in Massachusetts in 1846.   Recent reports show at least 86 state schools.

[1] See Chap. XXXI, on organization, local and state.

The state department of education should make surveys of local needs, help to establish and then supervise local programs, control the state school, organize a program of placement and follow-up, and help in securing the passage of needed legislation. The two penal institutions are welfare agencies and only their educational program should be under the supervision of the state department of education. States now face the problem of deciding how far the preventive program shall operate, when the state shall assume responsibility for the youth, and which agency—educational or welfare—shall control these children when the state takes them over.

Problems and Questions for Discussion

1. How do the ideals governing a local program of caring for the socially handicapped differ from those governing a state program?

2. Trace in some detail the development of the state's program of caring for juvenile delinquents.

3. Should the educational or the welfare department control the state school? Why do you believe as you do?

4. What are the functions of the state with respect to educating and caring for truants and delinquents?

5. Should the state department of education have any administrative relation with the state's penal institutions? Why?

6. What is the problem that the state faces in dealing with the juvenile delinquent?

Selected Bibliography

HALL, W. CLARKE. *The State and the Child*, Chaps. I-III. The Pelican Press, London, England, 1917.

Is a brief, pointed description of conditions surrounding children in England, previous to the middle of the nineteenth century, who found themselves accused of crime; the changes taking place and the institutions later established to care for them are described.

FOLKS, HOMER. *The Care of Destitute, Neglected, and Delinquent Children*, Chap. XI. The Macmillan Company, New York, 1902.

Presents an interesting history of the development of America's institutions for caring for the delinquent.

FRAMPTON, MERLE E., and ROWELL, HUGH GRANT. *Education of the Handicapped*, Vol. I, "History," pp. 188–219. World Book Company, 1938.

Gives a brief account of the historical development of the socially handicapped.

MOSS, MARGARET STEEL. *Care of Juvenile Delinquents in Pennsylvania*, Department of Welfare, Harrisburg, Pa., 1927.

Presents a brief history of the state program for caring for truants and delinquents, with a description of present institutions.

SNEDDEN, DAVID S. *Administration and Educational Work of American Juvenile Reform Schools*, Teachers College, Columbia University, New York, 1907. 206 pp.

Gives a general survey of schools for juvenile offenders, including personnel, instruction, parole work, and results, as taken from the official reports of schools and personal visits to 12 of them. Has a good bibliography.

CHAPTER VI

THE STATE TRAINING SCHOOL

A change of name never changes the character of an institution. The latter demands a change in aims, type of personnel, and methods of managing; it requires a revolution in the whole spirit that pervades the institution. We have seen during the past century many shifts in the name attached to institutions for juvenile delinquents; it began with House of Refuge; later it was called House of Reformation, Reform School, Juvenile Reformatory, Industrial School, and State Industrial Home; now the name "State Training School" is being used.

A change in name that is not accompanied by fundamental changes in our whole conception of the institution will not change the institution. It is now said that these state institutions must be maintained as schools, that youths sent to them must be re-educated to fit them to adjust to society, and that a pupil should not be released unless this change has taken place.

What the character of this institution is ultimately to be will depend upon the state's solution of the problem of control. If control continues to be placed in the hands of welfare agencies, it is likely to remain a juvenile penitentiary—as some claim that it should be. If control is placed with the educational authorities of the state and if these authorities are granted the right to supervise the preventive programs of all local districts throughout the state, these institutions may become real agencies for reconstructing the state's socially handicapped.

1. GENERAL MANAGEMENT

The problems faced in organizing the state training school will now be considered. One of these concerns their general control and management. In addition to data concerning current practice, general policies will be suggested.

Control.—The general thesis is that these state schools are educational institutions. Their control should, therefore, be in the hands of educational authorities. The method of selecting the superintendent of the state school is indicative of the point where this control rests at present; reporting for 28 schools, Poe shows the method of

TABLE IV.—MANNER IN WHICH SUPERINTENDENTS OF STATE SCHOOLS ARE APPOINTED

Recommended by	Approved by	Number of schools
Governor of state............		4
Trustees....................	Governor.............	1
	Trustees.............	5
	Board of control......	4
Governor of state............	Board of control......	1
Board of managers............	State board of control.	1
	Board of managers....	2
Board of managers............	Full board............	1
Board of directors............		1
	County commissioners.	2
Civil service................		3
Civil service................	Welfare director.......	2
	Commission..........	1
Total...................	....	28

selecting that official.[1] The facts are presented in Table IV. In no instance are the educational authorities of the state made directly responsible for this appointment; it is possible, of course, that in some instances the trustees or the members of the board of control are appointed by the state's department of education.

Ages of Admission.—Some schools admit children at six years of age; others refuse to admit a youth over fifteen. The upper limits of 85 per cent of these schools were under twenty years of age. It is unfortunate that children six, seven, eight, and nine years of age should be admitted to any state school; the local community would be able to care for them if it were giving this problem serious consideration. If it were functioning properly, moreover, there would be little need of a state school for youths ten, eleven, and twelve years of age.

Causes of Admission.—By causes of admission we refer to those acts committed by the child which caused his placement in the state school. Before a youth can be helped, it is necessary, of course, that those who would help him shall know why he performed a given act. This point is not, however, the aim of the present discussion.

Table V shows the number of youths who were sent to 41 state schools for each of the listed charges. The list of charges, though

[1] DALE F. POE, *A Study of the Industrial Schools of the United States*, p. 62, unpublished Master's thesis at Ohio State University, Columbus, 1931. This thesis deals with a report of 44 industrial schools; with three exceptions all are state schools for juveniles. Both boys' and girls' schools are included.

informing, is much less so than one could wish. The table shows 3,877, or 38.0 per cent, reported for delinquency; delinquency, however, is all-inclusive. We do not know how these delinquencies showed themselves. Did the children steal? Were they immoral? What did they do? One does not know by such reporting.

TABLE V.—CHARGES WHICH RESULTED IN YOUTHS' BEING SENT TO STATE SCHOOLS.[1]

The Charge	Number of Youths
Arson	12
Assault	51
Auto theft	471
Burglary	372
Carrying concealed weapons	18
Delinquency	3,877
Destruction of property	36
Forgery	49
Housebreaking	196
Immorality	444
Incorrigibility	783
Intoxication	19
Larceny	292
Robbery	335
Stealing	695
Truancy	1,786
Other crimes	755
Total	10,191

[1] DALE F. POE, A Study of the Industrial Schools of the United States, p. 13, unpublished Master's thesis at Ohio State University, Columbus, 1931.

The analysis of stealing is more informing; auto theft, burglary, forgery, housebreaking, larceny, robbery, and stealing might all be classed as some form of theft. When these seven items are combined, we find that 2,410, or 23.6 per cent of the entire number, were admitted because of stealing. Aside from stealing (in all forms), truancy, incorrigibility, delinquency, and immorality, the other classifications contain relatively few cases.

These listed causes of placement merely represent the outward manifestations of an unhappy social adjustment. The school may well forget this outward manifestation and concentrate upon the situation that brought forth such behavior. Only as this is done, is there much hope of helping these youths to readjust socially.

Policies Regarding Discipline.—There are three general policies that may be differentiated with respect to discipline. The oldest of these is the penal; that the youth is bad and that badness must be punished are basic in this concept. There is, of course, the assumption that such punishment will induce the child to change his attitude toward society and its accepted standards and regulations; no attempt is made, however, to discover whether or not the punishment is likely to have such an effect.

Another policy is to establish a system of rewards. The theory is that if the child can be encouraged to act in prescribed ways by means of rewards, he will become habituated to these social reactions and will leave the school, ready to take his place in society. The psychology of such a policy might well cause the boy to respond to life situations in just the opposite manner; if the impelling motive in his conduct is solely the reward, he is well set psychologically to commit, upon release, any deed for which he is assured of a tangible and immediate reward.

A third policy is to discard all formal rules and regulations. Each child is to be handled as an individual; the attitude of the ideal home is the aim. Punishment is no longer the goal; rewards cease to play a vital part in the scheme of things; it is the individual who is the center of interest. An attempt is made to discover why the child misbehaved; the resulting action depends upon the circumstances leading to such misbehavior. The decision, as in the home, is to be in the hands of the housefather and the housemother. It is argued that a happy family group and capable, understanding house parents will eliminate most of the difficulties now found in our state schools.

Classification.—Of the 44 reporting schools, 10 do not classify their pupils for housing purposes; the remaining 34 do. Age is the basis for classification in 22 schools, contagious disease in 15, mentality in 10, color in 7, and the nature of the crime in 4; physical handicap and the loss of privileges are each used as bases in 3 schools; nationality, parole violation, and recency of admission are also used as bases, each in some one school.

State schools at present are being forced to accept two classes of students who ought not to be there. Due to an overcrowding of institutions for the feeble-minded, many youths who are feeble-minded and who have got into trouble have been sent to the state industrial schools because the local judges did not know what else to do. These youths clearly ought to be segregated if they are to be protected from brilliant, criminal-minded youth and if a program of work is to be provided from which they can profit.

Because so few localities make proper arrangements for taking care of youths who present problems of minor delinquency, judges frequently shift the problem of dealing with them to the state school. As a result, we find there boys and girls with minor delinquencies as well as those with vicious criminal records.   Youths who were merely caught in the dragnet and who had no direct part in the crime are sent to the school along with those who engineered the mischief.

Officials of state schools report the receipt of relatively innocent youths who before leaving have had their minds polluted by contacts at the school.   These officials appreciate their problem, but they are helpless.   We, the citizens of the state, prolong such vicious situations by our very penuriousness in refusing to staff and finance properly schools that we have established.   If youths who are sent to them are to be protected and aided in making a new social adjustment, they should be classified upon the basis of social attitude; this will put the vicious young criminals in one group and the relatively innocent pupils in another.

The Follow-up.—The follow-up work of most state schools is done in connection with what they call their parole.   It seems unfortunate that penal terminology should be used in connection with the education of the socially handicapped child.   When the school feels that a pupil has made a satisfactory adjustment, a conditional transfer might well be used instead of a parole.   Under the conditional transfer, the youth would be required to return to the school if his social adjustment proved to be inadequate.   In order that the child shall have aid in making that adjustment, a definite system of follow-up is needed. This follow-up would aim to prepare the home for the child's return; it would aim to reorient those agencies of the community that the boy would contact, with respect to changes in him, and so prepare them for his reception; if he is to go to work, it would help him find a job; it would contact him frequently until there was some assurance that his adjustment was satisfactory; it would, finally, allow him to be returned to the school if the adjustment proved unsatisfactory.

Of the 44 schools studied by Poe, 32 maintained their own field-workers to do this follow-up work; five maintained no follow-up; two placed it in the hands of those probation officers who originally had the boy, before his entrance into the school; and two relied entirely upon correspondence; one used the county superintendents of public welfare; and two used the state's parole workers.   The load per worker varied from 16 to 277 youths each.

Probably no work connected with these state schools is of greater importance than this follow-up service.   Often old friends must be given up if the youth is to make good.   Former neighbors look at him with suspicion and tend to refuse to allow their children to associate with him.   Too often, local social groups, such as the school and the church, turn a cold shoulder upon him. Employers tend to refuse employment. Youth itself points the finger of scorn and refuses to give the friendship that is necessary if the child is to be readjusted socially. The follow-up service needs individuals who have a large share of common sense, are full of human sympathy and understanding, have adequate technical training, and have a wide experience in the making of social contacts. Without such fieldworkers, the training given by even the best-equipped and best-managed state school is likely to fall far short of its real goal.

2. HOUSING

The method of handling the housing problem is indicative of the aims and character of the state school. There are two generally accepted methods, the congregate and the cottage.

The Problem of Definition.—I have seen fit to make a three-fold classification: the congregate, the modified congregate, and the cottage. Where the lines should be drawn separating them is subject to debate; some might see fit to recognize as different plans housing situations that are on the border line between any two of these.

As usually defined, the congregate plan houses and cares for all children in the school under one roof, whereas the cottage plan divides them into groups and these groups are housed in cottages. This definition sounds simple and reasonable but, when viewde critically, it is not very informing. One school may house all its children under one roof but have only 17 to house; another school may house its pupils in 10 cottages but have a total enrollment of 1,100. Which school is upon the congregate basis and which is upon the cottage basis?

A Suggested Solution.—It seems obvious that the definitions will have to be stated more concretely. It is here suggested that "the number of pupils housed" be used as the basis. What that number should be is not clear; certainly 10 pupils per unit would be recognized by all authorities as a cottage; whether a unit of 50 or 60 would be so recognized is questionable. Some schools report the use of cottages when these units house over 100 pupils each.

The original idea regarding the cottage system was that the life of the pupils should be made to resemble home life as much as possible. Home life implies loving parents, informed parents, perfectly free and happy association of parents and children, group give-and-take among peers, confidence in one another, and confidences given to each other. If this idea is to be accepted, are we not greatly in error when we designate as cottages dormitories that house from 50 to 125 or more youths apiece?

In order to give a basis for future discussion and future reporting, I am suggesting that any unit that houses fewer than 20 pupils be called a cottage; that a unit housing 20 to less than 50 be called a modified congregate; and that a unit that houses 50 or more be called a congregate.

Sleeping Quarters.—Another important variation in housing has to do with sleeping arrangements. Some cottages provide individual rooms; others provide one or more dormitories; the same variation applies to each of the other two types of housing.

3. PERSONNEL

If the ideals of personal contact and individual study are to govern the management of state schools, attention must be given to the number of pupils received each year, the average enrollments, the length of stay, and the type of officials who are chosen to manage the school and to instruct the pupils.

Admissions.—Reports from 84 state schools show that there is a wide range in the number of yearly admissions. Fourteen schools admit less than 50 yearly; 10 was the smallest number for any one of these schools. One school, on the other hand, admitted 1,050 during the year. The median number of admissions for the 84 schools was 113. Seventeen schools admitted 300 or more each; unless these schools are well staffed, it will be difficult to give these pupils the individual attention that they need.

Enrollments.[1]—When enrollments in these same 84 schools are noted, we again find a wide range. One reported 1,100; this, incidentally, is the same school that reported admissions of 1,050. One of the schools that reported fewer than 50 enrolled, had only 10 admissions. The median enrollment was 211; this should be compared with 113, the median admissions for that year. This means that these schools have on an average a complete turnover every 1.8 years, if we assume that enrollment is constant. One school had a complete turnover each 7.8 months; another, every 5.4 months. These data are significant. A school can hardly hope to effect material changes in these youths within so short a period.

Enrollment in Academic Schoolwork.—The total enrollment of 33 state schools as reported in 1929 was 12,247; of this number, 9,063 were enrolled in academic schoolwork. Table VI distributes these

---

[1] These data on admissions and enrollment were adapted from the *U.S. Bureau of Education Bulletin* 10, 1928, pp. 12–17. Only state industrial schools for boys or girls or both were considered; reformatories for young men and local and private schools were omitted.

pupils by grade. Grades 6 and 7 enrolled the greatest number of pupils. The junior high-school grades contained 36.2 per cent of the academic pupils; the senior high school enrolled 7.4 per cent; and the six elementary grades had 54.3 per cent.

TABLE VI.—ENROLLMENT BY GRADES IN 33 STATE SCHOOLS

Grade	Enrollment	Per Cent
1	390	4.3
2	417	4.6
3	539	5.9
4	949	10.5
5	1,195	13.2
6	1,431	15.8
7	1,434	15.8
8	1,178	13.0
9	666	7.4
Senior high school..	675	7.4
Special class.......	189	2.1
Total...........	9,063	100.0

Only three state schools saw fit to organize special classes, despite the fact that all of them reported large groups of youths who rated less than normal on intelligence tests. This lack is one more link in a chain of evidence which tends to show that state schools for the socially handicapped have not adjusted their program of schoolwork to the abilities of the youths that they enroll.

Senior high-school work was provided in only 16 of these 33 state schools; one school enrolled 184 senior high-school students. If one school can do this, then surely other schools with larger enrollments, admitting students of approximately the same ages, ought to find it necessary to provide similar work. These youths are not being given a satisfactory chance at social readjustment when they are refused an opportunity to obtain or continue high-school work.

Teachers.—Poe says that all schools which reported on the training of their teachers claim that they "have the same training as that required of the public school teachers by the state departments of education."[1] This is as it should be. Poe fails to state whether trade and industrial teachers were included in this group. Personal visitation of several state schools indicates that the men and women who direct shopwork and farm work are not considered teachers; that only those who instruct in the academic subjects are thus classified.

[1] POE, *op. cit.*, p. 44.

Superintendents of State Schools.—If state schools are to be primarily educational, the superintendents should gravitate from educational instead of from penal fields. The previous experience of

TABLE VII.—PREVIOUS EXPERIENCE OF THE SUPERINTENDENTS OF 35 STATE SCHOOLS[1]

Institutional		Noninstitutional	
Experience	Number of superintendents	Experience	Number of superintendents
Superintendent.............	7	Teacher...................	9
Assistant superintendent......	8	Pastor....................	1
Superintendent of school......	5	Principal of public school....	3
Teacher...................	4	Superintendent of county	
Psychologist...............	1	school....................	2
Community center teacher....	1	Y.M.C.A.................	2
Assistant superintendent of		Director boys' camp........	2
charities of state..........	1	Manager veterans' bureau....	1
Assistant physician..........	1	General practice in medicine..	1
		University teacher..........	1
		U.S. Army................	1
		Supervisor state fresh-air	
		schools...................	1
		Accounting...............	1
		Director public school at-	
		tendance.................	1
		County agricultural agent....	1
		War work................	1
Total....................	28	Total....................	28

[1] DALE F. POE, *A Study of the Industrial Schools of the United States*, p. 61, unpublished Master's thesis at Ohio State University, Columbus, 1931.

the superintendents of 35 state schools is shown in Table VII. Poe shows that 15 of the 35 have had direct contact with regular school problems. He does not show how many, if any, were trained in penal institutions before coming to the state school. It would seem that all prospective superintendents should have had some public school experience, plus experience in other state schools. Twenty-five superintendents reported data concerning their academic preparation. Of these, 8 had specialized in education, 12 in social service, and the remaining 5 in medicine, military management, mathematics, or agriculture.

If the superintendents of our state schools are to be adequately prepared, no candidate should be considered who does not have a master's degree in education and who does not have, beyond that, specialized training in the psychology and management of socially handicapped children. Such training, plus an experience requirement, ought to bring to the superintendent's position a type of man who will be able to make practical some of the ideals that are now held concerning the work of state schools. As long as these schools are politically controlled and as long as the management of them is placed in the hands of men untrained and unskilled for the task ahead of them, we cannot hope to find social readjustment taking place in the youths sent there; we shall, in fact, continue to have penal and not educational institutions.

4. PROGRAMS PROVIDED FOR PUPILS

Any program that is proposed has to be considered in terms of the staff that is to put it into operation. We assume in the following discussion a staff with the training necessary for realizing the ideals that have been suggested as those governing the work of our state schools.

Standardized Examinations.—The past decade has seen a remarkable growth in the methods of diagnosing school children. We have developed standardized tests for measuring the specific attainments and abilities of pupils. We have developed techniques for analyzing personality traits, character traits, and emotional stability. These instruments of measurement are being widely accepted in the public schools as a necessary part of regular school equipment.

State schools for the socially handicapped are especially in need of such measuring instruments. Poe reports that nine of 43 state schools completely ignore tests of mental ability; two other schools do not give tests, but they use the scores made on intelligence tests given prior to the pupil's admission. A comprehensive measurement of each pupil, mentally, emotionally, mechanically, and educationally is necessary if proper vocational and educational guidance is to be given.

Recreation in Cottages and Dormitories.—Reports from 44 schools show that 34 of them provide a recreation room in each cottage; one maintains a combined recreation room and library in each cottage; one has a central recreation room for all cottages. Of the 35 schools providing recreational facilities in cottages, such recreation is optional in half of them and compulsory in the remainder. Where it is compulsory, the period ranges from no specified amount of time to 1 to 3 hours daily. The fact that recreation is compulsory is partially indicative of the spirit of the cottage life. That such rulings have to be made is not consonant with happy home life.

Library Facilities in Cottages.—Of the 44 schools, 31 report libraries; 28 provide libraries in the cottages and 3 have central libraries. In 11 schools pupils are required to spend time in the library; in the other 20, the matter is optional. It would be ideal if every cottage could have its own library made up of interesting, informing, and inspiring books. The interest factor would seem to be vital if the library is to be useful; this may require the inclusion of books that would not be approved by a typical, literary-minded librarian. If house parents begin to function as real parents, however, they will gradually be able to interest the youths in more desirable reading material. If cottages cannot have their own libraries, they might organize smaller circulating libraries; certainly there should be maintained at least a central library from which books could be obtained by loan.

Academic Instruction.—There is a theory that all pupils in these state schools should be given trade training; that academic work is beyond their comprehension and can safely be ignored. Such a suggestion is, of course, in the same category with other glittering generalizations, in that it states a partial truth only. Many youths in these schools do have unique ability in work of a mechanical nature; others, however, have academic inclinations. Between is a group who have the ability to do either type of work and yet who have decided interests; there is still another group who will do neither type well.

The academic instruction of these state schools, therefore, should be sufficiently varied to meet the needs of all pupils. It should be possible, for those so interested, to pursue regular work leading toward high-school graduation. Others, not so interested, should be allowed to take the minimum essentials of particular subjects in which they manifest an unusual interest. For those who will profit little if any from present courses, there should be organized new courses of an academic nature that might well be called a curriculum in "citizenship."

Such a curriculum, as the name implies, would have as its goal the making of better citizens. Citizenship would be thought of as including the proper use of the ballot, the requirements of being a good neighbor, and ability to make excellent use of leisure time. A new course in literature that would start the youth reading at his present interest level would be a part of the program; the purpose would be to raise as far as possible the level of the literature that a given child would read with continued interest. The subject matter of all courses would be similarly revised to meet the real needs of these youths.

If such a program of academic instruction is provided, it would seem feasible to require that all children attend academic instruction in state schools until eighteen years of age or until they have completed high school or its equivalent in the number of hours of course work completed. This assumes that the special curriculum in "citizenship" would provide enough work to occupy the youth profitably for such a period; if it did not, the requirement would, of course, end with the completion of the work provided; vocational work organized as a definite course of instruction would count for credit in either this field or the regular academic field.

Vocational Training.—The special objective of vocational training might well be twofold. The pupil given an abiding interest in some work for which he has a particular aptitude, ought to be better able to adjust himself socially. Given a mastery of some one trade, he can become self-supporting, gain confidence in his ability to maintain himself, and thus become desirous of co-operating with society instead of combating it.

Vocational subjects have a unique place in the educational program of the socially handicapped, since some authorities maintain that such children are mechanically inclined and are sometimes really clever in solving mechanical problems. Slawson[1] presents evidence showing that their mechanical intelligence approximates that of children whose social reactions are perfectly normal. If this is correct, then a school for correcting social maladjustment should give much attention to its shopwork. There ought to be such a variety of work provided that the needs and interests of every boy attending could be met.

The current criticisms of the vocational work done in state schools are (1) it is conducted upon a maintenance instead of an educational level; (2) pupils are placed in vocations in accordance with the needs of the school and not in accordance with the interests of the youths themselves; (3) no study is made of the interests and the needs of the pupils; and (4) all pupils are required to emphasize industrial work, whereas there are some who like and want all they can get of regular academic work.

5. MORAL AND RELIGIOUS CARE

The Need.—Considering the type of youths received, moral and religious care and instruction are very important. The immediate objective is the elimination of antisocial habits and the establishment of a mode of conduct that will enable the child to live happily in society

[1] John Slawson, *The Delinquent Boy*, pp. 211–212, Richard G. Badger— The Gorham Press, Boston, 1926.

after his discharge.   A youth while in these state schools has no normal home influence brought to bear upon him which tends to give a better direction to his social reactions; there are no social gatherings or community groups setting moral standards.   This situation places upon the school the whole responsibility for developing its pupils; the responsibility is assumed by a large group of co-operating agencies in the normal life of a youth.

Despite the importance of this program, one should beware of attempting to separate too widely the various elements that go into the making of a complete program of education for the child.   Without doubt, the development of a strong, healthy body and the maintenance of play and health activities which will keep that body in fit condition is a prime prerequisite in any program of moral education. Writing as early as 1907, Snedden said, "Right conditions of physical hygiene constitute the first step in moral reform."[1]

A Proposed Program.—In order to change the conduct of these youths and to aid them in making a satisfactory adjustment upon leaving the school, the following suggestions are offered.

1. At the head of the list is placed the character and ability of the men and women who are responsible for their training; this includes the superintendent, his immediate assistants, teachers of academic, industrial, and manual subjects, housefathers and housemothers, guards, and workmen who have supervision of the boys at any time. If these officials are "on the square," if they are perfectly human, though strict, if they are not afraid of showing their human qualities, and if they have a love of youth, they become perhaps the most effective agency for good that the school can have.

2. Next in importance to the personnel of the staff is the program that is developed for knowing intimately each youth in the school. The responsibility for this might well be placed upon the housefather and the housemother in schools having the cottage system.   This implies, in addition to other commonly accepted requirements, a knowledge of methods of child study and a knowledge of child psychology upon the part of such fathers and mothers; it implies a system of individual pupil records available to them; and it implies the development of real cottages of family size, instead of large institutions called cottages.

3. There should be developed a program of placing responsibility upon the individual.   It seems entirely contrary to the rules of learning

---

[1] David S. Snedden, *Administration and Educational Work of American Juvenile Reform Schools*, p. 121, Teachers College, Columbia University, New York, 1907.

and common sense to attempt to prepare a youth for active life in a community wherein he must make proper social adjustments, entirely unsupervised, without giving him some training in the making of such adjustments. It is foolish to expect that these youths, after being held under a rigid disciplinary regime at a school where they are given no chance to assume responsibility, will, upon release from the school, assume such responsibility.

4. Adequate provision should be made for easy access to interesting and wholesome literature. Too often the few books which are available are not suitable. Speaking 30 years ago, Snedden said, "It would be amusing if it were not so educationally pathetic to look over the shelves in the libraries of some of these schools." This statement can be made with equal truth today. In a day when there are so many wholesome books of great appeal for youths, it is nothing short of criminal to impose so much trash upon these needy youngsters. Nothing would be easier than the development of a large interest in reading, if proper books were supplied.

5. Most schools are providing regular religious services. Services are held for the Protestants and for the Catholics; in many schools they are held for the Jews. These services are held at least weekly; some schools have chapel more frequently. Many schools depend upon neighboring pastors or Y.M.C.A. workers for their speakers; others have their own chaplains who conduct services for the student bodies.

Other Suggestions.—There are those who insist that moral reformation can come only as a result of the specific conversion of the individual. Snedden, discussing this point in 1907, said, "It seems to be generally believed that fairly mature girls committed to these institutions, who have gone wrong, are often most effectively reached by means of fairly concentrated religious instruction and appeal, producing the condition known as repentance or conversion."[1] There are still a number of individuals working with the socially handicapped who hold to this belief. It is entirely possible that much good can be done through conversion by those who believe most intensely in its efficacy. It is possible that there are youths who have intellectualized themselves into a firm belief that their own social response is entirely right; in these cases arguments might have little or no effect, but an emotional appeal of sufficient intensity might break down the logic of such an individual.

No one set procedure will be potent in causing all these pupils to reconstruct their social outlook; each child must be so studied that the

[1] *Ibid.*, p. 152.

most likely method of reaching him can be used. Our ordinary procedure of dealing with these children in the mass should cease. Such a change will increase the cost of maintaining state schools; it has the possibility, however, of reducing many times the ultimate cost to the state. The failure of state schools to perform their function of social reconstruction will undoubtedly place upon the state at a later date the greater cost of convicting and reconvicting a criminal and of maintaining him intermittently for the remainder of his life.

6. FINANCIAL CONSIDERATIONS

The point of view just expressed should not be forgotten when questions of cost are raised. To be sure, if money is not available, expenses cannot be made. It is usually, however, not so much a matter of no available money as a matter of the distribution of the money we have. This means that values must be considered; in considering the values of a properly organized state school, we must think of the ultimate consequences to society of a refusal upon our part to provide for the school adequately.

It is obvious that the cost of educating youths at state schools where board and lodging are provided will be greater than the cost of educating them in local schools. Since they are all special problem cases, it is obvious that more supervision will be required than at local schools; this likewise increases costs. Because they are problem children, an even greater degree of ability should be demanded of those responsible for supervision than is demanded of teachers and administrators in regular day schools. If this better type of supervision is to be provided, costs will again be correspondingly greater.

Salaries of Teachers.—Salary reports for the teachers of academic school subjects were received from 42 schools. Of these, 14 reported the annual salary range. The maximum salaries ranged from $850 to $3,830; the median of these maximums was $1,560. The minimum annual salaries for these 14 schools ranged from $600 to $3,250. With two exceptions, the range was from $600 to $1,900. The median of these minimums was $1,050. In only two instances did these annual salaries include maintenance.

These data show that many schools are still paying salaries that can neither attract the best teachers nor encourage those already upon the staff to continue their education in an endeavor to handle better the many problems that are bound to face them. Only an occasional able individual who loves this service and who is devoting his life to it could one hope to retain, as long as salary conditions remain as they now are.

Cost of State Schools.[1]—The per capita cost for current expenses for 128[2] state schools was $425 for the year 1926–27. The schools were located in 43 of the 48 states and in the District of Columbia. In a few instances, states reported their local schools for caring for truants and delinquents. In most states, however, these data referred to state schools. The per capita expenditure for all purposes was $518 for 152 state schools within the United States in 1926–27.

7. UNIQUE PROVISIONS FOR GIRLS

State schools for girls differ little from similar schools for boys. The general ideals that govern them should be the same; the general control and administration can be the same; the housing facilities, educational facilities, and disciplinary and parole measures will not differ greatly. There are, however, a few provisions needed in the schools for girls that serve to differentiate them.

Maternity Service.—One of these provisions is maternity service. Although some state schools refuse to accept girls who are pregnant, the majority do accept them. A study[3] of 57 schools for girls, 54 of which reported on maternity service, showed that 37 of them received pregnant girls; during one year these schools cared for 316 such girls.

Methods of taking care of them differ. Previous to confinement, some schools allow them to live in the regular cottages with other girls; sometimes they live in the hospital or in the administration building, apart from the rest of the school; only one state had organized a separate school for them.

Such girls ought to be cared for by our state schools. Just because they are suffering so directly the results of previous misconduct, they should not be deprived of the aid that can here be secured. If the school is to be of greatest service, however, it would seem wise to provide separate housing facilities. One of the school's problems in dealing with these expectant mothers is to develop upon their part a normal, happy, wholesome attitude in looking forward to the coming of their babies; this may be made more difficult if they are in constant and intimate contact with girls of low ideals who are not in this condition.

[1] FRANK M. PHILLIPS, "Industrial Schools for Delinquents 1926–27," *U.S. Bureau of Education Bulletin* 10, p. 11, Washington, D.C., 1928.

[2] The number given in *U.S. Bulletin* 10 is 127, although 128 are actually listed on p. 11, col. 6.

[3] MARGARET REEVES, *Training Schools for Delinquent Girls*, p. 221, Russell Sage Foundation, New York, 1929.

Care of Babies.—At the time of her study, Reeves[1] found that only six girls' schools made provision for caring for babies. Sometimes the baby sleeps with its mother; sometimes a separate dormitory is provided. Various arrangements are worked out when the baby is not retained. Sometimes the girl goes home with him; sometimes she works and earns enough money to keep him; sometimes she works and pays his board at some institution; and sometimes she returns to the school and he is placed in a home.

The procedure to be followed should be based upon the most careful case study. The infant's ultimate welfare should be paramount; if there is genuine mother love or if there seems any likelihood of such love being developed, mother and baby should by all means be kept together. If, therefore, it seems advisable to retain the girl at the school, arrangements should be made to care for her baby. Since these girls are young and need unbroken rest, the babies should sleep in a dormitory under the supervision of a night nurse. The young mother would assume the care of her baby during the day. If she is in good physical condition, she should nurse it. This mother care will not only be beneficial to the baby but ought to make it possible for the school to be of greater help in the final social readjustment of the girl herself.

Social Hygiene.—This problem is uniquely, although not exclusively, related to schools for girls, owing to the fact that more girls than boys have been received at state schools because of illicit sex experiences. Boys are sent for stealing, incorrigibility, and truancy, and not so frequently for sex offenses.

This does not mean that girls are more lax sexually than boys. Girls become delinquent at a later age than boys; they reach the adolescent stage earlier and are sexually awakened earlier; they form associations with older boys of eighteen or nineteen, or with men. The men and older boys are often not apprehended, whereas the girls are. The younger boys in our state schools are not sexually excited so early; they are active, energetic, and roving; they find money loose and cars not locked; they want excitement; they steal and are sent to the state school.

As a result of promiscuous sex experience, a great many of these girls have one or more of the venereal diseases. The per cent so afflicted depends somewhat upon the attitude that has been assumed in sending them to the state school. If it is uniformly considered a "place of last resort," a place where the girl is sent when everything else has failed, more of them will have had such miscellaneous sex

[1] *Ibid.*, p. 222.

experience and consequently many more will be diseased. There must be definite provision for the segregation of all active venereal cases; there must be provision for immediate rigid physical examinations; and there must be adequate provision for the proper treatment of all cases. While all of this should be done at schools for boys, the problem is intensified in schools for girls, for the reason just stated.

Reeves[1] reports in her study, "It was not unusual for a school to have one-fifth to one-sixth of its pupil population under treatment for gonorrhea or syphilis." She further suggests that in many schools one-fourth are so treated and that some schools have a much larger percentage under treatment. These facts serve to re-emphasize the suggestion that the examination for and the treatment of venereal disease is a unique problem in schools for girls.

Even though the school provides adequate medical attention, it has not met the challenge presented by these girls until it has helped them to the attainment of a healthy, normal attitude toward sex. This problem of sex education is even more important than the data above indicate; although from one-sixth to one-half of the girls are victims of venereal disease, the proportion who have had illicit sex experience reaches the 100 per cent mark in some schools, according to statements that have been made by superintendents.

Sex education has before it the problem of avoiding two extremes. The girls have allowed normal sex desire to take extreme control of their actions. They must be helped to develop inhibitions, just as an individual must establish inhibitions over his love of gain, love of acclaim, or love of position. These desires are all normal, but there are generally accepted norms of social conduct that set the limits within which these desires are given freedom. The desirability of such norms should be explained, and the girls should see clearly the personal as well as the social dangers of ignoring the accepted standards of sex conduct.

At the same time, the problem should be handled with such care that no sex taboos are established. Sex desire, she should come to understand, is just as natural as any other impulse that the individual has; it is, in fact, the foundation stone of the loveliest elements in the life of a human being; it furnishes the drive which makes for success in business, politics, art, science, and religion. It is not, therefore, the sex desire that is to be thought of with shame; it is the lack of control over that desire which brings shame. This whole problem of the right attitude is without doubt the biggest problem in the sex education of these girls.

[1] *Ibid.*, p. 210.

If this attitude is to be secured, the school must provide a proper outlet for sex surges; they have previously resulted in antisocial sex acts; they must now be utilized in other ways. The sensible house-mother will provide the girl an opportunity to show her creative ability in decorating the cottage, in making her own pet dishes for the household, or in organizing some stunt or game for the enjoyment of the group. The wide-awake teacher will allow the pupil's creative ability an outlet in various kinds of problem work connected with any and all courses. The manager of the shops will provide an opportunity for her to work on projects of her own conception, as well as requiring her to do routine work. The supervisor of the farm, the gardens, the orchards, the poultry, and the animals will find many an opportunity for her to engage in valuable and interesting projects. The director of games and health education will encourage her to propose her own amusements and to plan, organize, and conduct them. The opportunities for diverting those sex drives that result in antisocial conduct into action of a wholesome social character are innumerable.

Recreation.—A school activity that presents great opportunity for sublimating sex drives is recreation. Schools of all types need a recreation program; such a program can be made unique in schools for delinquent girls, because it gives the school authorities an opportunity to utilize these drives. The girl with a single unfortunate sex experience may so live over and over again that experience in imagination that it becomes habitual. Such daydreaming may be successfully counteracted by active, interesting play.

It should be the aim of the school to develop an interesting program of play for each pupil. Many of these girls never had adequate play opportunities in their old home life. Not only is recreation necessary for the good of the girl during her process of re-education but, if that re-education is to be made permanent, a program of recreation must be developed for each girl, so that when she leaves the school she will automatically put that program into operation for herself.

Prevocational Training.—The only thing that makes prevocational training unique is the fact that most of these girls will never go into business or industry but will get married. Reeves says that "A very large proportion will become homemakers." It is doubly important, therefore, that girls in these schools be given home training. But few of the girls have wholesome concepts of good housekeeping, personal cleanliness, the care of children, the repair and making of clothing of even the simpler kinds, or the preparation of plain but wholesome foods.

Particular emphasis should, therefore, be placed upon such courses as domestic science, homemaking, general housework, canning, care of children, home nursing, plain sewing, dressmaking, needlework, and physical health and hygiene. For girls who will be working for a few years before establishing a home, such courses as hairdressing, typing, stenography, filing, and beauty culture will need to be emphasized. It should be repeated, however, that, since vocational training is not the major aim of the school, these courses should be looked upon as a means of studying, treating, and helping the girl to readjust her outlook on life; if at the same time she can be given definite aid in doing better some of those things that she will be called upon to do at a later date, the work of the school will be just so much more worth while.

Decentralization.—In schools for girls, feeding is more decentralized; instead of big central kitchens and dining rooms, as in many schools for boys, girls' schools tend to have cottage dining rooms and cottage kitchens. The need for such decentralization is evident, of course, if the girls are to be taught home management, home cooking, and serving.

There seems to be a tendency to decentralize sleeping quarters in girls' schools. A great many of the newer cottages in schools for girls are providing single rooms in the place of dormitories. The tendency is not so evident in boys' schools. It is argued that the girl needs a place of privacy where she can go for quiet thought and meditation; that she needs a spot she can call her own, where she can read or study or work without interruption. If this argument justifies single rooms for girls, perhaps the same reasoning would justify such sleeping quarters for boys. There seems to be a general agreement that the room housing two individuals is not ideal.

8. SUMMARY

Any change in name of state schools, to be worth while, must be accompanied by changes in aim, personnel, methods, and spirit. The management of the schools should be in the hands of educational authorities. Problems of admission, housing, discipline, classification, trained personnel, type of program provided, and character of moral and religious instruction challenge administrative authorities. State schools for girls are faced with such unique problems as maternity service, care of babies, social hygiene, recreation, prevocational training, and special problems in physical care, clothing, and decentralization. These problems are all most real and challenge the best educational leadership if they are to be solved satisfactorily.

Problems and Questions for Discussion

1. Is the name of the state school an important consideration? Explain your answer.

2. What important problems of management arise? State your solution for each.

3. Draft in some detail the training and qualifications you would demand of state school officials.

4. Propose a program of study, work, and management that will help these youths make the best and quickest social readjustment.

5. Can one hope to provide effective moral and religious instruction? If not, why not? If so, describe how you would do it.

6. Secure data concerning the cost of educating the socially handicapped at state expense.

7. What unique problems are faced in educating girls in these state schools? How would you propose solving them?

8. Are many of the girls' problems sex problems? What evidence can you secure on this point?

9. In what ways do state schools for the socially handicapped constitute a challenge to the state's educational and political leadership?

Selected Bibliography

BURLEIGH, EDITH N., and HARRIS, FRANCES R. *The Delinquent Girl.* The New York School of Social Work, New York, 1923. 118 pp.

An excellent description of parole work, of systems of parole, and parole work as developed in Massachusetts.

REEVES, MARGARET. *Training Schools for Delinquent Girls.* The Russell Sage Foundation, New York, 1929. 455 pp.

A brief history of the development of schools for the socially handicapped and an excellent survey of 57 schools for girls made by personal visitation.

WEBB, L. W. *An Analysis of the Statutory Provisions concerning Truancy and Delinquency in the United States.* An unpublished Master's thesis, Ohio State University, Columbus, 1929.

As the title states, this is an analysis of the laws of the 48 states concerning truancy and delinquency.

POE, DALE F. *A Study of the Industrial Schools of the United States.* Unpublished Master's thesis, Ohio State University, Columbus, 1931.

Presents the results of a questionnaire study of 44 industrial schools; deals with commitments, housing, discipline, training, follow-up, and personnel.

CHAPTER VII

TYPICAL STATE SCHOOLS

Theory, if it is to function effectively, must constantly be checked by daily experience; at the same time, current practice must seek the rigorous criticism of intelligent theory. Nowhere are these suggestions more applicable than to theory and practice in dealing with the socially handicapped; they are particularly appropriate as related to the state schools. Administrative officials responsible for managing state schools are severe in their condemnation of theorists who try to tell them how to do their jobs; to the extent that the theorist assumes that he knows how to administer the school in order to achieve certain goods, this criticism is justified.

Theorists are just as stinging in the censure which they heap upon administrative officials; to the extent that the latter have allowed their vision to become obscured by real or fancied difficulties and have become content with a mechanical administration of the school, these sharp rebukes are needed. The criticisms of both groups are necessary if the state school is to become an agency for social good worth preserving; they must not stop at that point, however; they must co-operate in the development of a workable organization that can achieve such a goal. The last chapter discussed theory; this chapter undertakes to describe how a number of the state schools are organized, how they are administered, and what they are accomplishing. The data to be presented are those which the schools themselves have presented in printed reports or which they sent to the writer in manuscript form as a means of making these descriptions accurate and up-to-date.[1]

1. MINNESOTA STATE TRAINING SCHOOL

The State Training School at Red Wing was opened in 1868; the present institution was begun in 1889. Its capacity is 375. The

---

[1] The choice of schools to be described in this chapter was based largely upon chance. Correspondence with workers in the field unearthed a number of schools; a survey of literature discovered others. This chapter presents data on only a few of the schools thus discovered. Doubtless other schools are doing just as good work and some may be doing better work than those described. This

grounds occupy 560 acres, of which 106 are under cultivation. There are 80 officers and employees.

Classification.—Each incoming boy receives a rigorous health, educational, and psychological examination, and lives in a cottage of new boys. After an adjustment period of about six weeks, he is assigned to a different cottage, and a complete educational program is developed. At present there are eight cottage groups, which the school recognizes are seriously overcrowded for achievement of the best type of remedial work. Judicious segregation is employed in organizing these cottage family groups. Two cottages care for parole violators and boys who do not adjust well to their fellows and to the school. There is a cottage for subnormals, one for fifteen-year-olds, one for thirteen- and fourteen-year-olds, one for boys of twelve and under, one for older boys, and a receiving cottage.

Instruction.—Academic instruction is given in grades 1 through 11. There are two semesters of 19 weeks each; all grades are in school during this period. Certain elementary classes who need remedial attention have half-time summer schoolwork. Practically all elementary and some junior-high work is thoroughly individualized. All boys under sixteen do academic work, while those over sixteen enter classes if they wish. A remedial program for reading is in progress. In addition to academic instruction, the boys are given training in music, both vocal and instrumental; vocational training consists of auto mechanics, baking, barbering, blacksmithing, carpentering, cooking, laundry work, painting, pipefitting, plumbing, printing, tailoring, and shoe rebuilding. Entertainments are given, athletic teams are organized, a swimming pool is provided, motion pictures are given in the auditorium, a well-equipped library is available, and each cottage is provided with a large, well-lighted reading room for the use of the boys on long winter evenings.

Parole Work.—Parole work is maintained by four agents working under the direction of the school. An office is maintained at the school. A number of organizations in various communities throughout the state furnish big brothers for the boys placed in those communities. This is a feature which the school hopes to develop further. An attempt is made to visit every boy on parole at least once a month. The home of each boy at the school is also visited within a month after

---

chapter will have served its purpose if it gives the reader a little better conception of what such schools are doing for socially handicapped youths. No attempt is made to describe each in detail. Rather, the intention has been to pick out significant items in their programs without repeating similar items for successive schools.

his arrival, and prior to his return. The parole officers try to adjust, for all boys on parole, difficulties in the home, in the schools, and at places of employment.

2. THE CALIFORNIA PLAN

The Plan.—There are two schools in this state. The Whittier State School admits boys under sixteen years and over eight years of age; the Preston School of Industry admits boys sixteen years of age and up to twenty-one years. On Feb. 22, 1937, Whittier had an enrollment of 350, the largest it had ever had; the enrollment at the Preston School was approximately 665.

The Whittier School.[1]—The plant at the Whittier State School has 221 acres of ground and 26 major buildings; its estimated cost is approximately $2,000,000. The cottages, with one exception, are new and modern. They house on the average 30 boys each. A splendid gymnasium has been recently erected.

A boy upon entrance to Whittier spends 6 weeks at the receiving cottage. While in this cottage, he is taught the fundamentals of etiquette, cleanliness, neatness, personal appearance, boy scout laws, honor-club program, and calisthenics. At the end of this period, he comes before the superintendent's clinic; the personnel of this clinic consists of the superintendent, assistant superintendent, head supervisor, school principal, psychologist, and director of physical education. The complete history of the boy is reviewed. Upon the basis of the data presented he is assigned to a trade and a cottage; he remains in the cottage during the rest of his stay at the school.

Whittier attempts to make real trade training primary, and maintenance of the school by student help, secondary. The boy's program is so arranged that he spends half the day at school and the other half at vocational training; the only exception to the preceding statement is that a junior boy spends the entire day in the academic school. The schoolwork is based on the contract plan and permits the boy to progress as rapidly as he chooses.

In the fall of 1928 a general shop was established which gave each boy an opportunity to try out in various occupations. Electrical work, carpentry, and mechanics were among those provided. Each boy received approximately 4 months' training in each of these trades. The vocational director and the psychologist during all this period studied each youth. In the final vocational placement of the boy

---

[1] Based upon typed material received from the Whittier State School and upon the *Fifth Biennial Report of the Department of Institutions*, California, 1931.

consideration was given to the type of job that would likely be open to him when he left school.[1]

At present the academic work and vocational training are closely correlated; in his academic schoolwork the boy is given special problems pertaining to his trade. The school appreciates that perhaps most of these boys must have some trade training. The work is so given that every boy who works at a trade is prepared to be at least a good helper or apprentice in the area in which he has chosen to specialize.

An assumption that governs the work at Whittier is that the boy is more likely, upon release, to fail during his leisure hours than during his working hours. Whittier's recreational program, therefore, gives considerable attention to all kinds of games. The director of the program attempts to utilize every boy in the school at least 45 minutes per day in some kind of activity; he has an eight-team intramural schedule planned, in which practically every boy participates. The school has a central radio broadcasting station so installed that broadcasts can be given to the various cottages. The boys participate enthusiastically in group singing; a well-organized band is functioning and is in great demand by outside agencies.

Two months before the boy is to leave, he is passed by the clinic as being eligible and worthy of entering the placement, or honor, cottage; he spends his last months at the school in this cottage. During that time he has more leeway and latitude than previously; he is placed more or less on his honor; it is felt that this 2-month period lessens considerably the gap from strict 24-hour supervision to the very little or no supervision which he will have upon leaving the school. At the end of the 2-month period, if his conduct has been satisfactory, he is eligible for placement. A placement breakfast is given in honor of the graduates. Interested citizens from civic, educational, and business life are guests; each boy is called upon for a few remarks; he gives his name, age, cottage, trade, and home town; he then gives his reactions to the work of the school.

The school has five men who give their entire time to helping these boys adjust happily in their out-of-school placement. Such follow-up service demands well-trained men; they need not only academic training but an understanding of the problems of these boys and an ability to contact various communities and place the boys with employers who will be interested in helping them make a satisfactory out-of-school adjustment.

The Preston School of Industry.—Some of the improvements to be noted recently at the Preston School of Industry are: (1) better

[1] For a listing of typical trades, see p. 91.

placement of boys in schoolwork and in the trades as a result of the work of the classification committee; (2) greater individualization of classroom work; (3) organization of more special evening classes; (4) special work planned for unusual disciplinary problems; (5) inauguration of boy scout work for specially selected boys; (6) special training classes for boys who are due for parole; and (7) the organization of a council, made up of boys from each company, which meets with the school superintendent to consider various school problems.

Trade training is given more emphasis than academic schoolwork, although the latter is provided for all boys of superior mental ability who show any inclination to continue with their academic studies. The trades include auto mechanics, baking, blacksmithing, butchering, cabinet-making, carpentry, concrete work, cooking, dairying, electrical work, garment making, farming, horticulture, landscape gardening, laundering, masonry, millwork, painting, plumbing, poultry raising, printing, sheet metalwork, shoe-making and repairing, steam fitting, swine husbandry, tailoring, and vegetable gardening.[1]

Parole is not granted to any boy until he has completed a special parole course. The course lasts 1 month. Problems of right living, of personal efficiency, of obedience to law, of duty to parents, and of home and social relations are considered. The boys are taught how to go about securing employment, to budget their money, to live within their income, and to buy clothing and other necessities. Suggestions concerning recreation, social contacts, and attendance at religious services are given.

When on parole, the boy may be promoted or demoted. At the time of parole, he is classified as average; he may be promoted to "above average," and then to "superior"; or he may be demoted to "below average," and then to "inferior." To reach and remain in the superior classification, the boy must become well established in a job, send in regular reports, save money, and keep out of trouble. The school now has six men giving full time to parole work; the case load for parole officers ranges from 100 to 150.

3. THE VENTURA SCHOOL FOR GIRLS (California)

General Data.—The California School for Girls was provided for by legislative enactment in 1913. The site finally chosen was 125 acres of land 3 miles north of Ventura. It is a hilly region. In June, 1916, enough buildings were completed to house 71 girls; these were transferred from the Whittier State School. It was not until May 22,

---

[1] These specific classes of work are typical of schools of this kind.

1925, that the legislature changed the name to the Ventura School for Girls.

Of the 125 acres, 20 are given over to the campus, orchards occupy 47, and 12 are planted in vegetables. A dairy and a piggery are maintained; these provide most of the meats and all the dairy products needed. Apples, peaches, citrus fruits, walnuts, and berries are grown for the use of the school.

The Cottages.—In June, 1930, there were six cottages housing 25 to 30 girls. The girls sleep in dormitories on the second floor of each cottage; the first floor has living room, dining room, kitchen, and laundry. One of the cottages is called Alta Vista; it is the honor cottage. The girls in this cottage are free to go to beach parties and to entertainments in Ventura during the year; they are not locked in at night; they have no night officer; each year for 2 weeks they go to a summer camp, where they are free to swim, fish, and enjoy the woods; they are given the honor assignments in all detail work.

Staff Personnel.—In addition to the superintendent, who is a woman, the school has a woman business manager, who supervises men and women employees. The woman physician has a graduate nurse and three or four student nurses to help her. The dentist is employed on part time. The school department has a principal, four regular teachers, and four specialty teachers—in sewing, weaving, music, and gymnasium. Each cottage has a housemother, an assistant, and a night watch. Other women are hired to relieve the house officers on days off or on yearly vacations.

Pupil Personnel.—Of 219 admissions, 201 were of white American parentage. All but 55 of the girls were first commitments. The school's report stated that 75 per cent of these girls came from broken homes and that many of them had had sex difficulties; this latter is indicated by the fact that 118, or 54 per cent, of the 219 girls were suffering from venereal disease.

Instruction.—The younger girls who do not have eighth-grade standing attend school 5 hours daily. Many of them are able to complete the grade 8 during their stay at the school; when they meet the local county requirements, the diploma of Ventura County is given to them. These girls are allowed to proceed at their own rate. One girl, who entered the grade 6 in the fall, did such good work that she was given an eighth-grade diploma the following June. The older girls may take (1) commercial training 3 hours daily, (2) instruction related to their work in the kitchens 2 hours daily, or (3) academic work 3 hours daily. The program is altered every year to fit the needs of those enrolled.

The general training consists of practical cooking experience and baking, the preparation of the dining room for meals and serving, general housekeeping, laundry work, sewing, the selection of dress materials, gardening, weaving, and basketry; each girl spends at least 3 months at each of these types of work. Sewing and cooking are frequently taken for much longer than 3 months, as the girls want this training. A few of the girls receive nurses' training; they are chosen upon the basis of ability and of their conduct record.

Parole.—Most of the girls are committed until twenty-one years of age; as soon as any girl's conduct and training are satisfactory, however, she can be released on parole. Of 208 girls so released, the average length of stay had been 18.6 months. When a girl is paroled, an attractive wardrobe consisting of dresses, colored underwear, aprons, a coat, and a hat are given to her. There are two full-time supervisors on the school's staff whose duty it is to find suitable homes, meet girls at their destinations, place them in the new homes, and supervise them. These girls become mothers' helpers; get positions in stores, telephone offices, factories, or laundries, and in general offices; and do general housework. Many of them marry while on parole. As soon as a girl shows by her actions that she has made a satisfactory adjustment and is capable of managing her own affairs, she is released from the school.

The School's Success.—The success of the school is shown by data concerning 97 girls who left it between July 1, 1927, and June 30, 1928. At the time of the report the girls had been out of the school from 2 to 3 years. Of the 97 girls, 43 had excellent records, 10 were above average, and 22 were average. Fifty-one of the girls had been happily married. Only four had been returned to the school; these were paroled a second time and three of the four are doing nicely. Of the original 97, about two-thirds were discharged from parole for satisfactory adjustment.

4. EL RETIRO SCHOOL FOR GIRLS[1] (California)

El Retiro and Its Beginning.—This school is strictly a county institution and has a local function; it is a good illustration of what

[1] From a typed annual report of the El Retiro School for Girls of Los Angeles County, Calif., for the year ending June 30, 1931.

This report is unique among the reports of institutions. It presents forcefully and clearly the life of the school, its defects, its difficulties, as well as its successes. The reader continually had the feeling that this school was succeeding in helping its pupils, despite the fact that its failures were discussed. The staff evidently has a clear vision of what its problems are and sets a very high standard for successful adjustment.

might be done within a state if, instead of one large state school, our state programs were to call for a number of schools serving various districts within the state. The school serves Los Angeles County, Calif.. The site comprises 10 acres; the buildings are located in a grove of olive trees. This grove and the natural beauty of the landscape give to the school an attractive appearance.

El Retiro was originally used as a private sanitarium. The venture failed and the county supervisors purchased the plant in 1919 as a branch of Juvenile Hall (the county detention home) and started a girls' school in August, 1919. It is the aim of the school to give these girls, who are wards of the Juvenile Court, a chance to adjust.

A Complete County Plan for Dealing with Juvenile Delinquency. Juvenile delinquents in Los Angeles County are under the general supervision of a county probation committee of seven members, which is appointed for 4 years by the board of supervisors. This committee has general supervision of Juvenile Hall (detention home), Juvenile Hall Hospital, and El Retiro.

In 1927 money was appropriated for the hospital and for a school building for Juvenile Hall. The hospital houses the behavior clinic, which gives to each admission a physical examination, a mental examination, and, where time allows, a psychiatric examination. This tends to emphasize care and treatment instead of confinement. The new hospital is the pivot about which all the work of Juvenile Hall is centered.

Juvenile Hall and Juvenile Hall Hospital.—The staff at Juvenile Hall and Juvenile Hall Hospital includes psychiatrists, physicians, psychologists, nurses, attendants, teachers, and general staff personnel. Owing to the large number of admissions, it is not yet possible to give each one the necessary careful study that the staff would like to provide. During a 5-year period, there were 25,266 admissions. Another handicap to extensive study is the short stay; a recent study showed that the average for boys was 23 days; the average for the girls was 18 days. The average daily population was 188.[1]

A Theory of Dealing with Delinquency.—There seems to be unmistakable evidence that Los Angeles County assumes that a boy or girl is not necessarily all bad just because he or she has transgressed some social law or custom; that in any given instance of delinquency, it is the bad that predominates; and that in order to help the child, we must study to discover why that bad has predominated in directing his actions.

[1] Report of the Los Angeles County Probation Committee from July 1, 1929, to July 1, 1935, p. 43, Los Angeles, Calif., 1935.

After thorough study, some children are returned home, some are put out in foster homes, some are sent to private schools, some go to the state schools, and some of the girls are retained in El Retiro.

El Retiro Itself.—El Retiro in 1937 had a staff of 12 officers and employees. It has five cottages; these are the Mary Lyon, the Susan B. Anthony, the Jane Addams, the Florence Nightingale, and the Administration Building. The unit in the Administration Building houses the honor girls. Each cottage has its housemother and an assistant. Every girl is given individual attention with respect to academic schooling, vocational training, ordinary home and table manners, health, the development of ideals, and the development of initiative and self-respect.

Each cottage has its own dining room, kitchen, laundry, living room, sewing room, and a very attractive patio. In these cottages girls are given a chance to plan, cook, and serve meals; check laundry and wash and iron linens; clean woodwork, floors, and furniture; and do general housework. The home supervisor, known as "mother," awakens each girl by name in the morning, advises and confers with each one concerning her duties for the day, listens to her worries and griefs, hopes and aspirations, and tries in every way possible to be a real mother to her.

Admissions.—El Retiro exists primarily for those girls who need training and who desire further schooling. In the placement of girls in the school, preference is given, therefore, to those who have ability and who need and desire further training. The average I.Q. in 1937 was 102. Of 57 girls received, only 12 had had a normal home life in that both parents were alive and living together; the home conditions of some of the 12 were far from desirable.

Leisure Time.—People from the churches of San Fernando call every Sunday for girls who wish to attend services of worship. The girls go to the theatre, to picnics, and on hikes with various members of the staff. Honor-cottage girls are allowed to attend afternoon or evening church functions or services; they also have the privilege of taking unchaperoned walks about the campus.

The recreational director has all girls in the gymnasium from 6:00 to 7:00 P.M., except Friday and Saturday. They have dramatics, basketball or volley ball, and social dancing. Such social activities are important. Too many of the girls do not know how to play; their leisure time has previously been spent quite differently. Sometimes they have to be coaxed, urged, and even compelled to enter the play life of the group. A former superintendent reports that one of the happy things about her work in the school was the receipt of letters from former pupils who stated that they had left the school with the idea of returning to the old life but that they had found the old crowd disappointing. Interests developed and habits formed at El Retiro had actually superseded former interests and habits.

A Conclusion.—It is thus that all our local and state schools for socially handicapped youths must ultimately function if they are to command the support and respect of the taxpayer. On the other hand, we as taxpayers must realize that more adequate support must be given to most of the schools that we have at present if they are so to function.

5. SUMMARY

This chapter can hardly be summarized without doing violence to its original purpose. It was included in order that the reader might get a better picture of how particular schools were organized and administered; it aimed at showing the almost infinite variations in practice; it has sought to be particular and not to generalize. Any attempt to summarize these reports will force us to digress, therefore, from the central theme of the chapter; despite this danger, perhaps a few generalizations will be helpful.

It is interesting to note that, despite the multitudinous variations discoverable in the organization and administration of the schools, most of them are accepting the theory that punishment is not the goal; theoretically, at least, they profess to be interested in helping the child to adjust; they claim that he has been "more sinned against than sinning"; they assume that, if enough can be learned about him, he can be helped; and finally they recognize and accept the principle of causation in dealing with these handicapped youths. It is hoped that the details regarding management which have been presented in this chapter will serve to emphasize the importance of these principles and will make a bit clearer the ways in which certain schools are undertaking in a practical way to put some of these theories into operation.

Problems and Questions for Discussion

1. What reasons can you give for the seeming conflict that so frequently appears as between practice and theory? Apply your comments to the specific problem of dealing with the socially handicapped.

2. Should a state provide two state schools, one for boys from eight to twelve years of age, inclusive, and another for boys from thirteen to sixteen, inclusive? Defend your answer.

3. Criticize the Minnesota plan of classification. Justify your criticisms.

4. What is Whittier's plan of vocational training? Criticize it and justify your comments.

5. What is your opinion of the parole proceedings of the Preston School of Industry? Defend your ideas.

6. Criticize the report made by the Ventura School for Girls on its success in dealing with its girls. Show why it is good or where it is weak.

7. Why is parole work or follow-up work needed in these state schools?

8. What is the Los Angeles County Plan for dealing with delinquency? Criticize it.

Selected Bibliography

MONTEGRIFFO, HELEN A. *Annual Report of the El Retiro School for Girls for* 1929–30. A typewritten copy secured from the superintendent. 68 pp.
An excellent description of the physical plant and its surroundings, together with a good description of the girls received at the school.

MONTEGRIFFO, HELEN A. *Annual Report of the El Retiro School for Girls for* 1930–31. A typewritten copy secured from the superintendent. 60 pp.
An excellent description of the problems faced in the school based upon the day-to-day contact of teachers with pupils. A much clearer realization of human problems is disclosed than is shown by the reports of most schools of this type.

Report of the Los Angeles County Probation Committee on Juvenile Hall and El Retiro, 1924–1929. 31 pp.
An excellent description of the way one county is attempting to care for its socially handicapped youths.

Reports of Department of Institutions: Fifth Biennial Report, 1930, pp. 100–157. *Appendix to Journals of Senate and Assembly,* California, Forty-ninth session 1931.
A good description of the work of the Preston School of Industry, the Ventura School for Girls, the Whittier State School, and the Department of Juvenile Research; a brief history of each is given.

CHAPTER VIII

THE CHALLENGE OF THE SOCIALLY HANDICAPPED

The real challenges of life consist of a vivid realization of the vital facts of life. Youth is stirred by the passionate appeal and the spirit of conquest; the aggressive nature of maturity is aroused by the presentation of facts that show the existence of wrongs, needs, or dangers. The fact that children are hungry brings a supply of food; the suffering and the deprivation occasioned by storm and flood bring thousands of dollars for relief; facts concerning the need of play space, school buildings, and medical aid for children bring a generous response. Not oratory but information presents the greater challenge to the adult population.

Throughout the preceding six chapters data concerning the socially handicapped have been presented in detail. These facts constitute the challenge. Vast numbers of school children are actually socially handicapped or potentially socially handicapped. The White House Conference says that 3 per cent would be a conservative estimate; 3 per cent of the approximately 25,000,000 elementary school children in the United States is 750,000 or three-quarters of a million children who need either preventive or remedial attention if they are to have a happy social adjustment. The size of the problem is anything but insignificant.

In addition, there is an indeterminable number of youths who do not need placement in special schools or classes but who need the help of teachers, principals, or pupil-personnel workers if they are not to become severe problem cases. When one considers (1) the great cost of special education, (2) the even greater cost of providing complete maintenance for the more severe cases, (3) the dangers to society in allowing these severe cases to develop, and (4) the agonies that these handicapped youths undergo if they are not given aid in making early adjustments, no other facts are needed to bring realization of the greatness of the challenge.

We now recognize that problem children are as they are because of some condition or situation that has the possibility of being discovered; that the condition or situation has the possibility of being removed; and that, thus studied, the child is a most likely candidate for complete recovery. In order that we may operate upon this basis, it must be recognized that the primary problem in handling a given child is the discovery of the cause or causes of his condition. The implications that these suggestions have for a training program constitute a further challenge to both local and state school authorities.

1. CAUSES OF TRUANCY AND DELINQUENCY

An analysis of the plans that are used at present in dealing with truants and delinquents indicates with some degree of clearness the differences in basic assumptions as to the causes of these social handicaps. Any program proposed for educating and caring for truants and delinquents ought to be based upon the best that is known concerning causes. This is particularly true if the program is to involve prevention as well as cure.[1]

Inheritance.—There are those who claim that traits of truancy and delinquency are inherited. The boy is truant or delinquent because he has in his original nature an inheritance that causes him to do the specific act that brands him as a truant or a delinquent. The high-school principal who said that such boys "are naturally bad. They were born that way. All we can do for them is to shut them away from our well-behaved normal youngsters" believed in the direct inheritance of truant and delinquent traits; he believed, furthermore, that such a trait could not be modified or materially changed. A belief like that points directly to the method of treatment. Granting his assumptions, his conclusions were correct.

Lack of Intelligence.—There are others who believe that there are inherited traits which give an ideal background for the growth of truancy and delinquency. One of these traits is low intelligence. Many investigators have reported the intelligence ratings of youths who are confined in schools and institutions for the truant and delinquent; these reports show that a large per cent of those young people are much below normal.

Criticisms have been made of these reports. It is claimed that (1) The examinations are often made by incompetent persons. (2) The attitude of the inmates toward the tests has invalidated the results. (3) Inmates of institutions represent a selected group, in that there is a tendency to place on probation the brighter individuals.

[1] There will be no attempt in this brief section to do more than summarize briefly some general points of view concerning the causes of truancy and delinquency. Those interested in a further and more detailed discussion may turn to references by Glueck, Healy, Scheidemann, and Slawson listed in the selected bibliography at the close of this chapter.

(4) The sixteen-year mental age has been taken as normal for the average adult population, whereas it should be rated considerably lower.

If these criticisms are taken into account, intelligence becomes much less of a factor in truancy and delinquency than its advocates have claimed. In a statistical investigation involving 1,664 boys from four institutions of New York State that cared for truants and delinquents, Slawson[1] concludes that intelligence has been greatly exaggerated as a factor causing truancy and delinquency.

Lack of Adjustment.—Other writers claim that lack of intelligence is not so much a factor in causing delinquency as is the lack of adjustment. If we demand more or less of the individual than his ability warrants, he is inclined to rebel against the situation in which he finds himself. His rebellion may show itself in any one of many forms. If he is attending school and tasks beyond his ability are required, he may become incorrigible; if he dislikes putting up a fight, he may run away and thus become a truant. If the pupil is brilliant and no work is demanded that challenges his ability, he may hate the monotonous grind and cut his classes, or he may bend his energies toward disrupting class routine.

This lack of adjustment may apply to the home situation, to his play life among the children of the community, to his school associates, or to the job he later holds. If the child is not adjusted, there is constant irritation; he is not happy and seeks to avoid the unpleasantness of the situation. In his attempt to do this, he may fight, brawl, run away, steal, or even kill. Thus it is claimed that lack of adjustment causes the delinquency.

Emotional Instability.—While admitting that criminal tendencies are not inherited, some state that a tendency to emotional instability is inherited and that such a trait is fertile soil for the development of truancy and delinquency. We may be uncertain about the extent to which such instability is innate or acquired, says Slawson, but we are reasonably sure of the "intimate association between psychoneurotic responses and male juvenile delinquency."[2]

Other Inherited Traits.—There are other inherited traits or characteristics which, it is claimed, have a part in causing delinquency. Some of these traits are insanity, physical inferiority, superabundance of physical energy, and abnormal psychic tendencies, appetites, and instincts. These traits are found in such varying degrees and are

---

[1] John Slawson, *The Delinquent Boy*, pp. 442–444, Richard G. Badger—The Gorham Press, Boston, 1926.

[2] *Ibid.*, p. 444.

combined so differently in individuals that the dispositional patterns of no two individuals are the same.   It is the abnormal combination of these traits that causes truancy and delinquency, these advocates claim.

Environment.—There is another group which claims that whether or not any of these traits make for delinquency depends upon the kind of environment in which the child is reared.   Given the proper environment, any child, they claim, can be raised as a normal social being.   Certain it is that many children of low mentality, children emotionally unstable, children physically inferior, and children with a surplus of physical energy have not been truants and delinquents. Equally certain is it that children from unspeakable social surroundings have likewise not been truant or delinquent.

Those who consider environment as the chief cause of delinquency are not agreed as to which environmental factor is of greatest importance.   Some studies indicate that the marital conditions of the parents are of chief importance; others, that general home conditions are responsible; others, that the gang life of the child exerts more influence; and others, that the type of school attended is responsible.

Certain Conclusions.—1. Perhaps the best general conclusion that can be reached is that, when it comes to dealing with an individual, no general law can be laid down; therefore, no general administrative schemes will solve all problems in truancy and delinquency.   Original human nature is complex; motivation in human conduct is exceedingly complex.   Those who seek simple problems to solve must look elsewhere for a vocation than to the field of preventive and remedial work for the socially handicapped.

2. Every child must be studied individually; final treatment must be just as individual.   All children who play truant must not be handled identically; treatment must depend upon what is discovered as to cause, as to the child's present attitude, and the like, based upon the most complete case study possible.

3. A complete and adequate record of each individual pupil should be kept and it should be readily available to classroom teachers.   This is seldom done.   Occasionally, an adequate record is kept by the principal, but rarely is it so available to classroom teachers that they can use it.

4. Since intelligence seems to be a material factor in causing the social handicap if schoolwork is not adjusted to the pupil's ability, the administrative staff of the school system should take whatever steps are necessary in order to make these adjustments possible.

5. Since environmental factors have a material bearing on the amount of delinquency, general measures that will help to control

the gang life of a neighborhood and give children healthy occupations during leisure hours should be undertaken. Organized playground work, supervised expeditions, more complete utilization of the school plant, and well-governed club work of all kinds will be of material aid.

6. No institution for boys of the truant and delinquent type can hope to serve such boys effectively which does not provide a staff that is qualified to study them as individuals. Qualifications requisite for a member of the staff are (a) a high degree of common sense; (b) love and understanding of boyhood; (c) a physique that commands admiration; (d) training in psychology, psychiatry, and physical hygiene; and (e) a complete mastery of the particular task for which he is responsible.

7. No one should attempt to deal with children of this type who is not interested in discovering the causes back of the overt acts committed. Neither should anyone do so unless he is willing to develop the child's program in terms of what is likely to aid that child most in making a real adjustment in his social relationships. It is the writer's fear that much of what we do at present in trying to aid the child tends to hinder, instead of aid; that, due to our ignorance of his needs, our efforts tend to drive him further and further into the realm of antisocial attitudes.

2. A PROGRAM FOR LOCAL SCHOOL DISTRICTS

The program for local school districts will be presented in brief outline form.

The Task of the Regular School.—The goal of the regular school is to work with each pupil under its supervision so that no child need be referred to any other division of the school system for management. One school principal rather crudely expressed this goal as follows: "We believe that every school district should clean up its own back door yard and we try to do this by not calling upon other agencies to solve pupil problems which we can solve ourselves."

If this goal is to be achieved, the following provisions would seem necessary: (1) Demand that each teacher on the staff have not only a mastery of teaching methods but a mastery of the art of understanding children. (2) Install an adequate "Pupil's Cumulative Record" which is readily accessible to all teachers. (3) Make constant use of standardized tests—mental, mechanical, prognostic, social, and subject matter—in order to have at hand objective data concerning pupil abilities. (4) Adopt methods of so adjusting schoolwork to the abilities and interests of the pupils that maladjustment will be eliminated. (5) Provide within the schools field service of such excellence and amount that all extreme problem children may be given early and continuous supervision. (6) Maintain a program of guidance that will reach all pupils and will be accepted as a regular part of the duties of the entire staff. (7) Develop a health and physical-education program of such scope that the school facilities for play will be utilized the entire year, including vacation periods, Saturdays, and afterschool hours. It will take sane, challenging, and determined leadership in each and every locality if these preventive measures are to be put into effect.

The Task of the Pupil-personnel Department.[1]—The goal of the pupil-personnel department or division will be so to contact pupils referred to it that within the shortest possible time, conducive to successful work, every such child can be restored to its school without the necessity of sending it to some other special agency, either within or without the school system, for adjustment.

If this goal is to be achieved, the following provisions are necessary: (1) The fieldworkers (attendance workers or visiting teachers) should have mastery not only of social service work, but also of teaching and of the art of understanding children. (2) A continuous census should be maintained. (3) The function of placement and follow-up should be assumed for all children certificated for work. (4) The functions of testing, guidance, clinical service, medical service, and health service should be developed. (5) All special education for the district should be assumed as a function of the department. The size of the department would vary, depending upon the size of the school system.[2]

The Task of the Local School Board.—The goal of the board of education will be to set up such local agencies that it will be unnecessary to send any child out of the district in order to help him make proper adjustments to the social group in which he lives. This would demand that the board take the following steps:

1. Take whatever action is necessary to enable local school principals and their staffs to carry out the program outlined for them.

2. Take whatever action is necessary to enable present pupil-personnel agencies to reorganize as a single department or division of pupil personnel.

3. Project a school building program which will in time eliminate all small school units or buildings; this is necessary if each school unit is to organize so as to provide more adequately for individual differences among its pupils.

[1] For a description of its departmental organization, see Chap. XXXI.
[2] For a discussion of this problem, see Chap. XXXI.

4. Establish a special centralized industrial school of the type of the Thomas A. Edison, of Cleveland, or the Montefiore, of Chicago. These could be established in all cities of 100,000 population or more; near-by districts might make arrangements to send pupils to the city schools. Smaller cities might arrange with the county in which they are located to develop a county school centrally located. Two or more counties might unite in the organization of such a school.

5. Establish a farm or parental school. Two or more city, town, or county school districts might co-operate. The organization of such a school, except in a city large enough to maintain one of its own, should be done under the leadership of the state department of education and as the result of a survey of needs.

3. A STATE PROGRAM

Most of the elements of a thoroughgoing state program are implicit in the discussion of Chaps. V, VI, and VII. These elements will now be drawn together into outline form, without discussion or defense.

State Control.—The principle upon which this state program is based is that all the educational work of the state should be under the control and supervision of the state department of education. This principle is followed by the assumption that any program of caring for socially handicapped youths under twenty-one who are normal mentally is educational and not penal.

It is proposed, therefore, that (1) all state industrial schools for boys and girls be placed entirely under the control of state departments of education; (2) this state department will determine the minimum training and experience that will be demanded of all employees; (3) it will establish standards that local communities should meet in attempting to take care of their own problems of truancy and delinquency; (4) it shall supervise the work of probation for these schools; (5) it shall maintain a continuous survey of the probable number of truants and delinquents who will need to be cared for by state schools; and (6) it will be responsible for proposing legislation that will make possible the preceding program.

Character of the State Schools Proposed.—The fundamental principle governing state schools should be that of social readjustment. Each youth should be so aided that when he is released he will be a self-directive and self-adjusting citizen; his antisocial attitudes will have been displaced by socially co-operative ones.

It is proposed, therefore, that (1) housing facilities of the cottage type be provided;[1] (2) several small schools, instead of one huge

[1] See pp. 71–72.

institution, be organized within the state; (3) the farms be just large enough to care for these smaller groups; (4) adequate clinical facilities be supplied; (5) a regular academic program be provided through high school; (6) a completely revised academic course be developed for those of lesser mental ability, which will give them some concept of social organization and social responsibility; (7) vocational work be planned that will help each youth to do better those things that he will be likely to do when he leaves the state school; (8) a program of pupil management be instituted that will tend to develop initiative, self-reliance, and self-control; (9) love of sports and the liking for reading, art, and music be developed as a means to the better employment of leisure time; and (10) pupils be classified so that those of similar mental and social traits will be kept together in their training program.

Relation of State Schools to Local Schools.—The relationship of these state schools to local schools is based upon the theory that each locality is to do all it can in taking care of its own truants and delinquents. The state department of education will set the minimum standards that localities must meet.

When the local schools have done their best and failed, the court may then transfer the child to the state school; he is thus withdrawn from old associates and old associations. The state schools receive, therefore, youths who are more hardened or who have found it utterly impossible to readjust as long as they remained in constant contact with old associates or in close proximity to them. Aims and ideals in dealing with pupils in the two situations are essentially the same.

4. SUMMARY

The program of caring for and educating its socially handicapped children is one of the community's biggest problems. The numbers needing preventive work are large; the resulting financial savings may be great; the lessening of individual mental anguish is almost inestimable. Regular public school teachers and principals are essential factors in any comprehensive program of prevention. Pupil-personnel workers do preventive work in relationship to special education; their job is remedial with respect to the work of teachers and principals. Special local schools and classes do remedial work for the district, but preventive work for the state.

The entire program of prevention is based upon the search for causes. No single factor seems pre-eminent in causing truancy and delinquency; many factors seem to be related to them, if not actually the cause of them. Low intelligence, emotional instability, and bad environment seem to be among the most significant causes. Possible causal factors are so numerous and so interrelated that each child must be studied individually if proper measures to aid him are to be discovered.

State schools have the task of trying to succeed where the local schools failed. If state schools are to function educationally, they must be placed under the control of the state department of education. The entire emphasis of the training program should be that of social re-education. The requirements suggested mean the spending of more money than many states have thus far seen fit to spend upon the rehabilitation of their social misfits. This greater expenditure, however, will bring greater dividends to the state in terms of greater social efficiency upon the part of a large group of citizens who would otherwise not only be dependents but who would cost the state untold sums of money in later prosecutions and in life maintenance.

Problems and Questions for Discussion

1. What is the challenge of the socially handicapped? Wherein are these facts a challenge?

2. When is a program of care and education for the socially handicapped preventive and when is it remedial? Illustrate.

3. What are the causes of truancy and delinquency?

4. What lesson does the study of causes of truancy and delinquency have for the worker in the field? Explain.

5. What do you consider the single chief cause of truancy and delinquency? What data can you present in the support of your answer?

6. Describe in outline form what you consider a community's task in caring for the socially handicapped.

7. Describe in outline form the state's task in educating the socially handicapped.

8. Describe in detail what your own community and your own state do for the socially handicapped.

Selected Bibliography

BAKER, HARRY J., and TRAPHAGEN, VIRGINIA. *The Diagnosis and Treatment of Behavior-problem Children*, The Macmillan Company, New York, 1936. 393 pp.
  The title is eloquently descriptive of its content; a most worth-while contribution.
BENTLEY, JOHN EDWARD. *Problem Children*, pp. 165–366. W. W. Norton & Company, Inc., 1936.
  A good presentation of many of the problems involved in educating the socially handicapped.
CABOT, FREDERICK P., Judge, Chairman of Committee. *White House Conference* 1930, pp. 341–353. The Century Co., New York, 1931.
  Discusses the size of the problem of delinquency, suggests new approaches to the solution of the problem, and outlines briefly a program.

COOLEY, EDWIN J. *Probation and Delinquency*, Chaps. XV–XVI. Thomas Nelson & Sons, New York, 1927.

An interesting analysis of the causes of crime and its treatment.

GLUECK, SHELDON, and GLUECK, ELEANOR T. *One Thousand Juvenile Delinquents*. Harvard University Press, Cambridge, 1934. 341 pp.

Reports a study of 1,000 delinquents sent by the Boston Juvenile Court to the Judge Baker Foundation for examination; studied the family, educational, industrial, and leisure-time activities of these youths. Despite discouraging results, insists that "path of progress does not seem to lie in the direction of abandonment of juvenile clinics and courts." Suggests ways of improving the situation.

HEALY, WILLIAM, BRONNER, AUGUSTA F., BAYLOR, EDITH M. H., and MURPHY, J. PRENTICE. *Reconstructing Behavior in Youth*, Chaps. I–III. Alfred A. Knopf, Inc., New York, 1929.

A discussion of the place of the foster home in a program of caring for the socially handicapped; argues that even difficult types of children may be handled very successfully by this method.

MARTENS, ELISE H., and RUSS, HELEN. "Adjustment of Behavior Problems of School Children," *U. S. Office of Education Bulletin* 18, Washington, D. C., 1932. 78 pp.

Describes and evaluates the clinical program at Berkeley, Calif.; describes organization; compares behavior of problem children who were under intensive treatment for years with (1) nonproblem children and (2) problem children who had no such treatment. Concludes that "prolonged intensive study and clinical attention" changed for the better the "overt problem behavior of children."

MATEER, FLORENCE. *The Unstable Child*, Chaps. XII, XIX, and XXI. D. Appleton and Company, New York, 1924.

Gives an interesting analysis of the delinquent as a deviate; causes of delinquency are considered.

SCHEIDEMANN, NORMA V. *The Psychology of Exceptional Children*, Chap. XV. Houghton Mifflin Company, Boston, 1931.

Discusses types of offenses, cause of delinquency, physical and intellectual condition of delinquents, and the outcome of treatment.

SLAWSON, JOHN. *The Delinquent Boy*, Chaps. I and VII. Richard G. Badger— The Gorham Press, Boston, 1926.

Discusses briefly methods of studying causes of delinquency and presents the general results of his use of a statistical technique in the study of causes. The study is based upon 1,664 cases from four institutions in New York State.

THRASHER, FREDERIC M. *The Gang*. The University of Chicago Press, 1927. 571 pp.

Reports a study of 1,313 gangs in the city of Chicago; certain causes of delinquency are implied throughout the report.

PART II

THE EDUCATION OF THE PHYSICALLY HANDICAPPED CHILD

CHAPTER IX

THE EDUCATION OF THE CRIPPLED CHILD[1]

A greater challenge could hardly be presented to the physically fit than to observe the happiness and optimism of a class of crippled children. It challenges many of our personal attitudes toward life and our interest in doing everything possible to improve the opportunities of those who physically are so far less fortunate than ourselves and yet who can keep so happy.

1. WHY A PART OF SPECIAL EDUCATION

Administrative Reasons.—Children who are crippled represent one important unit in a program of special education, because they require special facilities for physical care that cannot be provided in regular grade classes, and because unusual attention must be given to the selection of a vocation. Greater attention to the latter problem is necessary since opportunities for the vocational placement of crippled children are limited. The special school must know each child's handicaps, how they will affect his efficiency in given vocations, and what their effect will be upon men responsible for hiring.

Psychological Reasons.—Psychologically, one might defend the inclusion of crippled children in a program of special education. In a regular class, the handicap of a crippled child is constantly noticed, because it is unique; he becomes self-conscious. In a special school he is one among many who are similarly handicapped. He sees other crippled children play and have good times; he joins their activities. He is shown no particular sympathy and is, therefore, less inclined to feel sorry for himself. His teachers expect performance of him and he responds to that expectation; they also instruct the parents in regard to proper attitudes to take toward him. For the first time in his life, the crippled child finds that school and home respect his ability and demand of him things that he can do; therefore, he does them.

2. DEFINITIONS

The term "crippled child" is restricted to include those children who cannot walk or who cannot walk without the aid of crutches or a cane.

[1] Dr. J. W. Larcomb, M.D., read all chapters dealing with the physically handicapped. He gave particular attention to those sections dealing with preventive measures and with causes.

Horizontal and Vertical Limitations.—At present, there is not sufficient agreement as to definition. Lack of agreement is both horizontal and vertical. Horizontally, one must know the types of physically handicapped children that are included. Vertically, one must know to what extent the youth must be handicapped in order to be considered a cripple. Both limitations should be agreed upon and accepted. Until this is done, statistics concerning the size of the problem of educating cripples will not be accurate. It is easy to double the number of cripples by merely taking away certain limitations, horizontal or vertical.

Need for a Better Definition.—Some suggest that vertical limitations are not necessary. They claim that, regardless of the degree of deformity in bone or limb, anyone so deformed is a cripple and should be kept indefinitely in the special school. Others exclude children who manage to get around satisfactorily at a regular school. Some keep such a pupil if he occasionally needs physical attention; others, if he needs psychological help; and still others, if he needs to develop habits of taking care of himself. For purposes of special education, therefore, some schools put rigid limitations upon their definition of a crippled child, while other schools have few such restrictions, if any. More careful definition is needed; those who have the interests of crippled children at heart and who have the necessary technical training should establish a definition that could be used uniformly. Comparative statistics cannot be obtained without such a definition.

3. GUIDING PRINCIPLES

In educating crippled children, we must realize that they have the same ambitions, desires, and mental abilities as have children who are not crippled. They differ in that it is impossible for them to be as active physically as others.

1. Equality of Educational Opportunity.—Equality of educational opportunity for the cripple has been and is still being ignored in most communities. Our state laws ignore it when they refuse to provide transportation for crippled children; they ignore it when they exempt such children from school attendance. Schools must be provided that will meet the physical needs of these children, and transportation must be provided so that they can attend.

2. Educational Program Must Recognize Handicaps.—The educational program provided must not ignore the handicap from which a given child is suffering. Each child must be helped to realize the problems he will face in entering occupations where his physical condition interferes with his work.   Certain types of physical deformity make it difficult for him to enter any occupation or profession where personal contacts are important.   The child's physical handicaps are, therefore, important in deciding his educational and vocational program.

3. Develop Initiative and Self-reliance.—Initiative and self-reliance must be developed.   This is important, since the past experience of the child has often emphasized just the reverse.   Parents and friends have often done everything for him; as a result, he has been invalidized far more than was necessary.   Crippled children must be taught to do things for themselves and to assume initiative in the development of school projects and this teaching must not stop at the doors of the school building.   The teachers must maintain a constant and intimate contact with the home; parents must be encouraged to accept this new attitude toward the child.   Constant and close co-operation between home and school can develop such initiative and independence.

4. Retain the Child as Long as Help Can Be Given.—Retain the child at the school as long as he needs its help; it may be able to help him not only physically and educationally but emotionally.   Retain the child, therefore, as long as the handicap is a source of embarrassment to him when with physically normal children, even though treatments are unnecessary and even though he is able to attend a regular day school.   No child should be forced into a school situation that continually upsets him emotionally.

4. HISTORY

Some writers describe roughly four stages in the treatment of crippled children: (1) extermination, (2) ridicule, (3) physical care, and (4) education.   Such periods have existed but they are far from being mutually exclusive.

Extermination and Ridicule.—Primitive peoples in their fight for survival were unable to carry with them the crippled and the aged.   The fight for existence was too strenuous.   Naturally, they allowed these groups to die.   The policy of the Spartans regarding the destruction of the physically imperfect was more consciously put into effect.   Its purpose was group survival through the development of a race having bodily perfection.

Little is known about the cripple during the Dark Ages.   Conditions for his care, however, could scarcely have been different from those of earlier times.   Even as late as the eighteenth century, Watson reports that "over 70 per cent of the children born in London died before they reached the age of five."[1] During the Middle Ages cripples were scarce; they had come into their own as jesters. The greater the deformity, the greater the mirth and laughter. Courts sought them. A scarcity of them increased their value to such an extent that during those times parents are reported to have crippled their own children in order to enhance their value.

Physical and Educational Care.—Not until the nineteenth century were the third and fourth stages of the treatment of crippled children ushered in. The greater part of that century is noted for physical care. Duchenne in France, Stromeyer in Germany, John Little and Hugh Owen Thomas in England, and John Ball in America were prominent orthopedic surgeons who devoted their effort and thought to the prevention and remedying of crippling conditions.

The century came to an end with emphasis still placed upon physical care. Education occupied a minor place in any program for taking care of cripples. In the realm of physical care, prevention was given little practical thought and even hospitalization was far from adequate. Constantly increasing numbers of crippled children, however, gradually served to enlist wide public interest in an educational program for them.

Education in the Public Schools.—The first public school class for crippled children was organized in London, England, in 1899.[2] By 1927, England had 62 schools, with a capacity of 5,875 pupils.[3] Good special day schools were also to be found in Birmingham, Leeds, Liverpool, Manchester, and Sheffield. The second public school class was organized in Chicago; it was arranged for in 1899 but was not opened until 1900. The responsibility for educating crippled children was very gradually accepted by boards of education.

A letter from a school superintendent written in the second decade of this century well illustrates the process. He said:

Our school for cripples is the culmination of a process of evolution. It began with an organization of women known as the Sunbeam Circle, who gathered together a few crippled children in a school and furnished for them a teacher. The next step in the evolution was that the board of education furnished the teacher. Then the board of education built a suitable building to accommodate these children. Meanwhile, the Sunbeam Circle transported them from their homes to the school and back again. This function is now performed by the

[1] FREDERICK WATSON, *Civilization and the Cripple*, p. 3, John Bale, Sons and Danielsson, Ltd., London, England, 1930.

[2] DOUGLAS C. McMURTRICE, "Home Teaching for Shut-in Crippled Children," *New York Medical Journal* (April 19, 1919), Vol. 109, pp. 680–682.

[3] EDITH REEVES SOLENBERGER, *Some Agencies and Institutions for Cripples in Various European Countries*, p. 18, The International Society for Crippled Children, Inc., Elyria, Ohio, 1931.

board of education. The Sunbeam Circle still continued to furnish lunches for the children; now the board of education furnishes everything, the children's lunches, transportation, general equipment, . . . the school for cripples is a part of our organization.[1]

The movement once begun, spread with considerable rapidity. By 1928, classes had been organized in at least 88 cities of the United States with populations of 10,000 or more; these cities reported 10,038 crippled children as being educated in public schools. Chicago had established four schools for the cripple; they enrolled 1,624 pupils. New York City was educating 3,583 crippled children; Detroit, 672; and St. Louis, 252.[2] By 1936, the Office of Education reported 233 cities[3] of over 10,000 population that were educating a total of 24,385 crippled children; Chicago reported 3,043 pupils; New York City, 3,383; Los Angeles, 2,639; and Detroit, 1,117.[4]

Present Needs.—Despite the extensive increase in classes for crippled children, there is still a great need. Of 153 cities which had organized classes or schools for crippled children, 35 were located in Ohio, 11 in New Jersey, 22 in Michigan, 10 in California, 11 in Illinois, and 16 in New York; thus 105, or 68.6 per cent of these cities were located in only 6 states. The remaining 48 cities were scattered throughout 20 states; no classes were reported in 22 states.

5. METHODS OF CARING FOR CRIPPLED CHILDREN

Home Instruction.—The 22 states that did not report classes or schools for crippled children may be educating them by means of home instruction. Such instruction is necessary as a part of any complete program. It ought to be a rare instance, however, where home instruction would be the only means used. Massachusetts, Michigan, New Jersey, Ohio, Oregon, and Pennsylvania require home instruction under certain conditions; California and New York specify that home instruction is authorized.[5] The remaining states legislatively ignore this method of educating cripples.

[1] EDITH REEVES SOLENBERGER, "Public School Classes for Crippled Children," *U. S. Bureau of Education Bulletin* 10, p. 9, Washington, D.C., 1918.

[2] ARCH O. HECK, "Special Schools and Classes in Cities of 10,000 Population and More in the United States," *U. S. Office of Education Bulletin* 7, pp. 1, 27–29. Washington, D.C., 1930.

[3] This included 80 cities which gave home or hospital instruction but which had no public school classes.

[4] FOSTER, EMERY M., and MARTENS, ELISE H., "Statistics of Special Schools and Classes for Exceptional Children," *U. S. Office of Education Bulletin* 2, pp. 27–45, Washington, D.C., 1938.

[5] WARD W. KEESECKER, "Digest of Legislation for Education of Crippled Children," *U. S. Bureau of Education Bulletin* 5, p. 2, Washington, D.C., 1929.

Hospital Instruction.—Instruction at hospitals is used for children who have to remain in the hospital for an extended period of time. Some suggest that such instruction, by occupying the mind agreeably, assists the child in regaining his health or in rebuilding that part of his body which has been deformed or which has undergone an operation. Teachers are provided by the public schools. The hospital furnishes the schoolroom and the necessary equipment. There are many such schools throughout the United States. Although this service is necessary, it can by no means supplant the work done by special schools and classes.

Local Schools.—Local schools are organized for crippled children in many public school systems; every child who has some deformity or orthopedic defect is segregated so that more specialized care and treatment can be provided. These schools are often located close to a hospital or clinic so that the very best provisions can be had for treatment and care.

Some cities plan their school program for cripples almost solely upon the basis of central schools. Of 88 cities reporting in 1930 a program for educating cripples, 17 reported schools only; 8 of these cities, however, had schools of only 2 or 3 classes each. The other 9 cities—Chicago, Minneapolis, St. Louis, Jersey City, Cincinnati, Cleveland, Columbus, Oklahoma City, and Pittsburgh—reported fairly large schools. The Spaulding School at Chicago was the largest; it had an enrollment of approximately 1,000.

Local Classes.—Other cities have a decentralized plan of giving instruction to their cripples. Philadelphia reported 22 special classes with an enrollment of 484 pupils; it reported no central school.[1] New York City approximated a decentralized program; it had one school with 460 pupils, but it had 146 classes scattered throughout the city enrolling 3,123 children. All small cities organize upon a class basis, since they have enough children for only one or two classes.

These classes enroll from 8 to 20 crippled children. The class is located in a regular school building. The principal of the building supervises the work of the class. Sometimes two such classes are housed together; this makes for better classification. The organization of classes reduces the problem of transportation but makes inadequate the equipment for treatments and physical care.

State Schools.—Massachusetts in 1904 established the first state school for cripples.[2] It was called the Massachusetts School and Home for Crippled and Deformed Children and provided for both

[1] HECK, *op. cit.*, p. 29.
[2] KEESECKER, *op. cit.*, pp. 1–2.

physical care and education.   Minnesota was the first state to pass legislation concerning the public care or treatment of crippled children; this legislation was passed in 1897.   Education was not added until 1907.[1]   New York established a state hospital in 1900.   Nebraska followed suit in 1905; schooling was included later.   In 1922 North Carolina introduced schooling for crippled children at its state hospital.

6. THE COST OF EDUCATING CRIPPLED CHILDREN

It is difficult to find data that give a satisfactory picture of the cost of educating crippled children; this is especially true when attempts are made to compare figures for different communities. Even when we have figures covering costs, we do not have information

TABLE VIII.—COSTS OF MAINTAINING REGULAR SCHOOLS AND SCHOOLS FOR CRIPPLED CHILDREN COMPARED

City	Elementary schools	Entire system	Schools for cripples	Ratio of elementary to schools for cripples
San Francisco, Calif.........	$112.60	$128.46	$354.85	3.1
Fort Wayne, Ind...........	92.00	105.60	593.50	6.4
Grand Rapids, Mich........	103.75	104.46	388.36	3.7
Hamtramck, Mich..........	79.90	106.31	274.47	3.4
Highland Park, Mich.......	......	157.48	452.85	
Saginaw, Mich.............	103.07	126.62	319.13	3.1
Jersey City, N.J............	96.00	120.00	368.46	3.8
Newark, N.J...............	77.67	129.37	431.01	5.5
Barberton, Ohio............	47.06	68.40	186.88	3.9
Cleveland, Ohio............	91.49	......	428.88	4.6
Dayton, Ohio..............	75.04	92.08	220.33	2.9
Lima, Ohio................	76.00	89.50	292.76	3.8
Piqua, Ohio................	48.96	......	259.00	5.2
Springfield, Ohio...........	66.32	......	268.54	4.0
Struthers, Ohio.............	75.18	......	281.14	3.7
Warren, Ohio..............	57.00	71.83	190.18	3.3
Philadelphia, Pa...........	72.40	90.61	275.73	3.8
Smallest amount...........	$ 47.06	$ 68.40	$186.88	2.9
Largest amount............	112.60	157.48	593.50	6.4
Median amount............	76.84	105.60	292.76	3.8

covering services rendered.   A large class group, a poorly paid teacher, little or no medical attention, no special equipment, and the use of a

[1] KEESECKER, op. cit., pp. 1–2.

regular classroom reduce the cost materially.   The provision of all needed services on the other hand makes for a high cost.   The following figures should be examined with these limitations in mind.

Report of 17 Cities.[1]—A report on 17 cities showed a median cost of $292.76; the range was from $186.88 to $593.50.   This is shown in Table VIII.   The ratio between the cost of regular elementary education and the cost of educating crippled children varied from 2.9 to 6.4.   The median ratio was 3.8; thus the cost of maintaining a school for cripples was on the average nearly four times the cost of maintaining a regular elementary-school program.   The ratio for Philadelphia was the median for the group; Cleveland's ratio was 4.6, and Newark's was 5.5.

7. SUMMARY

Crippled children found in public school classes are a happy lot; much of the credit for this situation is due to the work done by the teachers of these classes.   That fact is one of the reasons for including the education of cripples as a part of the school system's program of special education.   Other reasons are (1) the child needs special physical care, (2) it makes possible an adequate educational program, (3) initiative and self-reliance can be better developed, and (4) work adapted to the handicap can be provided.

Although the history of the care of the crippled child reaches back far into the centuries, the first public school seems to have been opened in London in 1899; the second was organized at Chicago in 1899, but not opened until January, 1900.

Problems and Questions for Discussion

1. Why is the education of crippled children an essential phase of any program of special education?

2. What problems do we face in attempting to define what is meant by a "crippled child"?

3. What guiding principles, if any, are there that should govern the education of crippled children?

4. Trace briefly the history and development of the education of cripples.

5. What means are being used at present to care for and educate crippled children?

6. How widely have special public day schools and classes been organized for the education of crippled children?   How widely have state schools been organized?

7. Justify, if possible, a program of education for cripples that costs so much more than the regular school program.

8. Is there much need at present for facilities for educating the cripple?

[1] ARCH O. HECK, "Education of Crippled Children," *U. S. Office of Education Bulletin* 11, p. 36, Washington, D.C., 1930.

Selected Bibliography

FRAMPTON, MERLE E., and ROWELL, HUGH GRANT. *Education of the Handicapped*, Vol. I, "History," pp. 112–145. World Book Company, Yonkers-on-Hudson, New York, 1938.

An interesting historical account of the education of crippled children. The book also contains a brief account of the development of educational programs for other types of physically handicapped children.

HADLEY, HAZEL C. *Educating Crippled Children in Ohio.* State Department of Education, Columbus, Ohio, 1927. 134 pp.

A description of the work done in Ohio. Methods of financing, standards of admission, methods of conducting class, teaching qualifications, ways of transporting, and the kind of care, training, and education given are discussed. Present needs are mentioned and descriptive reports of the work done in various cities are presented.

HECK, ARCH O. "Education of Crippled Children," *U. S. Office of Education Bulletin* 11, Washington, D.C., 1930. 57 pp.

Brief history of the education of cripples and definition; description of the work in 27 cities and in 36 schools. Organization and management, pupil personnel, and special facilities are the major topics.

HECK, ARCH O. "Special Schools and Classes in Cities of 10,000 Population and More in the United States," pp. 27–29. *U. S. Office of Education Bulletin* 7, Washington, D.C., 1930.

Survey of 736 of the 762 cities of the United States, showing the number of classes and schools for crippled children.

KEESECKER, WARD W. "Digest of Legislation for Education of Crippled Children," *U. S. Bureau of Education Bulletin* 5, Washington, D.C., 1929. 13 pp.

Extracts from state laws governing the education of crippled children. Brief features of laws shown in a table. Only 21 states have legislation.

McDONALD, ROBERT A. F. *Adjustment of School Organization to Various Population Groups*, pp. 58–63. Teachers College, Columbia University, New York, 1915.

Gives a brief history of the education of cripples, describes briefly ways of educating them, and discusses the educational offerings.

SOLENBERGER, EDITH REEVES. "Public School Classes for Crippled Children," *U. S. Bureau of Education Bulletin* 10, Washington, D.C., 1918. 52 pp.

A discussion of such problems in educating crippled children as aims, buildings, equipment, food, mental progress, organization of classes, and transportation.

WATSON, FREDERICK. *Civilization and the Cripple.* John Bale, Sons and Danielsson, Ltd., London, 1930. 120 pp.

Good historical background. Describes the education and training of cripples in both England and America. A good discussion of prevention and rehabilitation is given.

CHAPTER X

PROBLEMS FACED IN EDUCATING CRIPPLES

Excellent educational theories often fail to bear fruit because the practical problems of putting them into operation are never faced. This statement does not imply that less thought should be given to problems of theory; it means that problems of organization and administration are of profound importance. Failure to deal with them adequately means that the theory itself will not function. If the cripple is poorly housed, if the medical attention provided is inadequate, if the educational program is limited, if poorly equipped teachers are hired, and if equipment is meager and poorly selected, the program as operated will be anything but ideal. This chapter proposes, therefore, to consider in some detail the practical problems of organizing special schools and classes for the education of crippled children.

1. THE LOCAL SCHOOL BUILDING

Number of Stories.—There is no unanimity of opinion as to whether each of these buildings should have one story or two or three stories. The one-story building eliminates stairways, elevators, and ramps. It is argued that construction costs are reduced, since foundations need not be so substantial, less care need be exercised in making buildings fireproof, and the cost of ramps and elevators need not be considered. It is also argued that distances which the children must travel in going about the building are reduced.

Advocates of multistory buildings claim that the difference in cost is negligible. One-story buildings require much more ground space and more roofing. The further claim is made that many crippled children ought to be required to climb stairs or go up ramps as a part of their training. Another argument is that distances which the crippled children have to travel may be reduced; by means of elevators near the center of the building, pupils can be easily moved from floor to floor with but minimum distances to travel.

The Sunbeam School at Cleveland, the Christopher School[1] at Chicago, and the Dr. Charles H. Oakman School[2] at Detroit are

[1] R. W. YARDLEY, "Building Schools for Crippled Children," *The Nation's Schools*, No. 5 (November, 1930), Vol. 6, pp. 55–64.

[2] NEAL M. DUNNING and others, "Two New Schools Widen Educational Activities of Michigan Cities," *The Nation's Schools*, No. 6 (June, 1929), Vol. 3, pp. 58–60.

beautiful examples of one-story school buildings; the Spalding and Robert Louis Stevenson schools[1] at Chicago and the School for Crippled Children[2] at Cincinnati are splendid illustrations of multistory buildings. If the building is to house only 100 to 350 pupils, a one-story building may be best. If it is to house 1,000 or more, the multistory building will undoubtedly be chosen.

General Plan of Construction.—The one-story building, almost square and of the open-court type, is a favorite modern structure. Sometimes the classrooms occupy the outer sides of the building, while offices, treatment and examination rooms, storerooms, rest rooms, bathrooms, and toilets are located about the inner court; at other times, the classrooms are found upon three outer sides of the building and on the three corresponding sides of the court, while the special rooms occupy the entire fourth side of the building.

Another type is built on the plan of a modified rectangular structure. Classrooms occupy the two ends and one side; a concrete court and bus entrances dip into the other side, giving the building a somewhat U-shaped appearance. The bus entrances open into a hallway that runs the length of the building. In the center are the auditorium, a playroom, a lunchroom, and the physiotherapy rooms.

A third style is the long rectangular building with a hallway through the center. Classrooms and all special rooms are, of course, located on either side of the central hallway. This style is common in two-story structures. Examinations and treatments all take place on one floor.

Special Rooms.—A school for crippled children has many special rooms that are not found in regular school buildings. Among these are solaria equipped with cots for resting; often the window glass used is of the type that permits the sun's ultraviolet rays to penetrate. A suite for the orthopedist is frequently included; it consists of an examining room, a treatment room, and a plaster room, where casts are made or changed and where splints are supplied. A suite is arranged for the pediatrician, too. In many cases there are also a dentist's room, a darkroom for developing X-ray pictures, and a special room for ultraviolet ray treatment.

Toilets and Water Fountains.—The toilets should be readily accessible to all pupils. A few years ago it was considered necessary that every classroom have its toilet. In some schools there are two

---

[1] YARDLEY, *op. cit.*, pp. 55–64.

[2] ELDRIDGE S. HANNAFORD, "Where Crippled Children Are Taught to Lead Normal Lives," *The Nation's Schools*, No. 3 (September, 1930), Vol. 6, pp. 65–68.

toilets for boys and two for girls on each floor; other very modern
buildings have toilet facilities placed between every two rooms. A
toilet for every two classrooms would seem to be satisfactory. Many
authorities insist that every classroom should have its own washbasin
and its own drinking fountain. This reduces to a minimum the
necessity of having the children leave the room.

Classrooms.—The classrooms will need to be slightly larger than
rooms in regular school buildings if class groups are of approximately
the same size. The floor space per child must be greater, in order to
allow for specially built seats and desks, for wheel chairs where the
children need them, and for abundant cloakroom space. Space for
wraps in the classroom makes it possible for the teachers to give their
pupils prompt assistance with the removal and the putting on of
heavy winter wraps.

Floors.—The flooring should be of material that will reduce to a
minimum slipping and falling. One school recently installed materials
that were thought to be nonslipping; too late it was discovered that,
when wet, the floors were positively dangerous. Mastic tile, linoleum,
specially prepared composition, and cork are materials used.

Entrances and Steps.—The entrances where the busses unload
pupils should be on a level with the bus floors. Some authorities
insist that there should be no steps, either without or within the
buildings; others claim that steps are advantageous because the child
is thus forced to do what he will have to do later, unless he is to be
invalided for life. If steps are kept, there should be ramps as well,
so that children who find it utterly impossible to climb steps will be
able to manage themselves without continual assistance.

Corridors.—All corridors should have handrails; if there are stairways, both sides should have handrails; they encourage the children
to walk on all possible occasions with the minimum of assistance from
crutches. In many schools full-length mirrors are placed at the ends
of all corridors. They assist the pupils to see what they must do in
order to have erect carriage.

Corridors in a number of these schools are much wider than those
in regular school buildings; the argument usually given is that they
are used for play. Another reason that might be urged is the need for
space to use wheel chairs and crutches in the hallways.

Other Features.—A multistory building should have ramps and
elevators. The building must be so planned that these features can
be placed where they will give the maximum efficiency; they ought to
help reduce travel to the minimum. Stairways will be built, as well,
and children who need training of this kind will be urged to use them.

Closets are provided in the vestibules for the storage of wheel chairs. The vestibule itself may be so built that when the bus backs up to the vestibule door, the children can enter the building without being exposed to the weather.

2. SPECIAL EQUIPMENT NEEDED

Tanks.—The tank has an important place in connection with treatment; it may vary in size from one measuring 4 by 6 feet to the larger pool used both for swimming and for treatments.   Perhaps the ideal arrangement for treatment is to have a tank, in a room adjoining a standard swimming pool.   The tank and the pool are connected. In the tank, attendants give treatments on tables under water; pupils who have considerable physical development are allowed to take their exercises in the pool.   Tanks facilitate muscular treatments, since in water the bodily weight is lessened and the corrective exercises can be much more easily given.

Equipment for Exercises.—The school at Newark, N.J., reports 6 massage tables, 6 gymnasium mats, 3 Burdick bakers, 2 stall bars, 2 benches, 2 horizontal bars, one pair of rings, one balance beam, and one large mirror.   For spastic paralysis cases, colored cubes and Holgate travel blocks and junior building blocks are provided.   For active play there are badminton, shuffleboard, indoor balls, paddle tennis, clock golf, ping pong, rubber suction darts, bowling (giant pegs), and basketball goals (soft balls).   For quiet play, they have carom boards, flinch, lotto, monopoly, parchesi, dominoes, checkers, jacks, soft balls, ball-on-string, sand equipment, and miscellaneous card games.

The Sunbeam School at Cleveland has designed two unique pieces of equipment.   The "walker" is used by pupils to help them relearn to walk, or at least to give them aid in using leg muscles needed in walking which they could not use otherwise without the continuous assistance of an attendant.   Another piece of equipment, a muscle stretcher, enables the pupils to exercise certain thigh and leg muscles.

Much of the exercise arranged for the pupils is found in participation in games; children who cannot take part actively are used as umpires and timekeepers.   The chief object is so to interest the children that they will enter joyously and wholeheartedly into the spirit of the game.   Illustration 5 shows crippled children at play in a Los Angeles school.

Miscellaneous Equipment.—The ultraviolet ray equipment is almost universal in the large schools.   Bakers, balance rails, Seguin ladders, head-suspension frames, and stall bars are other types of equipment frequently used.

3. TRANSPORTATION

The need for transportation facilities in connection with schools for crippled children is due to the fact that most of them must travel great distances to the central school or class.

Methods.—Some cities use busses that are owned by the board of education; private companies are sometimes engaged; individuals are occasionally employed; sometimes the police provide transportation;

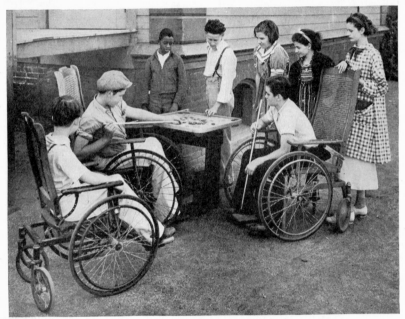

ILLUSTRATION 5.—Recreation is not neglected at the school for cripples at Los Angeles.

and sometimes the board of education and a private company co-operate in supplying it. When private individuals or companies transport, sometimes busses and sometimes taxicabs are found to be satisfactory. Los Angeles has reported that "through a system of private contracts, using the services in nearly every case of the *mothers of crippled children*," 70 pupils were brought in private cars to the day schools. Illustration 6 shows crippled children arriving at school in Los Angeles.

Those in favor of using public school busses claim that the private company or individual does the job solely for profit and that proper care of pupils cannot be assured. They claim, further, that if the city owns its busses they can be used for other purposes when not needed by the special school. One city has a complete system of scheduled visits by various school groups to places of interest within the city; its school busses are used as a part of this system of visiting.

Those who object to the use of the bus claim that it jolts and is uncomfortable and that pupils have to spend too long a period in transit. The busses are large enough to accommodate a great number of children and must travel great distances to gather a load.   As a result,

ILLUSTRATION 6.—Crippled children transported to school by automobiles at Los Angeles.

some children must spend daily as much as 2 hours going to school and 2 hours returning home.   Instead of busses, they hire taxicabs.   The cabs can collect children at a considerable distance from the school and transport them quickly, safely, and comfortably.

The chief objection to the taxicab service is the claim that it is more expensive.   This claim is not so well buttressed with facts as it might be.   In fact, one city that uses taxi service makes the claim that it has cheaper service than many cities using busses.   It does not provide statistics, however, in support of its claim.

Some cities are supplied with enough busses or taxicabs to transport all the children at one trip.   This makes it possible to begin school for all pupils at the same hour.   Other cities allow each bus or taxi to make two trips; Newark, N.J., does this.   The first group of children reaches the school at 8:30 A.M. and leaves at 2:30 P.M.   The second group reaches the school an hour later and leaves an hour later.   The first group receives individual help during the first hour of the day; the second receives such help during the last hour.

Attendants.—Most cities provide attendants on each bus to see that the children are transported in safety and to help them get on and off the bus.   This assistance in many cases involves carrying the child to and from the bus.

Some cities use these attendants only for the ride to and from school.   Other cities keep them busily occupied throughout the day at school; they assist the children at the toilet, in getting to the rest room, and in making the necessary trips about the building.

Cost of Transportation.—A report from 17 cities shows comparative costs of transportation.   The lowest per pupil cost was $30.71; the greatest cost was $126.16.   The median cost is $83.55.   These per pupil rates are based upon the roll at the close of the year for which the report was made.   We need a study of costs that will analyze services rendered and the efficiency of those services, as well as the number of pupils served.   Such a study would enable one to judge better what would be a reasonable cost for specified services.

4. PHYSICAL CARE PROVIDED

Care by a Physician.—No uniform procedure is followed.   If the child is under the care of a family physician, the school follows his advice with regard to needed exercises and treatments.   If he insists upon special treatments at outside clinics, these are arranged.   Sometimes the physician is perfectly willing to have all exercises and treatments given by the school, with the child reporting to him for examination at stated intervals.

No child should be treated except under orders of a physician. In Ohio, the physician in charge of special classes must be approved by the state department of health; he must co-operate with the physician in charge of the inspection of regular classes.   In no case are family physicians ignored; they are allowed complete supervision of the care and treatment of their own cases.

Examinations.—Most schools admit pupils upon the basis of a physical examination by an official representative of the board of education.   After this examination, the frequency of further examinations depends partly upon whether or not the parents leave the child under the supervision of the school physician or hire their own.   In case their own is retained, the school will likely give an examination at yearly intervals for the purpose of record. If the school physician is to supervise the case, the examinations by the school will be more frequent.

A recent study[1] of 24 schools showed that only 16 had regular physical examinations throughout the term. Only 11 of these 16 schools reported the length of the interval between examinations. One school makes examinations weekly; one does it monthly; three have it done three times a year; three do it at the beginning of each term; one makes examinations annually; and two do it biennially. The eight schools that do not have regular examinations arrange to have them upon the request of a teacher, the parents, a nurse, or a clinic.

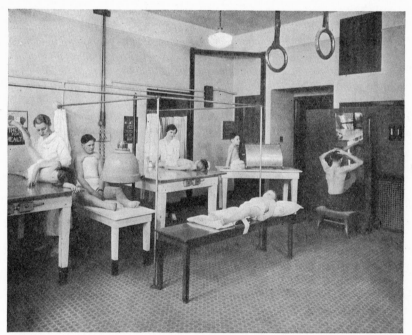

ILLUSTRATION 7.—Exercises, stretching, baking, and massage at the Leland School, Detroit.

Exercises.—Upon the basis of such examinations, exercises to meet the needs peculiar to each pupil are determined by the school or family physician and usually are carried out by the school's physio-

---

[1] Arch O. Heck, "Education of Crippled Children," *U. S. Office of Education Bulletin* 11, pp. 25–26, Washington, D.C., 1930.

therapists. Occasionally the exercises are given under the direct supervision of the family physician at his own office or at some clinic recommended by him.

Sometimes two or three children are treated at the same time. More frequently, the cases are so unlike that each child must be treated individually. This means that a single physiotherapist cannot care for a great number of children. The time allotment per child depends upon his condition; it may vary from 15 minutes to an hour for a single treatment. By overlapping the undressing and the baking of one child with the exercises of another, some time is saved. Illustration 7 shows exercises, baking, and massage being given.

Baths.—Schools in city systems provide baths for their pupils; both showers and tubs are used. Many exercises are taken in tanks, with the pupils submerged. When the pupil is thus supported by water, it is found that withered muscles more easily obey the impulse from the brain; this reaction is further augmented by the muscular relaxation induced by the warm water of the bath. The Christopher School in Chicago has a small swimming pool that is used for these tank exercises.

Light baths are just as frequently used and just as important. At the Christopher School "Heliotone lights and electric bakers are used to stimulate by heat the muscles that are given rebuilding massage and exercise." The quartz lamp is used for patients suffering with bone tuberculosis. The lamp gives an ultraviolet ray which makes possible, according to some authorities, an increased absorption of calcium and phosphorus from the intestine; this facilitates the healing process necessary for curing tuberculosis of the bone.

In the Spalding School at Chicago, provision has been made for natural sunlight baths. These are taken in the roof gardens on the third floor. In Cincinnati the sun baths are given in the two solaria, located on the southeast and southwest corners of the second floor. These rooms have great window areas covered with a glass that permits the penetration of the sun's ultraviolet ray.

Sleep and Rest.—Rest rooms are an important feature in the physical care of crippled children. Such children need rest that will enable the bodily forces to function rapidly in rebuilding the affected parts. The ideal situation is one in which each child uses his own cot and blankets. The Christopher School in Chicago makes this ideal type of provision for younger children and for heart cases. Many schools have cots for every two pupils; other schools are content if they have a cot for every four children. The state standards for

Ohio say that "cots may be in an adjoining room, but there shall be at least one cot to every 4 pupils. Where room is available a larger number is advisable."

Some schools have located the rest rooms so that they are very convenient to the pupils who are to occupy them. The Spalding School, however, has its rest rooms on the third floor. This takes them out of the noise and the atmosphere of the street level and gives the advantages of all the sunshine available. Without question, in a choice between traveling a short distance and having quiet, fresh air, and sunshine, one would choose the latter, just as Spalding did.

In Cincinnati, where the school is in a thickly populated section, the rest room is on the third floor, where sunshine and fresh air are abundant. One-story buildings are frequently located in beautiful spots, where quiet, sunshine, and fresh air are assured without reaching up into the air for them. The Sunbeam School at Cleveland is a shining example of a situation of this kind.

Food Served.—Schools for cripples find it necessary to serve meals, since the children are not able to go home at noon. Practice varies with respect to the number of feedings. Some schools serve just the noon meal; others serve a light lunch as soon as the children arrive in the morning and a midday meal; others, in addition to these two feedings, provide a light lunch shortly before the children leave school in the afternoon.

There is no unanimity of opinion concerning payment for this food. Many schools supply it free of charge; this is made possible either by the board of education or by some one of the numerous organizations that have interested themselves in the care and education of crippled children.[1] Other schools insist that all children pay for their food; this payment need not be made in money; it may be paid by allowing the child to help with the serving, to clear the tables, to wash the dishes, or to run various errands.

The Christopher School in Chicago serves cocoa and crackers to each child upon arrival. At noon a hot lunch is served without cost; it consists of a meat dish, a vegetable, bread, butter, fruit, and milk. The food is varied daily and is prepared and served by four luncheon attendants. At Newark, N.J., the children pay 15 cents apiece for lunch; the Kiwanis Club pays for the lunches of about 10 children. The Sunbeam School in Cleveland serves light refreshments upon arrival in the morning, a hot noon lunch, and milk in the afternoon. These excellent measures for the feeding of crippled children are essen-

[1] *Ibid.*, p. 26.

tial if maximum benefits are to be derived from the physical treatments and exercises to which they are submitted.

Recreation.—By no means the least important of the measures that should be taken for the physical care of crippled children is an adequate program of recreation. Ball games can be played; some of the children play on crutches, some in wheel chairs, some on foot. Such games as pin ball and basket-toss are favorites. The school at Newark, N.J., provides a 15-minute period twice a week in all class-rooms, where games are taught; frequently, these are the games that are played daily during the free play periods.

In cities where the cost of additional ground near the buildings makes adequate outside playgrounds prohibitive, space can be arranged on the roof. Many buildings have corridors wide enough to allow play space. In some buildings the solarium is used as a play-room. Crippled children need play in the open air, but such play must be supervised so as not to become too violent for individual pupils. These children should be taught games and encouraged to participate freely as long as their physical condition is satisfactory.

5. THE EDUCATIONAL PROGRAM

The educational program is very similar to that of the regular day schools; crippled children, mentally, are typical school children. They have the ability to do regular academic schoolwork and they should have an opportunity to do it.

The tendency to put crippled children into the trades at an early age, upon the theory that they must be taught to be selfsupporting, is vicious. We must, of course, help them to get a clear picture of the handicaps they will face in attempting to enter certain professions or occupations. This is the plainest common sense. But they should be given a chance at academic study through high school and college, if their mental ability and academic interest warrant it. They will, to be sure, take trade subjects at any time during this course, just as any normal child would. If their interest is predominantly in the trades, that interest should be encouraged, just as in the case with children who are physically fit.

Regular Curriculum.—The regular academic schoolwork too frequently is provided only through the elementary grades. Illustration 8 shows a primary class engaged in regular school activities. This is typical of the school activities of crippled children. If the child is not able to stand the boisterous hilarity of the regular high school and if his parents can not afford a tutor, he is often deprived of further education. Many crippled children are in this latter class; this means that at the outset the child is forced into the trades if he is to become selfsupporting.

The Spalding School at Chicago is now organized so that children can enter in grade 1 and remain until they are high-school graduates. Los Angeles has developed a special school for pupils of secondary-school level. Every school district should give crippled children an

ILLUSTRATION 8.—Crippled children of a primary class engaged in regular school activities.

opportunity to secure a high-school education. Of 22 cities which reported concerning the course of study used in the classes for cripples, every one stated that the regular course was adhered to for children normal mentally. Some of the larger schools provided a revised course for cripples who had low mental ability; the Spalding School did this.

Household Arts.—As in the case of regular grade schools, we find many special schools giving courses in household arts for the girls, often in an apartment consisting of kitchen, dining room, living room, and bedroom, fitted up for their practice in housekeeping. Girls are taught to plan, cook, and serve meals; they are taught the proper care of kitchen, dining room, and living room; and they are taught the

niceties of home etiquette.   In Illustration 9, girls are ready to serve
a meal they have just prepared.

Sewing courses are given.   These are not restricted to dressmaking
but include interior decoration, as well.   The girls not only get the
general theory of decoration but are taught to make curtains and
draperies that are to be used as a part of the decorative scheme.

ILLUSTRATION 9.—Homemaking emphasized at the Leland and Oakman Schools,
Detroit.   The group is preparing to serve a meal which they have just prepared.

These decorative plans may be quite simple, but some of the simplest
designs add considerable beauty to the home.

Practical Arts.—Some schools emphasize the learning of a trade as
the most important element in the education of a crippled child.
McDonald, writing in 1915, recommended " . . . the making of
reed articles, engraving, the jeweler's trade, mechanical drawing,
wood carving, cobbling, typewriting, printing, cooking, sewing,
embroidery, and dressmaking,"[1] as types of work in which persons
with limited strength might well engage.   Los Angeles teaches typewriting in its educational program for cripples; Illustration 10 presents
a class that is learning to type.

In a recent study of 36 schools,[2] 13 reported that they offered no
practical art subjects.   Among the remaining 23 schools, 19 types of

[1] ROBERT A. F. MCDONALD, *Adjustment of School Organization to Various
Population Groups*, p. 62, Teachers College, Columbia University, New York,
1915.

[2] HECK, *op. cit.*, pp. 24–25.

industrial work were provided.   However, many of the specific trades suggested by McDonald in 1915 were not found among the offerings of the 36 schools reporting in 1928.   The later types of industrial work are more generalized.   Actual practice tends to emphasize therapy and the development of healthy attitudes toward vocations rather than skills in some narrow field.   Illustration 11 shows children in an occupational therapy class in Los Angeles.

ILLUSTRATION 10.—Crippled youths learn typing at Los Angeles.

Results.—Evidence as to the results of the educational program that is provided for crippled children is very scarce.   We have instances of unusually fine results.   Some have graduated from college and technical schools with honors; a large number are high-school graduates; and some have gone into business and become successful. We do not know what proportion of the entire group have made good or are at least self-supporting.

The needed evidence is not easy to secure.   It costs money to follow up closely the aftercareer of the graduates of these schools. Since, however, the cost of educating crippled children in special classes and schools is rather high, it would be a wise expenditure of money to sustain a system that would make an adequate follow-up possible. If costly school buildings and equipment are failing to produce results, another plan might be evolved to accomplish what we feel ought to be done for these cripples. If present programs are

ILLUSTRATION 11.—Crippled children in an occupational therapy class, Los Angeles.

effective, the evidence obtained could be used to help preserve and broaden them.

6. FOLLOW-UP AND PLACEMENT

When crippled children complete grade 8 they are usually too young to find employment, even if they were prepared for it. Many of them need continued physical care; and often the parents are not familiar with the measures that are required to ensure this continued physical improvement. Failure to provide the necessary aftercare may easily neutralize all the beneficial effects of the school's physical care. There is a definite need for a continuous follow-up of each such crippled child.

Follow-up and placement are just as pressing in those school districts that make educational and vocational provision for cripples through a 12-year or a 16-year, instead of an 8-year program of study. Securing a position is not always easy, even though the crippled youth is perfectly capable of doing the work required. The fear that he might be more easily injured and therefore become a liability to the employer undoubtedly accounts in part for this difficulty. The schools should take the lead in the development of a local organization that will make possible placement and follow-up. The Rotary Clubs, Kiwanis, Lions, and the Shriners should be linked up with this program. A program of education should make leading businessmen cognizant of the ability to be found in those who are crippled.

A recent study of 36 schools[1] showed that only nine of them took definite steps that would assure the child who leaves them of proper physical care. The care provided in these nine cases was quite varied. Highland Park, Mich., provided treatments for children who entered high school; in San Francisco the school nurse was responsible for the follow-up; in Jersey City the medical examiner of the school and the school nurse were responsible.

At Elyria, Ohio,

the social service department of the hospital in which the school is located keeps in touch with the child after he is sent home; the county district nurse keeps the child under observation; the parents are instructed how to care properly for the child; directions concerning food and rest are made specific; the children are returned to the hospital for clinical examination at regular intervals; and this watchful care is often continued for several years.[1]

If the program of special education is included, in each city and county district, as a part of a complete pupil-personnel program,[2] the leadership necessary for adequate placement and follow-up will have been provided. Under such leadership, the assistance of all local organizations can be secured and a program can be put into operation that will make possible the placement and follow-up of all the cripples of the community.

7. THE RURAL PROBLEMS

One of the biggest problems to be met in educating crippled children is that of providing adequately for those in rural, village, and very small city districts. Various attempts have been made in the effort to solve the problem. One of the most recent is the establishment of a class for cripples at Chillicothe, Ohio, for Ross County. This class, in addition to serving the entire county, serves a few crippled children just outside the county boundaries.

[1] *Ibid.*, p. 28.
[2] For this recommendation, see pp. 468–473.

It was organized Oct. 16, 1935. A survey[1] made in the county 3 years before had indicated the need for such a class. The Rotary Club at Chillicothe co-operated with the local county and city boards of education in establishing it. The author of the survey aided materially in interesting these groups in the project. His research was made available to them. Two rooms in one of the city school buildings were specially equipped for crippled children; a special teacher and a physiotherapist were employed full time; and all cripples in the

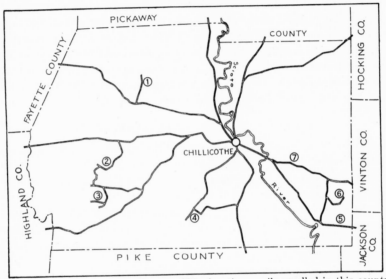

Fig. 1.—Outline map of Ross County, Ohio, locating pupils enrolled in this county's class for crippled children, January, 1938.

county were contacted. When the class was organized, 18 children were enrolled.

By January, 1938, the class had an enrollment of 26 students. Five of these are children from other counties who are boarded in Chillicothe in order that they may enjoy the advantages of this special class. Fourteen of the children reside in the city of Chillicothe. Among these, however, are several whose parents previously lived in the rural districts but moved into the city so that their children might live at home and attend the special class. The remaining seven children are from rural areas of the county. Three are boarded

[1] MERLE R. SUMPTION, "A Survey to Determine the Number and Location of Physically Handicapped Children of School Age in Ross County, Ohio, and a Proposed Plan for Their Education," unpublished Master's thesis, Ohio State University, Columbus, 1932.

in the city and four are transported daily by automobile to and from school. All crippled children of the class are transported to the door of the school building by taxicab.

An outline map of Ross County is shown in Fig. 1. The homes of the seven children from the rural areas of the county are spotted and numbered from 1 to 7. Those numbered 1, 2, and 3 board in Chillicothe and go home each week end; those numbered 4, 5, 6, and 7 are transported daily. Only the county roads leading to the homes of the seven children are shown. The five who live outside the county and are boarded in Chillicothe live 20, 35, 100, 100, and 100 miles respectively from the city. What is being done in Ross County, Ohio, can undoubtedly be duplicated in many other rural sections just as soon as hard roads are built, and as soon as the need is clearly understood and someone assumes the responsibility for making clear the need and for handling the many problems involved in organizing such a class.

8. DESCRIPTION OF SELECTED SCHOOLS

Cincinnati's School for Cripples.—This school was first opened in 1928. Previous to that date the cripples had been treated and educated in the general city hospital. The present building is a three-story structure; it is equipped to house 250 children. Stairways and elevators are provided, toilets are between every two classrooms, handrails are placed along the corridors, and vestibules are arranged so that busses can back up to the entrances and unload their pupils without exposing them to the weather.

The first floor is similar to a regular school building; the second floor contains special-treatment suites, the solaria, domestic and practical art rooms, and examination rooms. The basement floor has the tank room, pool, and lunchroom. The school cares for crippled children from the entire city; the children are given medical, dental, nursing, and physiotherapeutical care. Educationally the work parallels that of the other public schools; graduates enter the regular high schools. The school supervises the work done for crippled children in three hospitals and one convalescent home; five teachers give home instruction to as many as 45 children.

Oakman School.—This school is a one-story structure of the open-court type. It is shown in Illustration 12. It is located in Detroit and is designed and equipped to care for 300 children. The building occupies an entire block and has four entrances, one at the center of each side. These entrances lead to main central corridors, 13 feet in width, which run the length of each side of the building. Handrails are located on either side of all corridors.

The classrooms occupy the outer walls, with doors opening on a terrace where outdoor classes are held in fine weather. All special rooms surround the inner court, except the cot room, the playroom, the lunchroom, and the auditorium; these four rooms occupy the four outer corners of the building. The auditorium has a separate entrance for public use; a ramp makes the stage accessible to children in wheel chairs. The physiotherapy department gave 12,029 treatments during the school year 1935–36.

ILLUSTRATION 12.—A typical modern one-story building for crippled children. The Oakman School, Detroit.

Spalding School.—This school is located in the heart of the great West Side of Chicago. It was the first of the centers that Chicago has developed for the education of crippled children. The original building at its maximum housed about 600 children; the new Spalding houses over 1,000 pupils. This new building "is a modified Maltese cross with four wings of classrooms leading out from certain centralized facilities."[1] Ramps, elevators, and stairways have all been provided.

The school is unique in its treatment section. It has a series of small rooms in which treatments are given. Each is large enough to accommodate two pupils and contains massage table, washbasin, set of stall bars, full-length mirror, small desk, chair, and electrical outlets. There are both shower and tub baths. There are dressing

[1] JANE A. NEIL, "Chicago's Laboratory, the Jesse Spalding School for Crippled Children," *Bulletin of the City of Chicago Municipal Tuberculosis Sanitorium* (June, 1927), Vol. 7, No. 6, p. 10.

rooms, lockers, washrooms, and a waiting room in connection with the central treatment office, where parents may observe the treatments and exercises.

Shops are equipped for actual training; they make it possible for pupils to enter apprentice courses. In the lunchroom·pupils are fed upon arrival at school; the usual noon meal is provided. The kitchen is large, modern, and very well equipped. The corridors are 14 by 75 feet and are large enough to be used for play.

Sunbeam School.—This school is located in the eastern part of Cleveland. The board of education was fortunate in securing a location on a high knoll, apart from heavy traffic, and well secluded from the observation of passers-by. There are no factories near by to bring noise and soot; but there is plenty of fresh air, as well as quiet. The building was opened in September, 1923. Before that time, crippled children had been housed in a temporary frame building. The total capacity is 250. The building is fireproof and is of the one-story type. The single story was decided upon in order to eliminate ramps.

The rooms are so arranged that the kindergarten and the lower grades are near the rest room, the playroom, and the gymnasium. The upper grades have a rest room near by, as well as the manual training and domestic science rooms. There are 10 classrooms; each has two exits, one to the corridor and the other to the school grounds. There are a manual training and a domestic science department but no attempt is made to train for a specific vocation. One of the domestic science rooms is divided into four units, to serve as a model housekeeping apartment with kitchen, dining room, bedroom, and sitting room. There are in addition, a large kitchen and a large dining room for feeding the children.

An auditorium seating 450 is provided. Next to the auditorium is a playroom which, with the auditorium, dining room, gymnasium, and treatment suite, occupy the center of the building; hallways completely surround these units. Most of this central space can be used for free play and is so used. During good weather, however, many of the children play in the large cement court on the side of the building where busses drive in to unload and load the children.

9. SUMMARY

Practical problems of organization and administration in the education of crippled children must be met and overcome, if theoretical considerations are ever to be achieved. The type, general plan, and special features of school buildings for cripples; needed equipment;

methods of transportion; the program, both physical and educational; and the need for and ways and means of providing for placement and follow-up are practical problems that must be solved. Central schools for educating cripples have many unique features. These include such things as ramps, elevators, numerous toilets, handrails in corridors and on stairways, full-length mirrors in hallways, wide halls, wheel chairs, specially made desks, tanks, equipment for strengthening various muscles, swimming pools, baths, solaria, sleeping rooms, light treatments, frequent feeding, close medical supervision, and transportation.

Problems and Questions for Discussion

1. What may be one of our chief difficulties in putting admirable theories relative to the education of cripples into effect? Explain.

2. In what unique ways should a school building for crippled children differ from regular school buildings? Why?

3. Describe some regular school building you have visited; explain what remodeling would be needed in order to adapt it to the use of crippled children. Draw sketches to show present plans and the proposed changes.

4. Describe special equipment that will be needed in a school for cripples. Show how it will be used and why.

5. How are crippled children transported to school? How should they be transported? Why?

6. Describe the methods used in the physical care of pupils in schools for cripples.

7. Does the educational program for cripples differ in any essentials from that provided for other children? Should it? If so, how? If not, why not?

8. What seem to be the great gaps in programs for educating crippled children?

9. Be able to describe in some detail one or more special schools for crippled children.

Selected Bibliography

CHRISTIANAR, ALICE. "Sunbeam School: A Public School for Crippled Children," *The Nation's Health*, No. 5 (May 15, 1924), Vol. 6, pp. 303–305, 360.

Describes the building in some detail, as well as the use to which each part of the building is put. The origin of the school is explained briefly. Several splendid illustrations accompany the account.

DUNNING, NEAL M., and others. "Two New Schools Widen Educational Activities of Michigan Cities," *The Nation's Schools*, No. 6 (June, 1929), Vol. 3, pp. 58–60.

Describes the Charles H. Oakman School for Crippled Children at Detroit. The uses to which each unit of the building is put are described and floor plans are given.

"Handicapped and Underprivileged Children: Special Schools and Special Care," with *The Thirty-sixth Annual Report of the Superintendent of Schools*, pp. 106–180. Board of Education, New York City, 1934.

A descriptive account of what New York City does for its physically handicapped children, of the aims and purposes of the work, and of the follow-up of the careers of these children.

HANNAFORD, H. ELDRIDGE. "Where Crippled Children Are Taught to Lead Normal Lives," *The Nation's Schools*, No. 3 (September, 1930), Vol. 6, pp. 65–68.

Gives description of the school for crippled children at Cincinnati, Ohio, accompanied by beautiful illustrations; the provisions for physical care and education are discussed.

HECK, ARCH O. "Education of Crippled Children," *U. S. Office of Education Bulletin* 11, Washington, D.C., 1930. 57 pp.

Describes in some detail various ways in which local districts meet the numerous administrative problems involved in organizing schools for crippled children.

LORD, ELIZABETH EVANS, and CROTHERS, BRONSON. *Children Handicapped by Cerebral Palsy*. The Commonwealth Fund, New York, 1937. 105 pp.

A psychological study of more than 300 cases of cerebral palsy treated at the Children's Hospital in Boston; gives attention to mental testing and mental development and notes the relation of these to problems of parents and teachers.

McLEOD, BEATRICE. "Teachers' Problems with Exceptional Children. V. Crippled Children." *U. S. Office of Education Pamphlet* 55, Washington, D.C., 1934. 18 pp.

Discusses such problems as who the children are and how crippled; what the educational provisions, treatments, and the like are; has a good reading list.

ROGERS, GLADYS GAGE, and THOMAS, LEAH C. *New Pathways for Children with Cerebral Palsy*. The Macmillan Company, New York, 1935. 167 pp.

A most interesting account of methods used in the treatment of spastics. The authors believe that "the spastic requires a treatment entirely different from other cripples." They give attention to such problems as relaxation, muscle training, toys, apparatus, body mechanics, surgical treatment, and the responsibilities of parents.

"The School for Crippled Children, Part I," *Newark School Bulletin* 5, Newark, N.J. (January, 1926), Vol. 6, pp. 87–94.

Explains the purpose of the school; describes the building, and transportation system, and the schools' various activities.   Illustrations are given.

"The School for Crippled Children, Part II," *Newark School Bulletin* 6, Newark, N.J. (February, 1926), Vol. 6, pp. 111–117.

Describes the physical care provided for cripples, as well as treatments that are given.

YARDLEY, R. W. "Building Schools for Crippled Children," *The Nation's Schools*, No. 5 (November, 1930), Vol. 6, pp. 55–64.

The Spalding and Christopher schools for crippled children in Chicago are described; floor plans and pictures of the buildings are given. The uses to which each unit of these buildings is put are described.

CHAPTER XI

THE CHALLENGE OF THE CRIPPLE

Ignorance blocks many a program aimed at helping the unfortunate. The crippled children of our country have suffered and continue to suffer for this reason. An investigator recently undertook a survey of such children within a county school district. County authorities discouraged the plan, because of a belief that the county had not enough crippled children to make a survey worth while. The survey, however, was made and disclosed a great many cripples unknown to school authorities and local social agencies. All these youths had been ignored educationally and many of them had had no medical attention for months. This is typical of what happens whenever complete and accurate surveys are made to discover the number of crippled children within a given community.

1. THE SIZE OF THE PROBLEM

The New York State Commission[1] used 2.5 as the number of crippled children under eighteen years of age for every 1,000 persons in the general population. The White House Conference claims that in the light of various state and local surveys this ratio seems to be conservative. New Jersey discovered 11,671 cases, which represent a ratio of 2.9 in terms of the 1930 census figures. New Jersey cities of over 100,000 varied from 1.24 to 4.07 cripples per 1,000 of the general population; cities of 30,000 to 100,000 varied from 1.70 to 9.79; cities and towns under 15,000 varied from 1.19 to 5.10.

If the 2.5 ratio is approximately correct and if we estimate the total population of the United States at 130 millions, there would be 325,000 crippled children under eighteen in this country. If 2.9 is the ratio assumed, there would be 377,000 cripples. The White House Conference[2] estimated that there were 300,000 crippled children in the United States and that 100,000 of them needed the services of a special school or class. This means that every community of 50,000 population has from 125 to 145 crippled children under eighteen years of age; it means also that one-third of them, or from 42 to 48, need a

---

[1] White House Conference, *Special Education: The Handicapped and the Gifted*, p. 24, The Century Co., New York, 1931.

[2] *Ibid.*, p. 5.

program of special education. Upon this basis, a school district of 5,000 population in general will have about 5 crippled children in need of special education.

These facts present a clear challenge to every community to study its child population; it should maintain a continuous census that would show who its children are and where and under what conditions they live. For one who is interested in reducing the suffering of children, in eliminating crippling conditions, and in helping the crippled child to become self-supporting, there can hardly be a greater challenge than that of discovering them and of planning a special program for their education and care.

But an even greater challenge faces us when another series of facts is considered. The White House Conference says, "An analysis of the onset of crippling conditions in 1,531 cases in Chicago disclosed the fact that 83 per cent of the children under twenty-one years of age had been crippled under the age of six years."[1] When crippled children under six years of age are found and given medical and surgical attention at once, many can be cured. Thus the need of special education for them will be prevented.

Again quoting the White House Conference,[2] "Experience has shown that at least 50 per cent of crippling conditions occurring at this period are curable if taken in time." If, of the 100,000 crippled children in the United States who now need special education, 80 per cent were crippled under six or seven years of age, and if 50 per cent of these 80,000 could have been cured, we are at once faced with the possibility that 40,000 of our present group of cripples could have been cured by the time they had reached the age of entering school. This would have meant less need for special education, less suffering upon the part of the unfortunate children, and greater opportunity for them to become self-supporting and to contribute to the social welfare of all. This challenge of prevention will be even more impressive when the various possibilities for preventing the conditions that result in orthopedic defects are once considered.

2. THE CAUSES OF ORTHOPEDIC DEFECTS[3]

No program of prevention can be planned without first giving some thought to what causes orthopedic defects. While these causes are innumerable, a few are clearly of major importance. The facts shown in Table IX have considerable significance. Infantile paral-

[1] *Ibid.*, p. 26.
[2] *Ibid.*, p. 27.
[3] Referred to often and less technically as crippling conditions.

ysis[1] is clearly shown to be the chief cause; the range in per cent is from 25.4 at Los Angeles to 82.0 at Newark. The number of cases at Newark is, however, small. The per cent of infantile paralysis cases for the entire 9,982 cases is 35.0.

The rest of the table is less informing. The total per cent for spastic paralysis cases is only 3.2, whereas, with one exception, the individual surveys ranged from 5.6 per cent to the 18.5 per cent, with a median of 8.5. The report on tuberculosis is significant. With

TABLE IX.—CAUSES OF ORTHOPEDIC DEFECTS

Causes	Reports from various sections						
	Christopher School at Chicago	Los Angeles	Ohio		Newark, N.J.	State of New Jersey	Total
			1925–26	1920–30			
Infantile paralysis....	38.2	25.4	36.7	29.8	82.0	37.0	35.0
Spastic paralysis.....	18.5	8.0	8.5	5.6	10.0	.....	3.2
Tuberculosis.........	13.9	9.1	16.9	18.6	.....	3.3	9.6
Cardiac condition....	9.4	10.3	8.4	.....	.....	.....	1.3
Accidents..........	.....	12.3	.....	.....	.....	12.6	7.5
Congenital deformities	.....	2.4	8.5	20.7	.....	26.0	21.4
Acquired deformities.	.....	.....	.....	21.6	.....	.....	6.0
Miscellaneous........	20.0	32.5	21.0	3.7	8.0	21.1	16.0
Total............	100.0	100.0	100.0	100.0	100.0	100.0	100.0
Cases............	330	252	886	2,757	50	5,707	9,982

two exceptions, the individual reports range from 9.1 per cent to 18.6 per cent. Nonuniform methods of classifying the causes evidently occasion some of these variations.

3. PREVENTION OF ORTHOPEDIC DEFECTS

The prevention of orthopedic defects is the most significant of all the problems we meet in dealing with cripples. If it could be solved completely, the problems of discovering, examining, curing, educating, and placing the cripple would no longer exist; not only would they be solved, but the agony, both of body and of mind, undergone by these little sufferers would be eliminated.

The task of preventing orthopedic defects, however, is the most difficult and baffling of all the problems that confront those interested

[1] More accurately described as acute anterior poliomyelitis.

in the cripple. It is difficult for many reasons: (1) It requires the co-operation of many people. (2) Since most of these people are not familiar with their part in the program, it demands a widespread program of education. (3) Since poor hygienic conditions are related to the frequency of many diseases that cause orthopedic defects, we need for all families a standard of living that will permit of the best hygienic living conditions. The general economic status of the entire social group becomes, therefore, a factor in the elimination of orthopedic defects.

Specific Suggestions.—It has been shown that infantile paralysis[1] is the chief single cause of orthopedic defects in children. We now know that it is caused by a filterable virus; we have reason to believe that individuals not infected may be carriers of the virus to others. The virus apparently enters the body through the nose and throat, travels through the olfactory nerves to the brain, and from there extends down the spinal cord. While infantile paralysis is now considered to be a systemic infection, it is in the spinal cord that most of the damage is apparent. It is the destruction of nerve tissue here that results in the paralysis of various muscles.

If the disease is epidemic, no increase in temperature and no indisposition should be allowed to exist without attention by a physician who is familiar with the diagnosis and treatment of this condition. If the case is taken early, before paralysis has occurred, the administration of human convalescent serum or whole blood from either of the parents appears to abort some cases. Even in the early stages of paralysis, most authorities advocate this treatment, in the hope that the disease will be arrested and the damaged nervous tissue allowed to regenerate.

The probable mode of entrance of the virus of poliomyelitis into the body has suggested a means of prophylaxis. Schultz and Gebhardt[2] report that the application of a defined strength of zinc sulphate solution to the olfactory nerves prevented entrance of the virus into the brains of monkeys. This method was extensively used in the summer and fall of 1937. No figures are yet available that would indicate its efficacy in man.

In an epidemic, parents and older members of the family should keep out of crowds just as strictly as the younger children are kept from them, since adults may be carriers. It should also be remem-

---

[1] See footnote, p. 144.

[2] E. W. SCHULTZ, M. D., and L. P. GEBHARDT, M. A., "Zinc Sulfate Prophylaxis in Poliomyelitis," *The Journal of the American Medical Association* (June 26, 1937), Vol. 108, pp. 2182–2184.

bered that, while children are more susceptible to the disease, adults frequently succumb to it.

A considerable number of children in schools for cripples have spastic paralysis; this is caused by some defect in brain centers. A hemorrhage due to prolonged labor at birth may cause the condition; infectious diseases, such as meningitis, may bring on a condition of this kind later in childhood. A child in this condition moves the affected muscles with difficulty; walking, standing, and arm movements are awkwardly made. The muscles seem stiff and work rather spasmodically.

Too much care can not be taken at birth to prevent prolonged labor, forceps delivery, and prolonged asphyxia. The most skilled physician possible should be secured in all obstetrical cases. In meningitis cases, if they are detected early, there is a serum which "is believed by most observers to be of value. . . . "[1] The White House Conference report says that personal cleanliness and the elimination of overcrowding are important measures in the prevention of this disease. Healthy persons may be carriers; this is particularly true during epidemics. The past year has been marked by an advance in chemotherapy in meningitis. If later reports substantiate present work, the chemical sulphanilamide promises to supplant serotherapy.

Tuberculosis is another of the diseases that result in orthopedic defects. The disease attacks the tissue of the bones and joints; it may thus affect the spine, the knees, the ankles, shoulders, and hips. It operates very slowly, and in many cases parents hardly realize that anything is wrong with the child until the deformity appears. The child may get the disease from parents who have tuberculosis of the lungs, from the milk of tubercular cows, or from living conditions of squalor and filth. The preventive measures are thus self-evident. The whole social program of eradicating slums, with their filth and dirt, will help. Parents who suspect any tubercular trouble should have immediate medical advice and follow it. Milk should not be used unless it has been pasteurized or unless the cows have been recently tested.

Many common deformities can be prevented to a great extent if treatments are begun early in the life of the child. Club feet should be treated in infancy while the bones are soft and pliable. Dislocated hips, if treated as soon as discovered, can be cured. Deformities resulting from fractures and joint injuries may be prevented to a considerable degree by prompt, skilled treatment.

[1] White House Conference, *Communicable Disease Control*, p. 150, The Century Co., New York, 1931.

General Suggestions.—The most valuable of all the suggestions of a general nature for the prevention of orthopedic defects is that a program of education be undertaken and be eternally continued. The object of the program will be to acquaint every home with what physicians now generally know concerning the means of preventing these defects. Specific information concerning what parents themselves can do should be included.

Quarantine methods should not relax. All physicians should be made responsible and liable for reporting immediately cases that ought to come under quarantine. Every physician should be required to report in some detail the results of his examination of the newborn child. Should orthopedic defects be detected, the health department should immediately contact the physician to lend the aid of any of its agencies in helping to correct the defect. Each political unit should provide physicians for the care of indigent maternity cases. Midwives should be licensed and should be made responsible for calling a physician of the health department if there is no family physician in charge.

Laws relating to birth control now on many statute books should be repealed. Measures should be taken to give to married persons and to those about to be married full information, sensible and wholesome, concerning the sex act, the rearing of children, and general physical hygiene. Such preventive measures as are suggested in this section should become a vital part of any city's program of education, both special and regular. The extent to which cities now fail to do this directly will be evident in the following section, if printed reports of what they do can be trusted to tell the entire story.

4. THE CITY SCHOOL DISTRICT'S ADMINISTRATIVE PROGRAM

City school districts have followed no uniform procedure in educating their crippled children. The system used by a given city may not represent the best thought of that city; it may represent just the growth of a program, with many adjustments to the exigencies of the occasion. It will, nevertheless, be referred to as the plan of the city in question.

The New York City Plan.—In 1927–28, New York City had one large central school for crippled children that housed 460 pupils. The remainder of the cripples in the public schools were housed in regular school buildings; this latter group consisted of 3,123 children, organized into 146 class groups. The total number, 3,583, was 1,069 more cripples than were being educated in New York City during the school year of 1920–21. By 1934, 4,547 crippled children were cared for.   The report of 1934 did not mention a central school and Table X shows a scattering of pupils among a great number of the city schools.

TABLE X.—ORGANIZATION PROVIDED FOR CRIPPLED CHILDREN IN NEW YORK CITY (1934)[1]

Type of case	Register	Teachers	Schools and annexes	Location
Crippled.........	1,296	59	32	Elementary Public School classes
Crippled.........	422	..	20	Vocational High School,
Crippled.........	620	6	9	Elementary and High School physiotherapy centers
Cardiopathic.....	1,239	54	39	Elementary Public School, and convalescence homes
Crippled.........	970	46	26	Hospital and convalescence homes
Total.........	4,547			

[1] Adapted from "Handicapped and Underprivileged Children: Special Schools and Special Care," p. 110, a special report submitted with the *Thirty-sixth Annual Report of the Superintendent of Schools*, New York City, 1934.

Home instruction has been provided since December, 1918; this was found necessary in order to educate all children mentally capable and yet physically too helpless to be transported and educated in a special class.   In June, 1921, 33 home teachers gave instruction to 173 crippled children.   Each full-time teacher spent six 6-hour days each week in home instruction.   By 1934, 786 pupils were taught in homes; 126 teachers and a few part-time teachers gave this instruction.

The aim in this educational program for cripples is to enable home cases to enter special classes as quickly as possible and to lessen the orthopedic defects of children in these special classes, so that they may be returned to regular classes at the earliest opportunity.   Large school buildings equipped with elaborate paraphernalia are frowned upon; the preferred course is to take all necessary steps to reduce physical handicaps without building monuments celebrating the education of the cripple.   The aim is to have all children in regular school classes.

The Chicago Plan.—Chicago maintains four large, well-equipped elementary schools located at strategic centers for crippled children; there are no classes organized in regular school buildings.   In 1927–28, the enrollment for these schools was 1,624.   The Spalding School alone can care for over 1,000 children; the Christopher can house 500.

In addition to the elementary schools, two special schools of high-school grade are maintained, which are rated as branches of regular high schools. The services in all schools are practically the same, "although the facilities for treatment at Spalding are more elaborate than those in other schools."

Recognition at present is given to the idea that these children need long and continuous care and that, if they are to be given an opportunity equal to that of their more fortunate brothers and sisters, this physical care and their education must go hand in hand. The best of equipment for physical treatments has been provided. The authorities intend that nothing shall be neglected in trying to bring to these children the highest degree of physical fitness possible. It is recognized that in many cases several years of persistent care and treatments are necessary to accomplish the maximum recovery. It is this maximum recovery that the plan seeks to emphasize.

The Cleveland Plan.—Cleveland has one central school building; there are no classes in regular school buildings.[1] The Cleveland theory seems to be that crippled children should attend regular schools as long as they can do so without physical discomfort or injury to themselves; this means that as soon as the physical condition of children in the school has improved sufficiently, they are returned to the regular day schools. A Cleveland report says, "So far as possible, crippled children are encouraged to attend classes with normal children. Approximately 1,300 are thus enrolled in regular schools, learning to 'stand up to' life without expecting special privileges."[2] This seems typical of what we have here called the Cleveland plan.

The Los Angeles Plan.—Los Angeles has organized classes in three regular public schools and in four hospitals; about 848 pupils are thus cared for. In addition, about 506 more children are being taught at home. According to a report in 1936, there were to be three school buildings "in the use of crippled children exclusively"[3] by Jan. 1, 1937. Los Angeles is unique with respect to its high-school program for cripples. High-school work was begun in 1925 at the Orthopaedic Hospital. During the school year, 1935–36, the average enrollment of cripples at the Metropolitan High School was 70; there were 136 others who received instruction at home or in hospitals.

[1] See p. 139.

[2] Report of the Superintendent of Schools to the Board of Education of the City School District of the City of Cleveland, p. 103, School Year, 1927–28.

[3] "Education of the Physically Handicapped," p. 20, Los Angeles City School District, *School Publication* 281, Los Angeles, Calif., 1936.

To teach these crippled children, 50 elementary and 11 secondary teachers are employed.

Suggestions.—The reports dealing with these city programs gave clear and forceful statements concerning that part of a program of special education which deals with remedial measures. Needed preventive measures were not emphasized. This is the point at which workers who are interested in crippled children face a real challenge. Have they the daring, the vision, and the ability so to organize a state and local program of special education for crippled children that preventive as well as remedial measures will be included and put into operation?

5. STATE LEGISLATION

The Census of Crippled Children.—The White House Conference,[1] reporting in 1930, showed that by law 15 states took a census of the crippled at the time they took the regular school census; 12 other states could do this by ruling of the state department of education. Six additional states, as well as 9 of the preceding 27, provided also a special census or survey of cripples. One other state, in addition to 16 of the 33 just listed, provided local and district clinics. Two more states, plus 5 listed above, required the reporting of children at birth. Of these 36 states with some provision governing a census of cripples, 3 require an annual registration of such children by their parents.

It should be clearly understood that this census ought to aim at securing more than a bare list of youths who are badly crippled. Again and again the idea of prevention has been emphasized; if anything really worth while is to be accomplished, there must be data concerning those whose physical condition is such that physical deformity is sure to follow unless immediate correction is available. Any census of the crippled should make sure that all such children are listed.[2]

Rules Governing the Establishment of Classes.—Only 20 states, according to Steiner, had specific legislation governing the establishment of classes for crippled children in 1928.[3] Six of these states set up no regulations governing curriculum, state aid, or supervision; they simply granted local boards the right to establish such classes.

---

[1] White House Conference, *Special Education: The Handicapped and the Gifted,* pp. 30–31, The Century Co., New York, 1931.

[2] See suggestions regarding census program, pp. 499–500.

[3] JESSE W. STEINER, *The Legal Provisions for the Education of Crippled and Feeble-minded Children in the Forty-eight States,* pp. 22–26, an unpublished Master's thesis, Ohio State University, 1928.

State Financial Aid and Its Effects.[1]—Of the 20 states that had legislation pertaining to the establishment of classes for crippled children, only 12 made provision for helping finance such a program.[2] It is interesting to note the relation between the provision of state aid for the education of crippled children and the number of cities in the various states that reported having schools and classes for their education. There were 88 cities that claimed to have classes or schools for the crippled.[3] The 12 states that provided state aid had 71, or 80.7 per cent, of the cities of the United States that had organized schoolwork for crippled children. The remaining 17 cities were located in 11 states. The situation is shown clearly in Table XI.

Undoubtedly, state aid is not the only factor; the number of large cities within the state is also a factor. Nevertheless, Tennessee, Texas, and Massachusetts have a number of large cities, and these states had only one, two, and three cities, respectively, reporting schools and classes for crippled children. Those interested in the

TABLE XI.—RELATION BETWEEN PROVISION FOR STATE AID AND NUMBER OF CITIES PROVIDING SCHOOLS AND CLASSES FOR CRIPPLED CHILDREN

Provision of State Aid	Number of Cities Having Schools or Classes
12 states provide state aid	71
11 states do not provide aid	17
25 states do not provide aid	0
48 states	88 cities

development of special classes and schools for crippled children can well afford to give some thought to these figures. Incidentally, it is interesting to note that Ohio, which is most liberal in its special aid, had 25 cities with such classes.

6. A STATE PROGRAM

The care and education of crippled children should be considered just as much a part of the state's educational program as is the education of physically normal children. The state department of education will, therefore, supervise the education of all crippled children and co-operate with all agencies interested in educating them.

The State's Part in This Program.—The following outline indicates proposals to which the state department of education should give considerable attention.

[1] For discussion of methods of giving financial aid, see pp. 451–454.
[2] STEINER, *op. cit.*, p. 32.
[3] See p. 116.

1. A continuous census of all crippled children should be kept. Reports of deformities at birth should be required of physicians or of those in attendance at a birth. Reports of accidents or of diseases resulting in orthopedic defects should be required of physicians attending given cases.

2. A program of education aimed at preventing accidents, diseases, and conditions that are known to cause orthopedic defects should be planned.

3. A state aid program should be developed that would encourage local districts to provide adequately for their crippled children.

4. A series of clinics should be held yearly throughout the state for the purpose of discovering orthopedic defects or potential orthopedic defects.

5. A complete survey of conditions within given school districts (city or county) showing the need for new classes or schools should be made. The state supervisor in these surveys would secure the assistance of all local agencies who have or who might have an interest in such children.

6. Upon the basis of surveys, the feasibility of establishing one or more state or regional schools for crippled children will be determined. Any community able to provide satisfactorily for its cripples should be allowed to do so. There may be rural sections where this is clearly impossible; there may be unspeakable home conditions from which the child should be removed completely; the frequency of these cases will be a determining factor in deciding whether a state school, one or more regional schools, or no such schools should be established under state control.

The District's Part in the Program.—There must be someone in the local district (city or county) directly responsible for the care and education of crippled children.[1] He will secure the aid and co-operation of all local groups interested in the cripple, assist the state in developing an educational program aimed at the prevention of orthopedic defects, provide a continuing census of cripples, and co-operate with the state in conducting an annual clinic.

Districts with fewer than eight crippled children will provide home instruction for cripples living in satisfactory home conditions and able to receive all needed medical care at home; where either of these conditions is not met, the child shall be a candidate for a state or regional school, unless the parents prefer to place him in a local hospital at their own expense. If local hospitals are used, the local

[1] For a discussion of state and local administrative organization, see Chap. XXXI.

board of education should provide teachers for all who are physically able to study.

Every local district with as many as eight crippled children should establish a special class as a part of its system of public education; this implies the provision of such equipment as is necessary for the proper care, as well as the proper education, of these children. This requirement should apply to county school districts as well as to cities; in districts where medical care and treatment cannot be provided, the state school or the state regional schools could care for the children.

Large city districts should provide at least one central school where the best of facilities for physical care would be supplied; if the city maintains a hospital where such care is given free, such a hospital might substitute for the central school and the board of education could offer an educational program for the children at the hospital. The special school, however, if equipped properly, is preferred.

Whether all the crippled children within a city should be cared for and educated in large central schools or whether the one school should be supplemented by the organization of special classes is an open question. One should constantly remember that the goal of any program of caring for cripples is prevention. If success is attained in this direction, it might be hoped that not only the ratio but the present number of crippled children would diminish from year to year. If this be the case, it is possible that one or, at most, two big central schools for even our largest cities, supplemented by a varying number of special classes, might quite ideally meet their needs in trying to educate crippled children.

7. SUMMARY

The fact that we have at least 300,000 crippled children in the United States, that 100,000 of them need a program of special education, that approximately 80 per cent become crippled under six or seven years of age, and that 50 per cent of these cripples could be cured if discovered at once and treated promptly, thrusts upon school authorities in every local district a very real challenge. They must provide a continuous census; they must provide needed medical and surgical aid for all cripples from birth on; and they must develop a program of educating them from six or seven years of age through high school. Such a program must emphasize both preventive and remedial measures. The former unquestionably presents the greater challenge since, if successful, these measures would (1) immediately remove the greatest handicap to self-support, (2) prevent the agony and inferiority attitudes due to a crippled condition, and (3) make unnecessary the costly program of special education. The latter holds a real challenge of its own, inasmuch as an adequate program of special education will (1) materially lessen the orthopedic defects, (2) make the youth better able to support himself, and (3) give him an optimistic outlook upon life.

The outstanding causes of these orthopedic defects are (1) infantile paralysis, (2) spastic paralysis, (3) tuberculosis, and (4) congenital deformities. Preventive measures involve (1) early discovery, (2) education of the public, (3) early diagnosis of all colds, (4) greater care of maternity cases, (5) campaigns to eliminate dirt and filth, (6) supervision of the sale of milk and other foods, and (7) the provision of medical and surgical care as soon as the orthopedic defect is discovered.

A class should be provided in any district wherever eight crippled children are discovered who can profit from attendance at such a class; home instruction should be provided for those unable to attend class. A state or regional school may be necessary in some states for those in remote areas or where home conditions are miserable.

Problems and Questions for Discussion

1. What is the challenge of the crippled child? Explain.
2. What are the chief causes of orthopedic defects? Give your evidence.
3. How would you proceed in an attempt to prevent orthopedic defects? Illustrate.
4. Describe two or more methods used in large cities to educate crippled children. Which is best?
5. Outline the state legislation which you consider necessary in order that a state may organize properly to educate the crippled children.
6. If you were the superintendent of schools in a city of 25,000, what steps would you take in order to care for the crippled children of your city? If you were superintendent in a county school system, what would you do?

Selected Bibliography

BERRY, CHARLES SCOTT. *Special Education*, pp. 25–30. Detroit Board of Education, 1925.

Brief description of the organization of the work of educating cripples; describes the present program, the care given, and the educational work provided.

"Handicapped and Underprivileged Children: Special Schools and Special Care," pp. 106–138. A special report submitted with *The Thirty-sixth Annual Report of the Superintendent of Schools*, City of New York, 1934.

Describes program of educating its crippled children. New York emphasizes early discovery, immediate physical restoration, a good school program, social placement, and careful follow-up; programs for doing these things are described.

HORN, JOHN LOUIS. *The Education of Exceptional Children*, pp. 291–313. The Century Co., New York, 1924.

Discussion of the nature of the problem of educating crippled children, of the problems of organization and instruction, of three needs, and of the possibility of having state schools.

HOWETT, HARRY H. *Progress in the Education of Crippled Children*. The International Society for Crippled Children, Inc., Elyria, Ohio, January, 1930. 20 pp.

Brief discussion of origins, first steps in corrective education, and outline of modern special education. Programs operating in the United States, private and public. Three state programs described.

LISON, MARGUERITE M. *Care and Education of Crippled Children and Disabled Adults*. Wisconsin Association for the Disabled, *Bulletin 1*, Madison, Wis., July, 1928. 53 pp.

Short history of the organization is given; its activities are described; and statistics concerning the causes of orthopedic defects are presented. Laws relating to the medical care and education of cripples in Wisconsin are also given.

Report of the Temporary Commission for Inquiry Relating to the Distribution and Condition of Crippled Children. Report of New Jersey State Crippled Children's Commission, 1928. 47 pp.

Survey findings on the number of cripples, facilities provided for their physical care and education, existing legislation, and recommendations.

SMITH, MABEL E. *The Crippled Child: The Ohio Plan for Care, Treatment, and Education*. Crippled Children's Bureau, Division of Charities, Department of Public Welfare, State of Ohio, January, 1931. 55 pp.

Traces history of program in Ohio. Emphasizes the physical care of cripples and the work of the nurses, but practically ignores the program of educating and caring for them that the state has developed. Describes in some detail various diseases that cause orthopedic defects and suggests some things that can be done; the treatment follows closely the suggestions of the White House Conference report.

SOLENBERGER, EDITH REAVES. *Some Agencies and Institutions for Cripples in Various European Countries*. The International Society for Crippled Children, Inc., Elyria, Ohio. First issued in 1929, revised in 1931. 25 pp.

Gives some history, describes institutions, and reports the educational program developed for cripples in some 19 European countries.

STEINER, JESSE W. *The Legal Provisions for the Education of Crippled and Feeble-minded Children in the Forty-eight States*. Unpublished Master's thesis, Ohio State University, Columbus, 1928. 89 pp.

Describes provisions for census and defines cripples. Shows extent to which states have provided for special classes and state schools for cripples. Excerpts of a proposed state law are given.

The Special Schools and Curriculum Centers, pp. 103–109. Board of Education, Cleveland, Ohio, 1931.

A brief account of the development of the orthopedic department which cares for crippled children in Cleveland.

White House Conference. *Special Education: The Handicapped and the Gifted*, pp. 19–112. The Century Co., New York, 1931.

Extent of the problem, organization, and administration of the education of cripples in cities and in rural districts, housing facilities, education and care provided, and description of state institutions, private institutions, and state legislative policies.

White House Conference. *Communicable Disease Control*, pp. 99–214. The Century Co., New York, 1931.

Excellent analysis of contagious diseases with specific suggestions for prevention and control.

CHAPTER XII

THE EDUCATION OF BLIND CHILDREN

The direction of civilization's groping is indicated by its changing attitude toward its unfortunates. The blind portion of our population has been with us for ages; the whole tenor of an individual's life is changed when he suffers this handicap. Today, civilization is sympathetic toward the blind person; he is cared for physically, trained to be self-supporting, and given a general education commensurate with his abilities and in line with his interests. Formerly, the general population considered it impossible to educate such individuals and they were utilized as sources of merriment. Such a shift in sentiment is significant.

1. DEFINITIONS

The Problem.—This shift is even more pronounced when we note how educational programs for the blind have expanded. Instead of being interested only in those entirely without vision, we are interesting ourselves in educational programs for those with vision so impaired that they cannot do effective work in regular public school classes. This creates a problem in definition. State schools for the blind care for children who are properly candidates for sight-saving classes; many public school systems provide for the education of both types, but fail to distinguish between them. Romaker[1] found these two types closely associated. Legally, some states provide for the education of the blind; these statutes, however, have often been interpreted broadly so as to include children with defective vision.

Importance of the Problem.—The wisdom of making this distinction lies in the fact that children in sight-saving classes are sighted, not blind. To be sure the line of demarcation is hard to fix, since people are not either blind or sighted. The amount of vision is a variable, and a large unselected group of individuals will vary by almost imperceptible degrees from those with the most perfect sight to those who are totally blind. There must be fixed arbitrarily, therefore,

---

[1] C. C. ROMAKER, *A Study of Schools and Classes under the Control of Boards of Education Which Are for the Education of Blind and Partially Sighted Children in the United States*, pp. 2–3, unpublished Master's thesis, Ohio State University, Columbus, 1930.

a degree of vision below which an individual will be declared blind for purposes of education and above which he will be considered sighted.

The Technical Limits.—This dividing point is quite generally fixed as vision of 20/200 according to the Snellen chart. A blind child is defined, therefore, as a child with less vision than 20/200; such children are candidates for the schools and classes described in this chapter. Vision is so limited that it cannot be used in the educative process. Classes for the blind are frequently referred to as Braille classes, since a touch system known as Braille is used.

2. GUIDING PRINCIPLES

1. Despite the absence of vision upon the part of children in these schools, educators have broken away from the notion that all the blind can do is to cane chairs, weave rugs, and make baskets. They now tend to extend to him the same educational facilities that are open to all physically normal children.

2. Some occupations the blind cannot perform effectively; this definitely limits the range of choice in selecting a vocation or a profession.

3. Other things being equal, the local community and the home ought to care for their own problems to the full extent of their ability. There will, of course, be honest differences of opinion as to the extent to which "other things are equal."

4. Prevention should be the keynote of the entire educational program of the blind; overcoming the blind child's handicap by providing him an education is society's attempt to make partial restitution for allowing conditions that resulted in blindness. Obviously, then, the big job which society faces is that of preventing these conditions. The educational forces of the state can be made one of society's important agencies in such a program.

3. HISTORY

Beginnings.—Illingworth[1] presents evidence that the blind were being taught to read long before the establishment of the "National Institution for the Young Blind" at Paris. This school, established by Valentin Haüy, was the first organized attempt that we know of to educate blind children. The school was established in 1785. For some time Haüy had been experimenting with a young man named LeSeur and in 1784 had taken him to Paris, where the Academy of Sciences had examined him. The ability developed by this blind young man was so striking that the Philosophical Society of Paris,

---

[1] W. H. ILLINGWORTH, *History of the Education of the Blind*, pp. 1–4, Sampson Low, Marston and Company, Ltd., London, 1910.

which had been greatly impressed by the demonstrations, granted Haüy money with which to instruct other youths.[1] The following year, public exhibits were arranged and so much interest was created that the school was established.

Authorities differ as to the origin of Haüy's interest in the blind. McDonald finds that it was a blind Austrian singer, Maria Theresa von Paradis, who gave Haüy his first inspiration to help educate the blind.[2] According to Illingworth[3] Haüy's interest was first aroused by seeing at the entrance to one of Paris's numerous places of refreshment a band of eight or ten blind persons with musical instruments, who amused the guests of the place by playing a "discordant symphony"; coins collected from the guests supplied them with their living. Haüy argued that, if these blind could distinguish between coins and learn to know numerous other objects in the world about them, they could be taught the difference between musical notes, even between letters of the alphabet; in other words, they could be educated.

Early Type.—The first type used by Haüy was an italic. In 1831, James Gall originated the use of an angular Roman type; he considered his method the most nearly perfect that could be devised. In 1838, Lucas introduced a stenographic type of alphabet, which had wide usage. Moon used what was known as the "return line principle"; every other line was read from left to right and the alternate lines from right to left. Many forms of the Roman type were devised and used. In fact, every interested educator of the blind for a few decades seemed to think it his duty to devise a new and better method of instructing them. Most of these inventors of alphabets were sighted persons. Theoretically, many of their plans seemed ideal, but practically they were so difficult to learn that the attempt to educate the blind was a failure until the blind themselves undertook to solve the problem of devising their own system of instruction.

Braille.—The actual development of an acceptable system was worked out by Louis Braille, a blind Frenchman. He was born Jan. 4, 1809, at Coupvray, near Paris. His father was a harness maker; at three years of age the boy, in trying to use one of his father's tools, pierced an eye; the other eye suffered from "sympathetic inflammation," and the boy was soon blind. At ten years of age he was sent to the school for the blind at Paris. He progressed rapidly. In addition to regular academic branches, he studied music, at which

---

[1] *Ibid.*, p. 5.

[2] ROBERT A. F. McDONALD, *Adjustment of School Organization to Various Population Groups*, p. 29, Teachers College, Columbia University, New York, 1915.

[3] ILLINGWORTH, *op. cit.*, p. 8.

he excelled.   In 1826 he became a teacher at this school where he had learned to read and where they still used the old embossed Roman letters.

He spent much of his leisure time trying to devise a way whereby the blind could write in relief, studying many devices.   He finally selected M. Charles Barbier's scheme of dots as the best; Barbier in 1825 proposed 12 dots, six high and two wide.   Braille took six dots, three high and two wide, and constructed his alphabet.   His preliminary scheme was first produced in 1829, in 1834 it was presented in its final form, and 20 years later his method was adopted at Paris. He died in 1852, and thus failed to see his system given general acceptance.   This system was brought to America about 6 years later and introduced at St. Louis.   Older schools established in the Eastern states were using various styles of old Roman letters.

But Braille had its difficulties; various modifications were made by different schools from time to time.   By 1900, in America there were in use three systems of Braille; that year the Convention of Braillists in America met and appointed a committee of three to decide upon a system that they should recommend.   As a result, "American Braille" came into existence.   Not until 1916[1] did the workers of the world, interested in the education of the blind, agree upon a universal system of Braille; this is known as "Revised Braille" and is now generally accepted in all institutions.   The graduate of any school for the blind is now able to read by a universal alphabet.

Schools Developed.—Following the establishment of the French school in France in 1785, schools arose in the British Isles, Denmark, Germany, Holland, Russia, and Sweden in quick succession.   Haüy carried the idea to Germany and Russia, after the French school was temporarily disbanded during the French Revolution.

In the United States, John D. Fisher seems to have been the first person to propose that the blind be educated.   He had studied medicine at Paris and was acquainted with the work of the Paris school.   He returned to Boston in 1826.   In February, 1829, he called a meeting of those interested in educating the blind.   This resulted immediately in the passage of a bill by the legislature to incorporate The New England Asylum for the Blind.   As Fisher was unable to assume active leadership of the project, Samuel G. Howe was chosen as the first superintendent, in 1831.   He was sent to Europe for a short period of study, but returned the next year and immediately started his work with a class of six blind children.   The first state

---

[1] *The Blind in the United States*, 1920, U.S. Bureau of the Census, p. 12, Washington, D.C., 1923.

school for the blind was begun in Ohio in 1837. By 1875, there were 25 state schools and 5 private schools enrolling 2,000 pupils.

Development of Public Day Schools.—The U.S. Bureau of Education had in 1928 reports for 80 institutions; 47 of these were from state schools, 10 were private or semi-private schools, 2 were insular schools, and the remaining 21 were from schools in public school systems. The fact that city school systems are undertaking to care for their blind will naturally reduce the need for further state or private schools.

The first American city to organize a class for blind children was Chicago; this was in 1896.[1] Bruner says that official figures on enrollment were not available until 1900. In 1900 the average membership was 23, 10 years later it was 39.4, and in 1920 it was 50.3. Beginning in 1919, however, sight-saving classes were started, and these were included in the 1920 report. By 1922, the average membership had increased to 97.6.

Chicago's successful work encouraged other cities to organize classes for the blind. Cincinnati organized a class in 1906; Milwaukee did the same in 1907; and Cleveland, New York, and Racine, Wis., followed suit in 1909. By 1926–27, 22 cities reported the organization of such classes to the Bureau of Education at Washington.[2] The White House Conference reported in 1931 five cities as having classes that did not appear in the Bureau's report of 1926–27. The number of blind pupils actually enrolled in public school classes is not large. The White House Conference reported 423 pupils in public school Braille classes.

4. METHODS OF EDUCATING THE BLIND

The preceding historical review shows that three methods have been followed in an attempt to educate and care for blind children: private schools, state schools, and public school classes. A fourth plan, used in recent years, is to send a teacher to the home.

The Private School.—The private school represents the interest of individuals philanthropically inclined who have felt that more attention should be given to the education of blind children. Early attempts to educate the blind were of this character. Many of these pioneering efforts were later given state support and are now run as semipublic or as state institutions.

[1] FRANK G. BRUNER, *Report of the Director of Special Schools for the School Year 1922–23*, p. 93, Board of Education, Chicago, 1924.

[2] FRANK M. PHILLIPS, "Schools and Classes for the Blind 1926–27," *U.S. Bureau of Education Bulletin* 9, pp. 3–5, Washington, D.C., 1928.

The State School.—The state school was developed during a period when institutional care was accepted generally as the most practical method of caring for individuals who were materially different from their fellows.   It was developed at a time when the free public school was being born and when it was making a most strenuous fight for its very existence.   If the blind were to be educated, the state school was, therefore, the logical place for doing the work at public expense.

The Local Class.—After the free public school had won its fight, and after the public generally had begun to have a consciousness of responsibility for its own handicapped children, local school districts began to appropriate money for the establishment of public school classes for the blind.   Due to the relatively small number of blind children in a given population, however, the number of classes needed in even a large city was relatively small.   This scarcity of pupils hampered the development of classes in smaller cities and in rural school districts.

Home Instruction.—The sense of local responsibility has so increased that some cities, in addition to establishing special classes, have undertaken to provide an education for blind children who are not physically able to attend class.   A special teacher instructs the child at home.   Detroit, in addition to providing Braille classes, has home instruction for blind adults and blind children.   Two lessons of 1 hour each are given weekly to the children.   The number and length of the lessons for adults depend upon individual needs.

5. THE STATE SCHOOL

The biennial survey of education for 1934–36[1] reported 41 states with state schools for the blind.   Some of the states had two schools apiece—one for the Negroes and one for the whites.   Some states had more than one school for whites.   The blind and the deaf were both received in 18 state schools.   Seven states—Delaware, Maine, Nevada, New Hampshire, Rhode Island, Vermont, and Wyoming—were not listed as having state schools.   The 41 states reported 55 residential schools.   Maine reported a school in 1927.   The state school, since its first organization in Ohio in 1837, has been quite generally accepted throughout the country.   Only in recent years has a criticism arisen concerning this plan for educating blind children.

[1] EMERY M. FOSTER, and ELISE H. MARTENS, "Statistics of Special Schools and Classes for Exceptional Children," *U.S. Office of Education Bulletin* 2, pp. 122–127, Washington, D.C., 1937.

Administrative Control.—In 1927, Cowdery reported on the 37 states[1] which had state control and state support of their schools for the blind. In 12 states the control of the school was in charge of a board of trustees or a board of visitors; in 12 other states, control rested with the board of charities and correction, the board of control, or the department of public welfare; in the remaining 13 states, control was in the hands of the state department of education.

This last-named method of control is beginning to be generally accepted as the proper one.   Care of blind children is no longer charity; the problem is strictly educational.   These children have the same right to an education as have sighted children.   The state school assumes the responsibility for providing it.   Control should rest, therefore, with the state department of education.

Length of School Year.[2]—Only 11 states specified how long their state schools should be open during the year.   The range, with one exception, was from 32 to 40 weeks.   The state school is clearly not of the institutional type, since the pupils are not housed and kept through the entire year; they go home for summer and midyear vacations.

Enrollments.—The enrollments shown in Table XII represent the total number of children in state or state-supported schools for the blind.   Pennsylvania, with 423 pupils, had the greatest number.   Montana was lowest, with only 22 pupils enrolled in its state school for blind and deaf.   The median enrollment was 127.   Of the 41 states, 13 enrolled less than 100 pupils each.

There are many reasons for this variation in enrollment.   The most obvious is the state's population.   A scattergram, using the enrollments shown in Table XII and the populations of these 41 states as of 1930, showed a relatively high relationship.   New York ranked highest in population and next to highest in enrollment; Pennsylvania ranked next to highest in population and highest in enrollment; Texas was third in enrollment and fifth in population; and Ohio was fourth in population and fifth in enrollment.   At the lower end of the distribution, Arizona was sixth from the lowest in enrollment and ranked next to lowest in population; Idaho had the next to lowest enrollment and was third from lowest in population.

Other possible factors affecting enrollments are (1) the extent to which the state provides local facilities for educating the blind, (2)

---

[1] KATE LOUISE COWDERY, *The Legal Status of the Education of Blind and Deaf Children in the Forty-eight States*, p. 14, unpublished Master's thesis, Ohio State University, Columbus, 1927.

[2] *Ibid.*, p. 35.

TABLE XII.—ENROLLMENTS IN STATE SCHOOLS FOR THE BLIND BY STATES[1]
Public school classes not included

State	Enrollment	State	Enrollment
Alabama	207	Montana	22
Arizona	40	Nebraska	54
Arkansas	130	New Jersey	33
California	127	New Mexico	100
Colorado	60	New York	400
Connecticut	65	North Carolina	247
Florida	94	North Dakota	37
Georgia	128	Ohio	261
Idaho	23	Oklahoma	166
Illinois	238	Oregon	71
Indiana	135	Pennsylvania	423
Iowa	196	South Carolina	101
Kansas	110	South Dakota	36
Kentucky	189	Tennessee	197
Louisiana	119	Texas	356
Maryland	112	Utah	43
Massachusetts	275	Virginia	152
Michigan	200	Washington	105
Minnesota	128	West Virginia	131
Mississippi	74	Wisconsin	151
Missouri	115		

[1] Some private schools supported by state appropriation are included. The table is adapted from Emery M. Foster, and Elise H. Martens, "Statistics of Special Schools and Classes for Exceptional Children," *U.S. Office of Education Bulletin* 2, pp. 122–127, Washington, D.C., 1937.

the extent to which all blind are discovered and brought into school, and (3) the differences that actually exist in the proportion of the population that are blind.

School Costs.[1]—The cost of educating blind children at state schools varies greatly. The per capita cost for current expenses in Maine was $885, whereas the cost in Tennessee was $141. The average for the United States was $526. Most states ranged from $300 to $700 and were fairly evenly distributed throughout that range. There are numerous reasons for this variation. Enrollment is a partial factor. Provision for extensive industrial training increases costs. Provision for extensive library facilities and other special equipment increases the cost. A variation in physical and medical care or in methods of feeding will change cost figures. One cannot look, therefore, at per capita cost figures and determine whether a given state school is being wasteful; this can be done only in the light

[1] FRANK M. PHILLIPS, "Schools and Classes for the Blind, 1921–22," *U.S. Bureau of Education Bulletin* 51, Washington, D.C., 1923.

of what the school is doing for its pupils. One conclusion is clear, however: the cost of educating the blind at state schools is much greater than in local schools.

The Curriculum.—State schools usually provide a complete academic program of studies from kindergarten through high school. Music is emphasized; the piano, violin, trombone, and other musical instruments, as well as voice, are taught. As a vocation, piano tuning is a subject of instruction. The girls are taught sewing, plain and fancy, crocheting, knitting, and all kinds of needlework. The weaving of mats, rugs, and carpets is taught, and reed work is provided. Boys are given instruction in various types of industrial work; chair caning, basketmaking, and broom building are common. Some schools claim to teach these industrial subjects merely for their value in training blind children to use their hands effectively; others claim that many of their pupils become self-supporting through their mastery of these skills.

Many state schools have failed in their vocational program through ignoring the fact that many of their pupils could do effective service in business organizations. Business, however, will not be interested in finding positions for the blind. Those interested in educating these children must find the jobs and must then assist those who want to go into the industrial or business field to prepare for it.

Placement and Follow-up.—If the state school is to assume the responsibility for determining with greater accuracy the types of industrial and business positions that blind people are capable of filling, then it is in an ideal position to assist in placing the graduates. The business contacts formed through continuous checking on possible jobs for the blind ought to create such an interest upon the part of businessmen that they will be willing to secure the graduates of the school. This placement service must be matched with immediate and sane follow-up service.[1]

6. THE STATE SCHOOL VS. A LOCAL SYSTEM

The state school was the first to develop; it came into existence during the first half of the 19th century and spread rapidly. Only in recent years has any interest been shown in the organization of special day classes. Even now the development of such classes is not proceeding with great rapidity. One writer recently pleaded for

---

[1] For a more detailed account of this necessity for placement and follow-up service, see pp. 181–182.

the abandonment of both state schools and local classes; he urged the organization of central local schools.[1]

Arguments for the State School.—The Federal Census for 1920 shows 497 blind persons per 1,000,000 of the general population.[2] The number available for Braille classes is, therefore, not great.[3] On account of this small incidence, it is argued that there are not enough children to organize local Braille classes in sufficient number to provide an adequate classification of pupils. In a state school, where children come from an entire state, classification by grades is possible. Because of this larger enrollment, moreover, the school can develop a program of trade and industrial training peculiarly adapted to blind children, such as could not be presented in local classes. It can also develop a better physical-education program.

The state school has an even greater argument for its existence in the fact that the equipment needed for blind children is very expensive. The local district with few children can hardly afford to spend the money necessary to secure it. A raised map of the United States, for example, sells for $200. Much expensive equipment of this kind could hardly be provided for a local class of six or eight pupils, although a state school with 100 or more children could well afford to buy it. Textbooks, supplementary texts, library books, reference books, and educational magazines, when put into Braille, are very costly. An ordinary textbook selling for $1.50 may cost anywhere from $10 to $20 when written in Braille. Visits to local Braille classes reveal a decided deficiency in textbooks and in library facilities. The state school can have a library that will match fairly well the library facilities for sighted pupils. This line of thinking cannot be ignored. The blind child suffers a severe enough handicap in securing an education without having that handicap increased by being denied these facilities.

It is argued further that the state school allows a blind child a greater opportunity to make a selection in forming life friendships. In the local class his opportunity of establishing enduring friendships is so small, the argument goes, as to represent no opportunity at all. Sighted children may be glad to give aid and sympathy, but that is not what the blind want; they want to feel that they are accepted as equals. They are so accepted in the larger state school, and they have the happiness and satisfaction that come from constant association

---

[1] JOHN LOUIS HORN, *The Education of Exceptional Children*, Chap. XII, The Century Co., New York, 1924.

[2] *The Blind in the United States*, 1920, U.S. Bureau of the Census, p. 14, Washington, D.C., 1923.

[3] See pp. 217–218.

with a group of intimate friends. A local class, with 6 to 12 pupils distributed throughout the grades and varying in age from six to sixteen does not, it is claimed, provide such an opportunity.

The state school has a better opportunity to determine which occupations are best adapted to the blind. The size of the school makes the need for such service imperative. In similar fashion, the superiority of placement and follow-up service is argued; this service in a local community can be provided only incidentally by someone whose major interest is in another job. It is argued, moreover, that the local Braille class teacher has an almost impossible task and does not have the time to give even her small number of pupils adequate help, supervision, and instruction. In defense of this proposition are cited the detailed duties of such a Braille teacher.[1]

Finally, the argument goes on, many of the blind children come from homes that are unsanitary and where parents ignore the most elemental facts concerning cleanliness and health. Other homes fail in their understanding of the psychology of the blind; they make weaklings of children who could become independent and self-supporting. It is claimed, therefore, that most blind children would be better off if they were placed in a boarding school, where they would be supervised and cared for by persons well acquainted with their physical and mental needs.

Arguments for the Local Classes.—The chief argument in favor of the local class lies in the fact that the blind child is permitted to recite with sighted pupils. It is claimed that such recitation, by making possible competition with sighted pupils, prepares them for later competition; that in classwork they find they can do as well as the sighted; that self-confidence, initiative, and independence of action are thus developed; and that attitudes of self-pity and dependence that result from assembling the blind by themselves are destroyed.

This, it is argued, enables the blind child to develop a proper attitude toward the people of the community in which he must live. He has lived with sighted people; he has argued with them in class; he has listened to their points of view concerning the problems of home, community, state, and national life; these are things that he could never have gotten in a segregated school.

Even more important, the sighted children have learned to appreciate the blind child; they have seen him do better schoolwork than they were able to do; they have heard him argue given points in class discussion with fluency and great accuracy; they have seen him make his way about the building with a minimum of assistance; and they

[1] See pp. 179–180.

have seen him take part in many games and sports. These sighted children have thus been liberally educated.

This last argument leads to another. The claim is made that coeducation of the blind and the sighted will help to solve the later economic problems of the blind. The sighted businessman of tomorrow will know the abilities of his former blind classmates. He will be more willing than many have been in the past to hire those who have lost their vision.

Arguments for Either the Local Class or the Local School.—Advocates of local instruction have additional arguments that apply either to the organization of schools or to the organization of classes. (1) Costs will be less; board and lodging will not be needed. (2) It will eliminate, as one city report put it, the supporting of blind youths in state schools until twenty-one or twenty-four years of age in idleness. (3) The home life of the child can be preserved. (4) Institutionalization will be prevented, inasmuch as they claim children in a state school come to depend upon the school instead of upon their own drive and initiative. The proposition, as usually presented, fails to be very convincing because supporting evidences are lacking; this, nevertheless, is one of the lengthy arguments often produced in contending against the state school.

Arguments for a Local School.—Horn argues at considerable length for a local school.[1] In addition to the arguments just outlined, he says that it would ensure (1) better classification, (2) better industrial training, (3) better physical care, (4) better equipment, (5) better library facilities, (6) more adequate textbooks, (7) better association for the children with others of their own kind, (8) the formation of more lasting friendships, (9) a tendency to give more emphasis to pupil placement, and (10) elimination of the necessity for placing upon the Braille class teacher the almost insufferable task that now confronts her.

All arguments given for the state school can here be reaffirmed with the exception of one. The local school will not take a child out of undesirable home conditions; it leaves him there. Most of the arguments are based upon the assumption that the local school will have a fairly large enrollment. If city enrollments are too small, counties surrounding the city might be attached to the city district for purposes of organizing a local school for the blind. If this were done, undoubtedly many pupils would need to have rooming places provided for the school days of each week.

[1] J. L. HORN, *op. cit.*, Chap. XII.

The fact that a school is organized, however, in great part nullifies the arguments that were used for just the special classes. The advantages to the blind which, it is claimed, come from competition with the sighted are wholly lost; the sighted are not given an opportunity for real appreciation of the capabilities of the blind; thus, the later economic problems of the blind are not so well cared for; and the blind child does not in quite so direct a way learn to lead a useful life among sighted people.

Conclusions.—Most of these arguments are not based upon an objective type of evidence. The whole argument at present turns upon the general point of view that one holds respecting the relative values of different types of living conditions for those who have lost their vision. Those who believe in the maintenance of the home and in the association with sighted children will favor local classes. Those who believe that an association of blind children with one another provides the more healthy atmosphere will favor the state or local schools.

We greatly need objective data on a number of problems. Does life at a state school institutionalize its pupils? To what extent do pupils in local classes have the meat of their courses made lean, due to a scarcity of text materials and library facilities? Is the effect of coeducation of the blind and sighted beneficial or detrimental to one or the other or to both groups concerned? There are numerous other problems that need investigation. The succeeding chapter will discuss some of them.

7. SUMMARY

According to the Snellen chart, the blind are defined as those with vision of less than 20/200. The first school for such children was founded by Valentin Haüy in Paris in 1785; Fisher was responsible for the founding of the first school in America in 1832; Howe was its first superintendent. The first state school was established in Ohio in 1837; Chicago organized the first public school class for the blind in 1896. Braille, a touch system of reading, was devised in 1829 by Louis Braille when he was twenty years of age.

The blind are educated in private schools, in state schools, in public school classes, or at home. The state school has been established in most of the states. Arguments for such a school claim that it provides (1) better classification, (2) a better training program, (3) better equipment, (4) more adequate library facilities, (5) a better opportunity to form life-long friendships, and (6) more efficient placement and follow-up service.

Arguments for the local class emphasize the desirability of remaining at home, the values which come from living and studying among sighted children, lower cost, and the prevention of institutionalization.

Problems and Questions for Discussion

1. Who are the blind? Why is the problem of definition important?
2. What are some important guiding principles in caring for and educating blind children? Why are they important?
3. Trace briefly the history of caring for and educating blind children.
4. What is Braille? How was it devised? Why? Trace its development.
5. Describe the various ways of educating the blind. Which is best? Why?
6. What problems are being met today in operating state schools for educating the blind? How would you solve them?
7. What argument can be made in defense of state schools for educating the blind? Present specific data.
8. If you believed in educating the blind locally, what arguments would you use to support your proposal?

Selected Bibliography

BEST, HARRY. *Blindness and the Blind in the United States*, pp. 3–50, 299–342. The Macmillan Company, New York, 1934.

Data presented relative to causes of blindness; suggestions concerning the possibility of prevention. Brief consideration of the history of the education of the blind; general provisions for the education of the blind.

COWDERY, KATE LOUISE. *The Legal Status of the Education of Blind and Deaf Children in the Forty-eight States.* Unpublished Master's thesis, Ohio State University, Columbus, 1927. 85 pp.

An analysis of school codes, showing types of instruction provided, admission requirements to schools and classes, rules governing curricula, qualifications of teachers, and financial support provided; finally a compulsory educational law for deaf and blind is proposed.

FRENCH, RICHARD SLAYTON. *From Homer to Helen Keller*, pp. 31–170, 173–283. American Foundation for the Blind, Inc., New York, 1932.

An excellent historical treatise dealing with the education and care of the blind, in which problems of education, vocation, and avocation are raised.

HORN, JOHN LOUIS. *The Education of Exceptional Children*, pp. 231–238, 267–290. The Century Co., New York, 1924.

Describes the problems of the city day classes, the way that the work is organized, the need of local schooling, the dangers and good points of the state school, and makes a final argument for the centralization of city classes.

ILLINGWORTH, W. H. *History of the Education of the Blind.* Sampson Low, Marston and Company, Ltd., London, 1910. 167 pp.

Describes the first attempts to teach the blind, the work of Haüy, the development of systems of reading, and the development of equipment needed.

McDONALD, ROBERT A. F. *Adjustment of School Organization to Various Population Groups*, pp. 29–36. Teachers College, Columbia University, New York, 1915.

Gives a brief but good history of the development of the education of the blind; describes courses of study, equipment, method of reciting in public schools, and some evidences of the success of such education.

PHILLIPS, FRANK M.   "Schools and Classes for the Blind, 1926–27," *U.S. Bureau of Education Bulletin* 9, 1928.   7 pp.

Shows the increase in schools for the blind by 5-year periods since 1900; the 80 schools reporting are listed, showing name, number of instructors, roll, pupils per grade, library volumes, and value of property.

ROMAKER, C. C.   *A Study of Schools and Classes under the Control of Boards of Education Which Are for the Education of Blind and Partially Sighted Children in the United States.*   Unpublished Master's thesis, Ohio State University, Columbus, 1930.   134 pp.

Gives detailed study of provisions made by 39 cities to educate their blind; covers housing conditions, teachers provided, admission requirements, types of children in classes, the school program, special equipment, transportation, and costs.

CHAPTER XIII

LOCAL PROBLEMS FACED IN EDUCATING THE BLIND

Effective service can be given only when the problems to be met in rendering it are recognized. Local school authorities, to educate satisfactorily their blind children, must have a clear realization of the nature and the size of the problems that face them in their attempt to provide such instruction. These problems range all the way from the maintenance of a continuous census, through the work of organizing the special classes or schools, to the task of placing and supervising these youths in their afterschool careers.

1. PROBLEMS OF ORGANIZATION

Discovery of Blind Children.—If the local community is to educate all blind children, it must find them. This will demand a complete and continuing census of all blind children within the district. The regular school census and the follow-up work necessary to keep it continuous will not be enough. Arrangements should be made for the regular examination of the eyesight of all pupils; teachers can make a first rough check, if school nurses are not available. All cases of defective vision or of questionable vision should be referred by the teacher or nurse to the regular school physician or special eye examiner.

Location of Class.—After children in sufficient numbers have been discovered to organize a class, consideration must be given to its proper location. It should be centrally located for the district that it serves; if bus transportation is provided, this factor should be given considerable weight. The class should be located in a regular school building where the principal is alive to his responsibility for it; this is vital if the blind children are to find themselves in a congenial atmosphere and are to receive all the benefits claimed for special-class instruction.

If the children come by streetcar, nearness to the streetcar intersections of those lines that reach all parts of the district will be an important item. The availability of a room or rooms that will meet the physical needs of these blind children must not be ignored. Much of the criticism of the work done in the past in local classes has been based upon a failure at some one or more of these points.

172

Transportation.—Owing to the long distances that pupils have to travel, special arrangements must be made for transportation. Some cities provide carfare and the streetcars are used. When this is done, a sighted pupil is permitted to accompany the blind child to the central school and to attend the regular classes at that school. This general plan is followed at Cleveland and Chicago. Other cities transport the pupils. A Los Angeles report for 1936 stated, "About sixty pupils are transported to these classes daily, the Board of Education making provision for this service."[1] Braille classes were referred to. Both plans might well be used within a given city; transportation could be made available to those children who live great distances from the school or where streetcar travel would be roundabout, long, and tedious.

The Classroom.—Any good regular classroom is suited to the education of blind children. Since the classes are small, such a room will give plenty of space for needed equipment. It should provide a maximum of sunlight, devoid of glares, if the little vision remaining is to be preserved. Never assign small, dark basement rooms, or poorly lighted, irregular rooms to the Braille classes; this practice has been too frequent in the past.

Psychologically, the type of classroom assigned to Braille classes is important. Many blind children tend to have an inferiority complex. The school must place these children in a setting that will help to develop their ego rather than in a setting that will further strengthen those feelings of inferiority.

Administration of the Class.—This special class differs from a regular class group. The latter constitutes a unit for instruction and, in the elementary school, studies and recites in its home room. The former is composed of children from as many as four or five different grades; its enrollment may vary from as few as 4 to as many as 12 or 15; its pupils study in their home room, but they recite in regular classes with pupils who have normal vision. This demands most excellent co-operation between regular and special teachers. The former must continually remember the blind child and adjust their instruction to his needs; the latter must work out in detail a personal daily program for each member of her class.[2]

2. EDUCATIONAL PROBLEMS

Learning Braille.—Braille is the system of raised points which the blind now use universally for reading and writing. The history

---

[1] "Education of the Physically Handicapped," p. 16, Los Angeles City School District, *Publication* 281, Los Angeles, Calif., 1936.

[2] For further duties, see pp. 179–180.

of its development was traced in the historical section of the preceding chapter.[1] There have been several revisions, which for years were used simultaneously in various schools. Since 1919, there has been

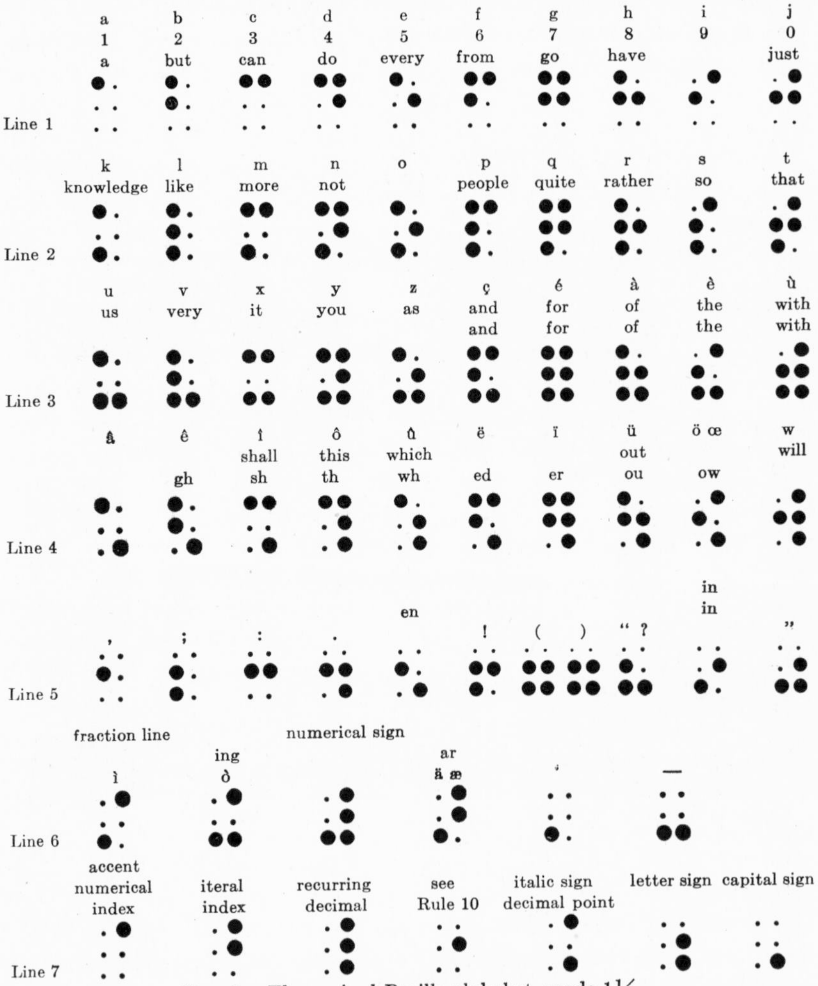

a	b	c	d	e	f	g	h	i	j
1	2	3	4	5	6	7	8	9	0
a	but	can	do	every	from	go	have		just

Line 1

k	l	m	n	o	p	q	r	s	t
knowledge	like	more	not		people	quite	rather	so	that

Line 2

u	v	x	y	z	ç	é	à	è	ù
us	very	it	you	as	and	for	of	the	with
					and	for	of	the	with

Line 3

â	ê	î	ô	û	ë	ï	ü	ö œ	w
		shall	this	which			out		will
	gh	sh	th	wh	ed	er	ou	ow	

Line 4

en (above), in / in (above w column)

Line 5: , ; : . ! ( ) " ? "

| fraction line | | ing | | numerical sign | | ar | | | |
| | | | | | | ä æ | | | |

ì / ð / ar / — (dashes and signs)

Line 6

accent / numerical index / iteral index / recurring decimal / see Rule 10 / italic sign decimal point / letter sign / capital sign

Line 7

FIG. 2.—The revised Braille alphabet, grade 1½.

almost unanimous agreement upon the use of what is called revised Braille grade 1½. England has revised Braille grade 1 and grade 2. Grade 1 has full spelling; grade 2 has a highly contracted spelling.

The basis for all Braille writing is 6 dots arranged rectangularly, three high and two wide. These dots arranged in various combina-

[1] See pp. 159–160.

tions represent not only the letters of the alphabet but letters with unique diacritical marks, such as ë, ï, ö, and ü. A single arrangement of dots, moreover, will represent not only a letter but a numeral and a whole word. Another arrangement will represent a letter, a whole word or a part of a word. Still other arrangements will represent whole words, part words, and punctuation. Thus, ⠃ represents the letter "b," the numeral "2," and the word "but"; and ⠥ represents the letter "u," and the word "us."

ILLUSTRATION 13.—Developing manipulative skill needed in learning to read Braille. The larger girls at the left are new to the city and have had no training. A class for the blind at Detroit.

The revised Braille alphabet grade 1½ is shown in Fig. 2. The child must learn this alphabet with its numerous contractions before he can become a proficient reader or writer. The reading is done by passing the finger tips over the raised dots. The child reads from left to right, just as he would in ordinary reading. Both hands are used; usually the left hand merely helps the reader to keep the correct place at the left-hand margin of the page; occasionally, a rapid reader will use the right hand to read the first line, while the left hand looks ahead on the second. In Illustration 13, pupils are developing the manipulative skill needed in order to learn to read Braille.

Equipment Necessary for Instruction.—In order to facilitate the learning and use of Braille, Braille slates and styluses, arithmetic slates, and Braille writers are needed. Other necessary equipment are typewriters, paper and wooden relief maps, a piano, work tables, large desks that will easily hold the large Braille books, and bookcases.

The Braille slate and stylus are used in writing Braille. These slates are the result of an evolutionary process. Illingworth says,

> The original method of writing Braille . . . was to impress it by means of a stylo on paper placed upon baize, rubber, soft leather, or other yielding substance, the guide consisting of a strip of brass containing one or two lines of oblong holes of the required size, similar to the upper half of the ordinary Braille brass guide.[1]

The present slate contains rows of cells; each cell is exactly the size of the basic six dots of the Braille system. On either side of the cell are three indentations, which represent the dots of this basic Braille unit. The slate frame is attached to the paper upon which a pupil writes. In writing, one begins at the right side of the paper and goes to the left. In order to read what has been written, the paper is taken out of the slate and turned over; then the copy is read from left to right.

The Braille writer is similar in some ways to an ordinary typewriter. There are, however, only six keys. Each key represents one of the dots of the basic Braille unit. If four dots are used to represent a given letter, these four keys must be struck at the same time. The Hall Braille writer was one of the earliest of the writers and is still one of the best; its base is 12 by 8 inches, and it stands about 4 inches high. The six keys are arranged in two groups of three.

The typewriter is needed in order that the pupils can learn to transcribe their Braille notes into English. This saves the special-class teacher much labor. The wooden relief maps have blocks of wood of the relative size and the exact shape of the various countries or states. These are contained in a wooden frame and may be taken out and replaced at need. The surface of the map has raised areas to represent high plateaus and mountains, and depressions to represent rivers, lakes, and broad lowlands along rivers and oceans.

Library Problems.—The problem of securing adequate reading materials is probably the most vexing of all that have to be met by the teachers of the blind. It is a problem that troubles all teachers, but for several reasons it is much more perplexing in schools for the blind.

---

[1] W. H. ILLINGWORTH, *History of the Education of the Blind*, p. 32, Sampson Low, Marston and Company, Ltd., London, 1910.

1. All the library books must be printed in Braille. The characters in Braille books are just as large as those used in writing in the Braille classroom. The books, therefore, are large, being frequently 11 by 11 inches; despite the size, it takes several volumes to contain the subject material of an ordinary library book. The biography of Abraham Lincoln by Carl Sandburg when put into Braille made 10 volumes. The *Adventures of Tom Sawyer* ran into four volumes; and the four books of *Ceasar's Gallic War* required 10 volumes. It takes a great amount of space to house what a regular library would consider a relatively small number of books.

2. Next comes the difficulty encountered in having needed supplementary material transcribed into Braille. The market for Braille books is relatively small, because its entire extent is limited by the number of blind people in the United States. Actual market possibilities are far less, since a large portion of the blind are too poor to have libraries of their own. Sales opportunities are, therefore, limited to Braille schools, library demands, and the needs of organizations interested in providing reading material for the use of the blind. As a result, commercial printing houses do not care to undertake the printing of Braille books. The bulk of the printing is done, therefore, at the American Printing House for the Blind, which is located at Louisville, Ky., and which is being subsidized each year by the Federal government to the amount of $75,000.

3. Another problem is that of cost. In spite of a Federal subsidy, the cost of these books is excessive on account of the bulk and the relatively small sale. Sandburg's *Abraham Lincoln*, which the Book of the Month Club sold for $3, sold for $23.50 when put into Braille. A handsome limp-leather edition of Mark Twain's *Tom Sawyer*, selling for $2, cost $11.90 when put into Braille. Allen and Greenough's edition of *Ceasar's Gallic War*, Books I–IV, when published in Braille, sold for $33.20.

These are problems encountered by any school system when it begins to build up a satisfactory library for the use of blind pupils. Public libraries will, of course, be in a position to assist in expanding the reading facilities of local schools. At best, however, library costs will be heavy if reading materials are to be adequate.

Textbook Problems.—The same problems arise in the matter of providing textbooks, and still another is added. Textbooks are being constantly revised and new texts are being continually published. These changes often represent improvements so important that they ought by all means to be made. This involves publishing the new book in Braille. Before this is done, the school must be very sure of the significance of the new points of view.   It is too costly to make changes only to find, within a year or so, that making the new adoption was a mistake.   As a result, textbooks tend to be used longer, and newer and better books are more slowly adopted.

Braille classes in the public schools have an additional textbook problem.   The public schools make relatively frequent changes; the blind pupils recite with regular class groups.   This means that in these classes the texts for the blind must be changed as frequently as are those for the sighted.   Often these books are not printed by even the American Printing House until several years later, if at all. As a result, the teacher of the Braille class has to prepare text materials, or else to read to her pupils.   Some teachers undertake the Herculean task of putting into Braille a newly adopted text for their pupils; this, however, they cannot do for all grades or even for all texts for a given grade.

The Elementary Curricula.—Braille classes in the public schools offer a program of schoolwork that is very similar to that provided in the regular elementary grades; arithmetic, civics, geography, history, language, reading, science, writing, fine art and manual art subjects are taught.   The differences lie in the means used.   Reading and writing are in Braille; arithmetic makes use of number slates, as well as relying upon mental calculation.   The latter is developed in some schools to a considerable degree of perfection.   The pupil is able to multiply even fairly long numbers without mechanical aids of any kind.

Curricula beyond the Elementary Grades.—The type of educational program which should be provided beyond the elementary grades is subject to debate.   There are three schools of thought. The older group emphasizes industrial training; blind children must be so educated that they will become self-supporting.   This group argues for industrial training in which blindness will be of little or no handicap; such simple skills as basketry and chair caning are emphasized.   As late as 1915, McDonald reported that "a limited number of the simple trades are taught, including needlework, chaircaning, basketry, making hammocks, brushes, brooms, mattresses, rugs, and carpets."[1]   A few schools provided business courses.

The second group urges the regular elementary school program, with a good basic course in general manual training.   The contention is that when the child reaches the age for entering a trade, a few months

[1] ROBERT A. F. McDONALD, *Adjustment of School Organization to Various Population Groups*, p. 33, Teachers College, Columbia University, New York, 1915.

of intensive training will fit him to enter it. The suggestion implicit in both these points of view is that the blind are fit to enter only the simplest of trades; theoretically, many who in practice accept this thesis would violently oppose it.

The attitude of the third group is that, while the blind should be so trained that their handicap will least hinder their efficiency at self-support, their opportunities for self-support are good. Members of this group see no reason for not allowing the capable blind who have an interest in scholarship to secure a high-school and a college education. The blind student should face frankly the actual difficulties in securing teaching positions or in entering other professions; he should not, however, be prohibited from entering such professions. There will, of course, be many less capable, who can succeed in only the simpler crafts; this, however, is true in the education of the sighted.

This last-mentioned point of view certainly seems the sensible one. High-school work should be made available; typing, music, piano tuning, and general shopwork should be open to those students who have some ability and interest in them; college work should not be refused to those who can profit from it. Teachers in Braille classes in the public schools have the problem of helping to discover types of shop and industrial work that the blind can do. The greatest original contribution that they could make would be to develop a broad program of practical activity for the education of blind children.

3. THE WORK OF THE SPECIAL TEACHER

The special teacher's task is by no means insignificant. Braille reading and writing must be mastered; the Braille notebook work of the pupil must be transcribed into script for the regular teacher until the pupil has learned typewriting; blackboard work in arithmetic and spelling must be transcribed into Braille for the pupil. Where textbooks in Braille are not available, the teacher frequently does a great amount of work in transcribing them into Braille.

Each pupil must have a detailed schedule of work arranged. The time of each recitation with the regular class must be known, and time for preparing his lessons must be planned. The teacher must assist in the preparation of these lessons. One teacher with considerable experience in public school Braille classes explained that pupils frequently get entirely wrong conceptions of the new assignments, as well as of the discussion, in the regular class groups. The special class teacher must discover these errors and correct them.

Because of the scarcity of Braille materials, a great amount of reading must be done for these children. Special assistance is needed in number work, where they have to be taught to use the specially devised number slates. If typing is begun in the grades, the special teacher will usually supervise this instruction, and she assists them with a great deal of the handwork that they are taught to do as a means of training hands and fingers to perform efficiently.

Most such teachers have their pupils learn and participate in numerous indoor games. If the teacher has from three to five or more grades in the special class, her task is correspondingly greater. Not only must the subject matter of each grade be known, but the amount of necessary reading and transcribing is further increased.

The very bigness of this job[1] is one of the reasons that Horn has advanced for organizing a central city school instead of attempting to teach blind children in isolated Braille classes, as is the common practice at present in our public schools.

4. HOME CONTACTS

The Need.—Some city school systems have felt the need of a closer relationship with the home than that which is provided by the occasional visits of the special-class teacher. Some homes are most unsanitary and are not fit to care for the children over night. In other homes, parents often deny the child the measure of independence of action that is necessary if he is to be fitted to take his place in a world of sighted people.

One Method.—As early as 1916, in Cleveland[2] this problem was recognized and a teacher was appointed whose duty would be to visit the homes of pupils in Braille classes. This teacher studied the home, tried to discover its particular needs, and assisted it to give the blind child the type of help needed. Such home contacts would seem necessary. The task of the school for many of its pupils is the development of a more healthy point of view regarding life, and this cannot be accomplished without the assistance of the home where the child spends so much of his time.

The Cleveland visiting teacher

interprets the blind child's nature and his needs to his parents, to his church school teacher, to boy and girl scouts, and other recreational organization heads. She encourages the parents to permit and to help the child to enter activities, and suggests to the leaders ways in which they can make the blind child's participation most worth while.[3]

[1] John Louis Horn, *The Education of Exceptional Children*, pp. 272–273, 284–287, The Century Co., New York, 1924.

[2] *Deaf, Braille and Sight-saving Classes*, p. 16, Report of the Superintendent of Schools to the Board of Education, Cleveland, Ohio, 1929–30.

[3] *The Special Schools and Curriculum Centers*, pp. 23–24, Report of the Superintendent of Schools to the Board of Education, Cleveland, Ohio, 1929–30.

5. OTHER PROBLEMS

High-school Instruction.—If the general thesis of this chapter—that the blind should be allowed to continue their academic training as long as their ability and interest warrant—is accepted, then provision must be made to give assistance to blind pupils in high school.

Since they have mastered Braille, the assistance needed will be that of a reader. High-school courses require considerable reading; not many high-school texts are in Braille. Therefore, readers become most important. State institutions are generally providing high-school instruction; if local districts expect to instruct their own blind, they cannot afford to ignore their responsibility in this respect.

Costs of Educating the Blind.—The costs, obviously, will be greater than those for educating sighted children. There are several reasons for the excess. Class enrollments are small; additional equipment is needed; textbooks, library facilities, and special equipment are costly; transportation must be provided; and lunch is sometimes free.

There are no adequate data on total costs. Romaker[1] in 1930 reported total per capita costs for 14 cities. These cities reported the costs of educating all children with eye defects. The lowest cost was $84.25; the highest was $412.37; and the median cost was $232.91. The White House Conference reported that per capita costs in public school Braille classes ranged from $120 to $590.[2]

Placement and Follow-up.—The home-contact service rendered by visiting teachers for pupils who are attending Braille classes must not be dropped as soon as the pupils complete the educational program provided for them in the public schools. If they are to become self-supporting, aid will be needed to place them in suitable employment. Businessmen seldom realize what the blind can be trained to do. This placement service will need to locate vacancies, to know which vacancies their blind protégés can fill successfully, and to sell businessmen the idea that the positions can be filled just as well by the blind as by the sighted.

In addition to placement service, there needs to be developed a follow-up service. If a pupil fails in his job, placement service must know why. Failure may be due to misunderstandings upon the part

[1] C. C. ROMAKER, *A Study of Schools and Classes under the Control of Boards of Education Which Are for the Education of Blind and Partially Sighted Children in the United States*, p. 108, unpublished Master's thesis, Ohio State University, Columbus, 1930.

[2] For data on instructional costs excluding supervision, see *U. S. Office of Education Bulletin* 2, pp. 46–51, Washington, D. C., 1937.

of employers as to what they should have expected of the employee; it may be due to a misunderstanding upon the part of the placement bureau as to the requirements of the position. In any case, an efficient follow-up would seem necessary. Only thus can prospective employers be retained; only thus can errors upon the part of the employer, the blind employee, the placement service, and the school in its training program be corrected.

Follow-up is necessary also where the pupil remains at home. At school the child has developed self-confidence, has learned how to use leisure time and how to care for himself physically. If these attitudes and activities are to be maintained, he must not be forgotten as soon as he leaves the special school. The follow-up should continue until a happy afterschool adjustment has been fairly well assured.

6. TEACHER PERSONNEL[1]

There may be some justice in the claim that the blind can best teach the blind. It is difficult for the sighted teacher to approach problems of instruction from the point of view of the blind. A sighted teacher tends to expect reactions that are typical of the sighted, not of the blind; children report, therefore, not their own experiences but what they know the teacher expects them to report. It is difficult, also, for the sighted teacher to talk to blind children in terms that they clearly understand. She tends to assume that they have the same background for understanding as sighted children have.

State schools frequently take sight into account in securing their staff. Some schools have one blind instructor for every two who are sighted; others have one for every three; occasionally there is one blind for one sighted. In public school classes, there are many difficulties involved in using blind instructors. An analysis of the duties of such teachers at once indicates what those difficulties are.[2]

Preparation.—In state schools, the teacher is frequently accepted direct from a regular college course. The new recruit is then closely supervised by the principal or by some one or more of the older teachers of the school. Fairly good results seem to be secured in this way. A local city system would probably find it much more difficult to give such training; therefore, teachers for the Braille classes should have the necessary special training before being appointed.

A teacher of blind children should have the same general academic preparation as teachers in the regular day schools. In addition, she ought to be familiar with the physiology and hygiene of the eye, with

[1] For personal traits, see p. 194.
[2] See pp. 179–180.

the best methods and practices in teaching blind children, and with the physical education program appropriate for the blind. She should have some facility in the various handicrafts. This should be specially true of those crafts that are generally used in classes for the blind as a means of training pupils to use their hands more readily. She must also know Braille and the best methods of teaching it.

Experience.—Eleven cities[1] reported public school teaching experience as a requirement of all candidates for teaching positions in the Braille classes; the extent of such experience required varied from 1 to 5 years. State schools, as previously indicated, occasionally accept college graduates without experience of any kind. Specialized study, as well as teaching under close supervision, is then required of them.

In city school systems, the supervision needed to train new recruits in the successful conduct of the class is difficult and often impossible to give. The classes are few in number in even large cities. The teacher is expected to know her job and to be the city's expert in the instruction of blind children. She must have not only adequate training but adequate experience. This experience should include both public school teaching and teaching in some school for the blind. It might well develop that state schools could act in part as training schools for teachers who are to serve in local districts which establish Braille classes.

The training received at the state school, if that plan were followed, should have been preceded by 2 or more years of public school experience. Such experience is important on account of the close relation that must exist between the work of the Braille teacher and the work of regular class teachers.[2] No relationship of this kind exists in central schools, local or state; therefore, the last-mentioned requirement is not so important for their teachers.

Salaries.—If the teachers of city Braille classes are to have the training and the experience suggested in this section, the minimum salary should always be considerably above the beginning salaries of regular teachers. This does not imply a differential in salary schedules. Any city that works consistently under a salary schedule need but apply that schedule with respect to the beginning Braille class teacher. If she has 4 years of public school experience and 2 years of teaching in a state school for the blind, she can be credited with 6 years' experience in accordance with the salary schedule; if, moreover, she is a college graduate and has done an additional year's work

[1] ROMAKER, *op. cit.*, p. 38.
[2] See pp. 194–195.

specializing upon the teaching of the blind, the 5 years of college work should be credited to her in placing her in the salary schedule.

7. PROGRAMS OF SELECTED CITY SYSTEMS

Los Angeles City.[1]—The first Braille class was organized in Los Angeles, Jan. 1, 1917. At present, such classes are located at the Thirty-second Street elementary school and at the John Francis Polytechnic High School. The local board of education transports about 60 pupils to these classes. The same course of study is followed as is used by sighted pupils. Piano lessons, typing, and special handwork are provided. The pupils are taught Braille in the home room. Elementary pupils attend regular classes for certain major subjects. In the high school all subjects are taken in the regular classes.

Since the textbooks received through Federal aid from the American Printing House of Louisville are not the same as those used in California, the special Braille teachers "make much of the material on Braille machines, a slow and tedious process." The school has 3,800 volumes in its library; this includes the books that the teachers have made during the past 20 years.

Cleveland.[2]—In January, 1909, the first blind children were accepted in the regular classes of the Stanard School for instruction. Such instruction was not authorized by the board until September of that year, when a class of six was organized. By the end of the first year, a second class was requested, and the second year a supervisor was employed. Within 8 years there were four Braille classes; special teachers in music, physical and manual training, and piano tuning were provided; a teacher of vocational guidance and a teacher to visit the homes of pupils had also been secured. The enrollment in Braille classes reached its maximum in 1919, when 48 pupils were enrolled. In 1935–36, there were 41 blind pupils, six of whom were in high school.

In order to provide more adequate reading facilities, many school-books have been put into Braille. The work was done at first by the special teacher. In 1912, the board authorized an assistant, who started a Braille print shop; textbooks essential to good instruction and not available at the American Printing House were thus duplicated. In 1916, the print shop began to use the revised Braille grade

[1] "Education of the Physically Handicapped," pp. 16–17, Los Angeles City School District, *Publication* 281, Los Angeles, Calif., 1936.

[2] *The Special Schools and Curriculum Centers*, pp. 15–24, Report of the Superintendent of Schools to the Board of Education, Cleveland, Ohio, 1929–30.

1½, which was formally adopted by the Uniform Type Commission a year later.   During 1916, the first visiting teacher was hired, and under her supervision plans were put into effect whereby preschool blind children were visited on Saturdays by Braille class teachers.

This was a preventive measure and proved most effective and economical because it made the preschool years of value in the blind child's training, provided a wholesome attitude both on the part of the parent and child toward his handicap, and prevented the formation of unpleasant habits, sometimes known as "blindisms," corrections of which would require school time later.[1]

Pupils admitted include those who are totally blind and all with insufficient vision to read 24-point clear type; they do not enter until they have reached regular school age.   No pupil is placed in the class except upon the recommendation of the school oculist.   Of the 41 pupils enrolled in 1935–36, 6 had no vision; 9 could distinguish light and gross objects; the remaining 26 had more vision, but not enough to read 24-point clear type even after correction by glasses.

The children use the streetcars; if brothers or sisters are not available, the board of education provides guides.   The classes are in centrally located school buildings; the rooms are of regulation size, with plenty of sunlight.   Each class is subject to building rules, just the same as regular classes.   The Braille room is a home room; the pupils recite in regular grade classes.   The regular curriculum is followed; in addition, typewriting is begun in the elementary grades; extra handwork and music are provided in the junior high school. Handwork and music are cared for by special teachers.   Music "includes singing, eurhythmics, and individual piano and instrument lessons for pupils of ability."[2]

Since Braille classes were started in Cleveland, 24 pupils have graduated from high school; 17 of these have gone to schools of higher learning and 6 of these latter have graduated from college.   Two have the Master's degree and one is working on his Doctor's dissertation.   Occupations of the high-school graduates are insurance selling, home teaching of blind adults, music teaching of the sighted, dictaphone work, music teaching in public schools, supervising in social case work, proofreading of Braille books, operating a lending library, playing in an orchestra, housekeeping, and factory work.

Nongraduates become housemaids, nursemaids, canvassers, Braille proofreaders, musicians, and dictaphone operators; they operate candy shops, magazine shops, tobacco shops, specialty shops, caning shops, broom shops, and shining parlors; they work in candy factories

[1] *Ibid.*, p. 20.
[2] *Ibid.*, p. 22.

and box factories, and do sewing, knitting, and basketwork in their own homes.

New York City.—The first Braille classes in New York City were started in 1909; three were begun that year in Manhattan and two in Brooklyn. By 1915, there were 18 classes; this was the peak. In 1920–21 there were only 11 classes; these were located at public schools 16, 45, 54, 77, 110, 127, 157, DeWitt Clinton High School, and Wadleigh High School. Public School 127 had three classes; the remaining schools had one class each.

A special license was being required of Braille class teachers in 1920–21. This was accompanied by a higher salary schedule. Pupils were being given mental examinations; it was the aim to make special provisions for those having the double handicap of low vision and low mentality. Eye treatments were given wherever there was the least chance that a child's vision might be improved.

By 1933–34, there were only eight Braille classes; six of these were in elementary and two in high schools. The school report of that year says "with the possible exception of one high school class for both boys and girls, this provision is adequate."[1] The report points out that in New York City are several institutions for the blind that have provided excellent programs of schoolwork.

8. SUMMARY

The local district must know the problems involved in educating blind children. These problems deal with (1) the discovery of the blind, (2) the locating of a center, (3) transportation, (4) the proper equipping of classrooms, (5) the development of proper relations between the special and the regular teacher, (6) the securing of an adequate number of library books and textbooks, (7) the development of home-visiting service, (8) the provision of high-school training, and (9) the selection of a capable teaching staff.

These special teachers should have the same training as regular classroom teachers; they should have, besides, special courses dealing with the physiology and the psychology of the blind; they should have experience in teaching in regular day schools; and if they cannot be closely supervised during the first year, they should have had a year's experience in a school for the blind under good supervision.

Problems and Questions for Discussion

1. Describe in some detail how you plan to discover all blind children in your district.

[1] "Handicapped and Underprivileged Children," a special report submitted with *The Thirty-sixth Annual Report of the Superintendent of Schools*, p. 10, Board of Education, New York City, 1933–34.

2. What are the chief problems of organizing a local class?   How would you solve each of them?

3. What are the important educational problems faced in teaching blind children in day classes?   What are the possible solutions of each?

4. Does the special Braille teacher have an easy task?   Give the reasons for your answer.

5. Is it wise to give the beginning Braille teacher a larger salary than a beginning regular teacher?   Defend your idea.

6. Describe the program followed in two or more cities for educating blind children.   Select cities whose program was not described in the text.

Selected Bibliography

ALLEN, EDWARD E.   "Special Features in the Education of the Blind During the Biennium 1918–20."   *U.S. Bureau of Education Bulletin* 16, Washington, D.C., 1921.   14 pp.
>   Describes new possibilities in industry for blind, the governmental subsidy for printing, and the development of day schools.

CUTSWORTH, THOMAS D.   *The Blind in School and Society.*   D. Appleton and Company, New York, 1933.   263 pp.
>   An interesting analysis of various problems faced by the blind; verbalism, phantasy, voice and speech, emotional life, problems of sex, and aesthetic life are considered.

HORN, JOHN LOUIS.   *The Education of Exceptional Children*, pp. 231–238, 267–290. The Century Co., New York, 1924.
>   Describes problems of city day classes, dangers of state schools, and the need of local schools in place of classes.

MAXFIELD, KATHRYN E., and IRWIN, ROBERT B.   *The Blind Child and His Reading.*   American Foundation for the Blind, Inc., New York, 1928.   215 pp.
>   Considers the special methods needed in teaching blind children to read; deals with the mechanics of Braille reading, tests used with blind children, and materials used in teaching Braille reading.

ROMAKER, C. C.   *A Study of Schools and Classes under the Control of Boards of Education Which Are for the Education of Blind and Partially Sighted Children in the United States.*   Unpublished Master's thesis, Ohio State University, Columbus, 1930.   134 pp.
>   A detailed study of local provisions made by 39 cities to educate their blind children; deals with housing, teachers, pupils, program, equipment, transportation, and costs.

Twenty-third Annual Report of the Superintendent of Schools 1920–21, pp. 115–118. Board of Education, New York City, 1922.
>   A brief account of the program of work in operation in New York City for blind children.   Especially interesting as a group of recommendations.

White House Conference.   *Special Education: The Handicapped and the Gifted*, pp. 241–274.   The Century Co., New York, 1931.
>   An excellent discussion of the problem involved in educating the blind, existing provisions, organization and administration of Braille day-school classes, and the course of study.

CHAPTER XIV

THE EDUCATION OF LOW-VISIONED CHILDREN

If it is agreed that the prevention of blindness and not the education of the blind is the supreme problem in dealing with children of defective vision, then the organization of sight-saving classes for children of low vision is a problem of great moment. We have had a glimpse of the extent to which a blind child is handicapped all through life, despite the best educational program that can be provided for him. This fact makes it important that every effort be put forth to preserve all the eyesight that a given child may possess; such a saving may well mean the economic independence of hundreds of boys and girls who would otherwise be forced to cope with economic problems under the most severe of physical handicaps—that of blindness. To preserve all existing sight for these youths is the chief aim of the sight-saving class.

1. DEFINITION

It should constantly be remembered that children in sight-saving classes are not blind; they can secure the education that they receive by the use of their eyes and not by the use of their fingers. Since children are not either blind or sighted, but vary in the degree of sight possessed, from no vision to perfect vision, there are many children whose sight is so near the point of demarcation between those considered blind and those considered sighted that classification is most difficult.

Candidates for sight-saving classes are arbitrarily defined as children whose vision ranges from 20/200 to 20/70 by the Snellen chart. The 20/200 vision means that children who have less can hardly be expected to read 24-point clear type. Children whose vision is less than 20/70 cannot read the type used in regular school textbooks without undue strain on the eyes and without constant danger of losing the little sight that they have. This latter limit is sometimes raised to 20/50 in the better eye; this is true in cases of children with corneal opacities, children with inactive keratitis, children with congenital or secondary cataracts, children having congenital malformation, and children having fundus lesions with no acute condition present.[1] It is assumed, of course, that these degrees of sight are those which exist after proper refraction has been made.

2. GUIDING PRINCIPLES

Save Sight.—The primary principle is the prevention of blindness. All children in sight-saving classes have less than normal vision; continued attempts to use regular texts would undoubtedly weaken the little vision they already possess. All materials used, classrooms selected, and work required will be determined in large part by the effect they will have upon the sight of the children for which they are intended. Sight conservation is without doubt the driving force that has made possible the widespread development of special classwork for children with low vision.

Prevent Failure.—The second principle aims at the prevention of failure. Many a child in the regular class group has seemed dull and even mentally slow only because of his inability to see board work which the teacher has placed before the group; his speed of reading, also, is frequently so slowed down that he has been unable to cover lesson assignments. As a result, children are found in the public schools who are failing their courses for no other reason than that they have poor vision.

Recognize That the Child Is Sighted.—The third principle recognizes the fact that children of low vision are sighted. They use their eyes and they read from books; they do not learn through their fingers as do the blind. The only differences between the educational program for those of low vision and for the sighted are (1) that greater care must be exercised to preserve vision and (2) that more personal attention must be given to the child in order to help him overcome his handicap.

Form Good Habits.—A fourth principle aims at assisting each child to form such habits of using his eyes, to follow such hygienic rules in caring for them, and to develop such skill in protecting them that at no time in his life will he seriously jeopardize the sight which he now has.

Return to Regular Class When Possible.—A fifth principle demands the return of all children to regular classes just as soon as the physical condition of their eyes will permit their return without any danger of further injury to their vision.

----

[1] HAZEL C. HADLEY, *Sight-saving Classes in the Public Schools*, p. 81, State Department of Education, Columbus, Ohio, 1927.

3. HISTORY

The history of the movement to provide a special program of education for low-visioned children is of short duration. Classes for such children originated in England in 1908. Through the efforts of Edward E. Allen, and "backed by the resources that Perkins Institution and Massachusetts School for the Blind had to offer," Helen Smith organized a sight-saving class at Roxbury, Mass., in April, 1913;[1] this was the first class of its type to be established in the United States.

Previous to the establishment of special classes, children of low vision were either ignored in the regular classroom, with whatever loss of sight or failure to pass school-work this occasioned; sent to state schools for the blind; or accepted in local classes for the blind. In the two latter cases they were being taught Braille because of their inability to read ordinary print.

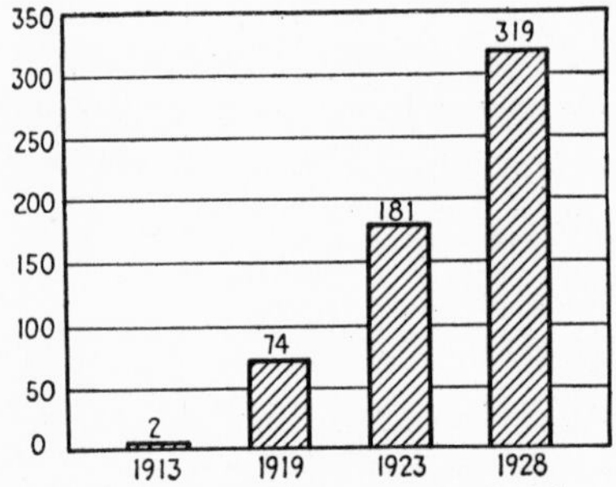

Fig. 3.—Increase in number of sight-saving classes.

The second class to be established in the United States was at Cleveland in September, 1913. The head teacher for the blind at Cleveland had for some time been challenged by the very serious problem of trying to teach sighted pupils by the Braille method. He had been experimenting for several years with various sizes of type for these low-visioned children. In January, 1913, the Ohio State Legislature passed a bill providing state aid not only for the blind but for children of low vision. The following fall the Cleveland Board of Education permitted the opening of its first sight-saving class.

The early classes tended to accept just the partially sighted; in a short time sighted children who needed special care, owing to dangerous eye conditions, were admitted and thus the term sight saving became appropriate. The development of sight-saving classes in Ohio has been steady; the state aid granted in 1913 encouraged them. Starting with the class in Cleveland in September of that year, there were 30 classes organized by June, 1922. During the year 1929–30, a total of 25 Ohio cities had organized 62 such classes; Cleveland by this time had 22.

[1] White House Conference, *Special Education: The Handicapped and the Gifted*, p. 118, The Century Co., New York, 1931.

The development of sight-saving classes in the United States from 1913 to 1928 is graphically presented in Fig. 3, taken from Myers.[1] The chart tells its own story.   The first 6 years after 1913 showed the organization of 72 classes; during the next 4 years, 107 more classes were formed; and during the next 5 years, 138 classes came into existence.

4. METHODS OF EDUCATING LOW-VISIONED CHILDREN

Some children of low vision are still being educated in state schools for the blind; the practice, however, is being rapidly discontinued. The superintendent of one of our large state schools said recently that in his opinion such children should not have a place in these schools for the blind, since they are sighted and the state school is primarily equipped for the blind.

The other method is the organization of special classes within the public schools.   They are supported by local boards of education, with certain aid from the state, and are organized similarly to public school classes for the blind, in that their pupils recite with the regular classes. They differ in methods of instruction and in equipment used.

A third method, which has been suggested but nowhere adopted, is the organization of a local school where all children of defective vision would be assembled and classified for instruction.   There are several reasons why such a plan might be worthy of a trial.[2]

5. THE RURAL PROBLEM

Using Berry's formula that there is one child with defective vision for every 2,000 of the general population, and using Ohio's minimum standard of eight pupils in a class, every city of 16,000 should maintain a sight-saving class.   If small cities were allowed to receive pupils with defective vision from the surrounding territory to a distance which pupils might easily travel daily by motorcar or bus, the size of cities that might support sight-saving classes could possibly be cut to 8,000 population.   There would still, however, be a great many children with defective vision in strictly rural districts who would not, by this plan, be given educational opportunities.

Plans for Meeting the Problem.—Several plans have been suggested that might well be used in giving such children an education.

[1] EDWARD T. MYERS, "A Survey of Sight-saving Classes in the Public Schools of the United States," p. 13, The National Society for the Prevention of Blindness, *Publication* 64, New York City, 1930.

[2] See pp. 168–169, 226.

1. Arrangements might be made whereby those who live too far from the city to make daily trips could be boarded during the week.

2. In those sections where large consolidated rural schools have been established, a sufficient number of children needing a sight-saving class might be found to organize one locally.

3. A county class might be established. Ohio has had such a class at Oak Harbor in Ottawa County. The pupils were transported daily to this central county school, which is located in a village of about 2,000 population. If children must be boarded, some suggest that the county class be organized in the city in which or near which the county children's home is located. The home, they suggest, would make an excellent boarding place.

4. Others suggest home instruction. Under this plan, a teacher would visit the home, both to assist the child with his schoolwork and to teach parents what they may do to help him with his studies and at the same time prevent him from doing further injury to his eyes. Such a plan may be utilized in isolated cases, but it is not generally recommended.

5. Berry suggests[1] that, where other arrangements cannot be worked out, children with eye defects could be cared for in the local school in a regular class group. If this is done, the regular teacher must have certain information about their needs. She should seat the children where there is sufficient light, but where it is not too glaring or too intense; she should train them in the proper use of their eyes; large-typed books should be provided; pupils with good vision might be prevailed upon to read aloud; the proper writing materials should be provided; a typewriter with large type should be made available; parents should be given all needed instructions regarding the care of the eyes; and the child should be encouraged to visit a competent oculist.

6. Another plan calls for the organization of a mixed class. There might be several of these classes within the county. A class of this kind might have in it three crippled children, one blind child, three children with eye defects, and two children with defective hearing. The difficulties involved in one teacher's trying to supervise the education of such a miscellaneous group are obvious.

The Need.—In most county-school districts, the need for classes of this type has not yet been fully recognized. Hadley has reported

---

[1] CHARLES SCOTT BERRY, "The Education of Handicapped School Children in Michigan," p. 10, *State Department of Public Instruction Bulletin* 11, Lansing, Mich., 1926.

for Ohio[1] 62 counties large enough, based upon a 1 to 500 ratio, to have at least 8 children in need of a sight-saving class. She has reported 28 counties large enough to have 12 children needing such a class. Of these 28 counties, there were 12 that had at least one city each with such a class; there were, however, 16 others where no provision had been made. Many of these do not realize how great is the need for sight-saving classes within their own boundaries.

A continuing census is needed. The teachers ought to be encouraged to report suspected cases of eye difficulty. Literature should be sent home which will call attention to the more obvious symptoms of eye defect; and the state department of education, through co-operation with the state department of health, might well arrange for clinics throughout the state. The state department of education would be fully justified in establishing clinics of its own upon the basis of the educational gain to the children discovered. We now know that many children are failing in school subjects because of undiscovered eye defects; it has been shown that placement in sight-saving classes has not only protected the child's vision but has often prevented further failure.

Ottawa County's Class.—Ottawa County in Ohio has organized a special sight-saving class for the children of its rural sections. Thirteen children were located who needed to attend such a class. Five of them lived at Oak Harbor, where the class was located. One traveled 12 miles by automobile, with other sighted pupils who attended school at Oak Harbor. A special school bus daily carried three pupils to Oak Harbor, a distance of 12 miles; one of the three had to travel 5 miles by individual automobile before taking the bus; another had to travel a short distance on a regular school bus before transferring to the special bus. Another student traveled 22 miles by traction morning and afternoon, in order to attend this class. The remaining three children with defective vision are not in the class, as they refused to make the necessary trip.

The class had two children in grade 2, three in grade 5, and one child each in grades 1, 3, 4, 6, and 8. Thus for 10 pupils 7 grades were represented. The attendance is good, and the children gain regularly in weight. All are of American parentage.

6. TEACHER PERSONNEL

Attention to the training of people to be teachers of sight-saving classes is of recent date. In Ohio, previous to 1925, teachers for such classes had no other preparation than that which a successful teacher

[1] HADLEY, op. cit., pp. 32–33.

in the regular grades might secure from reading or from personal conferences with a supervisor.

Personal Traits.—Resourcefulness and initiative are commonly mentioned as necessary in the special teacher. These are qualities that all teachers should have; but some claim that the teacher of sight-saving classes has a peculiar need for them. Often, she has either no large-typed texts or, at best, very few; yet the pupils must not read small print. In order to help these children master the material of their courses in the time allowed, the teacher will need all the resourcefulness at her command.

Poise and quietness of manner are needed. Many of these children have failed in their courses previous to admission to the class; they feel discouraged and beaten as the result of repeated failure. This special-class teacher has the task of changing these established attitudes toward life; a poise and quietness of manner that come from a knowledge and confidence that these children can succeed will do more to re-establish their confidence in their ability to succeed than perhaps any other single factor.

In addition the teacher must be well adjusted socially and able to get along with people. If instruction is to be put upon a co-operative basis, she will have a real job in arranging a satisfactory program of instruction for her pupils and at the same time keeping the good will and enthusiastic co-operation of regular classroom teachers. She will have contacts with the school principal, the school nurse, the oculist, and the parents of her group. Only through the united efforts of all these individuals can sight-saving classwork be most beneficial; the special teacher stands as the key that opens the door to this needed co-operation.

Preparation.—Most authorities agree in suggesting that the teacher should be required to have the same general preparation as that required of all regular teachers. In addition, she should know the physiology of the eye, have some acquaintance with the diseases of the eye that result in decreased vision, know what needs to be done in protecting eyes that have these varying defects, and know why unusual care must be given to the child who is suffering from progressive myopia.

Experience.—Most schools take, as teachers for sightsaving classes, successful regular classroom teachers with 2 or more years of experience. This practice is to be commended. The poise and self-confidence that come from several years of successful teaching experience are needed by the special-class teacher. She, moreover, has the unique problem of co-ordinating her special classwork with that of the regular school classes. Her load in the special class is heavy; she is likely to overemphasize her duties at the expense of the regular classes. Only a teacher who is fully alive to the unique problems of both situations can hope to co-ordinate successfully the work of the two groups.

If excellent supervision is provided, teachers may be accepted who have had no previous experience in sight-saving classes; candidates have to get such experience somewhere. If there is no supervision available, the teacher should have had actual experience in sight-saving work; the reasons are obvious.

7. PROGRAMS IN SELECTED CITIES

New York City.[1]—In 1920–21, the city of New York had 27 sight-conservation classes; with five exceptions, there was only one class in a building; the five buildings had two classes each. These 27 classes accommodated 522 pupils; at that time, however, more than 500 names were on the waiting list of those needing the services of a sight-saving class.

The city had nine eye clinics, which, with one exception, were located in public school buildings; these clinics were part of the city department of health. The clinics had a staff of expert ophthalmologists, who co-operated with the school medical inspection in discovering (1) contagious eye diseases, (2) refractive errors, and (3) candidates for sight-conservation classes.

These sight-saving classes were under the supervision of the departments of health and education; the former had the ocular work, the latter the educational program. The co-operative program was started about 1916. The work of the clinics was not confined to caring for the children placed in sight-saving classes. Hundreds of children were examined and, after treatment and refraction, were returned to regular classes without having to attend special classes. Such services are important and represent a greatly needed type of preventive work.

By 1933–34, there were 89 classes; the report says, "When the depression began to settle upon us and there was no money for additional classes we . . . increased registration to the maximum number of twenty children to a class."[2] There were at that time, moreover, 400 on the waiting list. During the calendar year of 1933, the clinics

---

[1] *Twenty-third Annual Report of the Superintendent of Schools*, pp. 115–127, Board of Education, New York City, 1922.

[2] "Handicapped and Underprivileged Children," a special report submitted with *The Thirty-sixth Annual Report of the Superintendent of Schools*, p. 23, Board of Education, New York City, 1933–34.

of the health department examined 300 children; hospital clinics and oculists practicing privately examined 295 others. Of the 595 examined, 511 were referred to sight-saving classes and 13 to classes for the blind, while 71 were discharged to normal classes. Despite this good service of co-operating agencies, the report asks for an eye specialist on the staff of the board of education. This would seem a most reasonable request; it seems hardly possible that extraschool agencies will be able to handle all of the school's problems in the prevention of loss of vision. Emergency cases constantly arise, calling for immediate care; lighting of special rooms needs to be checked for adequacy and avoidance of glare; and border-line cases need further follow-up.

There are two visiting teachers who serve children in Braille and sight-saving classes. They contact the family and other agencies when this is necessary for the good of the child. If parents hesitate in having eye examinations or necessary corrections, one of these teachers explains the reasons for such action; she studies the child and arranges, where necessary, for further physical and for mental examinations; she determines transportation routes and decides whether an escort is necessary.

Cleveland.[1]—The first class was started in 1913; there were three classes in 1914 and eight in 1918. During the year 1935–36, there were 21 classes with an enrollment of 376 children. Cleveland reports that about 45 per cent of these children need the class in order to preserve eyesight; the other 55 per cent need the class because they are unable to see the ordinary print and require the special methods used in the sight-saving class.

In 1935–36, of the pupils in sight-saving classes, 60 had been referred by hospital dispensaries, 100 by private oculists, and 216 by the public school clinics. Medical examinations are made as a matter of routine in the kindergarten and in grades 1, 3, and 5, in Cleveland. These usually reveal most eye defects. Thus, children are seldom referred to sight-saving classes from the upper grades. The pupils are 84 per cent white and 16 per cent Negro, and 96 per cent of them were born in the United States. However, the parents of 56 per cent of them were born in other countries.

The 1929–30 Cleveland report states that this is the only city known which classifies pupils with defective vision upon the basis of eye defect. That is not done 100 per cent, but there is an attempt to

[1] *The Special Schools and Curriculum Centers*, pp. 24–37, Board of Education, Cleveland, Ohio, 1931.

keep children with myopic conditions in classes by themselves. For some 10 years a segregated class for children with trachoma was maintained; at one time there were 20 children in the class. In 1926, however, the class was discontinued because it was not needed.[1]

San Francisco.[2]—The first class in San Francisco was organized late in the fall of 1922 under the combined auspices of the board of education and the board of health. San Francisco is unique, in that one of its three classes is for Chinese children; there were 14 of them at the time of the report in 1928. These children had always lived in a Chinese environment; they were taken from their home school and placed in the Jean Parker School.

It took at least three months of coaxing and humoring, such as striking the Chinese note in the decoration of the room, the wearing of jade and a Chinese coolie coat by the teacher, the bringing of Chinese objects of art from the home of the teacher, the burning of incense and an occasional ice-cream party before there was a sign of friendliness toward the teacher or the least letdown in the reserve of their attitude.[3]

This group of children set up the following rules that they were to observe as members of the sight-saving class.

(1) We should wear our glasses always. (2) We should keep our glasses clean. (3) We should sit up straight. (4) We should have our books raised. (5) We should have the light coming from the left side. (6) We should draw the shades or move our desks if the sunshine is on our work. (7) We should have the lights turned on, on dark days. (8) We should read large print only. (9) We should look away from our work when we are typing.[4]

These rules were composed within 6 weeks after the class had been organized. They are printed on a chart 22 by 36 inches in size. The pupils are much interested in them. From time to time they are retyped by some child of the group, but the rules remain a permanent fixture in the school.

Cincinnati.[5]—The work in Cincinnati was first organized in 1914 by Robert Irwin; during 1926–27, there were 95 children enrolled—approximately a ratio of 1 to 500 of the school population. In January, 1937, there were 130 pupils enrolled; they were assembled in seven classes, representing all grades from the first through senior high school.

[1] For discussion of visiting teachers, see p. 185.
[2] *Conservation of Vision*, Mimeographed Report, 28 pp., Board of Education, San Francisco, 1928.
[3] *Ibid.*, p. 14.
[4] *Ibid.*, p. 17.
[5] HADLEY, *op. cit.*, pp. 54–55.

Cincinnati in 1926–27 was unique, in that it did not confine its work of sight saving merely to those children who had defective vision; it gave this service just as other cities did. In addition, it had organized to do sight-saving work in all the public schools, in the interests of all children in the system. This plan began to take effect in the fall of 1926, when a department of sight saving was organized. The executive of the department was designated as a director.

The department organized a group of teachers from within the city as a means whereby sight-saving activities could reach every school in the system; one teacher from each school was selected to become a member of the group. Three or four times a year these teachers met with those educational and medical authorities who were interested more directly in the sight-saving program.

This group originated the idea of putting better lighting facilities in some of the older buildings; it assisted in the routine work of caring for eye cases; it helped develop school sentiment among all pupils who had need of glasses to wear them regularly and keep them clean. Such an organization might well have a very valuable function to perform in every community. It is to be hoped that this one is still active. Such work is prevention of the finest kind and should be given most hearty encouragement.

8. SUMMARY

Sight saving refers to all programs that tend to prevent the loss of vision; sight-saving classes generally accept children who rate between 20/70 and 20/200 according to the Snellen chart. The major aim of the whole program of these classes is that of saving sight. The first class was organized in England in 1908; in 1913, the first class was established in the United States. The development of sight-saving classes has been rapid since about 1920. The generally accepted method of educating these children is in classes using the co-operative plan.

Teachers need such personal traits as resourcefulness, initiative, poise, patience, sympathy, firmness, and excellent health; they need the training of regular teachers plus experience as regular teachers. Teachers of classes in small cities and rural sections will need the best of state supervision. Some cities are now reporting in detail the educational programs being developed for low-visioned children.

Problems and Questions for Discussion

1. What children should be admitted to sight-saving classes? Are standards universal? What problems arise?

2. What principles should govern the development and handling of classes for children with defective vision?

3. Trace briefly the history of sight-saving classes.

4. What suggestions have you to make for improving or broadening the methods used in educating children with low or defective vision?

5. To what extent is the rural problem of educating children of defective vision unique? What suggestions have you for educating them? Is the need great? Give evidence.

6. What are the preparation, training, and characteristics that you would hope a teacher of a sight-saving class would have? Why?

7. Describe the sight-saving programs of two or more cities that were not discussed in the text.

Selected Bibliography

BERRY, CHARLES SCOTT. "The Education of Handicapped School Children in Michigan," pp. 6–11. *State Department of Public Instruction Bulletin* 11, Lansing, Mich., 1926.

An account of the size of the problem of educating children of defective vision, the way to find them, classroom needs, size of class, subject material, teacher qualifications, the rural problem, and results.

BRUNER, FRANK G. *Report of the Director of Special Schools for the School Year* 1922–23, pp. 93–101. Board of Education, Chicago, 1924.

A brief account of historical development, equipment used, and results.

HADLEY, HAZEL, and HATHAWAY, WINIFRED. "Sight-saving Classes: Their Organization and Administration," *Publication* 30, The National Committee for the Prevention of Blindness, New York City, 1927. 50 pp.

An excellent description of aims, eligibility, problems encountered in organizing classes, costs, transportation, and the serving of hot lunches. Gives digest of legislation for each of the 48 states governing sight-saving classes.

HADLEY, HAZEL C. *Sight-saving Classes in the Public Schools*, presenting the Ohio Plan. State Department of Education, Columbus, Ohio, 1927. 90 pp.

A description of problems involved in organizing classes, of aims, of teacher training, of state supervision, of the rural problem, and of financial support. Describes in detail the work of some 23 Ohio communities in caring for and educating children with defective vision.

HECK, ARCH O. "Special Schools and Classes in Cities of 10,000 Population and More in the United States," *U.S. Office of Education Bulletin* 7, p. 30. Washington, D.C., 1930.

A list of cities which had organized sight-saving classes in 1929–30.

CHAPTER XV

LOCAL PROBLEMS FACED IN EDUCATING LOW-VISIONED CHILDREN

The local problem of educating children of low vision is important but difficult; so many people have to be convinced of its worth before action can be taken and many have so limited a view of life that the matter is not seen in the proper perspective. As a result, a few communities put into operation a program that solves the problem satisfactorily. But there are thousands of communities and each has to be convinced.

This is the situation that makes it so difficult to care for and to educate all low-visioned children in the United States. These children are not educated in state schools, and there is very little state supervision; each locality is forced to work out its own program. Such programs, as was pointed out in the previous chapter, have been developed in a number of cities. This development has been proceeding at a rapidly increasing tempo during the past 20 years. Despite this fact, thousands of communities have still completely ignored the problem.

Because of this situation, it has seemed worth while to discuss some of the problems which any community will face in organizing schoolwork for children of low vision. It is believed that the mere enumeration and discussion of these problems, together with suggested solutions, will assist the reader to get a clearer picture of the need for such an educational program.

1. ORGANIZING THE CLASS

Admissions.—In reporting the types of children who should be admitted to sight-saving classes in Ohio, Hadley lists the following:

1. Children who cannot read more than 20/70 on a standard Snellen chart in the better eye, or who cannot read No. 2.00 at 20 C.M.
2. Myopes who have more than 6 diopters of myopia and under 10 years of age.
3. Children who have 3 diopters of myopia which are progressive.
4. Hyperopes who have symptoms of asthenopia and whose vision in their best eye falls below 20/70.
5. Children who have an astigmatism of more than 3.5 diopters and whose vision cannot be brought up to more than 20/70, in the better eye.

6. Children with corneal opacities whose vision is 20/50 or less in the better eye.

7. Cases of inactive keratitis where vision is 20/50 or less in better eye.

8. Children having congenital cataracts, secondary cataracts, congenital malformation, or fundus lesions where no acute condition is present, with vision of 20/50 or less in the better eye.[1]

This writer then adds that the preceding conditions are assumed to exist after the child has been fitted with the proper glasses; she also states, "Any child who, in the oculist's opinion, would benefit by sight-saving training will be accepted subject to the suggestions of the oculist for treatment or training."[2] These suggestions broaden greatly the scope of sight-saving work and tend to justify the name which is now applied to these classes. Admissions are limited, however, upon the basis of mentality; but agreement as to the degree of mentality that will be acceptable is lacking. Some cities refuse to accept children with an I.Q. under 80; others set the limit at 70.

Incidence.—The number of children to be cared for can be estimated in a general way by considering that one child in every 500 of the school population will be in need of the services of a sight-saving teacher. In Ohio, where the minimum size of class is eight, this means that every city with a school population of 4,000 should be able to maintain such a class. Of 22 cities in Ohio from which data were available for the year 1926–27, only eight did not have enough pupils in these special classes to conform to this ratio.

Devices for Discovering Defective Vision.—In order to have specific information concerning need, an examination may be made of the school census records; they frequently record data concerning the vision of school children. In other school systems the pupils' cumulative record would provide the information. In cities that have regular physical examinations of all school children, data can be obtained by examining the school's physical record of the child or the records of the school physician.

Where records are lacking, reports will be required from teachers concerning children who have eye troubles. Specific suggestions will need to be made to the teachers as to what signs indicate probable eye difficulties.[3] If enough school nurses are available, they could make the preliminary examination of all children; if nurses are lacking, a good oculist could instruct the teaching staff regarding the essential points in the use of the Snellen chart. These rough surveys would

---

[1] HAZEL C. HADLEY, *Sight-saving Classes in the Public Schools*, p. 81, State Department of Education, Columbus, Ohio, 1927.

[2] *Ibid.*, p. 82.

[3] For such a list, see pp. 226–227.

be sufficient to bring to the oculist's attention the more serious cases. New York City has eye clinics in the Bureau of Child Hygiene of the Department of Health.

Where other measures fail, or even as a supplementary measure, it has been found helpful to examine all children who are continued failures. New York City examined 400 of these "habitually left back" children in one of their large schools and found 110 who needed glasses. When 100 members of the group procured the glasses prescribed, 98 of these "habitually left back" children passed their examinations successfully. Many skipped; one boy even skipped five grades. Of the 10 who refused to procure glasses, all but one failed. Thus, many children who need the services of a sight-saving class may be discovered by a careful examination of the failing groups each year.

After the organization of these classes, a continuous survey should be made of the sight of all beginning children. Continuous reports should be made by regular teachers concerning all children who seem to be developing eye troubles; early treatment and care are the surest preventions of serious sight handicaps and of blindness.

Care of the Eyes.—Despite the great importance of the educational program of sight-saving classes, without question their major aim is the care of the eyes. This care is provided by setting up conditions under which children with partial vision may be educated without additional injury to the eyes; it is provided by giving ocular supervision to each child and treating the eyes of each according to needs.

The housing, equipment, materials of study, and methods are all judged in terms of this aim. Every child should have a plan of treatment outlined for him by the oculist recommending him. This plan should be followed by the parents, the school, and the special teacher. A private oculist selected by the parents may supervise the treatments; the school oculist will do this in all other cases.

There should be in the hands of the special teacher a detailed individual record of each pupil, showing the amount of vision, the cause of any lack in vision, the nature of the disease that affects the eye, the specific ways in which care can be taken to protect the child's vision, and the time of the next examination. If glasses are needed or treatments are to be taken, details concerning both should be recorded. A statement should be given concerning the amount of eye work allowed, conditions under which it is allowed, and the question as to whether or not the eyes are likely to become worse.

There should be an arrangement whereby a close follow-up of all children placed in the special classes can be made by the oculist.

For many children a yearly examination will be far from adequate. The first examination will probably indicate which cases should be re-examined shortly; all pupils under constant treatment will, of course, be under close observation. Hadley states that progressive myopia cases should be examined every 6 months and that every 3 months would be better. Whenever a child shows signs of eye diffi- culty, the teacher ought to be free to call the oculist for an examination.

The Classroom.—A room to be satisfactory should be large enough so that seats may be rearranged in order to avoid glares or too-strong light; it should have plenty of sunlight. Adequate light devoid of glare requires eastern, western, or northern exposure; it requires a window space equal to at least 25 per cent of the floor area; it requires windows that reach to the ceiling and a room narrow enough for the light from the top of the window to light well the far side of the class. The room, in fact, should meet the requirements of all present-day standards for modern classroom construction.

Care should be exercised in seeing that shafts of light do not enter from the sides, due to narrow blinds, or between the rollers placed at the center. Artificial lighting should be provided, and it should be of the indirect type.

Blackboards.—Blackboard space is essential and should be plentiful. The individual schedules of pupils described in this section need to be kept constantly before the teacher, as well as before the pupils, if they are not to miss any of their oral recitations or be late at any. Such schedules can be built into a class program, showing the hourly responsibilities of each child; this program could be placed on the front blackboard, where daily changes could be made to fit the changes in the recitations of regular classes. One school allows to each child 3 feet of blackboard space where he is expected to place at the close of each day samples of his best work.

Equipment.[1]—Some of the equipment of a classroom for sight- saving work will be the same as that in regular classrooms. Seats and desks will be the same as in any other modern school building; it should, however, be particularly emphasized that modern equip- ment that will assist in maintaining good posture and in avoiding glares is especially essential in the special rooms where the preserva- tion of sight is important.[2]

More cupboard space is needed than in regular classrooms. The textbooks are larger than regular texts, and since books from the

---

[1] For excellent suggestions concerning needed equipment and means of making some of it, see *Methods of Teaching Sight-saving Classes*, by ESTELLA LAWES.

[2] For equipment needed for serving lunch, see pp. 211–212.

school library cannot be used, there will need to be more supplementary texts available; these, too, must be in the large, clear type. Sand tables and adjustable bookracks are useful. Typewriters are essential; they should be of a dull finish and have silence pads and blank keys. Maps and globes in strong outline are needed; but the ordinary charts for reading and arithmetic can be used for the elementary pupils. In Illustration 14 are shown the movable and adjustable

ILLUSTRATION 14.—A sight-saving classroom, Detroit.   Note shades adjustable from center, movable and adjustable desks, large-type books and wide-lined paper.

desks, large-type books, and wide-lined paper, as well as shades adjustable from the center.

A Manila paper, rough and unglazed, is commonly used; it is usually 9 by 12 inches in size. Lines should be heavy and an inch apart. Pencils with heavy, soft lead, and a sharpener to fit the pencils are needed. Soft chalk and pens that make broad, heavy lines can be used. Every precaution should be taken to make sure that the writing of the teacher and of the pupils is large enough to prevent eyestrain; this criterion should be followed in judging all equipment and all work demanded of pupils.

Records.—The regular public schools are more and more feeling the need of complete and adequate records of each pupil, if teachers and supervisors are to make satisfactory school adjustments for individual pupils. This need is even greater in classes for children with defective vision. The degree of defect varies greatly; the variation in kind of defect is nearly as great. No two children can be treated alike in the care of their eyes. Their other differences are just as great as in any unselected group of children with normal vision. Records, therefore, become a necessary equipment of the sight-saving class.

These records should be individual; they should be cumulative; and they should be readily accessible to the classroom teacher. They should conform in detail to the specifications of any modern pupil-recording system.

Administration of the Class.[1]—The sight-saving class is a unit of the regular school organization, just as any other home-room group is. The general rules of the school are applicable to the class; the teacher is responsible to the building principal, just as other teachers are; and she is considered a regular member of the school's faculty. If the city is large enough to have a supervisor of sight-saving classes, the special-class teacher will bear the same relation to such a supervisor as the art teacher does to the art supervisor.

Instead of assembling all children of these classes for special programs, many school principals are now encouraging them to take part in regular school programs with the regular class pupils. They are given parts of programs that they can do as well as children with perfect vision. They take part in many of the regular school contests in the languages and in spelling; they belong to the school band; some compete in games; and others compete in school exhibits. Thus the pupils of sight-saving classes have come to belong closely to the school; they are a completely socialized unit in it; they are no longer merely housed in the school building.

2. WORK OF THE SPECIAL TEACHER

Co-operation with Regular Teachers.—If the above relationship is to be effectively carried out, the special teacher has a real task ahead of her. She must be in contact with all regular teachers to whom her pupils are to recite; without being didactic or officious, she must help these teachers to visualize the problems encountered by the low-visioned child in securing an education. They must realize the necessity of proper lighting; they must help the pupil abstain from reading regular type and from writing without proper materials; they need to understand that all eyestrain must be avoided.

[1] See p. 173.

This program of educating regular teachers, to be successful, must be tactfully and skillfully managed by the special teacher.

Help to Pupils.—She must assist her pupils in lesson preparation. If books with large print are not available, she must do a greater amount of reading to them. In any case, considerable reading will be necessary, since in some courses none of the reference materials will be in large print. The work of programing her pupils will be no small task, since they will represent from four to six grade divisions. Individual programs must be so specific and detailed that each child will know exactly the time and place of each oral recitation, as well as the time for studying various subjects in the home room.

The teacher will be responsible for giving special quizzes and examinations. The regular class teacher will send the questions or problems to her. She must then recopy them in large writing so the child can easily read them, or she must dictate them. All blackboard or written work required during the regular class period must be handled in the same way.

Making Equipment.—Much of the equipment must be made by the special teacher. Globes and maps needed in geography can seldom be purchased, either because of lack of money or because of nonavailability. The teacher, however, can take old globes and, by using glue, putty, and coloring, make good relief maps. The ordinary colored wall maps have to be outlined in India ink, if suitable maps cannot be purchased. In order to meet the requirements of map drawing, the special teacher frequently makes from regular maps stencils of the countries to be studied; if these are of dark construction paper, the child has a means of making maps. Such tasks as these are indicative of some of the work that teachers of sight-saving classes must be ready to undertake.

3. PROGRAM MAKING

Gathering Data.—Program making is one of the teacher's important duties, early in the term. She must secure from each regular teacher in whose class her pupils will be reciting a complete program of the work that the regular grade pupils will be doing; this will show at what hours the regular classes will be busied in activities from which the low-visioned pupils will be able to profit.

Upon the basis of these programs, the special-class teacher will proceed to build a daily work program for herself, as well as for the pupils of each grade represented in her class. In building these programs, she has to consider the problem of covering for the pupils of each grade all the work that is being done in the regular class.

Arrangements have to be made for securing regularly an outline of the work to be covered daily by each grade. Sometimes this is managed by providing each grade group in the sight-saving class with a small notebook; in this notebook, some pupil of the regular grade class copies the assignments from day to day. The book is taken to the special teacher, and she assists the group for that grade to prepare the new assignment. Necessary reading and writing must be supervised by the special teacher, and any eye work of a close nature must be done under her supervision.

Rules to Observe.—The necessity of exercising great care in programing the work of the class, involving as it often does from four to seven or more half grades, is evident. The program must allow time for each pupil's independent study; it must provide time for the special teacher to work separately with each grade group; and it must permit the pupils to attend regular classes for that portion of their work from which they can hope to profit most by attending. At the same time, the program must keep a part of the pupils in the special classroom at all hours of the day. Equally important is it that some of the pupils should be attending regular classes each hour; this makes it possible for the special teacher to give the needed personal supervision.

The program should ensure to each pupil as much instruction in every subject as regular class pupils receive. In order to check her program before putting it into definite operation, the teacher should, according to a San Francisco report, check it in three ways. She must "see that every child has his share of time during the day," "see that the teacher is teaching only one subject at a time," and "see that there are no consecutive periods of eye work."[1] Other points that should be observed are (1) make each period demanding eye work as short as 20 minutes, (2) remember that these children need to work more slowly than do those with normal vision, (3) arrange that all required subjects are included, and (4) provide the necessary rest periods.

A Sample Daily Program.—A sample daily program is shown in Table XIII. "A," "B," and "C" indicate where the pupil does the work of the subjects listed. "A" means that he recites with the regular grade group; "B," that he recites with the special-class teacher and is receiving more or less personal direction and assistance from her; and "C," that he is studying in the special room preparing his own lessons. Instead of using letters, colors are quite generally accepted as a device for showing where the pupils do the work.

[1] *Conservation of Vision*, report to Superintendent of Schools, p. 16, Board of Education, San Francisco, 1928.

TABLE XIII.—MONDAY'S PROGRAM FOR GRADES 6B, 7A, 7B, AND 8A[1]

Hour	6B, 5 pupils	7A, 1 pupil	7B, 1 pupil	8A, 4 pupils
9:00	B. Oral sentence structure, punctuation	C. Written arithmetic	A. History	A. Geography
9:20	C. Composition typing	B. Oral arithmetic	A. History	A. Geography
9:45	C. Composition typing	C. History study	B. Oral grammar	C. Written arithmetic
10:00	B. Eye hygiene			
10:30	Physical education—nutrition—recess			
10:45	C. Written arithmetic	C. History study	A. Domestic science (cooking)	B. Oral arithmetic
11:05	B. Oral arithmetic	C. Typing		C. Written arithmetic
11:25	C. Finish composition	C. Written grammar		B. Oral grammar
11:45	B. Story reading by teacher (Book report)	B. Story reading by teacher		B. Story reading by teacher
12:00	Luncheon			
1:00	A. Geography	A. History	B. 1:00 Blackboard arithmetic 1:30 History study	A. Literature
1:45	Eye rest for entire class			
2:00	A. Chorus singing, Marshall School	A. Literature	A. Literature	B. History study
2:20	A. Singing	A. Literature	A. Literature	B. Oral grammar
2:45	A. Singing	B. Correct written grammar	C. Typing	C. History study

[1] *Conservation of Vision*, report to Superintendent of Schools, p. 9, Board of Education, San Francisco, 1928.

Such charts are prepared for each school day of the week. They are posted or drawn on the blackboard at the front of the special room; this makes it easy for each pupil to make sure of what he should be doing each hour of the day. Because the regular class teachers make frequent changes in their schedules, the special teacher has to make arrangements with them to have all such changes reported to her; in the light of these reports she must adjust her own schedules.

4. RESPONSIBILITIES OF THE REGULAR TEACHER

A regular teacher who has in her classes pupils from a sight-saving class assumes unique responsibilities. She ought to secure from the special-class teacher information concerning them.

Specific Rules.—The State Department of Education of Ohio sends the following suggestions to the regular teachers in those schools in which sight-saving classes are located. A pupil in a sight-saving class should

1. Take the same part in oral recitations as does the child with normal vision.
2. Do no written or other close eye work in the regular grade classroom unless special arrangements for such are made in consultation with the sight-saving class teacher.
3. Work with the light coming from above over the left shoulder, for right-handed pupils, and over the right shoulder, for left-handed pupils.
4. Conduct himself in the same manner as do children of normal sight in the classroom.
5. Enter and leave classrooms with the least possible disturbance.
6. Be kept informed of any changes in program, assignments, etc.[1]

General Suggestions.—If the regular teacher will merely remember that there is a low-visioned child in the class and, without attracting the attention of the group to him, encourage him to take part in all discussions, she will have done considerable to promote the child's education. A sympathetic attitude, plus an assumption that the child can do just as well as other children, will make for success in this special program.

5. EDUCATIONAL PROBLEMS

The Curriculum.—Preceding discussions have already indicated that sight-saving classes follow the same general course of study that is followed in the regular day schools. The children we are consider-

---

[1] HAZEL C. HADLEY, and WINIFRED HATHAWAY, "Sight-saving Classes: Their Organization and Administration," pp. 18–19, The National Committee for the Prevention of Blindness, Inc., *Publication* 30, New York City, 1927, revised by the authors in 1939.

ing are sighted; many of them are returned to the regular classes after their eyesight has improved.

The same examinations are used for children in sight-saving classes as are used in regular class groups. In only minor ways is the curriculum adjusted. Illustration 15 shows pupils at work on a rubber project; a geography lesson is under way in Illustration 16. Typewriting is taught in grades 4 and 5; vocational guidance is given considerable attention, in order that the pupils may be helped to avoid occupations where failure would be nearly certain; some schools

ILLUSTRATION 15.—A rubber project in a sight-conservation class. Public School No. 54, Brooklyn.

give instruction in the making of rugs, mats, and baskets; and others teach cardboard construction, clay modeling, freehand cutting, poster work, soap carving, and sand-table work.

Music, as a subject to be taught to the blind, has been emphasized. In some cities all classes are required to take a graded course in eye hygiene. This latter is important, since the child needs to know what to do to conserve the little vision he may have and to improve it if possible; but habits of sight conservation must actually be established so that, at school or out of school, he will put them into operation.

Textbooks.—The effort of the special teacher to keep the special-class pupils up to grade is greatly handicapped by an inadequate supply of clear-type textbooks. As late as 1930 Cleveland reported only

129 clear-type books for all grades. The reason is fairly obvious. These books are costly, because, printed in large clear type, as they are, the sale is limited. A geography text, for example, selling regularly at $1.72, when printed in clear type costs $25.

This scarcity of books puts additional work upon the special teacher. The pupils cannot read regular type; the teacher must,

ILLUSTRATION 16.—A lesson in geography in a sight-conservation room in Brooklyn.

therefore, do considerable reading. In arithmetic, the problems must be copied by the teacher. Despite the cost, it would seem that adequate textbooks and auxiliary readers in clear type might well be an economy, since larger enrollments could be handled. An even more important argument would be the development of good reading habits; they can hardly be established when reading materials are so scarce.

6. MISCELLANEOUS PROBLEMS

School Lunches.—In some schools, the lunch problem is adequately cared for by the regular school lunchroom. Many schools that have sight-saving classes, however, have no provision for serving lunches. The special classroom in all such cases should be supplied with an electric hot plate, dishes, pots, and pans to the extent necessary to serve one hot dish. The hot dish may be canned soup, boiled rice, boiled potatoes, tapioca pudding, milk toast, or macaroni with cheese or tomatoes. The essential thing to remember is that it should be nourishing and at the same time easily prepared. The children should bring sandwiches and fruit from home. Milk should be provided. The lunch is prepared sometimes by the teacher, sometimes by the older pupils. The small children can arrange the table.

The wise teacher makes the lunch hour not a chore but a joy hour to which the pupils look forward with considerable eagerness. Besides providing good, suitable food, it can serve several other purposes. (1) It permits the teacher to become acquainted, in the easy informality of preparing, serving, and eating the lunch, with each of her pupils, as she can never become acquainted with them in the classroom. She can get a clearer picture of home conditions and of the children's real interests; this is gleaned more frequently than otherwise from incidental remarks and conversations, rather than from questions directly asked and answered. (2) The pupils learn about nourishing foods through the group discussions of proposed menus. (3) Table etiquette can be taught, not to the group but individually. At first, the outstanding crudities of various members will be noted, and these in personal conference can incidentally be called to their attention. Thus the lunch hour can provide good food, a socially enjoyable time, and a liberal education to both the teacher and her pupils.

Transportation.—The transportation problem is similar to that involved in transporting the blind, only simpler. The incidence being larger, the centers are closer together; more children can walk and fewer will have long distances to go.[1]

Home Visiting.—Visits to the home are essential if the program of the sight-saving class is to succeed. Parents need to be acquainted with the objectives and purposes of the class. Many parents have a mental set against any kind of special class, since the term has been used so frequently in reference to classes for mentally defective children. Parents who have learned how children's vision has been improved and how their school progress has been quickened no longer have any hesitancy in backing the program.

Many parents do not realize that, even at home, strong light and glare should be avoided; glasses should be worn with the same regu-

[1] See p. 173.

larity as at school; and no reading should be done unless authorized, and then only in accordance with directions. They must realize that one evening's lapse might destroy all the beneficial effects of several weeks of treatment.

Some parents feel that they cannot afford glasses or treatments. Not realizing the seriousness of the child's condition, they neglect taking the steps necessary to preserve his sight. This visiting service is informative.   When the parents are informed, they are usually willing either to provide the glasses and treatments or to allow the school to provide them.   As home visiting is truly essential, it ought to be provided as a regular part of the services rendered to the children of sight-saving classes.[1]

The High-school Class.—In some cities there are no special high-school classes.   A very common practice, in fact, is for the child of high-school age with defective vision to attend all classes just as other children do.   The only difference is that they must have readers for a considerable portion of their work.   Some cities, according to one report,[2] assemble a number of pupils with defective vision in one high school; these children are all placed in some one home room with pupils of normal vision.   The home-room teacher is a sight-conservation teacher with experience in high-school teaching.

This teacher does not give the individual assistance in lesson preparation that is required of the special teacher in the elementary school.   The high-school pupil has a reader; some cities pay 20 cents per hour for such readers.   The selection of readers might well be based upon both ability and need; both the reader and the special student might be taking the same courses and be members of the same home-room group.   They could meet daily after school in some place where, under the supervision of the special teacher and under proper lighting conditions, lessons could be prepared for the following day.

The sight-saving teacher and the readers will have enough contact so that the latter can be of material assistance in guarding the child with defective vision from any improper use of his eyes.   By the time these pupils graduate from high school, they should be so familiar with their own eye difficulties and with the care and treatments necessary that they could be safely trusted thenceforth to manage this problem for themselves.

[1] See p. 180.

[2] Estella Lawes, "Method of Teaching Sight-saving Classes," p. 51, The National Committee for the Prevention of Blindness, Inc., *Publication* 28, New York City, 1926.

Costs.—The size of classes and the extra equipment and facilities needed to educate and care for pupils of low vision make it evident that costs per pupil are greater than in the regular schools. The costs seem to be less than those for the blind and the cripple; data, however, are not so extensive as for some other types of special class instruction. The White House Conference says average costs are $235 per pupil for year.

7. RESULTS OF LOCAL CLASS TRAINING

Educational Results.—Educationally, these children are being helped to complete successfully the elementary grades; great numbers are completing junior and senior high school; a considerable number have continued into college and successfully completed the work for a degree. Even more significant, educationally, is the change in attitude that takes place in them toward their schooling. Many of them had been failures in regular classes; they were discouraged and had come to the conclusion that they could not do the work. The sight-saving class changed that point of view entirely. So great, indeed, is the change that under the guidance of the special teacher many skip grades; this has helped to make up the loss of progress suffered in earlier years.

Physical Results.—Physically, the children have been given a knowledge of their eye conditions and of what must be done to prevent further injury. Some eye conditions that had been steadily getting worse maintain the status quo when these children enter the sight-saving class. Other children with poor eye conditions have had their eyes so improved that within a short time they were able to return to regular school classes. Detroit reported, "In many cases their eyes have improved so much, due to the relief from eyestrain, that they have been returned to the regular grades."[1]

Vocational Results.—A report from Cleveland in 1931 says that, since 1925, questionnaires had been sent yearly to former students, and that 65 per cent of those replying were employed. It is unfortunate that the report failed to show the per cent replying. It implies that an even larger per cent of sight-saving class graduates were employed, since those who had made the best adjustment did not need the placement service and had not been included in the study.

---

[1] *The Department of Special Education*, p. 20, Board of Education, Detroit, Mich., 1925.

8. SUMMARY

Excellent publicity is needed if local problems are to be solved adequately and rapidly. Failure to provide such publicity in the development of sight-saving classes is possibly the reason for our failure at present to care for all the children who need such classwork. More information about the problems of organizing such classes is needed. Those discussed in this chapter relate to such problems as (1) how to provide adequate texts and equipment, (2) how to administer the routine work of the class without friction, (3) how to find enough time for the teacher to do her work, (4) how to secure the hearty co-operation of classroom teachers, (5) what records to keep, (6) whom to accept, (7) how to build a satisfactory program for the special class, (8) how to provide lunches, (9) how to maintain home contacts, and (10) what results are actually being achieved. The relation between the special teacher and the regular teachers of the school is made clear.

Problems and Questions for Discussion

1. Is it difficult to organize sight-saving classes? Give any facts you have discovered that seem to support your theory.

2. What children should be admitted to a sight-saving class? Why do you set these limits?

3. Outline what you conceive to be the five most important problems in organizing sight-saving classes. Give reasons.

4. Plan in some detail a class program for a group of 10 low-visioned children. Make your own assumptions concerning the facts regarding your class and the local school situation. Present both the assumed facts and the plan.

5. Is it true that the teacher of a sight-saving class has an unusually big task? Give facts in support of your opinion.

6. What do regular classroom teachers need to know about the work of this special teacher?

7. What should the special class aim to do educationally and otherwise for the low-visioned child?

8. What relation should exist between the home and the special class? Why?

9. What evidence have you been able to discover relating to the worthwhileness of sight-saving classes?

Selected Bibliography

BERRY, CHARLES SCOTT. "The Education of Handicapped School Children in Michigan," pp. 6–11. *State Department of Public Instruction Bulletin* 11, Lansing, Mich., 1926.

A good but brief discussion of some of the problems of educating children of low vision.

HADLEY, HAZEL C. *Sight-saving Classes in the Public Schools*, presenting the Ohio Plan. State Department of Education, Columbus, Ohio, 1926–27. 90 pp.

Brief discussions of a great many of the problems faced in organizing sight-saving classes. Describes work done in 23 communities in Ohio.

HADLEY, HAZEL, and HATHAWAY, WINIFRED. "Sight-saving Classes: Their Organization and Administration." The National Committee for the Prevention of Blindness, Inc., *Publication* 30. New York, 1927. 50 pp.

The subtitle describes the contents; digest of state laws is also given.

LAWES, ESTELLA. "Methods of Teaching Sight-saving Classes." The National Committee for the Prevention of Blindness, Inc., *Publication* 28. New York, 1926. 60 pp.

An excellent description of sight-saving rooms, program making, and special methods of teaching arithmetic, reading, writing, and typewriting. Describes work done in regular grades, provisions for maps and posters, work in high schools, vocational guidance, and records.

White House Conference. *Special Education: The Handicapped and the Gifted*, pp. 115–240. The Century Co., New York, 1931.

An excellent presentation of the problem of educating children with defective vision, of giving physical care, of financing the work, and of appraising results.

CHAPTER XVI

THE CHALLENGE OF THE CHILD WITH DEFECTIVE VISION

The challenge of any problem depends upon the opportunity one sees in it for service. Too frequently vital problems are ignored because we fail to see these opportunities; they may go unrecognized because we are seldom brought face to face with them or because we are uninformed concerning the possibilities of handling them. The problem of educating children with defective vision is just such a problem. This is true for several reasons. (1) Despite the large number of such children for the country as a whole, the number per 1,000 is small. (2) They are seldom educated locally. (3) We seldom realize what can be done for them educationally. (4) The extent to which eye defects interfere with schoolwork is not yet properly appreciated; we are just discovering that much of school failure is due to these defects. (5) We have failed utterly as a social group to see the possibilities of preventing defects in vision.

The preceding four chapters should have made clearer the possibilities and the importance of educating children with defective vision. This chapter will show the extent to which they are being educated, point out ways in which states have shown an interest in them, and make clearer the possibilities of prevention. It is this possibility of prevention that presents the greatest challenge; it will demand the finest type of co-operation among all the social agencies of the community. With effective programs of prevention in operation, however, the reduction in serious defective vision among children may indeed be great.

1. EXTENT TO WHICH CHILDREN OF DEFECTIVE VISION ARE BEING EDUCATED

The White House Conference[1] estimated that there were 14,400 blind under twenty years of age; only 6,000 of these were being educated. It estimated 50,000 partially seeing children who need to be taught in sight-saving classes; only 5,000 were enrolled at that time. Figure 4 shows the per cent of school children who have defec-

[1] White House Conference, *Special Education: The Handicapped and the Gifted,* p. 5, The Century Co., New York, 1931.

tive vision.   Assuming an elementary school enrollment of 25,000,000 in the United States, this would mean 12,500 blind children, 50,000 who need to be in sight-saving classes, and 4,937,500 who have eye defects that can be corrected.   These figures, which are thought to be conservative, demand attention.   Over 50 per cent of the blind children of the United States are not being educated, and only 10 per cent of those who need to attend sight-saving classes are doing so.

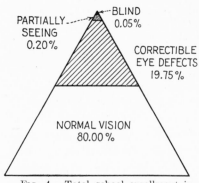

FIG. 4.—Total school enrollment in the United States classified by visual capacity.[1]

The third group, of nearly five million children, have eye defects that are correctible.   After correction, these children will have no visual difficulties in regular classes. In all cases, however, correction is needed; if this need is ignored, these children become potential candidates for special classes.   Just how much the percentages within these three groups of children with eye defects can be reduced, we are not sure, but evidences of success in dealing with individual cases indicate that well-planned programs of prevention in all communities would reduce them materially.

2. CAUSES OF EYE DEFECTS

Preventive work in the field of vision is impossible until one knows something about the causes of poor vision.   A brief review of these causes is all that will be attempted in this section; and upon the basis of these findings, an attempt will be made to outline a program for preventing eye defects.

Blindness.—The causes of blindness are grouped by Scheidemann under three general categories.[2]   Disease, which heads the list, causes, according to this authority, about four-fifths of all blindness. The other two suggested causes were heredity and accidents.

The more common diseases of childhood which may affect eyesight are measles, meningitis, mumps, smallpox, scarlet fever, typhoid fever, and venereal disease.   Babies' sore eyes (ophthalmia neonatorum) and granulated eyelids (trachoma) are found to be an important cause.   The report of a commission to study the blind in Pennsylvania

[1] *Ibid.*, p. 127.

[2] NORMA V. SCHEIDEMANN, *The Psychology of Exceptional Children*, p. 359, Houghton Mifflin Company, Boston, 1931.

showed that babies' sore eyes had caused the blindness of from 17.4 per cent to 32.5 per cent of the pupils admitted to two residential schools in that state.[1]

Best suggests that the total amount of blindness due to accidents and injuries is 17.9 per cent.[2] This includes such direct injuries as industrial accidents and carelessness; it also includes indirect damage through some injury to the optic nerve. Eyestrain, poisoning, exposure to heat, and foreign substances in the eye are included in the accidents listed.

A study of 29,242 blind persons reported in the 1920 census showed that 11 per cent, or 3,221 individuals, had blind relatives—either parents, brothers or sisters, children, or some combination of these three groups of near relatives.[3]

Children in Sight-saving Classes.—Children will be placed in sight-saving classes who have eye defects due to diseased conditions of the eye, to refractive errors, to an unbalanced condition among the muscles that govern the eye, and to other conditions of the eye that affect its proper operation. No one of these causes need appear singly. There may be a diseased condition plus errors in refraction. There are so many parts of the eye, any one of which may be diseased or in an unbalanced condition, that the variation in possible eye difficulties is very great.

Diseases.—In a study of 2,932 children in sight-saving classes in the United States, Myers[4] found that 42.2 per cent had diseases of the eye. Diseases of the cornea occurred most often, and diseases of the lens were second in frequency. He listed, in addition, diseases of the chorioid and the retina, of the optic nerve, of the iris and the ciliary body, of the conjunctiva or lids, glaucoma, and malformations. These do not nearly exhaust the list.

Refractive Errors.—Refractive errors result when the shape of the eye is abnormal in some respect, causing the light rays to focus improperly. If the eye is too long from front to back we have a condition known popularly as shortsightedness; technically, it is called myopia. If the opposite condition exists and the eye is too short, farsightedness results; this is technically called hyperopia. In the first case, the child can see only things that are close at hand; in the latter, things that are distant. A hyperope does not, however, see better at a

[1] Report of Commission to Study Conditions Relating to Blind Persons in Pennsylvania, p. 15, Harrisburg, Pa., 1925.

[2] HARRY BEST, *The Blind*, p. 173, The Macmillan Company, New York, 1919.

[3] U.S. Census, 1920.

[4] White House Conference, *op. cit.*, p. 128.

distance than can those with normal sight; he merely sees objects at a distance better than he does those close by. A third error in refraction occurs when the lens of the eye is irregular in shape; this condition prevents a perfect focus and sight tends to become slightly blurred, resulting in a condition known as astigmatism. The muscles of the eyes that operate to produce a proper focus are, as a result, overtaxed and the eyes tire very quickly. Myers reported that 68.2 per cent of children in sight-saving classes had refractive errors.[1]

Muscular Imperfection.—There are six muscles that govern the movement of a single eye. Any weakness or imperfection in one or more of these muscles will cause a certain lack of control needed in perfect vision. If such weakness results in a rolling of the eyes, the condition is called nystagmus; this rolling may be horizontal, vertical, or purely rotary. If the muscular weakness causes the lines of vision of the eyes to be other than parallel, the condition is known as heterophoria. If the line of vision of one of the eyes deviates from its proper direction, so that both are not directed simultaneously at a given object, the condition is commonly known as cross-eyedness; more technically, it is referred to as strabismus.

Myers[2] found in his study that only 22.6 per cent suffered from lack of muscular eye control. Of those with this defect, 59 per cent had nystagmus, while 31 per cent were cross-eyed. The remaining 10 per cent had some one of the other defects or a combination of some two of them.

3. WAYS AND MEANS OF PREVENTING EYE DEFECTS

Despite the importance of educating children with defective vision, a far greater problem is that of prevention; when the latter is solved, the former will not exist. If administrative procedures could be put into operation so that we could utilize universally what is now known about prevention, both problems would be materially reduced. The suggestions made in this section will be centered, for the most part, about those causes of defective vision that were enumerated in the preceding section.

Disease.—Probably the most important single suggestion concerning the prevention of eye disease is that every parent be given information which is now rather common knowledge among physicians regarding the prevention of those diseases that often result in blindness. If parents knew the possible aftereffects of such diseases as measles, mumps, and scarlet fever, they would use precautionary

[1] *Ibid.*, p. 133.
[2] *Ibid.*, p. 134.

measures more frequently than they do in guarding against them; there would also be less objection to vaccination for smallpox and to vaccine injections for typhoid. Some authorities suggest that children should be vaccinated for smallpox during the first few days after birth. In the case of epidemics, those likely to exposure should be revaccinated, unless successful vaccination is very recent.

In the case of measles, the disease is so common that people frequently look upon it as one of the unavoidables. It is very difficult, therefore, to enforce placarding or quarantine. Since the reporting of each case is entirely essential if measures to prevent the spread of the disease are to be taken, some suggest that the older practice of quarantining and placarding be abandoned; instead, the nurse who responds to the report will explain to the parents the possible dangerous aftereffects, and urge isolation. She will, in addition, visit throughout the neighborhood and explain the need of care in watching for symptoms and in reporting cases at once. Parents will usually respond sympathetically to this kind of approach, it is claimed, and thus measures can be put into effect to prevent the spread of the disease, as well as to protect those who have it from bad aftereffects. Human serum is frequently urged as a means of modifying and even of preventing the disease.

In the case of typhoid, the purity of drink and food is essential. A pure water supply and pasteurized milk are basic in prevention. Travel by auto through regions where the purity of the water supply is unknown has its dangers, unless the travelers abstain or carry their own supply. Well water should be tested at regular intervals. The best of sanitary conditions should prevail in and about the home in order to prevent the breeding of flies; they may be carriers of the disease. Obviously, those engaged in the sale and distribution of food supplies should strive for perfection in sanitation; such perfection should be assured through adequate legislation.

In the case of diseases such as babies' sore eyes and granulated eyelids, the physician should be called at once and his recommendations followed. It should be understood by parents generally that trachoma, or granulated lids, is spread by use of a common towel or washbasin. Such practices should be eliminated. Children should be led to understand the dangers involved in rubbing and wiping their eyes with dirty hands and fingers.

A great amount of blindness has undoubtedly been prevented in recent years by the care that physicians now exercise at the birth of a child. The baby's eyes are thoroughly treated; eye infection at birth, due to lack of care, was in the past a potent cause of blindness.

Accidents.—The inventor of the Braille system of reading and writing lost his eyesight as the result of an accident. Sharp tools, sticks, and pencils are not proper playthings for little children. They are especially dangerous for those who are just learning to walk, and even for a few years afterward.

Fourth-of-July celebrations with firearms and firecrackers are coming more and more under control; blindness from such causes should, therefore, be on the decrease. The increased attention of the schools to signs of eyestrain should more and more reduce blindness from that source. Despite such advances, however, our program of education must continue to emphasize these rather obvious causes and the measures necessary for eliminating them.

Heredity.—To suggest that blindness is hereditary does not imply that all individuals who are blind are doomed to have children who are blind. Much blindness, we know, is not either directly or indirectly hereditary. Loeb,[1] however, suggests 12 diseases that are found to have hereditary influences upon blindness. The three whose influence is shown the most frequently are cataract, atrophy of the optic nerve, and retinitis pigmentosa. Even in these cases, the percentage of children who are blind falls far short of being 100 per cent. For cataract, 60 per cent of the children of parents who were both affected were blind; where only one parent was affected, the percentage was 58.2; where the heredity was indirect, the percentage dropped to 42.1; but in cases which Loeb calls collateral heredity, the percentage increased to 61.8. These percentages are not small.

In all such cases, if blindness is to be prevented, procreation must not take place. If those afflicted with diseases that have such hereditary influences are permitted to marry and have children, we may expect to have with us perpetually the problem of caring for and educating the blind. Many people, these days, refuse to bring children into the world when they themselves are in a physical condition that is likely to affect seriously the well-being of their offspring. Hereditary blindness would seem to be such a physical condition.

There are two possible solutions of the problem. (1) We may as a social group see fit to legalize the teaching of the proper use of contraceptives. (2) We may encourage sterilization of those who are unfit for parenthood and who have no likelihood of ever being fit. Under either plan, young people should be informed concerning the possible meaning of their physical handicaps for their children. They should then be informed as to modern methods of preventing conception and the advantages of sterilization which would not detract from

---

[1] SCHEIDEMANN, *op. cit.*, p. 363.

the pleasures of the sex act. These young people could still adopt children and thus have them within the family.

When we reach the stage where we think a little more about the interests of newborn children, when we see more clearly the ill effects of uncontrolled propagation upon the social group, we shall be less concerned about certain usually accepted applications of the personal-liberty theory; especially will this be true when the application of the theory permits the continuance of so many serious social problems.

An Educational Program.—The general recommendations just made regarding the prevention of eye defects demand a program of education. This program must make parents more familiar with those ordinary precautions that must be taken if the eyesight of their children is to be preserved; unless the program is well organized, this cannot be done. The information to be given out must be prepared by expert oculists. The newspaper, the radio, school nurses, and teachers are excellent media through which parents may be informed concerning steps that they should take to prevent eye troubles.

The school administrative staff should plan just as carefully an educational program for its teachers, who should be taught to detect quickly all signs of eye difficulty. They should be well informed concerning the necessity of having good light, sufficient in amount and free of all glare. They should note all children who take unduly long to read material placed on the blackboard. If these children are seated in the rear of the room, they should be tried at other locations until they can see more easily the board work that they have to read.

A list of the names of all children believed to have defects of vision should be given to the principal, who should notify the parents by letter suggesting that the child's eyes be examined by a physician skilled in the diseases of the eye. In case parents are unable to provide such expert care, the taxing unit should be called upon to provide funds for the examination and for the purchase of glasses if they are needed. It is hoped that the time will come shortly when health service will be a permanent part of every public school system.

Care of Preschool Children.—If an extensive continuous program of education is maintained regarding eye conditions, parents can be encouraged to bring preschool children to a public clinic or to a private oculist for examination. All cases of defective vision should be reported immediately to the local school census department.

The school district should maintain a continuing census of all children from birth to eighteen years of age. This department should be charged with the responsibility of enumerating all children who have defective vision. Data concerning such children of preschool age should be referred to the city's public agency for making eye examinations; it would be the duty of this agency to follow up the case and see that proper care was provided.

Regular School Physical Examinations.—Some city school systems try to give physical examinations at regular intervals. Not many plan any definite follow-up of cases needing attention. If nurses give examinations and discover children with eye deficiencies, these children should be referred at once to the school oculist or to the eye clinic that is providing ocular service for the schools. Early discovery of eye difficulties, plus immediate treatment or proper refraction or both, may prevent a great amount of serious eye trouble later.

Proper Ophthalmological Staffs.—If the program just suggested is to function, the school system must either (1) provide its own oculist or ocular staff, (2) arrange with the department of health to provide such service, or (3) secure the services of private oculists who are willing to serve school children free of cost. It is the lack of such service that has in the past made our general physical examinations so farcical.

Such services are too often not related, in people's thoughts, to a program of public education. Not until the two are related shall we begin to approach that ideal of American education that we so fondly refer to as "an equal opportunity for every boy and girl to secure an education." As long as children potentially capable of being well educated are prevented from doing their best or are prevented entirely from securing a good education, through the failure of society to give them certain physical care, we cannot claim that we are providing American youth with this "equal opportunity."

Improved Schoolhouse Lighting.—Lighting in regular school buildings has improved materially during the past two decades. The frequency of poorly lighted buildings, however, is still great in most large cities and in all smaller communities where new buildings have not recently been erected. No school superintendent should be content until every classroom in his system meets standard lighting requirements. Principals of school buildings should be just as insistent that lighting requirements be met. The classroom teacher should, likewise, know and demand proper lighting facilities for any room in which she gives instruction.

It ought not be left to the medical profession, to school nurses, and to departments of health to force the hand of educators. The latter should be eager to meet the medical group more than halfway in an attempt to have ideal housing facilities for the millions of American youths who are forced to trust that the public school will not allow conditions that may injure their vocational, social, and educational prospects for life.

4. A STATE PROGRAM FOR BLIND CHILDREN

The entire state program of caring for and educating blind children shall be under the supervision and control of the state department of education; the immediate supervision of such work shall be given over to the division of pupil personnel. The state department of education should assume the leadership in putting into effect throughout the state both general and specific measures for the prevention of blindness; where legislation is necessary to make given preventive measures effective, the state department should sponsor the legislation.

State Supervision.—The division of pupil personnel will be responsible for setting up rules and regulations governing the taking and keeping of a continuous census of all blind children within the state. It shall make arrangements for the conduct of eye clinics at various centers throughout the state. The clinics shall make reports of their examinations to the school census department, as one means of keeping the census of the blind up to date.

Upon the basis of data from the entire state respecting the number and location of blind children, the feasibility of establishing various central schools as a substitute for or as a supplement to the present state school or schools will be considered. It shall be the duty of the state department to study the relative values of the local class or school vs. the state school as a means of educating blind children. It shall formulate rules that are to govern the establishment of local schools or classes; it shall set minimum qualifications for teachers of the blind; and it shall assist in the development of a program of studies to meet the needs of children who are without vision.

The State School.—This school shall be under the general control of the state department of education. Its superintendent shall co-operate in making more effective the work of any local classes that may be established within the state, and its teachers shall be certificated by the state department of education.

There shall be developed at the state school adequate library facilities and a good academic program of instruction through high-school grades; industrial and trade training shall be wide enough in scope to give the blind plenty of opportunity to enter business and industry.

This school shall make a special attempt to reach all blind children in rural school districts who for various reasons are not being cared for. It shall also make an unusual effort to reach blind children whose home conditions are so unsatisfactory that little can be done for them as long as they remain in the home environment.

The school shall have a placement department that will keep up a continuous study of business, trade, and professional opportunities for the blind; and it shall maintain a close follow-up after the placement of its pupils. It shall advise the supervisors of local schools regarding the best opportunities for placement. This placement service can be state wide in scope and value.

The state school shall become a definite training ground for prospective supervisors and teachers in the local school districts; it has a unique opportunity to serve the communities of the state in this way.

The Local City School.—In those states where unusually large cities are located, it would seem advisable to experiment in at least one city with the development of a local school. The state department and the local district should co-operate in developing the details of the plan. The experiment should not be forced upon a given city; it should be based upon a detailed survey of the blind within the city, as well as of those within a 15- or 20-mile radius. A small elementary school of 10 to 16 rooms, if there be such, might be used temporarily. If no such school exists or if it is located poorly, a sufficient number of rooms in a larger school building might be allocated to the use of such an experimental school.

The school should be maintained for a period of several years, until evidence can be secured concerning its effectiveness. Its own costs, the success of its pupils in school and in social adjustment, the breadth of training it is able to provide for its pupils are all factors that would be measured and compared with similar data for state schools.

The Local City Program.—The program will be under the direct control and supervision of the local department of pupil personnel. The local supervisor of the work will be either the principal of the local school or a head teacher who is responsible for the organization of classes in various centers.

This local department will co-operate with the state in maintaining a continuous census of all blind children within the district. Regular class teachers will assist in keeping such a census continuous and up to date. The children in question may be readily noted by such indications as "cross eyes, frowning, itching or smarting of the eyes, congested eyes, headache, blurred vision, sensitiveness to light, holding the book near the eyes, poor spelling, poor reading."[1]

---

[1] CHARLES SCOTT BERRY, *How the Teacher May Help the Exceptional Child,* pp. 6–7, Bureau of Special Education, Ohio State University, Columbus.

The regular class teacher can be of considerable assistance in preventing serious eye defects by instructing the children (1) to read only when they have good light; (2) to sit, when reading, so that the light comes over the left shoulder; (3) never to face the light when reading or working; (4) always to hold material parallel with the face when reading; (5) to do all reading while sitting up, never lying down; (6) never to read while riding on streetcars or in automobiles; (7) to rest the eyes from time to time when engaged in close work or in reading; (8) to abstain from reading when recovering from an illness; (9) to keep dirty hands from the eyes; and (10) to give the eyes plenty of rest during a severe cold.[1]

5. A STATE PROGRAM OF SIGHT SAVING

The program presented here for consideration is broader in scope than one of simply organizing classes. The suggestions that are given more or less in outline form will emphasize what the title implies—an attempt at real sight saving. It is a program that is being sadly neglected in all states, even in those that are most successfully conducting sight-saving classes.

The State Organization.—Sight-saving work shall be a responsibility of the division of pupil personnel in the state department of education. The department, through this division, will be responsible for formulating the educational, supervisory, special-class, and clinical programs in the field of sight saving.

An Educational Program.—This division will be responsible for setting up a state-wide educational program in the interests of sight saving, not necessarily just for the establishment of classes. The program should include means of informing (1) regular class teachers about their responsibility for saving the sight of regular pupils, (2) boards of education concerning lighting needs of their present school buildings, (3) parents concerning what they can do to help preserve the sight of their own children, and (4) children of rules for saving their own vision.

A Legislative Program.—It will assist in securing specific legislation, which will not only permit sight-saving classes by implication, interpretation, or enactment, but which will make mandatory the organization of such classes. It will see to it that the state provides (1) a continuing census of children with eye defects, (2) some method of assisting local districts to finance special classes, and (3) other legislation needed to round out the state's sight-saving program.

[1] *Ibid.*, p. 7.

A Special-Class Program.—The state's director of sight-saving classes will conduct local surveys in order to determine more adequately the need for classes and will assist in their establishment where need is shown. Near-by county territory will be incorporated in possible sight-saving class districts, where feasible. The development of county classes will be given more attention than at present. In the larger cities some experimental work might well be done with the central-school idea.

The Clinical Examination.—A program of eye examination should be so well developed and advertised throughout the state as to make it possible for all parents to have their children's eyes tested, properly refracted, and treated, even if they themselves are unable to have it done for them. The state provides an excellent educational program at public expense for all children with eyesight sufficient to enable them to accept it. These clinics will make it possible for more children to accept the advantages of that program, without resorting to the special classes. They will also protect thousands of other children from injuring their eyes while getting this education.

Where possible, boards of health might be prevailed upon to give this service; where that is impossible, the state department of education should be responsible for setting up an agency that will give the needed ocular examinations, corrections, and treatments.

The Local District's Program.—The local district shall assume the initiative in studying its problem in the light of the entire state program; it will study its school buildings from the point of view of lighting; it will organize to assist the state with its general program of educating the public, the parents, the regular teachers, and the children, with respect to sight saving; it will keep a continuous census of eye defectives; it will establish the needed classes; and it will co-operate with near-by districts in the establishment of union classes where there would otherwise not be a sufficient number of pupils for a class. The local director of pupil personnel will have immediate supervision over this program.

6. SUMMARY

Communities fail to realize how important it is that youths with defective vision be cared for and educated; the problem of preventing such defects has scarcely been recognized. With approximately 14,400 blind, 50,000 in need of sight-saving classes, and 5,000,000 with eye defects that are correctible, one can hardly say that the problem is insignificant. Despite these facts, state legislatures have been slow to do anything about it. Many states ignore the problem;

a few provide state aid to those local districts that educate these children; some provide state supervisors; and some few write into law specific regulations under which classes may be organized locally.

Disease is the principal cause of blindness, but heredity and accidents are not insignificant causes. Such common diseases as measles, meningitis, mumps, smallpox, scarlet fever, and typhoid fever may cause defective vision. Preventive measures include (1) education of the layman so that he will know what to do in order to prevent the diseases, (2) better care of preschool children, (3) regular physical examinations at school, (4) provision of adequate ophthalmological staffs in the schools, and (5) improved school lighting.

A state program should include (1) adequate supervision by the state through its pupil-personnel division; (2) a state school or, at least, small regional schools to care for the blind who cannot be cared for and educated locally; (3) local classes or, possibly, schools for those who have good home conditions and who live within transportation distance; (4) a state-wide educational program; (5) the making of local and state surveys of eye defects; (6) the establishment of clinics throughout the state; (7) local districts well organized to care for and educate the blind and partially seeing children; and (8) the whole program "shot through and through" with the one idea of trying to prevent eye defects. The challenge implied by such a program is by no means an insignificant one.

Problems and Questions for Discussion

1. Is there any real challenge to society in this problem of caring for and educating children of defective vision? Explain.

2. What facts have you been able to discover relative to the number of children with defective vision? What do these facts mean to you?

3. Outline the chief provisions of a state law which you think ought to be enacted in your home state in order to care for and educate children with defective vision. Why have such provisions?

4. What do you consider the best method of financing the education of children with defective vision? Explain why.

5. What relation, if any, exists between the type of legislation a state has for governing the education of children with defective vision, and the number of cities it has that educate these children?

6. Give any data you can find relative to the causes of eye defects.

7. Outline a program of prevention which you feel would reduce materially the number of children with eye defects.

8. Describe in detail a state program which you believe would satisfactorily care for and educate all children with defective vision.

9. Argue pro and con the proposal to enforce compulsory sterilization of those who have eye defects that are hereditary.

10. To what extent should the state control the education of the blind? Give reasons.

11. What are some of the unsolved questions with respect to the care and education of children with defective vision?

Selected Bibliography

ALLEN, EDWARD E. "Special Features in the Education of the Blind During the Biennium 1918–20." *U.S. Bureau of Education Bulletin* 16, Washington, D.C., 1921. 14 pp.

Lists the events of the biennium affecting the blind; describes new possibilities in industry, the work done for the war blind, the uniform type and the governmental subsidy for printing, and the development of day schools.

BEST, HARRY. *The Blind*, pp. 99–212. The Macmillan Company, New York, 1919.

A discussion of causes of blindness; relation of heredity, disease, and accidents considered. An excellent treatise.

COWDERY, KATE LOUISE. *The Legal Status of the Education of Blind and Deaf Children in the Forty-eight States*. Unpublished Master's thesis, Ohio State University, Columbus, 1927.

An analysis of the legal provisions made by the 48 states for educating blind children.

HADLEY, HAZEL, and HATHAWAY, WINIFRED. "Sight-saving Classes: Their Organization and Administration," *Publication* 30, pp. 32–49. The National Committee for the Prevention of Blindness, Inc., New York City, 1927.

An analysis of the legislative provisions of the 48 states governing the organization of sight-saving classes.

MYERS, EDWARD T. "A Survey of Sight-saving Classes in the Public Schools of the United States." The National Society for the Prevention of Blindness, *Publication* 64, New York, 1930. 105 pp.

The results of a questionnaire study of 319 sight-saving classes in the United States are presented; returns were gathered from 2,882 children representing 213 classes. A vast amount of personal pupil data is analyzed.

SCHEIDEMANN, NORMA V. *The Psychology of Exceptional Children*, pp. 358–402. Houghton Mifflin Company, Boston, 1931.

An excellent analysis of causes of blindness and a brief account of the training of blind children.

White House Conference. *Communicable Disease Control*, pp. 99–214. The Century Co., New York, 1931.

Very brief suggestion for the prevention and control of certain contagious diseases that often result in defective vision.

White House Conference. *Special Education: The Handicapped and the Gifted*, pp. 113–240. The Century Co., New York, 1931.

A discussion as to who are candidates for sight-saving classes, the amount of eye defect, types of eye defect, and care needed.

CHAPTER XVII

THE EDUCATION OF DEAF CHILDREN[1]

No man should ever despair who has become familiar with the education of the deaf. No other group with a single handicap presents, perhaps, so serious a problem as do the deaf, from the point of view of instruction. Certainly, in the education of normal groups we find no problem quite so complex and difficult. These children enter school with no language, and the attainment of a language must be achieved through other senses than that of hearing. Unless one has worked with children thus handicapped, this statement cannot be fully appreciated.

A normal child entering the public schools knows his name and age; he has an extensive vocabulary, so that new concepts can be explained in terms of this language. The deaf child has none of these advantages. The training must begin at a point which the child with normal hearing passed several years before. The deaf child, furthermore, cannot imitate the voices of others; he must imitate the less conspicuous movements of the speaker's face, throat, tongue, and lips which he can either feel or see. Anyone who has observed deaf children patiently struggle with these handicaps and overcome them must be obtuse indeed if he has not been inspired to believe that he can achieve far more than he had thought he could.

1. DEFINITION

Popularly, the deaf have been thought of as those individuals who have lost their hearing; no thought is given to the fact that losses in hearing vary. If a person does not hear ordinary conversation, he is called deaf. Technically, the definition includes only persons who have had no hearing since birth, who lost their hearing before they achieved speech, or who lost it so soon after achieving speech that the speech gained has been lost. (All individuals who lose their hearing after speech has been permanently achieved are classified as hard of hearing.) *– Not True !!*

---

[1] The chapters dealing with the deaf, the hard of hearing, and the speech defective were read and criticized by Professor Marie K. Mason of the Department of Speech at Ohio State University.

2. GUIDING PRINCIPLES

What Is Best for the Child?—There are many problems involved in the education of deaf children, such as (1) whether they should be taught in state or local schools, (2) what they should be taught, and (3) what methods should be used in instruction. Prime consideration should always be given, in answering such questions, to the way the solutions proposed will affect the child. Whatever is best for him ought to be the lodestar that guides us in making those decisions.

Equality of Opportunity.—The second principle demands equality of opportunity; but this does not mean identity of opportunity. It means that we are not to limit the opportunities of the deaf to a greater extent than his physical handicaps limit him. In the past we have tended to overemphasize printing and various kinds of handwork and to neglect his regular academic training. Also, many states have neglected to make compulsory the education of deaf children; others have made it compulsory only when provisions were made for such a program. Under such conditions the deaf are not being given an equal educational opportunity.

Education for Association with the Hearing.—The third principle suggests educating deaf children so that they can communicate with hearing people. Unless this is done, the deaf will be considered a group apart. The more effective we make intercommunication, the greater the blow given to barriers that tend to separate the two groups. The hearing must understand the abilities and capacities of deaf children; they must learn to react to them as to normal, hearing children. Unless this happens, the deaf will find it difficult in later life to get any jobs by which they can support themselves.

Prevention.—Fourth, the education of the deaf should emphasize prevention. This may be attained by educating parents and communities and by properly educating the deaf children themselves. All three groups should clearly understand the causes of deafness; they should know how to eliminate these causes.

3. EUROPEAN DEVELOPMENT

The ideas of Hippocrates and Aristotle regarding the deaf are still extant; we still hear the deaf spoken of as deaf and dumb; state schools are popularly referred to as schools for the deaf and dumb. These two Greeks—one a great physician and the other a famous philosopher—believed that those who were deaf from birth were also dumb. To them speech seemed a faculty inborn, not acquired by means of the ability to hear. If, therefore, the child did not develop speech, he was dumb and incapable of being instructed. The authority of these men continued to influence many centuries following the fifth and fourth centuries B.C. The deaf, therefore, were frequently classed with the insane and were denied the rights of citizenship. Roman law, likewise, considered the deaf and dumb as without intelligence, though the Code of Justinian differentiated between those who were congenitally deaf and those who became deaf after birth.

Earliest Attempts to Educate.—There are no records of attempts to educate the deaf until about the latter part of the seventh century of the Christian era. Bede, in his *Ecclesiastical History of the Charity of St. John of Beverly*, records an instance where St. John commanded a deaf-and-dumb boy to repeat letters, then words and sentences; his success in this effort is not reported. St. John died A.D. 721.

Centuries passed before other instances of attempts to educate the deaf were mentioned in any records we now have. Fay says, "The first instance in history of a deaf-mute who learned to read and write was that recorded by Rodolphus Agricola, who lived from 1443 to 1485."[1] Juan Luis Vives questioned the story, since it seemed impossible that anyone without hearing would have sense enough to learn to read and write. Cardano of Milan believed the story and set up the principle upon which such an education depended; he insisted that without sound people may be taught to associate ideas with written words. Cardano lived from 1501 to 1576.

The first regular instructor of the deaf about whom records are available is Pedro Ponce de Leon (1520–1584). He was a noble of the house of Arcos and taught the deaf sons of noblemen reading, writing, reckoning, Latin, Greek, and astrology.

Jacob Rodriguez Pereire became interested in the education of the deaf through work that he did in helping to educate his deaf sister. Later, he instructed d'Azy d'Etavigny with such success that he was invited to present this youth before the French Academy of Science at Paris in 1749. Pereire lived from 1715 to 1780.

The First School for the Deaf.—The honor of founding the first school for the deaf goes to Charles Michel de l'Épée who lived from 1712 to 1789. This school was founded in Paris in 1755.[2] Abbé de l'Épée was born at Versailles. In 1736 he entered the priesthood. Some years later he made contact with two deaf sisters who had been taught by a Father Vanin; at the Father's death, de l'Épée decided to

---

[1] EDWARD ALLEN FAY, *Histories of American Schools for the Deaf*, Vol. I, p. v, The Volta Bureau, Washington, D.C., 1893.

[2] A. J. WINNIE, *History and Handbook of Day Schools for the Deaf and Blind*, p. 5, State Department of Education, Madison, Wis., 1912.

attempt their instruction. This he did so successfully that he consecrated his life to the education of the deaf.

The school that he established in 1755 was made possible by using a portion of his personal income for its support.[1] He received poor and rich alike. This was in decided contrast to the work done by Heinicke in Germany and Braidwood in England; these two gentlemen kept their methods secret and were thus able to charge the rich substantial fees.

Some suggest that the good Abbé's practice of accepting poor children who were unable to pay for their instruction was the immediate cause of de l'Épée's work of devising a new method for instructing the deaf. It is said that his school drew so many pupils that he was unable to provide enough teachers trained in the oral method.

Others suggest that de l'Épée believed that only by means of signs could the deaf be taught. Regardless of the reason, we know that de l'Épée did devise a mimic language. He tried to make the signs conform as closely as possible to our conversational language in respect to vocabulary and syntax. Making use of the original mimic language adopted naturally by the deaf-mute, he devised the *methodical signs* or the present-day manual method of instructing the deaf.

This manual method of the Abbé's was known at first as the French System. Later, when the French schools changed to the oral method as they did between 1879 and 1886, some writers began to refer to the manual method as the American system and to the oral method as the European system.

German Schools.—Samuel Heinicke founded a school near Hamburg, Germany, about 1760; in 1778, at the suggestion of state officials, he moved to Leipzig. His was the first school for the deaf to be recognized by any government. Previous to starting this school, he had, as a student at the University of Jena, tutored deaf pupils. His school might well be considered the first public school for the deaf. He concealed his methods and only from letters written to the Abbé de l'Épée can they be even partially reconstructed. He believed the deaf could learn to read lips and be taught to speak; he insisted that as soon as they had learned to speak that they should be required to converse with other people. Heinicke is regarded by many as the father of the oral method.

Frederick Moritz Hill, who lived from 1805 to 1874, is referred to by some as the greatest of all educators of the deaf. He developed the truly German system. Born in Breslau, he was trained to teach under Pestalozzi, and received special training for teaching the deaf at Ber-

[1] HARRY BEST, *The Deaf*, p. 126, The Thomas Y. Crowell Company, New York, 1914.

lin's School for the Deaf.   His maxim was, "Develop speech in the deaf child in the same way that nature does in the hearing child."

English Schools.—Thomas Braidwood established a school at Edinburgh in 1760[1] and later one in London.   It is claimed that Braidwood used the oral method; he, however, never wrote anything describing his techniques.   For 59 years the Braidwoods had a monopoly on the methods of instructing the deaf in England, these methods being handed down to various members of the family.   Secrecy was demanded.

Later European Situation.[2]—Except for a brief period in France, the European countries have generally made use of the oral method of instruction.   By the opening of the twentieth century, 80 per cent of all deaf children in the European schools were thus taught.   In four countries—Germany, Holland, Norway, and Switzerland—100 per cent of all deaf pupils were taught by the oral method.   Only in Spain and Sweden were more than 50 per cent taught by the manual method.

4. AMERICAN DEVELOPMENT

The United States has been recognized for years as the stronghold for manualism.   As late as 1910, only 22 per cent of the deaf children taught in the United States were taught by the oral method; only 26 per cent were so taught in Canada.[2]   This divergence in practice, as between Europe and America, was due largely to accident.

A European Method Transplanted.—In 1815 the Reverend Thomas Henry Gallaudet went to England to study methods of teaching the deaf, in order to establish a school in America.   He immediately encountered "the Braidwood monopoly" and "was utterly unable to gain either an entrance to the British schools or any information as to their methods, except upon terms which he was obliged to decline."[3]

By accident, in London Gallaudet met the Abbé Sicard, who, when he heard of Gallaudet's mission to Great Britain and of that mission's failure, invited the young American to France.   Gallaudet accepted.   In France "he was given all the information that he desired, and . . . secured the services of Laurent Clerc, one of Sicard's most brilliant students, who returned with him to this country as a teacher."[4]   Thus,

---

[1] BEST, *op. cit.*, p. 127.

[2] WINNIE, *op. cit.*, p. 6.

[3] ROBERT A. F. MCDONALD, *Adjustment of School Organization to Various Population Groups*, p. 9, Teachers College, Columbia University, New York, 1915.

[4] H. VAN ALLEN, "A Brief History of the Pennsylvania Institution for the Deaf and Dumb," *Histories of American Schools for the Deaf*, Vol. I, p. 3, The Volta Bureau, Washington, D.C., 1893.

an accidental meeting led to the acceptance of the manual method of teaching in the first school for the deaf to be established in the United States.

The Hartford School.—Gallaudet's European experience, therefore, introduced the manual method into America, where it kept a firm hold through the succeeding century. It is by no means a discarded method even today (1940). The first school was established at Hartford, Conn., in May, 1816. It was opened for instruction on Apr. 15, 1817, with seven pupils, and by the end of the year, 33 had enrolled. The influence of the American Asylum, as the school for the deaf at Hartford was called, was soon felt.

The New York School.—The New York Institution for the Deaf and Dumb was incorporated on Apr. 15, 1817. The board of directors first wrote to England for a teacher, thinking that the Braidwood system of instruction would be better than that used at Hartford. No reply was received for a year; when it came, the demands were so exorbitant that they were turned down.

On May 20, 1818, Abraham O. Stanbury, who for one year had been at Hartford, was elected superintendent and teacher of the New York school. Thus the manual method of instruction was adopted. At a later date, Professor Léon Vaisse was brought from the Paris school to assist in improving instruction. In 1831 Harvey P. Peet, who had instructed at Hartford for 9 years, came to New York as superintendent and principal.

The Pennsylvania School.—The school at Philadelphia was officially started on May 15, 1820. A year later, Laurent Clerc was secured from Hartford to act as principal and to introduce the manual method of instruction. He was succeeded by Lewis Weld, who had been first assistant at Hartford.

The Kentucky School.[1]—The fourth school to be established was at Danville, Ky., in 1822; classwork started on Apr. 27, 1823, with three pupils attending. After several unfortunate experiences, John Adamson Jacobs was appointed principal in November, 1825. He had gone to Hartford on horseback in 1824 to study the manual method, taking private lessons from Clerc at 40 cents per hour, while he lived with the pupils and spent all his time in the classroom. He returned to Danville on horseback after 13 months of study.

The Ohio School.—The fifth school was opened at Columbus, Ohio, on Oct. 16, 1829. The first superintendent was Horatio Nelson

---

[1] CHARLES P. FOSDICK, "A Short History of the Kentucky School for the Deaf," *Histories of American Schools for the Deaf*, Vol. I, pp. 1–8, The Volta Bureau, Washington, D.C., 1893.

Hubbell, who had spent 18 months at Hartford preparing for his duties. The assistant teacher was Danforth E. Ball, a mute who had received his training at the Hartford "Asylum."

Other Schools.[1]—The Virginia school opened on Nov. 30, 1839, with Joseph D. Tyler, a teacher of experience from Hartford, as principal. Indiana established its school the first Monday of October, 1844, with William Willard as principal; he graduated from Hartford and taught at the Ohio school for several years. The eighth school opened at East Knoxville, Tenn. on Apr. 14, 1845; Thomas MacIntire, a teacher from the Ohio school, was the first principal. North Carolina drew its first principal from Virginia and opened its school on May 1, 1845. Illinois opened the tenth school in February, 1846, at Jacksonville; Thomas Officer was the first principal and came from the Ohio school, where he had taught for 5 years.

Georgia sent O. P. Fannin to Hartford to study before opening its school in May, 1846; Fannin was made principal. The first principal of the South Carolina school, which opened in 1849, got his training in the Georgia school. Missouri established its school in 1851; the new principal had taught in the Kentucky school for 20 years. When Wisconsin started its school in 1851, the first principal was John A. Mills, a graduate of the New York school. Louisiana secured the superintendent of the Indiana school as its first superintendent; the school was opened on Dec. 8, 1852. Mississippi chose a graduate of the New York school as its first principal and opened in 1854 as the sixteenth school in the United States for the deaf.

The Struggle of Two Methods.—The story could be continued with similar results. The school at Hartford was responsible for fixing upon America the manual method of instructing the deaf. The actual development of the whole program is not so simple as this brief sketch might lead one to believe. Efforts were made to introduce the Braidwood method, and offers to start schools were received from European scholars. After due consideration, however, every such attempt or offer was laid aside in those early days, and scholars interested in educating the deaf agreed that America should have but one method and that the program being developed by Gallaudet at Hartford should not be handicapped by the introduction of other systems.

Gallaudet's Interest.—A great amount of interesting history connected with the founding of each of these schools has to be ignored in this brief account. The founding of the Hartford school grew out of Gallaudet's interest in the deaf daughter of Dr. Mason Cogswell. He

---

[1] *Histories of American Schools for the Deaf*, Vol. I, The Volta Bureau, Washington, D.C., 1893.

devoted considerable time to Alice Cogswell's education and became so deeply interested in the study of this work that he was willing to go to England to prepare himself to accept the principalship of the first American school for the education of the deaf.

Oral Methods in America.—Horace Mann visited Europe in 1843, and when he returned, he reported favorably upon the oral method of instructing the deaf. This was resented by the manualists, who defeated the first attempt to secure state aid in Massachusetts for the establishment of an oral school. The controversy was so bitter that nearly a quarter of a century elapsed after Mann's report before the founding of the first oral school, known as Clarke Institute, at Northampton, Mass., in 1867.

Gradually the oral method has become established in America. Some schools began by setting up separate units for the two methods, the children being kept completely separated for both study and housing; even the teaching staffs were not allowed to overlap. In this way, the two methods were tried out and compared. At Philadelphia the oral method proved to be so successful that the school became distinctly oral. Other schools developed a practice of combining methods. The abler pupils were given the oral and the less able, the manual method. Oral methods are used almost universally by public school systems in educating the deaf.

5. DEVELOPMENT IN PUBLIC SCHOOLS

Public School Classes.—Boston was the first city to attempt to educate its own deaf; in 1869, the Horace Mann School there was opened. In Chicago the education of the deaf was begun under private control in 1870; the board of education in 1875 undertook this work as a part of its own program.[1] The manual method was followed until about 1900 when, through the efforts of Miss Mary McCowan, the oral method began to be used solely. St. Louis started its school in 1878. Cincinnati began its classes in 1882.[2] The Cleveland Day School for the Deaf opened in 1893 at the request of parents who wanted to have their deaf children educated at home. For its first teacher,[3] Cleveland secured from Cincinnati one who had been orally trained.

[1] McDonald, *op. cit.*, p. 11.

[2] *Eighty-first Annual Report of Public Schools of Cincinnati*, p. 61, Board of Education, Cincinnati, Ohio, 1910.

[3] "The Special Schools and Curriculum Centers," *Report of the Superintendent of Schools for the School Year* 1929–30, p. 52, Board of Education, Cleveland, Ohio, 1931.

Los Angeles started a school for the deaf in 1898; private contributions supported one of the two teachers.   Detroit in 1900 organized the Detroit Day School for the Deaf.[1]   New York City delayed until 1908 before opening its first school of this kind.   Newark, N.J., opened its own in 1910.[2]

A Possible Effect of State Legislation.—The first state to enact a day-school law for the deaf was Wisconsin in 1885.   It permitted the organization of public day schools and for each child enrolled provided $100 a year.   In 1893 this sum was increased to $125 and in 1897 to $150.   In 1907 the law made it compulsory for deaf children to attend some school for the deaf.   By 1890, three cities had established schools under the first law; during the next 10 years, 15 more cities had organized classes.   By 1908, 27 Wisconsin cities had established classes for the deaf.[3]

In 1930,[4] Wisconsin had 18 cities of 10,000 population or more with public school classes for the deaf.   Michigan, the nearest competitor, had only nine; California and Ohio had seven each.   On the other hand, Massachusetts and Pennsylvania had only two cities each and New York, only four.   There may be some relation between early encouragement of such a program and the extensiveness of its development.   This encouragement needs to be official as well as financial; an active, energetic state official can accomplish a great deal in encouraging local communities to establish special schools.

6. METHODS OF INSTRUCTION

Popularly, there are two methods of instructing the deaf—the manual and the oral.   Technically, we find four methods designated— the manual, the manual alphabet, the oral, and the combined.

The Manual Method.—This method makes use of natural signs or gestures and gross bodily movements to express ideas; it also utilizes the manual alphabet, or finger spelling, and writing as means of communication.   The aim is to develop the child mentally and to give him a mastery of written language so that he can read and so that he can communicate in writing with those who do not know the sign language.

[1] *Special Education*, p. 21, Board of Education, Detroit, Mich., 1925.

[2] Newark, *School for the Deaf, Monograph* 8, p. 4, Board of Education, Newark, N.J., 1921.

[3] WINNIE, *op. cit.*, pp. 32–73.

[4] ARCH O. HECK, "Special Schools and Classes in Cities of 10,000 Population and More in the United States," *U.S. Office of Education Bulletin* 7, p. 31, Washington, D.C., 1930.

The sign language "consists of gestures, bodily movements, mimic actions, pantomime, postures—and to carry a close shade of meaning, even the shrugging of shoulders, the raising of eyebrows and the expression of the face—all appealing graphically to the accustomed eye."[1] As can be seen, many of these signs are natural and can in a sense be said to be part of a universal language. The system is very expressive and can be rapidly and clearly understood by those trained in its use.

The Manual-alphabet Method.—This method eliminates signs. The manual alphabet is the means employed for communication besides writing, which, of course, is emphasized and used. Those employing this method place considerable emphasis upon the mastery of language; they believe that the use of signs tends to corrupt good style in the use of proper English. The manual alphabet is based upon the regular alphabet and so makes possible an excellent training in the mastery of good English. All the usual signs that creep into the speech of most normal hearing people will, naturally, be used by people who have been trained under this method of instruction.

The Oral Method.—The oral method bases communication upon ability to read speech and the ability to speak and write. The manual alphabet and the sign language are not supposed to be used by pupils, teachers, or other employees about the school.

The success of the method depends largely upon the ability that pupils develop in speaking; it depends, besides, upon the development of an ability to understand what is said to them by observing the movements of the face, the throat, and the lips of the speaker. These two tasks are by no means so simple as they sound.[2] These children have, as a starting point, no language and no means of knowing what the voice sounds like. Because of this lack of language, the teacher is unable to explain what she means to the beginner. The first step in the educational process, therefore, is to give the child a language.

The Combined Method.—The majority of state schools in the United States now use both the oral method and the manual or the manual-alphabet method. Their aim is to instruct by the oral method all who can profit by it, but to use the manual method for all others. Schools vary greatly in the proportion of those who, it is believed, need to use the manual method. The oral method in these schools is largely a schoolroom technique. The children employ signs almost exclusively about the school grounds, and assemblies are generally conducted in the sign language.

[1] Best, *op. cit.*, p. 278.
[2] See pp. 249–252.

7. ORGANIZATION FOR EDUCATING THE DEAF

In this country the methods of instruction used seem to be closely related to the type of organization set up to educate deaf pupils.   Best[1] reports that "the strictly private" schools are oral; that the denominational and the state schools commonly use the combined method; and that the public day school uses the oral method in 63 out of 65 cities, with two using the combined method.

Private Schools.—The first schools for the deaf were private ventures.   In some instances, an individual undertook to teach a few deaf children at his own initiative, and sometimes an association was formed, which then elected a board responsible for organizing and managing the school.   Often, this latter type of organization was given financial aid by the state; sometimes the state took over the management of the school.   According to the *American Annals*,[2] there were 19 such private (and denominational) schools in 1929.   The Office of Education reported 31 in 1937.[3]

State Schools.—As we have seen, state schools had the first extensive development.   A state school seemed the logical early development.   The proportion of deaf children in a single community was small; methods of teaching were difficult to master; and no law compelled the deaf to attend.   The Hartford school served all New England for some years.   The first attempts to start schools in the states of New York and Pennsylvania, even, were defeated because of a desire to give complete support to the Hartford school, which was then being organized.

By 1849, however, schools had been established in 12 states.   In 1914, Best reported schools in all states but Delaware, New Hampshire, Nevada, and Wyoming; there were at that time 65 state schools in 44 states.   The *American Annals of the Deaf* in 1929[4] reported only 64 public residential or state schools.   This slowing up in the number of institutions is not surprising.   A state may enlarge the capacity of its one school, but only infrequently will it establish additional schools. Four Eastern states—Connecticut, Massachusetts, New York, and Pennsylvania—have two or more schools each; a number of Southern states have established separate schools for Negroes.

---

[1] BEST, *op. cit.*, pp. 286–287.

[2] *American Annals of the Deaf*, (January, 1929), Vol. 74, pp. 25–27.

[3] EMERY M. FOSTER and ELISE H. MARTENS, *U.S. Office of Education Bulletin* 2, p. 10, Washington, D.C., 1937.

[4] *American Annals of the Deaf*, (January, 1929), Vol. 74, pp. 6–11.

Local Day Schools and Classes.—The first day school originated in 1869 at Boston; by 1914,[1] Best reported 65 such schools; in 1935, Foster reported 148 cities having programs for educating their deaf.[2]

In 1928, when the writer made a survey of cities of 10,000 and more,[3] he had reports from 96.6 per cent of all the 762 cities of that size in the United States. Of this group, 103 claimed to be educating their own deaf. One of the schools reported an enrollment of 421 pupils, another had 247, while five others enrolled from 100 to 149. The remaining cities had enrollments of less than 100 apiece and many of them had less than 25. Obviously, the public day schools have relatively small centers except in the large cities.

8. THE STATE SCHOOL VS. LOCAL SCHOOLS

Of the many discussions concerning the merits of state and local schools, a great number are largely theoretical; very little concrete evidence is advanced in support of either set of claims. The probability is that both methods of educating the deaf are necessary and that both function with reasonable satisfaction.

Institutionalization.—The claim is made that the state school institutionalizes the child. It assumes all responsibility for him, the home is lost sight of, and the child fails to develop a normal attitude toward the home. Home ties are weakened and broken; the child becomes tied to the institution and looks to it for support and continued assistance. These attitudinal changes, it is maintained, prevent these youths from functioning normally in society; they become in feeling and in attitude a "class apart" and so remain throughout life.

The answer often made is that these youths do make good in life, that they are able to maintain themselves, that they do establish homes and become a part of the normal social group. There is need of a follow-up of the graduates of both types of schools if we are to get a fair answer to this question of institutionalization.

Supervision.—It is claimed that the deaf are better supervised in a state school. They have here a genial, kindly supervision throughout the 24 hours of every day. This makes possible improved health, better morals, finer co-operation, and greater educational possibilities. In a day school the child is supervised only some 5 hours out of 24; the parents are not trained and have no understanding of the problems involved in educating the deaf. But all homes are not ignorant, says the public-school advocate; with present-day home contacts, parents

---

[1] BEST, *op. cit.*, p. 191.

[2] EMERY M. FOSTER and ELISE H. MARTENS, *op. cit.*, pp. 16–45.

[3] Unpublished manuscript in the author's personal library.

are being trained to supervise their own deaf. This they can do even more effectively than a big school. Perhaps, a halfway ground is the actual situation.

School Grading.—State school enrollments are sufficiently large to make possible good classification. In the smaller local schools a teacher will have to instruct pupils of from two to eight different grades. This, it is claimed, makes for inefficiency of instruction. On the other hand, some argue that the instruction of the deaf should be largely individual. If this be the case, highly graded instruction ceases to be of importance.

Education outside School Hours.—In the state school the child is continuously in contact with other children similarly handicapped; he is continuously in contact with teachers who are familiar with his needs. This means that methods developed in school enabling the children to communicate with one another will be continued; the pupils will have full-time practice in them, instead of merely the practice of the classroom, as in the day school. This, if true, is important. These children have a late start in getting an education and they need full-time practice in developing their methods of communicating with others. Though some public school people will admit that the argument has weight, others insist that many homes do give just the co-operation needed. The answer to the problem again is dependent upon the type of home from which the child comes.

Trade Education.—The residential school makes extensive provisions for all kinds of shopwork. This work can rarely be provided in local schools on account of the small enrollments, while most state schools do provide shops. It is claimed that these youths can expect to earn a livelihood by their hands alone; therefore, it is argued that this training, which only the state school can provide efficiently, is essential in the educational program of the deaf.

The other point of view suggests that we deal unjustly with the deaf when we assume that they must depend upon a living by the use of their hands. They have all the mental abilities of hearing children. They might make excellent research workers in almost any field. They have opportunities in the actuarial field.

Public Attitude.—The public school advocate also stresses the importance of the constant contact between the deaf and the hearing child. If the two groups are continually separated, the hearing group habitually thinks of the deaf group as so abnormal that it can have no place in the normal life of the social group. Lack of contact allows fantastic notions concerning the deaf child's handicap to grow; it keeps hearing people in ignorance of the abilities and capabilities of the deaf.

If these groups are educated together, and if the hearing, through these personal contacts, come to understand better the mental powers of the deaf, the task of securing jobs for the latter as adults will be greatly lessened.

Cost.—Finally, says the public school advocate, the cost of maintaining the public school class is less, in that housing and food do not have to be provided. This argument is not without considerable weight when we face average per pupil costs of $496[1] per year in these state schools.

9. SUMMARY

The problem of educating the deaf is not surpassed in difficulty by that of any other type of handicapped child. These children have been deaf from birth or before speech developed and have no language. Principles governing their education demand (1) that the child be given first consideration in the development of a program, (2) that equality of opportunity be not forgotten, (3) that these children be educated to associate with hearing individuals, and (4) that prevention be the core of the entire educational program.

The first school was organized by de l'Épée at Paris in 1755. He used the manual system of instruction; this system was brought to America by Gallaudet in 1816 and was adopted by all schools established here up to 1867, when the first oral school was started under the name of Clarke Institute. Two years later, the first public school was organized at Boston; this latter movement continued until, in 1929, there were 107 cities reporting such schools or classes. The public schools have used the oral method almost universally.

State schools provide careful supervision and give a better opportunity for classification. The day school makes it possible for the child to stay at home, it gives him an opportunity to live with and associate with hearing children, it keeps his home life normal, and forces him constantly to use what he learns at school in conversing with hearing persons on the playground and at home.

Problems and Questions for Discussion

1. Why is it so difficult to educate the deaf? Give examples.
2. Who are the deaf? Why are they thus defined?
3. State the principles you think should guide one in organizing to educate the deaf. Show how each applies.
4. Trace the development of the education of deaf children. What do you consider the significant phases of this development? Why?

[1] See p. 259.

5. What methods are used in teaching the deaf?   Describe in detail each of these methods.

6. If you had your choice and were starting a new school, which method would you use?   Why?

7. How do communities now educate their deaf?   What plan is used in your home community?   Which method should be used?   Why?

8. Plan a consistent argument for the use of state schools; plan one for using day schools.

9. What is meant by institutionalization?   How important is it as related to the organization of state schools?   Why?

Selected Bibliography

BEST, HARRY.   *The Deaf.*   The Thomas Y. Crowell Company, New York, 1914. 340 pp.

A very complete report, dealing with numbers, causes, treatment, economic condition, social organization and education of the deaf.   His report of their education deals with its history, organization, methods, cost, and attendance.

FAY, EDWARD ALLEN, Ed.   *Histories of American Schools for the Deaf*, Vol. I. The Volta Bureau, Washington, D.C., 1893.

A brief history of the beginning of the education of the deaf.   It contains also a series of articles giving the history of some 16 American schools for the deaf.

FUSFELD, IRVING S., and others.   "The Survey of Schools for the Deaf," *American Annals of the Deaf* (November, 1925), Vol. 70, pp. 391–421; (March, 1926), Vol. 71, pp. 97–135; (September, 1926), Vol. 71, pp. 284–348; (January, 1927), Vol. 72, pp. 2–34; (November, 1927), Vol. 72, pp. 377–414; (January, 1928), Vol. 73, pp. 1–36; (March, 1928), Vol. 73, pp. 184–201; (May, 1928), Vol. 73, pp. 273–299.

The report of a survey of 42 schools for the deaf—28 residential and 14 day schools; data were gathered by visits made to each of the 42.

McDONALD, ROBERT ALEXANDER FYFE.   *Adjustment of School Organization to Various Population Groups*, pp. 8–16.   Teachers College, Columbia University, 1915.

Gives brief history of the education of the deaf and describes current provisions for their education.

WINNIE, A. J.   *History and Handbook of Day Schools for the Deaf and Blind.*   State Department of Education, Madison, Wis., 1912.   130 pp.

A brief history of the education of the deaf; it also has brief descriptions of the development of Wisconsin's public schools and classes for the deaf.

CHAPTER XVIII

PROBLEMS FACED IN EDUCATING THE DEAF

Many a problem that seems unsolvable appears to be not nearly so hopeless after we have taken time to study it. The preceding chapter has emphasized the difficulties to be met in educating the deaf. Without minimizing them, it should be pointed out that the more familiar we become with them the less insurmountable they are likely to appear. Perhaps no one but the student of these problems rightfully appreciates how arduous they are; at the same time, no one else can so clearly see the opportunities available for overcoming them. Thus we have the paradox that he who most clearly sees the difficulties involved in educating deaf children is the one who is most hopeful of being able to overcome them.

In this chapter the many problems involved in educating deaf children will be discussed. Some of them will be applicable to any type of organization for educating the deaf; others will apply only to public school classes.

1. ORGANIZING PUBLIC SCHOOL CLASSES FOR THE DEAF

Admission.—Public school classes admit children who have a total loss of hearing; those who have sufficient hearing to be retained in a regular class or with the hard of hearing, but who have a diseased condition which indicates that a total loss will soon occur; and those who need continuous aid in preserving their present speech.

Children vary in degree of deafness from that of total loss to that of zero loss; there is a point on this scale below which a child cannot profit by regular instruction and where the development of speech has been defective, owing to the loss. City school systems often fail to state the point at which children are admitted to classes for the deaf.

Discovery of Deaf Children.—By definition, the deaf child is one who is deaf from birth or before he has developed speech sufficiently to have attained a permanent mastery of it. This means that most deaf children will have become deaf before reaching school age. We can locate, therefore, only a few of them through the public school; they must be discovered outside the school. If a permanent continuing census were maintained from birth, we could hope to locate the

246

deaf at an early age; this is important if parents are to be instructed as to what they can do to help the child develop language ability. Even more important, classes for language development could be organized for these children at three or four years of age.

Of course parents, physicians, nurses, and school officials report to the central office many children who are deaf. This, however, is too spasmodic to be satisfactory. California has a recent law that reads, "It shall be the duty of every attending or consulting physician, nurse, parent, or guardian having charge of any minor who is totally deaf or

ILLUSTRATION 17.—Rhythm work in a specially constructed room, School for the Deaf, Detroit.

whose hearing is impaired, to report at once to the superintendent of schools . . . the name, age, and residence of such minor."[1] Some such measure would seem to be necessary if complete information concerning the location of deaf children is to be secured.

The Building or Classroom.—A building erected for the education of the deaf will contain a music room where the children can develop a sense of rhythm. The acoustics should be as nearly perfect as possible. Such training is important for the development of good speech. This room is sometimes made soundproof and is a complete acoustic unit within itself. Illustration 17 shows such a room in the school at

[1] *Education of the Physically Handicapped*, p. 15, School Publication 281, Board of Education, Los Angeles, 1936.

Detroit. The hardwood floor is slightly elevated above the concrete foundation; the walls and floors are sensitive to the vibrations of the piano.

The school often includes space and equipment for shopwork and domestic science. A lunchroom must be provided, since most of the children have long distances to travel. The gymnasium with shower baths is considered essential. As in many regular elementary schools, an auditorium is now an essential feature. It is used as a central assembly for the pupils, as a place where parents can gather, and as a meeting place for the various clubs of the school. A clinic for diagnosing the problems represented by each child in the school is considered necessary as an aid in the placement of these children educationally.

New York City opened a new school building for the deaf in 1927. "It has 46 classrooms which are well lighted, seven trade rooms with the newest equipment, a medical unit, an auditorium with a motion picture booth, a gymnasium, a roof playground, a library, a radio-ear room, a model apartment, a lunchroom with special equipment, an exhibition room, and teachers' rest rooms." Although these classes are small, the classroom should be of the same size as a regular schoolroom. This makes it possible to provide unusual and needed equipment, to assemble pupils by groups, to shift desks so that good light may be had at all times, and to spend some time daily in games and exercises, even outside regular gymnasium hours.

The rooms should be well lighted. It is important that the sight of these children be protected, because they have to hear with their eyes; when sight is lost, they are doubly handicapped. If these children are to read lips, good light must be available, as only with the greatest care can certain words be distinguished from others.

A great amount of blackboard space is needed, for the instruction of the deaf requires considerable written work. The room should have numerous charts, toys, pictures, and other objects, especially in the lower grades; these are needed for teaching names and later for helping the children to develop language. In the development of speech, a large mirror has been found to be effective; for rhythm and the improvement of speech, a piano is required. In some schools the radio-ear is being used to try to develop more effectively the little hearing that the child may have.

Transportation.—Busses and streetcars are used to convey deaf children to the various centers. Los Angeles uses both methods. Drivers of automobiles are under contract to transport children at 40 cents per day per child; pupils who choose to travel by streetcar have their fare paid.   In the case of very young children, the board of education pays the fare of escorts.   Philadelphia "pays \$1 as well as carfare for an escort who takes the children to and from school."[1]

Size of Class.—McDonald reported in 1915 that classes ranged in size from five to ten; Berry, writing in 1926, said, "The average number of pupils per teacher enrolled in city day schools and classes for the deaf in the United States for the school year 1921–1922 was eight." In 1929 the new school in New York had 46 classrooms with 436 pupils enrolled; this was an average of 9.5 pupils per room.

The small size of class means that the per capita cost of educating the deaf will be large; this we have to face frankly.   There is, however, no single group of handicapped children where the results of instruction are so obvious and impressive.   Without instruction these deaf children remain dumb; they have no language, no means of communication, and so no ability whereby they can hope to maintain themselves.   Instruction changes this situation and converts virtually dumb animals into human beings.

2. INSTRUCTION

Speech Reading.—One of the major problems to be solved in teaching the deaf is the development of ability to understand the speech of others by means of speech reading.   What hearing is to the average child, speech reading is to the deaf.   The hearing child begins to store up impressions of speech and ideas derived from speech long before speech develops.   The deaf child has none of these impressions or ideas when his education begins; it is by means of speech reading that these are gained; its acquisition is, therefore, of prime importance.

Speech reading has been called "a subtle art."   It is more than a science.   It is a science, in that it relates certain definite lip, face, and throat movements to certain sounds and combinations of sounds. There are, however, certain sounds that have practically identical facial movements.   The ear detects the slightest variation in sound; these minute variations are not so easily or so frequently detectable by sight.   The letters *p*, *b*, and *m* look identical to the lip reader; *t*, *d*, and *n* likewise are indistinguishable; thus, such words as *dan, tat, nan, tad,* and *dad* look exactly alike.   The particular one used can be determined only by means of the context.   This demands more than skill in the use of specified tools; it requires the artist who can visualize the whole word picture and so reproduce in the minutest detail the

---

[1] *Division of Special Education*, p. 11, Board of Education, Philadelphia, 1926.

thought of the speaker. "A subtle art" would seem to describe very accurately the study of speech reading.

So important is this training that it should begin on the opening day of school. Work is started with nouns such as *ball* and *top*. A ball is held before the class and the teacher pronounces "a ball," "a ball"; she calls attention to the movement of the lips. This is done repeatedly. The top is then used in the same way. Then, putting the objects down, she says "a ball" as she points to it; this is done repeatedly. She does the same thing with the top. She then

ILLUSTRATION 18.¹—Teaching speech reading in Seventeenth Street School for the Deaf and Hard of Hearing, Los Angeles.

calls upon some child who apparently has caught the idea, to point to the object that she names. Pictures of these objects are then associated with the objects and with the lip's movements of the spoken word. Thus noun after noun is taken up. The verbs are developed by use of various commands represented by the simple actions of hopping, running, and skipping; the teacher performs an action and then gives the command "run" or "jump." As the children seem to grasp the idea, they are called upon to perform the action. In Illustration 18 children are being taught speech reading.

Speech reading is preparatory to all language work; it is quite independent of the development of speech. In developing language,

of course, the words learned in speech reading must be associated with
the printed and written words and thus reading and writing are
developed.

Speech Development.—Another major problem is teaching the
deaf to speak.   This begins in the first year at school.   As soon as
the child begins to relate the lip movements of the teacher with a
given word, he is encouraged to attempt the reproduction of those
lip movements and thus produce the sounds that represent the object.

ILLUSTRATION 19.—Teaching speech in Seventeenth Street School for the Deaf and
Hard of Hearing, Los Angeles.

The task involved at this point is not an easy one.   Though for
many years teachers of the deaf thought this step too difficult for most,
if not all, of the deaf, many now believe that "practically every deaf
child can be taught to speak."   The teacher assists the child in the
attainment of speech by leading him not only to imitate the lip movements of the teacher but to use the sense of touch as well as that of
sight.   The pupil places his hand on the teacher's throat as a word is
pronounced, then places it upon his own as he attempts to say the
word.   He is made to realize that the movements he feels must be
reproduced, as well as the lip movements that he sees.   Illustration
19 shows children in Los Angeles being taught speech.

None but the trained teacher can realize how difficult the development of good speech is for the deaf child. It demands constant and continuous repetition. Even with expert training, the voice of the deaf child will often be harsh and monotonous. The use of the piano helps to develop better inflection; methods, however, will have to be much further developed before anything like normality of speech can be secured. The most that is claimed at present is that the speech of the deaf can be developed to meet the "needs of social and business intercourse," and this is no little achievement.

ILLUSTRATION 20.—The use of hearing aids in Seventeenth Street School for the Deaf and Hard of Hearing, Los Angeles.

Unique Equipment.—Los Angeles has a radio-ear that accommodates 18 children. By means of it, sound is so amplified that children who cannot hear the natural voice are able to hear. It is hoped that this will aid them in improving the quality of their speech. Illustration 20 shows hearing aids actually being used. The new school building in New York City has a radio-ear room also; the children are given daily drill. The audiometer is one of the more common instruments of special value to the deaf; there are several kinds; the 2A and the 4A have been commonly used. Both are used to measure the amount of hearing possessed by the child.[1]

[1] For a more extended account of audiometers, see pp. 275–277.

Curriculum.—Deaf children spend the first 2 or 3 years in the development of speech reading, speech, and language ability. After this is done, the first grade of the regular course of study is started and the regular grade work continued thereafter; both speech and speech reading are continued.

In order that the pupils may acquire facility in the use of their hands, shopwork of various kinds is begun at an early age. There has been a tendency in the past to overemphasize shopwork. It was assumed that a deaf child could support himself only by manual labor. Our ideas are more liberal now. We believe that the deaf have a mentality which equals that of those who hear normally; we know that they do succeed in brain crafts; and so we are willing to grant them an opportunity to pursue a regular arts course.

3. THE TEACHING PERSONNEL

Without belittling the task of regular or other special teachers, one is inclined to the opinion that special teachers of the deaf have a task unsurpassed in difficulty by any of the others. The hours of necessary repetitive work required before the child develops speech call for the qualities of persistence and patience in a unique degree. The years of labor needed for the development of speech urgently demand enthusiasm and optimism. These traits plus a great love of the work are exacted of one who would be a successful teacher of the deaf. These children face so difficult a task that only the continuous optimism of the teacher can keep them from becoming discouraged.

Training.—The difficulty of teaching speech and speech reading suggests that there are techniques necessary for this instruction which are unique. The usual methods employed for teaching children who can hear are not sufficient. The deaf child has no language concepts; in place of hearing, he has to use sight and touch to gain these concepts. Since regular methods are based upon the assumption of hearing as well as upon the assumption of an initial language development, the technique of teaching during the first several years must adjust to these two deficiencies.

A common suggestion regarding teacher training asks for one year of technical instruction over and above that of the regular grade teacher. In addition to general courses that ought to be taken by all teachers in the field of special education, the White House Conference suggests 20 to 22 semester hours of study particularly applicable to the teaching of deaf children. The courses include (1) "Principles of formation and development of speech and rhythm for the deaf and training of residual hearing"; (2) "observation, participation, and practice teaching of deaf children"; (3) "methods of teaching language and reading to the deaf"; (4) "study of principles of teaching hard of hearing children, together with study of the anatomy and hygiene of the ear"; (5) "industrial arts for handicapped children"; (6) "speech improvement and correction"; (7) "mental hygiene."[1]

Experience.—One aim in the teaching of deaf children is to educate them so that they can live happily and successfully with hearing people. In order to do this it would seem quite essential that teachers of the deaf have experience in the teaching of hearing children. The number of years of such experience is not so important as the degree of understanding the candidate has of the problems involved in teaching hearing pupils. The White House Conference reporting on the preparation of teachers for the deaf recommends "at least two years of successful teaching experience with normal children."

Opportunities.—The well-trained, experienced teacher has many opportunities for service entirely apart from her classwork. Many communities have special classes that are considered experimental. They are not acquainted with the rich background of development that has preceded the organization of special classes within their own system. Such information imparted through personal contacts, lectures or talks, and newspapers would do much to give stability to special education.

Many parents need suggestions for taking better physical care of their children. At this latter point the teacher can render her greatest extraschool service. Too few parents recognize the close relation between deafness and such diseases as measles, diphtheria, scarlet fever, meningitis, and brain fever. Some of these diseases are commonly thought to be inevitable and not very serious. This is unfortunate, for they are largely preventable and are likely to cause deafness unless the patients are well cared for after the disease has been contracted. Even the common cold and catarrh may result in serious impairment of hearing unless care is taken to prevent such ill effects.

In a sense, what the teacher does in the matter of educating parents can be far more significant than anything she will do in the classroom. The classroom work is remedial; she tries to develop senses of the child that will compensate for the one lost. What she does by way of educating parents is preventive; she helps to keep children from becoming deaf.

4. OTHER PROBLEMS

Time Used to Cover the Eight Grades.—Because of the deaf child's lack of language, he is unable to complete the first eight grades

[1] White House Conference, *Special Education: The Handicapped and the Gifted*, pp. 567–568, The Century Co., New York, 1931.

in that number of years. Newark reports that 11 years are needed; the first year is given over almost entirely to the development of language, speech, and speech reading. The next 4 years are needed for the completion of the first two grades, or possibly for the first two and one-half grades. Los Angeles reports that the "deaf child is allowed 8 years to complete the first five grades." The remaining grades require only a year each.

Costs.—The costs of a program of education will be greater for the deaf than for the hearing. Costs are increased by the necessity of providing extra physical care, transportation, and equipment and by the necessity of having small classes. Per capita costs for four day schools reported by the *American Annals* were $228, $240, $363, and $375—or an average of $301 for the four.

Placement and Follow-up.—If so much money is to be spent on educating the deaf, they should not be forgotten as soon as they have completed their academic school program. One aim of special education is to make its pupils self-supporting men and women. Unless placement service is organized, many deaf pupils will not become self-supporting. This will be due not to inefficiency upon their part but to the fact that the general public has not been educated to understand their capability. Until such education has been accomplished, schools for the deaf must place their pupils vocationally.

During the first few years after graduation the deaf child, owing to difficulties peculiar to himself as well as to difficulties that confront all hearing children also, often finds himself poorly adjusted to his job. Unless the schools can provide a consistent follow-up during these years, many who might otherwise have succeeded in maintaining themselves will become dependent upon society.

5. SELECTED DAY SCHOOLS

Cleveland.—The Alexander Graham Bell School for the deaf was organized originally in 1893 as the Cleveland Day School for Deaf Children, the name being changed in June, 1923. Not until 1914 was the building that the school now occupies opened. "This building was the first in the United States, planned and built as a Day School for Deaf Children."[1] Children are admitted at four years of age and may complete eight grades, after which they enter grade 9 of a regular junior high school. The regular city curriculum is used, though modified to meet the needs of the deaf. Only deaf children are housed in this school.

[1] *The Special Schools and Curriculum Centers*, p. 53, Board of Education, Cleveland, Ohio, 1931.

The building has two stories over a basement; the first floor has a dispensary, the principal's office, a storeroom, and 13 classrooms; the second floor has an auditorium with seating capacity of 260, a rest room for teachers, a storeroom, a library, a drawing room, a sewing room and five classrooms; the basement has a cafeteria lunchroom, a domestic-science kitchen, a manual-training room, a laundry, two playrooms, shower baths, and the heating plant.

During the first 3 or 4 years, notebooks are kept by the pupils. Each June they are returned to the pupils and the parents are shown how they can continue some of the exercises with the children during vacation. They are told how to make object charts and to give commands so that the pupils can continue speech-reading drill. The school likewise tries to get the parents to understand that the deaf child can do things and can be taught that other people have rights.

Chicago.—Records show that in Chicago classes were organized for the deaf as early as 1875; then the manual method of instruction was used. The oral method was begun about 1900, and it finally became the sole method of instruction. No schools were organized until 1912; previous to that date, classes were housed in centers of one to three classes each. The Bell School, built in 1917, was named for Alexander Graham Bell. It was planned particularly for the deaf and was considered one of the best-equipped schools of its kind.

In 1921–22, Chicago had three well-equipped schools for the deaf— the Bell, the Parker, and the Beidler—with enrollments of 71, 132, and 102, respectively. One class of 6 and one of 10 were housed at the Perry and Kozminski schools. These all aimed to get deaf children into school at early ages. Many began at four, and an attempt was made to have them all in school by five years of age. This was not accomplished, however, since a report in 1921–22 said, "Every year we discover ten or a dozen deaf children, eight, nine or ten years old, who have never attended any school."[1] The goal is a worthy one.

Physical education was considered unusually important for the deaf, since they were barred from many of the sports of hearing children. They could play games but they had to be taught if they were to participate. Only the Bell School had gymnasium facilities. Boy Scout Troops and Camp Fire Groups were organized. The schools also emphasized dramatics and assembly participation. The deaf were encouraged to put on assembly programs for the hearing children.

Vocational work was emphasized; this was necessary "since deafness bars entrance into any of the professions or business life . . . "

[1] Frank G. Bruner, *Report of the Director of Special Schools* 1922–23, p. 73, Board of Education, Chicago, 1924.

This meant that "the deaf must find employment with the hands."[1] The Chicago schools, therefore, gave a great amount of handwork, such as basketry, clay modeling, cooking, millinery, pottery, printing, raffia and reed work, sewing, textile work, and woodwork. Chicago at that time seemed to find little difficulty in placing the deaf graduates. Many factories and printing establishments called upon these schools for workers.

By January, 1937, all the centers and classes for deaf children in Chicago had been furnished with the latest devices in hearing aids. Chicago's greatest advance during the school year 1936–37 was the establishment of high-school classes for the deaf, presided over by qualified teachers. These teachers serve not only to continue exercises in lip reading, but as coaching teachers in the various subjects that the deaf pupils take in the regular high-school classes.

Los Angeles.—A school for the deaf was established in Los Angeles, as an experiment, by the board of education in 1897. "One of the two teachers employed was supported by private contributions . . . " The present building houses hard-of-hearing and hearing children, as well as deaf pupils. Grade work from kindergarten through grade 6 is given. Sixteen rooms house the deaf and the hard of hearing; the hearing children have the rest of the building. This is considered a good arrangement, since the deaf can associate with the hearing.

Upon completing grade 6, pupils go to a junior high school where two special teachers have charge of their home rooms; their schedules are adapted to the regular departmental program. In senior high school a special class for the deaf is maintained, where the pupils receive special help; they recite, however, in the regular classes for hearing children.

New York City.—The school for the deaf in New York City was organized in 1908; it opened in September of that year with an enrollment of 47. It graduated its first class, numbering six, in 1911. Vocational work consisted of cooking and sewing; cocoa only was served for lunch; no children were being placed in positions; there was no doctor and there were no alumni associations; and the students had no outside activities.

Ten years later there were 106 graduates; every one who wished a position had been placed; an alumni association had been organized and met monthly at the school. The Parents' Association had a membership of 280. The school had an aurist for ears, eyes, nose, and throat; a doctor for regular examinations was in attendance, as well as a dentist and a nurse. In 1927 the present finely equipped building

[1] *Ibid.*, p. 81.

was completed and opened.[1] In 1929 it enrolled 436 pupils and was "the largest day school for the deaf in the world."[2] Children who were placed in positions after graduation were followed up, and their work was found to be so well done that no complaint could be made about it.

A report for the year 1933–34 showed a roll of 502. Busses brought children to the school from Brooklyn and Queens; carfare was provided, where necessary, for children from other boroughs; older children acted as guides for the younger ones. New York believes in a central school, instead of classes scattered throughout various schools, in order that more careful grading may be arranged.

The board of education, recognizing that skilled teachers are needed for the deaf, requires three years of teaching experience, one of which must be in the city schools. Upon application, candidates may be assigned to the school for the deaf for one year of training and practice teaching; at the end of the year, they must take an examination.

6. THE STATE SCHOOL

The first state school[3] was started by Kentucky in 1823. It had been organized the year before, but its actual opening had been delayed.[4] State schools differ from day schools mainly in their being residential, whereas pupils in day schools continue to live at home.

Control.—Most state schools are strictly public; they are supported by taxation and controlled by the legislature. In a few instances the state merely supports them financially; these semipublic schools are found in the Eastern states. In the strictly state school, the legislature permits the control of the school to rest with an appointed board or with a department of state government. At an early date, either a special board or the state board of charities was generally made responsible for visiting, inspecting, and supervising the school.

Cowdery's study[5] showed that in 15 states these schools were controlled by boards of visitors or boards of trustees. In 13 states they were supervised by the state board of charities or by the department of public welfare. In 14 states they were under the supervision of the

---

[1] For a description of this building, see p. 248.

[2] WILLIAM J. O'SHEA, *Progress of the Public Schools* 1924–29, p. 81, Board of Education, New York City, 1929.

[3] ROBERT A. F. McDONALD, *Adjustments of School Organization to Various Population Groups*, p. 9, Teachers College, Columbia University, New York, 1915.

[4] For development of the state school, see pp. 236–237.

[5] KATE LOUISE COWDERY, *The Legal Status of the Education of Blind and Deaf Children in the Forty-eight States*, p. 19, Master's thesis, Ohio State University, Columbus, 1927.

state department of education or the superintendent of public instruction; in 4 of these states, however, the department of education was assisted by a specially appointed board of control.

In recent years the tendency has been for state boards of education to be given general supervisory control of these schools. This is entirely logical; the school is an educational organization; its primary purpose is the better education of deaf children; all other problems are subordinate.

Enrollments.—The 64 residential schools that reported in 1928 had a median roll of 194. The two largest schools had 537 and 536, respectively; the two smallest were 14 and 26, respectively. Table XIV shows the distribution of enrollments for all 64 schools.

TABLE XIV.—ENROLLMENTS IN SIXTY-FOUR RESIDENTIAL SCHOOLS FOR THE DEAF

Enrollment	Number of schools	Enrollment	Number of schools
Under 50	4	300–349	7
50– 99	12	350–399	5
100–149	11	400–499	2
150–199	6	500–599	2
200–249	10	Total.........	64
250–299	5		

Costs.—The state faces a serious problem in the cost of educating deaf children in a residential school. For the school year 1921–22, the average per capita cost for 56 state schools located in 38 states was $496. The highest per pupil cost was $1,131 in Idaho; the enrollment was 62. Tennessee costs were $244—the lowest; the enrollment was 257.[1]

Curriculum.[2]—Of 28 schools reporting, 12 developed a course of their own; 6 followed that used by the public schools; and 10 adapted the public school curriculum slightly to meet the needs of the deaf. In 17 of the schools, the course covered 12 years; three schools had a 13-year course; the other schools had courses varying from 10 to 16 years in length. In 15 schools prevocational subjects, such as beginning woodwork, handicraft, sloyd, and construction work were provided; in 12 schools no such preparation was given.

The purpose of this shopwork is not money-making, according to about two-thirds of the schools; seven schools stated that some, if not all, of their departments earned money. In most cases the teaching

[1] FRANK M. PHILLIPS, "Schools for the Deaf," *U.S. Bureau of Education Bulletin* 52, p. 9, Washington, D.C., 1923.
[2] *American Annals of the Deaf* (September, 1926), Vol. 71, p. 284.

staff of the trades is used in repairing buildings and keeping grounds in good condition; in all schools pupils in the trades courses are used in repair work. This work may be of value for instructional purposes if properly handled.

Twenty-two of the schools give definite rhythm training; the same number have a systematic course in physical education. In all the schools there are well-organized sports. Baseball and basketball are provided for boys in each school; girls have basketball in 23 schools. Other sports are football, tennis, track, soccer, swimming, volleyball, handball, wrestling, hockey, and indoor baseball.

Teachers.[1]—A survey of the academic teachers in 29 state schools showed that 84 per cent were hearing and 16 per cent deaf; 16 per cent were men and 84 per cent women. Applicants for teaching positions were required to be at least high-school graduates in 5 of the schools; 17 other schools required additional special training or experience, usually for 1 year. Six schools demanded at least 2 years of normal or college work; and the other school insisted upon having normal-school graduates who had had special preparation for teaching the deaf.

The industrial teachers in these same schools were 60 per cent men and 40 per cent women; 42 per cent were deaf and 58 per cent hearing. Nine of the schools demanded only proficiency in the industries taught; nine required knowledge of the trade and ability to impart knowledge; three asked a fair command of English, as well as knowledge of the trades; and only four insisted upon a high-school education in addition to a mastery of the trades.

The average beginning salaries of academic teachers, without maintenance, were $165 for men and $118 for women. The average maximum salaries were $207 and $186, respectively. The industrial teachers, on the average, were not paid so well. Beginning men were paid $141 and women $98, the maximums being $193 and $159, respectively.

Placement and Follow-up.—Data secured concerning placement and follow-up are very inadequate. The schools give a little help in the placement of graduates; follow-up consists chiefly of the incidental reports which come to the school through friends and relatives or which are reported voluntarily by the pupil himself in letters or visits. Data available indicate that the vocations most frequently followed are printing, carpentry, farming, shoe repairing, and dressmaking. The survey of 28 state schools reported that "as a rule graduates enter the trades learned at school." It reported that 50 to 60 per cent of those who go to work enter such trades. There was no

[1] *American Annals of the Deaf* (March, 1926), Vol. 71, pp. 122–133.

information that told how many of the young people remained in these trades; the schools' follow-up program was too weak to make this information available.

7. SUMMARY

The problems of educating the deaf in the public schools center around which children shall be admitted, how they shall be discovered, where classes shall be located, what adjustments need to be made in classrooms to fit them for the use of the deaf, how the pupils shall be transported to centers, what the size of each class should be, what equipment is necessary, what the nature of the curriculum should be, what time is necessary for the completion of the elementary school; what the program will cost, and what training is necessary for teachers. The hardest task faced by the instructor is that of teaching speech and speech reading.   Just how to organize in order to give adequate placement and follow-up service has not been determined.

The tendency at present is for state schools to be controlled by state departments of education.   Admissions at these schools on the average are delayed until nearly eight years of age.   Shopwork and domestic science are emphasized.   The oral method of instruction is used in all state schools at present, but only two of them are strictly oral.   The minimum requirement for teachers is, on the average, high-school graduation with 1 year of special training.   Actual training averages higher than this.

Problems and Questions for Discussion

1. Why is it important to become well acquainted with the problems of any social enterprise?

2. List what seem to you to be the chief problems involved in organizing public school classes for the deaf.   How would you propose solving those problems?

3. What is speech reading?   Why is it important?

4. What unique problems are involved in teaching deaf children to talk?   Why teach the deaf to talk?

5. Describe some of the unique equipment required in schools for the deaf.

6. What kind of instructional program do you think ought to be provided for deaf children?   Defend your proposals.

7. Describe the ideal teacher for deaf children.   State needed traits, required preparation, and experience.

8. Do you consider that the teacher of the deaf has much opportunity for service?   Explain how.

9. Describe in some detail the work being done for the deaf in two or more cities other than those described in the text.

10. What do you consider the 10 most important things that should be true of the state school for the deaf in your own state?   Why would you make each of these demands?

Selected Bibliography

BRUNER, FRANK G.   *Report of the Director of Special Schools for the School Year 1922–23*, pp. 71–92.   Board of Education, Chicago, 1924.

A description of the educational program of the public schools of Chicago for the deaf.

COWDERY, KATE LOUISE.   *The Legal Status of the Education of Blind and Deaf Children in the Forty-eight States.*   Unpublished Master's thesis, Ohio State University, Columbus, 1927.   85 pp.

A study of the school codes of the 48 states relative to the education of the deaf; cites specific provisions made for education of deaf, age requirements and financial support given to local districts.

FUSFELD, IRVING S., and others.   "The Survey of Schools for the Deaf," *American Annals of the Deaf* (March, 1926), Vol. 71, pp. 97–135; (September, 1926), Vol. 71, pp. 284–348; (May, 1928), Vol. 73, pp. 273–299.

A study of residential schools for the deaf, covering management, financial support, pupils, parents, teachers, curriculum, methods of instruction, records, and occupations of graduates.

Handicapped and Underprivileged Children.   A special report submitted with *The Thirty-sixth Annual Report of the Superintendent of Schools*, pp. 225–238. Board of Education, New York City, 1934.

A discussion of the problems of the deaf child, the aims of the school, the city-wide program of educating the deaf, the training of teachers, and the results secured.

PHILLIPS, FRANK M.   "Schools for the Deaf," *U.S. Bureau of Education Bulletin* 52, 1923.   29 pp.   *U.S. Bureau of Education Bulletin* 8, 1928.   17 pp.

Statistics showing schools in the United States, their enrollments, receipts, and costs.

School for the Deaf, Monograph 8, Part II.   Board of Education, Newark, N.J., 1921.   43 pp.

Describes Newark's public school program for the deaf, outlines in some detail the course of study and discusses at some length the problems of speech reading and speech teaching.

The Special Schools and Curriculum Centers, pp. 52–61.   Board of Education, Cleveland, Ohio, 1931.

A description of the history and work of the Alexander Graham Bell School for the Deaf, one of Cleveland's public schools.

White House Conference.   *Special Education: The Handicapped and the Gifted*, pp. 277–346.   The Century Co., New York, 1931.

Reports number of deaf, methods of discovering them, and educational programs arranged for them.

CHAPTER XIX

THE CHALLENGE PRESENTED BY THE DEAF CHILD

The presentation of facts is the most effective way of focusing public attention upon an important problem. Such a presentation implies sincerity and honesty of purpose and constitutes a great challenge to those who are concerned with solving the problem. The problem of caring for and educating deaf children is no exception to this rule. The facts presented in the two preceding chapters concerning the deaf set forth fully the challenge. We have seen what can be done for them; we know how socially helpless they are when their education is ignored.

Three other problems will have to be discussed before the benefits derived from educating the deaf can be fully realized. We must realize (1) the size of the problem, (2) the reason why we have the deaf, and (3) the need for developing a program that will reduce the number of deaf children to the minimum.

1. HOW MANY DEAF CHILDREN HAVE WE?

The White House Conference estimated,[1] upon the basis of U.S. census reports, that there are 48 deaf persons in the United States in every 100,000 of the population; this means that about one person in 2,000 of our population is deaf. It estimated that over 37 per cent of these deaf are under twenty years of age. These estimates, the conference recognizes, are probably too low.

Using these estimates as a basis and using 130,000,000 as the total population of the United States, there are 23,088 youths under twenty who are deaf. Whether this represents only half of the actual number or approximates it somewhat closely, is not known. Approximately 18,212 youths are being educated in public, state, or private schools. There remain, under even the minimum estimate, about 5,000 who are ignored. Since failure to educate the deaf makes them entirely dependent upon society or relatives, the significance of educating these 5,000 becomes more apparent.

[1] White House Conference, *Special Education: The Handicapped and the Gifted*, pp. 279–282. The Century Co., New York, 1931.

2. CAUSES OF DEAFNESS

If deafness is to be prevented, we must know its causes; and prevention is most important. The education of a deaf child is very difficult; such remedial work is costly; at best, the youth finds it impossible to achieve as he might have done had his hearing been retained. Preventive measures, therefore, become the real challenge to one who is interested in a program for helping the deaf.

A New York City Study.—New York City, in reporting the causes of deafness for 326 pupils in special classes, says that 140, or 42.9 per cent, of the entire group were congenitally deaf. Table XV shows the

TABLE XV.—CAUSES OF DEAFNESS OF CHILDREN IN NEW YORK CITY

Causes	Number of children	Causes	Number of children
Congenital	140	Accidents	5
Spinal meningitis	45	Whooping cough	5
Measles	30	Typhoid fever	3
Catarrh	20	Prenatal troubles	3
Scarlet fever	17	Marasmus	2
Abscesses	12	Influenza	2
Convulsions	9	Brain fever	1
Diphtheria	7	Rheumatism	1
Paralysis	6	Malformation of ears	1
Pneumonia	6	Unknown	6
Mastoiditis	5	Total	326

distribution of the enrollment according to cause. Diseases that have high fevers are predominant. Children's diseases such as measles and scarlet fever are significant. Catarrh caused 6.1 per cent of these cases of deafness.

A Detroit Study.—On the other hand, Detroit officials report that a survey that they conducted "showed that seventy-six per cent of the pupils became deaf from preventable diseases."[1] These diseases, they say, were measles, scarlet fever, whooping cough, and other children's maladies; and enlarged adenoid tissue and tonsils added their toll to the number of persons having defective hearing.

Best's Report.—Best[2] says that approximately one-third of the deaf are congenital cases. The remaining cases of deafness are due to

[1] *Special Education*, pp. 22–23, Board of Education, Detroit, Mich., 1925.

[2] HARRY BEST, *The Deaf*, p. 41, The Thomas Y. Crowell Company, New York, 1914.

disease or accident, disease accounting for the vast majority of this group. The chief diseases that cause deafness, Best says, are scarlet fever, meningitis, brain fever, catarrh, disease of the middle ear, measles, typhoid fever, colds, malarial fever, influenza, diphtheria, pneumonia, whooping cough, and grippe, in about the order named. These diseases account for over 40 per cent of the deafness.

According to Best,[1] in children under two years of age, meningitis, scarlet fever, disease of the middle ear, brain fever, and measles are the chief diseases causing deafness. From two to five years, scarlet fever and meningitis lead; from five to ten, scarlet fever alone heads the list by far; from ten to fifteen, meningitis, scarlet fever, and brain fever followed by catarrh cause most deafness; catarrh and meningitis take the lead from fifteen to twenty; catarrh, colds, and typhoid fever are chief causes from twenty to forty; and after forty, catarrh is the leading cause.

3. PREVENTION OF DEAFNESS

Although the problem of deafness is not so great numerically as that of other types of handicapped children, it is perhaps more serious and more tragic. Even mental deficiency is less embarrassing to the child, since he lacks the mentality to be fully conscious of his loss. It is, therefore, important that deafness be reduced to the minimum.

Education of Parents.—The analysis of causes pointed clearly to the necessity of educating parents concerning the aftereffects of childhood diseases. Measles and whooping cough have generally been considered to be necessary ills of childhood. Their very frequency has tended to cause parents to minimize their effects. Parents should know the dangers to hearing that accompany lack of care in the case of all children's diseases. The physician should not have to distribute this information; many parents tend to discredit his word, since they think he is interested in creating a greater demand for his services.

Because the schools are vitally affected by an increase in deafness, they might well assume the responsibility for developing an educational program regarding this matter. Through the parent-teacher associations, the press, instruction in health classes, and a program of widely advertised lectures, the school system within a relatively short period might hope to educate parents to the need of exercising unusual care with regard to the hearing of their children.

Reporting Illnesses.—Laws in various states require that contagious diseases be reported to the health authorities. There is not

[1] *Ibid.*, p. 18.

yet an enlightened public opinion regarding the necessity of such reporting. Negligence respecting the enforcement of these provisions is not wholly a matter of lay ignorance; until state and local boards of health are adequately staffed, so as to make the fullest possible use of the reports, a great amount of prevention resulting from these efforts cannot be expected.

School Examination.—Health departments of the public schools should be so staffed that yearly physical examinations could be made of all children, and children with hearing defects could be given the necessary attention for preventing further deterioration, even if complete hearing could not be restored. In the past, the operation of such a plan has failed to follow up with personal attention the needs of individual cases. The need for such examinations and follow-ups is great during these days of posteconomic depression. Ways and means should be found for making such services available.

Prevention of Disease.—The diseases that cause deafness are largely preventable; vaccines and serums are fairly effective, if used properly. Any educational program should emphasize these facts and should encourage parents to see a competent physician the moment the first symptoms of disease appear. Some diseases can be guarded against even before that stage is reached. The necessary steps should be known and taken in all such cases. The development of further preventive measures will, of course, have to await further research upon the part of the medical profession.

Prevent Deafness.—Even after a disease has been contracted or primary ear troubles have got under way, deafness may be prevented. "It has been estimated that three-fourths of deafness from primary ear diseases, and one-half from infectious diseases, is preventable."[1] Immediate attention is the prime requirement in all cases where the ear shows any indication of being affected.

Reduce Birth Rate of Congenitally Deaf.—About one-third of all deafness is congenital; Best says that nearly half of these cases are born in families that have no known deafness. "The liability of deaf offspring depends in the greatest degree upon the presence or absence in the parents, deaf or hearing, of deaf relatives."[2] It is not true that all children of the congenitally deaf will be born deaf. However, if there are deaf relatives, there is likely to be a greater proportion of the children who will be deaf. If both parents have deaf relatives and are congenitally deaf, the likelihood of deaf children is still greater.

[1] *Volta Review*, Vol. 10, pp. 251, 348.

[2] HARRY BEST, *The Deaf*, p. 61, The Thomas Y. Crowell Company, New York, 1914.

If deafness is to be reduced, it is certain that measures for the control of propagation are needed.[1]

4. STATE PROGRAM FOR EDUCATING THE DEAF

Any legislation passed should make it compulsory that all deaf within the state be educated; it should also provide the necessary staff to enforce such a requirement.

State Supervision.—The staff needed to supervise the education of the deaf within a given state will depend entirely upon the problem within that state. In some states the official responsible for the education of other types of handicapped children can adequately care for them. In other states an official known as the director or supervisor of the education of the deaf will be needed.

It will be the duty of this official and his staff to press upon the legislature and the governor the educational needs of the deaf and to secure the passage of such laws as are necessary to provide them with the needed education. The legislature should keep up a continuous census of all children deaf from their birth; it should arrange for a reporting of all children who have physical ailments at birth, or later, that tend to cause deafness. Legislation should be passed permitting two or more districts to unite in establishing a class or school for educating the deaf. Districts should be encouraged to do this by means of liberal state grants; these grants should be controlled so as to prevent a wasting of money and yet should allow freedom in developing the educational program.

The state office will co-operate with local authorities in the organization of schools and classes. It will be responsible for the establishment of the state census for the deaf. Upon the basis of this census, children in need of physical care can be aided in getting it more quickly, and children who are deaf can be entered in a special school at an early age. This state office will be responsible for organizing a publicity program, the object of which will be the prevention of deafness. Educational materials will be provided by the office and a systematic educational program outlined.

The State School.—Another duty of the state office will be that of giving general supervision and having general control over the state school for the deaf. Such a school should be maintained as a means of caring for those deaf children whose home conditions are so unsatisfactory that they can never make progress in school while remaining at home. Unsatisfactory conditions, it should be said parenthetically,

[1] See pp. 222–223.

should never mean merely poverty.   If no love exists in the home, if the children hate to stay at home, or if it houses prostitutes, then the state should provide a home that will make it possible for them to profit from the education that is being provided at such great expense. The state school is necessary also in order that isolated deaf children may be educated.   There are many such children who are inaccessible to special local schooling facilities.

The Local Program.—Many larger cities have already organized schools or classes for the deaf.   This should be continued until every city has definitely provided a satisfactory school program for them. The county district surrounding such a city should make arrangements to transport its deaf to the city school or class, if hard roads are available; if not, arrangements might be made for housing these children throughout the week.   They might go home each week end.   The state should provide the money to house these children comfortably. A county that has no large cities should either co-operate with near-by counties in establishing a union school or, if it has enough deaf children, establish a school of its own.   The local officials will co-operate with the state in putting on an educational program aimed at the prevention of deafness.

5. SUMMARY

Deafness is largely due to disease and accident, although much of it is congenital.   Children's diseases are the chief causes of deafness up to about fifteen years of age; from then on, catarrh becomes a greater and greater menace.   Prevention depends upon the education of parents concerning the dangers of children's diseases and what they themselves can do by way of prevention.   The schools, by maintaining a regular system of physical examinations and by keeping proper records of those examinations, can assist in the prevention of deafness.

State legislation is not extensive enough to make possible a very complete program of education for the deaf.   We need legislation governing the census, compulsory education of the deaf, and a better general program of state support.   We also need legislation that will make possible the maintenance of a program of prevention.

We need state supervision of local programs for the education for the deaf.   The state school will need to be maintained.   Local districts will need supervisory aid in developing classes and schools; adjacent districts should be encouraged to co-operate in organizing them.   These needs point most clearly to the challenge that the deaf children of any community present.

Problems and Questions for Discussion

1. Which of the problems faced in educating the deaf constitute the greatest challenge to school people? Why?

2. How many deaf children do we have in the United States? Find any data available in addition to those given in this book.

3. What are the causes of deafness? How do the causes suggested in this book compare with those reported by other writers? .

4. What would you propose as a program for preventing deafness? Describe how you would proceed to administer such a program.

5. What relation has the registration of school children to the prevention of deafness? Explain.

6. What do you consider the one step which would be most effective in a program of prevention?

7. Outline what you consider the essential elements in a state legislative program dealing with deaf children.

8. Describe in some detail a complete state program for educating and caring for deaf children. Defend each proposal.

Selected Bibliography

BEST, HARRY. *The Deaf*, pp. 15–52. The Thomas Y. Crowell Company, New York, 1914.

Deals with causes of deafness.

White House Conference. *Special Education: The Handicapped and the Gifted*, pp. 277–346. The Century Co., New York, 1931.

Has data on the number of deaf, describes educational provisions and state laws.

CHAPTER XX

THE CARE AND EDUCATION OF HARD-OF-HEARING CHILDREN

The most serious problems are too frequently ignored. This is not deliberate but is the result of ignorance. How serious do most parents consider earache, running ears, imperfect speech, or the habitual request to repeat what has been said? Yet these are indicators, danger signals, that point to a loss of hearing. How many parents are greatly concerned by even an observable loss of hearing, as long as the child can hear by giving close attention? Parents, teachers, and youths need to realize that, at the first indication of ear trouble, the one so afflicted should immediately have the advice and care of a competent ear doctor. Society ought to make generous provisions for the early detection of all hearing defects; those discovered should be cared for immediately, either at the expense of the individual or at the expense of the state.

1. DEFINITION

For the average person, the term "hard of hearing" refers to those who hear with difficulty. Professionally speaking, however, there are included among the hard of hearing those who have completely lost their hearing after having learned speech. Sometimes the latter group is referred to as the deafened, but the recent tendency is to call them hard of hearing. This terminology is based upon the method of instruction recommended for the education of these groups. The hard of hearing do not need speech development; they need only speech reading and speech education, in addition to the regular curriculum. They have learned to speak and need only that training which will make it possible for them to understand more readily what others say to them and to retain the speech they already have.

2. GUIDING PRINCIPLES

1. Since most of the children in this group have partial hearing, and since the causes producing the partial deafness may lead to a total loss of hearing, all hard-of-hearing children should be discovered at as early an age as possible.

270

2. Since they have learned to speak, have heard the human voice, and have all the appreciation of speech that comes to the hearing child from hearing the speech of his fellows, the only special aid that such children need is instruction to enable them to read the speech of others by means of lip movements and facial expressions, to perfect their own speech, and to retain a normal voice quality.

3. Since these children are normal mentally, their schooling should be kept normal; they should attend regular classes and have continuous contact with hearing children. To segregate them with the deaf, where unnatural speech will be seen and heard and where school progress is slower, is to deal unfairly with them.

3. HISTORY

Recency.—The education of the hard of hearing is only now in the making. While the hard of hearing have always existed, only recently have attempts been made to provide them with an educational program that would at all meet their needs. Writing in 1927, Dr. Emily A. Pratt said, "We are in the pioneer days of lip-reading for school children who have a hearing defect."[1]

Beginnings.—A public school for hard-of-hearing children was organized in Berlin in 1902.[2] Norris reports that "Special lip-reading classes for them [the hard of hearing] became a reality in 1916."[3] Within the United States, Rochester, New York, and Lynn, Mass., hired trained teachers for such classes in that year. In 1921, Austria opened classes for the hard of hearing.[2]

In 1928, 12 cities in the United States were designated as three-point cities.[4] This meant that each of them (1) gave speech-reading instruction to hard-of-hearing children in addition to that given to deaf children, (2) used either the 3A or the 4A audiometer in testing the hearing of school children, and (3) used all clinics available for remedial work on the ears. These cities are Baltimore, Md.; Boston, Mass.; Detroit, Mich.; Fall River, Mass.; Rochester, N.Y.; San Francisco, Calif.; Somerville, Mass.; Springfield, Mass.; St. Louis, Mo.; Syracuse, N.Y.; Toledo, Ohio; and Washington, D.C. The first 10 were the original three-point cities.

Present Status.—The American Federation of Organizations for the Hard of Hearing reported in 1930[5] that in January of that year

[1] *Volta Review* (October, 1927), Vol. 29, p. 560.

[2] *The Hard-of-hearing Child*, p. 14, *U.S. Bureau of Education*, School Health Series, 13, Washington, D.C., 1927.

[3] *Volta Review* (October, 1932), Vol. 34, p. 517.

[4] *Volta Review* (November, 1928), Vol. 30, p. 708.

[5] *U.S. Office of Education Bulletin* 7, p. 32, Washington, D.C., 1930.

there were 44 cities in the United States which had employed special teachers as a part of the public school system to give speech reading to hard-of-hearing children. The 44 cities represented 23 states and the District of Columbia. A year later, the same federation reported 83 cities that had organized classes for these children; 26 states and the District of Columbia were represented. Classes had been organized in 15 cities in Wisconsin, 11 in Massachusetts, 8 in New York, 6 in Ohio, and 5 in California. Much of the increase represented newly organized classes for the hard of hearing.

Surveys Showing Need.—A committee of the National Education Association reported in 1902 a study of 57,072 pupils in seven cities, which showed that 3.6 per cent had defects in hearing. In 1908 a report by Gulich and Ayres concluded that 5 to 6 per cent of all children were defective in hearing. In 1926 Fowler and Fletcher by a sampling of a number of cities estimated that there were 3,000,000 hard of hearing in the United States. Further investigations led Fowler to report 2 years later that the first estimate was "approximately correct." The latter figures were reported by the White House Conference in 1931.

4. METHODS OF EDUCATING THE HARD OF HEARING

Until recent years, hard-of-hearing children were either continued in regular classes until the hearing defect became so great that they could no longer profit, or they were sent to a school for the deaf. We realize now that such procedures failed to meet the needs of these children. The hearing defect, though not great, resulted in failure to master the work of the regular grades when the child was so retained; this made for wasted effort, wasted time, and discouragement.

When sent to a school for the deaf, the hard of hearing suffered other handicaps. Most of these pupils still had some hearing. They had already developed satisfactory, or even excellent, speech. The school for the deaf tended to break down these good speech habits because so much of the speech heard at the school was not normal.

The Special Teacher.—A common procedure is to have a teacher, trained in speech reading, go from school to school; at each school she meets with hard-of-hearing pupils once or twice per week for sessions of a half hour to one hour. Speech reading is taught; speech education[1] must also be provided if these children are to retain their good speech. The special teacher contacts the regular teachers and helps them to realize some of the difficulties that their hard-of-hearing pupils have in mastering their studies. Misunderstandings are reduced, and

[1] For definition, see p. 279.

regular teachers come to appreciate much more the abilities of these handicapped children.

The Combined School.—Another method is to organize a center to which these children come. They usually travel by streetcar; the younger children are accompanied by older pupils. They and their escorts attend the regular classes of this school. The school also enrolls the hearing children of the district. There is a teacher of speech reading who is a permanent member of the school staff; she meets with small, classified groups of the hard of hearing throughout the day. Her entire time is spent at the one school.

The Special Center.—The hard-of-hearing children are enrolled in their own home-school districts. The special teacher stays at a given central school. At stated intervals the hard-of-hearing children from other schools come to this center for training in speech reading.

The Special Class.—The above methods demand of the special teacher instruction in speech reading and possibly instruction in speech education. Another method is to organize a special class in which the teacher also instructs in all the school subjects. The special room is the home room and classroom for the hard of hearing; there may be one or more such classes within a grade school which otherwise has none but normal hearing children. If hearing improves, or if speech reading is well mastered, and if speech remains normal, the pupils are allowed to return to the regular classes.

The Special School.—One city assembles its hard-of-hearing children in a separate school. It argues for the method by saying that it is attempting to relieve all regular teachers of children who are handicapped. These children are so hard of hearing that they cannot complete the work of one grade in a year's time. If continued in regular schools, they fail; but if sent to a special school, they can be taught so as to reduce failure to a minimum. In this school there are no normal hearing children; a few pupils may be deaf, but most of them are just hard of hearing.

A Recommendation.—Which of the above methods is used will depend upon several factors. Hays[1] suggests that the method might depend upon the degree of hearing. He groups the hard of hearing as (1) mildly deafened, (2) moderately deafened, (3) very deafened, and (4) hopelessly deafened.

The mildly deafened child, he says, "should be kept in the same classroom with the other children." He recommends a front seat

---

[1] "The Deaf Child in the Elementary Schools; The Economic and Educational Aspects," pp. 207–216, *Proceedings of the Ohio State Educational Conference*, Columbus, 1927.

and a teacher who remembers that such children are sensitive and easily discouraged. The moderately deafened, he says, will not succeed in the regular classroom unless special aid is given; this includes medical treatment and lip reading.

The very deafened children, he says, should be sent to a special class taught by a specially prepared teacher. These pupils should be encouraged to engage in all activities pursued by children in regular classes. The home should encourage the child to feel his own importance and thus reduce to a minimum the inferiority complexes so often developed in the hard of hearing. The hopelessly deafened, he says, should be sent to a special school for the deaf, where speech and speech reading can be taught; he believes that the school "should be a part of the general school system."

Another writer[1] has classified the hard of hearing into three groups. The "slightly hard of hearing" will have a hearing loss of from 10 to 25 per cent; they should stay in regular classes and be seated in the front of the room. A teacher should always know that hard-of-hearing children are enrolled and should become familiar with the rules[2] that should govern her procedure. The "moderately hard of hearing" have a hearing loss of from 25 to 50 per cent; these children will remain in the regular school but will attend a speech-reading class. The "definitely hard of hearing" are those with a hearing loss of 50 to 75 per cent; these children should be placed in a special school or class where they would receive all their instruction from a special teacher.

5. DISCOVERY OF THE HARD OF HEARING

One reason for the delay in organizing special schoolwork for the hard of hearing has been the inadequacy of methods of discovering them. A slight hearing defect is not obvious. In order that no child shall be neglected, all children should have their hearing tested; but a program of this kind is so huge that it was physically impossible of being accomplished by older methods.

The Watch Tick.—One of these methods—the watch-tick test—utilizes simple equipment. An Ingersoll watch is used. The normal hearing person can hear its tick at 48 inches. Only one child is tested at a time, and an experienced tester is needed. One ear is tested at a time; the child holds his finger in one ear while the other is being tested. The watch is placed at the child's ear and is slowly withdrawn until

---

[1] G. DE LA BAT, "The Hard of Hearing School Child," *Volta Review* (April, 1932), Vol. 34, p. 163.

[2] See p. 279.

he ceases to hear it. If he ceases to hear it at 24 inches, his hearing is recorded as 24-48. A reverse procedure is then followed. The two scores are averaged to secure the child's degree of hearing.

There are three difficulties. (1) The tester is never sure that the child actually ceases to hear or begins to hear at the instant he gives his report. It demands skill and ingenuity upon the part of the tester to eliminate this error. (2) Since we are interested in the child's ability to hear speech, it is doubtful that a measure of this ability is secured from the watch-tick test. (3) Only about 15 children can be tested in an hour; this makes impossible the testing of entire school populations.

The Whisper.—Another, older, method is the use of the whisper. A low voice is not permitted; the sound must be a whisper. This method requires an experienced tester. The whisper should be made after "emptying the lungs of all normal air and then whispering distinctly with the residual air." Only one child can be tested at a time. The tester is 20 feet from the child, who stands with his back to the tester. The child is to repeat what is said. If he does not, the tester gradually comes closer until the child does repeat the words whispered. If what is said can be repeated at 15 feet, the rating is 15–20.

The test has several difficulties. (1) It is not definitely standardized; some claim that those of normal hearing can hear a whisper at 30 feet. (2) Voices differ, and this prevents satisfactory standardization. (3) Since only 15 can be tested in one hour, it is practically impossible to test all children. One city recently tested 1,000 children, but it took the doctor 6 weeks, working five mornings each week, to do the job.

The 4A Audiometer.—This machine is sometimes called a phono-audiometer; it is a combination phonograph and telephone. The portable case is the phonograph, and attached to this are telephone receivers—one for each of the 40 children to be tested. One phonograph record produces a woman's voice that is repeating numbers consisting of three digits; her voice grows less distinct with each number until the number spoken can be heard by only those who have normal hearing or better. This record is repeated for each ear. Another record producing a man's voice that repeats numbers consisting of three digits is then used for each ear.

Each child is given a printed sheet and a pencil; the sheet provides a column for each of the four series of numbers. Children can be tested at the rate of 100 to 150 per hour. Some claim that the tester need not be experienced; if he reads the directions carefully, it is claimed, he can operate the machine easily and accurately. The machine is said to be foolproof and seldom needs repairing. This instrument can be used for all children above the grade 2; children of that grade and below require individual testing.

This method of testing was in use as early as 1926. It eliminates many variables that made it impossible to standardize other tests. It detects hearing defects long before such defects are generally noticeable and thus makes possible immediate preventive work. The rapidity of testing is so great as to encourage the belief that we may soon hope to have the hearing of all school children tested at fairly frequent intervals.

The 4B Audiometer.—This machine is a newer development of the phono-audiometer. It is a phonograph with telephonic apparatus added. It tests 40 persons simultaneously. The 40 headsets come in sets of 10. Only one set is a part of the 4B equipment; the other 3 sets must be purchased separately. It is claimed that 500 pupils can easily be tested in one day.

Two records are supplied, each double-faced. One is used for pupils of grade 5 and above; it produces eight series of three-digit numbers. Four series appear on each side of the record; two of the four are in a woman's voice and two are in a man's voice. Each series of numbers is arranged so that their intensity becomes less and less by small steps. The second record duplicates the first, except that it is composed of two-digit numbers and is used for children of grades 2A to 4A inclusive.

The 3A Audiometer.—This is an electrical machine in which an electrical current is generated and sent through electrical resistances so regulated by a dial that varying tones, from a very high pitch to a very low pitch, may be produced. These tones may also be varied in intensity by another dial. The examiner can detect whether or not an individual is hard of hearing at any point in the pitch range.

In order to test the child, the tester may tell him to say "now" every time the sound is heard. Another method is to have a push button attached to a light bulb. The light flashes when the button is pushed. The child is then seated where he cannot see the audiometer and is told to press the button whenever and as long as he hears the sound. The 3A was used as early as 1926. This instrument is especially valuable for making retests and for use in grades 1 and 2.

The 2A Audiometer.—This instrument is likewise individual and duplicates the essential features of the 3A. It has come into use in recent years.

The 6A Audiometer.—The 6A audiometer replaces the 2A. It is a very recent development. The claim is made that it provides all the good features of the 2A and, in addition, has the following advantages: (1) testing is possible at any frequency from 100 to 10,000 cycles per second; (2) testing of bone conduction is made possible; (3) speed tests can be made and this is important if electrical hearing aids need to be used; (4) a record of hearing acuity by air conduction and by bone conduction is provided; (5) it is so accurate that following tests show gain or loss in hearing acuity; (6) it is speedy and accurate and so is of value in legal cases; (7) even great hearing losses may be measured; (8) the machine is very easily operated; (9) the instrument is smaller and lighter in weight than the 2A; (10) it is operated by ordinary AC or DC currents.

The machine is enclosed in a walnut case; it is 8 by 15 by 8 inches in size and weighs only 23 pounds. The claim is made that, with this instrument, the otologist for the first time is able to measure accurately bone conduction; the attachment used for this purpose is the 100A audiometer masking attachment.

Other Equipment.—Other variations of the original 4A and 3A audiometers are in use. Some of the variations of the 3A do group work, instead of individual testing. In general, however, there are the two procedures. One uses the human voice; the other uses electrical vibration.

6. IMPORTANCE OF DISCOVERY

The need for developing an adequate program for discovering hard-of-hearing children can hardly be overemphasized. Norris says, "It is estimated that 80 per cent of the deafness of late life could have been cured if it had been taken in time."[1] She reports that in the Rochester clinics such foreign bodies as "beads, sticks of wood, glass tubing, macaroni, beans, wheat, peanuts, rice, oats, grape seeds, paper and cotton wads, flies both dead and alive, spiders, and stones" have been taken from children's ears. These conditions, if continued, are directly the cause of much deafness.

Such a program of discovery will reduce greatly the amount of failure in the regular schools. Many failing pupils are not backward mentally; they simply do not hear what is said in the classroom. Norris says that, while all repeaters are not deaf, "three and a half times as many hard-of-hearing children repeat as other children."[2]

There is another angle to this problem which is often ignored; it has to do with the psychology of the hard of hearing. The child is sensitive; he tries to compensate for his deficiency in hearing; he has

[1] *Volta Review* (September, 1926), Vol. 28, pp. 452–458.
[2] *Ibid.*, p. 454.

ability, yet cannot respond as other children do because of his lack of complete hearing; in order to gain attention, he may resort to anti-social acts of such a character that he is classed with the socially handicapped. Others meekly submit to the school regime, continue to fail, quit school early with no preparation for holding a position, often lose the poorly paid jobs that come their way, and finally, unable to maintain themselves, become a dead weight economically upon society.

7. PROBLEMS INVOLVED IN EDUCATING THESE CHILDREN

Discovery is one of the biggest problems in the whole program of educating the hard of hearing. The methods of discovery just discussed, however, are only a part of the solution of the complete problem.

Determining the Need.—There is at present a great variation in reports showing the percentage of school children who are hard of hearing. On account of these enormous variations, some school men are inclined to view rather skeptically recent reports which show that large percentages of children are hard of hearing. They openly insist that the figures must be padded.

These variations are due to three factors. Norris states that the type of home accounts for much of the variation. Her data show that one school, in a foreign section where parents were unable to provide medical care, had 25 per cent of its children classed as hard of hearing; another school in the same city where the people were equally divided between foreign and middle-class American had 15 per cent; another school made up entirely of middle-class Americans had 10 per cent; and a private school made up of children from wealthy homes had less than 1 per cent. Unquestionably, the financial and social status of the home is a factor in this variation.

The method of determining who have ear defects is a second factor. The older surveys and recent surveys using the older methods usually report relatively low percentages. Recent surveys in which the audiometer was used have generally reported the higher percentages. This is due to the greater reliability and to the greater sensitivity of this test; any slight defect will be noted and noted regularly. A third factor is the degree of defect that must exist before a child is reported as hard of hearing. If norms for determining who are hard of hearing and if a standardized implement for determining hearing defects can be agreed upon, then we may expect to eliminate two of the three elements that make for the present enormous variation in per cent of hard of hearing reported.

Speech Reading.—Since children who are deficient in hearing need aid if they are to understand satisfactorily all that is said to them in the classroom, they must be taught to read the speech of others. In order to do this, they must develop definite skills. This can best be accomplished through special instruction by a person skilled in speech reading. Such instruction takes time and is usually arranged for by omitting from the regular curricula music, auditorium work, or some other specialty. Selection of subjects to be omitted should be based upon the child's lack of interest or ability.

Speech Education.—There seems to be considerable evidence that points to a definite loss of perfect speech upon the part of the hard of hearing unless they receive help in maintaining their speech. Obviously, the speech development demanded by the deaf is wholly unnecessary, but aid needed in maintaining present speech and in improving it, which is here called speech education, is demanded.

Work of the Regular Teacher.—Every regular teacher should continually be on the lookout for children who have hearing defects. If periodic ear examinations are not held, these defects may be discovered only through her efforts. Berry[1] calls attention to signs of defective hearing that teachers should not ignore. They are earache complaints, running ears, stupid expression, imperfect speech, poor spelling, frequent asking that questions be repeated, one side of head turned toward the speaker, and a way of looking "at the speaker with a peculiar intentness."

When the teacher discovers such children, she should insist upon an ear examination. She might try out the watch-tick test. Children with defects should be given front seats; the side of the room should depend upon which ear has the greatest defect. The teacher in making remarks that are intended to be understood by such a child should stand where the best light will fall upon her face. These teacher habits can be made more or less automatic, so that they will not interfere with her regular work.

The teacher must constantly remember that the ordinary classroom makes many problems for the hard-of-hearing child. If the speech reading that the child is learning is to be used, the regular teacher must so seat him during recitation that he can watch the lips of the children as they recite, as well as watch the lips of the teacher. Further practice in speech reading may be had if the parents are instructed to speak slowly and distinctly; they, too, should face the child when speaking to him, so that the movement of the lips can be seen.

[1] CHARLES SCOTT BERRY, *How the Teacher May Help the Exceptional Child*, p. 8, Ohio State University, Bureau of Special Education, Columbus.

Work of the Special Teacher.—In addition to giving instruction in speech reading and speech education, the special teacher should instruct the regular teaching staff with respect to the opportunities of helping the hard of hearing. Most regular teachers do not realize that there is much of a problem. The children seem normal; continuous colds, even earaches, do not seem so very unusual and are seldom related to a lack of hearing, which may be causing poor work. If the special teacher can help regular teachers to see that defective hearing is a real school problem and if she can then aid them in the development of a day-by-day procedure for detecting and for helping these hard-of-hearing children, she will have indeed earned her salary.

She can assist regular teachers in securing the physical care needed by these newly discovered hard-of-hearing children; she can also help them to educate the home with respect to ways in which it can help the child to develop speech-reading ability and maintain his present speech. The wholehearted co-operation of all these agencies will materially assist in the development of self-supporting, self-respecting individuals.

The Medical Problem.—Too much emphasis cannot be placed upon the need for medical services, if hard-of-hearing conditions are to be prevented and if children with slight losses are to retain what hearing they have. Regular periodic examinations of the hearing of all school children is important in such preventive work.

Although recent figures tend to show that 14 per cent, or 3,000,000, of our school children have hearing defects, one authority suggests that of this number only 2 per cent now need speech reading. All in the group, however, do need medical inspection and care if the remaining 12 per cent are to be kept from needing speech reading. Bock has rather clearly shown that a great percentage of our hard of hearing need only medical care and that, if this is provided, the need for special education will be materially reduced.

Hays[1] reports that in three years in New York City he and his associates treated over 500 children; this involved over 5,000 treatments. Of these children, 60 per cent were either cured or improved; the remainder were properly placed in school.

Costs.—Actual data are scarce. Where pupils attend regular classes and receive special instruction in speech reading, only a rough estimate may be made. If we assume an average class of eight pupils who meet twice a week for 1-hour sessions, if we assume a teacher

---

[1] HAROLD HAYS, "The Deaf Child in the Elementary Schools; The Economic and Educational Aspects," pp. 210–211, *Proceedings of the Ohio State Educational Conference*, Columbus, 1927.

can handle four such groups daily, and if the teacher receives $2000 a year, the per capita costs would be $25 per year, in addition to the regular costs of instruction.   If periods are reduced to a half hour each and the teacher thus handles 20 instead of 10 different groups each week, the costs will be only half as great.   To these costs must be added the cost of discovering, examining, and giving medical service to these children.

8. TEACHER PERSONNEL

A major problem in the education of the hard of hearing is to determine how much preparation and training the special teacher should have.   At present there is considerable disagreement.

Preparation.—The White House Conference says, "It is possible for teachers who are otherwise adequately prepared to receive sufficient training to teach lip reading to hard-of-hearing children in a six weeks' course of recognized standing, or a college extension course of eighty to one hundred hours."[1]   Berry, in emphasizing the need for teachers of the hard of hearing, says that we do not need as teachers experts trained to teach the deaf.   "Our need," he says, "is for an intelligent sympathetic woman, qualified as a grade teacher, who can take a few months of specialized training in just the lip-reading side of the work."[2]

Others insist that too much emphasis is being placed upon the scanty preparation necessary for becoming speech-reading teachers. They point out that many children who need speech reading are discouraged and quit because they have had inefficient instruction and that the work has been retarded many years in some communities because it has been initiated by unqualified instructors.   Macnutt says, "Speech-reading, as much as any other art, needs special training in *practical work* as well as in theory, more, by far, than can be acquired only from a course of lectures."[3]

Although all would be in sympathy with higher requirements, the fact must be faced that there are relatively few teachers at present and that there are great numbers of children needing this instruction; a further fact to be met is that experienced and well-qualified teachers often cannot or will not spend a half year or more in study, just for the

[1] White House Conference, *Special Education: The Handicapped and the Gifted,* p. 307, The Century Co., New York, 1931.

[2] GORDON BERRY, "Problems of the Hard of Hearing," *The Volta Review* (March, 1928), Vol. 30, p. 131.

[3] ENA G. MACNUTT, "The Importance of the Qualified Teacher," *The Volta Review* (October, 1927), Vol. 29, p. 584.

sake of teaching hard-of-hearing children.   Many such well-qualified teachers might, however, take night or extension courses in order to prepare to teach them.   At present, serious difficulties are involved in demanding all the preparation that might well be required of special teachers for the hard of hearing.

Experience.—Most recommendations insist upon a year or more of successful experience as a teacher of normal children.   Ideally, it is perhaps not too much to suggest that the minimum experience ought to consist of 3 years of successful teaching in regular school classes and 1 year of supervised teaching of the hard of hearing. This year of apprenticeship could be done by the candidate as a temporary transfer from her regular school position.   If she made good, the transfer would be made permanent; if not, she could return to regular schoolwork where she had already made good.   Her work with the hard of hearing for the first year would be looked upon not as the work of an expert but as that of an apprentice.   In case she failed, her poor work would not reflect upon the whole program for the hard of hearing but upon her ability to give this unique instructional service.

9. WORK IN VARIOUS CITIES

Cincinnati.—In September, 1929, an itinerant lip-reading teacher was added to the school staff in Cincinnati; it was found that many pupils who were quite hard of hearing could, by means of lip reading and proper seating in their schoolrooms, overcome their handicap and compete with children of normal hearing.   Cincinnati defines the proper seating for a hard-of-hearing child as "the second seat in the section next to the window."   This enables him to turn in his desk and watch the faces of his fellow pupils, as well as his teacher's face. Being in the section next to the window, he does not face the light.

Since 1929, approximately 130 hard-of-hearing children have been cared for each year.   During this period, testing of the hearing children by means of the 4A audiometer has been carried on extensively throughout the system.   Children who are in need of medical attention for hearing conditions have been taken care of at the hearing clinic or by private otologists.   Cincinnati reports, "In the fall of 1934 the Cincinnati Telephone Game for testing the hearing of young children began to be developed as there had been no plan previously for testing Kindergarten, First and Second Grade children by means of 4A audiometer, as they were too young to write the numbers."   During 1936–37, there were from 200 to 300 children in the kindergarten, and in grades 1 and 2 tested every week.

Baltimore.—An aim of the division of special education in Baltimore is "to discovery *every* child in the public schools who has defective hearing." Special classes for those who are seriously hard of hearing and instruction in lip reading for those in regular schools who need it are provided. Children in the public schools who need these services are discovered by the 4A audiometer. Such testing began in 1928–29.

Teachers of lip reading give lessons twice per week for half-hour periods. In 1932–33 each teacher was "carrying a heavy schedule of 12 schools for the white and 10 for the colored. The groups are particularly large." The special classes began to operate in 1929–30; they serve the seriously hard of hearing. If children of the regular schools who take lip-reading lessons fail to make good, they are transferred to a special class for the hard of hearing.

Los Angeles.—The 1931 report showed that in Los Angeles a 4A audiometer was being used and that a program was under way to test the hearing of all public school pupils. During the year 1929–30, 3,120 pupils in 13 elementary schools and 1,769 pupils in 5 junior and senior high schools were tested. Medical tests followed in 915 cases. In 1935–36, 6,846 were tested. In addition, parents, principals, teachers, physicians, and nurses are required to report all hard-of-hearing cases.

In one hard-of-hearing group the hearing defect is so great that they attend the school for the deaf; when they reach junior high school, they may return to their home districts or attend the James A. Foshay Junior High School, which provides special help for them. Those hard of hearing whose defect is not so great stay in their home schools and are given speech-reading lessons twice each week by itinerant teachers.

10. REASONS FOR DEFECTIVE HEARING

The illnesses and weaknesses that result in deafness are also causes of hard-of-hearing conditions. A slight loss of hearing, moreover, is often the forerunner of complete loss, but this may frequently be prevented by finding children in the early stage and by eliminating the causative factors so that further loss is stayed, even though the hard-of-hearing conditions cannot be eliminated.

Bock reports that often when the ears of children are examined they are found to be filled with dirt so caked as to reduce hearing efficiency; they are also likely to be full of wax so hardened that hearing is temporarily affected. Earlier in this chapter[1] are listed the

[1] See p. 277.

numerous foreign bodies that are found in the ears of children who have had follow-up clinical examinations. Hard-of-hearing conditions resulting from the ordinary cold and from catarrh are fairly common when these diseases are long continued. It is obvious that definite losses in hearing may result from ailments that are so common as not to be taken seriously by the layman.

11. METHODS OF REDUCING THE PROBLEM[1]

Early Discovery.—Early discovery is important; if found at once, children who would otherwise have become school failures will be given a fair chance to succeed in their school-work. Such early discovery, in addition to ensuring the immediate removal of dirt, wax, and foreign particles from the ear, will serve to call the attention of the family and the school to the possible results of catarrhal conditions and the tendency to have colds for an indefinite period.

Education of Parents.—In many a home there is still the opinion that colds are unavoidable and necessary evils and that catarrhal conditions in given individuals are a part of their original constitutions. No great concern is felt about such conditions because they are accepted as a matter of course.

It is high time that parents realized, not only that such diseases are avoidable, but that they often result in physical defects that seriously handicap the child for life. The loss or partial loss of hearing is not the least of these possible handicaps. We know how effective natural sunshine is in the dissipation of colds. Children should get an abundance of sunlight. Doctors and clinics have lamps for giving sunlight treatments. If the children are dressed warmly, outdoor play on sunshiny days is far more healthful than play indoors in warm rooms.

Parents, further, should understand that a good general physical condition is essential to a reduction of colds. Late hours, irregular feeding, improper food, disturbed emotional conditions, and exposure are closely related to susceptibility to colds. It is the suspicion of the writer that emotional disturbances and their causes are quite generally ignored as factors affecting health. Every parent should understand these rather elemental truths.

Teachers Trained in Early Detection.—Each teacher should be trained to note hearing defects. Henry is inattentive. Why? Mary always turns one side of her head in my direction when talking to me. Why? Bill asks me to repeat so many questions. Why? Every teacher-training institution ought to include a required course in

---

[1] See pp. 265–267 on Prevention of Deafness. It should be reread at this point.

which some study would be devoted to this problem. This is particularly true for teachers in elementary schools. Such training would lead to the immediate examination of all cases of noticeable hearing defect. Reporting of this kind by teachers is needed even in cities where a regular yearly examination is made by means of the audiometer.

Regular Yearly Examinations.—Even where teachers are properly trained and where they report all observable cases, there will be many children with slight hearing deficiencies who give no outward indication of that condition. There ought to be instituted a method of detecting these very slight hearing defects; such early detecting will make even greater the likelihood of removing the causes of the defect.

Every school ought to have access to some one or more of the modern means of detecting hearing defects. The 4A audiometer is at present widely recommended. Undoubtedly the newer 4B audiometer should be given a trial. The importance of the yearly examination is emphatic if we are genuinely concerned about the prevention of hard-of-hearing conditions.

The Ear Clinic.—All these finding methods will, nevertheless, avail little unless some provision is made for the examination by competent ear specialists of all children who have hearing defects. The importance of this cannot be overemphasized.

Fowler says, "There is really no such thing as an 'ordinary cold.'"[1] Fowler's findings indicate that progressive deafness is often related to having continuous and successive colds. He says that even "Though the hearing appears to the family and the patient to recover its former acuity, the audiogram may show this is not so, but that the hearing is less than before the attack and progressively diminishes as the attacks of sinusitis persist or recur."[2]

He insists that such conditions in children may be not only arrested but cured. Arguing against promiscuous operation on the ears or noses of children, he says, "The aim of all treatment should be to restore the sinuses of the nose and ear to normal, and non-operative measures and careful management are always imperative, no matter what the surgical indications may be."[2] He further insists that careful examination and constant supervision of "remedial agents" can stop the disease and thus improve the child's hearing and general health.

12. A STATE PROGRAM

Supervision.—The state's chief function is one of supervision. This supervision, where programs are well developed, should be

[1] *The Volta Review* (November, 1928), Vol. 30, p. 655.
[2] *Ibid.*, p. 659.

independent of and separate from that given to the deaf. Those responsible for supervision in the two departments should co-operate fully, but the task of educating these two groups differs so widely that separate supervisory control should exist.

A second function is to secure the passage of appropriate legislation dealing with the hard of hearing. This, we have seen, is negligible. Provision should be made for the periodic measurement of the hearing of all school children. Local or traveling ear clinics should be provided; training in speech reading for all children with hearing defects should be made mandatory.

Another duty will be to assist in selling the program to local districts. Through local organizations, surveys will be made of the needs in various localities. The co-operation of all local groups interested in the hard of hearing will be secured and the state office will help them to get the needs of the hard of hearing before the community. This work will generally precede any attempt to secure the passage of state legislation. After legislation has been passed, the office will assist local school officials in organizing for (1) the measurement of hearing, (2) the medical examination of all with defective hearing, and (3) the establishment of special classes or schools.

The Local City Program.—Under state supervision the public schools will test annually the hearing of all pupils. Each school will have one member of its staff so trained that it can be responsible for its own testing program. The 4A or the 4B audiometer will be used. Every child with a 15 per cent loss or greater will be examined by an otologist; all children whom the otologist selects for speech reading will be placed in a special class.

The Local Rural Program.—The rural school districts of a county within which a city is located will co-operate with the city in its testing program; arrangements will be made so that all 15 per cent loss cases can be given ear examinations at the city clinic. Pupils needing the assistance given by classes for the hard of hearing will arrange to attend the city classes.

If the pupils reside in counties that have no cities, a special teacher will travel from school to school giving instruction in speech reading.

13. SUMMARY

The fact that hard-of-hearing people appear normal is undoubtedly the reason why so little concern is shown about them. Technically, the hard of hearing include not only people with partial hearing but persons who have lost all hearing since learning speech. The first class for hard-of-hearing children seems to have been organized in

Berlin in 1902; the first class in America was organized in 1916. In 1931 there were 83 cities in the United States that had organized such classes.

The educational program for hard-of-hearing children differs from that for normal children chiefly in that speech reading and speech education are added to the curriculum. The hard-of-hearing child may have an itinerant teacher come to his building or he may go to the special teacher for speech reading and speech education. Depending upon the degree of hearing, pupils of the same system may find it advantageous to have two or more of these methods of instruction open to them.

Failure to discover the hard-of-hearing children in time may result in their deafness; it may mean school failure for many capable pupils; and it sometimes results in truancy and delinquency and in the development of permanent antisocial attitudes. The work of the special teacher is important if this program is to be effective and if it is to sell itself to parents and pupils. Where co-operative arrangements are developed, the work of the regular teacher may mean much to the success of the speech-reading program.

Many parents fail, even yet, to realize the close relationship between catarrhal conditions or long-continued colds and hard-of-hearing conditions. We take colds for granted. General good health is the best antidote for colds, while sunlight, natural or artificial, is the next best preventive.

Early discovery of hard-of-hearing conditions, careful medical diagnosis by expert otologists, and the teaching of speech reading and speech education are the three important procedures to be put into operation in any program for the care and education of the hard of hearing.

Problems and Questions for Discussion

1. Just how big and how serious is the problem of the hard-of-hearing child? Explain.

2. When is the child hard of hearing? Why is he so defined?

3. What principles do you think should govern us in caring for and educating the hard of hearing?

4. Which is the best method of educating the hard of hearing? Explain.

5. Describe means of discovering the hard of hearing. Outline a plan you would propose for doing the job.

6. Why is it important to discover all cases of even slight hearing defect?

7. Enumerate several major problems involved in educating hard-of-hearing children. How would you solve them?

8. Draft a state law that you would propose governing the care and education of hard-of-hearing children.

9. Why do children become hard of hearing? Outline a plan for preventing this condition.

Selected Bibliography

BERRY, GORDON. "Problems of the Hard of Hearing," *The Volta Review* (March, 1928), Vol. 30, pp. 127–136.

Discusses the development of the Federation for the Hard of Hearing, the nature of the hard-of-hearing child, what can be done for such, and the need for funds to develop the work.

DURFEE, MARION A. "Public School Teaching of Hard of Hearing Adults and Children," *The Volta Review* (October, 1927), Vol. 29, pp. 565–572.

A report of work for the hard of hearing at Fall River, Mass.; contains a brief discussion of various methods of dealing with this group.

FOWLER, EDMUND PRINCE. "Progressive Deafness: Means Now Available for Prevention and Cure," *The Volta Review* (November, 1928), Vol. 30, pp. 650–663.

A brief synopsis of a study of 100 consecutive cases of ear disease in children. He pleads for a clinic in every community, which will emphasize "the cure and alleviation of deafness and especially its prevention."

The Hard-of-hearing Child, U.S. Bureau of Education, School Health Studies 13. Washington, D.C., July, 1927. 14 pp.

A good discussion of various methods of detecting hearing defects and of treating them, as well as suggestions for educating the defective in speech.

HUMPHREY, J. H. "Hard of Hearing Children in the St. Louis Public Schools," *The Volta Review* (November, 1928), Vol. 30, pp. 644–646.

A description of work done for the hard of hearing in the St. Louis public schools. Use of audiometer showed many children to have a hearing loss who were not known to be hard of hearing.

IDE, GLADYS. "Hearing Defects and Their Treatment in the Philadelphia Public Schools," *The Volta Review* (September, 1926), Vol. 28, pp. 449–451.

A fairly complete description of what Philadelphia was doing for the hard of hearing in 1926.

MACNUTT, ENA G. "The Importance of the Qualified Teacher," *The Volta Review* (October, 1927), Vol. 29, pp. 582–586.

In addition to education and training, love of people, love of the work, a constructive attitude, and cheerfulness are characteristics of a good teacher, she concludes.

MADDEN, RICHARD. *The School Status of the Hard of Hearing Child*. Teachers College, Columbia University, New York, 1931. 64 pp.

Defines the hard-of-hearing child, describes methods of testing hearing, and reports upon the intelligence, achievement, and personality traits of hard-of-hearing children.

MCLEOD, BEATRICE. "Teachers' Problems with Exceptional Children; IV, Deaf and Hard-of-hearing Children," *U.S. Office of Education Pamphlet* 54. Washington, D.C., 1934. 29 pp.

Problems dealing with definition, prevention, discovery, educational provisions, medical care, advice to parents, and occupations are considered.

NEWHART, HORACE. "Efforts toward Prevention of Deafness in School Children," *The Volta Review* (September, 1926), Vol. 28, pp. 440–449.

A discussion of the problems involved and the newer methods used in testing the hearing of school children. Shows the cost of repeating on account of defective hearing.

NORRIS, ANNE C. "Committee on the Hard of Hearing Child," *The Volta Review* (November, 1928), Vol. 30, pp. 707–714.

A good report on the work of the committee on the hard of hearing; calls attention to the three-point cities, and discusses briefly the use of the 4A audiometer.

NORRIS, ANNE C. "Committee on the Hard of Hearing Child," *The Volta Review* (October, 1932), Vol. 34, pp. 517–521.

A brief history of the work of this committee, a report of a survey of 275 officials of schools for the deaf in the United States and Canada, and recommendations based upon this survey.

NORRIS, MRS. JAMES F. "Committee on the Survey of Hard of Hearing Children," *The Volta Review* (September, 1926), Vol. 28, pp. 451–459.

An account of the program being carried on for the hard of hearing by various cities. It also describes the use of the new audiometer for testing hearing.

PALEN, IMOGEN B. "The Grade Teacher and the Deafened Child," *The Volta Review* (September, 1926), Vol. 28, pp. 437–440.

Discusses the importance of regular grade teachers' better understanding the problems involved in teaching pupils with defective hearing. She makes seven concrete suggestions as to information the grade teacher should have.

PRATT, EMILY A. "The Importance of Determining the Need for Lip Reading among Deafened School Children," *The Volta Review* (October, 1927), Vol. 29, pp. 558–563.

Develops briefly the history of the education of children with defective hearing; points to the need for measuring the hearing of children; discusses causes of defective hearing; and points to the importance of preventing deafness.

VAN DEVEER, BLANCHE. "The Hearing Survey of the San Francisco Public Schools," *The Volta Review* (November, 1928), Vol. 30, pp. 761–765.

A description of the work being done in San Francisco for the hard of hearing; describes in some detail the use made of the 4A audiometer.

WARWICK, HAROLD L. "Hearing Tests in Public Schools of Fort Worth," *The Volta Review* (November, 1928), Vol. 30, pp. 641–643.

An account of the testing of the hearing at Fort Worth, Tex., of 20,000 school children.

White House Conference. *Special Education: The Handicapped and the Gifted*, pp. 277–346. The Century Co., New York, 1931.

An excellent discussion of terminology, incidence, means of detecting, methods of educating, training of teachers, state laws relating to, and recommendations made dealing with the deaf and hard of hearing.

CHAPTER XXI

EDUCATION OF CHILDREN HAVING DEFECTIVE SPEECH

The seriousness of a defect must be measured in terms of its effect upon the child; this effect may be physical or mental, or it may be some combination of these two conditions. A defect that destroys the child's self-confidence may be worse than one that makes him a cripple for life. A crippled person may associate with people, assume leadership, maintain his self-respect, and contribute to the welfare of the social group. When confidence in self is lost and social relationships are avoided, a person may be neither self-supporting nor a contributor to group improvement; this is the situation that makes defective speech so serious a handicap.

The physical conditions of a speech defect are generally not nearly so serious as other kinds of physical handicaps. It is the psychological results of the defect that make it so serious a problem; these results are undoubtedly due to a too-common popular attitude toward it. Almost all other physical handicaps make great demands upon popular sympathy; such handicapped children are made to feel that they are important to the social group. But what happens to the child with unusual speech defects? Until recently, little if any special attention was given to his education; no campaigns were waged in his behalf. Instead, he was ridiculed by his playmates. This attitude is all too prevalent at present and is due to popular ignorance of the reasons for these speech troubles.

1. DEFINITION

Speech defect refers to those severe defects that usually require the assistance of a trained person to overcome. The term "is applied to those mispronunciations which are due either to malformation or to wrong use of the organs of speech."[1] Another writer says, "A speech defect may be defined as any acoustic variation from an accepted speech standard so extreme as to be (a) conspicuous, (b) confusing, or (c) unpleasant."[2] These defects include stammering and stuttering,

[1] IDA I. WARD, *Defects of Speech*, p. 1, E. P. Dutton & Company, Inc., New York, 1923.

[2] RICHARD C. BORDEN, and ALVIN C. BUSSE, *Speech Correction*, p. 126, F. S. Crofts & Co., New York, 1925.

lisping, lalling, cluttering, nasality, thick speech, baby talk, hoarseness, foreign accent, and other defects due to organic difficulties.

2. GUIDING PRINCIPLES

Motivation.—The child must first of all realize the urgency for correction. Until he does, he will not put forth the effort necessary for successful correction. Rogers tells of a boy with speech defects who failed completely to correct them. He left school and got a job. Two years later he applied for admission to a night class for speech defectives, having recently failed to get a promotion because of his speech difficulties. He was admitted to the class and soon overcame them. Motivation is important. These defects become well-established habits, and routine drill will have little effect on them unless a motivating drive accompanies the drill.

Do Not Overemphasize the Handicap.—In the development of this drive, we must beware of overemphasizing the difficulty of correcting the defect. Such a procedure may destroy the pupil's confidence in his ability to overcome the defect; his faith is necessary for successful correction. In fact, the building up of the child's confidence in his ability to do the work may be the only motivation that is needed.

Diagnose Carefully.—Methods of assisting a child to overcome his speech handicap should depend upon careful diagnosis. Cases have been reported where the cause was supposed to be organic and where an operation was deemed necessary, but careful diagnosis showed that the organs of speech were perfectly normal. Proper drill soon corrected the defect.

Adapt Exercises to Defect.—If no organic difficulty exists, the proper exercises and drills must be determined. These will be adapted to the defect and will require a knowledge of speech construction. The special teacher must know how speech sounds are constructed; this will enable her to construct the drills or exercises that are necessary for the correction of given speech defects. In order to choose or to create these exercises, the teacher must be able to recognize the wrong sounds in the child's speech; in order to use them, she must be able to point out the difference between the wrong sounds and the correct ones.

Eliminate Worry.—In correcting a defect, the child should be so engrossed with what he is doing that he will have no chance to worry about whether or not he will be able to say correctly the sound or sounds that are difficult for him. This principle is particularly applicable to stammering and stuttering.

Educate in Regular Classes.—Because these children are normal in all respects but speech and because most speech defects can be overcome, the school program for such children should be so organized that they will not think of themselves as a class apart. They should be kept in regular classes, if possible; where this is impossible, they should return to the normal group just as soon as is wise.

Avoid Embarrassing the Child.—Every precaution should be taken to prevent the child from encountering embarrassing situations in the public schools. This requires an understanding teacher and principal; they should help pupils with correct speech to develop a more humane attitude toward speech defectives; they should make it possible for the latter to recite only when the "spirit moves them."

3. HISTORY

Beginnings.—The first school to be organized in Europe for speech defectives was established in 1887 at Potsdam, Germany.[1] In the United States the first schools were private. In 1874 the American Vocal Institute was organized in New York City; it treated stuttering and other speech troubles. The Bryant School for Stammerers, opened in 1888, was an outgrowth of the former; this was a day school. A boarding school was started at Indianapolis in 1901 under the title "Bogue Institute for Stammerers." In 1904 the Northwestern School for Stammerers was organized at Milwaukee.

Developments in American Public School Systems.—A public school class was organized in New York City as early as 1908; J. F. Reigart, principal of Public School No. 2, was responsible for its establishment.[2] He selected a young teacher with normal training, had her do some special study, and placed her in charge of the work. During 1920–21, 8,757 children received training; 4,057 were entirely corrected and 3,226 showed "great improvement."

Chicago started speech correction in the public schools in 1910; when six teachers were appointed. Each teacher was made a supervisor of from four to six schools. Detroit, likewise, began speech correction classes in 1910. At first, stammerers only were admitted; later, centers were established where all kinds of speech defects were treated. The public schools in Los Angeles organized such classes in 1921; these were located in five well-distributed parts of the city. In 1931 classes were being held in 151 of the city's public schools. Providence started a class just as an experiment in 1923; a survey in 1924 showed that 740

---

[1] ROBERT ALEXANDER FYFE MCDONALD, *Adjustment of School Organization to Various Population Groups*, p. 85, Teachers College, Columbia University, New York, 1915.

[2] *Ibid.*, p. 88.

children needed speech correction. In February, 1925, a full-time teacher was appointed who gave instruction in seven different centers.

4. ORGANIZATION

Itinerant Teachers.—Under this type of organization pupils with speech defects remain in their own local schools. Each special teacher is assigned several schools, the number assigned depending upon how widely they are scattered and upon how many speech defectives there are in each. Every school is visited two or three times a week; each group of children is given 20 or more minutes of instruction at each meeting. This method of planning the work was used by Chicago in 1910, when classes for speech defectives were first organized.

The method has attained great favor among city school systems and is the usual way of organizing to eliminate speech defects. A report from 35 cities showed that 24 of them used this method. It keeps the child at home; it retains him in a normal speaking group; it does not overemphasize his defect; and finally, it gets satisfactory results.

Centers.—Another method assigns a special teacher to a given school, which is designated as a center for the correction of speech. Pupils are received from other schools; upon admission, they continue to recite in regular classes but report twice a day to the special teacher. New York City used this plan when it initiated classes for speech defectives in the school year 1908–09.

Of 35 cities reporting on methods of organization, only six used this plan. The center allows the child to recite with children who have good speech; makes possible a high type of co-operation between special and regular teachers; allows more aid in the correction of defects; is very effective in correcting defects of the most difficult types; and provides an opportunity to grade the pupils. The plan, however, creates a problem of transportation if children have to come any considerable distance.

Boarding School.—The theory back of the boarding school seems to be that, if the child is taken out of a situation in which he has suffered agonies of embarrassment due to his handicap, he will be better able to give attention to special instruction and so overcome his defects more easily. The method is used chiefly by private or semiprivate schools. It would seem to emphasize the handicap unduly.

Other Procedures.—Two cities reported that special aid was given by regular teachers within their classroom. Oklahoma City and Binghamton, N.Y., reported the use of this method. Three cities combined the two methods of itinerant teachers and school centers.

5. PROBLEMS INVOLVED

Number of Speech Defectives.—There is considerable disagreement as to how many children of public school age have speech defects; the number reported as stutterers varies much less. Gutzmann[1] reported that 1 to 2 per cent of the school children in German cities were stutterers; his report was made early in the twentieth century. In 1900 Boston[1] reported that 0.7 per cent had difficulty in speaking. Conradi,[2] in 1904, estimated, after a study of 87,440 children in six American cities, that 2.46 per cent of the school children of the United States were speech defectives and 0.87 per cent were stutterers.

Berry[3] reported that Grand Rapids, Mich., in 1926 had more than 3 per cent of its public school children enrolled in speech-correction classes; while Detroit, with 1.8 per cent enrolled, had a waiting list large enough to make the number about equal to the Grand Rapids percentage. In 1915 Wallin[4] studied 89,057 children in St. Louis. He reported 2.8 per cent defective in speech; 1.6 per cent were lispers and 0.7 per cent were stutterers.

Blanton[5] in Madison, in 1916, found that 5.69 per cent of the 4,862 children studied had speech defects; 3.27 per cent were lispers and 0.72 per cent were stutterers. Root,[6] as late as 1925, studied 14,072 children in South Dakota. He reported that 6.3 per cent had speech defects, 2.6 per cent were lispers and lallers, and 1.2 per cent were stutterers and stammerers. Root also reported a study made in Philadelphia, but not published, which showed that "10 to 12 per cent of the school population suffered from defects of speech."[7]

Stinchfield[8] in 1923 tested 340 freshmen college women by means of a standardized speech test. She discovered that 16 per cent required

[1] McDonald, *op. cit.*, p. 85.

[2] Edward Conradi, "Psychology and Pathology of Speech Development in the Child," *Pedagogical Seminary* (1904) Vol. 11, pp. 365–366.

[3] Charles Scott Berry, "The Education of Handicapped Children in Michigan," p. 28, *State Department of Public Instruction Bulletin* 11, Lansing, Mich., 1926.

[4] J. E. Wallace Wallin, "A Census of Speech Defectives among 89,057 Public-school Pupils," *School and Society* (February, 1916), Vol. 3, pp. 213–216.

[5] Smiley Blanton, "A Survey of Speech Defects," *The Journal of Educational Psychology* (December, 1916), Vol. 7, p. 583.

[6] A. R. Root, "A Survey of Speech Defectives in the Public Elementary Schools of South Dakota," *The Elementary School Journal* (March, 1926), Vol. 26, pp. 532–533.

[7] A. R. Root, "Special Education and the Speech Defective," *Educational Administration and Supervision* (April, 1927), Vol. 13, pp. 257–258.

[8] Sara M. Stinchfield, "The Speech of Five Hundred Freshmen College Women," *The Journal of Applied Psychology* (1925), Vol. 9, p. 112.

immediate speech correction and that 24 per cent more had such "ineffective speech" that correction would be needed during the sophomore year.   These percentages seem exceedingly high; they may be due to an unusually high standard for good speech established by the test.

The White House Conference presented data for 48 cities in the United States.   It showed that 6.2 per cent of the total number of children enrolled in these cities had defective speech.   The cities represented 18 states.   The percentages varied from 0.5 per cent for Detroit, Mich. to 21.4 per cent at Fresno, Calif.

These variations may be due to any one of several factors.   The standards used for determining speech defect are perhaps the most potent; one student ignores all but the most obvious speech defects, while another includes the slightest departure from good speech. Some investigators use tests in order to select children, others make individual personal examinations, while still others use a questionnaire. Some studies report conditions for the lower grades and others report for the upper grades; there are obviously more cases of defective speech in the lower grades.   The amount and effectiveness of the work already done within a system will be a factor; the general health and climatic conditions of a city are other likely and not negligible factors.

Upon the basis of the median of the 48 cities, there are in the United States 1,625,493 children with speech defects.   As the White House Conference summarizes, "In view of this evidence we have no hesitation in saying that there are 1,000,000 school children in America so defective in speech as to require remedial treatment."[1]

Early Discovery and Treatment.—The problem of early discovery and early treatment is important, since ease of correction is so dependent upon it.   Grade teachers should have training that will help them to detect immediately children with speech defects.   Where a special staff is available, all questionable cases should be referred to an examiner at the central office.   Cases of obvious and serious defect should be reported by parents even before the child enters school, and arrangements should be made to give whatever preschool aid is necessary.

A survey of 35 cities[2] showed that 32 of them had organized speech-correction work in the kindergarten and in the elementary grades. One city had organized it only in the kindergarten.   Unquestionably, any program of speech correction should be started in the elementary

---

[1] White House Conference, *Special Education: The Handicapped and the Gifted*, p. 357, The Century Co., New York, 1931.

[2] RAYMOND A. LEMMON, *The Status of the Education of Speech Defectives in Public Schools of the United States*, p. 48, Master's thesis, Ohio State University, Columbus, 1931.

grades and should be continued until the defect has been corrected or until it is decided that correction is impossible.

Types of Instruction.—Whether individual or group instruction should be used is not generally agreed upon. Twenty-eight cities[1] have reported their practice. Four have 100 per cent individual instruction, four have 100 per cent group instruction, four claimed that 75 per cent of their instruction was individual and 25 per cent was group, eight divide the instruction half and half, and the remaining eight cities allowed 25 per cent individual instruction and 75 per cent group. Undoubtedly, both types of instruction should be used. Children with severe defects will need a greater proportion of individual instruction. Since most speech defectives have relatively minor difficulties, it would seem reasonable to expect a considerable amount of group instruction.

Co-operative Assistance.—Since some speech defects have a pathological basis, the fullest co-operation of the school physician and school nurses is needed. Since many cases have a psychological basis, the report of a psychologist is essential. The survey of 35 cities showed that school physicians were consulted constantly in 21 of them; in 24 cities the school nurses gave material aid; psychologists and psychiatrists were called in for advice in 25 cities. The extent to which such aid was available by a given city was unfortunately not reported.

Eight cities used grade teachers in supervising the corrective exercises recommended by the teacher of speech correction; these regular teachers reported upon the progress made by the children. Omaha reported that eighth-grade students were used; they supervised the corrective exercises of younger children. Social workers and school counselors were used to help in organizing and supervising the work in one city.

Costs.—Fifteen cities reported per capita costs for this type of instruction. The costs ranged from zero in Binghamton, N.Y., where regular classroom teachers did the work, to $26.59 at Philadelphia. The median cost for these cities was $7.32. The costs covered the excess over and above that of the cost of regular school instruction. Meager equipment and the relatively high pupil-per-teacher ratio helped to account for these small excess costs.

Extent of Correction.—The success of this work must be judged by the per cent of correction. Gutzmann[2] in his early work with speech

---

[1] *Ibid.*, p. 50.

[2] G. STANLEY HALL, *Educational Problems*, Vol. II, p. 114, D. Appleton and Company, New York, 1911.

defectives reported a high per cent. From 1890 to 1896, he treated 1290 stammerers and claimed that 72.7 per cent were cured, 23.7 per cent improved, and 3.6 per cent were unaffected.

Lemmon in his study defined the term "corrected" as "pupils— entirely cured of their defects or whose defects were so corrected as to permit their withdrawal (or transfer) from speech correction classes."[1] He received data from 30 school systems. The percentage of correction at Bayonne, N. J., was lowest, at 7.3 per cent; Kalamazoo, Mich., and Sheboygan, Wis., had percentages of 73.5 and 69.2 per cent, respectively; the average for the 30 cities was 36.4.

These figures from Lemmon are based upon the number of cases enrolled for the year 1929–30 and the number actually cured during that year. Since many cases continue more than a year before correction is effected, these percentages would have been higher if all that were finally corrected could have been included.

Such results are impressive. When the misery and agony endured by the sufferer of such a handicap are considered and when the economic and social inefficiency that results is noted, the cost of this program of correction is small. Instead of having only a fractional portion of the million speech defectives in corrective classes, they all ought to be there.

6. TEACHER PERSONNEL

Training.—Every teacher of speech correction should have had the training required of a regular teacher. In addition, she should have had special training in speech correction. Rogers[2] has reported requirements at Madison, Wis. They comprise 3 semester hours each in (1) correction of speech disorders, (2) speech pathology, (3) advanced correction of speech disorders, (4) introduction to phonetics, and (5) psychology of speech. In addition, 4 hours is required in intelligence testing, plus 12 hours to be chosen from 44 semester hours of work which cover in general the fields of psychology, physiology, health, zoology, social case work, counseling, measurement of intelligence, and speech. These 31 hours constitute a minimum; the 12 optional hours are to be chosen from at least 4 different departments.

Teaching Load.—The load per teacher is reported for 38 cities by Lemmon.[3] This load ranged from 20 at West Allis, Wis., to 873 at New Rochelle, N.Y. The median load was 203. New York City

[1] LEMMON, *op. cit.*, p. 34.

[2] JAMES FREDERICK ROGERS, "The Speech Defective School Child," pp. 11–12, *U.S. Office of Education Bulletin* 7, Washington, D.C., 1931.

[3] LEMMON, *op. cit.*, p. 42.

had the second highest load with 629; 28 teachers gave corrective work to 17,612 pupils. Only four cities have a lower ratio than Philadelphia, where 56 teachers were provided to care for 5,938 pupils, or 106 pupils per teacher.

Unless individual work is to be reduced to the minimum and the length and number of periods per week are to be kept exceedingly low, the Philadelphia ratio would seem to represent what might be accepted as the ideal maximum. Upon the basis of 10 pupils per group and three group meetings of 45 minutes each, the teacher would be kept occupied 4½ hours daily with actual group instruction, under the Philadelphia plan. If time is to be allowed for individual work, for preparation of material, and for necessary consultations with other school officials, the teacher's week will be filled to overflowing.

The above suggestion is corroborated by Ward,[1] who says that 150 pupils per teacher are too many if successful work is to be accomplished. Lemmon reports that special teachers have to teach "in as many as sixteen and more different buildings." We need experimentation that will help to determine the optimum teaching load under varying types of organization. Even a Philadelphia load of 106 pupils will be too heavy for a teacher if she has them scattered in 16 school buildings.

7. THE ECONOMIC HANDICAP OF SPEECH DEFECTS

The problems discussed in the two preceding sections are of more than academic importance; they have an importance that extends even beyond that of making life more pleasant for the individual so affected; they have a social significance that must not be ignored.

Children with speech defects are just as normal in other ways as any unselected group of children who are free from speech defects. Were it not for this one defect they would be as capable of progressing through school, of entering the occupations or professions, and of succeeding in them as do other normal individuals. This means that the group as a whole, were it not for this handicap, would be just as capable of maintaining themselves and just as capable of making contributions to the social order as is the group with normal speech.

Many persons, owing to unusual qualities and abilities, succeed in life, are self-supporting, and make a real social contribution despite this defect. Rogers lists a remarkable array of distinguished men having speech difficulties. Their success could hardly be attributed to the defect; they succeeded in spite of it.

[1] *Biennial Report for* 1926–28, Department of Public Instruction, Wisconsin.

Certain it is that the speech defective, though of average intellectual ability, is more retarded than the nondefective in speech. We find that speech defect is less frequent in upper grades. This ·is partly due to the correction of many defects as the children become older; it is also due to the elimination of many of these children before they reach the upper grades. This elimination from school at an early age and at a low grade tells its own story of economic and social loss.

Youths with these defects are limited in vocational opportunities. If the defect is serious, salesmanship is not open to them, managerial positions are closed, and positions involving personal contacts and relationships are usually barred. There remain numerous "closed-alley jobs" and manual labor, both skilled and unskilled. When these economic handicaps are considered in relation to the personal embarrassment and agony which the speech defective suffers daily, we find a genuine argument for providing the funds needed to correct such defects just as early in the life of the child as it is possible to overcome them.

8. LOCAL CITY PROGRAMS

Baltimore.—Speech work was begun in 1923 in Baltimore and has had a consistent and steady growth. In 1926 the supervisor reported[1] that 650 pupils were under observation in 8 schools. The school principals reported that 5,000 children needed speech correction. During 1936[2] there were 1,150 children who received speech training; 800 were enrolled in 36 white elementary schools, and 350 in 12 colored schools.

Before starting work in any school, the entire enrollment is examined for speech defects. The defectives are then classified according to age, grade, and type of defect. The classes meet for periods of 20 to 30 minutes, twice each week. The more serious cases not otherwise cared for receive aid in a Saturday morning clinic at the school administration building.

A recent report says, "Massotherapy and thermal treatment develop better-toned muscles, while tongue exercises and drill in the mechanical processes of speech production make for better speech." The following data tell their own story. In 1928–29 there were 50 cases of speech defect corrected; during the following 4 years there were respectively 163, 253, 377, and 514 cases of correction.

[1] DOROTHY M. NEWKIRK, "Speech Correction and Improvement in the Baltimore Public Schools," *Baltimore Bulletin of Education* (April, 1926), Vol. 4, pp. 164–165.

[2] Data directly from the director of special classes.

Binghamton, N.Y.[1]—In this city special teachers for the correction of speech are not provided, but every regular teacher in kindergarten and in the primary grades is expected to prepare herself so that she can correct speech defects. Extension courses have been made available to these teachers by Syracuse University; the school system has paid all expenses. Ultimately speech correction will be provided in the upper grades. A record of each pupil is now kept, showing his difficulties and portraying his progress in correcting defects. This record is continuous and is passed from teacher to teacher.

Chicago.[2]—Classes were first organized in Chicago in 1910. In 1923 there were 12 teachers; they visited 107 schools and treated 2,304 cases. There were 1,280 major cases, that is, children who when trying could not speak reasonably well; this left 1,024 minor cases, that is, children who could speak correctly when their attention was called to the need of it. Cures or marked improvement were shown in 79 per cent of the major cases and in 88 per cent of the minor cases. The 12 teachers devoted their entire time to the correction of speech defects.

The Chicago department believes that all teachers entering the public schools "should be trained in the elements of speech correction." It recognizes that many children have physical difficulties that need to be corrected before they can make much progress in overcoming their speech defects. At the same time, it is convinced that most speech defects have a psychological basis. These children feel that they can never speak well. In order to help develop the right attitude toward correction, the pupils learn 10 commandments of speech. They are

1. I have no fear. I know that I can speak well.
2. I will think before I speak.
3. I will always speak quietly and calmly with all of the muscles relaxed.
4. I will always speak slowly and carefully.
5. I will stand or sit quietly and erect when speaking.
6. I will inhale quickly, deeply, without straining, and with the mouth open.
7. I will be very careful of the first two words in each sentence.
8. I will always lengthen and strengthen the principal vowels.
9. I will be especially careful to lengthen the short vowels.
10. I will be honest with myself and not try to avoid words that are difficult.

A teacher's typical schedule requires that she spend a half day at each of 10 schools during a week. At each school 10 to 15 children

[1] H. J. Hellman, "Some Educational Aspects of Speech Correction," *Quarterly Journal of Speech* (April, 1930), Vol. 16, pp. 221–225.

[2] Frank G. Bruner, *Report of the Director of Special Schools for the School Year 1922–23*, pp. 139–147, Board of Education, Chicago, 1924.

are treated. Approximately half of these are major cases. At each school the teacher is assigned either an unoccupied classroom, a doctor's office, the library, or some other room that can be vacated during her stay in the building. The children selected for her by the principal are sent in. She classifies them. From long experience she can tell within a few minutes whether normal treatment will help the child. If she decides it will not, he is sent to the school physician and later to the child study department for diagnosis.

All teachers of corrective speech meet the first Thursday of each school month with the director of special classes. The meeting lasts one hour, during which reports on speech work and accounts of problem cases are followed by discussion. Help is sought by teachers on the handling of problem cases.

Until 1921 no speech work was done in high schools; but 2 years later it was conducted in seven of them and there were insistent demands from others for an extension of the training. Training in high school is important. Because the pupils sense the defect more acutely at this age, they co-operate so well that results are secured quickly. Moreover, the correction is necessary if they are to continue in school or are to enter business.

Detroit.—In September, 1910, speech work was first started in Detroit. Since 1920, speech surveys to discover children with defective speech have been conducted each year. Of 21,918 children examined in April and May, 1930, 8,518 were found to have some type of speech defect. Only those with major defects were placed in classes; the others were observed and were placed in classes if the defect became worse. In classwork pupils check one another. This is shown in Illustration 21. The boys at the mirror are checking on lisping; the boys at the individual desks are checking their reading.

The department has organized a club called the "Knights of the Silver Shield." A small silver shield is given monthly to the child in each school who improves most in speech. The aim is to make all children proud of conquering defective speech rather than to allow them to feel ashamed of the defect. In June, 1936, there were 7,343 children in classes for speech improvement; there were 35 teachers and one supervisor.

New York City.—Classes were started in New York by one of the elementary schools in 1908. In 1933–34 there were 23,864 children under "the direct clinical care or the supervision of the members of the Department of Speech Improvement." Since there were 28 special teachers, this made an average of 852 pupils per teacher. Of the total membership, 3,544—or 14.8 per cent—were stammerers; 11,646—or

48.8 per cent—were lispers; 6,118—or 25.6 per cent—were cases of acute defective phonation; and the remaining 2,556 were distributed among 15 different types of speech defect.

The 28 special teachers are under the supervision of a director. The latter is directly responsible to the associate superintendent in charge of handicapped children. "The teachers are assigned to district superintendents" by this associate superintendent upon the recommendation of the director. Three district superintendents, in 1933–34, were without speech-improvement service. The teachers visit from 4 to 34 schools, each. If they do all the work of correcting

ILLUSTRATION 21.—Pupils check one another in a speech improvement class in Detroit.

defects, they visit fewer schools; if the regular teachers assist them, they visit many buildings.

In one district the special teacher visits 34 schools; there are 1,759 pupils needing correction in these buildings. Each school, however, has a regular teacher to assist with the work. The special teacher "interviews the new cases in the presence of the assistant teacher, diagnoses them, and prescribes treatment. Upon succeeding visits, she interviews each of the cases previously seen, checks the progress, and suggests modifications in the procedure."

During the year 1933–34, there were 8,057 of the 23,864 enrolled who had had their speech corrected; 12,287 had improved; 2,329 were discharged for various reasons; and 1,191 had, up to that time, not improved. During the 4-year period including and ending with 1933–34, there were 30,923 pupils discharged from these classes as having had speech corrected; this represented 30 per cent of the total number taught. There were also 47,770—or 53 per cent—who improved. Such data ought to answer once and for all the person who says, "You can't really do anything for these people, can you?"

Philadelphia.—Speech correction was begun in Philadelphia in 1922. It was provided from the kindergarten up through normal

ILLUSTRATION 22.—Speech-correction class at work at the Hayne School, Philadelphia. Note the use of mirrors.

school, with 50 teachers and one supervisor managing the work. The teachers served in 84 elementary, 13 junior high, and 7 senior high schools. During the year 1934–35, there were 7,093 children enrolled in speech classes. In the elementary schools there were twice as many boys as girls; but in senior high there were twice as many girls as boys. The elementary schools provide a half hour of instruction daily, with the periods so rotated that no child misses a given class continuously. Illustration 22 shows mirrors being used to aid pupils in the correction of speech. One half day weekly the teachers hold clinics where children in schools without speech classes may come for correction. The supervisors aid in conducting the clinics.

9. TYPES OF SPEECH DEFECT

The problems which a city school system faces in organizing to care for its speech defectives can hardly be appreciated without some knowledge of the variability in types of speech defect. If the whole program, for example, could center about stammering, the problem would be less difficult. Recent students of speech defects have continued to recognize more and more classes of defects. Swift suggested three classes—phonetic cases, stammering and stuttering, and others not included in these two. Blanton listed (1) delayed speech, (2) letter-sound substitution, (3) oral inactivity, and (4) stuttering. In other attempts at classification, as many as 40 to 50 different classes of speech defects are listed.

The White House Conference[1] groups all types of speech defect into four classes: (1) stuttering, (2) articulatory defects, (3) disorders of voice, and (4) aphasias. Under articulatory defects are included defects due to malformed teeth, tongue, palate, or nasal passages; defects due to some injury to nerve centers; as well as oral inactivity, sound substitution, and foreign or provincial dialects. Disorders of the voice include huskiness, shrillness, and any failure to make "smooth, even, vibrant vocal tones."

Stuttering.—This term includes what is sometimes called stammering. It is

A disturbance in the rhythm of speech, an intermittent blocking, from which, if the conversational situation is favorable, the child may at times be quite free. This blocking may be in the muscles of the face, lips, tongue, or jaw; in the throat or larynx; in the respiratory muscles; or it may be a mere hesitation in the initiation of sounds or their repetition when initiated.[2]

Some think of stammering as a complete stoppage of speech and of stuttering as a repetition of a given sound, word, or phrase. These are the common and obvious features of stuttering. Amoss[3] says that stuttering is the repetition of the first letter of a word as " p-p-paper," that stammering is not merely a hesitation before making the letter or sounds but that it is an inability to make it. This inability is due

[1] White House Conference, *Special Education: The Handicapped and the Gifted*, pp. 351–353, The Century Co., New York, 1931.

[2] *Ibid.*, pp. 351–352.

[3] HARRY AMOSS, and L. HELEN DeLaporte, *Training Handicapped Children*, p. 270, Ryerson Press, Toronto, 1933.

to a "muscle-bound condition," which prevents speech. In the case of stammering, peculiar movements of the body, uncontrolled breathing, and even "actual contortions" accompany it.

Lisping.—This defect is quite common and consists of a failure to produce correctly the sibilant sounds, such as *s*, *z*, *sh*, and *zp*. Frequently an imperfect *th* will be made in place of the *s*. Amoss[1] suggests that *s* combined with the consonant *m* or *p* is easier for lispers than *s* before a vowel, unless the vowel is a long *e* or a short *i*. He says that lispers may get the *s* sound correctly produced very quickly, but that it takes long and constant practice to eliminate the lisp from regular speech if the child has been afflicted very long.

Lallation.—This is sometimes referred to as baby talk. The lingual or tongue muscles fail to co-ordinate. Lalling speech is fairly common in children four, five, and even six years of age and may be temporarily ignored, as it will frequently be outgrown if it is not associated with mental deficiency.

Acute Defective Phonation.—This is an articulation of sounds so defective as to make the child's speech unintelligible. There is no structural defect, but the speech defect is due to poor speech habits. Most of these cases can be cured by regular classroom teachers.

Nasality.—The emission of sound through the nose during speech causes the peculiarity of sound known as nasality. A cleft palate, an excessive growth of the tonsils or hypertrophied tonsils, or even a habit due to design or accident may be the cause of such a defect. Amoss illustrates nasality by suggesting that the child hold his nostrils closed while he sounds any series of vowels. If a vibration is felt in the fingers, nasality exists; all English vowels, he says, are emitted through the mouth and not through the nose; the resonating chambers of the head serve only to reinforce these sounds. There are French vowels that are nasal.

A second kind of nasality is exactly the opposite of the type just discussed. Instead of an excess of nasal resonance, we here have a deficiency of such resonance. The consonants *m*, *n*, and *ng* normally should have a marked degree of nasal resonance; if a deficiency exists, these sounds are "stuffy" and "muffled." Children with such a deficiency are said to be afflicted with nasality of speech.

Aphonia.—This is loss of voice. Where the voice is not completely lost, it is a low whisper, often guttural, and will be a lifelong defect unless special care and attention are given to its correction. Aphonia may be due to (1) "acute laryngitis," (2) "extreme weakness of the muscles of the larynx following an exhausting illness," or (3)

[1] *Ibid.*, p. 267.

"laryngeal paralysis."[1] Borden and Busse suggested that patients so afflicted be referred to a physician at once.

Another writer suggests that aphonia is due to a lack of development of the vocal organs. Such cases, it is claimed, may be cured, and generally are if given regular exercises for developing the inefficient organs. The defect may not be organic, however, but due to a mental condition; in such cases, only the best psychoanalytic help can aid the patient.

Foreign and Local Accent.—This defect is an imperfection in speech due to carrying over from another language its peculiar accents or pronunciations. Localities sometimes allow a certain slovenliness to creep into their pronunciation. These defects are passed on by those who have them to others through association.

Letter Substitution.—The name implies the nature of the defect; a letter is substituted in various words for some other letter: t for k, d for g, f for th, s for th, w for r, w for y and sh for s, to mention some of the rather common substitutions.

Guttural and High-pitched Voices.—The defect, in this case, is that of improper pitch. The guttural defect is an unusually low-pitched voice; the high-pitched voice is sometimes called the feminine voice. These voices can be rather quickly trained to respond at a normal pitch. The defect is the result of habit and needs a bit of exacting direction in order to break the old and form the new speech habits. These defects are not the same as those resulting from "chronic laryngitis or newsboy's voice." The latter does not yield very readily to treatment; a guttural voice that results from injury to the voice apparatus is not easily cured, whereas one that is due to bad habits of speech responds readily.

10. CAUSES OF SPEECH DEFECTS

Two theories have been advanced to explain the occurrence of speech defects. One is based upon pathology, the other upon psychology. The former theory has many physicians as proponents; the latter is accepted rather widely by school people. The pathological theory assumes that some physical disturbance, disorder, or defect lies at the root of most speech defects. If these physical defects are cured, the speech defect itself will be relieved.

The school man admits that some speech defects result from a physical condition, but he does not believe that any great proportion of children with speech defects have physical ailments that can account for those defects. He suggests that the defects are due to emotional

---

[1] BORDEN and BUSSE, *op. cit.*, p. 277.

disturbances, to carelessness in the development of speech habits, and to an imitation of incorrect or defective speech. The development of speech is so largely a matter of habit formation that parents and elementary school teachers should give most careful attention to the speech development of children.

In the case of stuttering and stammering, some of the recognized "contributing causes are physical obstructions of speech, nervous habits, nutritional defects, lack of proper rest, unfavourable home conditions, and association with other stammerers."[1] Once stuttering has started, it becomes its own cause for further stuttering. The individual has a horror for the words or sounds that have caused him such extreme embarrassment. This fear so possesses him that any necessity for saying those particular words or sounds causes him to stutter.

In the case of nasality, organic defects play a great part in causing it. Amoss says that abnormal tonsils, a fallen soft palate, obstruction of the nasal passages, and a cleft palate may be causes of nasality. He lists, also, imitation as a possible cause.

Lisping is very likely to be caused by imitation, therefore, parents cannot be too careful of their own speech. If they are careless about the child's lisping during dentition, under the mistaken impression that the teeth are effective in speech, the habit may become fairly well fixed before they realize what has happened. Certain physical defects may cause lisping; abnormal tonsils, paralysis of the tongue, lingual inactivity, or a fallen palate are examples.

11. HOW TO REDUCE THE PROBLEM

With 1,000,000 children in the United States suffering from speech defects and with only 52,112 being cared for in special classes, one is impressed with the importance of prevention. A comprehensive program of prevention would undoubtedly be more significant than a comparative program of correction. The former, if successful, would save untold suffering and embarrassment; it would prevent much school retardation; and it would save the money now spent for correction. To make prevention effective, parents need to recognize the importance of stopping such defects before they get fairly started, and elementary teachers must be trained to detect and to cure minor defects before they can develop into major obstacles.

Education of Parents.—There are several golden rules that all parents should follow regarding speech. (1) Under no circumstances should they use baby talk in the presence of their children. (2)

[1] Amoss and DeLaporte, *op. cit.*, p. 271.

Clearness of enunciation and absence of slovenliness should characterize their speech. (3) They should constantly watch the child's speech to see that he says words correctly. Many words he hears incorrectly; if he had heard the correct pronunciation, he would have said that just as easily as he says what he did hear. If incorrect pronunciation is allowed because it sounds cute, then a habit pattern will soon become so fixed that correction of the defect will be very difficult. (4) In case more serious defects appear, parents should have an immediate conference with a speech specialist. If the defect seems to be structural in origin, a physician should be consulted. (5) Parents should always understand fully the importance of the best of physical care. This includes proper food, plenty of wholesome exercise, an abundance of sunlight, plenty of sleep, a happy home and play life, and loving but sensible parents.

Teachers Trained in Speech Correction.—All teachers should have as a part of their training some instruction in the detection and correction of speech defects. From the point of view of prevention, such training is doubly important for kindergarten and primary teachers. Some cities require that all teachers have speech-correction training. Cities whose teachers are not so trained frankly state that they give corrective work only to the worst cases; minor cases are watched and brought to the clinic or special class if the defect gets worse. This procedure eliminates those who gradually outgrow the difficulty; there are, however, too many who get worse and who could have been cured at the earlier stages.

12. STATE LEGISLATION

A recent survey shows that California had 16 and Wisconsin 10 cities holding special classes for children with defective speech. No other state had over six, and most of them only one, two, or three such cities. Elsewhere the correspondence between good state legislation for a given type of special education and the number of cities or communities that have undertaken to organize such special classwork has been noted.

This theory seems to hold for work with the speech defective. Rogers reported in 1931 only two states that had provided a state supervisor of classes for speech correction. California had organized a "bureau of correction of speech defects and disorders with a specialist and two assistants." A part-time specialist was provided in the state department of education in Wisconsin. No mention was made of special supervisors of speech defects in any other state. In addition to California and Wisconsin, Indiana, Minnesota, Michigan, Pennsylvania, and Washington were reported as furnishing state aid to districts where special classes for children with defective speech were organized.

13. A STATE PROGRAM

The State's Responsibility.—Legislation should be passed making specific provision for the correction of speech defects, and this legislation should provide for state supervision and for some state support. Local classes should be made compulsory where surveys show that five or more children need such correction. The method of organizing to care for these defectives should be subject to the approval of the state supervisor.

The supervisor and his assistants should be held responsible for making speech surveys throughout the state; he should assist local school authorities to show the need for such classes; he should fix the standards for acceptable teachers; he should be responsible for making final recommendations regarding state support; he should hold conferences for speech-correction workers; he should supervise instructional activities; and he should annually propose problems for study and assist local workers in setting up techniques for the study of their own individual problems.

The Localities' Responsibility.—Working under the state office, each locality should arrange for a continuous survey of its speech defectives. School authorities should encourage every teacher to take at least one course in speech correction. This would make possible the quick discovery of potential cases of defective speech and an immediate attempt to correct these incipient cases.

After the survey, local classes should be established; enough teachers should be supplied so that personal attention could be given to each child. There is some evidence for believing that, if individual attention could be given and if corrective work could be done frequently, the handicap could be overcome before the child has become discouraged by the slowness of his progress.

There are other important factors governing progress in speech improvement. If the child refuses to co-operate and does not take seriously the corrective program suggested or if the parents fail to understand what they can do to assist in correcting his speech, progress will be slow, despite the time spent on correction. Local authorities need to realize, therefore, the importance of pupil and home co-operation and must definitely seek to gain it. This may be done, in most cases, by simply informing both the child and the parents concerning the purpose of all remedial suggestions and helping them to believe that correction is possible.

The Rural District's Problem.—The problem of the rural district is unique merely in that there are too few children to provide full-time employment for even one person. If there is centrally located a group of small towns and villages with enough children having speech defects to occupy a full-time teacher, these districts might co-operate.

In isolated villages, it may be best to have one of the grade teachers secure special training at the expense of the board of education and have her devote part time to the correction of speech defects. In villages where a teacher for the hard of hearing has already been provided, she may have the time and preparation to care for those defective in speech. Another village that is organizing for the first time may find that it has enough cases to keep one teacher busy if she is prepared to handle two or more types of handicapped pupils.

In a state that has a great many one-room districts, all rural teachers should be required to have had speech training before being certified. If hard roads are general, the county, town, or parish office may provide one or more traveling teachers, who will visit all schools where there are several cases of speech defect and thus supply the needed correction. These supervisors can institute training courses so that gradually all rural teachers will be able to care for all but the more serious cases of speech defect.

14. SUMMARY

Despite its seriousness, people generally have been more amused than sympathetic on observing any speech defect in others. That attitude may account for the fact that public schools ignored the problem until 1908, when New York City started speech-correction classes. A recent survey showed 96 cities that had instituted such classes. Recent estimates place the number of children having speech defects at 1,000,000—a figure that is considered very conservative. No city among the 96 would claim that it handles all of its cases; most would state that they handle a comparatively small number of them.

The itinerant teacher and special centers are the customary methods of organizing to correct speech defects. In a few instances, regular teachers do this work. Early discovery and treatment are important; teachers, principals, parents, pupils, physicians, and nurses assist in making early discovery possible. Some cities make all their instruction individual, others use only group instruction, while many combine the two methods.   The percentage of correction is so high as to encourage the development and extension of this work. Teachers with a minimum of technical training are able to do fairly effective work in correcting defects.   Teaching load can average 100 with hope for a fair degree of success.   The teacher's biggest task is perhaps that of giving the child an assurance and confidence in his ability to acquire correct speech; once this is achieved and the child begins to strive for correction, the task is half done.

Stuttering, lisping, lallation, acute defective phonation, nasality, aphonia, foreign and local accent, letter substitution, and guttural and high-pitched voices are some of the defects of speech which are referred to when defective speech is mentioned.   Defects that have a high frequency are lisping, stammering, and defective phonation. There is fairly general agreement that causes of defective speech are much more psychological than pathological.   Parents and elementary teachers can do much to reduce defects in speech; they need to be better educated with respect to specific causes, preventive measures, symptoms, and early remedial treatment, if the severer cases are to be prevented.

Problems and Questions for Discussion

1. Is the problem of educating children with speech defects a serious one? Give reasons for your answer.

2. What are speech defects?   How are they classified?

3. What important principles govern the correction of these defects?

4. Trace the history of educating and correcting children with speech defects.

5. How do cities at present organize in trying to educate children with speech defects?

6. List the various problems involved in trying to educate children with speech defects.   Which are the more important of these problems?   Why do you consider them so important?

7. What plan would you propose for discovering children with speech defects? Why do you think it would work?

8. What evidence have you been able to discover showing whether or not a special program of education for children with speech defects is worth while?

9. What demands should be made of teachers who seek to correct speech defects in children?

10. Is it important that we try to educate children with speech defects?   Give in some detail your reasons for answering as you do.

11. What are the causes of defective speech?

12. What can be done to prevent speech defects?

13. Draw up a state law that would ideally provide for the education of children having speech defects.

14. Outline in some detail the program you would attempt to carry out if you were supervisor of the education of children having defective speech in your home state.

Selected Bibliography

AMOSS, HARRY, and DeLAPORTE, L. HELEN. *Training Handicapped Children,* . pp. 261–308. Ryerson Press, Toronto, 1933.

An account of methods of organizing speech-correction classes, of various speech defects giving causes and methods of correction, and of vowel exercises for speech improvement.

BENTLEY, JOHN EDWARD. *Problem Children,* pp. 36–73. W. W. Norton & Company, Inc., New York, 1936.

An interesting consideration of many of the problems involved in the education of the speech defective.

BORDEN, RICHARD C., and BUSSE, ALVIN C. *Speech Correction.* F. S. Crofts & Co., New York, 1925. 295 pp.

Presents an explanation of the mechanism of speech, discusses the sounds of speech, and describes in great detail some seven types of speech defect.

Handicapped and Underprivileged Children, a special report submitted with *The Thirty-Sixth Annual Report of the Superintendent of Schools,* pp. 25–54. Board of Education, New York City, 1934.

Describes the organization for correcting speech defects, types of speech disorder, the afterschool clinics, methods used in correction, the training of teachers, ways of co-operating with various agencies, and present problems and limitations.

LEMMON, RAYMOND A. *The Status of the Education of Speech Defectives in Public Schools of the United States.* Unpublished Master's thesis, Ohio State University, Columbus, 1931. 64 pp.

Shows extent of speech correction in the public schools and considers methods of organizing, methods of selecting speech defectives for class work, equipment, costs, preparation of teachers, and the success of such work.

ROGERS, JAMES FREDERICK. "The Speech Defective School Child," *U.S. Office of Education Bulletin 7,* Washington, D.C., 1931. 31 pp.

Defines speech defect, lists kinds, gives frequency of each kind, and relates defects to mentality, age, race, and sex. A good survey of the way city school systems manage speech correction, what states do to support it, and what rural districts can do.

Twenty-third Annual Report of the Superintendent of Schools (reports on special classes), pp. 155–159. Board of Education, New York City, 1922.

A brief description of common types of speech defect, size of problem in New York, progress, and needs.

WARD, IDA C. *Defects of Speech.* E. P. Dutton & Company, Inc., New York, 1923. 79 pp.

A detailed description of various types of defective speech, of illustrative cases, and of remedies. Numerous diagrammatic pictures are given showing positions of lips, teeth, and tongue in the making of different sounds.

White House Conference. *Special Education: The Handicapped and the Gifted,* pp. 349–381. The Century Co., New York, 1931.

An excellent presentation of data showing the size of the problem, the types of disorders, what is being done, the costs, and what should be done.

CHAPTER XXII

THE EDUCATION OF DELICATE CHILDREN

1. INTRODUCTION

Seldom do we recognize the significance of conditions that are commonplace. Constant contact with whooping cough, mumps, and measles has dulled our powers of discrimination. Familiarity has developed a disregard for them as instruments of destruction. Such an attitude is due also to the fact that the damaging aftereffects are usually slow in making their appearance.

It is for these reasons, undoubtedly, that the delicate child has been ignored until recent years. Every generation has had its delicate children; every individual could enumerate rather quickly many children who were not strong, who were frequently ill, and who were not able to participate freely and strenuously in all kinds of games. Many of these youths failed to get a good start in school because of illness, and as a result quit at an early age. Others died of diseases from which a healthy youngster would have recovered. So frequent has been our contact with such children and so mild have their ailments appeared to be that we as a social group have tended to ignore their needs both physically and educationally.

Definition.—The delicate child has been referred to by different titles; he has been called the anemic, the child of lowered vitality, and the tubercular. Our title is a broad designation intended to cover that host of children who are not in perfect health, who cannot stand the strenuous play of the average child, and who need additional physical care if their systems are to become rugged enough to overcome disease and to meet all the demands of the play and work life of the average youth.

This group includes those who are malnourished; those who are represented by the "tired child," who either just overrates his strength and works beyond it or who is not endowed with the ability to do the work that the average child can do; and cases of incipient tuberculosis that are not active. Some class heart cases with this group, and this seems appropriate since heart cases need rest. Youths in a weakened physical condition resulting from influenza or pneumonia would be included. The term includes any child not ill enough to remain at

313

home but so weakened physically that he needs the physical care which it is proposed shall be given to the "delicate child" in the public schools.

Guiding Principles.—1. The schools today are responsible for the social and physical, as well as the mental, development of all children. We attempt to realize this ideal for the physically normal child through gymnastics, free and controlled play, and athletics, both intercollegiate and intramural. Pupils who do not have the vitality to engage in these activities have been rather generally ignored. Many cities organize small groups of delicate children and care excellently for them. Many others are ignored who should have had considerable attention given to their physical development.

2. We must again recognize as fundamental the principle of prevention. Many malnourished children in schools have no serious physical deficiencies or weaknesses; their run-down condition, however, is an excellent breeding spot for disease. If the entire preventive program of special education is to be made effective, the best of care must be given to these delicate children.

3. This program of care and education must deviate from the normal as little as possible. These children should not get the impression that they are unusual. If a special school is found to be necessary, the aim should be to bring the child to a normal physical condition as quickly as possible so that he can return to the regular school. If special rooms give effective remedial care, they should be provided in all regular schools; pupils would then become so habituated to them that placement in such a class would seem the appropriate procedure for any child who is delicate and malnourished.

2. HISTORY OF OPEN-AIR SCHOOLS AND CLASSES

The term "open-air school," or "class," is a title that has often been applied to the type of school organization which provides for the care and education of delicate children. It is sometimes termed a fresh-air school or class instead.

The Charlottenburg School.—The first such school to be established was the Open-air Recovery School at Charlottenburg, Germany, a suburb of Berlin. It was opened in 1904 and was for school children who had "lung trouble, heart disease, anaemia and scrofula"; they were too ill to do all the regular schoolwork and yet not ill enough to be kept at home. This school had been preceded in Germany by sanatoria for men, later by sanatoria for women, and finally by sanatoria for children. Because in the children's sanatoria a meager bit of schooling was given, they might be considered the parents of the first open-air school.

The Charlottenburg school[1] was located in a forest. The grounds covered 5 acres and were 3 miles from the city. The soil was sandy; the pine trees gave the place a fragrant odor. There were three sheds 81 feet long and 18 wide. One of these was used for rest on rainy days and was closed on the north but open on the south side; the other two had completely enclosed classrooms and teacher rooms for use in cold rainy weather. There were also two very large sheds nonenclosed, where the children studied and ate their lunch. These were used in warm weather and served as protection against both rain and sun. In addition to these five buildings, there were, scattered throughout the grounds, small open sheds capable of seating five to six pupils apiece. These had lockers where the children's rugs and raincoats were kept. Shower baths, a kitchen, and a shed for wraps were also available.

After a breakfast of hot cereal and bread and butter, half the pupils went to class at 8:00 A.M. A lunch of milk and bread and butter was served at 10:00 A.M. A brief 5-minute "stretch" was allowed each half hour. After lunch these pupils played, had gymnastic exercises, did manual work, or read. The other half of the school followed the same program in reverse order. A dinner of meat, potatoes, and green vegetables was served at 12:30 P.M. This was followed by a 2-hour sleep in steamer chairs—a siesta that was indulged in under the trees in nice weather but under the shed when it was rainy. From 3:00 to 4:00 P.M. they studied; a lunch was then eaten, and the rest of the day was spent in play. At 6:45 P.M. supper was served and the children went home. The poorer families had streetcar fare furnished. The pupils attended 7 days each week.

At the initial opening of the school, 95 children enrolled, and the number was gradually increased to an enrollment of 240. The school physician, assisted by principals and teachers, chose the children. There were nine teachers, six men and three women. The regular course of study was followed. Each child cultivated a garden; the girls did needlework, made baskets, and helped prepare vegetables for dinner. All were under the constant care of the school physician. The school nurse saw to it that his prescriptions were carried out. She weighed the children, brought to the physician's attention those needing further examination, and served five meals daily.

---

[1] NEIL S. MACDONALD, *Open-air Schools*, pp. 18–23, McClelland, Goodchild & Stewart, Toronto, 1918.

The school had considerable success. Weight increased, on the average, a half pound per week; behavior improved; personal habits of cleanliness, punctuality, and orderliness were much better; and a great many of the children were permanently cured of the physical ailments that brought them to the school. It was open for 3 months in 1904, 6 months in 1905, 8 months in 1906, and finally was opened permanently on a 12-month basis. Its success was quickly broadcast throughout Germany and within a short time open-air schools had "become an integral part of the German elementary school system."[1] These German schools were called *Waldschulen*, since each city that organized an open-air school picked a site in the midst of the woods.

Open-air Schools in England.—The first open-air school in England was established in July, 1907, at Bostall Woods near London. This move was the result of a visit to Charlottenburg. The school was located in the center of a 20-acre plot of ground; a space 70 feet in diameter was cleared, and two large sheds each open on one side were built. Except in wet weather, the sheds were not used, since in fair weather meals and instruction were both given outdoors. The school was open from 9:00 A.M. to 6:00 P.M., daily except Saturday, for 13 weeks of 5½ days each. One-third of the time was spent at school-work and two-thirds in eating, sleeping, playing, or wandering in the woods. Four meals were served daily—at 9:00 A.M. and 12:30, 3:30, and 5:30 P.M. The daily program was very similar to that followed at Charlottenburg. By 1918, day open-air schools had been established at Birmingham, Bradford, Bristol, Darlington, Halifax, Kettering, Lincoln, Norwich, Sheffield, and York.

Scotland established an open-air classroom in 1907 at the Willowbrae School in Edinburgh; one was started at the Duncan Street School in 1910; and the third was begun in the village of Humbie about 20 miles from Edinburgh in 1912. The Scottish schools, or rather classes, differ from the schools established in England and at Charlottenburg in that they are usually housed in regular school buildings within the city, whereas the others are specially constructed schools within the woods.

Open-air Schools in Canada.—Open-air schools in connection with hospitals opened in Canada, as early as 1910, at the Children's Hospital on Toronto Island. The Toronto board of education started an open-air public school in May, 1913; this was the first of its kind in Canada. It was located at Victoria Park, a short walk from the end of the streetcar tracks. On July 15, 1914, Toronto opened its second school at High Park. These were both forest schools of the

[1] *Ibid.*, p. 23.

Charlottenburg type; each cared for about 100 pupils. Four meals were served daily, except Sunday, at 8:00 A.M., 12:00 M., 3:00 and 5:30 P.M. In good weather, meals were served and studying was done in the open. The school term started in May each year and lasted for 6 months.

Special attention was given to personal hygiene. Each child had to have a toothbrush, and after every meal the children were given tooth-cleaning drills. Each toothbrush was numbered and had its own staple. Washing before meals was supervised. Tub baths were required at least weekly. Eyes, ears, and throat were given constant attention. The schools had a full-time nurse and a doctor who made regular visits. Improvement in the children extended beyond gain in health; they became more attentive, behaved better, and showed decided advance in academic achievement.

Open-air Schools in the United States.—In Providence, R.I., the first open-air school in the United States was started in January, 1908. The board of education allowed an unused school building in the center of the city to be taken over for its establishment; a room on the second floor was used. The brick wall on one side was removed and windows, extending from ceiling to floor, were substituted; these were attached with hinges at the top so that they could be raised to the ceiling leaving the whole side of the room open. Two stoves furnished heat, so that the temperature was rarely under freezing. The children sat in bags which enclosed feet and legs. In the coldest weather, heated soapstones were used to warm the feet. Pupils arrived at 9:00 A.M.; at 10:30 A.M. they were served hot soup; at 12:00 M. they had lunch. The teacher did the cooking. The regular school program was followed. The children gained an average of 5 pounds; they gained also in attention, truthfulness, and academic achievement.

In July, 1908, an association for the relief and cure of tuberculosis started a "school for outdoor life" on Parker Hill at Roxbury, a short distance from the center of Boston. This was immediately taken over by the school board and in January, 1909, was moved from its tents in the apple orchard on Parker Hill to Franklin Park. Here a building 20 feet long and 15 feet high was converted into an open-air school. The dining room and kitchen were on the first floor; the rest room was on the second; and a classroom was provided on the roof. As this room had no heat, the children used bags and blankets. On the sides of the classroom were curtains that could be lowered on stormy days. Three meals were provided daily. The children arrived at 8:30 A.M. and left at 5:00 P.M. The results indicated such great success that a committee of the board of education recommended that, "in all future school buildings, a room especially adapted for open-air schoolwork shall be included in the plans accepted by the School Committee."[1]

In December, 1908, New York City started its first open-air school on an unused ferry boat. This differed very little from the schools at Providence and Boston, except that its location made it unique. It was a success, and four other schools were opened; three were located on ferry boats and one on the roof of the Vanderbilt Clinic at Sixtieth Street. So successful were these schools that the board of education authorized the remodeling of classrooms as open-air rooms. Large corner rooms were usually chosen. In 1918 New York had 65 classrooms remodeled into open-air rooms for anemic children. The board of education had also established 250 classrooms of the open-air type for normal children.

3. METHODS OF ORGANIZATION

The methods of caring for and educating delicate children differ greatly; moreover, the terms used in describing these methods are not uniform.

Open-air Schools.—An open-air school qualified to be so named must have two or more class groups housed independently and supervised and administered apart from other normal or special groups. The housing facilities must be those peculiarly adapted to caring for delicate children. These schools may be specially constructed buildings located within the city or in wooded lands outside the city. Such a school is shown in Illustration 23; this one has four classrooms, a dining room, a clinic, a shower bath, and a sun room.

Complete Open-air Class Units.—These units differ from the school in that they are linked administratively with other class groups regular or special. They share the time of a single supervisory staff. There may be one or more classes. Special provisions, such as a nurse's room, a medical clinic, a dining room, a kitchen, a rest room, and a playroom are furnished. The complete unit may be located on the roof of a regular school, it may be secured by remodeling a section of such a school, or it may be constructed as an integral part of a regular school building. These are open-air units in the sense that one or more sides of each classroom can be thrown wide open.

Open-air Classes.—This type of organization differs from the preceding in only one thing. It lacks many special facilities for the physical care of children that are provided in the former. It is, for all

[1] MacDonald, *op. cit.*, p. 43.

essential purposes, merely a regular classroom or a specially built room that can be opened on one side or more. If medical services are supplied and if food is served, these children are cared for in just the same way as children in regular classes.

Open-window Classes.—These classes differ from the preceding only in the matter of remodeling classrooms. No remodeling is needed in this type of organization. The windows are kept open. Otherwise, a visitor would not be able to distinguish between a classroom of regular pupils and an open-window room.

ILLUSTRATION 23.—A typical open-air school, Detroit. Its capacity is 140 pupils.

4. PROBLEMS INVOLVED

How Many Delicate Children Are There?—According to the White House Conference, 382,000 children are listed as tubercular, 850,000 are suspected cases, 1,000,000 have weak or damaged hearts, 375,000 have serious heart defect, and 6,000,000 are malnourished. Four of the above groups are frequently reported as delicate children. Without allowing for duplication, these five groups equal 8,607,000— a number that·is approximately one-third of all the school children of the United States.

Each community will need to determine how many delicate children it has. It must decide how much of a variation from normal must be allowed before a child will be classified as malnourished, tubercular, or a heart case. Such a problem cannot be solved by laymen; the medical profession must establish standards if surveys in different communities are to be comparable.

The Discovery of Cases.—The attempt to discover delicate children will fail unless a systematic program is developed for checking the entire school population. Anything less than this is guesswork. The method must be continuous and efficient. Some cities have an annual physical examination of all school children; records are kept and tendencies are noted before the child becomes ill. Some cities have a regular daily or weekly inspection by classroom teachers, who report children that seem tired, worn out, and sickly.

New York City[1] uses the preceding methods and also reports from all agencies which in any way contact pupils. Reports come from baby-health centers, preschool age clinics, hospitals, convalescent homes, family physicians, medical specialists, and social workers. The attendance office has records of pupils discharged on account of physical disability. The board of education requires health certificates of all new pupils as well as the "thirteenth year health examination," which provide additional information concerning children who are delicate and who need the services of an open-air school or class.

Keeping Pupils Warm.—The problem of keeping pupils warm depends both upon the climate and upon the belief of local school authorities with respect to the curative value of a cold atmosphere. When the open-air school was first opened, it was held that fresh, outdoor air was essential to perfect health. Early reports showed that heat was supplied only during the coldest weather. One report said that the temperature was seldom allowed below freezing in the classroom and that heat was never used in the sleeping rooms. In colder climates, children had to be supplied with heavy caps, sleeping bags for sleep and study, mittens, blankets, heavy woolen slippers, and heavy soapstone foot warmers. Later practice has raised the temperature of the open-air school considerably; the minimum temperature in many schools is now 60° Fahrenheit. If the more recent suggestions concerning temperature are followed, open-air schools will merely be duplicating the temperature conditions of the modern classroom and the expense for extra clothing for classroom use can be eliminated.

Feeding.—One of the important tasks of the open-air school is feeding. Malnourishment is a result not only of lack of food, but of improper food as well. What a child likes to eat is largely a matter of habit. These children need nourishing food; they need to develop

[1] White House Conference, *Special Education: The Handicapped and the Gifted*, pp. 391–392, The Century Co., New York, 1931.

an appetite for such foods as milk and green vegetables. Unless such new habits can be established at the school and unless the home co-operates in the maintenance of them, the child will, after his transfer to a regular school, quickly return to his former physical condition.

One city reports that its teachers eat their meals with these delicate children. Thus, by example as well as by precept, the children are encouraged to eat wholesome foods. One school reports the following sample 5-cent lunches: Lunch 1 consisted of meat loaf, rice and gravy, bread and jam, milk and apricots; lunch 2 was meat stew

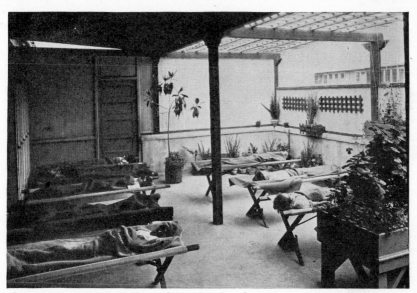

ILLUSTRATION 24.—A sunshine adjustment class during its rest period, Los Angeles.

with potatoes and carrots, bread and sirup, milk, and chocolate cornstarch pudding; lunch 3 provided baked beans, bread and butter, milk, and gingerbread; and lunch 4 included spaghetti and tomato sauce, bread and butter, milk, and raisin pudding.

Rest.—Although rest has been recognized as important in the daily program of the open-air school, it is frequently relegated to second place. Undoubtedly, improper and scanty food is a big element in malnutrition; however, lack of sleep and rest are just as important. The best of food may be eaten but, if the blood supply is immediately and heavily drawn upon for physical and mental energy, the stomach will not have a sufficient supply to digest it properly. For that reason, open-air schools make a practice of allowing a rest period immediately after the lunch hour. This period frequently extends from 1:00 to 3:00 P.M. if the lunch is over at 1:00 P.M. In Illustration 24, can be seen a Los Angeles class during one of its rest periods; the name "sunshine adjustment class" is given to this kind of class.

Many schools have a shorter period. Rogers reports[1] that, in 28 schools where only one rest period is allowed, 1 hour is the usual length. Fourteen schools allow two periods for rest, distributed variously as to length; seven of them allowed 1 hour per period. Two schools each had three rest periods; one granted 30 minutes per period; the other allowed one period of 15 minutes, one of 30 minutes, and another of 180 minutes. A fairly long period of rest immediately after the noonday meal seems logical and justifiable.

Curricula.—The curricular problem is similar to that of the regular schools. Many open-air schools make no adjustment, but the more frequent practice is to shorten the periods allowed for regular school subjects. Many open-air schools omit shopwork and domestic science in order to have time for the academic subjects. These schools undoubtedly feel under pressure to emphasize the academic, since they are urged to keep the children up to grade so that they will not be held back when they return to the regular school.

If these children are to take the time needed for feeding and rest, the regular school program will have to be reduced. Since it is the aim of the special school to return these children to regular classes as soon as possible, there is some argument for insisting that the academic work be stressed. If their stay in the special school is for a year or less, they can maintain their regular grade standing and still have time after they return to the regular school for shopwork and domestic science. This suggestion applies particularly to those children who can profit from academic instruction.

Medical Care and Treatment.—Previous to being enrolled in the open-air school, each child is given a thorough physical examination. After admission, he is under medical observation until a good picture is secured of his general bodily conditions. Any difficulties such as adenoids, bad tonsils, decayed teeth, or anemia are noted and steps are taken to see that they are remedied. Parents are consulted and arrangements are made for treatments, operations, or both.

Practice varies in the matter of physical examinations; a few schools make them annually, whereas a few have them weekly. The most common method is to give examinations at the beginning and at the close of each year. Most schools hold dental examinations for

[1] JAMES FREDERICK ROGERS, "Schools and Classes for Delicate Children," p. 25, *U.S. Office of Education Bulletin* 22, Washington, D.C., 1930.

all pupils yearly, weigh the pupils each week, and take a child's temperature only when directed by a physician, or not at all.[1]

Every school from which data were received by Rogers reported a part-time or a full-time nurse or nurses included in the staff of the open-air school. In most cases, the full-time nurse was employed. Her work is to visit the home and try to secure the co-operation of parents in maintaining at home the individual health program started at the special school. She is responsible for a frequent inspection of all children enrolled.

Hygienic Way of Life.—The open-air school is not just a place where children are fed, given plenty of rest and fresh air, and placed under the care of physician and nurse, as well as under the instruction of a teacher. These things are important parts of the school's program, but they may all be most carefully planned and carried out and still the school will have failed unless it has given the child a different point of view concerning health. This new point of view has been called the hygienic way of life. Not only are the ideals of cleanliness, of proper bodily care, of correct feeding, and of regularity in sleep and exercise necessary, but the appropriate and detailed habits that accompany these ideals must be established to the extent of habituation.

This task is the biggest that the teacher of an open-air school faces. She must break down life habits and, in place of them, build up others. Many of them are tied up with strong emotional attitudes, which must be recognized and dealt with rationally before the habit can be destroyed. This effort enters the sacred precincts of the home. Home practices are, at least indirectly, criticized. For the best results, parents must co-operate. In the case of people who know that there are better ways of living, but who have not known what they are, immediate co-operation can be expected. Where the parents hold a strong belief in their own way of doing things, the problem is difficult; and where the family has no interest in the children and no ambition to better itself, the task is nearly hopeless. Despite these difficulties, the implanting of a working ideal for the "hygienic way of life" in the thinking of these children is a real goal of the open-air schools.

Work of the Teacher.—The teacher of an open-air class has many duties that the regular teacher does not have. She must make arrangements for meals for her pupils; she serves milk and crackers or cocoa at lunches; and at noon she directs the preparation and serving of the meal. She supervises the cleaning of teeth and plans and supervises rest periods. She weighs the pupils at stated intervals; she inspects

[1] *Ibid.*, p. 24.

them constantly to discover those needing medical attention; and she makes sure they are comfortably clothed.

Equipment.—Types of equipment usually suggested for open-air schools are cots, extra clothing, and blankets. The cots are often so light that the pupils can manage them for themselves. Scales are needed for weighing the children. A cookstove, cooking utensils, tableware, kitchen cupboards, storage space for blankets, foot warmers,

ILLUSTRATION 25.—Pupils at work in a Detroit open-air classroom. Note windows on three sides and movable desks which allow changing positions in the sunlight.

filing cabinets, a typewriter, dining-room tables and chairs, and a refrigerator are some of the special pieces of equipment that will be needed. Baths, both shower and tub, should be provided; nurse's equipment should be available; the extra clothing may include a heavy overcoat, a sitting-out bag, two blankets, a knitted cap, and warm gloves. Eskimo suits are often used. Window space is abundant; Illustration 25 shows windows on three sides of a classroom.

Extent of Cure.—This is a crucial problem. Its answer holds the key to the determination of the value of open-air classes. We are interested both in the number of cures and in the permanence of those cures.   Data on the number cured are scarce, and on the permanence of cure they are practically unattainable.

New York City in June, 1921, reported 3,515 children enrolled during the preceding year in open-air classes.   During that year, 298—or 8.5 per cent—were discharged as cured.   This does not give the number out of the 3,217 who were retained and who were finally released as cured within the next 2 or 3 years.

Chicago's report in 1923 showed that 304 of the 2,045 children enrolled had been transferred to regular schools as cured; this was 14.9 per cent.   The report states, "In general, no child's residence is prolonged beyond the point where he is found physically sound and ready to work under the conditions prescribed for children in the regular grades."[1]   It also states that about 3 per cent of the children in open-air schools have to be retained over 2 years.   This implies a rather high percentage of cure.

When we ask about the permanency of these cures, we have even less data.   The permanency of the cure, of course, depends upon the child's ailment.   If he has symptoms of tuberculosis, permanency is less likely, unless the child can continue to have good food, rest, and sunshine after he leaves the school.   Myers[2] of Minneapolis says that, unless these cases remain much longer than they usually do, the trouble will soon recur.   He reports many children who have had relapses and died, and he recommends that the pupils remain in the special school until grade 8 has been completed.

As early as 1913, Newark, N.J.,[3] reported that, for the preceding 2 years, 60 per cent of the children in their open-air pavilions for tubercular pupils were cured, 39.5 per cent had improved, and 0.5 per cent had failed to improve.   Reports for the same city showed that 62.5 per cent of the children in open-air classes had been cured, 32.3 per cent had improved, and 5.2 per cent had not improved.

Follow-up.—Principals and teachers in schools for delicate children can point to cases that have returned after having been dismissed as cured.   We do not know, of those who do not return, the number that should have done so.   The return of such conditions may be due to a failure of the child or the home or both to have achieved that "hygienic way of life" which the special school is supposed to have developed.   It may be due to inability, financially, to put that way of life into operation.   Social conditions as well as personal attitudes are

---

[1] FRANK G. BRUNER, *Report of the Director of Special Schools for the School Year* 1922–23, p. 45, Board of Education, Chicago, 1924.

[2] ROGERS, *op. cit.*, p. 21.

[3] MACDONALD, *op. cit.*, p. 83.

factors in determining the permanence of the cure. If the latter are at fault, the school has failed; if the former are responsible, society has a responsibility for making it impossible to deprive youths of their birth rights—health and education. We need follow-up studies that will determine the permanence of the cure and the factors responsible for any lack of permanence.

Costs.—In most American school systems, the cost of supporting open-air classes is carried by the school district; outside agencies may help to provide medical services or food, or both. Tuberculosis associations have assumed a considerable portion of the additional expense during experimental periods. In Chicago, the Elizabeth McCormick Memorial Fund at first paid all costs except the teachers' salaries. The extras included medical services, nurses, matrons, cooks, helpers, food, milk, cots, blankets, Eskimo suits, and foot boots. With a few exceptions, local boards of education have now assumed the entire cost of maintaining these schools. An office of education report[1] in 1930 gave the average per pupil cost of open-air classes as $178. The range varied from $52.77 to $380.

5. REPRESENTATIVE CITY PROGRAMS

Columbus.—The first open-air school in Columbus started in the fall of 1914. The Society for the Prevention and Cure of Tuberculosis had tried from 1911 to get a good location for such a school. A committee of the society proposed to the board of education on Mar. 18, 1913, a co-operative plan for managing an open-air school; the society was to erect a building according to prescribed plans and provide physician, nurse, cook, food, clothing, and any other supplies not specified as a responsibility of the board; the board was to provide teacher, janitor, schoolroom supplies and equipment, light, heat, and water.

The board approved the plan and the building was built. This co-operative arrangement lasted for 2 years. In October, 1916, the society proposed that, if the board would assume full charge of maintaining the school, they would give up all claims to the property. On Nov. 1, the board accepted the proposal. The old building soon failed to meet the needs of the city. In November, 1928, the present building[2] was completed; it is a beautiful structure attractively located on the east bluff overlooking the Olentangy River Valley. This building cost $101,226.16; the equipment cost $6,260.51.

[1] ROGERS, *op. cit.*, p. 14.
[2] For description, see pp. 330–332.

Los Angeles.[1]—The sunshine adjustment class is Los Angeles' contribution to the care of delicate children. It is for the child

. . . who shows failure to gain; who has an irregular school attendance due to illness; who catches cold easily; the listless, tired child who does not care to play; the nervous and irritable child; the one who makes poor recovery from acute illness such as measles; the one who has come in contact with open cases of tuberculosis; and the debilitated child who comes from the home of extreme poverty.

ILLUSTRATION 26.—Study on a sunny roof at Los Angeles. A sunshine adjustment class for physically deficient children.

Before his placement in the school, a complete physical examination is made of each child, causes of the condition are pointed out, and recommendations are made by the physician to both parents and nurse for effecting the necessary corrections. In addition to the usual program in such classes, the children are given "fundamental instructions in health-giving habits." Illustration 26 shows a Los Angeles class studying on a sunny roof. It is a sunshine adjustment class for physically deficient children.

New York City.[2]—The delicate child is cared for in special classes in New York City. A report in 1921 showed 117 open-air classes,

[1] From data received from the superintendent's office early in 1937.

[2] *Twenty-third Annual Report of the Superintendent of Schools*, 1920–21, pp. 102–114, Board of Education, New York City, 1921. Also "Handicapped and

with a registration of 3,217 children.   In 1933–34 there were 192 classes, enrolling 4,659 pupils and 23 outdoor classes in day camps, enrolling 552 tuberculous pupils.   The open-air classes were organized primarily for pupils who "are tuberculous contact and history cases and are positive tuberculin reactors."   Schools not having enough such children to organize a class admitted malnutrites.   Most of the children in these special classes are of the latter type.   Malnutrites include (1) the malnourished due to insufficient or unsuitable food, (2) the malnourished due to infection from "tonsils, sinuses, teeth, and other infections and parasitic infections," (3) the "tired child," (4) the congenitally weak, and (5) the anemic.

Open-air classrooms are confined to the first three floors.   Corner rooms are used, preferably on the south side of the building; this gives sunshine and cross ventilation.   The mean temperature is 45° Fahrenheit.   A classroom will contain 25 adjustable movable seats, 25 folding cots, and scales.   Eskimo suits are provided; each includes a hood and mittens attached to the coat, bloomers, and leggings.

An attempt is made to establish good personal and home health habits.   Health inspections are made each morning.   Milk, whole-wheat bread, and butter are served to all each morning; a hot lunch is provided for the needy.   Reporting in 1934, the assistant director of health education of the New York City schools says,

One out of every five children in regular classes in the city, and one out of every three in Manhattan should have special study and adjustment directed toward improving his physical condition.   Nevertheless, many thousands of children are compelled to take part daily in mental and physical activity programmes which aggravate the conditions from which they are suffering.[1]

Even as early as 1920–21, a city report stated that a great portion of the city was not reached by open-air classes.   It estimated that 560 open-air classes would be needed to care for all pupils exposed to tuberculosis in their own homes.   "The ideal solution," says this report, "for an adequate supply of open-air class accommodations would be to have at least one class of each grade in every school an open-air class."[2]   The classes would be filled by pupils physically

---

Underprivileged Children," a special report submitted with the *Thirty-sixth Annual Report of the Superintendent of Schools*, pp. 138–144, Board of Education, New York City, 1934.

[1] "Handicapped and Underprivileged Children," a special report submitted with the *Thirty-sixth Annual Report of the Superintendent of Schools*, p. 141, Board of Education, New York City, 1934.

[2] *Twenty-third Annual Report of the Superintendent of Schools*, 1920–21, p. 111, Board of Education, New York City, 1921.

normal if enough delicate children were not available. The suggestion was further made that the next step to be taken after all delicate children are cared for properly would be to have open-air classes for all pupils. This is the "ultimate solution for preserving the physical condition of our school children and thereby rearing a healthy nation."[1]

Later in 1933–34, we find the assistant director of health education urging as an emergency measure that "open-air classes should be organized in every school district until there is at least one open-air class in every public school building to care for the most urgent and serious cases."[2] The city in 1933–34 was constructing these special classrooms in new buildings.

6. HOUSING FACILITIES

The first school buildings erected to house delicate children were rough sheds; sometimes one side was left open, and frequently there were no sides. The roof protected the children from the rain and the hot rays of the sun. As the work of the open-air school extended into the winter months, arrangements had to be made to protect the children against extreme cold. This was accomplished at first by having siding on at least three sides of the shed or schoolroom and by providing stoves and extra wraps. As experimentation continued, it was discovered that excessively cold temperatures were not so conducive to good health as were more moderate temperatures. This led to the modern open-air school building, which can be entirely enclosed, but which has an excessive amount of window space, so that the rooms can be thrown wide open.

Open-air Rooms.—If open-air classes only are to be provided, the housing problems are relatively simple. A room in a regular school is selected as the home for the class. If it has adequate window space, no change is made architecturally. It is frequently shut off from the regular ventilation system and the windows are opened so as to prevent drafts. Window space is provided on at least two sides and, where possible, on three sides of the room.

Unique Features of Buildings.—Buildings for open-air schools differ greatly in design, but there are certain features that characterize most of them. They contain, in addition to classrooms, a kitchen, a dining room, a clinic room, showers, tub baths, and usually a sun porch and sleeping rooms.

[1] *Ibid.*, p. 111.

[2] "Handicapped and Underprivileged Children," a special report submitted with the *Thirty-sixth Annual Report of the Superintendent of Schools*, p. 142, Board of Education, New York City, 1934.

The windows, as a rule, are different from those in ordinary schools. Some swing from the center, some are large, sliding windows; some are hinged at the side and swing in; some are hinged at the top and swing upward to the ceiling; some are in three or more vertical sections and pivot about a horizontal center; others swing open full length; and still others open out from the bottom. Those hinged at the side or the top and swinging in or up have been reported to be less successful than the other types.

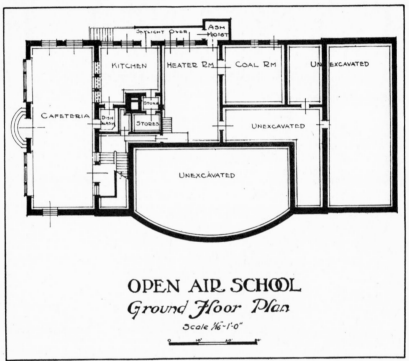

FIG. 5.—Basement floor of the open-air school at Columbus, Ohio.

Building Plans.—Columbus has a unique and attractive open-air school. The floor plans for this school are shown in Figs. 5, 6, and 7. Figure 5 shows the dining room in the basement on the west side of the building. The kitchen opens upon the outdoor ramp and into the storeroom and the dining room.

The first floor has classrooms in double units at the west and east sides of the building, as shown in Fig. 6. A wide corridor connects these two units. A large sheltered play porch is on the south side, facing the playgrounds. The principal's office is on the north center, with the clinic, the consultation room, and the storerooms on either

side. At either end of this north central section and adjoining the
class units are the girls' and the boys' toilets, situated on the west and
east ends respectively; the toilets both have shower and tub baths.

The second floor, as shown in Fig. 7, likewise has two class units,
with double rooms; between these rooms is a large sleeping room, with
a southern exposure, which can be cleared for play in bad or cold
weather. The terrace can be used in any but stormy weather; it

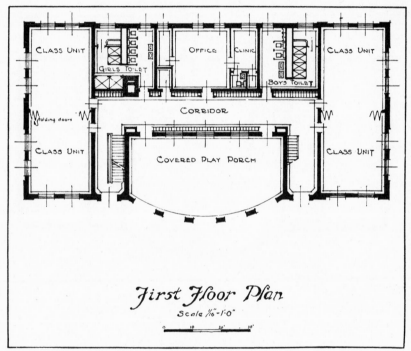

Fig. 6.—First-floor plan of the open-air school at Columbus, Ohio.

has a 5½-foot parapet around the outer edge for safety. Toilets both
for boys and for girls are also on this floor.

7. CAUSES OF THE CONDITION OF DELICATE CHILDREN

Of those groups under which delicate children may be classified, the
largest is that of the malnourished. The primary cause of such a
condition is failure to take proper care of the body; this includes overwork, lack of sleep, and insufficient or improper food. Deficiency in
food is undoubtedly the most important of the three. Malnutrition
may be due, besides, to decayed teeth and tonsils, hookworms, ascaris,
and malarial parasites; or it may be due to poor assimilation of food or

to weakened conditions resulting from various diseases from which recovery was not normal. There are children whose malnourishment can be assigned to no particular causes; it may be due to inheritance. Nonrobust parents, through faulty nutrition during the prenatal period, may account for this condition.

Another large group of delicate children is made up of those who are tubercular. Active cases are not accepted in the special schools.

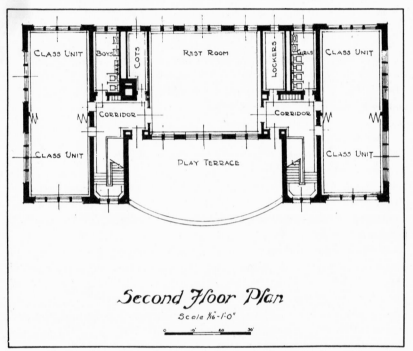

FIG. 7.—Second-floor plan of the open-air school at Columbus, Ohio.

Contact cases and cases predisposed to tubercular conditions are accepted. These conditions, as implied, may result from contact with other cases. They may develop after severe cases of pneumonia, influenza, asthma, chronic bronchitis, whooping cough, or any acute systemic infection.

A third group, consisting of cardiopathic children, shows results from various severe contagious diseases where proper aftercare has been neglected. Influenza may affect the heart; overexercise habitually carried to the point of exhaustion may cause trouble; or the difficulty may be inherited.

8. PREVENTION

Knowledge of Food Values.—If insufficient and improper food are the chief causes, as the preceding section would seem to indicate, then two separate and distinctly different steps must be taken if prevention is to be effective. The first step is one of education. Parents must know food values. Even now great numbers do not. The diet of their children too frequently lacks the elements necessary for good physical development. Much is being done at present; physicians, nurses, and teachers are helping to inform parents and children. These efforts need to be more systematized if all are to be reached.

Food Made Available.—Next, it must be possible to get the needed food. Since 1929, this problem has assumed enormous proportions. Schools and relief organizations have provided food for millions but, despite the zeal and energy of these workers, many children have gone without. What has been done during the past few years must be continued, but a better organization for doing the job must be developed and more money for such relief must be made available, or the number of delicate school children will materially increase. If the unemployment of the thirties proves to be the normal situation during the several decades to come, these relief agencies must become a permanent part of our social organization if children are to be made and kept healthy.

Medical Examination.—Since infections seem to affect the physical condition of children detrimentally, they should be constantly checked upon. This implies regular examinations by nurses and doctors if the work is to be preventive. These examinations should be so frequent that serious conditions will not have time to develop during the intervening intervals. In addition, teachers should have sufficient training to be able to report to the school nurse or the school physician children who require immediate attention.

This program cannot be operated with the present staff of school nurses and physicians; there are not hours enough during the day for examining regularly and keeping records of these examinations for all children. To examine, moreover, is useless unless something is done about the conditions that are found. This means a follow-up to see either that parents provide the medical care necessary or that they permit the school physician and nurses to do it. There are many implications of such an extensive program of physical supervision. If the state is to compel parents to correct the physical defects in their children that are reducing the social efficiency of those children, then the state should provide the medical care necessary to that end.

Some suggest that doctors and nurses become state officials on salary. If the state ought to assume the responsibility for the physical well-being of our school children, and does so, then it may be that the larger program, whereby all medical service becomes a function of the state, should be put into operation.

Care of Prospective Mothers.—If delicate children are the result of faulty nutrition during the prenatal period, another demand for extensive education is to be met. If well-fed healthy mothers bring forth husky, healthy babies, whereas the ill-fed, overworked mothers do not, we need to give wide publicity to all facts available about the physical needs of prospective mothers. Despite such knowledge, many prospective mothers will be unable either to have such food or to stop work long enough to secure the needed rest. A school man suggested recently that all prospective mothers should be under the supervision and care of state physicians during the prenatal period; further, he suggested that, in families where the mother works, the state should supplement the family income by the amount of her wages, so that she need not overwork during this period. If the state is to assume responsibility for the health of children after birth, the logic of this school man's argument would seem sound. Such prenatal care might materially reduce the postnatal care needed.

Education of Parents Concerning Common Ailments or Diseases of Children.—Another program in prevention is closely linked with a suggestion previously made for the prevention of every other type of physically handicapped child. Parents too seldom realize how dangerous the aftereffects of many of the ordinary contagious diseases of children are. The physical deficiencies of many delicate children have originated from the aftereffects of just such diseases. The common cold, catarrh, and influenza are also sources of ailments that make children delicate. Too much emphasis cannot be placed upon this one idea of educating parents regarding common ailments and diseases.

9. STATE LEGISLATION

State legislation governing the care and education of delicate children is noted for its rarity. A few states indirectly, under general legislation, provide for special classes. Rarely are these children legislated for as such. Four types of legislation should be passed in order that they may be cared for adequately. (1) There should be state regulations governing the finding of delicate children; a continuous census would become the basis for such discovery. (2) Adequate medical services should be mandatory. (3) Regular teachers should be required to take a 2- or 3-hour course that would help them to detect quickly the symptoms of disease and physical defect. (4) The law should make mandatory special educational facilities for delicate children. If a school district is too small to maintain a class, it should be required to combine with other districts. Very small districts, however, can make arrangements for their delicate children by building a small ell to even a one-room schoolhouse; glass partitions may separate the two units; the ell can have cots and desks for the few children who are to be given special care. Specific provision should be made by state law for the administration and supervision of these classes.

10. A STATE PROGRAM

The following are the essential elements in a state program of caring for and educating delicate children. (1) There should be a state supervisor who will help to develop and supervise their instruction. (2) There should be a census of these children, maintained as a part of the whole school census. (3) State support should be provided. (4) Every district should have its school nurse or nurses and school physician or physicians, who will assist in maintaining the census. (5) All teachers in regular classrooms will aid in keeping the census up to date. (6) Every district shall make special arrangements for the education of delicate children. Most delicate children can be best cared for by having special classes within the regular building. If the children found in certain sections of a city require the care of a specially equipped building, that should be provided. (7) A follow-up program should be established in each local system to determine the effectiveness of such a program of special education.

11. SUMMARY

Delicate children are frequently ignored because there are so many of them. The group includes the malnourished, the nonactive tubercular, and heart cases. These children should have unusual care given to their physical development. An educational program for them began in Germany at Charlottenburg, in 1904; such a program was introduced into England in 1907, into the United States in 1908, and into Canada in 1910. Forest and regular schools, open-air rooms and open-window rooms are among the methods used in public schools to provide for them. There are 8,607,000 delicate children in the United States. A suggestion comes from New York City that there ought to be one open-window room in each grade in every large school. If at any time there are only a few who are delicate, these rooms can be filled with normal children.

Discovering these children early, transporting them, keeping them warm, feeding them, giving them adequate rest, providing needed medical care, developing as an ideal the hygienic way of life, securing home co-operation, getting proper equipment, and checking the success of the work—these are a few of the problems to be solved in establishing a special educational program for delicate children. Columbus and Detroit have established open-air schools; Chicago and New York City have organized a great many open-air rooms and open-window rooms.

If prevention is to be effective, we need school physicians and school nurses; we need regular teachers who can detect physical ailments; we need an educational program that will cause parents to consider more seriously the common contagious diseases; we need some method of providing better prenatal care; and we need authority to compel parents to provide needed medical aid or to allow the state to do so.

Problems and Questions for Discussion

1. What makes the problem of caring for and educating delicate children a treacherous one? Explain.

2. Who are the delicate children? How many of them are there?

3. What principles should govern the education of such children? Why?

4. Trace briefly the history of the education of delicate children. What significant changes, if any, have taken place in the theory and method of caring for and educating these children?

5. How did and do these schools for delicate children differ from schools for physically normal children?

6. What differences, if any, existed between early European schools for delicate children and early American schools?

7. What methods of organization are used at present in caring for and educating the delicate child? Which is best? Why?

8. Enumerate the chief problems to be met in caring for and educating delicate children. What is your suggested solution for each?

9. Do you believe that the fresh, cold outdoor air is essential to the restoration of delicate children to perfect health? Why?

10. What is the significance of the expression "the hygienic way of life" in the training program of the delicate child? Why do you believe thus?

11. What data are you able to discover relative to the effectiveness of open-air schools and classes?

12. What unique structural features do we find in the school buildings that house delicate children?

13. What are the arguments for classes vs. schools? Which method do you believe to be the best? Why?

14. What causes lie back of the existence of many delicate children?

15. What suggestions do you have to make for the prevention of conditions that lead to our having so many of these children?

16. Do we need more state legislation covering the care and education of delicate children? Why?

17. What kind of state organization do you conceive as necessary if the best work is to be done?

Selected Bibliography

Amoss, Harry, and DeLaporte, L. Helen. *Training Handicapped Children*, pp. 209–214. Ryerson Press, Toronto, 1933.

A brief statement of who may enter open-air classes is given; a description of open-window classes, open-air schools, and forest schools and of the equipment for them is presented. The feedings are described, as is also other physical care which is given the pupils.

Bruner, Frank G. *Report of the Director of Special Schools for the School Year*, 1922–23, pp. 33–50. Board of Education, Chicago, 1924.

A brief account of the origin of open-air schools in Chicago is given; schools are described; work of co-operative agencies is explained; and data on weight gains are given.

MacDonald, Neil S. *Open-air Schools*. McClelland, Goodchild & Stewart, Publishers, Toronto, 1918. 127 pp.

A good historical account is given of open-air schools in Germany, Great Britain, Canada, the United States, and other countries. Good descriptions of typical open-air schools, dealing with site, buildings, equipment, staff, pupils, food, sleep, and curriculum are presented. Open-air schools for normal pupils are discussed.

McDonald, Robert Alexander Fyfe. *Adjustment of School Organization to Various Population Groups*, pp. 78–84. Teachers College, Columbia University, New York, 1915.

Presents a brief history of open-air schools, describes very briefly current practice in the management of such schools, and presents some results.

McLeod, Beatrice. "Teachers' Problems with Exceptional Children: VI. Children of Lowered Vitality." *U.S. Office of Education Pamphlet* 56. Washington, D.C., 1934. 16 pp.

Problems of definition, discovery, prevention, causes, education, summer care, and physical care are considered.

Rogers, James Frederick. "Schools and Classes for Delicate Children." *U.S. Office of Education Bulletin* 22. Washington, D.C., 1930. 66 pp.

Deals with many administrative aspects of open-air schools and classes; such topics as buildings, organization, care of pupils, educational program, and results are considered. Discusses also preventoriums, nutrition classes, and health camps. Describes open-air schools abroad.

White House Conference. *Special Education: The Handicapped and the Gifted*, pp. 385–436. The Century Co., New York, 1931.

Describes types of cases, purpose of classes, how to find cases, incidence, need for special classes and schools, what is being done, and what should be done.

PART III
EDUCATION OF MENTALLY EXCEPTIONAL CHILDREN

CHAPTER XXIII

THE EDUCATION OF CHILDREN OF LOW I.Q.

1. INTRODUCTION

Financial depressions disrupt past thought patterns. The more serious the depression, the more radically are those patterns changed. Questions that would have been rank heresy earlier are raised with engaging frankness. Deprivation of jobs, of homes, and of conveniences thought essential to well-being brings critical faculties to the fore. Social practices are examined and re-evaluated.

Thus it is that individual profits, individual control, and private ownership of business are being weighed in the balances. Despite the real values they have, if the greater social good can be achieved only in other ways, these institutions must go. No social institution can escape this critical analysis if the depression is severe enough and lasts long enough.

Those interested in public education must be just as concerned that the social values of universal education shall be known and understood as is the advocate of private business that its values shall be noted. School men are asking, for example, where the proper balance is between a program for children who are normal mentally, physically, and socially and a program for those who deviate widely from that normal state. Some question the advisability of caring for, protecting, and educating at excessive cost these deviates at the expense of the large normal group. They point to the millions required by state institutions and by public schools to educate and maintain these unfortunates; they suggest that the attempt to bear such a financial burden means bankruptcy and the annihilation of the present social order.

There are others who, though they see a real social value in the care and education of the social and physical deviates and of the children of high I.Q., seriously question present-day programs of educating children of low I.Q. They point to high birth rates among this group and to low birth rates among those of high I.Q.; they decry the desecration and pollution of the "social blood stream."

Thus it is that, among all the groups of children for whom special education is provided, perhaps none needs to have its cause presented

341

more clearly and carefully than does the group designated as children of low I.Q. Those interested in such a program must not expect other educational workers to make these defenses, but must, themselves, present the needs of their program and must make clear its value both to the individual and to the larger social group.

2. DEFINITION

A Common Misapprehension.—Frequently, children are referred to as bright, average, and subnormal, as though there were three clearly distinct and separate groups of children. Certain terminology used at present may help to give the lie to such assumptions; the terms "high" and "low," for example, are relative. The high hill of one section of the country would be low in another; the high mountain of one range would be a pigmy in another. Such variations are common. Perhaps, therefore, the use of high I.Q., average I.Q., and low I.Q., will assist the layman in visualizing not three distinct groups of children but a single group—one that varies by the minutest of changes, from those of unusual academic ability to those of very meager ability.

The Importance of the I.Q.—The term "I.Q." is satisfactory because it is one of the measures for determining the extent to which a child is able to master academic school requirements. Although data concerning the child's physical condition, his emotional stability, and his home conditions will be needed, the I.Q. will be an important factor in leading up to this decision.

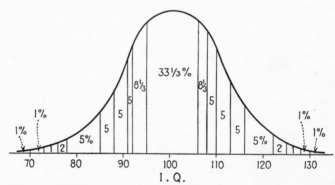

Fig. 8.—Percentage distribution of I.Q.'s of 1,000 children. (*Adapted from Terman.*[1])

A Child of Low I.Q. Defined.—Children rated upon the Stanford revision of the Binet-Simon test approximate a normal distribution if the group is nonselected and if there are enough cases. Terman

[1] LEWIS M. TERMAN, *The Measurement of Intelligence*, p. 78, Houghton Mifflin Company, Boston, 1916.

measured 1,000 "representative children." They distributed themselves as shown in Fig. 8. One-third of the group ranged from 95 to 106 I.Q.; 1 per cent had I.Q.'s of 70 or less, and 1 per cent had I.Q.'s of 130 or above. The variations from 100 for equal percentages to the right and the left are not identical, but they are nearly so. The distribution is approximately normal. This figure shows how children vary continuously from a very low I.Q. to a very high I.Q. For the purpose of forming special classes, the White House Conference says that 70 is the usual point for making this grouping, but that 80 is sometimes used.

3. GUIDING PRINCIPLES

Equality of Opportunity.—The program for such pupils must provide equality of opportunity, not identity. Their academic ability is too low to enable them to profit from the regular school program; neither content nor methods would be suitable. When forced to compete with children of average or high I.Q., these pupils fail; they develop a failure complex toward life; ambition is either destroyed or never developed. They are virtually taught that they cannot succeed.

Yet such children can succeed even with academic schoolwork if the steps are developed slowly, if constant repetition is made, and if methods are concrete and direct. Earlier there was a tendency to eliminate academic instruction. Now we know that most of these youths can achieve an ability to read children's stories of third- and fourth- and even fifth-grade level; that the simple fundamental operations of arithmetic can be taught and the use of these applied to the making of change; that history and geography, rewritten in simple story form, can be taught.

Self-support.—A program that will assist in making these children self-supporting should be planned. This can be done in normal times. During a financial depression, which puts millions of men out of work, the problem becomes more acute. This does not mean that we must give them technical vocational training. The work that these children will do as adults will be some type of unskilled labor, the technical part of which they can easily learn in a few hours' time.

It is possible, however, to habituate these children to regular habits of work, so that any work they can do will become a pleasure to them. If they are given schoolwork within their ability, the delight of successful achievement will contribute further to their desire to work. Care in choosing a job that lies within the range of their ability is all that is needed later on to keep them happily occupied.

Much of the simple industrial training given at present is often criticized as not practical. The critic must constantly keep in mind the objectives. We must first establish regular habits of work. We must then habituate these children in the use of their hands and fingers; hands that are clumsy must be made less clumsy if they are to succeed in industry.

Good Conduct.—Next, these children must form habits of good conduct. They must be trained to live happily among their fellows. This involves the establishment of habits of personal cleanliness, of not disturbing the property of others, of self-control, of ignoring strangers, of helping friends, of speaking kindly, and of telling the truth.

Avoid Stigmatization.—Finally, this special work should not stigmatize the child. This is impossible to accomplish 100 per cent, since the child himself so often carries with him those characteristics that automatically set him apart from normal children, regardless of whether he is in a special class or a regular class. Every effort should be made, however, to eliminate a disparaging attitude. Such expressions as "dumbbells," "feeble-minded," "subnormals" should be eliminated from the vocabulary of public school teachers and officials.

4. HISTORY

The education of children of low I.Q. is more recent than that for several types of physically handicapped children, despite the fact that the number now receiving education far exceeds the number being educated in any of the groups of the physically handicapped. This is due partly to the numbers involved and partly to the seriousness of the handicap, which makes it virtually impossible for children of low I.Q. to succeed in the regular grade classes.

Beginnings.[1]—Itard, about 1800, made the first attempt of which we have any record to educate a feeble-minded child. He was at the time the medical director of the National Institute for the Deaf and Dumb at Paris. This child, when about eleven years of age, was found wandering in a French forest; and was literally a wild man. For 5 years Itard sought to educate this youth; but so little progress was made that he decided the child was a hopeless idiot and gave up the task.

Doubtless Itard was too close to his problem to appraise his results correctly. At least the French Academy of Science praised him for his contribution to the science of education. It pointed to numerous changes that had taken place in the boy during his period of training.

[1] W. E. FERNALD, "History of the Treatment of the Feebleminded," *Proceedings of the National Conference of Charities and Correction*, 1893.

He had been taught numerous words, he could write, and he could make known through writing things that he wanted.   Thus, instead of failing, Itard had succeeded in demonstrating the principle that idiots have traits and characteristics similar to those in normal human beings; they differ in the degree to which they have them.   Given time and careful training, the idiot can be taught over a broad horizontal range, though he never reaches very high on any vertical scale of ability.

Edward Seguin, a pupil of Itard, appreciating fully the significance of Itard's contribution, started in 1837 a school in Paris for mental defectives that was supported by his own funds.   In 1846 he published a book dealing with idiocy, for which he attained considerable note. His work at Paris was so successful that other countries soon started schools for the mentally deficient.   He later came to the United States and in 1878 started a private school in New York City; later it was moved to Orange, N.J.

American Beginnings.—The American Asylum for the Deaf and Dumb at Hartford did the first educational work for the feeble-minded in America.   This was being done as early as 1818.   In 1842 Horace Mann visited schools for the feeble-minded in Europe; he was impressed by what they were doing and urged that such schools be established in America.   As early as March, 1846, a bill was brought before the New York legislature proposing the establishment of a school for the feeble-minded of that state.   The senate passed the bill, but the assembly turned it down.

Massachusetts, under the leadership of Samuel Howe, established a school for indigent feeble-minded youths in 1848.   The school was opened on Oct. 1 of that year, and was located at the Perkins Institute for the Blind, where Howe was superintendent.   After 3 years it became an independent school under the title of the Massachusetts School for Idiotic and Feeble-minded Youth.

H. B. Wilbur, in the July preceding, had opened, at Barre, Mass., a private school for the feeble-minded.   His, therefore, was the first school in the United States for the feeble-minded.   It was established on the family basis and proved very successful.   The second school was started near Albany, N.Y., as an experiment by the state legislature; Wilbur was brought from Barre, Mass., to be the superintendent.   Three years later the school was transferred to Syracuse, where the city had donated a site.   McDonald says this was "the first purely state institution in this country."[1]

[1] ROBERT ALEXANDER FYFE McDONALD, *Adjustment of School Organization to Various Population Groups*, p. 45, Teachers College, Columbia University, New York, 1915.

Public School Provisions.—Public school provisions for children of low I.Q. were considerably delayed. It has been suggested that this was due to lack of compulsory school-attendance legislation. As long as the children were not compelled to attend, those of low I.Q. seldom continued long in school; many never started.

Only two states had passed compulsory attendance legislation previous to 1870. During the seventies and the eighties, a great many states passed compulsory attendance laws; it was not until the nineties, however, that provisions began to be made for the enforcement of this legislation. It was during that closing decade of the nineteenth century that cities began to establish their first special classes for children of low I.Q.

The special class for children of low I.Q. seems to have started at Providence, R.I., in 1896; and in 1898, Springfield, Mass., organized a class. In November of the same year, Boston hired its first teacher for a class of mentally defective children. The class actually began work on Jan. 30, 1899, at "the Appleton-street Primary School house."[1] By 1906, seven classes had been started, with an enrollment of slightly under 100 pupils.

In the fall of 1900[2] Chicago opened its first class for children of low I.Q. at the Schiller School, with 15 pupils enrolled. A second class was organized in the Marquette School in 1902. There were classes in four other schools by 1906. One of the difficulties that faced teachers of the first classes organized for children of low I.Q. in Chicago was early recognized by school authorities. In 1914 the superintendent's report says, "We have in the divisions for the subnormal a 'hodge-podge' made up of children suffering from"[3] physical ailments and nervous disorders as well as from permanent mental retardation.

In 1911, so great was the general interest in the education of subnormal children that 222 different cities were reported as having classes organized for backward and mentally defective children.[4] By 1913 there were 284 cities in the United States which had special classes of this type in operation. The number had increased, by 1914,

---

[1] Report of the School Committee, Document 17, pp. 36–38, Boston, 1906.

[2] *Report of the Director of Special Schools*, p. 7, Board of Education, Chicago, 1924.

[3] *Sixtieth Annual Report of the Superintendent of Schools*, p. 367, Board of Education, Chicago, 1914.

[4] JAMES H. VANSICKLE, LIGHTNER WITMER, and LEONARD P. AYRES, "Provision for Exceptional Children in Public Schools," *U.S. Bureau of Education Bulletin* 14, pp. 71–88, Washington, D.C., 1911.

to at least 300.[1] In 1930[2] a study was reported showing 354 cities of 10,000 population and greater in the United States which had organized schools or classes for subnormal children.   There are, doubtless, many cities under 10,000 that have instituted classes of this type. The total number of cities in the United States with such classes is undoubtedly well over 400 and may be considerably higher.

5. TYPES OF ORGANIZATION

There are two major types of organization.   One involves the establishment of classes in regular school buildings and the other requires the establishment of a separate school with an independent administrative organization.

The Special Class.—The greater part of the educational program in the United States for children of low I.Q. has taken the form of special classes.   Of 354 cities reporting either schools or classes, 39 failed to report which they had, 47 had schools only, and 268 stated that they had organized classes.   Of the 47 reporting only schools, 31 had small schools of four classes or less.   Of the 268 cities reporting classes, 33 reported schools also, but only 19 of them reported over four classes per school.   The total number of pupils enrolled in classes was 41,660; the schools reported 13,494 enrolled.

Classes are organized in two ways.   An early method was to establish a separate department for children of low I.Q., with a director at its head.   When a class was organized, the teacher of the class was made directly subordinate to the director; the children of the class were no longer members of the school in which they were housed, because the principal ceased to have jurisdiction over them.

The other method of organizing retains the class as a part of the regular building organization.   The teacher is a member of the regular school staff, is directly responsible to the school principal, and owes allegiance to the director of special classes in just the same sense that the teacher of reading owes allegiance to the reading supervisor. The children are usually housed in the regular building, can be provided with a room adapted to their needs, and come to be accepted as a part of the regular school organization in sports, in play, in auditorium exercises, and in various extracurricular activities.

---

[1] McDonald, *op. cit.*, p. 50.

[2] Arch O. Heck, "Special Schools and Classes in Cities of 10,000 Population and More in the United States," *U.S. Office of Education Bulletin* 7, pp. 6–12, Washington, D.C., 1930.

The province of Ontario,[1] Canada, has arranged for some differentiation in plans, depending upon the size of the city and the age and sex of the child. The basic class for children of low I.Q. is the "mixed auxiliary training class." It is for boys and girls of any school age; a maximum enrollment of 16 is suggested. It is recommended that this type of class be organized in communities having a population of 3,000 to 6,000, in larger cities starting their first class, and in cities where divisions are relatively small and badly scattered.

In larger centers the regulations recommend that a vertical division be arranged whereby boys' auxiliary training classes and girls' auxiliary training classes are organized. The former take boys of any age, the latter girls of any age; enrollment may be allowed to reach 18. Some cities may find it necessary to continue the basic class even after the vertical subdivision has been made; this is particularly true for the less thickly populated areas of the city.

As the work progresses in population centers of 20,000 to 100,000, a division may be made upon the basis of adolescents and preadolescents. The suggested age for making this division is thirteen; those who are of this age and above are placed in boys' auxiliary promotion classes, and girls' auxiliary promotion classes. The younger children are organized without reference to sex into junior auxiliary training classes. In cities of over 100,000 the junior classes continue, but instead of classes for the adolescents, schools called "boys' special industrial" and "girls' special industrial" are formed.

Many cities in the United States have organized upon a similar basis, but use a different terminology. Detroit has its special A and B classes.[2] Chicago, likewise, has classes for the adolescent and for the preadolescent. Although these children vary a great deal in both ability and achievement, very little attention is given to such factors in the organization of special classes.

The Special School.—In order to classify more effectively children of low I.Q., some school districts bring them together in large central schools. The difficulties involved, however, have caused most districts to avoid this type of organization, despite its many educational advantages. Of 384 cities that reported schools or classes for children of low I.Q., only 80 reported the schools; only 44 reported schools of four classes or more. When a school unit of considerable size is organized, an opportunity is given to classify the pupils upon the basis of ability and achievement. Many of the cities reporting

[1] HARRY AMOSS and L. HELEN DeLAPORTE, *Training Handicapped Children*, pp. 22–25, Ryerson Press, Toronto, 1933.
[2] See pp. 351–353.

schools clearly did not have centers large enough for grading these children extensively.

6. TYPICAL PROGRAMS[1] FOR EDUCATING CHILDREN OF LOW I.Q.

Baltimore.[2]—The Division of Special Education of the Baltimore Public Schools, which was organized in 1929, serves all types of handicapped children. All first-grade children are given an intelligence test early in their first semester. Those who have an I.Q. of 90 and over are entered in the regular 1B grade. Those with an I.Q. of at least 110 and usually 120 and over enter, when they have finished grade 1, fast-moving groups, which complete the first six semesters in five, with no skipping of work allowed. Beginners of 89 I.Q. and lower enter slow-moving groups, which complete the first six semesters in eight by taking three semesters for each of the first two grades, with no repeating necessary. Although exceptions are allowed, the foregoing represents the procedure used in dealing with children of sufficient ability to do the work of the regular grades.

Upon this base, Baltimore has built a program for educating its children of low I.Q. This program includes (1) special center classes, (2) primary opportunity classes, (3) intermediate opportunity classes, (4) shop centers, and (5) advanced shop centers. Classes and centers of these five types developed rapidly between 1929 and 1939. Table XVI shows the changes.

TABLE XVI.—NUMBER OF TEACHERS FOR AND NET ROLL IN CLASSES FOR MENTALLY HANDICAPPED CHILDREN OVER A TEN-YEAR PERIOD

	1929	1931	1933	1935	1937	1939
Number of teachers...............	66	92	136	190	235	247
Net roll......................	1,137	1,773	3,193	4,500	5,573	5,827
Pupil-teacher ratio...............	17.2	19.3	23.4	23.7	23.7	23.6

Special center classes accept children with an I.Q. between 50 and 64 and a chronological age of six and thirteen, inclusive. These children do not read until ten, eleven, or twelve years of age. About one child in 200 belongs to the group. Academic work of grades 1 and 2 only is mastered; at fourteen years of age these children are transferred to the shop centers. Some children with an I.Q. of 65

---

[1] In the brief space allowed, it has been impossible to describe the good work being done in all cities; neither is it possible to describe in detail all the interesting things done in the cities mentioned.

[2] Taken from a mimeographed report from the office of the director of special education, dated Oct. 22, 1935.

to 70 may reach these classes. Children with a mental development lower than members of the special center classes become institutional cases.

The primary opportunity classes are for children who have an I.Q. between 65 and 85 and whose chronological ages vary from six to eleven inclusive. One child in 25 belongs to these classes. These pupils enter the intermediate opportunity classes at twelve years of age. Children from the regular grades who are failing and who are retarded 2 years or more are also admitted to the intermediate classes. At fourteen years of age they are promoted from here to a shop center.

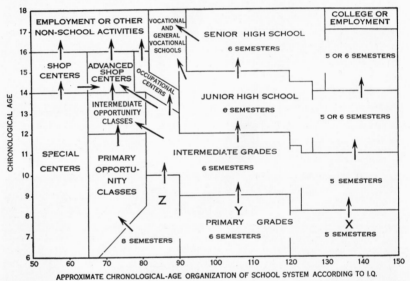

FIG. 9.—Relation of Baltimore's special education program for children of low I.Q. to its entire educational program.

The shop centers receive children with an I.Q. of 50 to 85 and a chronological age of fourteen and fifteen. The academic work is generally of fourth-grade level, though many of the pupils are still at second- and third-grade levels. Woodwork is the main shop activity. Most of the boys leave these centers to go to work. A few who are of fifth-grade level are promoted to an advanced shop center. Shop centers for girls prepare for child care, cooking, laundry work, and sewing.

The advanced shop centers are for youths of fifth- and sixth-grade level; they began in September, 1936. A few pupils from the shop centers register; the greater number are received directly from grades 5 and 6. Junior high-school pupils, in general, should not be sent.

The boys have woodwork, sheet metal, simple electricity, and household mechanics; the girls continue at a higher level work done in the shop centers.   From these centers both boys and girls quit formal schooling and get jobs.   Figure 9 shows the relation of Baltimore's program of special education for children of low I.Q. to its general educational program.

Detroit.—Classes for children with an I.Q. under 75 in Detroit are of two types.   The A special classes are for pupils under thirteen years of age, while the B classes are for children over thirteen years of

ILLUSTRATION 27.—Boys in the Jacoby and Lyster Special Schools in Detroit learn to repair shoes.

age.   There were in June, 1936, the grand total of 1,622 pupils and 69 teachers in the A classes and 2,040 pupils and 83 teachers in the B classes.   Two additional classes are organized for defective cripples; three classes are maintained for children under five mentally.   The A classes are located in regular and special schools, with usually a single class to a building.   The B classes are organized in units of at least two teachers and 50 pupils; there are 16 centers for boys and 9 for girls; five of these centers have 6 or 12 rooms each and four of the five are special schools.   Illustration 27 shows boys in one of Detroit's special schools learning to repair shoes.   Both the Jacoby and Lyster schools provide this training.

Pupils are placed in the classes by the psychological clinic and are taught in small groups. The groups are formed by the teacher upon the basis of the results of achievement tests. The regular course of study is not used; new outlines of work have been prepared in arithmetic, cooking, geography, health, manual training, reading, and sewing. Everyday needs and actual life situations are stressed; health habits are emphasized especially. Younger children spend an hour daily at handwork; work with general art materials and all

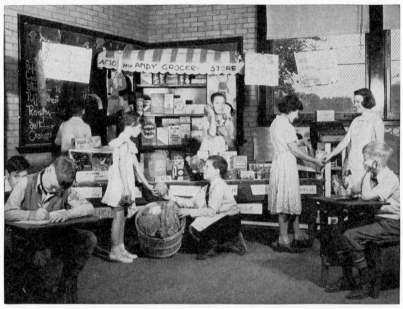

ILLUSTRATION 28.—An Amos and Andy grocery store in a Detroit school for retarded children.

kinds of activity projects are the chief occupations; Illustration 28, showing an Amos and Andy grocery store, is typical. The older children in B classes spend one-third of their time in shops or domestic science and art laboratories. They learn to repair broken furniture and make useful articles for the home. Illustration 29 shows a group of boys engaged in repairing furniture and making useful household articles.

In addition to the above, there are eight units for children of low I.Q. in the intermediate schools; 258 pupils are enrolled. The special teacher supervises the academic work; the pupils enter the regular classes for shop, auditorium, gymnasium, art, music, and the like. Pupils from the special B classes are promoted to these units at sixteen

years of age if, in the judgment of the previous teacher, they can fit
into the intermediate school organization. Children who have the
physical earmarks of being defective are not considered suitable for
these units. A certificate of work, similar to the intermediate school
diploma, is granted upon graduation. This enables the high-grade
defective to enter industry with a better standing. The units are
very popular among parents and children; the latter strive to get a
recommendation to attend them.

ILLUSTRATION 29.—Learning to repair broken furniture and make useful articles for
the home in a Detroit class for retarded boys.

Every attempt is made to eliminate all stigma from membership
in these classes. They are a part of the regular school organization;
hours of opening and closing are the same; the children have a part
in such regular activities as auditorium, library, and safety patrol;
the teachers belong to the regular school staff and are bound by all
the regulations governing that staff; and the principal of the building
has direct control over the class or classes.

Los Angeles.[1]—An educational program for the mentally retarded
began in Los Angeles in the elementary schools in 1917; it was started

---

[1] Taken from typed material received early in 1937 from the assistant supervisor
in charge of mentally retarded children. The elementary classes are known as
development centers, and those in high school, as orientation units.

in the high schools in 1925.   In 1934 there were 240,000 children in the Los Angeles public schools.   Upon the basis of the White House Conference estimate of 2 per cent, there should have been 4,800 mentally retarded children.   There were actually enrolled, in 1936, in classes for the mentally retarded, 3,864 pupils.   There were 11 centers; 9 of them were especially designed and equipped to educate subnormal children; 2 were separate units in regular elementary schools.   In addition, there were 42 separate development classes in the elementary schools.

ILLUSTRATION 30.—Learning to make dresses in one of Los Angeles' elementary development centers.

The Coronel subcenter is different from the other centers.   Children under fourteen years of age are not accepted.   Those are accepted who are too old for elementary schoolwork but who have not the ability to do work in the junior high school.   Since the latter's policy is to accept fourteen-year-olds with I.Q.'s of 65 and over, this center receives children of fourteen with I.Q.'s under 65, compelled by law to remain in school.   The children come from the entire city and represent all races and classes.   The buildings that house these centers, with two exceptions, are one story high and semifireproof.   They have a home economics unit, a manual education unit, a handwork unit, and an administrative unit. Illustration 30 shows girls in a Los Angeles class learning to make dresses.

The objectives of this program of work are (1) to remove remediable physical defects; (2) to develop to the limit the physical well-being of the pupils; (3) to develop desirable and healthful living habits; (4) to assist the pupils to make proper social adjustments; (5) to provide an essential academic program; (6) to develop a fund of useful practical information; (7) to equip the pupils with certain vocational skills; (8) to prepare the boys and girls for self-support; (9) to provide appropriate leisure-time activities, of which Illustration 31 is an excellent example; and (10) to develop standards of cleanliness, health, beauty, and harmony.

ILLUSTRATION 31.—An orchestra in one of Los Angeles' high school orientation units.

New York City.[1]—Ungraded classes were organized in New York City as early as 1902. A report in 1921 showed that there were 258 ungraded classes, with an enrollment of 4,896. The report estimated that 1,000 classes were needed to care for the problem in accordance with state law; it asked for the appointment of 30 additional psy-

[1] *Twenty-third Annual Report of the Superintendent of Schools*, 1920–21, pp. 78–101, Board of Education, New York City, 1921; also "Handicapped and Underprivileged Children," a special report submitted with the *Thirty-sixth Annual Report of the Superintendent of Schools*, pp. 55–105, Board of Education, New York City, 1934.

chologists for the following year.   Table XVII shows the development of this work since 1923.

TABLE XVII.—NUMBER OF CLASSES, PUPILS, AND SUPERVISORY WORKERS FOR
UNGRADED CLASSES ANNUALLY BETWEEN 1923 AND 1939

Year	Number of classes*	Number of pupils*	Medical inspectors	Inspector and assistants	Visiting teachers	Psychologists
1923	267	5,197	2	3	3	3
1924	302	5,898	2	3	3	3
1925	317	6,298	2	3	3	3
1926	361	6,648	2	3	3	4
1927	371	6,989	2	3	3	4
1928	386	7,825	2	3	3	5
1929	402	7,999	2	3	5	10
1930	437	8,035	2	4	6	11
1931	448	8,685	2	4	6	12
1932	472	8,911	2	4	6	12
1933	472	9,706	2	4	5	12
1934	472	9,297	2	4	5	12
1935	501	9,763	2	4†	5	12
1936	535	10,215	3	4	7	16
1937	570	10,349	3	4	7	16
1938	590	10,700	3	4	7	16
1939	608		3	4	7	16

* Data as of Oct. 31.
† Title changed to Director.

The department of ungraded classes has two functions: (1) to examine and adjust retarded children and (2) to educate them in ungraded classes.   Those who diagnose and recommend are, therefore, responsible for carrying out the recommendations.   The 16 psychologists are responsible for keeping in touch with the children they assign to ungraded classes; when necessary, re-examinations are made. These children are studied thoroughly.   An attempt is made to know the child so well that the best of help can be given him in making a satisfactory school and life adjustment.

In 1934 there were 452 ungraded classes and 20 for children of low I.Q.; these enrolled 9,706 pupils.   There were from one to six of these classes in a building, and they were distributed throughout the five boroughs.   Classes were organized upon the basis of sex, mental age, and chronological age, the older children being grouped according to sex.   All teachers of ungraded classes met on the first Monday of each month.   This was part of the whole plan of supervision.   The

20 classes for children of low I.Q. were for children seven years of age or older who had mental ages under five or I.Q.'s under 50.

Philadelphia.[1]—In 1899 there was established in Philadelphia a class for backward children. It was not for imbeciles but for pupils who could not progress properly in the regular grades. It was approved by the board but was privately supported; not until 1901 did the public schools assume this responsibility. By 1912 there were 86 classes enrolling 1,690. No supervisor was appointed until 1920. The report made by the first supervisor, a year later, showed 105 classes for backward children. By 1935 there were 383 classes for the "orthogenic-backward" or for children who had difficulty with school-work.

A great change has taken place in housing conditions during the past 15 years. All rooms now have electric lights; walls are cream colored, and the children like to keep them clean; sanitation is much improved; and paper napkins are regular equipment for lunch periods. One modern building has been specially built for backward pupils.

It is found in Philadelphia that, if the backward child works hard, after 10 years he may hope to read with fourth- and, perhaps, even fifth-grade ability. His English and spelling may equal that of third-grade children. He will do fairly well in addition, subtraction, and multiplication, but be "hopelessly lost" in division except for simple problems. He can learn simple fractions, but the remainder of arithmetic is pure waste.

St. Louis.[2]—Special classes for children of low I.Q. were first organized in St. Louis in 1908. At first pupils were assigned upon the basis of pedagogical retardation and of special need. In 1913 the board of education established a "psycho-educational clinic," which examined children by means of psychological tests. This practice is still in operation, although in 1921 the clinic was merged with the division of tests and measurements.

There are at present 14 "special schools." The local city board of education receives from the state $750 for each teacher employed in these classes. In order to receive this aid the following standards must be met:

(1) The number of pupils assigned to each teacher must not be less than ten or more than twenty; (2) Each pupil assigned must have a mental age above three years, but not over nine at the time of admission; (3) The intelligence quotients

---

[1] Based upon a mimeographed report dated 1935 received from the director of special education.

[2] *Eightieth Annual Report of the Board of Education*, pp. 40–41, Board of Education, St. Louis, Mo., 1934.

for pupils assigned must range between thirty and seventy; (4) These mental measurements must be determined by standard tests properly administered.

In recent years the admission of pupils under 50 I.Q. has been discouraged.

When the classes were first organized, they were housed in buildings separated from the regular school buildings; sometimes private residences were leased. More recently it has seemed wise to use classrooms in the regular schools. This has lowered the cost of instruction and has kept the children nearer their homes.

7. SUMMARY

It sometimes takes a severe financial depression to force us to examine critically currently accepted social practices. The schools and, in particular, special classes for children of low I.Q. have not escaped such examination during recent years. Those believing in the worth of such classes must assemble known facts concerning the problem and see to it that these facts are made generally available.

These classes admit children of I.Q.'s ranging from 50 to 70 or 80; practice varies. Other factors, such as school progress, irregularity of achievement, and lack of social control, are generally used in the placement of pupils. Principles governing such special classwork demand (1) equality of opportunity to develop whatever abilities these children may have, (2) a program of training that will materially assist them in becoming self-supporting, (3) recognition of the necessity of helping them form habits of good conduct, and (4) the development of a program that will not stigmatize them.

As early as 1800, Itard spent 5 years trying to educate a feeble-minded youth found running wild in the forest. A school for educating children of low mental ability was established by Seguin in Paris in 1837. In America some work was done for idiots at the Hartford Asylum for the Deaf as early as 1918, but the first American school was not organized until 1848. The public school class did not start until 1896, when one was organized at Providence, R.I. By 1930, 354 cities, of the 762 with a population of 10,000 or greater, had established a class or classes for children of low I.Q.

Problems and Questions for Discussion

1. What relation, if any, has a financial depression to the problem of educating children of low I.Q.?

2. Who are the children of low I.Q.? Approximately what proportion of school children are so classified?

3. State the principles you believe should govern the education of children of low I.Q. How do these compare with the principles suggested in the text?

4. Trace briefly the history of the development of schools and classes for educating children of low I.Q.   How does its history compare with that of other types of handicapped children?

5. Who were Itard, Seguin, Howe, and Edwards?

6. What relation, if any, existed between the development of compulsory school-attendance legislation and the development of public school provisions for educating children of low I.Q.?

7. How widely are special classes organized throughout the United States?

8. What methods have been followed in the organization of special classes? Which is better?   Why?

9. What is a "school" for children of low I.Q.?   How widely is it used in the United States?

10. Describe the work of educating children of low I.Q. in two or more typical school systems within the United States.   What are the significantly strong points of each?   Explain why.

Selected Bibliography

AMOSS, HARRY, and DeLAPORTE, L. HELEN.   *Training Handicapped Children*, Chap. II.   Ryerson Press, Toronto, 1933.

Describes in detail the organization of classes and schools for early mental variants in the schools of Ontario, Canada.

FRAMPTON, MERLE E., and ROWELL, HUGH GRANT.   *Education of the Handicapped* Vol. I. *History*, pp. 165–187.   World Book Company, Yonkers-on-Hudson, N.Y., 1938.

A historical account of the education of mentally handicapped children.

HECK, ARCH O.   "Special Schools and Classes in Cities of 10,000 Population and More in the United States," pp. 6–12.   *U.S. Office of Education Bulletin 7*, Washington, D.C., 1930.

Lists all cities reporting special schools or classes for subnormal children. Gives the number of schools, classes, pupils, and teachers.

McDONALD, ROBERT ALEXANDER FYFE.   *Adjustment of School Organization to Various Population Groups*, pp. 43–57.   Teachers College, Columbia University, New York, 1915.

Gives a historical account of the education of the feeble-minded; describes ways of educating them and the extent of the development of special classes; tells what finally becomes of these feeble-minded.

The Special Schools and Curriculum Centers, pp. 37–52.   Board of Education, Cleveland, 1931.

Deals with history, selection, housing, aims, organization, curriculum, recreation, and placement of subnormal and overage children.

TERMAN, LEWIS M.   *The Measurement of Intelligence*, pp. 78–104.   Houghton Mifflin Company, Boston, 1916.

Discusses briefly the significance of various intelligence quotients and shows what per cent of the population, on the average, have these quotients.

CHAPTER XXIV

PROBLEMS FACED IN EDUCATING CHILDREN OF LOW I.Q.

Any program of worth must be based upon sound theory. Regardless of its soundness in theory, however, little progress will be made in achieving its goals until basic administrative problems have been solved. Such problems as selection, organization, instruction, developing right attitudes, costs, teacher personnel, schools vs. classes, and evaluation must be considered.

1. WHO ARE THE CHILDREN OF LOW I.Q.?

This problem raises such questions as (1) How shall we select the children? (2) Who shall be admitted? (3) Who are actually found in such classes? (4) How many are there?

Selection.—The teacher and the principal should make recommendations for placement in the special class or school, and these recommendations should be checked by the psychologist. If the city is large and if great numbers are being recommended, a group classification test may be given first. All who succeed in this test as well as the average of their age group should not be placed in the special class; they should be recommended for further study, in order that it may be discovered why they have been doing poorly in their schoolwork.

Those who do poorly on the group test should be given individual examinations; the Stanford Revision of the Binet-Simon is commonly administered for checking the child's ability to do academic schoolwork. Other tests to determine academic accomplishment and mechanical or motor ability may also be given. A physical examination should be given; the child's school record studied; his social reactions at school and at home noted; and other factors that might be affecting his school progress examined. Upon the basis of such a study, the psychologist should make recommendations concerning the placement of each child.

The procedure indicated above is satisfactory if the aim is to select those cases that need help most. If the aim is to select all children who need special classwork, then arrangements should be made to give group tests to all pupils of the school, as well as to get the judgments of teachers and principals as to who ought to be transferred to the special class.   All pupils who rate as satisfactory by both criteria will not be considered special-class candidates; those who rate as unsatisfactory by either method should be continued for study; and those who are rated as unsatisfactory by both methods should be given individual tests.   From this point on, the procedure will be identical to that just outlined.

In no case should the formation of the special-class group be hurried.   It should never be necessary to take children from regular classes on suspicion and place them in the special class in order to keep it at maximum enrollment; neither should children be so placed in order that a class may be started by a given date.   Proper planning will make both procedures unnecessary.

Who Are Admitted?—Doll says that children of 70 I.Q. are usually placed in these classes, although many of 80 I.Q. are thus placed.[1] Wallin[2] shows the variability in state regulations regarding the way these children are designated.   Some states merely refer to them as "educationally exceptional"; others include all those who are 3 years or more retarded; and Minnesota restricts class membership to children with I.Q.'s from 50 to 80.   Missouri has 2 types of classes.   One is for the feeble-minded with I.Q.'s from 30 to under 70; the other is ungraded and has children of I.Q.'s from 65 to 90.   New York regulations demand I.Q.'s of 50 to 75 and mental ages from five to ten.

It would seem that the Missouri procedure which attempts to differentiate between the feeble-minded and the inferior normal should be followed.   Special classes are needed for both, but the educational program will be different.   Whereas there are 2 per cent feeble-minded, there are 5 per cent in the second group.[3]   Both groups at maturity have mental ages from eight to twelve, according to Doll.   The former, however, are mentally deficient, whereas the latter are only verbally deficient.   On performance or on nonlinguistic tests, the latter may be normal or even exceed normal; they have insight and understanding, which the feeble-minded do not have.

Size of the Problem.—Amoss says that from "one to five per cent of the children in any community . . . are non-academic minded."[4] For these pupils his auxiliary classes are organized.   Terman shows

[1] White House Conference, *Special Education: The Handicapped and the Gifted*, p. 447, The Century Co., New York, 1931.

[2] *Ibid.*, pp. 448–449.

[3] *Ibid.*, p. 453.

[4] HARRY AMOSS and L. HELEN DeLAPORTE, *Training Handicapped Children*, p. 12, Ryerson Press, Toronto, 1933.

that approximately 1 per cent have an I.Q. under 70, that 3 per cent are under 76, and that 5 per cent are under 78. The White House Conference says that there are "450,000 pupils enrolled in elementary grades who are mentally retarded to such a degree that they require special education to make the most of their possibilities."[1]

There is not unanimous agreement as to the limits that should be set for including children in special classes. We need experimentation that will demonstrate the point at which pupils are unable to do the minimum essentials of the regular course of study. This point, if it can be determined, might well be the dividing line between special-class instruction and regular instruction.

2. PROBLEMS OF ORGANIZATION

Problems of organization include such specific questions as (1) Where should the center be located? (2) What should be the size of the class? (3) What equipment is needed?

Choosing a Center.—The choice of a center is a problem of major concern. If stigmatization is to be minimized, too much care cannot be exercised in the choice of schools where special classes are to be established. A class should never be placed in a school where, because of lack of training or good common sense, the principal does not have the ability to develop upon the part of the community and staff a real respect for it; he needs also to develop in the pupils a respect for themselves.

The schools chosen should represent well the schools of the system. If morale is to be developed, castoff buildings and castoff rooms should not be the only ones assigned to special classes. The children of such classes should feel just as proud of their school building or classroom as children of the regular classes; this is important in developing respect for the class.

Size of Class.—The size of the class will depend upon such factors as age, sex, and grade. If boys and girls of all ages and all grades are assembled in a single class, instruction becomes individual and covers such a range of materials that only a small number of pupils can be cared for adequately. Ontario limits such classes to 16; if boys and girls are separated, the maximum is 18; and if classes are restricted to children under thirteen, then 20 is the maximum. If children of thirteen or over are divided by sex, 20 are permitted; if two rooms of boys or of girls are at a given center permitting classification, 24 is the limit; if three rooms are so assembled, then 30 becomes the limit.

[1] White House Conference, *op. cit.*, p. 6.

Some method of adjusting the size of the class to the type of class organized seems sensible. The more closely pupils are classified, the more group instruction can be utilized. The New York suggestion would seem to be correct, if no attempt has been made at classification; otherwise classes can be larger. Little or no objective evidence seems to be available upon which to establish the best size of class.

Equipment.—Not all the equipment required can be enumerated. That which is more or less unique can be suggested as illustrative, rather than as being in any sense complete. To a standard equipped classroom, there should be added cupboard space for special tools and supplies, sink and running water, rack for lumber and reed, a sand table, a worktable, manual-training benches, tools, a sewing machine, a mirror, a shoe-cleaning outfit, and a phonograph with march, dance, and special music records.

Specific equipment of a smaller type, such as dominoes, colored beads, crayons, plasticine, pegs for pegboards, and toy money will be found useful.[1]

3. INSTRUCTIONAL PROBLEMS

Problems related to instruction include the following: (1) What should be taught? (2) What is typical of the daily schedule? (3) Do methods of instruction differ? (4) What are the responsibilities of the special teachers?

Curricula.—Children in these classes are not held to the regular grade requirements academically; they do have academic work. Such work is simplified and reduced in amount; it tends to emphasize attitudinal development instead of informational material. Illustration 32 shows a group of boys doing academic work at one of Los Angeles' elementary developmental centers.[1]

In history and civics, for example, biography may be used to emphasize courage, courtesy, industry, kindness, loyalty, neatness, and truthfulness. The class may talk about and dramatize the helpfulness of the policemen, the firemen, the judge, and the "Big Brother" and "Big Sister." The hospital, the clinic, the savings bank, the Y.M.C.A., the Y.W.C.A., the church, the Sunday school, the boy scouts, and the girl reserves may be discussed and their work dramatized.

The upper age groups may discuss in simple, nontechnical terms political, financial, and social co-operation; they may dramatize the government of the school, the municipality, the state, and the United

[1] See AMOSS and DELAPORTE, *op. cit.*, pp. 51–59, for extensive lists of useful equipment.

States. The importance of choosing good representatives should be emphasized. These pupils should understand something of the banker's job and come to realize the need of receiving his advice concerning savings, credit, mortgages, notes, loans, insurance, stocks, bonds, and all kinds of investments. They should also realize the dangers of accepting the advice of strangers, salesmen, or uninformed friends. They should get a clear picture of how social agencies function and come to have a high regard for the advice of regular social workers.

ILLUSTRATION 32.—Boys doing academic work at one of Los Angeles' elementary development centers for children of low I.Q.

In arithmetic, the mastery of the fundamental processes is sought. Money, time, liquid and linear measures, surface measurement, weight, and accounting based upon store bills, wage sheets, and marketing may be covered in very elementary fashion. Simple practical measurement problems, fractions using $\frac{1}{2}$, $\frac{1}{3}$, and $\frac{1}{4}$, and simple interest and discount are often taught. These simple concepts, it has been suggested, may be mastered by the time the child has reached the age for shop training. Household and personal budgeting may also be included.

Other revised academic subjects are reading, spelling, composition, geography, and nature study, business habits and attitudes, and writing; writing is often emphasized by constantly supervising all their written work either in their exercise books or at the blackboard. Music, art, science, physical training, and health are usually given considerable emphasis.

In addition to the courses usually taught in the elementary school, we find considerable handwork.   Detroit reports that younger children spend an hour daily weaving, sewing, and building; the older pupils spend a third of their day in the shops.   The boys have carpentry of the rougher type, drawing, cement molding, and repairing books; the girls have cooking, laundry, needlework, and sewing.   The girls

ILLUSTRATION 33.—Learning to cook and serve in a high-school orientation class in Los Angeles.

make their own aprons, caps, and house dresses; help to plan and prepare the noon meal; and do the school laundry work for their group. Illustration 33 shows girls who are learning to cook and serve in one of Los Angeles' high school orientation classes.

In Toronto[1] manicuring and hairdressing have an important place in the schedule.   The health, cleanliness, and personal habits of the children demand this in the lower grades; in the upper grades only those pupils who hope to make a livelihood in that way take these courses.   Illustration 34 shows a Los Angeles class in cosmetology. The girls are members of a high school orientation class.   Toronto

[1] AMOSS and DeLAPORTE, op. cit. pp. 104–116.

also provides reed and raffia work, weaving and rug making, metalwork, bookbinding, paper work, cardboard work, leather work, typewriting, shoemaking, cleaning and pressing, and agriculture.

Not all of these things can be done in a single school which proposes to organize a mixed class of all ages and grades. The proposals point to possible types of work that may be provided for children of low I.Q.

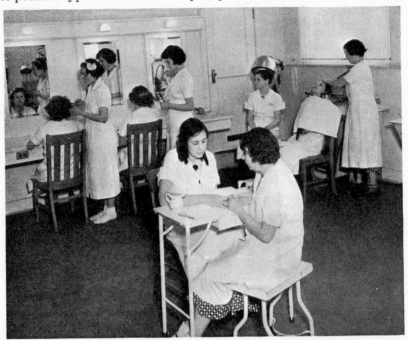

ILLUSTRATION 34.—Girls learning cosmetology in a high-school orientation unit in Los Angeles.

Methods of Instruction.—Differences in methods of instruction for special-class and regular pupils are not revolutionary, but they are marked. They are due, not to essential changes in aims, but to differences to be found in the children themselves. Children of low I.Q. are not lacking in ability to understand abstraction and to think; as compared with that of normal children, however, their ability along these lines is meager. It is not the lack of these abilities that necessitates changes in method, but the difference in degree to which they are held. The term "low I.Q." expresses this fact. A child of 50 I.Q. has all the abilities of the average child but to a much lower degree. These differences suggest that methods of teaching must differ.

1. There must be more repetition, in order to habituate children of low I.Q. to correct responses to given situations. The appropriate

verbal response to the combination of letters *g r e e n* will be achieved only by much repetition; the response "seven" to the situation "3 + 4" is made habitual only by much repetition. The methods used must take into account this necessity for repetition.

2. Long theoretical discussions are not appropriate. Specific and direct application of what is being taught must be made. The teacher cannot depend upon the child's making the application. This adds to the difficulty of instruction, because so many more specifics must be emphasized than are required in teaching normal children.

3. In literature and in the social sciences, attention will center largely upon events and characters; the relating of a social trend to various events has little likelihood of "getting across." The factual part of history can be ignored. The story of the discovery of America can be told and the child can be presented with the picture of a man with courage. Through a constant repetition of stories of men and women in American and world history, representing a few of the dominant and worth-while character traits, these children may be helped to establish such traits in themselves.

4. In geography and civics, we can ignore to a great extent foreign countries and center upon the home city, county, and state. Emphasis will again be given to the observation of concrete situations and to the telling of stories full of the human interest element. Trips that help the child to see the policeman in ordinary action are good; stories that emphasize the job of the policeman as one who helps direct traffic, who helps protect children, and who helps to give us a safe place in which to live give enough concreteness to the learning situation to fix in the mind of these children the dominant idea of the helpfulness of the policeman. Other public officials may be dealt with similarly.

By these methods we use the factual material as a means of establishing certain habitual reactions upon the part of the child to given situations. He will be trained in the doing of specific things to keep himself clean, to preserve his health, and to protect himself from accident; he will be trained to look for certain traits in individuals who are to be his leaders. Although whatever ability these children have for thinking will be utilized, one must not close his eyes to the fact that such ability is meager in amount; if, therefore, children of low I.Q. are to adjust to the present social order, they must be habituated to many forms of social reaction.

Work of the Teacher.—This revamping of methods of instruction presents a challenge to the initiative and originality of the special teacher. Many general suggestions are available, but the specific, concrete illustrations that are needed for instructional purposes are less frequently put into written form. If repetition could be simply repetition, with no embellishments, the task would not be so great; the repetition required, however, must be such that interest is sustained.

Many of the children are physically mature, have experienced life widely, and yet have mental ability equivalent to that of a child seven or eight years old. The academic materials used for the normal child of seven are not adequate, consequently, for the special-class child with a mental age of seven and a chronological age of twelve or fourteen. The latter has already attempted the mastery of these materials; even if he had not, they would not be adapted to his interests and his experiences. Attempts to make such curricular adjustments are not easy; the required materials are usually not available. This is true even of the handwork to be done. Youths of fourteen resent working upon identical materials with children of eight or nine. The same operations may need to be taught, but the materials used should differ.

The teacher has also the problem of dealing with the regular teacher, the principal, other children, and parents. She should be the one best fitted to assist in avoiding the development of prejudice against the class and in destroying whatever prejudice may already have been formed regarding it. Through willingness to co-operate, through clear-cut explanations as to reasons for such classes, and through a sane presentation of the achievements of such classes, she can do a great deal to give stability to this special educational program.

4. THE DEVELOPMENT OF RIGHT ATTITUDES

Avoiding Prejudice.—The point to be emphasized is the need for some means of referring to the organization of such classes without attaching a stigma to them every time reference is made to them. A class designated as for morons, for feeble-minded children, for subnormals, or for mental defectives, although these terms describe well enough the type of child we mean, carries a stigma that immediately establishes in the popular mind prejudice against it. Parents, as a result, if they do not openly resent the placement of children in these classes, are inclined to feel stigmatized by having a child in such a class. This feeling may easily make the child feel discouraged and hopeless about ever achieving, and may make him develop school antagonisms and become a lasting problem for society.

Despite the fact that I.Q. is an abbreviation for "intelligence quotient," the expression has come to have a significance of its own. The author believes that it does not arouse such popular prejudices as accompany the other terms just mentioned. This, if correct, would perhaps justify the use of the expression "children of low I.Q." in the title of this chapter; the expression also is descriptive of the children enrolled.

A more serious factor in developing such a prejudice is the attitude occasionally exhibited by the principal and the teachers of the school in which the class is located. Not maliciously but through ignorance or thoughtlessness, they may explain to visitors in the presence of other pupils, "We have a dumbbell group that I want you to observe," or "This next group is feeble-minded; they just don't know anything." Such expressions are sometimes used by teachers of these classes even in the presence of their pupils. The children may not have high academic ability, but they have intelligence enough to sense keenly these disparaging remarks.

Such prejudices may further be prevented by differentiating as little as possible between the special and regular class in all matters of routine administration. For this reason Detroit makes the school hours of the special group conform to regular school hours. The children participate in regular school activities, and the teachers belong to the regular teaching staff.

5. TEACHER PERSONNEL

Training.—Some suggest that the minimum training requirements should be graduation from a 4-year high school or its equivalent and approximately 2 years of additional training on the college level; they suggest that the 2 additional years be about equally divided between (1) academic training, (2) general professional courses, and (3) special professional courses, plus 10 semester hours of nonrequired work. These requirements would seem to be entirely too modest. The teacher for subnormal children needs a richer background in the academic subjects at the college level than the 20 hours recommended; the 20 hours of general professional work are too meager; and, clearly, the amount suggested as special professional work is far from adequate.

When one reflects that teachers of children of low I.Q. should have had experience in teaching normal groups and that the requirements for teaching regular grades are being materially advanced, the suggestions just mentioned are plainly seen to be too low for qualification. In the future, no person should be considered as a teacher of these classes who does not have a Master's degree. The work for the degree should be divided so that 3 years are devoted to academic training, 1 year to general professional training, and 1 year to special professional training.

Experience.—There should be at least a year of successful teaching experience as a regular teacher, although 2 or 3 years would give the candidate a better chance to become familiar with the problems of dealing with normal children. Such experience is essential if she is to evaluate properly the achievements of children of low I.Q. This experience, moreover, will give the beginner an opportunity to show whether she has an interest in problem children and an ability to work with them.

Any additional experience she may have will be all to the good. Training and experience as a clinical examiner will aid her in understanding children. Training and experience as a visiting teacher will give her the technique for making the many needed home contacts and a better understanding of children whom she finds in undesirable home and community situations. Training and experience as a school nurse will give her a clearer insight into the difficulties that entangle pupils who come from ill-kept homes; who are undernourished; who have ear, eye, nose, or throat troubles; and who have never known what it was to keep themselves clean, to keep regular hours, or to eat regularly.

Traits Needed.—When one undertakes to enumerate the traits of character needed by a teacher of these special classes, as a rule, just those traits are named that even a layman would demand in a regular class teacher. This suggests that the necessary traits are, perhaps, not so different in kind; if there is a difference, it is likely to be in the degree to which they are developed and the understanding with which they are used.

It is frequently suggested that the special-class teacher needs an unusual amount of patience. The children she must teach learn slowly; explanations must be repeated over and over again. She must have an unusual ability to see problems from another's point of view, even when that point of view is radically different from one's own. She must have in a high degree contagious enthusiasm; this is needed for arousing the interest of children of low I.Q. in the work that they have to do. Their lack of mental inquisitiveness tends to cause them to have less interest in things, in people, and in affairs than is shown by their more inquisitive neighbors in the regular classes.

6. SPECIAL SCHOOLS VS. SPECIAL CLASSES

Stigmatization.—Bruner,[1] in discussing special schools for children of low I.Q., says that there are several objections which he considers

[1] FRANK G. BRUNER, *Report of the Director of Special Schools for the School Year* 1922–23, p. 8, Board of Education, Chicago, 1924.

insuperable. He says that when children who are subnormal are segregated in a single building they are likely to be branded as defective and socially unfit; this makes it difficult to get employment for them after they leave school. This argument is frequently used. Segregation of any considerable number of children of low I.Q. seems to place upon them a definite stigmatization, which is not felt if they are assembled in small groups within the school buildings of their own districts.

Agreement is not unanimous, however. A former director of special classes says that they frankly call their centers schools for subnormals and that, until the present depression began, they had no difficulty in placing the graduates of these schools. After the placement service was well organized those industries that had employed the graduates began to call the placement office voluntarily for workers whenever vacancies occurred or whenever jobs of the type these youths could do were available.

Some critics charge that, even where these children are assembled in classes, stigmatization results. It is possible that stigmatization cannot be avoided in either case. Whether or not such an effect is felt depends, I believe, almost wholly upon the attitudes held and the attitudes developed by those who have been responsible for organizing the classes. If people understand that all children differ widely and that these differences extend to innumerable qualities, abilities, and interests, if they realize that children lacking in one attribute may have a good share of another, and if they are shown what children of low I.Q. have accomplished, much of the prejudice against such class groups and schools will materially lessen.

It must be remembered that these children do not escape stigmatization even when they attend regular classes. The child who fails constantly, who never is able to recite in class, and who has little or no opportunity to be seen by his classmates working at a job in which he excels is clearly not free from stigmatization. We need evidence of a more objective nature to help us decide which type of organization will be less embarrassing to the children who attend it and which will make the work of placement easier when the pupils are ready to go to work.

Classification.—Clearly, if the group is larger, better classification may be made. This argument is an effective one in favor of the special school. If small groups are assembled, children widely divergent in age, ability, and interests are held together. An answer to this argument is that the instruction of children of low I.Q. should be individual. The suggestion has merit, for certainly a great amount of individual attention is necessary. Some group work, however, is needed, even with individual instruction.

Provision for the Arts.—Children of low I.Q. need a greatly expanded curriculum. From one-third to one-half or more of their time is given to handwork and shopwork. All such work, if it is to be of value, requires considerable equipment. Practical arts, fine arts, and household arts cannot be well taught in a classroom minus equipment. To provide such equipment for scattered classes is difficult; but where the children are assembled in a school, the problem is not so great.

The suggestion is made occasionally that this problem is not really serious. It is claimed that little or no need exists for such special work among children under thirteen years of age, and that the special-class children thirteen years old and older, if they are placed in junior high schools or in elementary schools where shopwork and domestic science are provided for the regular grade pupils, can be adequately provided for without being assembled in large centers.

7. EFFECTIVENESS OF SPECIAL-CLASS WORK

Woolley and Ferris, in 1923,[1] reported results secured with a group of 16 special-class children in Cincinnati. All the children were first-grade failures; nine were neglected children, four were high-grade defectives, two had special defects, and one was psychopathic. While none of them had an I.Q. under 70, and practically all were in the eighties, they had had serious learning difficulties. It is significant that the work of the class was conducted under many of the practical difficulties that would be encountered in any average school situation; equipment, housing, and facilities for study were far from ideal. An attempt was made, however, to select the best possible teacher. Some of the significant conclusions are the following:

1. If the task can be properly adjusted to the degree of ability of the child, it is possible for many of the inferior children to experience the same love of learning and the same desire for independent work which is characteristic of the higher levels of accomplishment.[2]

2. In every instance, except those of the children who were ultimately shown to be feeble-minded, and one of those who was suffering from special disabilities, the intelligence quotient rose while the child was in the observation class and fell after he left it.[3] [This is interpreted as meaning that] the constant, personal, stimulating influence of the teacher infuses into the children an alertness and a

---

[1] *U.S. Bureau of Education Bulletin* 1, pp. 102–107, Washington, D.C., 1923.
[2] *Ibid.*, p. 102.
[3] *Ibid.*, p. 103.

capacity for comprehension which they can not command when thrown on their own resources.[1]

3. The most striking moral of the tale of our observation class is that of the many lines of evidence and information necessary to a real understanding of problem children. . . . The determination of mental level is one important element in the diagnosis of these cases, but it is only one.   To give it its just value in relation to physical, social, educational, and hereditary factors is one of the important tasks of applied psychology.[1]

4. The general conclusion which we can draw is that the combination of good health, good school opportunities, and a good home with bad academic failure of two or more years, means a very unfavorable prognosis in spite of some striking special abilities, and an intelligence quotient somewhat above the usually accepted limits of defect.[2]

There are five points to be considered in working with these children, the report says: (1) the child's mental level, (2) his academic history, (3) his state of health, (4) his heredity, and (5) his general mental tone and attitude.[3]   The last point is very important, yet it is the most difficult to determine.   Any anxieties, conflicts, obsessions or fears, special disabilities, character defects, or psychopathic conditions must be discovered and treated.   The important thing to note is that, when these factors were considered in dealing with these problem children, improvement was remarkable, and that, when they were thrown upon their own after a short period with the class, they again seemed unable to do their best.

Several questions press in upon us as we consider these results. Would a continued stay in the special class have so developed attitudes toward study, work, and society that the child could have become self-reliant?   Would the stay at least have fixed habits of responding to various situations so that he would henceforth have been able to maintain himself in the social group?   This, of course, is what the investigators believe.   If so, the answer is clear; many more special classes are needed.   This need exists not only for the feeble-minded but for the greater group of low normals who, for the reasons enumerated above, are failing to progress normally in grades 1, 2, and 3.

A study of the employment histories[4] of 1,069 boys and girls who had attended special classes showed that 94 per cent had been employed after leaving school.   These youths had left school between the years 1916 and 1920.   In 1923 they were interviewed.   Complete

---

[1] *Ibid.*, p. 105.

[2] *Ibid.*, p. 107.

[3] *Ibid.*, pp. 109–110.

[4] ALICE CHANNING, "Employment of Mentally Deficient Boys and Girls," pp. 66–69, *U.S. Department of Labor, Children's Bureau Publication* 210, Washington, D.C., 1932.

records were secured for 949 of the 998 who had worked. At the time of the inquiry, 61 per cent were then gainfully employed; the percentage was 71 for boys and 43 for girls. Marriage explains why the percentage was so low for girls. Positions were held for a fairly long period of time. Of the boys, 74 per cent had held a job for at least one year and 37 per cent for 2 years; the corresponding percentages for the girls were 69 and 37, respectively.

Of course, the study tells very little about the effectiveness of special-class work. We need to be shown what children of this type would do who never had had special-class training. From what we know of the changes that take place in attitudes after children have been placed in special classes, we should expect them to adjust much more satisfactorily than they would have done without the training. Definite evidence of this is needed.

8. PLACEMENT AND FOLLOW-UP

The studies reported in the preceding section either cover a limited period of time or are made by a special investigator. What is needed is a continuous long time follow-up of all members of special schools or classes, as a part of the regular routine of educating and caring for these groups. Some very good placement and follow-up service has been reported. Cleveland, previous to 1930, was able through such service to place a large proportion of the graduates of their schools for "subnormal" children. Detroit in 1930 reported two placement officers; one worked with boys and one with girls. In 1923 Bruner[1] reported studies in Chicago, Cincinnati, Cleveland, and New York City showing that most graduates of these special classes are able to adjust industrially and to get jobs at good pay. Unskilled labor and repetitive factory work took care of most of these youths; they got considerable pleasure from it and adjusted themselves very happily to social life at that level.

Such placement and follow-up ought to be considered essentially a part of the whole program of caring for children of low I.Q. The training they receive at school establishes habits of conduct that will make for satisfactory social adjustment, provided they can get jobs commensurate with their ability, to keep them busily and happily occupied. If, however, no assistance is given in placing them, many will not get jobs; they will become loafers subject to the wiles of the brighter-witted street-corner loafer. Just as the schools establish good habits, so an adverse environment can fix bad social habits upon these adults who have the mentality of children. The entire

[1] BRUNER, op. cit., p. 17.

benefit of an 8- or 12-year school program can be counteracted by a period of extended, unsupervised idleness. A program combining placement and supervision would, therefore, seem quite essential in order to capitalize upon the original investment.

9. SUMMARY

There are many problems that must be faced in the development of a program of caring for and educating children of low I.Q. Selection of such children should be based upon all available data, interpreted by trained persons. There are about 2 per cent of the population who are feeble-minded and in need of special-class work. Another 5 per cent are the border-line normals who need individual attention and would profit from instruction in special classes. The range in I.Q. is from approximately 50 to 72 or 73 and to 80 if the borderline normals are to be included.

Class size varies from 15 to 30, depending upon the money available and the extent of classification. The principal of a school is the key person in determining the success of the special class. He is responsible for its proper housing; for the attitude taken by teachers, parents, and pupils toward it; and for adequately equipping it.

Despite a belief that academic work should be banned, these children can benefit from such instruction when it is properly adapted to their abilities; methods emphasize the use of concrete materials and a plan of instruction that places great emphasis upon repetition. Obviously, where classes are organized that include both sexes, all ages, and all grades, the teacher's task is very arduous and resembles that of one-room rural teachers.

No problem in the organization of these special classes is more important than that of developing the right kind of attitude toward the class upon the part of teachers, parents, regular grade pupils, and special-class pupils. The past has too frequently seen those responsible for these classes foiled at this point; as a result, the work has failed. It is suggested that every teacher shall have a Master's degree and 2 years of teaching in regular classes; the 5 years of training shall consist of 3 years devoted to academic study, 1 to general professional training, and 1 to specialized training related to an understanding of the problems of dealing with children of low I.Q.

Evidence as to whether special schools are better than special classes or vice versa is inadequate and inconclusive. From the point of view of classification and adequate provision of the manual arts, the school seems to have some advantage. Transportation and distance to be traveled, on the other hand, favor the class. We need

evidence as to the relative value of these two methods.   We also need
to evaluate the entire program of special education for children of low
I.Q.   Better placement and follow-up procedures would help immeas-
urably in solving this problem.

Problems and Questions for Discussion

1. Who are the children of low I.Q.?   How many are there?
2. Outline a satisfactory method of discovering all such children of school age
within a given community.
3. What factors should be considered in determining the size of class?   Explain.
4. Is the selection of the school or class center important?   Why?
5. Describe in some detail the equipment you consider essential for the teacher
of the special class.
6. What are the important curricular problems to be met in educating children
of low I.Q.?   Why are they so important?
7. Will methods of instruction differ essentially from methods used in regular
classes?   Why?
8. What do you conceive to be some of the unique responsibilities of teachers
of these special classes?   Why?
9. What can be done to "sell" the idea of the special class to parents, teachers,
and pupils?   Illustrate.
10. Outline in some detail the training and preparation you would demand of
teachers of special classes for children of low I.Q.   Defend your proposals.
11. Which do you think are better—special classes or special schools—as a
means of educating children of low I.Q.?
12. What evidence have you been able to discover that shows the effectiveness
or lack of effectiveness of these special classes?
13. Criticize the above evidence.   Show how you would proceed to secure
more adequate evidence.

Selected Bibliography

ANDERSON, META L.   *Education of Defectives in the Public Schools.*   World Book
Company, Yonkers-on-Hudson, N.Y., 1922.   104 pp.
     Considers the best ways to select children for classes, the curriculum needed
by defectives, trade classes, and the place of the special class in the public
school system.
CHANNING, ALICE.   "Employment of Mentally Deficient Boys and Girls," *U.S.
Department of Labor, Children's Bureau, Publication* 210.   Washington, D.C.,
1932.   107 pp.
     Reports employment of former special-class pupils in Newark, N.J.;
Rochester, N.Y.; Detroit, Mich.; Cincinnati, Ohio; Los Angeles, San Francisco, and Oakland, Calif., giving wages, occupations, continuity of work, and
success on the job.
DESCOEUDRES, ALICE.   *The Education of Mentally Defective Children.*   D. C.
Heath & Company, Boston.   312 pp.
     Presents data concerning the early development of their educational
program, methods of selection, present-day educational programs, governing
principles, methods, and instructional materials.

Fernald, Walter E. "The Burden of Feeble-mindedness" (Delivered before Massachusetts Medical Society in 1912). *Massachusetts Society for Mental Hygiene Publication* 4. 16 pp.

A vivid portrayal of the size of the problem; discusses cause, present tendencies relative to size, burdens placed upon society, and suggestions for reducing the problem. Education of the public is stressed as probably the most effective way of lessening the problem.

Fernald, Walter E. "What Is Practicable in the Way of Prevention of Mental Defect" (Read before N.C.C.C. in 1915). *Massachusetts Society for Mental Hygiene Publication* 6. 11 pp.

Summarizes evidences showing need for prevention and presents reasons for segregation; cites objections and concludes education is "most effective method" of reducing feeble-mindedness.

Goddard, Henry H. *School Training of Defective Children.* World Book Company, Yonkers-on-Hudson, N.Y., 1923. 97 pp.

A report on the "ungraded" classes of New York City. It was originally published in 1914 and shows conditions in that city, as of 1912, relative to ungraded classes; shows what is done for the children, the equipment provided, kinds of teachers, supervision provided, and the way the children were chosen.

Ingram, Christine P. *Education of the Slow-learning Child.* World Book Company, Yonkers-on-Hudson, N.Y., 1935. 419 pp.

Describes the mentally retarded child, his educational objectives, the way to select him, instructional methods and materials, and a program for adjusting him to the community.

Martens, Elise H. "Teachers' Problems with Exceptional Children: III. Mentally Retarded Children," *U.S. Office of Education Pamphlet* 49. Washington, D.C., 1934. 42 pp.

Problems of definition, discovery, education, vocation, parental guidance, and instructional materials are considered.

Metzner, Alice B., and Engel, Anna M. *Course of Study for Special Classes.* Board of Education, Detroit, 1926. 95 pp.

Detailed outline of course of study for special classes "A" and "B" in arithmetic, geography, handwriting, reading, and spelling.

Phillips, Frank M. "Schools and Classes for Feeble-minded and Subnormal Children," *U.S. Bureau of Education Bulletin* 5. Washington, D.C., 1928. 21 pp.

A list of cities with such classes, giving the number of teachers, pupils by sex, and enrollment by some 5 subjects of study.

Wallin, J. E. Wallace. *Problems of Subnormality.* World Book Company, Yonkers-on-Hudson, N.Y., 1921. 485 pp.

Describes changing attitudes toward the subnormal; tells who they are; outlines principles and facts to be considered in trying to educate them, and suggests provisions that various states should make.

White House Conference. *Special Education: The Handicapped and the Gifted,* pp. 439–488. The Century Co., New York, 1931.

A good report covering state laws, extent of the problem, methods of selecting pupils, types selected, ways of organizing, materials taught, costs, appraisal, relation of public school work to state institutions, and recommendations.

WOOLLEY, HELEN THOMPSON, and FERRIS, ELIZABETH.   "Diagnosis and Treatment of Young School Failures."   *U.S. Bureau of Education Bulletin* 1. Washington, D.C., 1923.   115 pp.

A good description of the work done for 16 children in Cincinnati's first "observation" class.   The 16 case studies are quite complete and very instructive.   Subjective conclusions point definitely to the value of this special-class work.

CHAPTER XXV

THE CHALLENGE PRESENTED BY CHILDREN OF LOW I.Q.

1. THE CHALLENGE

The opportunity of doing a great constructive piece of work is a challenge to human ingenuity and action. It implies power; it is dynamic; and it makes demands upon those positive, aggressive traits in human nature that we have been taught to appreciate most. Many such activities are most spectacular. We build a skyscraper or we break a world's record. Such action stirs the popular imagination. Other activities are much less spectacular but no less important. World workers in these latter areas take the mediocre and make the maximum use of it; they are found in every occupation where an opportunity to serve is found. Their activities are vital to human progress, but they stir the imagination of the populace not at all. The teacher of children of low I.Q. may be such a worker.

Improvability.—There is no great stir of the imagination upon the part of the average visitor to special classes for children of low I.Q.; the immediate program is likely to appear prosaic, even dull and monotonous. The meager academic abilities of these youths develop slowly; from prospective social incompetence, they are helped after long years to become self-supporting. In the finished product of the special class, the casual observer sees youths just able to earn a living; the critic has eyes but he fails to see the transformation. From a near brute to a human being, each of these youths has been changed. Who can say which is the greater—such a change in human life or the production of a masterpiece of art or industry.

Itard was so discouraged with his attempt to educate the wild boy of the forest that he considered his 5 years of effort wasted; not so the French Academy of Science. They remembered the original boy; they saw the changes in him. We have considerable evidence today of successful work with children of low I.Q. Instead of remaining helpless beings, demanding complete support for life, they become partially or even wholly self-supporting; they take an interest in living; and they tend to become happily adjusted, despite being forced to live at what many would consider an unbearably low economic and social level. The fact that helpless human beings have the possibility of being so aided is indeed a real challenge.

379

The Size of the Problem.—If only a few children were involved, we might ignore the problem, despite the possibility of such improvement in their social and mental development. The numbers, however, are great. If we estimate the school population in the United States at 30,000,000 and if we assume that there are 2 per cent feeble-minded and 5 per cent low normals who need special-class work, we have the impressive total of 2,100,000 youths who ought to be given the advantages of a program of special education adapted to their needs. These two millions will in great part have the right to vote; they constitute a social and political menace unless educated.

Other Problems That Challenge the Conscientious Worker.— Every problem discussed in the preceding chapter sets up its own challenge to those trying to educate children of low I.Q. This chapter will deal specifically with the problem of prevention, based upon a study of causes, and with the problem of developing a state program of special education for preventing, as well as educating, children of low I.Q. If steps can be taken to prevent the birth of children of so low a degree of ability that they are forever doomed to exist at economic and social levels that can hardly be called existence, a great forward step has surely been taken in race improvement.

2. CAUSES OF LOW I.Q.

Aside from heredity, very little is known, says Bruner,[1] about the causes of subnormality in children. He calls attention to the possible relationship between the action of endocrines (ductless glands) and mentality. More recently, Mayers[2] has indicated a relationship between the endocrines and mental ability.

Heredity.—There is great divergence in estimates concerning the importance of heredity as a cause of low I.Q. It has been suggested that 90 per cent[3] of the feeble-mindedness found in children is due to heredity. Numerous textbooks report heredity as the chief cause of subnormality.

Bruner says[4] that, when school children just above the grade of feeble-mindedness are examined, heredity seems to play a small part. Of over 10,000 children examined in his laboratories, less than 4 per cent were cases of neuropathic heredity "as far as their immediate

[1] FRANK G. BRUNER, *Report of the Director of Special Schools*, p. 21, Board of Education, Chicago, 1924.

[2] LAWRENCE H. MAYERS and ARTHUR D. WELTON, *What We Are and Why*, Dodd, Mead & Company, Inc., New York, 1933, 340 pp.

[3] C. P. LAPAGE, *Feeblemindedness in Children of School-age*, p. 179, University of Manchester Press, 1911.

[4] BRUNER, *op. cit.*, p. 18.

parents" were concerned; this was less than 7 per cent when "collateral lines of ancestry were included."

He criticizes earlier studies in that they investigated children coming from institutions.   He suggests that in the public schools cases are just as serious; the difference is that home conditions are better.   He concludes that the institutional cases will, for the most part, be children whose parents or relatives are also mentally subnormal.   In order to study causes of subnormality fairly, we must, he says have studies in the public schools "where the ancestry of all who are school failures or social problems are studied."

Endocrines.—Little is known concerning the causal relations of the endocrines to low I.Q.   Bruner reports an experiment in which the products of certain ductless glands were fed to children of low I.Q.   Physical examinations, X-ray plates, blood tests, serum tests, and neurological examinations were made; individual mental and achievement tests were given before and after the treatments.   Metabolism tests were made.   Some children were given tablets containing hormones of the anterior pituitary; others were fed hormones of the thymus, the thyroid, the parathyroid, the ovary, or the pineal daily for a year.

The results were interesting.   Bruner says that they "seemed too good to be true."   The original I.Q.'s of the children treated ranged from 48 to 75; they had had a mental growth of from 6 to 9 months each year.   Tests showed that one girl gained $2\frac{1}{2}$ years in 1 year, two boys gained 2 years each, five children gained $1\frac{1}{2}$ years each, twelve gained 1 whole year, and only six showed no gain in rate of growth.   School work was excellent, though the improvement was not so striking.

Other Causes.—Some claim that feeble-mindedness results from apoplexy, epilepsy, insanity, and paralysis; in these cases, feeble-mindedness is not found among immediate ancestors.   There is also acquired subnormality; it is claimed to be the result of subnormal conditions of the mother during gestation, accident at birth, alcoholism in parents, syphilitic or tubercular condition of parents, head injuries in early infancy, acute infectious diseases, convulsions, and undernourishment.   Other writers discredit most of these suggested causes of acquired subnormality, claiming that they are very unlikely to be direct causes; if, however, a predisposition toward feeble-mindedness exists, these may indirectly be very real causes.

3. PREVENTION[1]

When the problem of prevention is raised, one finds considerable difference in point of view.   Some believe that no social program can

[1] For a more extended consideration of prevention, see pp. 489–494.

be accepted that violates the individual's right to care for his own person or for his children. Others believe that when the social good is at stake the individual must be subordinate. Differences in point of view regarding prevention are also due to differences in belief as to what are the causes of feeble-mindedness.

Sterilization.—Students of subnormality have for many years suggested that sterilization of all feeble-minded persons is necessary if the problem of caring for them is to be materially reduced. The difficulty is to secure such legislation in a country where personal freedom, liberty, and equality have been so emphasized. The general public is beginning to realize that the only way the idea of personal equality can be accepted is in the light of an opportunity to develop abilities and capacities to the maximum, as long as they do not obviously work to the detriment of the social group.

As this shift in point of view takes place and as the general public becomes permeated with the facts concerning the cost of caring for, educating, protecting, and even prosecuting these subnormals, perhaps it will be possible to put into operation regulations governing the sterilization of the mentally unfit.

A serious objection is that so little is known about the causes of subnormality. If experimentation with the hormones of the ductless glands should prove that subnormality of certain kinds can be eliminated, then we might expect to go more slowly. These findings so far are not conclusive, and we are meanwhile faced by a tremendous and accumulating problem of caring for these defectives. Compulsion may not be necessary. If the machinery were set to work and if information concerning the advantages of the operation and the ease of performing it were made general, we might find sterilization being accepted as a godsend.

A second objection must not be ignored. Some physicians claim that there are no detrimental physical or mental results from current methods of sterilization. Mayers emphasizes, however, the extremely close relationship between the ductless glands. It is known that a serious derangement of one gland has effects upon other glands; it is not clear, however, that the operation involved in the sterilization of either the male or the female constitutes in any sense such a derangement. If it does not, there would seem to be no objection to the proposal and very many excellent reasons for putting it into operation.

Medical Treatment.—If the hormones of ductless glands should prove to be effective in causing normal mental development, it would become important to discover children of retarded mentality at the earliest age possible. The treatment probably should not be delayed until the child enters school.

Segregation.—Segregation has been used and has long been advocated. It has failed as far as prevention is concerned; besides, it is costly. Despite huge expenditures, institutions cannot begin to house all who should be segregated.

Birth Control.—Present policies regarding birth control are not satisfactory; it is easy for the rich and the educated to secure information. The group that needs the facts most does not get them. They ought to be made available to every couple at the time they are married, if not before. Such information should be made free and available to all.

4. STATE LEGISLATION

Two aspects of state legislation governing the education and care of the feeble-minded will be considered. What provisions are made for public school classes and for sterilization? If feeble-minded children are to be educated in the public schools, sterilization becomes of increasing importance.

University of Washington Study.[1]—In 1914, 10 states had legislation governing the sterilization of the feeble-minded. The laws are interesting. With monotonous regularity they say that (1) if procreation is likely to produce defective children, (2) if the patient's condition is not likely to improve, and (3) if his physical and mental conditions are likely to be improved by it, then sterilization may or shall take place. Two other states provided for the sterilization of moral perverts, but ignored the feeble-minded as a class.

Hamilton and Haber's Study.[2]—State laws in 1917 concerning the feeble-minded dealt mostly with state institutions. Slight attention was given to special education and slightly more to sterilization. Iowa, Michigan, Montana, New Jersey, Oklahoma, Oregon, and Virginia were the only states that had state legislation dealing even indirectly with special education. New Jersey was the only state that had a specific program for educating feeble-minded children in local schools. It permitted local districts to provide schools for delinquent and dependent children under sixteen years of age, pro-

[1] "A Summary of the Laws of the Several States Governing the Feeble-minded, the Epileptic, and the Insane," pp. 16–35, *Bulletin of the University of Washington* 82, University of Washington, Seattle, 1914.

[2] SAMUEL W. HAMILTON, and ROY HABER, *Summaries of State Laws Relating to the Feebleminded and the Epileptic*, The National Committee for Mental Hygiene, Inc., New York, 1917, 240 pp.

viding they had the consent of the state board of education; by implication this included mental defectives.

Fourteen states had legislation relating to the sterilization of the feeble-minded and other classes, such as the insane, idiots, recidivists, and moral perverts. Thus, four more states within 3 years were added to the group that proposed the sterilization of the feeble-minded. Of these fourteen states, nine stated that sterilization may be required; five, that under certain conditions the feeble-minded must be sterilized.

In two states the sterilization board had to examine all cases reported by certain officials of the institution; if the board found the patient likely to produce feeble-minded children, or if the patient was not likely to get better, or if the operation was likely to help the patient, then the law demanded that the patient be sterilized. Another state demanded that all feeble-minded patients up for parole be sterilized if the board found that offspring would inherit feeble-mindedness. The other two states demanded that feeble-minded and epileptic inmates of state institutions be sterilized if the examining board found that they would produce feeble-minded children or if their condition would not improve.

White House Conference Report.[1]—In 1931, 15 states had legislation governing the schooling of children of low I.Q. Table XVIII shows the dates of the passage of such legislation.

TABLE XVIII.—YEARS WHEN LEGISLATION GOVERNING EDUCATION OF MENTALLY HANDICAPPED CHILDREN WAS PASSED IN 15 STATES[1]

State	Date	State	Date
New Jersey	1911	Wyoming	1919
Minnesota	1915	California	1921
Illinois	1917	Connecticut	1921
New York	1917	Utah	1921
Wisconsin	1917	Louisiana	1922
Massachusetts	1919	Alabama	1927
Missouri	1919	Oregon	1927
Pennsylvania	1919		

[1] Adapted from White House Conference, *Special Education: The Handicapped and the Gifted*, p. 439, The Century Co., New York, 1931.

Only five of these states made the establishment of special classes compulsory; in one it became mandatory upon the request of the parents of 10 or more pupils.

[1] White House Conference, *Special Education: The Handicapped and the Gifted*, p. 439, The Century Co., New York, 1931.

Certain Conclusions.—Despite the fact that 354 cities[1] report classes for subnormal children, present state laws deal with the problem very inadequately. State legislation is needed that will guarantee the child of low I.Q. an education commensurate with his abilities. At present such children too frequently are ignored or excluded. Instead of being treated so thoughtlessly, these children should be given most careful attention.

Legislation is needed that will make psychological service in city and county school districts compulsory. This service, aided by trained regular teachers, will make possible a continuous survey of children of low I.Q. Legislation governing the establishment of special classes should be passed. At present local boards are allowed to organize classes without specific legislation; the ineffectiveness of this is seen in the fact that, although 41 states had cities with such classes, 8 of them had only 1 such city each, and 10 others had only 2 or 3 such cities each.[2]

5. A STATE PROGRAM

Institutions for the segregation of children of low I.Q. are outside the scope of our problem, although they cannot be ignored in any state-wide program of caring for the feeble-minded. The possibility of education for the idiot and the imbecile is so limited that they can be cared for only in institutions; this is done at present in large institutions or in colonies with modest, though modern, housing facilities.

There is a much larger group of high-grade feeble-minded who can be cared for in classes in the public schools. There is an even larger number of low normals who need special-class work. These are the groups for whom a program of education and care is to be suggested.

The State's Responsibility.—If all children of low I.Q. are to be cared for and educated, the responsibility should not rest solely upon the shoulders of the local community. A few communities will do the task well; many more will ignore it. There must be in the state department of education at least one individual who knows this problem and who will have the authority to organize classes for mental defectives wherever such are needed. In some states a fair-sized staff will be required to organize and supervise this program properly.

The duties of this state supervisor and his staff will include the following: (1) to propose and urge the passage of legislation governing

[1] ARCH O. HECK, "Special Schools and Classes in Cities of 10,000 Population and More in the United States," *U. S. Office of Education Bulletin* 7, pp. 6–12, Washington, D.C., 1930.

[2] *Ibid.*, pp. 6–12.

the education of children of low I.Q.; (2) to keep a continuous census of all such children; (3) to plan a program of educating the general public to see the need of educating these children; (4) to assist local communities to organize classes; (5) to supervise the work done locally in caring for and educating children of low I.Q.; and (6) to supervise the educational part of the program which is carried on in the state institutions or colonies for the feeble-minded.[1]

Local Responsibility.—In connection with the local continuous school census, a census will be maintained of all children of low I.Q.; the state's program for doing this will be adhered to.

The local supervisor of these special classes will inform the public concerning (1) the number of such children, (2) the causes of such conditions, (3) the effect of ignoring the problems involved, (4) procedures that have been suggested for reducing the problem, (5) evidences of the effectiveness of various procedures, (6) methods of caring for and educating children of low I.Q. who are now with us, and (7) the values resulting from up-to-date methods of handling such children.

Local schools and classes will be established in all districts in accordance with need. If the incidence of 2 per cent or greater is correct, every school district of 500 pupils in the elementary grades could expect to establish its own special class. As small districts continue to disappear and larger school units are organized, the problem of educating children of low I.Q. will become less and less difficult.

6. SUMMARY

Any serious consideration of the problem of educating children of low I.Q. forces upon one the realization of its importance; he sees that the progress made by these children, when thought of in terms of their original capacities, is great; he sees the size of the problem in its proper light when he realizes that perhaps 2,000,000 or more children in the United States need special classwork.

The real challenge comes to those interested in children of low I.Q. when they face the problem of how to prevent such conditions. If it is solved, all the problems of educating these youths will have been solved; the expense to society of educating them will end; the dangers to society due to the ease by which these millions may be controlled by unsocial individuals will be lessened; and the misery of these millions, due to their inability to provide for themselves the essentials of life, will be minimized.

[1] For discussion of the state's administrative staff, see Chap. XXXI.

Prevention depends upon the removal of causes. Heredity has many advocates; some have suggested that the action of the endocrines is related to low I.Q.; others claim that apoplexy, epilepsy, insanity, and paralysis are causes; other suggested causes are subnormal conditions of the mother during gestation, accidents at birth, alcoholism in parents, syphilitic or tubercular condition of parents, head injuries in early infancy, acute infectious diseases, convulsions, and undernourishment.

Suggestions for prevention include sterilization, use of the hormones of certain ductless glands, segregation in institutions, and a wide distribution of data on birth control. If these methods are to become effective, state legislation making some of them legal will be needed.

Problems and Questions for Discussion

1. Why is it difficult to secure strong popular approval of an educational program for children of low I.Q.?
2. What challenge does the education of children of low I.Q. really present to us?
3. What do you conceive to be the chief cause of low I.Q.? Defend your ideas.
4. What is the possible significance of the ductless glands in dealing with children of low I.Q.?
5. Do you approve of sterilization? If so, under what conditions and why? If not, why not?
6. What legislation do we now have governing (a) sterilization, (b) birth control, and (c) special classes for children of low I.Q.?
7. Outline a state program that you would approve as a means of caring for this whole problem dealing with low I.Q. Defend your proposals.

Selected Bibliography

GODDARD, HENRY H. *Feeble-mindedness: Its Causes and Consequences.* The Macmillan Company, New York, 1914. 599 pp.
    A consideration is given to causes of feeble-mindedness. A vast amount of illustrative data is furnished.
HAMILTON, SAMUEL W., and HABER, ROY. *Summaries of State Laws Relating to the Feebleminded and the Epileptic.* The National Committee for Mental Hygiene, Inc., New York, 1917. 240 pp.
    Summary of state laws dealing with the feeble-minded; it deals with state institutions, special education, sterilization, and marriage.
MAYERS, LAURENCE H., and WELTON, ARTHUR D. *What We Are and Why.* Dodd, Mead & Company, Inc., New York, 1933. 340 pp.
    An excellent discussion of endocrine physiology and its possible relation to abnormality. Discusses sex, personality, cycles of life, giants, dwarfs, childhood diseases, and obesity, in relation to the endocrines.
PRESSEY, SIDNEY L., and PRESSEY, LUELLA COLE. *Mental Abnormality and Deficiency,* pp. 267–312. The Macmillan Company, New York, 1926.
    Considers causes and treatment of abnormal mental states.

Report of 1915 *Legislative Committee on Mental Deficiency and the Proposed Institution for the Care of Feeble-minded and Epileptic Persons.* Whittier State School, Whittier, Calif., 1917. 68 pp.

Discusses colony care of the feeble-minded, eugenics and euthenics, the social problem, their mental age, number in the schools, relation to delinquency, and studies made in New York State and in Missouri. Copy of the proposed law in California is included.

SCHEIDEMANN, NORMA V. *The Psychology of Exceptional Children,* pp. 181–230. Houghton Mifflin Company, Boston. 1931.

A consideration of causes of feeble-mindedness, its psychological and physical characteristics, and the training needed.

"A Summary of the Laws of the Several States Governing the Feeble-minded, the Epileptic and the Insane." *Bulletin of the University of Washington,* 82, Seattle, 1914. 87 pp.

Summary of state laws dealing with the marriage and divorce of the feeble-minded, their sterilization, admission to and discharge from state institutions, and an excellent discussion of these laws.

White House Conference. *Special Education: The Handicapped and the Gifted,* pp. 439–442, 477–478. The Century Co., New York, 1931.

A brief discussion of state laws governing the care and education of children of low I.Q.

CHAPTER XXVI

THE EDUCATION OF GIFTED CHILDREN

The danger of universal public education is mediocratization of a nation's leadership. The task of providing it is so great that children are handled en masse. Instruction lacks individualization because the course of study is developed to fit the average child. The more nearly education is made universal, the lower is that average. Selection ceases when all children continue through the grades, high school, and college. Since administrative authority frowns upon low promotion rates, either standards are lowered unduly or so much attention is given to the handicapped that the capable are ignored.

In one of Pearl Buck's stories of Chinese life, Wang the Tiger says, "The thing to do when one kills a centipede is to crush its head and then its hundred legs are in confusion and they run hither and thither against each other and they are harmless." If we neglect the brilliant children of this nation, may we not find ourselves to be a nation with a hundred well-trained legs, but without a head that would make effective the work of those legs?

The training provided for prospective leaders must be just as carefully planned and as thoughtfully administered as is the program for the followers. The notion that ability will push up of its own accord, that the capable child can take care of himself, is wrong. A vast amount of potential leadership has been lost entirely by being thus ignored. There are many instances of those who have made good, despite lack of help; what is nowhere described is the tragedy of those thousands of potential leaders who have failed to overcome economic or social handicaps. The public schools need to give the gifted child an opportunity to develop his ability as adequately as other children are permitted and helped to develop theirs.

1. DEFINITION

A Limitation.—The term "gifted child" refers to a child of high intelligence quotient. Such a child may at the same time have some other special ability; this latter is not, however, a prerequisite to classifying him as gifted. Regardless of how talented a child may be along a particular line, if he does not have a high intelligence quotient,

389

he is not considered gifted in the sense in which the term is used here.[1]

Variability.—Cleveland has included children over 120 I.Q. in its "major work groups."[2] Some children, however, with I.Q.'s slightly below 120 fit satisfactorily into these groups, whereas some slightly above do not. In addition to the given intelligence quotient, there must be drive, originality, and initiative for unusual success in academic achievement. Some cities include any child above 110 I.Q. in their classes for the gifted; many authorities raise the limit as high as 130 and even 140 I.Q.

2. GUIDING PRINCIPLES

Equal Opportunity.—The principle of equal educational opportunity is violated as long as we proceed upon the theory that we need not worry about the bright child, that he will succeed despite all handicaps. School practice of planning programs for the average child and of giving aid to slow-moving pupils in mastering those programs, while no special attention is given to the gifted group, is evidence of our failure to operate upon the basis of this principle.

Avoid Development of Conceit.—Gifted children should not be educated in such a way as to make them conceited. This is just what has happened when such children have been taught in regular classes; it may result, too, when special classes are organized unless care is exercised to prevent it. When children discover that they have exceptional abilities, they may easily become conceited unless they are helped to realize the responsibilities that their abilities place upon them. The average teacher with a large miscellaneous group of children finds it very difficult to give the assistance needed in orienting them properly with respect to these added responsibilities.

Social and Physical Placement.—That a child has unusual academic ability is no reason for misplacing him socially and physically. That a ten- or eleven-year-old child is academically able to compete with high-school pupils is not evidence that he will profit most by being placed in high school. An enriched program of studies that would keep him with youths of his approximate social and physical development would generally be much more satisfactory.

Worth-while Enrichment.—This program of enrichment must be worth while. Simply more work of the same type is not the enrichment needed. These children, indeed, need less of drill and of

---

[1] The specially gifted child will be discussed in Chap. XXIX.

[2] Major work groups are the same as classes for gifted children, as defined in this chapter.

easy reading materials than do children of lesser ability. They need a program in which they are given more opportunity to carry on investigations of their own.[1]

Avoidance of Bad Social Habits.—If the program provided does not challenge the child's ability, he may develop into a loafer; he may become the center of all disciplinary problems, since he must have some outlet for his surplus unused energy; he may, through lack of proper supervision, become cynical, develop antisocial ideals, and concentrate upon a program that later will make him a menace to society.

All-round Development.—School studies should not be allowed to absorb the child's entire attention or even the major part of it. The physical, the social, and the moral aspects of the lives of these children are of the greatest importance.

This does not mean that they are originally less well developed physically and socially than other children; they are likely to be even better developed. It means that some of them become so absorbed in academic interests that they tend to neglect other phases of life. It means that, because they are so capable, they owe it to themselves and to society to prepare themselves in such a way that the maximum good can come from their academic achievement. This does not mean equal development in all fields; it urges that other important areas shall not be ignored in the program of instruction.

Individual Study.—Pupil programs should be based upon a careful case study of each gifted child. Ideally, this is urged in these days for all school children, but the immensity of the task has prevented putting the ideal into operation. Since the training of the gifted child may affect profoundly the entire social group, every effort should be made to give such pupils the best preparation for life that society can afford.

3. HISTORY

The history of the development of an educational program for gifted children is less definite than that of the growth of practices to be used with other special groups. The fact that the gifted child is defined in terms of academic ability means that such children were probably taught as early as the arts of reading and writing began.

Plato's Plan.—Whipple[2] relates the idea of a program of education for the gifted to Plato's ideal republic; in this republic were artisans

[1] See pp. 394–397, 408–414.

[2] National Society for the Study of Education, *Twenty-third Yearbook*, pp. 1–2, Part 1, 1924.

and laborers, warriors, and magistrates. The first group was to learn a trade; the second group was to be trained in music and gymnastics; the third was to be taught the sciences, philosophy, and metaphysics. Children of the first class would be allowed entrance to the other classes if they had the necessary ability; on the other hand, children of magistrates, if they had no |ability, must be artisans and laborers. This was clearly an attempt to set up a program of education in terms of the academic ability of youths.

Gifted Individuals.—Literature is sprinkled with accounts of the education of gifted children. These children generally have been educated by either parents or tutors. Christian Heineken,[1] born in Germany in 1721, was so precocious that when he was ten months old a tutor was hired. His tutor claimed that by the age of four years he could give 1,500 Latin proverbs, answer any question in history and read German. Shortly after a visit to Denmark, where Christian had entertained the king, he died, being four years and four months old. Karl Witte read German, French, Italian, Latin, and Greek at nine years of age; he received the Ph.D. from the University of Leipzig before he was fourteen. Lord Kelvin and his brother James Thomson learned to read and spell as they learned to talk; they entered the University of Glasgow at ten and twelve, respectively. John Stuart Mill never knew when he learned Greek; he was told that he had learned it by the age of three years. The story of the world's gifted might be continued at great length.

Public School Beginnings.—Educating the gifted was not ineffective when the schools were small and when the teacher had an opportunity to become personally acquainted with each pupil. Under those conditions the conscientious teacher could discover the able child. Since what this child needed was an opportunity to do things, those early schools at least had a chance to give material aid to the gifted. But as enrollments increased and personal contacts between teacher and pupil became fewer and weaker, these conditions made it less possible for the gifted to be recognized and given an opportunity to do things.

As early as 1868, Harris of St. Louis reported upon promotion plans used in that city as a means of better caring for both the subnormal and the gifted. Promotions were made at first semiannually, later quarterly, and finally at five-week intervals. In Elizabeth, N.J., pupils of each of the elementary grades were grouped, and each group was allowed to advance as rapidly as it could. This permitted unre-

[1] *Ibid.*, pp. 2–4.

tarded advancement of the abler pupils. The plan was initiated in 1886.[1]

The Cambridge plan[2] of caring for superior pupils was originated in 1891. When first organized, it applied to grades 4 to 9, inclusive. One course covered these grades in 6 years, the other in 4; the work could be done in 5 years either by completing the first three grades under the first plan and the last three grades under the second plan, or vice versa.

Other methods of caring for the gifted that were early devised and are still used are (1) vacation schools, (2) the helping teacher, (3) double promotions, (4) credit by examination, (5) individual instruction, (6) some plan involving projects, and (7) special classes.

Public School Classes.—McDonald[3] says that probably the first special school for gifted children in the United States was organized at Worcester, Mass., in 1901. Pupils were selected from all over the city and were gathered at centers under superior teachers. The pupils did the regular work of the grades and began such high-school subjects as Latin, French, German, and algebra. Despite this relatively early beginning, there are not yet a great number of classes for gifted children in the United States. In 1930[4] only 30 cities reported schools or classes or both, although replies had been received from 736 cities in the United States. These cities reported a total of 135 classes, enrolling 3,883 pupils. Cleveland, Los Angeles, and Worcester, in the order named, led in the number of pupils enrolled; they had 518, 450, and 440, respectively.

4. TYPICAL CITY PROGRAMS

Cleveland.—According to Goddard, enrichment classes "began in the public schools of Cleveland, Ohio, about 1920." They are called major work groups. Originally children of 120 I.Q. and up were accepted; a few with lower I.Q.'s were admitted. More recently, only children of 125 I.Q. are accepted. An attempt is made to keep the class enrollment at 25 or less. About 3 years after these classes were first organized, Cleveland experimented with classes of 35. After

---

[1] *Ibid.*, p. 8.

[2] ROBERT ALEXANDER FYFE McDONALD, *Adjustment of School Organization to Various Population Groups*, pp. 94–96. Teachers College, Columbia University, New York, 1915.

[3] *Ibid.*, p. 99.

[4] ARCH O. HECK, "Special Schools and Classes in Cities of 10,000 Population and More in the United States," pp. 20–21, *U. S. Office of Education Bulletin* 7, Washington, D.C., 1930.

a year's trial, there was general agreement that the larger class was unsatisfactory.

During the school year 1935–36, the elementary major work classes had an average daily attendance of 536. There were 621 in major work groups in the junior high school. Despite the extensiveness of Cleveland's program, she still has much to do before all children of 125 I.Q. and above are cared for in special classes.

Cleveland's aim is to have children of high I.Q. progress through the first nine grades at the rate of one grade per year. The work of these grades is so enriched that all can profit by the time spent in them. This enrichment is not merely an "adding-to" process. More material is added, but far more significant is the change in method. The pupils are not taught en masse; neither is instruction completely individualized. The teacher becomes a guide in helping the children to localize and find problems; the pupils are given great freedom in working out these problems.

Modern language study and typing enrich the course. The writing of original prose and verse is encouraged. The children make collections of butterflies, insects, stamps, and stones, becoming quite expert in the field of study selected. Dramatization is important; they learn to interpret accurately what they read. They are encouraged to do something as a result of reading. They may simply report what they have done, tell the story of what they have read, or give a critical analysis of what they have studied.

The teachers are free to work out their own programs after the children have mastered the regular school curriculum. The teachers generally feel responsible for helping these children to develop socially and physically as well as mentally. Any child inclined to ignore his physical or social development is given special attention; this is imperative if he is to be able to make the maximum use of his academic ability.

Los Angeles.[1]—The first class for gifted children in Los Angeles was started experimentally in 1915–16. For 4 years the work was continued upon this basis. The teacher of the class was then made the supervisor and other classes were developed. By 1927–28 Los Angeles had 15 classes for gifted children, called opportunity A rooms.[2] By Jan. 1, 1937, there were 21 classes enrolling 630 pupils in the elementary schools. Two junior high schools also had some experimental groups.

[1] Most of the data came directly from the office of the supervisor of special classes for the highly endowed in January, 1937.

[2] *Third Yearbook*, Division of Psychology and Educational Research, pp. 23–43, School Publication 185, Los Angeles, Calif., 1929.

Children are selected after most careful study. An intelligence or a reading test is first given to all pupils of those grades from which children are to be chosen. Any child who rates 2 years ahead of where his chronological age would place him is a possible eligible. All such pupils are then given a group intelligence test. All who approximate an I.Q. of 125 are usually given the Stanford revision of the Binet; all primary pupils and about half the upper grades are thus examined. The remainder of the latter group are placed upon the basis of the Terman Group Test.

ILLUSTRATION 35.—A group of gifted children having an academic assignment dealing with astronomy and its contribution to civilization in a Los Angeles opportunity class.

Additions to the eligible list are recommended by school principals, parents, social agencies, and psychological clinics. Occasionally, children with I.Q.'s under 125, but of marked success in academic achievement, are admitted.

The program provided is essentially an enriched course of study. This enrichment is secured by (1) adding subjects, (2) selecting more difficult materials, (3) introducing many more supplementary books, (4) offering "opportunities for increased contacts with interest-arousing institutions, events, and people." Illustration 35 represents a class dealing with an academic assignment on astronomy's contribu-

tion to civilization.   Mere description fails to paint the picture fully.
The school is a "workshop in which children experience purposefully."
An understanding of the traditional school does not adequately aid
one in interpreting the picture.   "The day might begin with a conference—a discussion of progress and of plans for the next step.
When the conference comes to an end, groups and individuals begin
work on some aspect of the unit of study.   Possibly half the day is
spent on the problem."

This major problem may not engage all their interests.   Clubs
are, therefore, organized.   The pupils carry on research along many
lines; this may not have any relation to the central class problem.
The program varies from room to room and is dependent upon the
interests of the groups.

Some of the major problems used are given below.   They "represent movement and growth"; they provide many "why" and "how"
questions, which the pupils have to answer.

1. The magic city of Yang-Na (Los Angeles).   How did our city begin?   (See
Illustration 36)[1]
2. The development of civilization as shown through a study of sports, games,
and physical education.
3. The development of the people of Great Britain as shown in their literature.
4. What has a knowledge of astronomy contributed to civilization?   (See
Illustration 35)
5. Music as a picture of the history of people.   (See Illustration 40)[2]
6. What did Europe contribute to our government?
7. How people tell time.   (See Illustration 38)[3]

The child is encouraged to express himself in his own unique way;
models of what adults consider good verse or prose are set aside.

Dramatic play, free dramatization, that sometimes is preserved in the form of
play, pageant, or operetta; prose, that may take the form of speech, essay, or story;
art, that illustrates or decorates a poem or book, or expends itself on murals or
stage scenery; music, that becomes a part of a song repertoire; poetry, that finds
its way into the school periodicals[4] or into odd corners of various activity by-prod-
ucts; all these are used avenues of the urge to create.

These changes in method aim at securing as "much pupil activity"
as possible and in developing "all possible pupil initiative."   Various
projects are constantly under way and are always related to one
another.   Pupils establish a relationship with new words and then

[1] p. 409.
[2] p. 414.
[3] p. 411.
[4] See Illustration 39, p. 412.

use them on all possible occasions.   A modern language is studied in every room where a capable teacher can be found to supervise it.

Pupils are encouraged to read widely, as well as intensively, so that they may not (as adults too often do) fail to familiarize themselves with many of "the wonders of literature," because of concentrating interest on some one field.   With the gifted "little is necessary except a systematic exposure to reading material of the desired type." Teachers, supervisors, and librarians constantly give this problem attention.

New York City.—New York has not organized a city-wide special-class program for its gifted, as have Cleveland and Los Angeles.   This does not mean that the gifted child is ignored.   It does mean that the responsibility has been placed upon regular teachers for finding him and adjusting schoolwork to his needs.   The report on educating superior students[1] shows clearly that teachers and principals in New York City high schools give a great amount of attention to gifted children.   X, Y, Z classes are formed.   Special assignments are made, freedom from regular requirements is allowed, greater use of libraries is permitted, field trips are encouraged, more intensive study of typical class problems is secured, and more books directly applicable to courses in question are provided.   The methods used in the numerous high-school subject-matter areas in an attempt properly to educate the gifted are legion.

.The report shows that high-school teachers and principals are not yet satisfied with their methods of meeting the needs of gifted pupils. Some of the recommendations made are both informing and interesting. The group representing Art concludes that

A Central Arts High School should be organized, in which might be gathered all the aesthetically gifted children of the city.   It should be planned to cover industrial arts and crafts, graphic arts, such as painting, sculpture, and architecture, and also music, and the dramatic and literary arts.—It should have open shops, laboratories, and studios where children might meet on school days and Saturdays to unfold their precious gifts.—The ultimate aim should be the development of the artist-citizen of superlative creative ability, of cultured and inspired leadership.[2]

The biology group urges that "superior students in biology should be segregated in all schools."[3]   The economic group calls for greater

[1] HELEN LOUISE COHEN, and NANCY G. CORYELL, eds., *Educating Superior Students*.   Copyright.   Used by permission of American Book Company, New York, 1935.   340 pp.

[2] *Ibid.*, p. 13.

[3] *Ibid.*, p. 29.

library facilities, in order to provide adequately for their gifted.   To
aid selection of students for special work in English, it is recommended
that the junior high schools "send as much personal data as possible
for their pupils entering senior high school."[1]   It is suggested that in
grade 9 the English teacher retain her selected group for the entire
year.   The mathematics committee urges classification and suggests
that "superior teachers be assigned to classes of gifted pupils."[2]

The final chapter, on conclusions and recommendations, says that
the numerous reports of this survey of New York City high schools
are evidence of the "conviction of the teachers and supervisors" that
boys and girls of superior ability must "receive an education commensurate with their abilities."[3]   It says, further, "In order that
such leaders may be developed, it is generally agreed that the intellectually superior should be sought out and grouped in special classes."[4]

5. THE DESIRABILITY OF THE SPECIAL CLASS

The desirability of organizing special classes for children of high
I.Q. is questioned by many individuals when they first consider the
problem.   Habituation to a given method of classification makes
a change in method seem revolutionary and unworkable.   In the
past, children have entered grade 1 upon the basis of chronological age.
Special education proposes to classify mentally exceptional children
upon the basis of mental ability.   All that is done in organizing classes
for gifted children is to change the basis of classification.   Many of
the criticisms of such classes are based upon misunderstanding.   Such
misunderstandings must be dealt with if special schools and classes
for the gifted are to be encouraged.

Objections Frequently Raised.—1. A common criticism is that
when gifted children are segregated they become conceited.   Whether
or not this happens seems to depend upon the method followed in
organizing the class.   If the children are told that they are gifted,
it is likely, that they may be flattered into self-conceit.   If, however,
they are grouped according to ability to do their schoolwork as shown
by classification tests, and if this classification is accepted as a routine
part of school procedure, the likelihood of developing conceited children is very slight.   Goddard, who spent 2 days each month visiting
Cleveland's special classes for gifted children over a 5-year period,
reports, "It doesn't happen."   When organized in special classes,

---

[1] *Ibid.*, p. 90.
[2] *Ibid.*, p. 212.
[3] *Ibid.*, p. 316.
[4] *Ibid.*, p. 318.

these children encounter real competition, whereas in regular classes they usually are given excellent ratings with an expenditure of little effort. Regular teachers have seen too many likable children become unbearably conceited in this situation.

2. Another criticism is that such a plan is undemocratic. The problem here is one of definition. The critic often defines democracy as *identity* of school offerings; he insists that the special class brings the bright child into contact with opportunities that are withheld from the larger group of children. If democracy is defined as *equality* of opportunity, where an attempt is made to adjust the school program to the abilities and the interests of each child, then perhaps the special class is a more democratic way of dealing with gifted children than is the customary procedure.

3. It is claimed that such classes create an intellectual aristocracy; a chasm is developed between those of high mental ability and those of average ability. If it were proposed to assemble gifted children in a monastery completely out of touch with the average individual, there might be some basis for the claim. Special classes merely assemble these children for a few hours of each day for study in a group where all have relatively similar ability. They play with other children in and out of school; they co-operate with other children in all school projects; and they associate with other children in various neighborhood organizations.

4. Some hold the opinion that children in the regular classes become jealous of the children of greater ability. Convincing evidence that this is so has not been given. Observation of schools in which such classes are organized inclines one to the belief that when these gifted children are segregated for classwork they are less resented than when they recite daily with children of average ability. Goddard says of gifted children:

Mentally they are more alert, they think quicker, they are more observing, they can see relationships more promptly. They have more good habits and fewer detrimental ones. They have a better use of language. They seem to have more appreciation of social responsibility. They have more curiosity and more energy. They see the end from the beginning more promptly.[1]

If jealousy is to enter the picture, constant association in class discussion would probably develop it more quickly that segregation of the gifted.

5. The claim is made that these children would tend to overwork. Evidence, other than reports of teachers in charge of gifted children,

[1] HENRY HERBERT GODDARD, *School Training of Gifted Children*, p. 35, World Book Company, Yonkers-on-Hudson, New York, 1928.

is meager. These reports do not verify the claim. The gifted child is likely to be healthier than other children; he can do his academic schoolwork with greater ease. It is reasonable to expect that he would accomplish more than the average child and do it without undue mental strain.

6. Again, it is said that fewer leaders would be developed. Before grouping, every class had one or more able leaders. When these leaders are all assembled in one class, it is claimed that only three or four develop, whereas there were 30 or 40, before. One may note several misconceptions. It is assumed that all children of high I.Q. were leaders in their original groups. Some of them, owing possibly to group jealousy, were anything but leaders; they might have been leaders in the field of their special interest if this interest had been developed. The special class gives such a child a much greater opportunity for the development of leadership.

It is assumed that only three or four members of the special class would have an opportunity to become leaders, whereas each member of the group may be a leader. Each child in his own special field of interest may be a real leader in the special class. No potential leaders are lost. It is assumed that the regular classes would not develop other leadership after the children of high I.Q. were withdrawn. An interesting result of the organization of classes for subnormals is the fact that a very real leadership is developed where least expected. When the brighter children withdraw, others who were temporarily suppressed come to the fore.

7. Another contention is that the regular grade children are losers when the gifted are withdrawn. It is assumed that the average and slow child learns from the gifted. We have no very conclusive evidence of this. It is assumed that a grade group with abler students in it can progress more rapidly. If rapidity of progress is measured by the rate the abler students can achieve, then this is true; it is upon this basis that regular teachers too often proceed. When the bright children are taken from the group, the rate of progress is much slower, more explanations must be made, and more repetition is required. This probably means that the group is now proceeding far more understandingly than before and, in terms of successful work, even more rapidly than when handicapped by having several abler pupils in the class.

8. There are those who say that implements for selecting the gifted are inadequate. This can be frankly admitted. Those employed today, however, are better than those used 20 years ago. Furthermore, if a mistake is made and discovered, adjustments can

be made at any time.   If it is worth while to organize special classes, then possible errors in placement that can be picked up later should not prevent their being organized.

9. A serious practical difficulty is the matter of cost.   The per capita costs will be greater if the advantages of a smaller teacher load and of greater facilities for an enriched program are to be offered. This fact must be weighed against the advantages that seem to come from the organization of special classes for gifted children.

Advantages Frequently Suggested.—1. An advantage very often pointed out is that the special class provides the child with an opportunity to work to the level of his superior ability.   His progress is not set at a slower tempo than his ability would permit.   The greater ability of the group makes possible a more rapid development of projects that are part of the common curriculum; this makes possible the development of many common projects that could not be added to the regular course of study because of lack of time.

2. The child does not develop habits of carelessness and slothfulness in doing his work.   Many a child of unusual academic ability has wasted that ability because he never had to exert himself during his days in the public schools.   He refused to work, gave up school early, and, it may be, became one of society's malcontents.   Although the special class cannot ensure that all will succeed, it will give an opportunity to the able child to work instead of loaf, and encourage him to do his best.

3. The enrichment program not only keeps the child profitably occupied, but makes it possible to adapt schoolwork to his unique abilities.   The numerous projects undertaken give ample opportunity for making these adjustments.

4. The enriched program makes it possible for these children to progress through the grades normally with respect to chronological age.   They do not reach senior high school by eleven or twelve. To the extent that social and physical age correlates with chronological age, they are likewise better adjusted in these respects.   It is recognized that children who are accelerated by a year or even 2 years may be perfectly adjusted physically and socially, but, if that acceleration reaches 3 or more years, the situation is questionable.

5. The special-class program may prevent social maladjustment. Superior children who attend the regular school are content to remain idle.   Their alert minds are likely to seek an outlet through other channels if they are not kept occupied by a school program that challenges their efforts.   Among truants and delinquents are children of unusual ability who, because of too little to do, dislike school and

seek to escape its boredom. Some play truant, meet undesirable characters, and finally become young criminals; others misbehave in school, become the school's bad boys, and finally are classed as delinquents.

6. The special program helps the child put forth his best efforts. He sees in his group other youths who respond in class as quickly, who lead in discussion as ably, and who show as much initiative as he has ever shown. He realizes that he must work. Even more important is the challenge given him by the discussions of the group. He becomes interested because interesting things are being discussed. Thus, without any external pressure, forces within himself demand that he really achieve.

7. These youths secure a definite training for leadership along many lines. One boy may be a poet, one a prose writer, one a dramatist, one a linguist, one a botanist, one a geologist, one a historian, one a musician, and one an artist. Each would be recognized as a leader in his own area; each would have worth-while material to present to the group. From grade 4 or grade 5 up, the teacher might find that she would frequently have to refer certain questions to the class leader in his particular field.

8. Gifted children, as Goddard puts it, "are made of finer stuff than the majority." The fact that they are more alert and think quicker creates a classroom problem when they are combined with normals. The fact that they are more observing and see relationships more readily creates problems in stimulating both the average and the bright when they are taught as one group. These differences alone might well be the only reasons needed to justify the organization of special classes for children of high I.Q.

6. SUMMARY

If we center attention educationally upon the average and the subnormal child to the exclusion of the superior, society may discover to its sorrow that it is saddled with mediocre leadership. One method suggested for avoiding such a condition is the organization of special classes for the education of children of high I.Q. Cleveland and Los Angeles have done significant work.

The following principles are important in planning an educational program for these children. (1) It should provide the gifted with the same opportunity to develop their talents that is provided for the average child and for the child of low I.Q. (2) It should guard against the development of conceited individuals among the gifted. (3)

It should provide for social and physical placement, as well as for proper mental placement. (4) It should develop a real enrichment program. (5) It should prevent the development of wasteful and bad social habits. (6) It should seek for each gifted child a sane, all-round development educationally, socially, physically, and morally. (7) It should be based, in the last analysis, upon the most careful study of each child.

The gifted have always been with us. There are many stories and biographies telling of the education of geniuses. Practical plans for selecting gifted children and adapting the public school program to their needs are quite recent. Harris gave the problem his attention as early as 1868. Worcester, Mass., organized the first special school for the gifted in 1901. As late as 1930, however, only 30 cities out of 736 had started such classes.

Objections to the special class are: (1) The pupils become conceited. (2) It is undemocratic. (3) It tends to create an intellectual aristocracy. (4) It results in jealousy upon the part of the average child. (5) It causes the gifted to overwork. (6) Fewer leaders are developed. (7) Average children lose educationally. (8) Implements of selection are inadequate. (9) The cost is prohibitive.

The advantages are: (1) The child is permitted to work to the level of his superior ability. (2) The child does not develop habits of carelessness and slothfulness. (3) The class provides an opportunity to adapt instruction to the needs of the child. (4) The child can proceed normally through the grades and still have a worth-while program of study. (5) It prevents social maladjustment. (6) It forces the child to exert himself if he is to make good with the group. (7) The child secures definite training for leadership in specific areas. (8) It permits the use of materials and methods adapted to the unique ability of these youths.

Problems and Questions for Discussion

1. What relation does Wang the Tiger's saying have to the problem of educating gifted children?

2. Who are the gifted children? How many are there?

3. Outline the principles you think should govern the education of gifted children. Why are they important?

4. What answer, if any, can be given to each of the arguments commonly made against public school classes for gifted children?

5. What answer, if any, can be given to each of the reasons usually advanced in favor of such classes?

6. Do you favor the organization of special schools and classes for gifted children in your own public school system? Defend your point of view with any evidence you are able to discover.

Selected Bibliography

COHEN, HELEN LOUISE, and CORYELL, NANCY G., Eds. *Educating Superior Students.* American Book Company, New York, 1935.   340 pp.

A most interesting account of what public schools in New York City are doing for gifted children.

DANIELSON, CORA LEE.   "Special Classes for Children of Superior Mental Ability in the Elementary Schools," *Third Yearbook* of the Division of Psychology and Educational Research, pp. 23–43.   School Publication 185, Los Angeles, 1929.

Brief description of Los Angeles Plan for educating gifted children.   Provides statistics on I.Q. and M.A.   Lists many original poems written by these children.

DANIELSON, CORA LEE.   "Special Classes for Highly Endowed Children," *Fourth Yearbook* of the Division of Psychology and Educational Research, pp. 67–87. School Publication 211, Los Angeles, 1931.

Discusses reasons for opportunity A rooms, type of teachers selected, methods of selecting pupils, instructional procedure, and the high-school success of graduates from these classes.

GODDARD, HENRY HERBERT.   *School Training of Gifted Children.*   World Book Company, Yonkers-on-Hudson, New York, 1928.   226 pp.

A descriptive account of the work done at Cleveland, Ohio, in classes for gifted children, plus Dr. Goddard's very excellent analysis of the theory that evidently underlies the work done in these classes.

McDONALD, ROBERT ALEXANDER FYFE.   *Adjustment of School Organization to Various Population Groups*, pp. 90–101.   Teachers College, Columbia University, New York, 1915.

A brief historical development of the education of gifted children is given, plus a description of many recent methods of educating them.

National Society for the Study of Education.   Report of the Society's Committee on the Education of Gifted Children.   *Twenty-third Yearbook*, Part 1.   Public School Publishing Company, Bloomington, Ill., 1924.   443 pp.

Deals with history, selection, organization, administration, curricula, characteristics, achievements educationally, results of putting gifted children into special classes, and case histories.

CHAPTER XXVII

PROBLEMS FACED IN EDUCATING GIFTED CHILDREN

An appeal to the emotions is far more potent in securing popular approval than is an appeal to the intellect. This fact is recognized by the preacher, the philanthropist, and the practical politician. It is this fact that creates the greatest problem for the educator interested in the education of the gifted child. The crippled child or the blind youth invokes the emotional appeal automatically, whenever seen; enthusiasts for the education of these unfortunates have not hesitated to make use of it.

Even the socially handicapped and the mentally handicapped are not without a very strong emotional appeal. Visit schools or institutions for such handicapped and observe how quickly the sympathy of the average layman is aroused. Not one word need be spoken; the object lesson is sufficient. There is something pathetic in the mere observation of youths thus handicapped.

This fact has been so well capitalized that today we find a strong, developing program of special education for all types of handicapped children. This appeal the educator who is most interested in the education of the gifted does not have; he may build up an argument for such classes with a strong emotional appeal in it, but the mere presence of a gifted child at his side while he makes his plea will not strengthen that plea.

1. WINNING A PLACE IN THE PUBLIC SCHOOL PROGRAM FOR THE SPECIAL CLASS FOR GIFTED CHILDREN

Data Needed.—The most difficult problem faced in developing a program of special education for gifted children is that of convincing the public that there is need for it. Lacking the emotional appeal, the educator of gifted children must depend upon an appeal to the intellect. He needs data concerning gifted children. How many are there? What proportion have been making good? What happens to those who complete the regular public schools? What happens to those who study throughout the first nine grades in special classes? Does the latter group adjust better, succeed better, become more public spirited, assume more leadership socially, educationally, philanthropically, and politically than the former? The advocates of special classes believe that the answer to the last of these questions can be answered affirmatively. The public, however, wants facts. Such facts must be provided.

Size of the Problem.—Although national surveys have never been made, data based upon nonselected groups of children make possible a rough approximation of the number of gifted children in a given state or in the nation. If Terman's "genius" group are the gifted, there would be 100,000 gifted children within the United States. If Hollingworth's 1 per cent can be called gifted, there would be 250,000 in the United States. If Goddard's suggestion[1] that all children with I.Q.'s of 120 and above be accepted in the special classes, there would be 60 gifted pupils out of every 1,000—or, in the United States, the grand total of 1,500,000. The size of the problem obviously depends upon the point where the line is drawn between high normal and gifted.

2. SELECTION

Even though 120 I.Q. is accepted as the approximate point for determining admission to the special class, several other problems are to be met in actually making the selection. How are these pupils to be discovered? Must every child admitted to the class have a Binet test? If so, must every child in the system be given the Binet? The cost in time and money may prohibit this procedure. The importance of correctly selecting the children who are to enter, however, is so great that there is general agreement that every pupil entering these classes should pass a Binet.

The discovery of candidates for these classes may be based upon (1) teacher recommendation, (2) previous school marks, (3) results of achievement tests, (4) results of a group mental test, or (5) a combination of some two or more of these procedures.

Group Mental Test.—The use of the group mental test, supplemented by the other procedures, is perhaps best. The group test, while a fairly reliable measure of ability for most pupils, may be in error for some. Failure to understand directions, lack of rapport, and a mental disturbance are possible reasons for the child's failure to achieve results which satisfactorily represent his ability. To the pupils selected in this manner, should be added those who have done unusually good work on achievement tests, who have exceptionally good school marks, and who are rated high by teachers. This group will be given the Binet before actual placement in the special class.

[1] HENRY H. GODDARD, *School Training of Gifted Children*, pp. 64–75, World Book Company, Yonkers-on-Hudson, New York, 1928.

If the cost of group tests makes this plan impossible, the three methods suggested above as supplementary may be used. In this case, high achievement on subject-matter tests should become the chief basis for selection; the other two methods would be used as aids. If standard achievement tests have never been given, school marks and teachers' estimates of mental ability may be used.

Teachers' Estimates.—When teachers' estimates are used, the teachers should be given specific instructions for making such judgments. Certain errors tend to creep into these judgments. They are (1) failure to note overageness and thus to rate the pupil too high; (2) failure to note underageness and thus to rate the pupil too low; (3) tendency to overrate a pupil with bright sparkling eyes and a happy face; (4) tendency to underrate the surly, cross, troublemaker; (5) tendency to underrate the poorly clothed, uncared-for urchin; (6) tendency to overrate the child who likes the teacher and does everything possible to help her; and (7) tendency to underrate those who obviously dislike the teacher and who do everything in their power to make life miserable for her.

The Binet.—The procedures just noted provide candidates for the special class. It is this smaller group of pupils who are given the Binet. If the child has an intelligence quotient of 120 or greater by this test, he generally becomes a member of the special class. If, however, he is physiologically or socially immature, if his health is unsatisfactory, or if he is unstable emotionally, his acceptance may be delayed until an adjustment is accomplished that will make his success more sure.

3. PROBLEMS OF ORGANIZATION

Avoiding Prejudice.—Too little attention is given to the avoidance of prejudice in the organization of special classes for the gifted. The children may become conceited; the parents may be similarly affected; other children in the school may become jealous of the group; teachers may be led to expect the impossible of these special-class pupils; people of the community may, through unwise publicity, look upon these children as freaks of nature.

The teachers must understand that the special class is organized to give members of this group a better chance to develop their one common outstanding trait—academic ability. Since this ability is basic to the mastery of the subject matter of the schools, and since the schools are the instruments whereby academic subject matter is utilized in the all-round development of the child, such a classification of children can well be justified. Teachers must remember that there are children of unusual ability in other respects and that socially these other pupils may accomplish just as much as do the children of high I.Q.

When children, teachers, parents, and school patrons understand that the organization of the special class is just a part of the professionalized program of providing a more suitable classification or "grading" of school children, this problem of avoiding prejudice will be eliminated.   For years the public has accepted the grouping of school children in grades from the first through the twelfth; just so will special classes for the gifted be accepted as soon as the public understands what is being done.

Location of the Class.—In selecting the school in which to locate classes for gifted children, no factor is more important than the attitude of the principal.   If he is not sympathetic with the idea, his school should not be chosen, regardless of all other favorable factors.   If, however, though honestly questioning its value, he is able and willing to experiment, we have a wholly satisfactory situation.

4. PROBLEMS OF INSTRUCTION

Curriculum.—The most pressing problem to be dealt with by the teacher after the class has been organized is: What shall I have them do?   Two radically different practices have been followed.   Rugg[1] estimated in 1924 that 60 per cent of the schools provided rapid advancement, 25 per cent enriched the curriculum, and 15 per cent tried to use both methods.   The 60 per cent included two groups, of which one gave no special thought to an organized program of caring for the gifted and the other—a smaller group—planned definitely to provide rapid promotion as the best way of handling the problem.

For the past decade special classes have experimented with an enriched course of study.   Classes begin at the first grade and continue through junior high school.   One grade is completed each year and only occasionally does rapid advancement take place.   The regular course of study is mastered.   Other things have been accomplished, such as the mastery of French and typewriting, the development of skill in writing prose and poetry, ability in playwriting and acting, development of special interests, training in social co-operation, knowledge of the local trades, industries, and arts and of the local political and educational institutions.   An opportunity class in Los Angeles produced "The Story of Los Angeles"; Illustration 36 shows

[1] National Society for the Study of Education, *Twenty-third Yearbook* Part I, p. 97, 1924.

two boys of this class working on a reproduction of a mission built by the early Indians.   This listing presents briefly the vast possibilities open to the pupils who pursue an enriched program of instruction.[1] This curriculum is not merely the regular course of study plus.   The scope of the work covered is definitely broadened but both the old and the new are woven into a comprehensive unitary program.

ILLUSTRATION 36.—Reproduction of a mission built by Indians—"The Story of Los Angeles" by an opportunity (gifted) class.

New methods are used.   Dramatization is emphasized; an opportunity class in Los Angeles is shown, in Illustration 37, as it dramatizes "Snow White"; the dramatization is given in French.   In the sciences, pupils are encouraged to question previous experimental work and to suggest better methods; each child is encouraged to develop and follow up any problem in which he may have an intense interest.   Pupils are encouraged to read widely; this reading may be general or related to a specific field of interest.   They are encouraged to take certain projects and become thoroughly informed with reference to them.   One child may be interested in geology, and he will gather all kinds of geological specimens; another may be interested in botany; another may find that his interest lies in the study of butterflies.   In each case these children gather a considerable amount of technical

[1] See pp. 395–397.

data about their specimens.   If their interest is in the social sciences, they may study governmental problems, social conditions, and industrial organization.   Those who are aesthetically inclined may study about music, painting, sculpture, and writing.

ILLUSTRATION 37.—The opportunity class of Los Angeles dramatizes "Snow White" in French.

Methods of Instruction.—These children do not need constant supervision, once their interest is awakened; they need, rather, to be brought face to face with challenging problems and given a chance to work them out. Some of these problems will involve the group in co-operative undertakings; others will be individual; both will be reported upon from time to time before the class group.   Illustration 38 shows an opportunity class delving into the problem of "How People Tell Time."

The still too-frequent page-by-page lesson assignment and the customary recitation will be displaced by the development of a program of group work directed by the teacher. The group will be confronted by such problems as (1) What information do we need?   (2) How may the data be secured?   (3) What action needs to be taken?   (4) What persons shall be responsible for performing the various tasks? Group meetings will be necessary to report on facts discovered and actions taken; in the light of new facts, changes in plan may be necessary.   The point to be stressed is that old methods of instruction must be greatly changed if these gifted pupils are to have their chance to develop their abilities to the maximum; methods that force uniformity of achievement upon all will not accomplish this.

ILLUSTRATION 38.—Gifted children study "How People Tell Time" in a Los Angeles opportunity class.

Equipment.—If the preceding methods are to be used, the customary fixed desk has no place in these classrooms; chairs and tables will be used instead.   One writer suggests that a big conference table be provided; smaller tables, of course, could be put together to serve that purpose, and this is perhaps the preferable procedure for most special classes.   Illustration 39 shows a use to which such a table could be put; an editorial staff of an opportunity class is at work.

Too much emphasis cannot be placed upon providing adequate library facilities.   These are vital if the educational program just suggested is to be successfully carried out.   Reference books and supplementary material in considerable quantity should be housed in the classroom.   These materials become the actual textbooks of the pupils.   Several dictionaries and standard encyclopedias should be permanent room fixtures.   Many other reference books will be needed for short periods of time; these can then be returned to the regular school library and others be secured.   Pupils working on individual projects will use the school library and the public library.   In addition to the above, there should be atlases, dictionaries of the foreign languages studied, maps, nature-study references, and poetry in considerable quantity and kind.

Since the children are encouraged to gather specimens, shelving and cupboard space should be provided.   Many specimens will have to be mounted, others will need to be displayed in such a way that the successive steps in the development of the plant, the organism, or the

ILLUSTRATION 39.—The editorial staff of an opportunity class in Los Angeles at work.

product can be shown.   Cotton in various stages of growth and manufacture is an example.   Collections of butterflies, coins, eggshells, insects, leaves, moths, pictures of cathedrals, stamps, and stones are examples of the collections for which some provision will have to be made.

Bulletin-board space on which to post current pictures and news items will be needed.   Curtains, a movable platform, and materials for costumes should be provided for dramatization.   Typewriters are usually supplied.   Globes, pictures, a piano, a phonograph, stereoscopic views, and occasionally a lantern-slide machine with slides are among other items provided.

Excursions.—The city hall, art galleries, certain major industries, and some of the larger business concerns will be visited by the class;

certain very specialized industries and business organizations will be visited by individual pupils as their projects or their interests demand.

Visits have been reported by these classes to art museums, auditors' offices, aviation fields, bakeries, banks, brickyards, city courts, city dispensaries, city prisons or workhouses, city waterworks, clothing stores, court of domestic relations, dairy farms, department stores, electric light plants, gas company plants, historical museums, ice cream factories, insurance companies, foundries, mayors' offices, natural history museums, newspaper plants, post offices, public libraries, radio broadcasting stations, refrigeration plants, telephone exchanges, theaters, treasurers' offices, and zoos. It is obviously impossible to enumerate all the institutions or places of interest that have been or could be visited.

Many cities provide transportation for regular school groups that wish to visit places of interest. Where such plans are not in operation, street cars or school busses are used; sometimes volunteer transportation is secured.

Work of the Teacher.—When such visits are made, the teacher of gifted children has important duties not usually assumed by the regular teacher. Officials of the institution visited must know what is the purpose of the trip, how many are to be expected, and when they will come. The pupils must be prepared for the excursion by being shown the purpose of such a visit; they must also understand how to conduct themselves upon the trip, if they are to get what they want from it. All this preparation, as well as such specific matters as securing transportation, setting the time of starting, fixing the time of arrival, and arranging for the trip with the superintendent's office, must be undertaken by the teacher.

Since these children are exceptional in their abilities, a case study should be made of each child. Home data, school data, health data, facts secured through personal conferences should all be utilized in trying to understand him. While the case study should, ideally, be conducted for all school children, it is imperative that it be made in the special class.

The teacher must act as a co-ordinator for all activities carried on in the class. Both group and individual activities need to be so related that each has a contribution to make to the program being developed by the entire class. Each child must realize this necessity and be willing to take the steps necessary to achieve the ultimate result. In addition, the teacher has all the duties and responsibilities of any other good modern teacher in the regular grades. Illustration 40 shows an opportunity class at work on a group project in music.

On the whole, of course, the work of these teachers is not so different from that of the regular teacher as is the work of teachers for the physically handicapped. A modern regular teacher, were she permitted to follow her ideals concerning management and method, would probably duplicate much of the methodology of these special teachers for gifted children.

ILLUSTRATION 40.—Creative music and musical instruments.   An opportunity class in Los Angeles.

5. TEACHER PERSONNEL

The White House Conference passes by the problem of teacher personnel with the suggestion that regular teachers are usually selected for this type of special classwork, that they are thought to be best fitted for the work, and that they are familiar with the methods used by progressive educators. To the professional group interested in the education of gifted children these suggestions are not misleading and imply an adequately trained teacher. Perhaps the average layman might misconstrue them and conclude that any good average teacher would ideally serve these children. Such a construction would likely work havoc with special-class work for the gifted.

---

[1] White House Conference, *Special Education: The Handicapped and the Gifted,* p. 545, The Century Co., New York, 1931.

Training.—In general, a teacher will be needed who has had the training required of the regular grade teacher, for she will encounter the same instructional and personnel problems. She must, however, realize that in teaching gifted children she will have an unusual problem, in addition. These children should be guided in frankly recognizing their superior ability to grasp intellectual problems without becoming conceited and without allowing themselves to become impatient and critical of the slower responses of the average child.

These teachers need a training that will emphasize at least three kinds of study: (1) the psychology of the child of high I.Q., (2) methods of instruction that take into account the mental make-up of these children, and (3) a detailed survey of the changes that can be made in the materials of instruction if enrichment is to be the goal.

Experience.—For the special-class teacher experience is particularly important; this experience should have been gained, at least in part, with regular class groups. The candidate needs experience with regular-grade school children sufficiently long to help her to interpret properly her results with special-class children. While 2 years in regular schoolwork may not be advisable in all situations, such a period ought to give the prospective teacher of gifted children a sound background for judging the attainment of children of high I.Q.

Traits That Aid the Teacher.—The traits demanded of a teacher of gifted children are those that one hopes to find in regular classroom teachers. Among them, however, are a number that need to be developed to a higher degree if the candidate expects to teach successfully children of high I.Q.

1. Foremost among the prerequisites would be unusual ability. Situations that will challenge these children must be set before them, and one factor in the development of these situations is contact with a teacher of such outstanding talents along at least some one line that the pupils find in their instructor a challenge to do their best.

2. The candidate needs to be honest in her claims of ability; any attempt to pose as an expert along all lines is doomed at the beginning. A frank admission of lack of knowledge and a willingness to lean upon the class group for such knowledge will win their respect and co-operation. As long as the teacher can show a mastery in some one or more fields, she need not worry about admitting ignorance in others. These children will learn very quickly that no one can hope to be an authority in all fields.

3. The candidate must have a sufficient amount of originality to enable her to recognize worth, in spite of the fact that the product has not been shaped by customary molds. Teachers are needed who

can recognize fine work even though it is unusual. Genius thrives under encouragement rather than under unconstructive and damping criticism.

4. The candidate cannot be without a great amount of drive and initiative. Old procedures are not satisfactory; new methods, new devices, new materials must be planned. The responsibility for doing this new work rests upon the teacher. She should possess not only an originality that will enable her to recognize that trait in others and help her to see various ways of meeting a new problem, but also unusual ability in putting all the well-laid plans into operation.

5. The candidate will need special qualities of social leadership. She will be making contacts with innumerable groups of individuals all of whom will have questions to raise concerning her work. Parents will be interested in the class to which their children have been sent; other parents will want to know the reason for such a class; her fellow teachers will question the advisability of such a plan; visiting educators will observe her work and talk with her about her program; and the local administrative staff and the local board members will be wanting the teacher's reaction to many questions concerning such a class group. Despite her success in teaching the class, its ultimate acceptance as a permanent part of the school organization will depend very largely upon how well she sells the idea to these various groups; it will depend upon her social leadership.

6. It is important that she should have an attractive personality. Although many of the factors involved in this trait are included in traits previously mentioned, there are specific elements not noted before that should be present. One of these is an attractive personal appearance. Many an otherwise drab personality has been turned into an engaging one by careful grooming; neatness, cleanliness, a touch of color have been known to revolutionize not only the appearance but the attitude of a person. Deficiencies in proper attention to these matters are quickly noted by gifted children. If the teacher, in spite of negligence of this kind, wins the children's good will, they are too likely to adopt a similar attitude under the mistaken impression that as long as they "have ability and succeed, personal appearance is not important." Other elements of an attractive personality would include a kindly attitude in dealing with people, being considerate of the feelings of others, a willingness to recognize the worth of different points of view which might be held by others, and a spirit of friendliness that rings true.

7. The candidate must be free from jealousy of the gifted child. She must approach her teaching just as objectively and in a spirit

as free from personal bias as the experimenter approaches his problems. If she cannot do this, she should not seek to teach such groups. Hollingworth says that, although this warning might seem rather absurd, "Nevertheless, emotional bias against the bright, identified as such by tests, does appear among teachers."[1]

6. THE FOLLOW-UP

As with other groups of exceptional children, no provision is made for an adequate follow-up. It is a common experience, when anyone is urging the importance of providing more adequately for gifted children, to have this question raised. "What happens to these gifted children? We hear frequently of such children in school and later hear nothing more about them." The implication back of the question is that these children may have unusual academic abilities but that socially they are not very important individuals.

There are several ways of accounting for such a situation. These very same individuals may be doing high-grade work of a kind that does not attract popular attention; they may have been ruined by the school regime ordinarily provided for them; or they may not have the social attributes that would bring them into social prominence. Whatever the explanation, we need a more adequate answer than we have at present. Terman and his workers in California are making a follow-up study of many gifted children; other studies ought to be made.[2] Every city with well-organized schools or classes for gifted children should put into operation some method of following up all the pupils in these classes.

A follow-up should be relatively simple in their case. They have nothing to hide, as do the delinquents; as a group, they are from good homes. It should, therefore, be easy to secure the co-operation of these children and their parents in making follow-up studies. Some agency of the public school system must be made responsible for the follow-up studies. A file with a folder for each child to be studied should be maintained; arrangements should be made with the home for reporting regularly all changes of residence; the family should be so contacted that it understands the importance of prompt reporting; at

[1] LETA S. HOLLINGWORTH, *Gifted Children*, p. 306, The Macmillan Company, New York, 1929.

[2] A study of 328 graduates of Cleveland's major work groups has just been completed by Merle R. Sumption, an assistant at Ohio State University; the study is entitled "An Evaluation of the Cleveland Public School Program for the Education of Gifted Children"; it reveals material differences between graduates of the special program and graduates of the regular school program in attitudes, behavior, and ideals. The study was completed in January, 1940, but is not yet published.

stated intervals, facts concerning what these children are doing and how they are succeeding should be assembled.

The time should come when a given community can say of any member of the 1 per cent of its children with I.Q.'s above 130, that Henry, who is now 59 years of age, is doing thus and so and these are his achievements since leaving school. Of course, in order to test, in terms of social values, the efficiency of special schools and classes for the gifted, we should need a similar follow-up of children of equal intelligence who had attended regular school classes.

7. SUMMARY

The biggest problem faced in organizing special classes for gifted children is that of convincing the lay public that these classes are needed. Neither the mental, the physical, nor the social condition of these children lends itself to making an emotional appeal upon their behalf. Workers are forced to depend upon an appeal to the intellect; this situation is, doubtless, one very real reason why special education for the gifted has not been so widely developed as has that for handicapped children.

Defined in terms of Terman's genius group, there are approximately 100,000 gifted children in the United States. Based upon Cleveland's definition, there are 1,500,000. Provisional selection of the gifted is based upon (1) teacher recommendations, (2) previous school marks, (3) achievement tests, and (4) group mental tests. Final selection is based upon the results of a Binet test, physiological and social maturity, health, and emotional stability.

Such specific problems as (1) avoiding prejudice, (2) selecting a home for the class, (3) planning the curriculum, (4) adapting methods of instruction to the members of the group, (5) determining needed equipment, (6) making provision for excursions, (7) keeping costs reasonable, (8) selecting an adequately trained teacher, and (9) planning a follow-up of each pupil, represent some of the more significant problems which must be solved by any superintendent if he plans to establish special classes for gifted children.

Problems and Questions for Discussion

1. Is it possible to make the same emotional appeal for classes for the gifted as can be made for a similar program for the handicapped? Give reasons for your answer.

2. Why is it difficult to convince the lay person that special classes should be organized for children of high I.Q.?

3. Outline what you consider a satisfactory plan for selecting the children of high I.Q.? Why is it good?

4. Why is it important to avoid prejudice in the organization of classes for the gifted? What is meant by avoiding prejudice in this connection? How do you propose doing it?

5. Outline in detail a program of studies for such a class.

6. How, if at all, would methods of instruction differ from those used in regular classes?

7. What equipment should be available?

8. Describe the teacher you would want for a special class for gifted children.

9. Is follow-up important? If so, why? Outline a plan for making a complete and accurate follow-up of the gifted children of a city of 50,000 population.

Selected Bibliography

BENTLEY, JOHN EDWARD. *Superior Children.* W. W. Norton & Company, Inc., New York, 1937. 331 pp.

A consideration of the physiological, psychological, and social development of superior children.

BURDICK, W. H. "The Bright Pupil—An Enriched Course in Place of Acceleration," *The Fourth Yearbook Bulletin of the Department of Elementary School Principals*, pp. 262–271. National Education Association, Washington, D.C., 1925.

Description of the way gifted children are cared for at Schenectady, N.Y. Gifted are defined, curricula discussed, and data given showing how enrichment functions.

GODDARD, HENRY H. *School Training of Gifted Children*, pp. 51–125. World Book Company, Yonkers-on-Hudson, New York, 1928.

An account of the way Cleveland is meeting the problems involved in organizing classes for gifted children.

HOLLINGWORTH, LETA S. *Gifted Children*, pp. 267–338. The Macmillan Company, New York, 1929.

Discussion of the experimental education of gifted children, qualifications of teachers, equipment, some activities of the special class, and suggestions for the curriculum.

MARTENS, ELISE H. "Teacher's Problems with Exceptional Children, II Gifted Children," *U.S. Office of Education Pamphlet* 41, Washington, D.C., 1933. 45 pp.

Twenty questions about gifted children are raised for consideration and are answered. They deal with discovering gifted children, their characteristics, how they should be handled, what the teacher can do, and what the small school can do.

National Society for the Study of Education. *Twenty-third Yearbook*, Part I, pp. 25–121. Public School Publishing Company, Bloomington, Ill., 1924.

Reports dealing with the selection of gifted children, problems of organization, administrative problems, and a proper curriculum.

White House Conference. *Special Education: The Handicapped and the Gifted*, pp. 537–550. The Century Co., New York, 1931.

Considers briefly definition, methods of grouping, extent of education, different methods of educating, selection, teachers, costs, nomenclature, results, and certain conclusions and recommendations.

CHAPTER XXVIII

THE CHALLENGE OF THE GIFTED CHILD

1. THE CHALLENGE

If the point of view represented by the data and the arguments in the two preceding chapters is essentially sound, then the provision of special classes for gifted children ceases to be of purely local concern. The state immediately has a very real interest in what is being done for them.

A democracy must have leaders of statesmanship caliber as well as educated followers. Such leaders should have a high degree of academic ability as well as being outstanding socially and physically. As a society we have been very prodigal of our intellectual inheritance. If poverty, if other social handicaps, or if lack of physical fitness prevents a child of unusual academic ability from making the most of such a trait, society at present does little or nothing about it.

Schools are specially organized to assist the mediocre child in achieving to the limit of his capacity. They have organized even to enable the academically unfit to push their achievement as far as possible. They have continued generally to ignore children of superior academic ability. Because this group is of great importance to a democratic social order, steps should be taken (1) to discover the gifted, (2) to provide an educational program adapted to their needs, from grade 1 through college, (3) to encourage them to take advantage of it, and (4) to supply state funds to assure the maintenance of such a program and to enable the gifted to take advantage of it. This is the real challenge to those who want to provide more adequately for gifted children.

2. LEGISLATION

Discovery of the Gifted Child.—Unlike the handicapped, all gifted children are expected to enroll in school at some time during their elementary school career. In order to discover them, we only need to set machinery in motion that will examine all children who enroll, year by year, in public, private, or parochial schools; this examining must be done with unusual care and at the elementary level. Many public school systems already give their pupils one or more psychological examinations during their school career. Private and parochial schools are discovering that these examinations are essential.

We have state laws compelling children of certain ages to attend school. To enforce these laws, cities have established attendance departments staffed by 50 to 100 or more people. In many states every county and city school district is required by law to have at least one attendance officer who is responsible for enforcing these attendance laws. Without such legislation there would doubtless be untold thousands of children who would today be deprived of the benefits of any kind of education.

If the law provides officials for enforcing school attendance, ought it not to have, also, school officials to study the incoming group of children and to make to the superintendent recommendations for proper placement? If it is important to require that all children attend school, it would seem far more important that these children be thoroughly and expertly studied upon their entrance to school.

Just as every city has its attendance officers, so every city should have its psychological division. As counties are required to have attendance officers, so they should be required to have psychologists. Unquestionably, we are coming nearer the time when all types of pupil-personnel service will be included. State legislation is needed that will require every school district to have a psychologist. Minimum requirements should be fixed at first, and these should be gradually extended over a 10-year period. Each such official would organize a psychological testing program that would provide group mental tests for all children periodically and individual tests for all problem cases. Such an organization would make it possible to discover all gifted children.

Establishment of Classes.—In order not to give undue publicity to the organization of special classes for gifted children, the state law should merely call attention to the advisability of all districts' making satisfactory arrangements for educating children of high I.Q. Every district would be encouraged to make its own plans. These plans would have to be approved by the state department of education if state aid were to be secured.

Establishment of Scholarship Funds.—As soon as all gifted children are discovered, it will be found that there are many in the older age groups who do not have funds with which to continue in school. These children should be assisted by means of state scholarships. The amount of the scholarship should depend upon the need. One boy may have only himself to care for; another may have a mother, brothers, and sisters to support.

State Support.—In addition to founding scholarships, the state should encourage the organization of special classes by granting the local districts state aid. This aid could well be granted upon the basis of excess costs. The plan would eliminate one of the first reasons often given for failure to organize special classes; no longer would the district be able to claim that it could not afford them.

3. A STATE PROGRAM

State Supervision.—All classwork organized for the education of children of high I.Q. should be under the direct supervision of the state department of education. There should be a supervisor of classes for the gifted; the size of his staff will depend entirely upon the development of the work within a given state.

The duties of such a staff are numerous. It should develop a sensible plan for discovering all gifted children. If the state law provides for a psychologist or a psychological staff within each school district, it would work with these psychologists in developing such a plan, which would include the systematic giving of mental tests.

The state staff should receive the test results from all school districts throughout the state, as well as regular reports concerning all special classes organized for the education of gifted children. These reports would show whether or not given districts were providing adequately for their gifted.

If any district were to neglect its gifted, some member of the state staff should visit it and present the needs of these children to the local school authorities. It should be the aim to "sell" the idea to local educators so that the steps necessary for organizing these special classes would be taken voluntarily and without any undue publicity. The classes should develop as a part of the regular school routine to make more adequate provision for individual differences among children.

It will be noted that this procedure differs considerably from that often used in organizing classes for the physically handicapped. This difference is necessary if we are to avoid undesirable publicity concerning the ability of these children. There is so much popular misunderstanding concerning the nature of high academic ability that undue publicity concerning the placement of children in these classes might decrease the effectiveness of such classwork.

The state staff should have the authority to approve all requests for the establishment of special classes for the gifted. Data concerning the mental ability, previous school success, physical condition, and social adaptability of all candidates should be received and studied. Facts concerning the proposed housing of the class, the equipment provided, the program to be offered, and the instructional methods used should be on file. Data concerning costs, including facts upon which the estimate was made, should be available. Approval should be necessary, if state aid is to be given.

The staff should then help the various districts put this approved plan into operation and help them keep it operating as near as possible to 100 per cent effectiveness. The state supervisor should locate both excellent and poor work and study the methods of both groups. The former will help him to readjust his own thinking from time to time; the latter will enable him to give constructive criticism.

The state staff must arrange to receive reports of those gifted youths who need financial assistance in order to remain in school. It will prepare the blanks to be used in reporting such youths. Upon receipt of these completed blanks, scholarships will be approved for all who meet requirements. It will be the aim of the state to provide such scholarships for all youths of high I.Q. who are not financially able to continue their schooling.

The Local Program.—If the city is large and has a complete program under way for educating its gifted, it will need a separate supervisor for that work. In smaller places one supervisor may have to care for all problems in the entire field of special education. If the state law requires a psychologist in each school district, city or county, within the state, this official may supervise the special classes for mentally exceptional children within the smaller districts.

The local district will arrange to give at stated intervals group mental tests to all school children. Reports will be sent to the state office of all children having I.Q.'s of 120 and above. Reports will be sent also of those pupils who have rated consistently high in all academic work and those who are reported by teachers as being unusually capable. Accompanying these reports will be the results, wherever possible, of an individual test, together with the examiner's analysis of the case and her recommendations concerning placement in a class for gifted children.

The local school authorities will check with care the social background of all gifted children and have at hand the data necessary for determining whether these children will need state scholarships to continue in school. They will also determine how much help will be needed. Will tuition alone be needed? Will books and clothing be needed? Will the family have to have support as well as the child? The aim is that every gifted child should have an opportunity to remain in school.

Is the Program Unusual?—From the point of view of acceptance as a state program, the preceding group of suggestions is entirely unusual. It is not unusual in the sense of being wholly new and of never having been given a trial.

Cincinnati may be cited. (1) It has for a number of years been giving city-wide group tests to all first-grade children, to fourth-grade pupils, and to sixth-graders. (2) It has a system for selecting gifted children who need scholarships in order to continue their schooling. (3) It has a high school dedicated to the use of gifted children. Pupils who rate high on intelligence tests and who do good work in the grade schools are sent to this high school.

4. SUMMARY

The education of children of high I.Q. is a challenge to all who recognize society's need of capitalizing upon all available ability as a means of furthering social improvement. At present, schools are organized for the child of average ability; the handicapped, even, are being cared for adequately; it is the gifted youth who has become the forgotten child.

We need adequate psychological help to discover the gifted; we need special classes; we need state aid to encourage local districts to give attention to the gifted; we need a state department to help local districts solve their many problems in organizing to educate the gifted; and we need to provide scholarships for all youths who are gifted and who are economically unable to continue their schooling.

None of the needs are being met upon a national or even a state-wide basis. We have examples of a few cities that try to put some of these ideas into operation. What could not be done during the next half century for the betterment of society, if our schools should properly meet this challenge by finding and truly educating 100 per cent of these gifted youths?

Problems and Questions for Discussion

1. Give in some detail the state legislation now in existence governing the education of gifted children.

2. Outline a plan that might effectively discover all gifted children within a given community.

3. Why have state legislation governing the education of gifted children?

4. Draft a state law governing this problem of dealing with gifted youths which you would consider satisfactory for your state. Defend your proposals.

5. Do you believe in providing scholarships to enable gifted youths to continue their schooling? Why?

Selected Bibliography

Fourth Yearbook. Division of Psychology and Educational Research, pp. 67–87. School Publication 211, Los Angeles, 1931.

Gives a description of work done in the city of Los Angeles for its gifted children. Some data on success given.

GODDARD, HENRY HERBERT. *School Training of Gifted Children,* pp. 14–39, 103–125. World Book Company, Yonkers-on-Hudson, New York, 1928.

Presents a justification of the special class for the gifted; talks to parents about the problem; and considers high I.Q. in relation to temperament.

HOLLINGWORTH, LETA S. *Gifted Children,* pp. 278–338. The Macmillan Company, New York, 1929.

Gives an account of experimental classes for the gifted in the public schools. Describes the organization of and curriculum for classes for gifted children.

White House Conference. *Special Education: The Handicapped and the Gifted,* pp. 548–550. The Century Co., New York, 1931.

Gives a brief outline of recommendations with reference to the future of educating gifted children.

CHAPTER XXIX

EDUCATION OF SPECIALLY GIFTED CHILDREN

Society is, in general, quick to recognize unique and special talents. There is a familiar saying that the world will make a well-worn pathway to the doorway of him who makes the best of any kind of article, even though it be only a mousetrap. This is society's way of telling the specially gifted individual that it approves of him; talent must, however, not only be present but it must be used effectively to secure this approval.

1. DEFINITION

General Concept.—It is entirely possible that the gifted and the specially gifted may be one and the same individual. The two classes are not mutually exclusive. There are, however, gifted children who have no special talents; there are others who have special gifts but who are only average from the point of view of academic ability.

It should be understood, of course, that, in general, positive correlation exists between academic ability and special talent. Obviously, we hardly expect to find a musical genius in a class of feeble-minded children; neither do we expect a poet of great note to come from such a group. As McCall uniquely puts the problem, it is correlation, not compensation, that governs the traits existing in individuals. The fact that a child has low mental ability is no reason for thinking that he will be compensated by having a special talent of some kind; it is much more likely that he will be relatively low in all traits.

Types Described.—Included among the specially gifted are those artistically inclined, those of musical ability, those with mechanical talents, and those with a flair for writing either poetry or prose. To be classed as talented, youths must be much better than average. In general, perhaps, there would be as many children who could be considered gifted in a special trait as there are who could be rated as gifted academically. This judgment is based upon the assumption that a nonselected group of individuals would distribute themselves normally with respect to any and all of these traits. Terman says that persons of 140 I.Q. and above are geniuses or near geniuses; the percentage of the general population above 140 I.Q. is 0.4 of 1 per cent. If our previous assumption is correct, 0.4 of 1 per cent of a given population is in the genius class musically; likewise, 0.4 of 1 per cent would be poetic geniuses.

Musical ability of the kind referred to above may be illustrated by describing briefly what such specially gifted children have been able to do. Mozart had published four sonatas by seven years of age, had had his first operetta given at twelve, and his first Italian opera at fourteen.[1] By three or four years of age he "began to invent musical ideas"; at this age he would remember music that he heard. "On one occasion, before his fifth birthday, he learned at half-past-nine at night and in half an hour a minuet and a trio, pieces requiring independence of the two hands and some musical comprehension."[2] Beethoven enjoyed music from an early age; he began taking lessons every day when six years old.

Among the artists, we find that Rembrandt by fourteen or fifteen was so eager to paint that he set aside his parents' plans in order to do so.[3] Michelangelo, despite his father's opposition, devoted much of his school time to painting and constantly sought the company of the artists of his day and of those interested in art.[4] Cox reports other outstanding artists who loved painting from an early age.

The poet Tennyson wrote poetry at eight years of age.[5] Lord Byron composed the "Epitaph on a Friend" at fifteen,[6] and Cowper's gift for poetry was apparent at fourteen.[7] Emerson wrote "The History of Fortus, a Chivalric Poem" when he was ten.[8] Goethe, before he was nine years old, wrote "morning salutations in German, Latin, and Greek" that "express charming sentiments in artistic form."[9] Longfellow's first printed verses appeared when he was thirteen.[10] Sir Walter Scott translated Latin poems at eleven years of age and wrote "The Conquest of Granada" at fifteen.[11]

[1] CATHARINE M. Cox, "The Early Mental Traits of Three Hundred Geniuses," *Genetic Studies of Genius*, Vol. II, p. 593, Stanford University Press, Palo Alto, Calif., 1926.

[2] *Ibid.*, p. 593.

[3] *Ibid.*, pp. 255–256.

[4] *Ibid.*, pp. 543–544.

[5] *Ibid.*, p. 622.

[6] *Ibid.*, p. 562.

[7] *Ibid.*, p. 397.

[8] *Ibid.*, p. 518.

[9] *Ibid.*, p. 697.

[10] *Ibid.*, p. 589.

[11] *Ibid.*, p. 604.

2. IMPORTANCE OF THE PROBLEM

The preceding section, perhaps, has already impressed the reader with the importance of giving more than customary thought to methods of selecting specially gifted children and to methods of educating them. This whole problem is important because of the effect upon specially gifted children of ignoring them and because of the losses that society will sustain under a laissez-faire method of educating them.

As Related to Educational Theory.—Educational theory has been calling attention to a number of needed changes in current educational practice. It has been demanding that the school program of study be so varied that the interests of all children can be cared for; that the program be so adjusted that children of any ability or capacity can find work which will be of profit to them; and that methods of instruction be so altered that education will cease to be a preparation for life but will be life. These demands are closely related to a good program of special education. Any such program is special education, because it has been adjusted to meet the interests and capacities or abilities of a particularly selected group of children.

As Related to the Child.—One of the reasons for these changes in educational practice has undoubtedly been pragmatic. Maladjusted youths by the thousands have been discovered in the public schools. A study of these cases has convinced us that this maladjustment has frequently been the result of forcing children to work at tasks in which they had little or no interest, as well as the result of using methods that have failed to arouse latent interests and abilities.

As long as present policies are pursued in dealing with specially gifted children, the schools are failing to deal fairly with all pupils. They say, in effect, that provision will be made for youths of all degrees of academic talent, but that the child who is artistically, poetically, musically, or mechanically inclined will have to shift for himself. These talented children are not given the same educational opportunity as other children.

Because of lack of opportunity, many of these children never develop their talents; because of nonunderstanding parents, they are frequently forced into lines of endeavor where their talents are wasted and where they are unhappy and poorly adjusted; because of lack of money, they are forced into unskilled trades in order to win the necessities of life. The personal unhappiness and misery thus caused are undoubtedly greater than any of us realize and more devastating than we like to contemplate.

As Related to Society.—Society, too, sustains a great loss. The propositions that follow seem sound. (1) Genius in any line is a most precious asset to society. (2) Talent is so rare that, wherever found, it ought to be given special care. (3) Society depends upon genius to lead the way in scientific, industrial, artistic, and social developments. (4) Society's advance in literature, in sculpture, in painting, and in great music depends upon the opportunities she grants her geniuses to develop. (5) Without these achievements society loses in culture, in happiness, in beauty, and in contentment.

If these propositions are correct, it is imperative that special talents be discovered; it is essential that society and the individuals with such talents both realize that they have definite social responsibilities for seeing to it that these talents are fully developed. Millions of dollars are spent yearly by the courts, the schools, and the state in an effort to apprehend and re-educate those who offend against society. Vast sums are spent in aiding the mentally unfit to become at least partially self-supporting. This program is worth while, but an active constructive program of social improvement that emphasizes the maximum development of the fit is also needed.

3. HISTORY OF THE EDUCATION OF THE SPECIALLY GIFTED

In the light of the foregoing, it is safe to say there is no history of the education of specially gifted children. Children with special gifts have existed since the beginning of the civilized era and these children have been educated, but no definite program of special education has been developed and organized to care for such youths in the same sense that schools and classes have been developed for the blind, the deaf, the crippled, and the subnormal. The history of education for the specially gifted is, therefore, a thing of the future.

Selection.—In recent years, methods have been developed for selecting specially gifted children more accurately. Seashore has devised tests for measuring the musical capacities of children. Recently tests have been developed in the field of art for measuring artistic ability; Lewerenz published such tests in 1927. In the field of poetry, White has devised tests of poetic talent. These were reported as late as 1928.[1]

Organization.—To the extent that children of special gifts are also academically gifted, we find, it is true, more than usual attention being given to them. This does not, however, constitute a special educational program for the child of special talents. His academic

[1] For further details on selection proposed for current practice see pp. 430–432.

talents have brought him into the special class; the methods used in this class have helped to develop his special gifts.

A few children who are fortunate enough to have had their gifts attract attention have had individuals or organizations provide the money necessary for their education. Obviously, this method of solving the problem is inadequate. Many children with remarkable gifts remain undiscovered; others, though discovered, are not fortunate enough to attract an individual or an organization that has money to spend for such a purpose. Some specially gifted children have parents or relatives who provide the funds needed for the proper development of their talents. None of these methods constitutes a public program of special education for the specially gifted.

4. PROBLEMS INVOLVED

If such a program is to be well developed, two problems confront those who are interested in developing it. (1) A system of finding all such children must be put into operation. (2) Provisions must be made for giving the children selected a real opportunity to have their talents developed.

Discovery.—No longer can accident be depended upon for the discovery of children of unusual gifts. Every known means of discovering them must be systematically put into operation. As soon as cumulative pupil records are kept properly for all children, one necessary step in finding quickly the specially talented child will have been taken. This record should begin as soon as the child enters school. At that time an account of the child's preschool activities, interests, and abilities should have been secured from the home. If the child draws, paints, sings, plays musical instruments, writes stories or poetry, has a workshop and sundry mechanical contrivances, or takes toys apart and successfully puts them together again, these items will be properly recorded.

The record will also contain the continued observations of the child's teachers from year to year regarding unique or unusual abilities that he seems to possess. Talents that parents failed to discover may thus be noted. The problem of discovering these specially gifted children should be discussed by the teaching staff; teachers who have discovered unusual talent should give brief case histories showing how they discovered the child and should present illustrations of his creative ability. The very act of considering such problems will make the teaching staff more alive to them and will materially aid in the discovery of more nearly 100 per cent of the specially gifted.

A systematic testing of all school children should be arranged. In systems unable to give these tests universally, a systematic selection should be made of all pupils who seem to have some talent, based upon the cumulative record and upon teacher observation; these pupils should then be tested. This problem of discovering children with special gifts is important if talent is not to be lost. Not all children have had the opportunity to show their ability. Not all parents or teachers recognize how unusual the abilities of certain children are. This is why it is important that objective tests be used as a check. In the past children of marked musical or mechanical ability have been discovered, by means of tests, who have not been so recognized by either teachers or parents.

Seashore reports the cases of Viola and Jean. These two girls rated high on tests of musical ability. Each was 12 years old. The experimenter did not know any of the children who were being tested. When he reported these two girls to the school authorities, he learned that Viola was "a girl who had enjoyed most excellent musical advantages, came from one of the best families of the city, and was scheduled for a public recital for the following Sunday afternoon."[1] With Jean the situation was quite different. " . . . . it was discovered that she was the daughter of very poor parents, had enjoyed no musical advantages, and, indeed, had been irregular in much of her school work on account of her poverty."[2]

Jean had been rated by her teachers below average in general intelligence and superior in musical ability. These ratings had been sent to the parents, but neither parents nor teachers had taken the marks as meaning that Jean was markedly outstanding in musical ability; she was, therefore, for all practical purposes a real find. The school superintendent was so impressed by the discovery that he brought the matter to the attention of "a woman's club which expressed its willingness to guarantee that Jean should have the opportunity of trying herself in a musical education."[3]

Selection.—In the illustrations just presented, selection was based upon unusual musical ability and poverty. No one thought of giving assistance to Viola. She came from "one of the best families in town." The principle involved is old in American educational history. There was a day when education was a private function.

[1] CARL EMIL SEASHORE, The Psychology of Musical Talent, p. 24. Copyright, 1919. By permission of the publishers, Silver, Burdett Company, New York.
[2] Ibid., p. 26.
[3] Ibid., p. 27.

The first compulsory education law in America placed the responsibility of educating children upon parents. Many parents could not afford to do this and so laws were passed granting aid to such. These "charity schools" continued to operate for many years—schools in "which free tuition was to be provided only to the children of the deserving poor."[1] In the case of Viola and Jean a return is made to the old charity idea of education. Viola's parents could afford to provide a special musical education for their daughter; Jean's parents were unable to do so. A private agency, therefore, volunteered to educate Jean, since she was a pauper.

Obviously, education in America is not universal and free. It will not be until the public schools are equipped to educate all children, instead of the academically minded alone. In selecting children who are specially gifted, the financial status of parents should not be considered. If the child has unique talents, he should be eligible for special instruction; this instruction should be provided by the public schools as a part of their program of educating 100 per cent of all children of school age.

Organization.—A grouping of specially gifted children upon the basis of these abilities is not advocated. They should fit into whatever organization the system maintains for academic instruction. There will be no special schools or classes within a city where all the musically inclined will be educated from the grade 3 or grade 4, up; neither will there be such schools for budding artists.

The organization to handle this type of education can be built upon the basis of a type of administrative organization already found in many cities. They have music and art supervisors. These supervisors have well-trained music and art teachers who give group instruction to all children within the public schools. Such systems would need to give more attention to the discovery of real talent; they would need to provide more individual instruction for children of unusual ability. This would mean that, in some instances, the staff would need to be increased. As the work developed, the system would perhaps find it necessary to employ, part-time, persons of outstanding ability to continue the instruction of the school's most gifted children. The plan would guarantee to every child with talent an opportunity to develop that talent to the limit.

Curriculum.—No attempt will be made to set up a curriculum for children of special talents; rather, certain principles will be suggested that might govern the development of such a curriculum.

[1] ELLWOOD P. CUBBERLEY, *Public School Administration*, p. 9, Houghton Mifflin Company, Boston, 1922.

1. Children of outstanding special talents will, for the most part, have average or greater than average academic ability as measured by intelligence tests; therefore, these youths should be expected to master the regular academic course of study. No child should be deprived of the richness of experience that can come from having been brought in contact with various social developments as represented by the subjects of the regular course of study.

2. Despite the desirability of such universal experiences, the regular course of study should be critically evaluated in terms of the interests and unique abilities of these specially gifted children. If the child is academically gifted as well, the problem is not so compelling. Adjustments that meet the needs of the academically capable will meet this problem well enough. Such a child will master quickly the regular academic program and still have plenty of time to give to the development of his special talent. If the child is of only average academic ability and has special abilities in some field, the problem of adjusting the regular course of study is greater. Clearly, if no adjustments are made, the child will have but little time to develop his special talent.

This may mean that much of arithmetic would be eliminated for some; for others, some of the more formal aspects of grammar and of geography would be dropped; for others, some of the special subjects for which the child shows no aptitude whatever could be eliminated. That part of the elementary curriculum which emphasizes human relations would continue to be an important part of the program for all specially gifted children. In high school, mathematics, foreign languages, or special fields in science might be omitted; the social sciences would be given special emphasis; and credit would be allowed for extended study in his field of special interest.

3. If courses are given in these special fields and if, on account of unusual talent, given students already have more ability than the average pupil will have at the close of the course, such students should be given full credit for the course and not required to take it.

4. Provision must be made for individual instruction along the line of the student's speciality. Such instruction should give the pupil an opportunity to progress at his own rate of speed; it should be adapted to his ability and interests, and should make unnecessary parental or private aid in continuing the child's musical or artistic education.

The Teacher.—Such a program of instruction need not require a special teacher in the early elementary grades. The regular teachers in art or music or literature to whom these children are assigned, however, should be able to appreciate originality in these fields and should permit these young geniuses to wander from the well-worn paths of tradition. It will be the teacher's responsibility to see that the traditional is known, understood, and, perhaps, appreciated, but on the side of original contribution they must not be bound by it.

As soon as the child has mastered the fundamentals of his specialty, he should have contact with someone within the field who has unique ability. It should be someone whose genius is real enough to recognize talent and whose vision is so broad that the most radical departure from traditional ideas will not blind him to real merit in a production.

Few specialists have all these traits. These suggestions are ideals to be striven for in the selection of individuals to instruct our youthful genius. Not many such teachers will be needed, since there are not many geniuses to instruct. If a former premise is correct—that there are possibly as many geniuses in music as there are in academic ability—there would be 0.4 of 1 per cent of the school population gifted in music. This would mean 80 such children in a city of 100,000 population, if 20 per cent of the population are of school age. If these specially gifted children do not reach the special teacher until junior high school, there would be only 40 for whom he would be responsible. These 40 would be divided into many groups. Some would be interested in voice, some in piano, and some in violin.

A given child would need only one or possibly two contacts per week with the special teacher. The number of special teachers to serve a large city would, therefore, be small for each of these specialties. In music there might be only five or six of the genius class for whom special lessons in voice would need to be provided. It is possible that among the voice teachers of the public schools there would be an instructor who had the traits and accomplishments required of a special teacher.

Any school system, therefore, that already provides an extensive program of instruction in these various specialties is in a position to educate more adequately its specially gifted children. It will need a system of discovering all such children; it will need to readjust its teaching staff to provide expert teaching for those of unusual talent; and it may have to add a few new members to the staff.

5. A STATE PROGRAM

State Supervision.—The first step in a state program must be the clear-cut recognition of the state's responsibility for educating children having special talents. This responsibility must be placed upon some individual within the state department of education. At the beginning, it might be placed upon the official who is charged with the responsibility for developing other phases of special education. It is desirable to place it in the hands of a person specially appointed for the job.

Such an individual would be responsible for the discovery of specially gifted children. No attempt would be made, at first, to work with the entire state. Specific suggestions could be sent to all school districts, indicating what they might do to educate children of unusual talents. Contact could be made immediately with those districts that seemed unusually interested; in such, the plans recommended by the state could be tried out under close and competent supervision.

The Local Program.—What can be done by the state supervisor depends upon what the local district is willing to do. It should co-operate with the state in accounting for its specially gifted; it should reorganize its staff to the extent necessary to bring its talented children in contact with talented instructors; it should add whatever staff members are needed to provide adequately for all such children. No specially gifted child should be denied an opportunity to develop his talents to the limit.

State's Responsibility for Further Study.—This last objective cannot be achieved by simply providing special facilities within the public schools. These facilities will give the youth an excellent beginning. The cost of continuing specialized training increases greatly and is not within the province of the local public school system. It is, however, a problem that the state office cannot ignore, if youths having talents of tremendous worth to society are to have them fully developed. A plan should be developed whereby every talented child would be assured of an opportunity to continue his education beyond high school. Perhaps, the state could provide scholarships of such size that these pupils would be able to continue their schooling.

6. SUMMARY

Society, though quick to recognize well-developed talents, has been slow to provide an opportunity for all children to develop them. The talents referred to are musical, artistic, poetic, mechanical, and the like. Indications of these talents frequently appear at very early ages; perhaps, if observed closely enough, they would all be noticeable in early childhood. Pupils who have high I.Q.s only are not included in this group.

How many children are specially gifted is not known. If the same percentages hold as hold for the academically gifted, there would be approximately 0.4 of 1 per cent. The theory that education is life and not a preparation for life emphasizes the need of making adjustments in subject matter and method which will better meet the needs of all children. Reasons for these changes are not purely theoretical. The tremendous maladjustment among school children due to the school's failure to meet their needs is recognized.

Specially gifted children have been educated for years. This education, however, has been that regularly provided all children, plus what parents and private agencies could do to develop these special talents. There is no regularly developed program for finding all specially gifted children and for giving them the special training needed to develop their talents.

In attempting to set up a program, such problems are faced as (1) discovering these children, (2) determining a basis for selecting them, (3) organizing within a school district to educate them, (4) developing a curriculum for them, (5) selecting a proper teacher, (6) keeping costs within reason, and (7) financing the program.

The state office should help to organize local programs for educating the specially gifted. Emphasis at the beginning should be placed upon selling the idea through personal contact with local school people and showing them how to gather data that will help them to see the need. The tactics often used in organizing classes for the physically handicapped would not be so successful if used here. People are not so interested in the individual gifted child as they are in the individual deaf, blind, or crippled child.

Questions and Problems for Discussion

1. Who are the specially gifted children?

2. Presumably, how many specially gifted children are there? Upon what do you base your answer?

3. Have we ever educated these specially gifted children in the past? Explain.

4. Enumerate the problems involved in attempting to establish a program of education for specially gifted children within a given school district. How may they be solved?

5. What devices or methods would you use in trying to locate all specially gifted children within your own school district?

6. Outline the type of organization that you would recommend for properly educating specially gifted children in a city of 500,000; in one of 100,000; in one of 25,000; and in a county school district (town, township, or parish).

7. Describe special features of the curriculum you would provide for those talented musically, poetically, artistically, and mechanically.

8. Should the financing of a program of education for specially gifted children differ any from that for handicapped children? If so, why? If not, why not?

9. What responsibilities should the state assume for developing an educational program for the specially gifted?

Selected Bibliography

Cox, Catharine Morris. *Genetic Studies of Genius*, Vol. II. "The Early Mental Traits of Three Hundred Geniuses." Stanford University Press, Stanford University, Palo Alto, Calif., 1926.

Most interesting case studies based upon available data of 301 eminent men; particular attention given to the early development of these men. Upon the basis of these studies of behavior and performance the intelligence of these men was rated. The book is rich in illustrative detail.

Hollingworth, Leta S. *Special Talents and Defects*. The Macmillan Company, New York, 1923. 216 pp.

Good discussion of relationships between special abilities and general intelligence; special abilities and defects in reading, spelling, arithmetic, drawing, music, mechanical and social adaptability considered. A very brief consideration of the relation of this to an educational program.

Scheidemann, Norma V. *The Psychology of Exceptional Children*, pp. 268–289. Houghton Mifflin Company, New York, 1931.

Discusses the musically, artistically, and poetically gifted child; gives illustrations of these talents showing themselves during youthful years. These talents are analyzed in considerable detail.

Seashore, Carl Emil. *The Psychology of Musical Talent*, pp. 1–29. Silver, Burdett & Company, New York, 1919.

Suggests a method of identifying musical talents. Reports cases of children discovered to have musical talents by means of tests. Discusses the values of systematic surveys of musical talents.

PART IV
PROBLEMS OF ADMINISTRATION

CHAPTER XXX

FINANCING SPECIAL EDUCATION

The theorist is frequently very much irked when he comes face to face with the practical problem of financing his more or less idealistic plans. Yet there is perhaps no problem in education that involves more of idealism than the development of adequate and sound educational financing. Providing funds for special education is so closely related to financing all public education that it is thought worth while to enumerate and briefly discuss several theories concerning the financial support of the latter. The essential idealism of these plans will be self-evident.

There are in the United States three general theories concerning the financing of public education. They are (1) local support, (2) state support, and (3) Federal support. Regarding state support, four questions are always raised: (1) Should it equalize the burden? (2) Should it stimulate local enterprise? (3) Should it provide the whole of a minimum program? (4) Should the state exercise control over the funds granted to local districts? The local theory, plus partial state support, operates widely in most of the 48 states, despite the fact that for several decades we have theoretically accepted the idea that education is a state function.

1. THE LOCAL-SUPPORT THEORY

The local-support theory places the entire support of education upon the local district. The Ordinance of 1785, relating to the Northwest Territory, granted the sixteenth section of each township for the support of public schools. When Ohio was admitted to the Union in 1803, the grant of each section was actually to the local township for the support of its own schools. Clearly, the support of education was conceived to be local. Each local district determined what its schools would cost and then did its best to secure a local tax that would cover those needs.

2. THE STATE-SUPPORT THEORY

It was found, however, that local districts varied greatly both in wealth and in the number of children to be educated. These variations were not minor. Often the district with the greatest number of

441

pupils was the one with the smallest tax duplicate. Tax duplicates reaching into the millions were found in local districts with only a few children. Some districts provided excellent educational opportunities at a very low tax rate; others with tax rates two or more times as high were unable to supply a decent educational program. Such conditions forced the acceptance of the theory of state support.

Shall State Support Partially Equalize?—Some claimed that state support should partially equalize educational opportunity. They pointed out that many local districts were financially unable to meet the minimum requirements of the state department. They insisted that the state should help support the local program for those districts too poor to meet state requirements.

They pointed out also that some districts had more children to educate than did others. They insisted upon equalizing the burden by having certain state monies distributed to local districts upon a per-child basis. In the first case, only a few local districts received state aid; in the latter, all districts received some aid. Under neither of these plans did local districts receive a great part of state funds.

Shall State Support Stimulate?—Others claimed that state support should be used as a stimulant. There develop from time to time educational programs which are worth while, but which for various reasons do not appeal to the general public as essential. The state may decide that a given program is imperative if children are to be adequately cared for and educated; at the same time, the state may hesitate to make it mandatory for all districts. The hesitation may be due to a realization that the public is not ready to accept the program; it may be due to the thought that it ought to be experimented with in order to smooth out crudities of organization and administration.

There has developed, accordingly, the theory that these new programs should be stimulated by the granting of state funds. Under this plan many wealthy local school districts receive state funds because they have put into operation such projects. The method seems to be effective. Local supervisors report that their success in getting the new work approved has been due to the fact that it did not cost local districts any more than the regular program of education had been costing them.

As long as state support is merely a means of supplementing local support, stimulation makes possible the initiation of many worth-while educational projects that would not be accepted for many years upon the basis of local support.

Shall State Support Finance the Basic Program?—Increasingly, sentiment is shifting from the idea of partial state support to that of state responsibility for the whole of a basic program of public education. The lay public is beginning to realize, what the school man has known for decades, that local support and even partial state support for public education is very unfair. A farmer whose land lies on the north side of the road pays almost no school tax; his neighbor just across the road in a different school district has an almost confiscatory school-tax bill. It is not uncommon that the children of the former have the better school facilities.

There has thus developed a group who believe that the entire basis of public school support should be changed. They believe that the state should determine the basic school program to be provided for all school children; they then insist that the state pay the cost of this minimum program. Despite the problems involved with respect to methods of raising the money, distributing it equitably, and making sure that the minimum program is provided, the theory is tenable, if one believes that education is in reality a state function.

Theoretically, one can believe that education is a state function and still believe in local support. Actually, education is hardly a state function unless a local district can be forced to develop the type of educational program that the state asks it to develop. As long as education continues to be supported locally, just so long will the people in each locality consider that they are their own boss respecting the nature and kind of educational program they provide. If they refuse to start a new project, despite its proved benefits, they consider that they have that right.

In the past, the concept of "education as a state function" has operated in many ways. Legislatures have passed laws governing school attendance, length of school term, qualifications of teachers, subjects to be taught, and the construction of school buildings. One could enumerate a host of other items that are now demanded of local districts by the state. Court decisions have time and again supported the idea that education is a state function. When, however, it comes to legislative action governing the support of the public schools, we have hedged; generally, we have allowed local districts to pay the bills. Only recently has there been anything like a concerted movement to support the public schools at state expense.

Among those urging state support are two groups with somewhat differing theories. One group is concerned primarily with the idea that state support be provided; they are not concerned about how the local district spends the money; they see the iniquities of local support and urge a program of state support.

Shall the State Control the Expenditure of State Funds?—Theorists of the other group want some control over the money sent into a local district. As a superintendent of schools in district A, am I to be allowed, with the consent of my local board, to spend the state's money to build far beyond the needs of the district? Am I to be allowed to spend a lot of money in developing a program of schoolwork for a few which could have been provided much more reasonably in co-operation with other school districts? Shall I be allowed to erect high schools for small groups of children of high-school age when a number of districts might have united in erecting a large adequately equipped high school? This latter group answers these questions most emphatically in the negative.

Theoretically, the demand for state control of the funds to be supplied by the state is based upon good common sense and logic. There is implicit in the demand, however, the assumption that the state department of education will be professionally prepared to meet satisfactorily and efficiently the demands placed upon it by such control. The department should be adequately staffed by well-trained men; a meager staff of politically appointed, untrained persons with such power would cause untold damage. At present, too many state departments do not have an administrative setup that would adequately protect the department from inroads by the unscrupulous politician. Such inroads in the past have been kept to a minimum because the department has been unimportant politically.

If, however, the state department becomes the administrative agent of the public schools of the state, with supervisory control over the total spendings of these schools, then the department becomes important. It is necessary, therefore, that present educational financiers become educational administrators and help the public schools establish a state administrative organization that would be relatively free from politics. When this is done, those who believe in state support will probably be willing to take the final step in a program to finance adequately the public schools.

3. THE FEDERAL-SUPPORT THEORY

Federal support calls for the expenditure of Federal funds for the support of public education throughout the United States. Such support is not unknown. Land grants under the ordinances of 1785 and 1787, money grants as in the distribution of the surplus revenues, and the land and money grants of the Morrill acts are illustrative of financial support of the Federal government to public education. There is an increasingly greater demand that Federal funds be used to equalize the burden of education among the various states. There is an abundance of evidence that states differ in their ability to educate their children. So great are these differences that equality of opportunity can hardly be claimed for youths who are born and raised in different states. Many still fear the dangers of Federal control, which they insist would inevitably follow such support.

As long as youths are free to move from state to state and have citizenship in the state in which they choose to reside, it becomes a matter of concern to all states what kind of educational opportunities a given state shall provide. A state that provides excellent public schools and thereby makes possible a group of fine citizens, well-educated, progressive in thought, and socially minded, is not eager to accept thousands of uneducated, unsocially minded people from other states. This possibility creates a problem for the Federal government. If such conditions come about from inability to support an adequate program of education, then Federal support must be received; if they are due to a lack of interest upon the part of authorities within a state, then the final step of accepting some Federal control should be taken. This is necessary if all children within the United States are to be given that equality of opportunity about which we have talked so much.

4. LOCAL SUPPORT AND SPECIAL EDUCATION

Local support places the entire cost of education upon the local community. If special provision is made for exceptional children, local communities everywhere must be convinced of the need and of the value of such a program. Not all of the values of such work can be objectively stated; results are not so immediate as are the effects of given fertilizers upon the yield of corn.

If special education is provided for the truant and delinquent, it is difficult to secure immediate evidence of the effect of such schooling. It is difficult to follow given children over a period of years and note changes. Even if they are followed, it is difficult to say what would have happened if these youths had not had the special program offered. In the case of children of low mentality, only the specially trained teacher can properly evaluate the worth of special training. Laymen would be unable to contrast what was being accomplished in these classes with what the situation would be without them.

These cases show how difficult it is to convince lay people of the importance of special education. It can be done, but the process is very slow and laborious. Attention has frequently been called to the fact that special education has developed very slowly in those states where that development has had to depend entirely upon local initiative and local support.

A second reason why local communities hesitate to organize these special classes is the added cost. It has been shown that special education cannot be provided at as low a cost as regular schoolwork. The local district will not levy additional taxes to support a new program of education unless it is well assured of the value of that program. Even when such assurance is given, the district sometimes refuses to make the needed additional levy. If the program could be tried out for a year or more without increasing school costs, it would, in many instances, be given the trial. The increased cost stands in the way of any such experimentation.

5. STATE SUPPORT AND SPECIAL EDUCATION

State Support as Stimulation.—In the light of the preceding, it is understandable why so many states have a program of state support as a means of stimulating special education. State funds are allocated to the support of a particular type of schoolwork. They are granted, generally, either upon a per-pupil or a per-teacher basis. If different groups of exceptional children are being educated, funds are granted to just those groups for whom the school law makes provision. Frequently the state bears the entire excess cost.

Even such liberal provisions are not sufficient incentive to interest all local districts in the organization of these classes. Most compulsory-attendance laws grant exemption to children who are physically or mentally handicapped. Thus the local district can argue that the state should pay the entire cost. If special classes are not organized, many of these handicapped will not attend school; if special classes are organized, those who are able must attend. The district, therefore, that thinks only of saving money will neglect to organize the special class.

State Support as Partial Equalization.—This situation demands that the state cease to think of special education as a program that can be taken on and later dropped, as the local district sees fit. These exceptional children have a right to an education. State laws should make as specific regulations governing special education as they make concerning the regular educational program. All children capable of leaving home for any type of schoolwork should be required to attend school. Such legislation would place squarely upon every local district the responsibility for providing for all of its educable children.

If such legislation were passed, state stimulation would cease to be important. The education of exceptional children could then be supported upon exactly the same basis as the regular public school program is supported. If partial equalization were operative, state funds would be granted to just those districts that needed such aid in order to provide the minimum program required by the state.

Argument for Special State Support.—Some claim that special funds for the education of exceptional children should be granted, regardless of legislation governing attendance, because some communities have a much greater group of these children than do others. Moreover, they say, the proper education of such groups is of great importance to society. Since some localities are so greatly burdened with cases, and since the entire state will be affected by what is done for them, the state, they claim, should bear the expense. There is excellent logic in the argument. The same logic applies, of course, to the state's responsibility for supporting all public education. It is questionable whether any greater differences exist in the number of exceptional children to be educated than exist in ability to pay for a program of general education.

If the argument implies a greater difference, several factors would need to be checked. Such a situation might be due to neglect. One city may have developed pupil-personnel services represented by the visiting teacher, the school counselor, the school psychologist, the school psychiatrist, and the school nurse. It may have provided a rich regular program of studies, which meets well the varying needs, abilities, and interests of the entire pupil group; and it may have made excellent provision for the out-of-school activities of school children. Such a city, other things being equal, should not have so many handicapped children as a city that fails to make these provisions. Such a situation should not, however, be used as an argument for asking the former city to help care for handicapped children in the latter by giving special state aid.

A real defense for special aid is found, at present, in the fact that where it is given special education develops much more rapidly than in states where such aid is not given. The White House Conference[1] reported that, in the District of Columbia and in the 19 states that had legislation governing special education for children of defective vision, there were 339 classes organized; in the remaining 29 states only 11 classes had been organized. Of the 19 states with legislative provisions, 5 provided no state aid; 3 of these 5 had no classes, 1 had 3 and

[1] White House Conference, *Special Education: The Handicapped and the Gifted*, p. 196, The Century Co., New York, 1931.

the other had 5; this left 331 classes in the 14 states providing state aid.

There are, moreover, two groups of exceptional children for whom special state funds should be asked; these are the gifted and the specially gifted. Any program planned for them must exceed the basic program. The very nature of the gifted child demands this. The need for educating gifted children cannot be reduced by anything local school authorities might do. No one wants to reduce the need; all are interested in having gifted children to educate. These children, moreover, are not of value just to the locality; they are of the utmost importance to the entire social group. From them society gets its artists, its writers, its painters, its inventors, its business geniuses, its statesmen, its scientists, and its outstanding professional leaders. Society cannot afford to lose a single genius.

Regardless of the adequacy of attendance laws, special funds should be granted to local districts for the education of gifted children as long as local support is basic in the financing of the public schools. It will be needed under state support until such time as state control becomes an actuality. When this occurs, the state will be able to see to it that all gifted children are educated to the limit of their capacities.

State Support for a Basic Educational Program.—A financial program for the support of special education can be thought of as standing upon exactly the same basis as the regular program of education. At present this latter is based largely upon local support. While many states are thinking in terms of state support, most of them hesitate to follow the logic of that point of view 100 per cent. The financing of state programs for special education, therefore, has had to depend upon local support, state support as stimulation, or state support as partial equalization. An adequate financial program for special education will not be obtained until "state support for a basic educational program" is accepted and until present ideas of this basic program of public education at both the elementary and the secondary school level are materially broadened.

Further compulsory-attendance requirements have been meager during the past few years. This means that, unless these youths voluntarily attend school, they are forced to loaf wherever industry refuses to accept them. Despite the need of having these youths enrolled in schools and actively occupied, one hesitates to pass legislation compelling such attendance until the schools are more adequately prepared to receive them. Certainly if all youths are to be required to attend school until eighteen or possibly until nineteen or twenty years of age, our concept of a basic program of public education must be greatly revised.

The regular academic curriculum, as we now know it, is not a basic program. These youths need a program broad enough in scope to care for that vast breadth of interest, capacity, and ability which will be represented. In the past, it has been relatively easy for local support to maintain the narrow academic curriculum; it has failed miserably in maintaining a program that would meet adequately the needs of that great group of nonacademically minded youths who have been brought into school by present attendance laws.

Specialized services have been recently developed within the public schools that have been very effective in helping boys and girls solve various home, school, and personal problems. At the same time, these years of depression have greatly augmented the need for adjustments among school children. Parents have lost their jobs, money, and homes; children have suffered the resultant feeling of insecurity; parents have separated, and the emotional life of the child has been completely upset. These children need help in adjusting to the changing conditions—changes which for some children have been no less than cataclysmic in nature. Methods of helping most of them to make a happy adjustment are known; what is lacking is sufficient personnel, properly trained, to give the needed aid. These special agencies are not included in the basic programs usually described.

Because of failure to put into operation plans of prevention, the past few years have seen the need for special education become greater and greater. This is not included in the thinking of most advocates of a program of state support. This special program should be cared for, just as secondary education is cared for, by a larger appropriation per pupil per year; each type of exceptional child should be considered separately in determining the sum needed. When this broader concept of what is meant by a basic program of education is generally accepted, the support of special education can be placed upon exactly the same basis as that of general education.

State support should aim at providing the same proportionate amount of the cost of special education as it aims to provide for elementary and secondary. In dealing with these three types of public education, the essentials should be thought of as covering far more than the minimum academic program. They should take care of all children with the same degree of efficiency that we have usually hoped to achieve in educating the well-adjusted, academically minded child. Such a program will demand a more diverse program of study than is usually provided and will require the specialized services of many groups of pupil-personnel workers, in addition to the regular teachers, principals, and supervisors.

Until this broadened conception of an essential program of public education is accepted, the educational needs of great masses of children will be ignored. Such a policy is not democratic; it is academically aristocratic, selfish, and extremely bigoted. Why should a child of good average academic intelligence who is happily adjusted, owing to a happy home and community life, be furnished an ideal school program, whereas the child of nonacademic ability or the child who has unfortunately not become happily adjusted is forced through the same educational routine and given little or no aid in becoming adjusted? We have talked a great deal about "equality of opportunity" without knowing or without sensing many of its implications.

The Locality's Place If the State Provides This Basic Program.— Local support should not be necessary until all groups of children have been granted a school program adjusted to their needs and until aid has been supplied to help each child make the necessary adjustments to his school and home life situations. After this has been done, the local district can go as far as it wishes in enriching these programs. In music the state would see that all children with such ability were educated; the local district could broaden the program so that a great group might have the same musical opportunities, even though they never could perform effectively. The state guarantees a program of education that best fits the needs of all groups of children. What is provided over and above that could become the local district's responsibility. This does not mean that the nonmusical person can have no music except at local expense; he will continue to have what is thought to be necessary as a part of his whole educational program; he will not be given training beyond this point, however, except at local expense.

State Control and Special Education.—Obviously, to set up a basic program of education and supply the funds, with no assurance that the program will be carried out, would be unwise. Special education as a part of this program would be particularly liable to suffer under a system of complete local control of funds provided by the state. At least the same controls that the state puts upon the expenditure of funds for the general program will need to be applied in the case of special education.[1]

6. FEDERAL SUPPORT AND SPECIAL EDUCATION

The Federal government has thus far not seen fit to give financial support to the development of special education. There is, at present,

[1] For a brief discussion of state control, see p. 444.

a bill before Congress which proposes Federal support. It proposes a sum of $11,580,000 annually to be used by the states in establishing, extending, and improving educational programs for physically handicapped children.

This money would be used in three ways: (1) The sum of $40,000 would be given to each state and to each of the territories; this would use $2,080,000. (2) The sum of $9,000,000 would be distributed upon the basis of the number of inhabitants five to twenty years old, inclusive. (3) The Office of Education would be granted $500,000 for the "purpose of making studies, investigations, and reports pursuant to the provisions of this act."

The $40,000 would be used especially in rural areas. The $9,000,-000 would have to be matched by funds from the units participating and would be used to pay excess costs. In order to participate, each unit must provide (1) data concerning the number of its handicapped, (2) an equitable distribution of the funds between rural and urban areas and between the various handicapped groups, and (3) an adequate plan for administering and supervising the program.

7. PRESENT STATE PLANS OF FINANCIAL SUPPORT

Most states continue to ignore special education from the point of view of financing it. Those granting funds follow six different methods: (1) the excess-cost plan, (2) the teacher basis, (3) the pupil basis, (4) the class basis, (5) a plan based upon cost of the regular program, and (6) some combination of these methods.

Excess Cost.—The basis for determining excess costs is not uniformly agreed upon. Most states do not define by state law this basis. Michigan, in discussing aid for crippled children, says that the costs shall be based upon that of special equipment and instruction.[1] Wisconsin includes teachers' salaries, board and transportation of pupils, special books and equipment, and other expenses approved by the state superintendent.[2]

Most states base this excess upon the actual cost of the regular elementary program of the school districts in question within the state. This procedure makes for great variability. If one city provides inadequately for its regular schools and thus has low per capita costs, but is forced to meet the same state standards for its special class as other cities meet, it receives more excess than other cities as long as it does not surpass the maximum allowed.

[1] *General School Laws*, Sec. 455, pp. 146–147, Michigan, 1934.
[2] *Laws of Wisconsin Relating to Common Schools*, Sec., 41.03, Wisconsin, 1934.

When each district determines its own excess costs upon the basis of the cost of its regular elementary school program, the state faces the difficulty of having all costs figured upon a comparable basis. Methods of keeping a record of school expenditures vary so greatly that comparative costs under any circumstances are hard to secure. When these figures are to be used as a basis for securing state school funds, their comparability may be questioned still more.

Doubtless these difficulties caused Wisconsin to fix by state law the basic, regular costs used in determining the excess at $70 per year per child. The Wisconsin law sets limits above which the state will not pay excess costs; the limit is $300 for pupils physically disabled and $250 for those who are deaf or blind.[1]

The amount of excess granted varies among the states. California allows one-half the excess cost up to $100 per child for physically handicapped pupils.[2] Michigan grants excess costs to the amount of $200 for the blind, crippled, and deaf.[3] Illinois grants $110 for the deaf, $250 for children with defective vision and $300 for crippled children.[4] Ohio grants $300 for the cripples and the deaf and $375 for the blind; the hard of hearing and the children of low vision are also included.[5] Indiana pays three-fourths of the excess costs without setting limits.[6]

There are several advantages in this excess-cost plan. It takes into account variations in the cost of maintaining an educational program in different school districts. It encourages the local district to keep the teacher load small in order to keep up per-capita costs; the small class is necessary if instruction is to be efficient.

A Given Sum per Pupil.—Minnesota uses a per pupil basis without reference to the cost of the regular program of education. The state pays local districts $100 for each subnormal child in special classes, $250 for each crippled and deaf child, and $300 each for children who are blind.[7] In the case of speech defectives Minnesota deviates from the per-pupil basis.

This method has the advantage of simplicity. A record of daily attendance at these special classes is sufficient to determine the money that the state owes the local district. The method, moreover,

---

[1] *Laws of Wisconsin, op. cit.*, Sec. 41.03a.
[2] *School Code*, Secs. 3.620, 3.621, and 4.1, pp. 148, 149, 171, California, 1929.
[3] *General School Laws*, Sec. 455, pp. 146–147, Michigan, 1934.
[4] *The School Law of Illinois*, pp. 158, 160, Illinois, 1931.
[5] *Ohio School Code*, Secs. 7,758 and 7,760, pp. 502–503, 1935.
[6] *School Laws*, Sec. 230, p. 91, Indiana, 1932.
[7] *Laws of Minnesota Relating to the Public School System*, Sec. 250e, p. 73, Minnesota, 1927.

has the effect of encouraging regularity of attendance. It fails completely to take into account differences in the cost of providing exactly the same program in various communities.

It has the disadvantage of encouraging the local officials to keep all special classes at maximum capacity. The fewer the teachers, the lower the costs; the more pupils per teacher, the greater the amount of state aid. Despite certain seeming advantages, the plan has such fundamental weaknesses that it ought not be used except under such a rigid system of state regulation and inspection that the size of the class would be kept to a minimum.

A Given Sum per Teacher.—The teacher basis is used in several states. Minnesota grants $1500 per teacher in educating children having speech defects. Missouri[1] grants $750 per teacher, provided that sum is not over two-thirds of the teacher's salary. This grant is made to teachers of crippled children and to teachers of children with defective vision; teachers of mentally defective children receive $300. Pennsylvania grants one-fourth of the minimum elementary salary of $1,200 in districts of the first class and three-tenths of the minimum elementary salary of other districts.[2] Upon a per pupil basis, there is some temptation to keep the class group large. Upon a per teacher basis the reverse would probably hold.

A Given Sum per Class.—The per class basis probably differs very little from the one just discussed. Usually one teacher has one class and vice versa. In school systems, however, where a program of departmental instruction is organized the number of teachers giving full time might be difficult to determine, whereas there would be a fixed and definite number of class groups in the school.

Maryland grants aid upon a class basis.[3] The grant is $2,000 per class, provided not fewer than 10 children are enrolled; this grant is extended to all classes for physically handicapped children. Massachusetts provides $500 per class for sight-saving work, plus $250 the first year for initial equipment.[4]

Unless class groups are clearly defined, this method presents many difficulties. It is difficult for the state department to check local districts upon the accuracy of their reporting. If a local district wishes to increase its revenue, what is to hinder it from reporting its

---

[1] *Revised School Laws*, pp. 15–17, Missouri, 1933.

[2] *The School Law*, Sec. 1210, Pars. 2, 5, 6, 7, 19, pp. 86–89, 93, Pennsylvania, 1931.

[3] White House Conference, *Special Education: The Handicapped and the Gifted*, p. 99, The Century Co., New York, 1931.

[4] *Ibid.*, p. 196.

36 children as three class groups of 12 each, whereas in reality they were taught as two class groups of 18 each?

Perhaps the most serious objection to both of the latter plans is the difficulty of securing from state legislatures large enough grants for special-class work. Under these plans, only two states at present grant over $750 per teacher or per class. Upon the basis of 15 pupils per class, this would mean $50 per year per pupil. The minimum amount granted upon the basis of excess costs or a per pupil basis was $100 per child; this grant was as high as $375 per pupil. Upon this basis a class of 15 pupils would be receiving $5,625 per year as a maximum, which is nearly three times the amount any legislature has ever seen fit to grant upon the teacher or class basis.

A Multiple of the Regular State Support.—This plan is used in the state of Washington. The state appropriates annually an amount equal to $20 per child of school age.[1] This sum is distributed upon the basis of days of attendance. All schools for defectives are allowed five times their actual attendance in determining the state funds due them.[2] The multiple used is obviously arbitrary, though it probably was determined upon the basis of comparative costs. The plan is subject to all the difficulties involved in determining a "day of attendance."[3]

Combined Plans.—New Jersey represents a scheme of combining some of the above plans for granting state aid. Under the New Jersey law $500 is granted per teacher; this is supplemented by a sum equal to 50 per cent of the excess cost.

8. INCREASED COSTS JUSTIFIED

Financial Argument.—Society has long accepted the theory that it must provide food, clothing, and shelter for its indigent, helpless, and feeble-minded. This theory is humane and in keeping with the ideals of a civilized society. But society has come to realize that the practice of reaching out and gathering up such groups and supporting them for life is a costly practice. Special education, moreover, has an ever-increasing amount of evidence tending to show that much of this institutionalization is unnecessary. It has shown that the blind and the deaf can be educated; it has shown that when so educated they can become self-supporting. Despite increased costs for educat-

---

[1] *State Manual of Washington*, p. 158, Sec. 760, State Department of Education, Olympia, 1927.

[2] *Ibid.*, p. 163, Sec. 770.

[3] The attorney general's opinions in the state manual makes the difficulties quite apparent. See *ibid.*, p. 160, Sec. 765.

ing such children, society saves money every time such a child becomes self-supporting instead of remaining a burden on society.

The cost of special education for the socially handicapped is great. This cost is insignificant, however, in comparison with the cost to society of capturing, convicting, and housing the youth who, through lack of contact with special education, becomes the criminal of tomorrow. Special education has shown that children of low I.Q., who otherwise need institutional care or find themselves upon relief rolls, can be made self-supporting. Previous to the depression, the great majority of subnormal children of an Ohio city, upon graduation from its special program of study, were placed in industry and were able to maintain themselves successfully. Without this help, the same children would have been a burden upon society. The financial gain to society of developing an educational program for gifted and specially gifted children may well be incalculable. It is not merely a financial saving that results; it is a gain through the contributions of the genius to society.

Social Argument.—The financial gains are by no means the most important reasons for being willing to support the increased costs of a program of special education. Society is improved if the changes suggested under the preceding argument actually take place. A society that decreases dependency and increases self-support is a society fired with more energy, ambition, and drive; it achieves more; it undertakes greater tasks than it otherwise would. Beggary, shiftlessness, and contentment in being supported at public expense tend to decrease.

During these postdepression days, when work is still difficult to find, the greatest danger society faces is the pauperization of its people so that they expect, as a sacred right, to be supported and maintained. When the numbers thus pauperized become too great, present democratic institutions will be jeopardized. A part of society cannot indefinitely continue to house, clothe, and feed another considerable part of that social order. Special education emphasizes the necessity of becoming self-supporting. To the extent that it inculcates these ideals into the idealism of large groups of growing youths, it has strengthened the hold of society upon democratic institutions.

Individual Argument.—The act of freeing the individual from a condition of dependency by making him able to feed, clothe, house, and entertain himself gives him a greater ambition, greater enjoyment in life, and a greater degree of self-respect than he ever had before. It is just such traits that seem to be disappearing among large groups of our population in these days. Families which would have considered the acceptance of relief a disgrace, only a few years ago, now actively seek it as a God-given right. Too frequently such families make little or no effort to become self-supporting again. Any program that will help to combat these tendencies is of great social worth.

9. SUMMARY

There are three theories governing the financing of public education: (1) local support, (2) state support, and (3) Federal support. Questions raised concerning state support are: (1) Shall it equalize? (2) Shall it stimulate? (3) Shall it cover the basic educational program? and (4) Shall the state control funds granted? At present, special education is largely financed upon the basis of stimulation. It is suggested that ideally there should be no difference in principle between financing a regular program of education and financing special education.

State support has been based upon (1) excess costs, (2) the pupil, (3) the teacher, (4) the class, (5) some multiple of regular costs, or (6) a combination of some two or more of these plans. Increased costs are justified to the extent that this schooling saves society the cost of feeding, housing, and clothing these youths for life. Exceptional children, moreover, frequently have a contribution to make to society in the form of inventions, writing, and so on.

It is urged, therefore, that public education be financed by the state to the extent of providing a program essential for the education of all groups of children. This essential program is to be thought of in terms of educating all pupils in accordance with interest, abilities, and capacities. What is done over and above this for the various groups may be provided by the local community.

Problems and Questions for Discussion

1. What are the reasons for local support of public education? What are the essential weaknesses of the plan?

2. Argue state support as partial equalization as a satisfactory solution of our financial educational problems. Give the pros and cons.

3. Is it necessary to have state control if we are to have a satisfactory system of state support for public education? Give the arguments.

4. Why is state support, as a stimulation to special education, necessary at present?

5. What would you recommend as the ideal plan of financing special education? Why?

6. Describe present plans of providing state support for special education. What are the advantages and disadvantages of each?

7. Why is special education so much more costly than the regular educational program?

8. In what ways can the high cost of special education be justified?

9. If the state undertakes to support a basic program of education, what should that basic program include? Why?

10. Do you believe in state control of educational financing? If not, why not? If so, why?

Selected Bibliography

CUBBERLEY, ELLWOOD P. *School Funds and Their Apportionment.* Teachers College, Columbia University, New York, 1906. 255 pp.

Gives an early and most excellent analysis of the financial support of public education. Is rich in illustrative material showing gross inequality of ability to support public education among local districts.

LEHMAN, CLARENCE O. *The Legal Status of State Aid for Special School Projects in the United States.* The Ohio State University, Columbus, 1929. 167 pp.

Discusses the development of financial support for public education and makes an analysis of state aid for special school projects, including the education of handicapped children.

MORT, PAUL R., and others. *State Support for Public Education,* pp. 32–188. The American Council on Education, The National Survey of School Finance, Washington, D.C., 1933.

Discusses the evolution of principles underlying state school support, the minimum program of public education, local needs educationally, local ability to support, equalizing the burden, and provisions for local initiative.

REEDER, WARD G. "Proposed Modification of the County Tax Law for Ohio Schools," *Educational Research Bulletin* (Jan. 6, 1926), Vol. 5, pp. 1–9. Ohio State University, Columbus.

Calls attention to dangers that are present in any plan of stimulation. Suggests some details of the Ohio law governing state financing of public education that need to be changed.

UPDEGRAFF, HARLAN. *Rural School Survey of New York State,* Financial Support, pp. 110–118. Wm. F. Fell Co., Printer, Philadelphia, 1922.

Gives a brief account of the development of the theory of financing public education in the United States. Suggests a basis for state support.

White House Conference. *Special Education: The Handicapped and the Gifted,* pp. 94–112, 193–202, 439–441. The Century Co., New York, 1931.

Gives brief accounts of state aid for educating several types of handicapped children.

CHAPTER XXXI

STATE ADMINISTRATION AND CONTROL

The germ of an idea often originates in a remote center and its development may be due to the work of essentially unrelated forces; the development of special education does not deviate in this respect from developments in other fields. Various agencies have initiated some program of special education; in many instances private groups have begun the work; sometimes an individual has seen the need and has tried to meet it. City school districts seldom have a unified program of special education; often no one person is responsible for the entire program; there may be as many as four or five administrative officials in the larger cities who supervise various parts of the program.

The same situation exists within the various states; even a comprehensive program of special education may be lacking in effectiveness because of a lack of unity in the state administrative organization. Part of the program may be administered and supervised by one department, another part by a second, and so on. Departments may, of course, co-operate effectively and so provide a splendid program of special education. The fact remains that present allocations of responsibility frequently are not based upon any principle governing function but purely upon accident of original discovery of need and of an attempt to meet that need.

1. STATE DEPARTMENTS RESPONSIBLE FOR SPECIAL EDUCATION[1]

This section will consider those state departments that perform functions essential to the development of a program of special education. An attempt will be made to describe what now exists without any attempt to discuss a recommended state organization.

Department of Education.—Martens[2] reports 13 states that have organized bureaus for the supervision of special education in their state departments of education; not all these bureaus supervise the same types of exceptional children. The states are Alabama, Cali-

[1] ELISE H. MARTENS, "Organization for Exceptional Children within State Departments of Education," *U.S. Office of Education Pamphlet* 42, Washington, D.C., 1933. 35 pp.
[2] *Ibid.*, p. 13

458

fornia, Connecticut, Delaware, Maryland, Massachusetts, Michigan, Minnesota, New York, Ohio, Pennsylvania, Wisconsin, and Wyoming. The extent to which different types of special education are cared for by these bureaus is shown in Table XIX. In Alabama the bureau serves three groups: the mentally defective, the gifted, and the socially maladjusted. Twelve different types are served by one or more of these bureaus. In only one state does the bureau serve all 12 types. Four other states serve 11 of these types; they omit in each case the malnourished.

TABLE XIX.—TYPES OF EXCEPTIONAL CHILDREN CARED FOR BY EACH OF THE THIRTEEN STATES[1]

Name of type	States													Total
	Alabama	California	Connecticut	Delaware	Maryland	Massachusetts	Michigan	Minnesota	New York	Ohio	Pennsylvania	Wisconsin	Wyoming	
Blind		x	x	x	x	x	x		x	x	x	x	x	11
Cardiac		x	x	x		x	x	x	x		x	x	x	10
Cripple		x	x	x	x	x	x	x	x	x	x	x	x	12
Deaf		x	x	x	x	x	x	x	x		x	x	x	11
Defective speech			x	x	x	x		x	x	x	x	x	x	10
Gifted	x	x	x	x		x					x		x	7
Hard of hearing		x	x	x	x	x	x	x	x	x	x	x	x	12
Malnourished				x										1
Partially sighted		x	x	x	x	x	x	x	x	x	x	x	x	12
Socially maladjusted	x	x	x	x	x	x			x		x		x	9
Subnormal	x	x	x	x		x		x	x	x	x	x	x	11
Tubercular			x	x		x			x		x		x	6
Total	3	9	11	12	7	11	6	7	10	6	11	8	11	

[1] Adapted from ELISE H. MARTENS, "Organization for Exceptional Children within State Departments of Education," pp. 20–32, U.S. Office of Education Pamphlet 42, Washington, D.C., 1933. Applicable to just the bureaus responsible for special education under the state department of education.

Not one of the 12 types of exceptional children was served by all 13 bureaus; the cripple, the hard of hearing, and the partially sighted, were served by 12 of these bureaus. The malnourished group was reported by only one bureau; the tubercular, by six; the gifted, by seven; and the socially maladjusted, by nine. The differences in services rendered are far greater than are shown by this table. States reporting the same number of types cared for differ greatly in the extent to which they work at their job.

Department of Health.—Of the 13 states just discussed, six report that their departments of health have specific responsibilities for special education. In California this department organizes tuberculosis clinics and provides for the medical care of needy crippled children. In Massachusetts, it supervises hospitals that maintain schools for crippled children. In New York it supervises the "State Reconstruction Home for Crippled Children." In general, the department examines physically handicapped children and provides surgical and medical attention.

Department of Welfare.—Six of these states report that welfare departments have duties with respect to special education. In California the department gives advice to county probation officers; in New York it has an extensive program for the prevention of blindness. The other four states have these departments supervise and administer state schools for the delinquent; three of them supervise and administer state institutions for the feeble-minded and epileptic; one controls its state hospital school for cripples and approves all cases of home teaching of crippled children. One of the four also has administrative control of the state schools for the deaf and blind; another provides "traveling clinical service for child guidance," clinical services for crippled children, and aid for preschool children if parents cannot afford needed care.

This enumeration of duties aims at listing only those functions that have some relation to problems of special education.

Department of Mental Hygiene.—Two of these 13 states have departments of mental hygiene, with responsibilities for special education; they are New York and Massachusetts. Both departments supervise and administer their residential schools for the mentally handicapped. In Massachusetts the department supplies the public schools with traveling clinical service; aids the local communities in supervising their mental defectives; and examines delinquent youths. Both states assist in developing local child-guidance clinics. In New York the department examines children who are to enter special classes.

Other Departments.—California has a department of institutions, which has control of its state schools for delinquents, mental defectives, and epileptics, and which supervises its bureau of juvenile research. This bureau provides traveling clinics for child guidance. New York has a department of correction, which administers its program of educating and caring for delinquents in state schools.

Boards.—Five of the 13 states use, in addition to the department of education, special boards to care for certain special education functions. Alabama has boards of managers that administer all state residential schools; these boards are responsible to some state official. Delaware has a board of charities, which supervises the state mental-hygiene clinic and inspects the state schools for the delinquent, epileptic, and mental defective. The clinic operates traveling clinical service for the public schools. Minnesota has a board of control with functions similar to Delaware's board of charities; the supervision of state schools for the blind, crippled, and deaf are added. Wisconsin has a board of control, which administers the same state schools as Minnesota's board, with the exception of the one for cripples. Wyoming's board of charities and reform administers state schools for delinquents, epileptics, and mental defectives.

Conclusions.—The nonuniformity of practice with respect to administering special education is clearly evident. Each of these 13 states, in addition to its special bureau, has one or more other state departments or state boards or both, which perform many functions very closely related to a complete state program of special education. This scattering is due to the laissez-faire development of these functions; many of them developed long before they were thought of as educational and long before anyone dreamed of establishing a bureau of special education within the state department of education.

2. PRESENT ORGANIZATION IN STATE DEPARTMENTS OF EDUCATION

Of the 13 states that have provided bureaus or divisions of special education within the state department of education, 9 have, in each case, centered all special education activities in the hands of one person, whose sole responsibility is that of promoting and supervising the department's special education program. Other state departments carry on special education functions, so that the program for the entire state is not always centrally supervised and controlled within these nine states, even though the work within their state departments of education is thus supervised.

The State Director.—The title assigned to the person responsible for the department's special education program varies. Michigan, Pennsylvania, and Wyoming call him the Director of Special Education; Minnesota calls him the Director of Special Classes and Defectives; Maryland, the Supervisor of Special Education and Vocational Rehabilitation; Alabama, the Director of Exceptional Children; and Delaware, the Director of the Division of Special Education and Mental Hygiene. These seven states have a relatively simple organization, with a chief and, in two instances, an assistant.

Connecticut has a Director of Field Service and under his supervision are two supervisors, one of health and another of special education. California has a Chief of the Division of Special Education and under his supervision are four chiefs: (1) Chief of Bureau of Mental Hygiene, (2) Chief of Bureau for Education of the Deaf, (3) Chief of Bureau for Education of the Blind, and (4) Chief of Bureau for Correction of Speech Defects. The workers in each of the four bureaus are responsible, through their chiefs, to the chief of the whole division of special education.

None of the remaining four states has any one person responsible for co-ordinating all the special education functions of the department. The departments of education within these four states have developed programs of special education more extensive in some cases than those

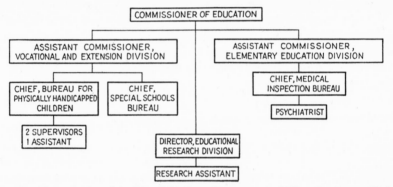

FIG. 10.—Organization of the New York State Department of Education to provide for handicapped children.[1]

found among the other nine; responsibility for the program is divided, however, except as the commissioner takes the time to co-ordinate the work. Massachusetts under the Commissioner of Education has a Supervisor of Special Schools and Classes and a Director of the Division of the Blind; Ohio has a Superintendent of the State School for the Blind, a Superintendent of the State School for the Deaf, and a Director of Special Classes; Wisconsin has a Clinical Psychologist and Supervisor, a Supervisor of Physically Handicapped Children, and a Supervisor of Deaf, Blind, and Speech Defective.

The situation in the New York State Department of Education can best be shown by Fig. 10. The chief of the bureau for physically handicapped children is responsible for the education of cardiacs, hard of hearing, partially seeing, speech defectives, and tubercular children. The chief of the special schools bureau supervises the

[1] MARTENS, *op. cit.*, p. 28.

education of the blind and deaf. Both of these bureaus are subordinate to an assistant commissioner of education who has numerous duties and functions entirely outside the field of special education.

The director of the research division is responsible for organizing and supervising classes for subnormal children; he has numerous other functions. The chief of the medical inspection bureau and his psychiatrist examine all children referred to them; the chief is responsible to the assistant commissioner in charge of elementary education.

Relation to Other Pupil Services.—A department of education will sometimes have a division, a bureau, a department, or several such, responsible for various specialized services for pupils. These services are designated by such titles as (1) attendance service, (2) counseling service, (3) psychological service, (4) psychiatric service, (5) health service, and (6) measurement service. Sometimes one or more of the services is related administratively to that of special education. The usual situation is to find them organized separately and independently of the whole special education program.

3. A PROPOSED STATE ORGANIZATION

There has been a tendency in American education to overstress buildings, curriculum, equipment, and teachers, and to forget the child. Teacher-training institutions have tended to overemphasize methods; school administrators have given an overwhelming amount of time and thought to finance and material equipment; teachers have tended to think too much in terms of subject matter. It has thus happened that the child—the real center of this whole program—has been forgotten; we have tended to allow the means to become the end of our educational endeavors and the real end of these endeavors has been ignored.

Present-day administrative organization of public school work has followed a similar pattern. In city school systems and in state departments of education we find an assistant superintendent in charge of finance and building, another to supervise elementary education, a third to supervise secondary education, occasionally a fourth in charge of curriculum reconstruction, and sometimes still another responsible for the system's staff personnel, including teachers and all other board employees. Seldom do we find a type of organization that gives direct and real attention to the child. Indirectly, the business department is supposed to do this, but too frequently it ignores him. Its major aim is to save money and keep within its budget. Even those in charge of supervision and curriculum tend to forget the child and to give their attention to the building of "bigger and better" curricula.

To be sure, teacher-training institutions are talking about child-centered schools; the curriculum-minded teacher is considered quite old-fashioned; and a great deal is said about changes in method and curriculum that will enable the teacher to be of greatest aid to the child. Within the public schools we have even found it necessary to develop a number of specialized services in order to help the teacher better understand the needs, interests, and capacities of her pupils.

We find that some cities already have most of the agencies needed for pupil study; they have modern attendance service, visiting-teacher service, health service, psychological service, psychiatric service, counseling service, advisory service, special schooling, placement service, and so on. The difficulty is that the work of these pupil-personnel agencies is not well correlated. One division of the school system has seen a need for some one of these services; the need has been recognized and the service has been established. Another division has seen the need for a second service and has been allowed to establish it. Thus, at present all these services are available within a given system, but each in turn has been tacked on to the regular duties of some already overburdened administrative officer.

These agencies are closely interrelated with respect to function; as now organized, they often develop as competing agencies instead of a well-organized group of co-operating agencies. The result is that we have the unhappy paradox of a number of agencies, established for the benefit of children, actually operating upon the basis of self-preservation.

The more limited field of special education has similarly suffered. In some states and in several cities an extensive program of special education covering all types of handicapped children has been established. The cripples, however, are supervised by one school department, the gifted by another, the subnormals by a third, and possibly the socially handicapped by a fourth. We find, thus, an administrative setup that makes it very difficult to think solely of the child and his good; it tends to put the good of the organization above that of the child. It is with the hope of correcting such situations that some of the following proposals are made with respect to state organization.

Administrative Relationships.—Figure 11 shows the proposed administrative relationship of various pupil-personnel services. Such an organization (1) will give due emphasis to the child as the important element within the public school system, (2) will so relate, under one administrative head, all pupil-personnel agencies that better co-operation may be secured, and (3) will associate with one another agencies that have common aims and purposes. Thus organized, these agencies will be able to co-operate to the maximum in getting all needed data concerning pupils to those teachers who need them. Such an organization can eliminate the overlapping of functions and the duplication of labor, and thus be able to accomplish far more with a staff of the same size.

Field service includes all duties involving visits to parents, relatives, or friends of pupils; it includes the necessary contacting of school, church, court, or social agencies of the community in handling a given child's problems. This service may be rendered by modern attendance officers, visiting teachers, social workers, or psychiatric social workers. The name by which such a worker is called is not nearly so important as the fact that we have the service and that it is performed by well-

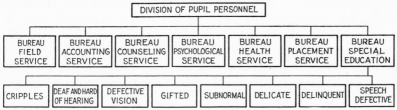

FIG. 11.—Chart for a state department of education showing an ideal administrative relationship between special education and other pupil-personnel services.

qualified and well-trained persons. Service of this kind is needed constantly by the teachers of exceptional children; these children are often handicapped in making a proper recovery unless the parents understand their own duties in aiding such recovery.

Accounting service includes taking the census, keeping it continuous, making age-grade-progress studies, studying attendance, handling court cases, and supervising the system's pupil recording and reporting procedures. Such services are necessary if all children of school age are to be educated. It has been noted again and again in earlier chapters that a big problem in ensuring the education of handicapped youths is to discover them. Parents hesitate to report them and frequently do their utmost to hide them. Only the most complete system of registering all children from birth until they are eighteen or twenty-one years of age will make it possible to educate all handicapped children.

Counseling service is here defined as limited to those individuals on the school staff whose sole function is that of conferring with pupils and gathering and distributing data that will help them make, more intelligently, certain important life decisions. The happy, normal, well-adjusted child finds it relatively easy to make most of these decisions; it is the child who has suffered severe social, physical, or mental handicaps who finds it very difficult to make many of them. A close relation exists, therefore, between the work of this bureau and that of special education.

Psychological service, although necessary for all children, is basic to the selection of mentally exceptional children in the development of a special education program. The same is true of health service. No educational program for physically handicapped children would be complete without the most careful attention to the child's health.

Placement service is gradually being recognized as more important in public school work. It is a service thought of as peculiarly necessary for those who are handicapped socially, physically, or mentally, if they are to secure jobs and become self-supporting members of society. The reasons for this have been emphasized in earlier chapters.[1]

Special education is peculiarly related to all these agencies, moreover, in another way. For the most part, such agencies are dealing with and surveying continuously the entire pupil population. They are responsible for accounting for all pupils of the community and for helping unadjusted children to make better adjustments. Their aim is to help all children so to adjust that they can pursue their schoolwork in a normal manner. Many children deviate so greatly from the normal, however, that this is undesirable, and even impossible; if the child is to profit, he must be provided with a special program of education. It seems, therefore, both advisable and logical that the bureau of special education shall be under the supervision of the pupil-personnel division.

Staff Personnel.—Personnel for the proposed state organization is a vexing problem. There are many factors that must be taken into consideration when one is considering the immediate steps to be taken in organizing such work within his own state. There are (1) the size of the state, (2) the proportion of the school population needing special education, (3) the program already in operation, (4) the extent to which the people will agree to provide special education, and (5) the existing amount of state supervision. Where nothing has been done, it might be wise for the state, as a temporary measure, to appoint a general supervisor with a secretary, to undertake the task of developing its entire program of special education. Where the state has already developed a program involving all types of exceptional children, it may be feasible to have a supervisor appointed for each of the

[1] See pp. 37; 50; 56; 63; 70–71; 134–135; 165; 181–182; 255; 325–326; 374–375; 417–418.

eight types noted in Fig. 11, supplemented by necessary assistants and clerical help.

Ultimately, only one factor would determine the size of this administrative staff. That would be the population of the state. Every state should be willing to accept its responsibility for educating all handicapped children. This would mean that each state, with the possible exception of a few of the smaller ones, would ultimately have a staff to supervise special education similar to that outlined in Fig. 12.

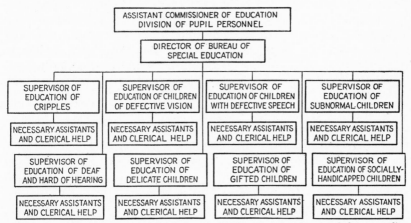

Fig. 12.—Chart for a state department of education showing in skeleton outline the staff necessary to ideally provide state supervision for a special education program within the state.

If handicapped children are adequately educated and cared for and if the pupil-personnel agencies are competently and effectively manned, the head of the state's division of pupil personnel should be an assistant commissioner of education.[1] The director of the bureau of special education would be co-ordinate in authority with the directors of each of the other pupil-personnel agencies shown in Fig. 11. The eight supervisors of various types of special education should be directly responsible to him and through him responsible to the assistant commissioner in charge of pupil-personnel work.

The big problem in special education is to care for and educate all exceptional children; it is generally recognized that we have barely begun to accept that responsibility. The vast differences among states with respect to the extent to which they have assumed this responsibility have been noted. The relationship between the number

[1] In some states this would be an assistant state superintendent of public instruction and in others an assistant state director of education.

of cities organizing special classes and the establishment of bureaus of special education to assist in organizing such classes has been noted. It seems reasonable to suppose, therefore, that this problem of educating exceptional children will not be met until the proper administrative staff is provided by the state department of education.

4. A PROPOSED LOCAL ORGANIZATION

The administrative organization for developing a local program of special education will follow, in general, the outline proposed for the state. There should be an assistant superintendent in charge of the division of pupil personnel wherever the local district is sufficiently large to have an assistant superintendent. All the functions outlined in Fig. 11 should be assigned to him. He should be free to give his entire attention to the development and utilization of these services. The size of his staff will depend upon the size of the district.

The City of 500,000 or Greater.—Figure 13 shows for a city of a half million or more population the major staff members of a division of pupil personnel; it shows in greater detail the staff members of the division's bureau of special education. Obviously, in the bureau of special education many services will have to be performed that are not provided for in the chart. Many of them will be cared for by the other bureaus of the division.

Many large cities now include practically all the services suggested by this chart. The chief difficulty has been that these services are not well co-ordinated; they are not under the supervision of one individual who can give his entire thought to the problem of securing co-operation among the staff members responsible for the services.

Many cities have ignored some of these vital services. Too frequently, field service is available only for the non-attender. Accounting service is often confined merely to the taking of a census by "hired enumerators." Counseling service is frequently the incidental conferring of teacher or principal with pupils; it may be somewhat systematized, but confined solely to what regular teachers are able to do. Even where a city has full-time counselors doing excellent work, too often such service is available to only a limited number of schools within the city. Too frequently the whole school system has to depend upon one or two persons for its entire psychological service, while placement service is largely ignored. Health service is, perhaps, most adequately performed, but all too frequently it is provided by authorities who merely co-operate with the schools and over whom the schools have no administrative control.

In the field of special education, many handicapped children are ignored. It is hoped that Fig. 13 will not only be suggestive of how these services should be administratively controlled but that it will call attention to services that are vital if all children within a community are to have a fair chance of being educated.

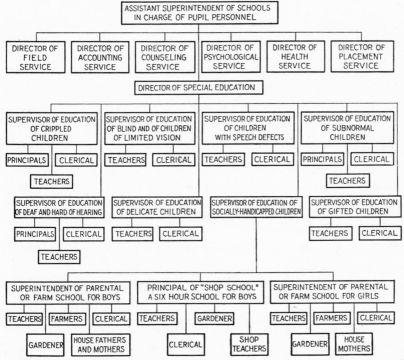

Fig. 13.—Chart for a city of 500,000 population or more showing major staff members of its pupil-personnel division and most of the staff members of the division for the bureau of special education.

The City of 100,000 to 500,000.—Figure 14 shows the major staff members proposed for the pupil-personnel division of a city of 100,000 to 500,000 population; it suggests most of the staff members proposed for the bureau of special education. All the functions proposed for a city of 500,000 are retained; however, the number of bureaus has been reduced from seven to five, the number of supervisors in the bureau of special education has been reduced from eight to three, and the parental school for girls has been dropped.

City school officials in the lower population ranges may feel that such a staff as here proposed is too large. As city school systems are now organized, the feeling will be justified. Several points must be considered before a final decision concerning the size of a city's pupil-personnel staff is reached. (1) Are the functions proposed legitimate and needed? (2) Are they being adequately performed? (3) If not, what staff is needed to perform them? (4) Is your community cognizant of the importance of these functions?

Be sure of your answer to this last question. It is a sad commentary on a city's educational leadership when it lags behind the demand of the community's more intelligent leaders. It may be that these leaders are ready to go with you much further than you think in providing modern pupil-personnel services. It may be that a city

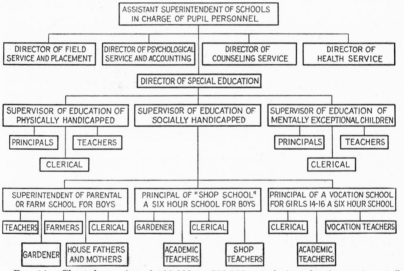

Fig. 14.—Chart for a city of 100,000 to 500,000 population showing major staff members of its pupil-personnel division and most of the staff members of the division for the bureau of special education.

of 100,000 can organize effectively with a smaller staff; the setting of limits is arbitrary. If a city of 100,000 needs such a staff, a city of 99,000 might likewise need such a staff. The organization chart for cities of 25,000 to 100,000 may for some time meet the needs of cities just over 100,000 in population. Each city must study its own problems and be ideal as well as practical in that study. If it finds a way of unifying and of administering adequately these services with a smaller staff, nothing more can be asked.

The City of 25,000 to 100,000.—Figure 15 shows that the functions of the pupil-personnel staff are the same whether the city be large or small. The personnel has been greatly reduced. The director is responsible for four functions; these functions in the large city were handled each by a separate bureau with a director in charge; he is not only responsible for co-ordinating all functions but must directly supervise the work of these four.

Owing to the close relation between health and psychological service, as well as their importance, they have been combined under a special supervisor. All special education is under a second supervisor.

Farm schools have been omitted. Local special schools for shop or industrial work for boys and for vocational work for girls are

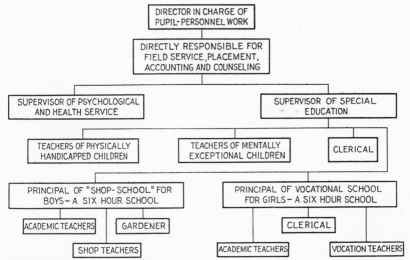

Fig. 15.—Chart for a city of 25,000 to 100,000 population showing major staff members of its bureau of pupil personnel and most of the staff members responsible for the bureau's special education program.

retained. The suggestions made concerning the organization chart for cities of 100,000 to 500,000 are applicable here.[1]

A County School System or a City under 25,000.—It is assumed that pupil-personnel services are just as necessary for children in rural communities as for children in larger cities. This assumption is not always made. Where it is, the additional assumption, that the district is too small to justify such services, is often made. Before the development of hard roads, it was true that a program of special education in most county school districts was not possible. Previous to the report of the White House Conference on Child Welfare in 1931, it was even assumed that very few counties where hard roads were available would have enough handicapped to organize central county

[1] If you doubt the wisdom of a staff of this size, reread pp. 469–470

classes or schools. The White House Conference, however, gave us some very startling facts.[1]

If one assumes that the United States has a total school population of 25,000,000, if one assumes that a county or a city having 5,000 population has 1,000 school children, and if one assumes further that the proportion of handicapped in this district is the same as for the country as a whole, there would be the following number of children

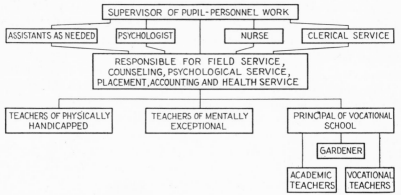

Fig. 16.—Organization chart for county school districts or for cities under 25,000 population showing major staff members needed to handle its pupil-personnel work.

with the various types of handicap in a school district having a population of 5,000.

Impaired hearing	120
Defective speech	40
Crippled condition	12
Weak and damaged hearts	40
Malnourished state	240
Behavior cases	27
Mentally defective condition	18

Obviously, such a district needs to give considerable attention to the problem of educating its handicapped. The problem is not insignificant as we have often been led to believe. There are several reasons why we have failed to recognize its bigness. (1) Accounting procedures have been antiquated. (2) Parents have a feeling of guilt and tend to hide handicapped children from official eyes. (3) Certain handicaps are taken too much for granted by parents who realize neither their seriousness nor the possibilities of cure. (4) Smaller districts have failed to provide health services, and so the children have been undiscovered. (5) Teachers have not been so sensitive to these

---

[1] See p. 6 for estimates of the number of handicapped children in the United States.

handicaps as have the teachers of larger school systems where pupil-personnel agencies force them to be on the lookout for all types of problem children. As a result, local school superintendents feel that they have no need for special education; they have no handicapped children.

A type of organization that would give some assurance that the exceptional child within the smaller school district would not be completely ignored is shown in Fig. 16. A supervisor is placed in charge of all pupil-personnel work; there is also a full-time psychologist and a full-time registered nurse; teachers are added to the staff as they are needed for the special classes or schools. This is a minimum organization; as the work develops, the needed assistants will be added.

The chart emphasizes the following: (1) Functions related to serving pupils are co-ordinated by making one person responsible for all of them. (2) Greater emphasis is placed upon the urgency of abundant psychological service within the public schools. (3) The advisability of placing health service under the supervision of the schools is pointed out. (4) The possibility of more effectively caring for and educating the physically and mentally handicapped is noted. (5) The advisability of providing a central vocational school for the education of boys and girls who never expect to do, are not interested in doing, or have not the ability to do, regular academic schoolwork is reemphasized.

5. SUMMARY

State departments such as education, health, mental hygiene, and public welfare have assumed in varying degrees some responsibility for special education programs in the various states; in some states, boards have been established to administer and control specific phases of the work.

State departments of education vary greatly as to the degree to which they assume responsibility for special education. Some have well-developed departments responsible for the special education provided by the public schools of the state; others have no departments and no legal provision whereby they can provide special education.

The powers of the state departments of education relative to special education vary greatly; some have none, some merely determine needs; some control only public day schools and classes; and others control and supervise the state schools. Many states limit their program to the blind, the deaf, and the crippled; others include all the physically handicapped; others directly or indirectly have supervision of all types of exceptional children.

Only 13 states have departments of special education. These departments are usually unrelated to the other pupil-personnel agencies, such as (1) field service, (2) accounting service, (3) counseling service, (4) psychological service, (5) health service, and (6) placement service. It is recommended that state departments reorganize to the extent necessary to place not only all types of special education but all pupil-personnel agencies under the supervision of one person in the state department of education, with the title of Assistant Commissioner of Education in charge of Pupil Personnel.

The local school district shall have one person solely responsible for all the district's pupil-personnel services, thus relating more closely its program of special education with that of those agencies established to solve more effectively all the special problems of school children. The larger cities will have in each an assistant superintendent in charge of this entire division; cities of 25,000 to 100,000 will each have a director in charge; every county district or city district of less than 25,000 will have a supervisor.

Problems and Questions for Discussion

1. Why do we find different types of special education administered and controlled by different state agencies? By different local agencies?

2. Would it be wise to consolidate all special education activities under a single agency? State specifically your reasons for your answer.

3. What types of the exceptional child should be provided with a special educational program under public control and at public expense? What are your reasons?

4. Should special education be administered as an independent school problem? State your reasons.

5. What would be the pros and cons of considering special education as one of the six or more pupil-personnel services and thus administered and supervised by the same person who administered and supervised these services?

6. What evidences, if any, are there of the need for special education in a county school district or in a city school district with a population under 25,000?

7. What types of state organization do we find administering the state's program of special education? What weaknesses, if any, do you note in each of these?

8. Is it practicable and feasible to establish a special vocational school in a county school system or in a city under 25,000 for boys and girls who have, for various reasons, no interest in the usual academic school program? What evidence have you to submit in support of your conclusions?

9. Is it practicable to establish a farm (or 24-hour) school for boys and girls in a city of 100,000 or more? What evidence have you to submit in support of your conclusions?

Selected Bibliography

MARTENS, ELISE H. "Organization for Exceptional Children within State Departments of Education." *U.S. Office of Education Pamphlet* 42, Washington, D.C., 1933. 35 pp.

An excellent analysis of the administrative organization for caring for and educating exceptional children within those 13 states that have already established a special bureau or division within the state department of education for this purpose.

WALLIN, J. E. WALLACE. *Problems of Subnormality*, pp. 382–416. World Book Company, Yonkers-on-Hudson, New York, 1921.

A summary of the work of the Missouri Children's Code Commission, containing recommendations for caring for, on a statewide basis, the state's feeble-minded, epileptic, crippled, blind, deaf, speech defectives, and the unstable and psychopathic.

White House Conference. *Special Education: The Handicapped and the Gifted.* The Century Co., New York, 1931. 604 pp.

Scattered through the text are numerous suggestions relative to present and proposed ways of organizing to care for the exceptional child; pp. 583–593 bear directly upon this problem.

CHAPTER XXXII

A PROGRAM OF PREVENTION

1. INTRODUCTION

The copybook maxims of our school days need to be examined with care. Not always is it true that "A bird in hand is worth two in the bush." Such a philosophy tends to blind us to the rich possibilities of the future and to bind us to the actualities of the present. A person ruled by this philosophy has little interest in spending money in the hope of preventing future possible catastrophes.

Businessmen become emotionally upset when brought face to face with little children who are badly crippled; they are willing to give their time and money and to provide means for remedying these defects. It is far more difficult to convince them that money should be spent on a program tending to prevent such conditions. The stark reality of a hopelessly crippled child forces them to face a real need; the idealism back of a program designed to keep children physically fit is a thing of the future; no need exists, since the children that the program is designed to help are healthy and well.

Theoretically, lip service is given to the idealism of prevention; practically, little is done about it. One can, of course, enumerate many things that are being done to prevent ills in human life; yet, in proportion to needs in the whole field of prevention, we are just beginning such programs. This is particularly true in the field of education. Attendance workers talk about preventing truancy and delinquency, and yet the bulk of their work centers about remedial procedures dealing with those already truant and delinquent. This remedial work, to be sure, may prevent the youth from becoming worse. Our difficulty is that the preventive program began so late.

Special education is no exception to these generalizations; in a peculiar way the entire special education program for handicapped children is a remedial program; it is only preventive in that it aims to prevent further maladjustment.

The immediate task of special education, therefore, is remedial. The workers in this field, however, recognize the relative hopelessness of their task if it ends there. Cities are finding, in their classes for subnormals, children whose parents and grandparents were in these same classes 18 to 36 years ago. Leaders in special education recognize that not only must the handicapped be cared for and educated, but they realize that steps must be taken to reduce the number needing special education. These workers are unusually well fitted for assuming a responsibility for such preventive programs; not only should they be given the responsibility, but school superintendents should see to it that they assume that responsibility.

2. WHY EMPHASIZE PREVENTION

There are several reasons why it seems advisable to emphasize a program of prevention. Unless specific attention is given to it, the fear is that little will be accomplished.

Costs.[1]—The cost of educating handicapped children is greater than that of educating normal children. If all the handicapped were being educated, the additional money needed would amount to a very large sum. When, therefore, a preventive program is questioned because of costs, it might be well to point out that the cost of re-educating the socially handicapped in parental or farm schools is several times the cost of the regular elementary school program. Crippled children are educated at a cost that ranges from three to six times that of educating the noncrippled. If we recognize the right of these handicapped children to an education, we must expect to continue to pay large sums for remedial work or an effective program of prevention must be put into operation.

Suffering of the Individual.—In considering the feasibility of a program of prevention, we must not ignore the handicapped child himself. When we see how the crippled child suffers, we are willing to give the money needed to relieve that suffering. What we forget is that, if we had been willing to spend that money or a part of it on prevention, much of that suffering would have been eliminated. We cruelly permit the handicap and then, when it is too late, do what we can to rectify our mistake.

If physical suffering were all that the child had to endure, the damage would not be so great; such pain is often the minor part of what is actually suffered. The handicap may disfigure the child, and frequently the disfigurement is permanent. The child is different from other children; bars are raised that prevent him from entering normal child activities. The mental suffering that results is impossible to estimate. Even if the child, under careful supervision, is able to

[1] For detailed data on costs for the different types of handicapped, see pp. 49–50; 81; 117–118; 164–165; 181; 255; 259; 280–281; 296; 326; 454–456.

adjust and accept his handicap, there is the inescapable continuous realization of what he might have been if proper preventive measures had been maintained by the social group.

On account of his handicap he finds that, even though he is well trained, it is difficult to get a job. The reasons are made clear by the prospective employer. The cripple may, therefore, be forced to depend upon others for a living. The psychological effects of such a situation are devastating in the extreme; whatever pride, initiative, drive, or ambition he may have had are in a fair way of being annihilated.

Loss to Society.—Society suffers very definite losses. As just pointed out, some handicapped children never become self-supporting. As a result, we find them being given custodial care, supported by relatives, or cared for by local public funds reserved for the indigent. This complete support may continue throughout life. The cost of such long-time support may well exceed many times what it would have cost to provide the best kind of preventive program.

Because of inadequate preventive measures for controlling delinquency, other individuals become antisocial. Again, society may lose more in actual money than would be needed to maintain the most nearly ideal program of prevention. The socially handicapped frequently hurt society in this way. Once a child suffers from such a handicap, he overcomes it with the greatest of difficulty. This is due to (1) the fact that attitudes and habits are stubborn and hard to change, and (2) the fact that society does not readily forgive or easily forget actions violating its accepted rules of conduct.

As a result, those youths who honestly want to about-face find the doors closed tightly against them. Church members hold aloof, businessmen do not want a former thief in their employ, and homes hesitate to accept the girl who has broken the moral code. Schools dealing with youths of this type find all kinds of difficulty when they undertake their placement. So difficult is this adjustment that great numbers of the socially handicapped are literally driven by society into further antisocial acts.

Once the socially handicapped youth becomes actively antisocial, he is a continuous expense and menace to society. For crimes committed he must be caught, convicted, and then supported at public expense; the cost of doing this over and over again represents, in the lifetime of even one criminal, a fortune. From the point of view of the good of society, the prevention of the social handicap is perhaps the most important type of preventive work we can hope to develop.

When preventive programs are ignored, moreover, children who might have made constructive contributions to society are prevented from making them. The blind person, despite his ability to do many things, cannot use his powers as effectively as he might have done. Many a brilliant boy with a real social contribution to make has not only failed to make it but has helped to lower the general social level because of antisocial acts. The need for a well- co-ordinated program of prevention is surely evident.

3. GENERAL SUGGESTIONS ON PREVENTION

Education of the Social Group.—No program of prevention will be effective without parental and community co-operation. Such co-operation can be had only when parents and other members of the community realize how important the program is and how they can co-operate in putting it into effect. A realization of its importance will come as soon as parents know how frequently children of school age suffer from these handicaps and how great that suffering is.

The community must realize also how much handicapped children cost. The cost is there, regardless of whether special education is provided or not; it is ultimately much greater when no such education is given. Parents and the community need all the facts we have to offer, if they are to co-operate fully.

The community must understand more clearly the causes of various types of handicaps. The discussion of causes should be concrete, direct, and well illustrated; a differentiation must be made between the specific things for which the home, the school, and the social group must assume responsibility. Publicity must be planned with care. The schools, the department of health, and the welfare agencies of the community should unite in planning and carrying out the program. Among all the methods of insuring a reduction of handicapped children, this is without doubt basic.

State Legislation.—Better publicity will make it easier to secure the legislation needed in order to provide an adequate program of prevention. Many children are handicapped from birth, on account of improper care at the moment of their arrival in this world; legislation is needed to govern such care. Laws controlling the marriage of handicapped persons are not satisfactory. Sterilization is suggested as one means of reducing the problem, but again legislation is inadequate. If birth-control information were readily available, programs of prevention would be aided. At present, most legislation dealing with this problem is opposed to such measures.

We need additional legislation dealing with public education. School districts are too small; pupil-personnel workers are lacking; school buildings are used only 5 to 6 hours of each 24. One might continue to enumerate these needs, many of which could be met by local authorities. Without further legislation, a considerable portion of any good program of prevention will be futile.

Adequate Pupil Cumulative Records.—Among well-trained teachers who put the child first in all their thinking, the pupil's cumulative record becomes a most essential and significant implement; it gives a complete school, home, social, mental, and physical history of the child. Such a record in the hands of the teacher on the opening day of school makes possible immediate adjustments to meet the child's mental, social, and physical peculiarities. This, in turn, would make for greater satisfaction upon the part of the child and for greater success in his schoolwork. Hosts of pupils now drawn into truancy and hence into delinquency by the route of poor school adjustment could be saved the agony and despair resulting from this type of handicap by adequate records in the hands of well-trained teachers.

Child Accounting.—In addition to the intimate personal record of each pupil, just described, the superintendent's office should maintain a cumulative census card for each child within the district from birth until the age of eighteen—possibly, twenty-one—years. Such a record kept up to date gives the community an exact accounting of every child. Then children of school age cannot so easily play truant; when one of them begins to do so, his reasons for it can be ascertained and steps can be taken to remove the causes. Such a record will make it difficult for parents to deprive their children of education by putting them to work; it will bring to the attention of proper authorities children with abnormalities which, if uncared for, will make permanent cripples of them; it will help to uncover potential blind, deaf, and tubercular children; and it will prevent parents from hiding away the mental defective, thus depriving him of any chance for mental development.

4. PREVENTING THE SOCIAL HANDICAP

A Program of Individual Study.—A program of individual study is of unusual importance if social handicaps are to be prevented. Attitudes, training, personal experiences, ambitions, deep-seated desires, and one's basic, original nature play dominant roles in determining the child's reactions to social situations. Stealing is due to varied and sundry conditions; a specific act is likely to be due to a combination, in varying degrees, of several or even of a great many conditions; until the specific situations that lead to stealing can be determined, little can be done to prevent the development of more serious difficulties. Such study of all school children will make possible the prevention of many of the first steps toward truancy and delinquency.

There are various agencies now provided by the public schools which tend to make individual study possible; at present, they are provided neither generally enough nor adequately. Attendance officers tend to overemphasize the legal aspects of their job and to ignore all problem cases who are not non-attenders. Visiting teachers and home visitors are meeting the problems of all children more squarely, but there are too few of them. Some teachers do such effective visiting service that they undoubtedly prevent much delinquency, but too few of them have time to devote to this work.

The services of psychologists and psychiatrists are needed if a correct picture of the child's abilities, aptitudes, capacities, and motivating urges is to be obtained. If a child has real mechanical ability and no interest in academic studies, he is on the highway to delinquency when he is forced to master academic subjects that are clearly beyond his ability. The schools need expert psychological service if these facts are to be known.

Most schools now provide school physicians, dentists, and nurses. Excellent work is being done. Too frequently such services are not supervised by the public schools. All too often, facts concerning the child are merely recorded in the office of the doctor or the nurse; the teacher may have no access to these facts, and the needed follow-up to improve the child's ailment is ignored. We are discovering many children who fail in school and come to dislike school, with all the resulting possibilities of becoming delinquent, whose failure is caused by defective vision, defective hearing, or poor physical condition. Health services need to be revitalized in terms of correcting quickly all remediable physical defects.

School counseling is being developed. It takes into account all the data unearthed by pupil-personnel agencies, adds school data collected from teachers and pupils, and helps the child to determine a general life program that he will enjoy. This program will include not alone his educational and vocational activities, but his social, leisure-time, physical, aesthetic, and civic activities. Such counseling as is provided, at present, is extremely limited, both in reference to the number of pupils reached and the scope of the service provided.

Service of this kind, when well developed, ought to prevent much of our present truancy and delinquency.[1]

Parents Retaught.—Data available show a close relation between home conditions and truancy and delinquency. Included in home conditions are (1) the relation of parents to one another, (2) the relation of parents to the child, (3) the manner of "handling" the child at home, (4) the physical conditions under which the child lives, (5) the amount and kind of food provided, and (6) in general, the whole attitude of the parents toward the child. A fieldworker who makes a happy home contact and who wins the confidence of that home is perhaps the most effective implement that can be provided for reteaching the parents. Many places have organized classes in adult education for the study of problems faced by parents in dealing with children of different ages. The important thing to remember is that some method of re-educating parents is necessary if a program of preventing social handicaps is to be most effective.

Supervision of Pupil Management.—The supervision suggested here is not different from what is now provided in good school systems; it would add supervision of the management of pupils to what we have at present. Some teachers have no disciplinary problems and no cases of truancy; their pupils like them and like their classwork. These children go to other teachers, and immediately the principal's office has numbers of these previously well-behaved youths reported to it for sundry and numerous offenses.

I know a high-school teacher who handles her pupils so well that she never has had to report to the principal even the youths who are being constantly reported by other teachers. She knows her pupils; she studies the office record; she visits the home; and she confers with the children themselves. She is vitally interested in the interests of these youths; they feel that interest; they think of her as a personal friend. She finds many ways of helping them to meet and overcome difficult problems. She has ceased to be "Miss Smith, the math teacher"; she is one of the group and is so accepted.

If principals would give more attention to the way teachers manage pupils and would help them to do a better job of managing, just as they help them to improve in methods of instruction, the public schools would absorb and manage satisfactorily a great many pupils who are now being turned over to the attendance officer, the juvenile court, the parental school, or the state industrial school, for salvaging. Principals need to help teachers think of ways of managing human

---

[1] For a description of the proper organization for such services, see pages 463–473.

beings wherein authority is laid aside and wherein the children respond to inner instead of outer compulsions.

Administrative Adjustments.—Administrative officials must make certain changes if the teacher is to care for individual differences among her pupils. First, many types of schoolwork must be added to the academic curriculum of the traditional school. The broadening of this curricular base must include more than just providing a variety of courses, such as (1) academic, (2) scientific, (3) commercial, and (4) industrial, wherein basic academic subjects are still an essential part of all four courses and wherein youths with low academic ability are not wanted.

There should be courses of a practical nature that will make it possible for boys and girls to learn to do better those things they will likely be doing after they have left school. This will make necessary not only special courses in automobile mechanics, woodwork, foundry, metalwork, painting, electricity, plumbing, commercial work, cooking, dressmaking, millinery, and home management, but it will involve a complete revamping of course materials in present-day academic subjects. History, literature, mathematics, civics, geography, biology, and physiology need to be revised entirely for those of low academic ability; logical organization must be dropped and subject matter used in dealing simply and directly with vital problems of daily living. In addition, data dealing with (1) baby care, (2) personal hygiene and health, (3) cosmetics, (4) sex hygiene, (5) child psychology and management, and (6) household financing should be added to the school curriculum.

Such a program of studies is needed if we are to accept a responsibility for educating 100 per cent of our children, instead of educating only those able to digest the academic diet usually placed before them. Until this is done, we shall continue to have great numbers of truants and delinquents. Boys and girls of spirit will not sit by patiently for 8 to 12 years doing work in which they have no interest, for which they see no reason, and for which they have no talent.

If a revised curricular program such as that suggested is to be put into operation, steps will have to be taken to form larger school units in both rural and city school districts. Aside from tradition and the immediate costs of a revised building program, there is no reason why large cities should not form these larger school units. In the rural and village school districts, however, three steps at least will have to be taken first. (1) The construction of adequate hard roads will have to be completed. (2) Transportation of pupils will have to be provided. (3) District control as we have known it for decades will have to give place to at least county control. With state control, school districts could be formed, upon the basis of state-wide surveys, large enough to make possible a wide curricular school offering.

One objection to the large elementary school district is the fact that small children, five, six, seven, and eight years of age, have to travel too far. The objection is a valid one. This suggests the possibility of a third administrative adjustment. We have at present the 8-4, the 6-6, the 6-3-3 and other forms of school organization. None of these is sacred, as their multiplicity shows. The suggestion is made, therefore, that our schools be organized on a 3-6-3 basis. This would permit small primary units near the homes of the pupils; it would allow senior high schools to operate as at present; and it would permit the organization of large middle schools, or grammar schools. This would permit, from grade 4 up, an adjustment of school-work to meet the needs of individual pupils through the provision of the proposed enriched curricular program. Since we have very little truancy and delinquency before the ages of nine or ten, there is no need for so great a variety of courses at the primary level as from grade 4 up.

Even when the three preceding administrative changes have been made, we may find that it is too expensive to provide all the new courses that will be needed in each of the large middle schools. It is suggested, therefore, that certain of these schools become centers for certain types of work and that youths interested in or needing such work be transported to the appropriate centers. Much of this new work, such as sex hygiene, personal hygiene, household financing, cooking, and certain shopwork could be given in all these middle schools. Courses of special interest that are needed by a relatively small per cent of the student group would be provided in the centers.

A fifth suggestion demands the inclusion of an adequate placement division for those youths who have to go to work as soon as the law permits or who go to work upon the completion of the various special programs of training provided for the nonacademically minded. These youths need work if they are to stay out of trouble; their limited academic schooling handicaps them in getting a job; their youth, inexperience, and general inadequacy to face and overcome general social problems demand the constant supervision that such a place-ment division could give during the period while the youth is adjusting to the new work program.

If minor delinquencies are to be cured, a sixth suggestion should receive most serious consideration. Many large cities have provided parental schools where boys and girls who are delinquent, but who are not vicious, are housed and educated. Many of these youths are unfortunate. Home conditions are vicious; understanding, not punishment, is what is needed. Such parental schools might save thousands of dollars of expense later and, in addition, present society with members able to make a real contribution of their own to the social group.

Greater Utilization of School Plant.—Not enough thought has been given by school people to the possibility of reducing truancy and delinquency through a greater utilization of the school building and its equipment. The close relation between delinquency and the out-of-school environment of the child has been noted.[1] Is it not possible for the school to revolutionize that environment if it chooses? Some of our larger elementary city schools and most of our secondary city schools are equipped with shops, libraries, auditoriums, playrooms, playgrounds, and even swimming pools. These facilities are available for school children 6 hours daily. During that time they have one type of environment; in the poorer city districts, they have an entirely different environment for the remaining 18 hours of the day.

At a minimum cost, these children could have the better environment for a much longer period daily. The library could be kept open each evening; interclass games might be arranged in the gymnasium; the swimming pool could be in constant use; the auditorium could be used for amateur plays; and the shops could be made available. Such an extension in the use of the school's facilities will, as we have already seen,[2] break up the night gang life of the streets, provide excellent supervision of the youths of the district, and materially reduce the problem of delinquency.

Summer Playgrounds.—The utilization of the school plant is only partially cared for if its use during vacation periods is ignored. Some day society will recognize that here are public facilities that lie idle, a dead loss to the community, for 3 to 4 months each year. Many of these schools have commodious playgrounds well equipped. Too frequently, despite a great need for play space, the grounds are not used during vacation periods. The school board should seek to facilitate the development of the summer playgrounds; making available the schools' playgrounds and equipment would be one way of doing so. This would, undoubtedly, be a big factor in the prevention of delinquency.

Sterilization.—Even a brief discussion of the prevention of delinquency cannot be abandoned without calling attention to steriliza-

[1] For causes of delinquency, see pp. 99–102.
[2] See pp. 24–25.

tion proposals. Few, if any, believe that delinquency is inherited. A child is not born a thief, a sex pervert, or a liar; these are learned responses. There are, however, hereditary traits that seem to facilitate the development of situations that aid materially in bringing about these unsocial responses.

Studies of the causes of delinquency suggest that among the most important are (1) defective home discipline, (2) general emotional instability, (3) morbid emotional conditions, and (4) a family history of vice and crime. Since these seem to rest upon traits that are hereditary, some insist that the habitual criminal, the sex pervert, and the habitual delinquent should be sterilized.[1]

5. PREVENTING THE PHYSICAL HANDICAP[2]

Four agencies have specific responsibilities for the prevention of physical defects. This discussion will merely enumerate the responsibilities of each of the agencies if physical handicaps are to be materially reduced. These suggestions will duplicate many of the recommendations made in earlier chapters; here they are reorganized upon the basis of agencies responsible and are listed with a minimum of discussion.

The Home's Responsibility.—Parents should become informed concerning the dangers of infectious diseases. Measles, mumps, whooping cough, influenza, colds, catarrh, abscesses of the ear, granulated eyelids, and light cases of scarlet fever are too frequently accepted as the inescapable lot of childhood; they are considered to be annoyances that must be endured. Seldom are they recognized as childhood plagues, which may deprive children of sight, hearing, and general good health.

Parents need to accept proper standards of cleanliness. The absence of screens, the collections of filth both within and without the home, the absence of baths, and the utter lack of the simplest principles of personal hygiene result in disease, which may bring death or permanent physical handicaps that will destroy the child's chances of becoming a capable or even a self-respecting member of society.

Parents need to recognize the dangers attending improper care of the mother, both at the time of confinement and during the months

---

[1] A more extended discussion will be given of this problem on pp. 489–494.

[2] Somewhat detailed discussions of prevention as related to specific types of physical handicap are to be found on the following pages: cripples, pp. 144–147; those with defective vision, pp. 220–225; the deaf, pp. 265–267; the hard of hearing, pp. 284–285; the speech defective, pp. 307–308; and the delicate, pp. 333–334. This discussion attempts to give general suggestions, covering all types of physical handicap, to four separate agencies.

immediately preceding confinement—a period that can be and should be the happiest of the prospective mother's life. This can be made possible by proper care and by an understanding home.

These three suggestions point to specific things that the home can do. (1) Illness should be reported immediately to the family physician. (2) The common cold and catarrhal conditions should be fought rigorously. (3) Infectious diseases should have the best of care until the physician releases the case; too many well-informed parents fail utterly at this point. (4) Homes should be well screened; debris should be removed from the home and premises; and facilities for regular washing and bathing must be provided. (5) Great care should be exercised in the feeding of the children, with careful attention to amount, kind, quality, and preparation of food.

The School's Responsibility.—The school must provide a trained staff; regular teachers must be trained if they are to aid in preventing physical handicaps. They should contact daily every child in school. They should help in detecting eye defects, ear defects, and general physical weakness; they should help children in the lower grades to overcome speech difficulties before bad speech habits are too firmly fixed.

School officials, such as physicians, dentists, oculists, otologists, and school nurses, have more direct opportunities to help in the prevention of physical defects. Two difficulties obstruct the rendering of the most effective service. (1) The services are often controlled and supervised by health departments instead of by boards of education. (2) Too few are available. Dentists, oculists, and otologists, particularly, are very scarce.

The following suggestions represent specific things that the technical staff, in co-operation with other school officials, may do in a program of prevention.

1. Each child should be given an annual physical examination.

2. Records of the examination should be kept.

3. A program of remedial work should be initiated, following the examination.

4. If children have no family physician, the school staff should correct defects discovered.

5. Teachers, under the supervision of the school nurse, should check the physical condition of the children daily; suspicious cases should be sent to the nurse.

6. If the child is ill and the family cannot afford proper attention, the school physician should attend the case.

7. Problems of health and hygiene should be studied by all pupils; the courses should be more practical than many of those now provided.

It may be found advisable to have a 1-hour course required throughout 2 or 3 years of the secondary school, rather than a semester course of 4 or 5 hours.

8. If the preventive program is to be effective, needed medical attention must be given to all children from birth. This will demand a complete and continuous registration of all children from birth.

9. The school building should be planned so that various health problems can be met adequately and effectively; this would demand (a) proper lighting, (b) automatic heat control, (c) efficient ventilation, (d) adequate toilet and bathing facilities, (e) provision for needed feeding, and (f) office space for the medical and nursing staff.

10. A practical course in safety education should be provided. It could be built about projects in which data concerning accidents would be gathered and discussed. It could make possible the participation of members of the group in plans designed to prevent accidents.

The Responsibility of Physicians and Nurses.—Physicians and nurses have certain duties of law enforcement. They should co-operate in a humane enforcement of quarantine legislation; where there are laws governing vaccinations, they should help to enforce them; where there is no legislation, they should encourage the practice.

They have an educational responsibility. Every family called upon presents an opportunity. The method will depend upon circumstances. In certain cases, only indirectly will suggestions be presented; in others, a frontal attack on the problem should be made. The nurses have a great opportunity, inasmuch as they are freer from the criticism of trying to sell their own services. Since the physician and the nurse have whatever facts are available with reference to causes of physical handicaps and means of preventing them, they must assume a responsibility for educating the public.

The attitude taken by the physician with reference to cases he is called upon to care for is an excellent means of educating the public. If he takes seriously his diagnosis of the "ordinary" cold, if he checks the slightest fever for symptoms that might indicate infantile paralysis or meningitis, he is educating parents in the most effective way possible. If he pauses long enough to answer their interested questions in simple nontechnical language, the educational program is carried a step further.

Society's Responsibility.—Legislation is needed in an effort to prevent physical handicaps. (1) Schools should be compelled to meet building standards respecting pupil health. (2) Boards of education should be required to provide medical and nursing service. (3)

State support necessary to help districts comply with the requirements should be provided. (4) Rigid laws should be passed for food, milk, and meat inspection. (5) Freedom from the restrictions of present legislation on birth control should be granted. (6) Enforcible quarantine and vaccination legislation is needed. (7) The legalization of a sensible sterilization program should be sought. (8) State clinical service, to supplement community efforts, should be provided, so that no child need suffer from lack of medical attention.

The community, too, has responsibilities. Some local agency, possibly the schools, should take the lead in bringing together all other local agencies, such as the health department, the social service department, the safety department, and possibly the courts, in an effort to devise ways and means of reducing physical handicaps. This organized group could (1) sponsor an educational program to secure co-operation from the public, (2) assist in the establishment of a local health clinic, (3) provide the setup necessary for giving prenatal care to all expectant mothers, (4) make possible hospital care for all pregnancy cases, and (5) make plans for insuring medical care for all babies during the first 6 years following birth.

6. PREVENTING THE MENTAL HANDICAP

The problem of preventing social and physical handicaps demands that parents, the schools, and society take specific action, and children already born can be so protected that they need not suffer from these handicaps; prevention of the mental handicap generally must not wait until the child is born. In this latter problem heredity is an all-important factor.[1] The former problem looks to the improvement of the environment of the child; the latter emphasizes the restriction of the bearing of children to good, sound stock.

Goddard's Point of View.—Writing in 1914,[2] Goddard said that 2 per cent of the average school population were feeble-minded; revising his report in 1923, he stated that this percentage was approximately correct and presented considerable supporting evidence. He said that his studies in Vineland showed that 65 per cent of the feeble-minded in that institution had feeble-minded ancestry; this percentage, he said, was corroborated by Tredgold, who even accepted 80 to 90 as being the correct percentage.[3] Goddard's figure would, therefore, seem to be conservative.

---

[1] For a discussion of causes, see pp. 380–381.

[2] HENRY H. GODDARD, *School Training of Defective Children*, pp. 43–44, World Book Company, Yonkers-on-Hudson, New York, 1923.

[3] *Ibid.*, p. 51.

Discussing the problem of feeble-mindedness in the New York City schools, Goddard estimated that there were 15,000 feeble-minded children in the city. Applying the above per cents to this number, he said, "We find that from 10,000 to 12,000 or 13,000 of these children will, when they grow up and marry, produce defective children like themselves. It has further been shown that they produce children in large numbers, increasing at twice the rate of the general population."[1]

Realizing the size of the problem, Goddard suggested two methods of reducing it. One plan was to segregate the feeble-minded so that they could not become parents. He feared, however, that parents would never give their consent to being thus separated from their children. The second plan was sterilization. This too, he said, was not practical at that time because of parental objections.

He concluded that we must wait for more data concerning the number of feeble-minded children, what happens to them when they leave the special classes, and what the aftereffects of modern sterilization methods are. With this new body of data, he said,

. . . . it will not be difficult to take action looking toward the solution of the problem, not only for securing efficient and far-reaching laws for the sterilization of the unfit in a much more helpful way than any of the laws now in force, but also for showing parents that segregation in institutions is the wisest thing that can be done for their children, unless they are willing to have them sterilized, if that shall have proved a wise procedure.[2]

In the meantime, Goddard believes, institutions should be made so attractive that parents will be glad to place their feeble-minded children in them. Where this fails, these children must be trained to become just as good citizens as possible. Goddard continues,

If we can train these children so that they have some little skill, even though in only one activity, and not sufficient to enable them to earn a living, they have an occupation; this will make them happy and tend to keep them out of mischief and to make them as little a burden upon society as possible.[3]

Wallin's Point of View.—In an excellent discussion of prevention, Wallin states and defends four theses.[4]

1. Society should prevent degenerate matings. He quotes authorities who claim that 66 to 80 per cent of feeble-mindedness is due to heredity. He points out at great length the difficulties of so diagnos-

---

[1] *Ibid.*, p. 51.
[2] *Ibid.*, p. 54.
[3] *Ibid.*, p. 56.
[4] J. E. WALLACE WALLIN, *Problems of Subnormality*, pp. 417–462, World Book Company, Yonkers-on-Hudson, New York, 1921.

ing cases as to be sure they are not fitted for mating. The real problem lies in the diagnosis of those cases in the "twilight" zone between normality and feeble-mindedness. These are the individuals who are most numerous in number and who are far more likely to procreate than are the easily recognized feeble-minded. Despite this difficulty, he insists, "we should not forget that the most important factor, or at least one of the most important factors, in eugenical hygiene is the prevention of the propagation of inherently, that is, hereditarily, weakened, defective, and degenerate strains."[1]

2. "Society should adopt measures to prevent the syphilization of the unborn child."[2] He believes that "parental syphilis is one of the causes of feeble-mindedness."[2] He considers it of sufficient importance to recommend that laws be passed "requiring the registration of infected persons, together with the prohibition of marriage or intercourse between such persons until they are cured."[3] If this does not work, he recommends that persons who insist on miscellaneous sexual intercourse be forced to use prophylactics. He says, "Is not the enforced use of venereal prophylactics better than the wholesale slaughter of potentially robust innocents and the possible pollution of the race stream?"[3]

3. The alcoholization of parents and of the embryonic and fetal life imperils the bringing into the world of children who are sound mentally and physically. He admits at the start that data are "not conclusive." He concludes, however, that "children conceived in drunkenness frequently come into the world with diminished powers of mental and physical development . . . . ;" that "sometimes parental alcoholism slays the progeny outright; sometimes it dooms it to temporary or lifelong invalidism, inefficiency, dependency, and mental and moral bankruptcy."[4] "We must," he says, "make it impossible for persons to breed who suffer from transmissible defects, whatever the cause of the defects may be."[4]

4. "From the standpoint of the eugenic ideal," procreation should be prevented during "periods of physiological immaturity, and of involution . . . . ;"[4] likewise, too numerous and unwilling conceptions should be prevented. "The public at large," he says, "has no idea of the great number of unwelcome embryos which are murdered year in and year out."[5] He concludes, "These facts suggest the query

[1] *Ibid.*, p. 438.
[2] *Ibid.*, p. 443.
[3] *Ibid.*, p. 444.
[4] *Ibid.*, p. 456.
[5] *Ibid.*, pp. 459–460.

whether it is not in the interest of social morality to instruct people in the use of harmless regulatives or to encourage the practice of sterilization, especially in the harmless forms of vasectomy and fallectomy."[1] He continues, "The compulsory sterilization of all who ought not to beget children and the optional sterilization of those who do not want children may some day become the practice of the land."[1]

Writing at a slightly later date,[2] Wallin, commenting on sterilization, said:

In spite of its great merits, society is not ready for the practice of sterilization on any effective scale. It is therefore scarcely worth while to go to the trouble of engineering a strenuous state or national campaign for the enactment of sterilization laws. Even if enacted, there is little likelihood that they will be enforced. Until public sentiment undergoes a radical change, the practice will have to be confined to voluntary applicants.[3]

He reached the general conclusion that "in spite of all its hampering limitations, segregation is probably the most feasible and the least objectionable means at present available for attempting to check the increase of defective stocks."[3]

Woodrow's Point of View.—"The proper solution of the great problem of the feeble-minded," says Woodrow, "remains to be determined." He points out that some authorities are convinced that state and other institutions for the feeble-minded should be so increased that the entire feeble-minded population could be cared for. "This would mean," he says, "that the existing facilities would have to be many times increased, for only a small fraction of the feeble-minded persons in the country, certainly not over a fifth, are now in institutions."[4]

He shows that other writers propose permanent custody of all feeble-minded persons except those who have been sterilized. Such a plan, he thinks, would show great improvement within a few generations. He believes, however, that

For the present, we must admit that the idea of putting all feeble-minded children under the control of institutions, unless they are sterilized, is an idle dream. The public has not yet been educated to the point of taking the drastic measures that are necessary to cope properly with the problem. . . . Consequently, the immediately urgent thing, pending such education of the public, is to provide more

---

[1] *Ibid.*, p. 461.

[2] J. E. WALLACE WALLIN, *The Education of Handicapped Children*, pp. 308–320, Houghton Mifflin Company, Boston, 1924.

[3] *Ibid.*, p. 319.

[4] HERBERT WOODROW, *Brightness and Dullness in Children*, pp. 272–273, J. B. Lippincott Company, Philadelphia, 1923.

thoroughly than at present for the after-care of the pupils who leave the ungraded classes of the public schools.[1]

General Conclusions.—It is interesting to note how these three men in general agree that heredity is an important factor in feeble-mindedness; that segregation and sterilization are steps which ought to be taken; that the public would not at the time they were writing permit the effective enforcement of such a policy; and finally, that we must, regardless of cost, take care of the feeble-minded who are born and give them all the training, care, and happiness possible.

It has been nearly two decades since the reports of Goddard, Wallin, and Woodrow. Great changes have taken place during these years. We have passed through a period of what seemed at the time to be unparalleled prosperity. Money was no object. Millions were put into palatial school buildings; other millions were spent on equipment. Suggestions regarding the spending of millions, if necessary, to take proper care of the feeble-minded would not have been seriously questioned.

It is not surprising, therefore, that Goddard, in outlining a system of taking care of and training the feeble-minded, said, "At this point the question of expense is forced upon us. There is only one answer to the question of cost. *Whatever it costs, it must be done.* This problem is as fundamental to our social wellbeing as our courts, our sewerage system, or quarantine system."[2] All would undoubtedly agree that the problem is of fundamental importance; some might suggest, however, that the time has come to emphasize the more radical methods of handling the problem.

At another point in his report, Goddard says:

The question of expense must not enter into the consideration. We have these children [the feeble-minded].[3] They can only be dealt with in one way, and we must do it, whatever the expense. We must appropriate large sums of money to care for them, in order to save larger expense in caring for them later in almshouses and prisons, to say nothing of their numerous progeny.[4]

It is possible that Goddard is correct and that society must stand by quietly and see defectives continue to reproduce their kind during this generation and in generations to come. On the other hand, it may be that the time has come when radical solutions are possible. As the education that skilled workers have been giving the feeble-

[1] *Ibid.*, p. 273.
[2] H. GODDARD, *op. cit.*, p. 63.
[3] The words in brackets are inserted by the writer.
[4] *Ibid.*, p. 64.

minded during the past two decades is evaluated in terms of social worth, as the costs of providing this education are contrasted with its results, and as the effects of this large feeble-minded group upon the larger normal and superior group are studied, it may be that society will agree that a definite program of sterilization and of segregation of the nonsterilized would be the best social procedure.

During the period of the depression and since, values have been carefully scrutinized and every social procedure has been pitilessly re-evaluated in terms of its social good. The time may have come for those who believe in taking radical steps for keeping the social blood stream pure to take the lead; perhaps they should resolutely marshal all facts available from a rich past experience in dealing with the feeble-minded and present these facts to the general public. Data are available for estimating the financial outlay necessary to care for the problem under a laissez-faire procedure of controlling propagation.

If the social group, during this period of re-evaluation, can have its attention centered upon the entire problem of dealing with defectives, it may be possible that, under the weight of intensive interest in the financial questions involved, previous prejudices will give way to common-sense methods of dealing with the problem. It may be possible for the layman, under the present-day financial urge, to see the essentials in this issue as clearly as did Goddard, Wallin, and Woodrow nearly two decades ago.

Thinking people, in these days, voluntarily refuse to bring children into the world when they are physically unfit for parenthood or when they realize that they do not have enough money to provide for a child adequately. This is frequently done by means of contraceptives or voluntary sterilization. Such procedures represent the plainest kind of common sense. Yet society allows a great group of individuals, who have neither the will to carry through a definite program of social improvement nor the mental ability to realize the social injustice that they do by reproducing their kind, to bring into the world hordes of children whom they have neither the ability nor the will to care for; and these youngsters, in turn, will not have such abilities, even after being cared for and educated at great expense by the social group. So their lives proceed in a vicious circle.

We would do well to consider seriously a program of education with the end in view of informing the social group of the advantages of and the reasons for compulsory sterilization of confirmed criminals, vicious delinquents, those physically unfit for propagation, epileptics, the insane, and the feeble-minded.

7. SUMMARY

Society is much more willing to provide for the immediate and observable needs of children than to spend money on programs of prevention, which would ultimately mean far more to society and to our children; distant values seem hard to visualize.

There are several reasons why far more attention should be given to programs of prevention. (1) The costs of educating the handicapped are great. (2) The handicapped individual undergoes untold suffering. (3) Society suffers the loss of contributions which the handicapped might have made had he been normal. (4) Society gives custodial care for life to many of the handicapped. (5) They frequently become antisocial and thus are a greater expense to society.

General suggestions for prevention are (1) education of the social group with regard to the problem, (2) state legislation that will make possible preventive measures, (3) teachers trained to combat these handicaps, (4) pupil records which will make available to teachers facts about their pupils, and (5) a system of accounting for every child from birth until he is eighteen or twenty-one years of age.

Specific suggestions for preventing the social handicap involve (1) a program of individual study of children, (2) a reorganization of various pupil-personnel activities, (3) a program of reteaching parents in which child management will be emphasized, (4) the supervision of pupil management, (5) adjustments relative to curricular extensions, redistricting, larger administrative units, special centers, and placement service, (6) a greater utilization of the school plant, (7) the utilization of school playgrounds and equipment for summer play, and (8) a sensible sterilization program.

Agencies responsible for preventing physical handicaps are (1) the home, (2) the school, (3) physicians and nurses, and (4) society itself. Important procedures involve: (1) educating the community, (2) providing for adequate medical care, (3) recognizing the dangers of infectious disease, (4) launching a campaign for personal and community cleanliness, (5) providing prenatal and postnatal care for mother and child, and (6) the establishment of community clinics.

Many authorities recognize the need for having the mentally handicapped either segregated or sterilized; all the authorities recognize the difficulties. Laws preventing the marriage of defectives and sexual intercourse for those with venereal diseases have been proposed. Birth control measures have been urged. Sterilization and segregation would seem sensible procedures, and states should immediately take the steps needed to secure the passage of such legislation.

Problems and Questions for Discussion

1. Do you consider it difficult to interest people in a program designed to prevent handicapped children? What are your reasons for the answer you make?

2. Should more money be spent on measures planned to prevent handicaps among children? Why?

3. What is meant by "education of the social group" as a means of prevention? Illustrate.

4. What state legislation is needed in order to prevent more effectively the increase of handicapped children?

5. Can regular teachers help to prevent handicaps among children? If not, why not? If so, just how? If so, what specific training would be needed to enable them to do this?

6. Outline in some detail how you would go about making an individual study of a problem child. What difficulties do you face in making such a study?

7. Of all the specific methods listed as means of reducing the social handicap, which do you think would be the most effective? Why are they so effective? Have you evidence of their effectiveness?

8. Which has the greatest responsibility for preventing physical handicaps, the home, the school, the medical profession, or society? Defend your answer with any evidence you can discover.

9. Should society attempt to segregate all of its mentally handicapped children (feeble-minded)? State why?

10. Is society justified in demanding the sterilization of all of its feeble-minded? Why?

11. What other methods, if any, do you think should be used in order to reduce feeble-mindedness? Give your reasons.

Selected Bibliography

DAVIES, STANLEY POWELL. *Social Control of the Mentally Deficient.* The Thomas Y. Crowell Company, New York, 1930. 389 pp.

Consideration is given to sterilization, segregation, training, and community supervision.

GODDARD, HENRY H. *School Training of Defective Children.* World Book Company, Yonkers-on-Hudson, New York, 1923. 97 pp.

Describes conditions in New York City respecting defective children; suggests a program for "ungraded" classes; and discusses the importance of the problem and its solution.

WALLIN, J. E. WALLACE. *The Education of Handicapped Children,* pp. 306-329. Houghton Mifflin Company, Boston, 1924.

Gives a fine discussion of prevention as related to mental deficiency; enumerates various proposals for eliminating the mentally unfit and comments on each; discusses methods of support, control, and training now in existence; and describes the "essential requirements of a modern residential institution and colony for defectives."

WALLIN, J. E. WALLACE. *Problems of Subnormality,* pp. 382-462. World Book Company, Yonkers-on-Hudson, New York, 1921.

Presents a discussion of state provisions for defective children and of problems of preventing mental defects from multiplying so rapidly.

White House Conference. *Communicable Disease Control*, pp. 93–214.   The Century Co., New York, 1931.

Offers a discussion of methods which are recommended for controlling various diseases of children; terms are defined; some 52 diseases are listed and such items as source of infection, manner of transmitting, period of incubation, periods of communicability, and ways of controlling each are discussed briefly.

White House Conference. *Special Education: The Handicapped and the Gifted.* The Century Co., New York, 1931.   604 pp.

Contains, throughout, suggestions on prevention; see particularly the chapter on Organization, Administration, and Supervision, pp. 583–593.

WOODROW, HERBERT. *Brightness and Lullness in Children*, pp. 254–274.   J. B. Lippincott Company, Philadelphia, 1923.

Considers "the relation of education to heredity and growth," the necessity of special education for bright and dull children, methods of educating them, and ways of ultimately caring for the feeble-minded.

CHAPTER XXXIII

A STATE PROGRAM FOR EDUCATING EXCEPTIONAL CHILDREN

Program making may be a fad, but progress in education would be greater if more of it were done. Too frequently, because immediate needs are seen, action is taken without any thought of a long-time program. Buildings are built which would not have been built, equipment is purchased which would not have been purchased, and changes are made in courses of study which would never have been made, if a long-time program had been in operation. Such a program is not fixed with respect to detail. It will establish certain principles in the light of which the specifics of the program will be accepted or rejected; it will project into the future a program of action—a program to be carried out as time and money permit, with any changes that new data show to be necessary. If special education is to be approved and accepted as a responsibility of public education, the formulation of such a program for educating exceptional children would seem to be essential.

1. PRINCIPLES GOVERNING THE STATE PROGRAM

1. Of primary importance in the working out of a special education program is the conception that each child should be given the same opportunity to develop his capacities as is any other child. Despite lip service to this principle, we have failed to put it into operation. Laws have exempted handicapped children from attending school, instead of asking local authorities to provide the special schooling needed. Common-sense measures for preventing handicaps have been ignored, and thus hosts of children have lost capacities that they originally possessed. A curricular program for the academically minded is still deified, and little attention is given to the development of the unique capacities of those who are socially, physically, and mechanically minded; even when special education is given, the aid provided is so restricted that they fail to have an equal opportunity to develop. This principle needs to be given far more attention than it has been given in the past in making plans for special education.

2. Education is not a local but a state function. Here again, despite lip service to the contrary, action taken seems to assume that

498

it is local. Instead of mandatory legislation governing special education, a great amount of it is permissive; despite the importance of special education, the local district is free to do as it pleases with respect to providing it. Instead of providing state supervision and encouragement, most states give local districts no help in organizing and developing their special schools and classes. Instead of giving financial aid upon the basis of need and of meeting state requirements, the state is giving it as a subsidy to encourage the community to provide such schooling.

3. A decision for or against a given procedure should be in terms of its possible effect upon the child. This means a child-centered program. If evidence indicates that plan A is most beneficial, it should be accepted in preference to plan B, in spite of the fact that the latter seems more logical and consistent. When this principle operates, no decision respecting program planning will be made without consideration of its possible effect upon children. Many of the other principles are corollaries of this one, in that if this one actually operates, many of the others are automatically complied with.

4. Other factors being equal, an effort should be made to maintain the home; of all social institutions, the home is, perhaps, the most important. The individual needs sympathetic companionship; the home composed of those united by blood ties is well-adapted to meet this need. There may be a great amount of love and companionship even in the hovel, as those who know the poor and unfortunate can testify. Perhaps no greater crimes have been committed in the name of "social welfare" than the ripping asunder of the lives of loved ones who are unfortunate in being deprived of this world's goods. No program of caring for and educating handicapped youths will be satisfactory if it ignores this principle.

5. The program must make prevention its lodestar. It is a wonderful service to educate little crippled children, but it is most disheartening to see, year after year, new crops of cripples brought for instruction who need never have been crippled if proper precautionary measures had been put into operation. A society that ignores measures which might have prevented a large share of these crippling conditions is wantonly cruel, regardless of any program of special education for crippled children.

2. A SYSTEM OF ACCOUNTING

If all children are to be given an equal educational opportunity, we must know that they exist. This principle is violated if children remain undiscovered and thus uncared for and uneducated. Ayres[1] presented evidence that the maintenance of an accurate census of school children would uncover enough additional youths of census age so that the increased revenues from the state would more than maintain the census. Denver,[2] upon the installation of its continuous census, discovered over 12,000 youths of census age who had been lost to the schools previously. Recent county and state surveys of crippled children show that many cripples are discovered who were unknown to local county and city school officials.

These situations point clearly to the need of a more accurate system of accounting for the youths of the various communities of our state. The state department of education should make provisions upon a state-wide basis for the maintenance of a continuous census[3] in each local school district of the state. This census should begin at birth and be maintained until the pupil is eighteen or possibly even twenty-one years of age; such a census should record all exceptional children, and the nature of the handicap or the ability should be indicated. The state department would maintain a file of all exceptional children; constant reports from local school districts would serve to keep this file up to date. Each district would be held responsible for providing for the education of all such children.

3. ORGANIZATION DUTIES

Education of the Public.—The adoption of a program for educating handicapped children will be impossible as long as the public is ignorant of the physical, educational, moral, and spiritual needs of these youths. The only organization capable of educating the public on a state-wide basis is the state department of education. This function logically belongs to the state.

The public needs to be informed regarding (1) the size of the problem, (2) what is being done elsewhere, (3) what success is being attained in educating these groups, (4) how extensively they become self-supporting, (5) how much the program will cost, (6) the reasons for greater costs, and (7) what are likely to be the costs of refusing to provide special education.

Local Surveys.—Each local community must be convinced that the program is actually applicable to it. The best way of accomplish-

---

[1] LEONARD P. AYRES, *Child Accounting in the Public Schools*, pp. 22–26, 65, The Survey Committee of the Cleveland Foundation, Cleveland, 1915.

[2] *Organization and Work of the Department of Census and Attendance*, Monograph, p. 11, Denver, 1930.

[3] ARCH O. HECK, *Administration of Pupil Personnel*, pp. 143–183, "A Discussion of Proposed Plans," Ginn and Company, 1929.

ing this is to make a local survey.   If a continuous census is already maintained, all needed data are readily available.   If such a census is not available,[1] the survey becomes much more difficult.   Despite the difficulties, it must be made if the community is to provide for its handicapped and its gifted.   The state office is in a position to make the investigation and secure the facts required.

Co-ordinating the Activities of All Local Agencies.—The survey will require the co-operation of all local agencies.   They include (1) the schools, (2) the health department, (3) the social welfare department, (4) the police department, (5) the churches, (6) the Y.M.C.A. and Y.W.C.A., (7) the relief agencies, and the like.   These can assist in the house-to-house canvass, secure complete publicity regarding the survey, and help to make public all findings.   The state office is in a strategic position to secure the co-operation of all such groups, whereas the local school superintendent might have some trouble in securing complete co-operation from so many co-ordinate agencies.

Other Specific Duties.—Before classes and schools begin to function, the state must set up the regulations.   These relate to (1) size of class, (2) type of child admitted, (3) kind of educational program, (4) qualifications and training of teachers, (5) equipment, (6) health service, (7) lighting facilities, (8) construction of buildings, and the like.

The state must assume the responsibility for setting standards; it must then provide whatever funds are necessary, over and above what the community can afford, to put these standards into effect.

4. SUPERVISORY DUTIES

Supervision of Instruction.—The most obvious of its supervisory duties is that of improving teaching within the special schools and classes.   Frequently, at present, this is done superficially by state departments.   In many cases no provision is made for such supervision.   As a result, while we find some very excellent work being done for the feeble-minded, we also find a great amount of superficiality; we find aims varying from that of a real constructive educational program to that of just busywork.   Some teachers have a clear vision of the future possibilities of these academically subnormal

---

[1] A word of warning may be appropriate.   The investigator must have real evidence that the census is up to date; the statement of local authorities to that effect is not sufficient.   Recent county studies clearly indicate that many local authorities think they have a complete and accurate census when, in reality, it is anything but that.

children; others are apostles of doom and see no future for such children. Clearly, if the children are to benefit most, and if the work done is to be of a caliber that will continue to convince the public that it ought to be provided, the state must accept its responsibility for supervising instruction in special schools and classes.

Supervision of the Curricula.—The key to the success of the special education program is the type of work offered. This is particularly true for children of low and high I.Q. Segregation of these groups and no changes in their program of studies will accomplish but little; a reorganization of all curricular material is needed. Children of low I.Q. need reading, history, literature, civics, and geography. It must, however, be a different civics and a different literature; the abstraction must be made concrete; theory must give way to interesting stories that will motivate. Probably no greater problem faces those interested in educating the subnormal; local workers need the help of a live state department to assist them in solving it.

Other Supervisory Duties.—An effective way to supervise is to plan regional conferences for various groups of workers in special education; if the number of workers is not great, these conferences may even be state-wide. Such conferences make it possible for workers to confer with respect to the problems they must deal with; they are able to learn what is done elsewhere and to discuss with workers from other districts the advisability of various proposals. Such conferences, held annually or even quarterly, can become a most effective method of supervising the state's special education program.

Local teachers should be permitted to visit and see for themselves what is being done outside their own area. Only the state office can effectively direct this visiting; it knows where excellent, mediocre, and poor work is being done. The visits must be planned; a half dozen or more workers may visit a certain city or school on the same day; such a day of visiting should be concluded with a group conference, with some one of the conferees acting as chairman and with the teachers visited sitting in on the conference.

So much new material is being published with respect to the various fields that every worker should be on the outlook for it. The opportunities for doing this in county and small city districts are meager. They have not the facilities for discovering good material, nor the money to buy it if it is discovered. The state department should (1) compile lists of such printed material, (2) mimeograph and mail them to all workers in the state, and (3) establish a circulating professional library, which would contain the best of the most recent publications.

5. ESTABLISHMENT OF CLINICS

Both medical and psychological clinics, if provided, would become most valuable aids in the state's supervisory program.   The workers in such clinics could be used by the state office for lectures and as leaders of conference groups.   The personal contact between the special teachers throughout the state and the personnel of these clinics could hardly help being a means of making the special education staff more professional.

These clinics are necessary if all children in need of special education are to be discovered.   The larger cities already have physicians and nurses who serve the public schools.   The service, all too frequently, is woefully inadequate; rural districts and small cities and villages find it difficult if not impossible to provide any such service.   It seems, therefore, that the state should assume the responsibility for furnishing clinical centers, and some of them could be of the moving type.

Hardly less important is some provision for psychological service; if this includes psychiatric help, that is quite as important.   We are beginning to realize how great an effect the emotional life of the child has upon the work he does in school.   This fact has been forced upon us more and more during the years of economic disturbance and maladjustment.   We have seen, only too plainly, the effects upon school children of the worries and economic upsets of the home.

Psychological service is needed, not only to detect the subnormal, the border-line, and the gifted child, so that classes can be organized for them, but also as a matter of prevention.   Pupils should have guidance in overcoming their emotional difficulties.   Many a potential case of truancy and delinquency is thus prevented.   Such a service is especially needed by the physically handicapped; they often are prevented from doing what they most wish to do vocationally; they are limited in their social contacts; and they are restricted in their leisure-time activities.   They require the best of help in making the necessary mental adjustments.   The larger cities provide a limited service of this type; smaller cities and rural districts usually have none. The need for it is unquestionable; the realization of that need upon the part of the public is lacking.

The state should establish at various centers psychological clinics upon which the public schools could call for aid.   In addition, the state should encourage and in time make mandatory a provision for the services of one or more psychologists in every county, city, and exempted village district within the state.   State clinics should supplement the work of the local psychologists.

6. SPECIAL SCHOOLS AND CLASSES

With the establishment of an up-to-date accounting system and with needed clinical service, the state will be able to provide the special classes needed to care for and educate all exceptional children.

Cripples.—It should be compulsory that every crippled child be provided with an education and needed physical care. One district may have a special class; another will provide a school; another may have home instruction; and still another may have some combination of these three methods.

Rural districts and small villages may send their cripples to schools or classes in other districts; if the crippled child lives too far from a center to be transported daily, the state department should arrange for his board. Cripples who have no homes or who have such bad home conditions that they should be removed from them must be cared for by the state. It should establish homes capable of housing 10 to 12 such cripples at various centers within the state and near public schools for crippled children. It does not seem advisable to maintain a huge state hospital and school to educate and care for them.

Children with Defective Vision.—Every district with enough partly blind or blind children should organize sight-saving and Braille classes. Districts with not enough such children should co-operate, under state supervision, with neighboring districts in organizing such classes. Children with defective vision who live under vicious home conditions should be cared for by the state until the home conditions are improved. If such children have no parents and no relatives with whom they can reside, they, too, should be cared for by the state. Since most states have state schools for the blind, it will be necessary to utilize these facilities. As reconstruction becomes necessary, it is recommended that smaller centers be provided for housing these children at several places within the state, the centers to be located near public schools where classes are organized for children with defective vision.

Children with Defective Hearing.—Every city and county school district should give children who are hard of hearing training in speech reading. The school otologist or the otologist associated with the state medical clinic, where such are provided, will be responsible for the selection of children who need such instruction. He will, besides, give regular teachers instruction that will enable them to co-operate in selecting hard-of-hearing children.

The deaf children shall be taught in local schools, wherever the district is large enough to warrant such a school. The state will send to these schools deaf children from the more or less isolated sections of the state where there are no special schools. Ultimately the big state institution for educating the deaf should be displaced by the establishment of homes near the various local schools within the state, to house and feed those who must be given complete state care and supervision.

Children with Defective Speech.—Much corrective work for the speech defective could be done in the kindergarten and in grades 1 and 2, if the teachers were trained for the task. The state department of education should require such training. Cities will organize speech centers in the densely populated districts, and use itinerant teachers in the outlying districts. The rural districts can use the itinerant teacher most effectively.

Delicate Children.—The White House Conference estimates that there are 6,000,000 malnourished children. This is nearly 25 per cent of the estimated elementary school enrollment. Upon this basis, any elementary school that has four first-grade rooms of pupils would need one of them for the malnourished. One authority insists that every elementary school in her city ought to have one "fresh-air" room for each school grade in the building.

These demands at first glance seem extravagant; only as careful physical checks are made upon all children do we begin to realize the justice of them. The physical deficiencies of delicate children are due to poverty, poor feeding and eating habits, and neglect of ordinary health rules. The open-air schools are noted for fresh air, rest, and good food. These children can be cared for in the regular schools by adapting rooms to provide fresh air and by supplying the needed food and rest. In the case of intolerable home conditions, the state may find it necessary to house such children in state centers established for other types of handicapped children.

Children of Low I.Q.—The physically handicapped division does not contain great groups of custodial cases; children of low I.Q. may belong in either of two such groups, idiots and imbeciles. Members of these two groups never become independent workers; they cannot be effectively taught in the special classes of public schools, and are proper candidates for the state's custodial institutions. The state must, therefore, maintain some form of institution that will humanely and efficiently care for such low-grade defectives.

The state institution for the feeble-minded has been accepted as furnishing the proper method of caring for such groups. The suggestion is frequently made that the state establish colonies in the open country, where training adapted to their mentality could be provided, where their help, meager as it is, could be utilized in maintaining themselves, where they could enjoy the out-of-doors, and where life in cottages could be made more homelike and personal. In either case, the problem is not primarily educational; the management of such an institution should reside, therefore, in the hands of the welfare department.

The high-grade feeble-minded group can be taught in the public schools. In large cities, centers should be established for them in the more congested districts; in outlying districts classes should be organized for the younger children, and the older children should attend the centers. The county school districts should organize special classes for the younger children, while special centers should be established for the older children.

As a rule, no child should be sent to the state institution if there is any doubt concerning his inability to profit from the special work provided in the public schools. If, however, he has no parents or if he lives under bad home conditions, he should be cared for in the state school, but should be released as soon as home conditions become satisfactory or as soon as he shows the ability and is of the age to be self-supporting with a minimum of guidance.

Gifted Children.—Every city should establish centers for the education of children of high I.Q. These centers should be located in regular school buildings; there should be at least two—preferably, three or four—class groups at each center. This grouping should begin with grade 1 and continue through grade 9. The program for these children should be so enriched that they can spend a whole year in each grade. County school districts with hard roads could establish similar centers. If the county has a city within its boundaries, a co-operative arrangement should be developed whereby the county could utilize centers already established.

Socially Handicapped Youths.—The state now provides for the socially handicapped the state penitentiary, the state reformatory, and state industrial schools. The first two are definitely custodial in aim; they are maintained to protect society from the criminal. The state industrial schools, as administered in many states, are also custodial institutions. It is with the idea that this situation should be changed that the following suggestions with respect to a state program for the socially handicapped are presented.

Every city should maintain one or more industrial or vocational schools, with a rich program of studies, where youths unhappily adjusted to the regular academic program of studies could attend them. County school districts, likewise, should provide similar central schools; one of them might be largely agricultural.   Where possible, county and cities should co-operate in the establishment and use of such schools.

The state should establish, at various centers, farm schools to care for those youths whose lack of adjustment in the regular school is due to vicious home or neighborhood conditions and who need a sympathetic, homelike atmosphere and understanding supervision during 24 hours of the day.   Each of the farm schools would house the youths in cottages accommodating 10 or 12, with no more than four or five cottages under a single management.   The acreage need not be great; the 100- to 500-acre farms frequently used at present would not be necessary.   Gardening, fruit raising, farming on a small-acreage basis, raising poultry, raising pigs, keeping a few cows, and maintaining three or four horses to do the cultivating would represent the basic activities of the school, in addition to regular schoolwork.

The state should establish, within the cities near the local industrial or vocational schools, "homes" in which to house and feed youths who want the industrial instead of the agricultural training.   City youths who are given homes at these centers come from unsatisfactory situations in their own homes.   Rural youths in these centers differ from those sent to the farm schools only in that the latter are interested in farm activities and they are not.

The state is called upon to establish the farm schools and the homes, because they represent a large initial expenditure, because none but cities would need units of such size, and because they must receive youths from remote parts of the state.   If these facilities are to be provided for all youths in the state needing them, they clearly become state responsibilities.

When these plans are put into operation, large state industrial schools will not be needed.   None but the most vicious truants and delinquents would be sent to the central industrial schools.   The local centers, moreover, by making curricular and living adjustments as soon as they are necessary, ought to prevent great numbers from becoming vicious.   There will be needed, however, a small central state school for youths who cannot be helped locally.   This school should cease being the "boy's penitentiary"; it should be recognized as an educational institution and should be placed under the complete control and supervision of the state's department of education.

7. THE COSMOPOLITAN SCHOOL

A few cities have developed a central school for many kinds of exceptional children.   Battle Creek, Des Moines, and Baltimore have such schools. It has been suggested that a slight variation from this type of school might be established centrally for a county school system. The variation would consist of admitting exceptional children and normal children.

This may prove to be the most satisfactory way of educating exceptional children in rural territories. It would involve transportation over considerable distances; in terms of time required to make the trips, it would hardly be longer than some children now spend on city busses in being transported to central schools for crippled children.

8. FUNDS FOR THE EDUCATION OF GIFTED CHILDREN

Many gifted children are found in families too poor to finance much education; they complete grade school and then frequently go to work as soon as they are old enough. This means a great social loss. Society can ill afford to allow even one of these gifted children to neglect the development of his talents. The state should make it possible for all such children to develop their talents to a point where they can become self-supporting and thus are able to expand their abilities through their own efforts.

Such a program must be planned. Gifted children must be systematically sought out year by year. An efficient accounting system, plus a systematic testing program, will make this possible. When discovered, these youths should be reported to the state with complete family, physical, and social data. The financial aid needed to help them to adequate education should be provided at state expense.

9. PLACEMENT AND FOLLOW-UP SERVICES

All types of handicapped children find difficulty in getting work when they have completed their schooling. If, therefore, they are to become self-supporting, they must have help in getting jobs. Placement service has two tasks. It must convince employers that these youths are capable and can serve them effectively, and it must discover the specific tasks which children with given defects can perform. The state can assist local officials by keeping in touch with what is done elsewhere, by holding group conferences, and by planning long-time researches.

This placement staff has also the responsibility for making a complete follow-up of all placements. Card files should be maintained of all youths placed; contacts should be maintained at stated intervals; continuous contacts should be made with each problem case until the youth has made a reasonably good adjustment to his new work;

and employers should be encouraged to report periodically concerning the progress of the youths.

This follow-up should be maintained for all youths who have been in special schools. Data are needed concerning the effectiveness of such education. At present, it is meager, on account of a failure to keep informed of what happens to these children after they have left school. The biggest argument for special education is lost because of lack of follow-up. Placement workers should include this service in their program.

10. PREVENTION OF HANDICAPS

The state must put on a continuous educational campaign in the cause of prevention, teachers must be trained to meet the needs of handicapped groups, more and better records must be kept, individual pupil study must be emphasized, regular teachers must not be overloaded, medical service must be provided, psychological and psychiatric service must be given, food and clothing must be supplied, parents must be helped to manage and feed their children properly, curricular needs must be more adequately met, the school plant must be utilized more than it is at present, and segregation and sterilization must be recognized as essential to the good of society.

11. RESEARCH

No field is in greater need of research work than special education. The basic causes at the root of all the difficulties that these children have need to be known; the most effective means of eliminating these causes then need to be discovered.

In the field of care and instruction, hosts of problems are encountered. How best correct speech defects? How best teach the deaf? How best educate the blind? Must military rule be utilized in aiding the delinquent to adjust? Problems in the field of methodology are legion when one deals with handicapped children. Careful research is needed in order that the work of educating them may be of maximum worth.

Accurate follow-up means research. What happens to different groups of youths under different kinds of treatment? What happens to delinquents who have been re-educated under strict military discipline? What happens to those re-educated in schools that have banished such discipline? Carefully controlled experimentation is needed. More ought to be known about the long-time results of special education programs; this can come only by means of the most careful research.

12. SUMMARY

In broad outline, the major features of a state program of special education include (1) accurate accounting, (2) education of the public, (3) local surveys, (4) co-ordination of the efforts of all agencies interested in the problem, (5) planning of the curricula, (6) supervision of class instruction, (7) establishment of clinics, (8) formation of special schools and classes, (9) provision of funds for the gifted, (10) development of preventive measures, (11) research studies, and (12) placement and follow-up.

Problems and Questions for Discussion

1. What should be the basic principles in the development of a special education program?

2. How can a census be of worth in developing a program of special education?

3. To what extent should the state office supervise local special schools and classes?

4. What advantage can you see in the establishment of state centers to displace central state schools for the deaf, the blind, and the crippled?

5. What would be the reasons for and against the establishment of cosmopolitan schools for the handicapped?

6. How would you justify the establishment of county and city industrial, vocational, and agricultural schools?

7. Will it ever be possible to provide special education effectively for rural school children? State your point of view and defend it.

8. Is the state justified in appropriating annually a specific sum of money for the education of gifted children? Why?

9. Outline in some detail the measures you think should be put into operation in order to reduce the number of handicapped children.

10. If you were given a position in the state department of education, with sole responsibility for the placement of handicapped children, what program would you seek to put into effect?

11. Outline in some detail various researches that you feel should be initiated in the field of special education.

12. List the specific types of legislation that would be necessary in your home state in order to put into operation the recommendations of this chapter.

Selected Bibliography

WALLIN, J. E. WALLACE. *Problems of Subnormality*, pp. 382–416. World Book Company, Yonkers-on-Hudson, New York, 1921.

A discussion of legislation as related to various types of defective children.

White House Conference. *Special Education: The Handicapped and the Gifted*, pp. 583–593. The Century Co., New York, 1931.

Specific recommendations relative to the organization of special schools and classes for exceptional children.

CHAPTER XXXIV

THE CHALLENGE OF THE FUTURE

When you have helped a man to help himself, your accomplishment leaps into the realm of the sublime. Parents have, during all time, caught the essential truth of this idea; they have given of time, strength, and even life itself in order that their children might grow into young manhood and young womanhood with that ability. Teachers are happy, as they grow old in the service, in the thought of the boys and girls they have helped to grow in physical stamina, mental stature, and social power. The preacher, the social worker, the physician, and the kindly neighbor are continually performing similar services.

Special education is uniquely aimed at performing this function. The regular program of education has not been adapted to the needs of exceptional children. Many such children have been permitted by state law to remain out of school because of the very obvious inability of the school to care for them. Special education takes the cripple, the blind, the deaf, the truant and delinquent, the speech defective, the delicate child, and the subnormal and so cares for and educates them that they increasingly are becoming self-supporting; it takes the gifted and so develops their unique abilities that they attain their maximum potentialities. Self-maintenance and self-development are both personal and social goods; the individual, so helped, gains in self-respect, self-confidence, and ambition. This means happiness for the individual and his family; greater ability to master technical, social, and personal problems; a better living for the family group; and consequently, a larger contribution to the social good.

1. TECHNICAL PROBLEMS

In the field of special education there are numerous problems that must be faced and solved if the goal, just described, is to be attained. The solution of these problems constitutes the challenge of special education. Basic to them all is that of educating parents, teachers, and the general public; the successful handling of each problem will depend upon how well this basic task has been done. If parents know the causes of specific defects, if they know the serious results of certain diseases, and if they know how to avoid these diseases, there need not be so many handicapped children. If the public is informed as to the costs of lack of action, necessary aid in solving its problems can be expected. If teachers become aware of the exceptional child and understand better the causes of various defects, the more likely are they to co-operate in the solution of special education's problems.

The problem of prevention has taken a most important step on the way to solution when the public, parents, and teachers have been fully informed. Since children who are prevented from becoming delinquent, crippled, blind, or deaf have a much greater opportunity of maintaining themselves than they would if they became so hampered, prevention is an all-important goal in the field of special education. Every penny spent on prevention saves money needed in remedial work and makes much greater the possible achievement of those helped.

Discovery ranks high in importance. If the handicapped are not known, little can be done for them. Data on numbers are even yet too much in the nature of estimates. Nation-wide studies are not available. The White House Conference reports were based upon numerous studies of limited areas. Until a continuous census covering ages from birth to eighteen or twenty-one is maintained, we shall not know with any degree of accuracy how many exceptional children there are or where they are located.

When the three preceding problems have been solved, that of financing the education of exceptional children will be less difficult. Parents, teachers, and a public alive to the significance of special education make fertile ground for the seeds of financial understanding. Such a public will demand adequate financial aid for educating these children. A public which understands the necessity for preventing these handicaps and which accepts the responsibility for discovering them will not hesitate, despite the increased costs, to make provision for these youths commensurate with the educational program provided for all children.

Only as financial responsibility is accepted can all exceptional children be cared for and educated. This problem has not as yet been met by any school district; at least, the writer has been unable to discover one that even pretends to make such a claim. Some districts come reasonably near providing for 100 per cent of certain groups, but fail to provide for other groups. Some have made a start at providing for all groups, but make no pretension of reaching all children. Others have no program for educating their exceptional children. The problem to be worked out is that of reaching every exceptional child of the community and of seeing to it that a program of special care and education is made available to him.

Finally, among these more or less technical problems are those of providing adequate and proper facilities for the care and education of these children. Sufficient and well-trained teachers, equipment for the educational program, adequate and good housing, medical care, food and rest, transportation, and attention to personal needs, which can be supplied only by means of a program of individualization that ignores no single child—all these are essential.

2. PROBLEMS OF POINTS OF VIEW

Important as are these technical problems, there are others even more vital. The length to which society is willing to go in the solution of the technical problems will depend entirely upon its point of view with respect to others. (1) What, for example, is the nature of the aid needed by these children for whom special education is provided? (2) What is to be our attitude toward the service agencies of the future? (3) What is to be our attitude toward financing, taxes, and earnings? While, technically, the challenge of special education rests upon our solution of the problems raised in the previous section, the real challenge of special education depends upon our answer to the questions of this section. Do exceptional children need more than physical care? Are public service agencies still in their infancy? Do earnings of individuals and corporations belong wholly to them or partly to the social group of which they are a part?

Help Needed.—As has been pointed out again and again, special education has been provided most adequately for those children whose handicaps make a direct appeal to the senses. The layman has his sympathies touched when the pitifully deformed cripple is brought before him; he waxes sentimental in the presence of the blind; the inability of the feeble-minded makes the appeal of the helpless to the strong; while the youthful delinquent with his customary background of broken home, poverty, unhappy childhood, cruel parents, and unfortunate friendships provides all the instruments necessary for playing upon his heart strings. These conditions are obvious and pitiful. The human heart reaches out to such unfortunate children and wishes to do something personal for them. Personal appeals of this kind have been so utilized that considerable progress has been made. The appeal now needs to be so generalized that society will not only spend more for these exceptional children but that it will do the spending upon the basis of the larger social good, instead of upon the basis of a personal appeal to human sympathy.

Even more important is acceptance of the idea that the needs of these children may reach far beyond those of medical aid, rest, food, and mental development. They may need far more that personal, friendly, homely understanding of pal for pal which most nonhandicapped children have. They need the comfortable feeling that comes with the give-and-take of normal family life; they need the sense of security that comes with being in a position to help others and of knowing that these others want to and will back them to the limit, if need be.

In addition, workers in special education have the task of guiding these youths in the forming of attitudes. The handicapped youth must be helped to accept himself as he is; he must become resolute in doing all he can at self-improvement; he must not permit permanent, nonremediable handicaps to "sour" him against life and people. This acceptance of oneself is a problem for all youths, but it is much more acute for the handicapped. The problem must be sensed by all who deal with these children. Teachers can help materially if they are well trained; visiting teachers, psychiatric social workers, psychologists, and psychiatrists are necessary if this problem is to be fully met.

Service Agencies.—Whether or not such services are to be made available will depend upon the extent to which there is a realization of a need for them upon the part of the general public. Even more important in determining this issue is the degree of our acceptance of the idea that service agencies must utilize a far greater portion of the total population than they have ever utilized in the past. Production and distribution at one time demanded a great proportion of the members of the social group. But machines during the past half century have made appalling inroads upon the demands for human labor; even the past ten years have seen machines displacing men at an ever-increasing rate. Despite a general improvement of business since 1932, there are still, according to numerous newspaper stories, 10,000,000 or more unemployed. One of the latest mechanical substitutes for human labor is the cotton picker of the Rust brothers, which, when and if it is put upon the market, may displace hundreds of thousands of rural workers in the country's cotton fields; and the end is not yet.

Sensible people do not question the social value of these mechanical inventions. They welcome machinery that will lessen the backaches of millions of workers. They insist, however, since such inventions are worthless except as the social group uses them or their products, that the time has arrived when they must not be permitted to enrich a few and pauperize millions. The Rust brothers seem to appreciate this problem; the practical meeting of the emergency is not so clearly visualized. It may be that no plan can entirely prevent some hardships to individuals; it may be that all that can be achieved in the revolutions great and small which follow the creation and acceptance of various laborsaving devices is to reduce as much as possible labor displacements by means of gradual adoptions and by means of developing simultaneously various types of service agencies that can absorb the best of the displaced workers and all of the future workers who might otherwise have been utilized in production.

The need for a vast increase of workers in service areas is unquestioned. One has only to meet with the board of some social agency and listen for an evening to its deliberations to understand how inadequately staffed it is. One city of 290,000 has 56 such public agencies and some private agencies supported by the community fund; there are many private agencies not so supported. Contact with these agencies shows clearly the need of more workers if problems in their own fields are to be cared for.

Among the professional groups the inadequacy of medical and nursing service is well known. Physicians, dentists, oculists, otologists, orthopedists, and other specialists are needed by vast numbers of individuals who are not being reached at present. Undoubtedly, if adequate public medical service were to be provided, a great increase would be necessary in the number of such professional workers. Public-health nurses and school nurses are woefully handicapped by the lack of numbers; there are not enough hours during the day for these nurses to care for the urgent problems demanding attention, let alone being able to develop anything in the field of prevention.

The public schools suffer from overloaded teachers and a lack of those service agencies needed in helping children to solve their numerous personal problems. Despite our knowledge of the necessity of individualizing instruction and adapting it to pupil needs, we have seen, since the crash of 1929, schools forced to increase teacher loads to such an extent that little but mass instruction can result. Despite a general recognition of the need and worth-whileness of counseling service within the public schools, we find it totally ignored in many school systems; and even in those systems that are recognized as doing excellent work we find one counselor trying to serve 2,000 to 3,000 children within a given high school. Despite the excellent work of the counselor, she recognizes clearly the inadequacy of the program for the school. Health service within our public schools just touches the fringes of the program that ought to be in operation.

Psychological service is almost nil when compared with needs. A survey in September, 1936, showed that, in 89 cities of the 93 with populations of 100,000 and over in the United States, there were 145 psychologists in the employ of these boards of education. Of the 89 cities, 38—or 43 per cent—had no psychological help, and 22 others had only one person each. Detroit and Rochester reported 17 each; if these two cities need and effectively use this number, a slight idea can be gained of how meagerly we are meeting this one problem on a national basis. As a matter of fact, probably neither of these cities would claim that their present staff is at all adequate.

Psychiatric service, needed in dealing with the emotional problems of children, is even less adequately provided. Of the 89 cities, 67—or 75 per cent—had no such service. On the other hand, one city reported 8, another 4, two cities 2 each, and the remainder each had one psychiatrist, or one serving part time. Through the years of depression, with their resulting toll on emotional stability, we find little service of this type. The total number of such employees in the 89 large city school systems was 30, and 12 of these were found in two cities. Although the number of visiting teachers and attendance workers is much greater, in terms of the cases these fieldworkers should be helping, these areas are sadly short-handed. Obviously, in the skilled service areas, there are possibilities of utilizing vast groups of our population; these services are needed by all groups. At present, only the few receive them, either because individuals cannot pay for private service or because public service is so limited. All phases of special education are activities that fall within this service area. The future may, perhaps, see production largely accomplished by mechanical aids, so that great numbers of the human race will be free to devote themselves to the important service areas of life.

Beard, in "The Open Door at Home," calls attention to this same problem. Pointing to service activities as a means of providing employment, he says that in these activities

. . . . the intellectual, esthetic, and scientific forces of the nation must be employed —the artists, architects, teachers, doctors, nurses, and leaders in sports and recreation—employed not as derelicts out of jobs but as creative designers, directors, and servants of civilization. Already a vision of expansion in the domain of "service industries" is dawning in the consciousness of American thinkers, especially with the decline in the employment of children, the extension of the school age, the reduction of hours of work days, and the growing inability of men and women "over forty" to secure satisfactory occupations in high tension machine industry, with its stresses and strains.[1]

[1] CHARLES A. BEARD, The Open Door at Home, p. 229, The Macmillan Company, New York, 1935.

He further urges that these services must not be thought of as "dilettante and a side issue." He insists that they are vital to society and that "any planning for the future which ignores the rôle of the arts and services will as certainly fail, as must any planning that neglects the powers of technology and the use industries."[1]

Financial Responsibility.—If the future does point in this direction, we must revolutionize our thinking with respect to the earnings of production, the support of government, and the levy of taxes. Obviously, if production is performed by fewer and fewer people, if increasingly greater groups enter the service occupations, and if all are to benefit by these services, such services must be provided at public expense. Obviously, too, we must revolutionize our ideas with respect to taxation and the amount to be collected by taxation if such services are to be developed and are to be provided for all. No longer will a property tax be sufficient. No longer can great groups of the population be exempt from income taxes. No longer can the per cent of incomes applicable to taxes remain as low as it has been in the past.

Just what the taxation plan should be is not the present concern of the writer. It is apparent that present plans are wholly inadequate if the service programs suggested in this chapter are to be put into operation. It seems clear that every man should pay his tax; that this tax should take a relatively small portion of the laborer's income and a relatively high portion of the highest incomes. What the portions should be would depend upon careful study. Although a reasonable difference in allowed incomes to individuals is proper and right as representing differences in ability, prudence, and endeavor, there can be no justification for the huge differentials of the past and present. We greatly need a system of taxation sufficient to make possible the development of these rich areas of public service.

The writer believes that service agencies are due and ought to be materially expanded. Such services are needed for a strong, healthy, happy people; they can well take up in the next few decades a great portion of the dangerous slack in unemployment. They cannot be furnished, however, upon our past basis of governmental support.

Much is being done and will continue to be done for the exceptional child, regardless of our future attitude toward service agencies in general, and regardless of our attitudes toward taxation. When and if, however, we do accept as a social group the points of view suggested in this section, we shall no longer need to worry about reaching, caring for, and educating all exceptional children. This is the challenge of the future.

[1] *Ibid.*, p. 230.

INDEX

I

Ide, Gladys, 288
Illingworth, W. H., 158, 159, 170, 176
Impaired hearing (see Deaf children; Hard of hearing)
Improvability of children of low I.Q., 379
Incidence, for children of low I.Q., 361–362, 380
  for cripples, 142–143, 153
  for deaf, 263
  for delicate children, 319–320
  for gifted, 406
  for hard of hearing, 278
  for partial vision, 201, 217–218
  for specially gifted, 406, 434
  for speech defectives, 294–295
  for socially exceptional, 6
Indianapolis, 21
Individual differences, why important, 1–2
Individual study, 480–482
Infantile paralysis, 143–144, 145–146, 154
Infectious diseases, 146, 218–221; 264–266, 332, 334
Influenza, 265
Ingram, Christine P., 377
Inheritance, as related to truancy and delinquency, 99
Institutionalization, 168, 169, 242
Institution, methods of (see Methods of educating)
Instructional problems (see Curricula)
Intelligence, lack of, 99
Intelligence quotient, importance of, 342
Irwin, Robert B., 187, 197
Itinerant teachers, 293

J

Jean Parker School, 197
Jefferson Farm School, 21–22
Jersey City, N.J., 135
Justification of costs of educating exceptional children, 454–456

K

Kansas City, 22
Keesecker, Ward W., 115, 116, 117, 119
Kentucky State School for Deaf, 236
Kiwanis Club, 135

L

Lallation, 305
Lancaster State Industrial School for Boys, 61
Lapage, C. P., 380
Larcomb, J. W., 111
Lawes, Estella, 203, 213, 216
Legislation, and children of low I.Q., 383–385
  and cripples, 150–151
  and deaf, 267, 268
  and delicate children, 334–335
  and gifted, 420–422
  and hard of hearing, 286
  and its effects, 239
  and prevention, 479–480
  and sight saving, 227
  and socially handicapped, 63
  and speech defectives, 308–309
Lehman, Clarence O., 457
Leisure time, 95–96
Leland School for Cripples, 127, 132
Lemmon, Raymond A., 295, 297, 312
Letter substitution, 306
Library, 76, 176–177
Lighting (see Schoolhouse lighting)
Lions Club, 135
Lip reading (see Speech reading)
Lison, Marguerite M., 155
Lisping, 305
Local classes, for blind, 161–162, 167–168, 185, 504
  for children of low I.Q., 346–348, 370–374, 505–506
  for cripples, 116, 150, 504
  for deaf, 238–239, 242, 504–505
  for delicate children, 505
  for gifted children, 393, 421, 506
  for hard of hearing, 273, 504–505
  for partial-vision children, 191, 192, 193, 195, 213, 228, 504